Wake up your

SOCIOLOGY

course!

Sociology in Action inspires students to DO sociology by combining foundational coverage with an abundance of activities that emphasize hands-on work, application, and learning by example.

No matter what kind of introductory sociology classes you teach—large lectures, small seminars, online, or hybrid courses—**Sociology in Action** gives you everything you need to create learning experiences that have impact, in one student-friendly text.

Sociology in Action engages your students through a variety of activity types:

- Activities or exercises that ask students to reflect on their own **experiences and observations about the world**

- **Group activities** carried out by students during or outside of class meetings

- Activities or exercises that involve **analysis of a graph, map, or table of data**

- Activities or exercises that require **content analysis** of news reports, videos, advertising, social media, and other forms of entertainment and culture

- Short, guided research activities that ask students to **investigate a person, organization, or social issue**

- Survey activities that **poll students on what they know or believe** about a certain topic or about personal experiences

A COMPLETE Teaching and Learning Resource!

Sociology in Action includes an Instructor Resource site with more ways to WAKE UP your sociology course, plus the tools you need to use the text successfully.

Doing Sociology 9.1 Sorting People by Race
LO 9.1: Define race and ethnicity.
15-30 minutes
either in-class or outside of class

As part of a documentary series, "RACE – The Power of an Illusion," PBS created an online tool that allows you to sort a series of photographs of people by race, and then check your answers against what those people marked on the U.S. Census form.

Visit http://www.pbs.org/race/002_SortingPeople/002_00-home.htm and click "Begin Sorting" to get started. Once you have completed the activity, answer the following questions:

1. Was it easy or difficult for you to place the people into the categories they selected on the U.S. Census. Why?
2. Which of the people pictured might face racial discrimination in the U.S. today? Why?
3. Describe at least two things this exercise teaches us about racial and ethnic categorizations in the U.S. today.

Instructor's Note
This exercise shows just how difficult it can be for people to accurately determine people's race or ethnicity as assessed on the U.S. Census. This exercise could be done by individual students, pairs, or small groups. If done in class, pairs or groups can report back their findings and compare them, bringing home the overall key points (racial appearance does not always match racial identity, racial ~ is subjective, Census categories change over time, people ~ than one racial or ethnic category but this exerci~ the Census counts them as BOTH mul~ minority (or non-White) ~ face racial or e~

Instructor Resource
Korgen, *Sociology in Action*
SAGE Publishing, 2019

MCAT Standards Mapping

To instructors and students using this resource:
In 2015, the MCAT (Medical College Admission Test) began to include the social and behavioral sciences (Section 3 Psychological, Social, and Biological Foundations of Behavior). Sociological content constitutes thirty percent of Section 3. This material is organized under four Foundational Concepts with a range of subtopics known as "Content Categories." The four Foundational Concepts are:

- Foundational Concept 7: Biological, psychological, and sociocultural factors influence behavior and behavior change.
- Foundational Concept 8: Psychological, sociocultural, and biological factors influence the way we think about ourselves and others, as well as how we interact with others.
- Foundational Concept 9: Cultural and social differences influence well-being.
- Foundational Concept 10: Social stratification and access to resources influence well-being.

This guide links the four MC~ ~dational Concepts and Subtopics to appropriate text chapters. It is organized in ~ ~nner. It first summarizes the main topics covered in each chapter, ar ~ ~below the summary. Each chapter entry also contai~ ~ore specific topic areas in more deta~ journal articles. Some ~ that the MCAT includ~ connections to healt~ Because each chap~ material of Chapt~ chapters that foll~

SAGE ANIMATED VIDEO
Agents of Socialization

Family
Work
Sports
Religion
Media
Peers

- **An Activity Guide** with suggestions for assigning, carrying out, and assessing every activity.

- **Links to exceptional teaching resources from ASA's TRAILS** (Teaching Resources and Innovation Library for Sociology).

- **An MCAT Guide** that maps chapter content to Foundational Concepts and Content Categories in Section 3 of the MCAT test.

- **Assignable SAGE Premium Video** (available via the interactive eBook, linked through SAGE coursepacks) that explains core sociological concepts and offers a view of current events through a sociological lens.

- **Additional activities and exercises** to give you more options beyond the ones in the print text.

To all instructors and students who put sociology into action.

SOCIOLOGY IN
ACTION

KATHLEEN ODELL KORGEN

William Paterson University

MAXINE P. ATKINSON

North Carolina State University

Los Angeles | London | New Delhi
Singapore | Washington DC | Melbourne

$SAGE

FOR INFORMATION:

SAGE Publications, Inc.
2455 Teller Road
Thousand Oaks, California 91320
E-mail: order@sagepub.com

SAGE Publications Ltd.
1 Oliver's Yard
55 City Road
London EC1Y 1SP
United Kingdom

SAGE Publications India Pvt. Ltd.
B 1/I 1 Mohan Cooperative Industrial Area
Mathura Road, New Delhi 110 044
India

SAGE Publications Asia-Pacific Pte. Ltd.
3 Church Street
#10-04 Samsung Hub
Singapore 049483

Acquisitions Editor: Jeff Lasser
Editorial Assistant: Adeline Wilson
Content Development Editors: Nancy Matuszak,
                                                        Sarah Dillard
Production Editor: Tracy Buyan
Copy Editor: Gillian Dickens
Typesetter: C&M Digitals (P) Ltd.
Proofreader: Alison Syring
Indexer: Will Ragsdale
Cover Designer: Gail Buschman
Marketing Manager: Kara Kindstrom

Printed in Canada

Library of Congress Cataloging-in-Publication Data

Names: Korgen, Kathleen Odell, 1967- author. | Atkinson, Maxine P., author.

Title: Sociology in action / Kathleen Odell Korgen, William Paterson University, USA, Maxine P. Atkinson, North Carolina State University, USA.

Description: First Edition. | Thousand Oaks: SAGE Publications, [2018] |

Includes bibliographical references and index.

Identifiers: LCCN 2017039363 | ISBN 9781506345901 (pbk. : alk. paper)

Subjects: LCSH: Sociology—Study and teaching.

Classification: LCC HM571 .S6197 2018 | DDC 301.071—dc23
LC record available at https://lccn.loc.gov/2017039363

This book is printed on acid-free paper.

18 19 20 21 22 10 9 8 7 6 5 4 3 2 1

Brief Contents

Detailed Contents

CHAPTER 8

CHAPTER 9

CHAPTER 10

CHAPTER 11

CHAPTER 12

Preface

If you, like us, have found yourself searching for activities to bring into your classroom and engage your introductory sociology students, you know why we wrote this book. We knew we couldn't be alone in our quest to get students to do more than read the text—we want them to *do* sociology, to understand and apply the terms and concepts they read about and realize them in the real world. Over the course of writing and refining the manuscript, as well as reading the reviews of instructors excited to see activities that many of us have been cobbling together over the years now residing within a textbook, we became even more convinced that our approach is one that offers instructors material for how they want to teach and offers students the foundational content they need in sociology, as well as engaging activities that will help them *do* sociology.

Sociology in Action puts all the tools instructors need to create an active learning course into one student-friendly text. Active learning teaching techniques increase student learning, retention, and engagement with course material, but they also require more creative effort than traditional lectures. No other sociology textbook works to ease this load by providing full coverage of introductory content *and* active learning exercises fully integrated into the text (with clear instructions on how to use and assess them available through the instructor resources). *Sociology in Action* provides instructors of small, medium, large, and online introductory courses with the material they need to create learning experiences for their students, including creative, hands-on, data-analytic, and community learning activities.

A group of gifted instructors who use active learning techniques in their own classrooms has written the book's chapters. The contributors, focusing on their respective area of expertise, expertly weave together content material, active learning exercises, discussion questions, real-world examples of sociologists in action, and information on careers that use sociology. Together, we have created a book that requires students to *do* sociology as they learn it and creates a bridge between the classroom and the larger social world.

Organization and Features

The clear organizational style of each chapter helps students follow the logic of the text and concentrate on the main ideas presented. Each chapter opens with focal learning questions, and each major section ends with review questions to remind students of the emphasis in the presented material. In addition, the chapters contain an analysis of subject matter from both *major theoretical perspectives* and, where appropriate, *middle-range theories*. Chapters close with a conclusion, and end-of-chapter resources include a list of key terms and a summary that addresses the focal learning questions. The active learning activities and *Consider This* marginal questions throughout each chapter help create a student-centered class that engages student interest.

The book's rich pedagogy supports active learning and engagement throughout each chapter.

- *Learning Questions* start off every chapter, introducing students to the focus of the chapter and preparing them for the material it covers. These questions are tied to the learning objectives provided in the instructor resources. Each learning question addresses a main section of the chapter.

- *Check Your Understanding* questions appear at the end of every major section in a chapter, providing students with an opportunity to pause in their reading and ensure that they comprehend and retain what they've just read.

- *Doing Sociology* activities appear multiple times in each chapter. These active learning exercises enable students to apply the sociological concepts, theories, methods, and so on covered in the text. Each chapter contains a variety of exercises so that instructors can use them in class, online, or as assignments conducted outside of class. Reference the *Doing*

Sociology activities and the clear instructions on how to carry out and assess them—and on how they relate to the chapter objectives—in the activity guide available through the book's instructor resources. Additional exercises can also be found in the digital resources accompanying the text.

- *Consider This* questions are designed to spark deep thinking as well as classroom discussions.

- *Sociologists in Action* boxes feature a student or professional "sociologist in action" doing public sociology related to the material covered in the chapter. This feature provides examples of how sociology can be used to make a positive impact on society.

- *Key Terms* appear in bold where they are substantially discussed for the first time and are compiled in a list with page numbers at the end of their respective chapters. Corresponding definitions can be found in the Glossary.

- Every chapter concludes with a *Chapter Summary* that restates the learning questions presented at the start of the chapter and provides answers to them. This provides an important way for students to refresh their understanding of the material and retain what they've learned.

In addition, as appropriate, chapters include information on careers that relate to the chapter content. This allows students to recognize, even during their first sociology course, the wide variety of career options a sociology degree provides.

Digital Resources

We know how important good resources can be in the teaching of sociology. Our goal is to create resources that both support and enhance the book's themes and features. SAGE edge offers a robust online environment featuring an impressive array of tools and resources for review, study, and further exploration, keeping both instructors and students on the cutting edge of teaching and learning. SAGE edge content is open access and available on demand. Learning and teaching have never been easier! We gratefully acknowledge Sarah Dillard for developing the digital resources on this site.

$SAGE coursepacks

Our content tailored to your LMS
sagepub.com/coursepacks

SAGE COURSEPACKS FOR INSTRUCTORS makes it easy to import our quality content into your school's LMS.

For use in: Blackboard, Canvas, Brightspace by Desire2Learn (D2L), and Moodle.

Don't use an LMS platform? No problem, you can still access many of the online resources for your text via SAGE edge.

SAGE coursepacks include the following:

- Our content delivered directly into your LMS

- Intuitive, simple format that makes it easy to integrate the material into your course with minimal effort

- Pedagogically robust assessment tools that foster review, practice, and critical thinking and offer a more complete way to measure student engagement, including:

  o Diagnostic chapter pretests and posttests that identify opportunities for improvement, track student progress, and ensure mastery of key learning objectives

  o Test banks built on Bloom's Taxonomy that provide a diverse range of test items with ExamView test generation

  o Activity and quiz options that allow you to choose only the assignments and tests you want

  o Instructions that are given on how to use and integrate the comprehensive assessments and resources provided

  o An Activity Guide that details all activities from the print book, as well as supplementary exercises, the learning objectives they address, and notes to instructors

  o SAGE Premium video, with corresponding multimedia assessment tools, that brings core sociology concepts to life through original, animated videos and licensed news clips, increasing student engagement and appealing to different learning styles

  o **EXCLUSIVE,** influential SAGE journal and reference content that is built into course materials and assessment tools and ties important research and scholarship to chapter concepts to strengthen learning.

- Editable, chapter-specific PowerPoint slides that offer flexibility when creating multimedia lectures so you don't have to start from scratch but you can customize to your exact needs.

- Integrated links to the interactive eBook that make it easy for your students to maximize their study time with this "anywhere, anytime" mobile-friendly version of the text. It also offers access to more digital tools and resources, including SAGE Premium Video.

- All tables and figures from the textbook.

$SAGE edge™ for students
http://edge.sagepub.com/korgen

SAGE edge enhances learning in an easy-to-use environment that offers the following:

- Mobile-friendly flashcards that strengthen understanding of key terms and concepts and make it easy to maximize your study time, anywhere, anytime

- Mobile-friendly practice quizzes that allow you to assess how much you've learned and where you need to focus your attention

- Multimedia links to open web video and audio resources that allow students to dive deeper into topics with a click of the mouse

- Exclusive access to influential SAGE journal and reference content, which ties important research and scholarship to chapter concepts to strengthen learning

Acknowledgments

We would like to acknowledge the many people who worked with us on *Sociology in Action*. Our thanks, first and foremost, go to the contributors who wrote the chapters and helped us to create an active learning introductory sociology course in one text. Their exceptional ability to use active learning in the classroom has impressed and inspired us. We appreciate their willingness to share what they do so well and to collaborate with us on *Sociology in Action*.

The two of us would also like to extend our gratitude to the wonderful people at SAGE for their tremendous work on this project. Acquisitions Editor Jeff Lasser believed in the need for this text, brought us together, and is the chief reason this book became a reality. Nancy Matuszak, our content development manager, provided her great expertise in helping us to shape this book. Sarah Calabi showed us just what a top-notch development editor can do. Gillian Dickens made sure the book was copyedited beautifully, while Tracy Buyan engineered the transformation of the manuscript into real book pages. Editorial Assistant Adeline Wilson managed to keep everything on track and moving forward throughout this long process.

We are also deeply indebted to the following reviewers who offered their keen insights and suggestions:

Deborah A. Abowitz, Bucknell University

Rebecca Barrett-Fox, Arkansas State University

Chastity Blankenship Florida Southern College

Mark Braun, State University of New York, Cobleskill

Joslyn Brenton, Ithaca College

Jess Butler, Butler University

Linda Carson, Lander University

Susan Claxton, Georgia Highlands College

Steven Dashiell, Towson University

Jeffrey Debies-Carl, University of New Haven

Richard G. Ellefritz, Oklahoma State University

Sarah Epplen, Minnesota State University, Mankato

Michael W. Feeley, South Suburban College

Lisa George, Portland Community College

Danielle Giffort, St. Louis College of Pharmacy

Laura Fitzwater Gonzales, Pacific Lutheran University

Belisa Gonzalez, Ithaca College

Roderick Graham, Old Dominion University

Wendi Hadd, John Abbott College

Anita Harker, Whatcom Community College

Jodi A. Henderson-Ross, University of Akron–Wayne College

William Housel, Northwestern Louisiana State University

Aaron Howell, SUNY–Farmingdale

Suzanne S. Hudd, Quinnipiac University

Peter Kaufman, State University of New York—New Paltz

Michele Lee Kozimor-King, Elizabethtown College

Andrea Krieg, Lewis University

Ashley Lumpkin, John Tyler Community College

Lori Lundell, Purdue University

Elizabeth Lyman, Radford University

Sara F. Mason, University of North Georgia

Naomi McCool, Chaffey College

Cassandra McDade, Tidewater Community College

Stephanie Medley-Rath, Indiana University Kokomo

Marian J. Moore, Owens Community College

Madeline H. Moran, City University of New York–Lehman

Jonathan Ortiz, Concordia University

Doris Price, Houston Community College

Barbara Prince, Bowling Green State University

Carolyn Read, Copiah Lincoln Junior College

Nicole Rosen, Pennsylvania State Behrend

Matthew Schoene, Albion College

Naomi Simmons, Newberry College

Chelsea Starr, Eastern New Mexico University

Melissa Swauger, Indiana University of Pennsylvania

Lori Waite, Tennessee Wesleyan University

Jeremy White, Pikes Peak Community College

Joshua Wimberly, Spring Hill College

Susan Wortmann, Nebraska Wesleyan University

Kassia Wosick, El Camino College

Mariah Jade Zimpfer, Sam Houston State University

John F. Zipp, University of Akron

Finally, we offer our great thanks to our families for their support and patience as we devoted so much of our time to *Sociology in Action*.

—Kathleen Odell Korgen and
Maxine P. Atkinson

Kathleen Odell Korgen, PhD, is professor of sociology at William Paterson University in Wayne, New Jersey. Her primary areas of specialization are teaching sociology, racial identity, and race relations. She has received William Paterson University's awards for Excellence in Scholarship/Creative Expression and for Excellence in Teaching.

Maxine P. Atkinson, PhD, is a professor of sociology at North Carolina State University in Raleigh, North Carolina. Her primary area of specialization is the scholarship of teaching and learning. She has received the American Sociological Association's Distinguished Contributions to Teaching Award and the University of North Carolina Board of Governors' Award for Excellence in Teaching.

Mikaila Mariel Lemonk Arthur teaches research methods and other sociology courses at Rhode Island College. Her research focuses on the sociology of higher education. Prior publications include *Student Activism and Curricular Change in Higher Education* (2011) and journal articles on organizational change in higher education, social networks between colleges and universities, and the long-term outcomes of Rhode Island's comprehensive college graduates, as well as on teaching and learning in sociology.

Wendy M. Christensen received her PhD from the University of Wisconsin–Madison and is an associate professor of sociology at William Paterson University in New Jersey. Her research focuses on how inequalities (race, class, and gender) shape political participation. She's published articles on the political participation of mothers of U.S. military members, as well as the intersections of military recruitment campaigns and race, class, and gender. Her forthcoming book, *Our Families Your Freedom: How Military Mothers Support and Challenge the U.S. War on Terrorism,* examines how mothers of service members negotiate the politics of support through recruitment, deployment, and postdeployment health care. She is currently collecting data for a new research project on community political organizing and voter participation.

Sandra Enos, PhD, serves as associate professor of sociology at Bryant University. She earned a PhD from UCONN after a long career in public service. She is the author of *Mothering from the Inside: Parenting in a Women's Prison* (2001), *Service-Learning and Social Entrepreneurship in Higher Education: A Pedagogy of Social Change* (2015), and chapters in books and articles on women and mass incarceration, the history of child welfare, pedagogy in sociology, and higher education reform.

Carissa Froyum is an associate professor of sociology at the University of Northern Iowa. Her research focuses on the roles emotions and identity play in reproducing inequalities. She is the coeditor of *Inside Social Life, Creating and Contesting Inequalities,* and the forthcoming *The Handbook of the Sociology of Gender* (with Barbara Risman and William Scarborough).

Melissa S. Fry is the director of the Applied Research and Education Center (AREC) and associate professor of sociology at Indiana University (IU) Southeast. Dr. Fry's research has included work on poverty, education (early childhood through higher education), homelessness, systems thinking for community development, government contracting with nonprofits, work supports for low-income families, the impact of the coal industry in Central Appalachia, and payday lending. Dr. Fry's broad research agenda is to better understand how public policies are both shaped by and, in turn, shape social inequality and how nonprofit organizations manage the tensions between their missions, government contracts, and the interests of private philanthropies in their efforts to build resilient communities. Prior to joining the IU Southeast faculty in 2011, Dr. Fry was a research and policy associate at the Mountain Association for Community Economic Development in Berea, Kentucky.

Andrea N. Hunt, PhD, is an assistant professor of sociology at the University of North Alabama. Her teaching focuses on diverse families, race and ethnicity, gender, and social justice. Her research in the scholarship of teaching and learning focuses on gender bias in instructor evaluations, the role of academic advising in student retention, mentoring undergraduate research, and learning experiences that promote information literacy and cultural competency. Dr. Hunt has facilitated numerous workshops on academic advising for diverse student populations, preparing high school students for college, best practices for online learning, and techniques for teaching about social inequality. Her research has been featured in *Teaching Sociology,* the *International Journal for the Scholarship of Teaching and Learning,* the *Journal of Effective Teaching, Mentoring and Tutoring: Partnership in*

Learning, and *Innovative Higher Education*. All of her teaching, research, and service are centered on empowering students and faculty for success.

John Chung-En Liu is an assistant professor of sociology at Occidental College. He received his PhD in sociology from the University of Wisconsin–Madison, holds a joint master's degree in economics and environmental management from Yale University, and has a bachelor's degree in chemical engineering from National Taiwan University. His main research projects include a wide array of topics about climate change, including the construction of carbon markets, climate change skepticism, and climate change in higher education curriculums. He has research experiences in the United States, the European Union, China, Taiwan, and India.

Kathleen S. Lowney is a professor of sociology at Valdosta State University—or at least she will be until May 2018, when she will retire. Most of her published work falls under three broad research topics: the sociology of new religious movements, especially teen Satanism; media's role in the construction of social problems claims, such as her article on kudzu as a social problem or her book, *Baring Our Souls: TV Talk Shows and the Religion of Recovery* (1999); and the scholarship of teaching and learning. She and Dr. Maxine Atkinson have written *In the Trenches: Teaching and Learning Sociology* (2015) to help sociology teachers discover innovative ways to communicate the discipline we love to students. She has received several teaching awards at her university, from the University System of Georgia, and from the American Sociological Association.

David Rohall is the department head of the Sociology and Anthropology Department at Missouri State University (MSU). Prior to coming to MSU, he received the Distinguished Faculty Lecturer Award in 2014 for his teaching and research in sociology from Western Illinois University, where he taught for 11 years.

Amy Sodaro is an associate professor of sociology at the Borough of Manhattan Community College/City University of New York. She holds a BA in drama and classics from Tufts University and an MA and a PhD in sociology from the New School for Social Research. Her research interests include sociology of culture, memory, museums, and gender. She is author of *Exhibiting Atrocity: Memorial Museums and the Politics of Past Violence* (2018) and coeditor of *Memory and the Future: Transnational Politics, Ethics and Culture* (2010); *Museums and Sites of Persuasion: Memory, Politics and Human Rights* (forthcoming); and a special issue of *WSQ*, "At Sea" (2017).

Rena C. Zito is an assistant professor of sociology at Elon University. She received her doctorate in sociology from North Carolina State University. Her research focuses primarily on family processes in the production of crime/delinquency. Specifically, her work employs a life course perspective to examine how family structure histories and family formation shape gender processes, adolescent role exits, and law violation.

Sara Miller McCune founded SAGE Publishing in 1965 to support the dissemination of usable knowledge and educate a global community. SAGE publishes more than 1000 journals and over 800 new books each year, spanning a wide range of subject areas. Our growing selection of library products includes archives, data, case studies and video. SAGE remains majority owned by our founder and after her lifetime will become owned by a charitable trust that secures the company's continued independence.

Los Angeles | London | New Delhi | Singapore | Washington DC | Melbourne

Looking at this picture of Grand Central Station in New York City from a sociological perspective can help us see how people both shape and are shaped by the cities in which they reside.

Learning Questions

1.1   What is sociology?

1.2   What do the sociological eye and the sociological imagination allow you to do?

1.3   What key aspects of sociology make it a social *science?*

1.4   How can you tell the difference between a good generalization and a stereotype?

1.5   What are the core commitments of sociology?

1.6   How can sociology benefit both individuals and society?

Training Your Sociological Eye

Kathleen Odell Korgen

Have you ever wanted to know why more women than men graduate from college today? Why college tuition is so expensive? What you can do to improve your chances of landing a desirable job after college? Why the number of hate groups in the United States has increased by 30 percent since 2000? What types of jobs will be most available when you graduate? Why people vote for certain political candidates (or do not vote at all)? How you can make a positive impact on society? If so, you have chosen the right subject! Sociology can help you answer all these questions—and raise some new ones.

What Is Sociology?

So, what is sociology? **Sociology** is the scientific study of society, including how individuals both *shape* and *are shaped* by society. Notice in this definition that people are active beings, shapers of society, but they are also affected by society. It's important to remember that society influences us in myriad ways—how we think, what we notice, what we believe to be true, how we see ourselves, and so on. But it is simultaneously vital to realize that we help shape the society in which we live. This duality is at the heart of sociology and our daily lives—whether we are aware of it or not.

Shaping and Being Shaped by Society

The life of Malala Yousafzai, the youngest Nobel Prize winner in history, provides an excellent example of this duality. No one can deny that Malala is an extraordinary young woman. Her personal bravery and selflessness are awe inspiring. Just nine months after she was shot in the head by the Taliban for publicly promoting education for girls in Pakistan, Malala Yousafzai declared in an address to the United Nations Youth Assembly that "one child, one teacher, one book, and one pen, can change the world" (https://www.youtube.com/watch?v=3rNhZu3ttIU). Her organization, the Malala Fund, has provided the means for many other girls to gain an education. Clearly, Malala has shown the power of an individual to influence society.

How I Got Active in Sociology

Kathleen Odell Korgen

I slept most of the way through the SOC 101 course I took in college. The professor lectured and we took notes (or not).

That SOC 101 course was the last sociology class I took until I found a sociology graduate program in social justice and social economy that encouraged sociologists to put sociological tools into action. In that program, I learned that sociology could show me how I can change society. As a researcher, I have worked on issues related to race relations and racial identity, evaluated social justice efforts and sociology programs, and helped create introductory textbooks that get students to *do* sociology as they learn it.

As a sociology teacher, I want students to know—right away—all that sociology offers them—and society. A major part of my work has been to help students use sociological tools to make a positive impact on society. In my classes, from SOC 101 to Public Sociology and Civic Engagement, students don't just learn about sociology—they become sociologists in action.

Malala Yousafzai was shot in the head and, later, awarded the Nobel Peace Prize for her work promoting education for girls. Her life helps us see how we both shape and are shaped by our societies.

Nigel Waldron/Getty Images Entertainment/Getty Images

Malala, however, just like the rest of us, is a product of her society. Imagine if, instead of growing up in the Swat Valley of Pakistan during the time of the Taliban, she grew up in the suburbs of New Jersey. Her life would have been very different. She would not have been shot by the Taliban and she would not have created the Malala Fund. Indeed, the Malala raised in New Jersey may not have even been aware that girls in many areas of the world face violence for going to school. Sociology helps us understand the impact of society on us and how we can work with others, as Malala is doing now, to solve the social issues facing our societies.

> **Consider This**
>
> How have the time period and the nation in which you live influenced your life? How might your life be different if you lived during a different time period or another nation?

The Origins and Current Uses of Sociology

Sociology developed out of the need to understand and address social issues. The roots of sociology are based in efforts to understand and to help control the impact of major societal changes. In the eighteenth and nineteenth centuries, in Europe and the United States, organized people challenged monarchies and the dominance of religion. The Industrial Revolution dramatically changed where people lived and how they worked. Social change occurred everywhere, and philosophers and scientists offered new answers to life's questions. Many began to believe science could help leaders understand and shape society. August Comte (1798–1857), the French philosopher who gave sociology its name, envisioned that sociology would be the "queen science" that could help steer society safely through great changes.

How Can Sociology Boost Your Career?

In this activity, you will consider the ways sociology can be a benefit in any workplace.

No matter what your major or what you intend to do after graduation, sociology can help you. Sociology is useful in any organization and any professional field. Gaining a sociological perspective will enable you to better understand how society, organizations, and groups work; interact effectively with people of different genders, sexual orientations, ages, races, cultures, and economic classes; make and use connections with other people and organizations; and recognize and address issues of inequality and privilege.

Answer the following questions:

1. What career do you plan on pursuing? If you are not sure yet, think of any profession with which you are familiar (e.g., lawyer, marketing director, police officer, entrepreneur, Wall Street banker, environmental activist, social worker, teacher).

2. How can gaining a sociological perspective help you to succeed in that career?

Today, sociologists help us understand and address challenges like economic inequality, environmental racism, sexism, the social dimensions of global climate change, war, terrorism, and so on. Sociologists work in a variety of settings, including colleges and universities, nonprofit organizations (e.g., environmental groups, public health programs, and community-based organizations), government, and marketing, sales, social services, and the human resources departments of businesses and nonprofit organization. People in every profession benefit from sociological training, and employers value employees with sociological skills.

A survey of employers commissioned by the Association of American Colleges and Universities reveals that students who study sociology tend to gain precisely the skills employers seek. For example,

- Ninety-five percent of employers polled noted that they seek employees who can promote change in the workplace.

- Seventy-five percent of the employers in the survey said they wish colleges placed greater emphasis on teaching complex problem solving, critical thinking skills, and how to apply knowledge in real-world settings.

- Most employers surveyed encouraged colleges to teach students how to conduct research and evidence-based analysis (American Sociological Association 2014).

In this course alone, you will have the opportunity to learn *and use* many of these skills. In most sociology undergraduate programs, you can gain and use all of them!

Check Your Understanding

- What is sociology?
- What is the duality at the heart of sociology?
- Out of what need did sociology develop?
- In what types of settings do sociologists work?

Changing How You View the World

This sociology course will help you develop your sociological eye and your sociological imagination. Together, they allow you to notice and make sense of social patterns in ways that enable you to understand how society works—and to help influence it.

The Sociological Eye

A **sociological eye** enables you to see what others may not notice. It allows you to peer beneath the surface of a situation and discern social patterns (Collins 1998). For example, there is a woman academic who conducts evaluations of various academic departments every year. Often, she does so as part of a team. She has noticed that, whenever she is paired with a man, the clients always look at the man when speaking to them both. As a sociologist, she knows what she is experiencing is gender bias. In general, both men and women tend to defer to men and pay more attention to them, particularly in business settings.

Once you start paying attention to gender patterns (e.g., who talks more in classes or meetings, who interrupts whom, etc.) or racial patterns (e.g., who eats lunch with whom in the cafeteria, what student organizations tend to attract specific racial groups, who is more likely to be stopped by the police, etc.), you won't be able to stop noticing them. Noticing these patterns can make you more aware of how your campus and the larger society work. Once you have this awareness, you can then take steps to change these patterns, if you so choose. The woman we referred to earlier, for example, now often prepares herself to talk more (and more authoritatively) when paired with a man and teaches others to make an effort to pay as much attention to women as to men. You will learn more about *why* we tend to pay more attention to men in Chapter 8!

Consider This

Why do you think we need a sociological eye to notice some social patterns? Why aren't social patterns obvious to everyone all the time?

The Sociological Imagination

Once you develop your sociological eye, you can also expand your **sociological imagination,** the ability to connect what is happening in your own life and in the lives of other individuals to social patterns in the larger society. For example, you may be having a difficult time paying for college. This is a challenge for many individuals. You may address it by taking out loans (and more loans), working while going to school, transferring to a more affordable school, and so forth. So far, these are all individual responses to the problem of high tuition. Looking at the problem with a sociological eye, however, can help you see that this is not just a hardship for a few individuals. You will begin to observe a pattern—many college students across the nation face the same issue. Now you can use your sociological imagination to connect your personal problem (how to pay for the high cost of your college education) with the social issue of the high cost of college throughout the United States.

As Figures 1.1 and 1.2 show, approximately 70 percent of college graduates accept student loans, taking on an average debt of just over $35,000. As government support for higher education drops and wages remain stagnant, more students and families are resorting to loans to pay for college (Berman 2015).

Once you begin to look at the high cost of college as a societal issue, you can investigate its causes. You can then work with other students and families across the nation to press elected officials to develop state and national solutions to this societal problem.

C. Wright Mills (1959:1) developed the concept of the sociological imagination to describe how our individual lives relate to social forces. The sociological imagination gives us the ability to recognize the relationship between our own biographies and the society in which we live. Mills explained the impact of society on individuals this way:

> When a society is industrialized, a peasant becomes a worker; a feudal lord is liquidated or becomes a businessman. . . . When wars happen,

You can use your sociological eye to notice racial, gender, and social status patterns in the cafeteria scenes in the classic film *Mean Girls*—and in most real-life cafeterias.

A. F. Archive/Alamy

FIGURE 1.1

Higher Education Students Graduating with Loans

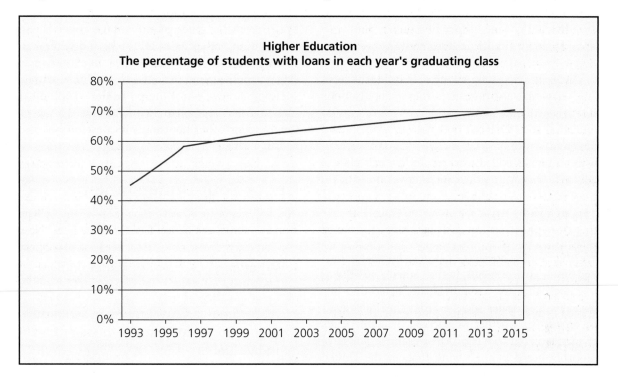

Source: Jeffrey Sparshot, "Congratulations, Class of 2015. You're the Most Indebted Ever (for Now)," *Wall Street Journal*, May 8, 2015. Reprinted with permission of Dow Jones Company.

FIGURE 1.2

Average Debt per Borrower by Graduating Class

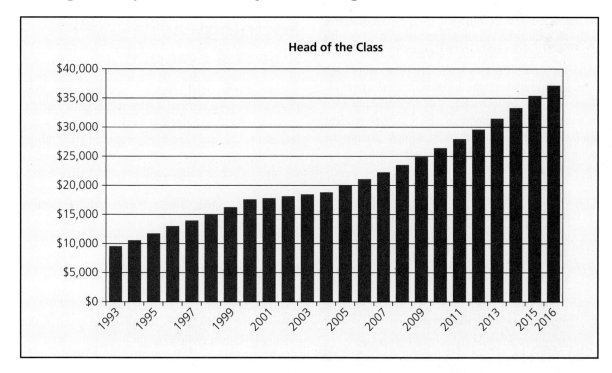

Sources: Jeffrey Sparshot, "Congratulations, Class of 2015. You're the Most Indebted Ever (for Now)," *Wall Street Journal*, May 8, 2015. Reprinted with permission of Dow Jones Company; Student Loan Hero, https://studentloanhero.com/student-loan-debt-statistics.

an insurance salesperson becomes a rocket launcher; a store clerk, a radar operator; a wife or husband lives alone; a child grows up without a parent. . . . Neither the life of an individual nor the history of a society can be understood without understanding both.

Our lives are shaped by the society in which we live. Yet, we can also help shape that society. Nations at war need individuals to fight in their armies. Industrial societies need both factory workers and investors. Postindustrial societies cannot succeed without highly skilled workers. Individuals choose how to behave within their social environments.

The Fallacy of the Individualistic Perspective

We often forget, however, that our choices are limited by our environments. In the United States today, the myth that we, as individuals, determine our own lives permeates society. From this *individualist perspective,* whether we succeed or fail depends primarily on our own efforts. For example, you have probably heard of the saying that, in the United States, anyone who works hard enough can "make it." A sociological eye quickly sees that this individualistic perspective is flawed. Some people have fewer hurdles and more opportunities in life than others. For example, take two students with the same level of innate intelligence. Both work hard but one goes to a school with many AP courses, where students are expected and encouraged to apply to selective colleges. The other student goes to a school with few AP courses, where teachers and administrators focus on preventing kids from dropping out of high school rather than on getting them into selective colleges. Chances are, the second student may not even be aware of all the schools to which the first student applies. His or her chances of "making it" are not the same—no matter how hard they both work.

Consider This

How would you address a lack of affordable healthy food for low-income people (a) from an individualistic perspective and (b) using your sociological imagination? Which would be more effective for the most people?

The sociological eye gives us the ability to recognize the impact society has on us and how the individualistic perspective works to prevent people from noticing that impact. Having a sociological eye, therefore, gives us advantages over those who cannot yet see societal forces and recognize social patterns. Those blind to the influence of society are unknowingly shaped by it. Those with a sociological eye—and therefore the sociological imagination—recognize the impact society has on them and have the opportunity to consciously shape society in turn.

Check Your Understanding

- What does a sociological eye allow you to do?
- What can you do with a sociological imagination?
- According to C. Wright Mills, what do you need to understand the life of an individual?
- How does the sociological eye help us to see the fallacy of the individualistic perspective in the United States?

Sociology as a Social Science

Sociology is a social science, a scientific discipline that studies how society works. As social scientists, sociologists follow rules that work to ensure that our research is transparent and replicable and that others can confirm or refute our findings. For example, as we seek to better understand how society operates, sociologists use theories and the scientific research process to formulate research questions and collect and analyze data.

Theoretical Perspectives

Theoretical perspectives are paradigms, or ways of viewing the world. They help us make sense of the social patterns we observe, and they determine the questions we ask. Different theories have different foci and ask different questions about the social world. Some ask questions about social order and

Channeling C. Wright Mills

In this exercise, you will research and explain to a peer how your life would have been different in a past century.

Recall what C. Wright Mills said about how the society in which we live influences our lives. Imagine you were living in the society you are in now 100 or 200 years ago (pick one). Look up information on your demographic group (people of your same age, gender, ethnicity, race, etc.) during this time period. The following websites may be useful resources:

www.quora.com/What-was-American-culture-like-in-the-1800s-in-comparison-to-the-1900s-How-much-had-changed-in-that-time

www.wic.org/misc/history.htm

http://pages.pomona.edu/~vis04747/h21/readings/Gutman_Work_Culture_Society.pdf

1. Using the information you found (be sure to cite your sources), describe how, if you lived during that time period, your life would be different in terms of how you would be perceived by (a) your parents, (b) other members of society, and (c) yourself.

2. Share your answer to question 1 with a classmate.

3. How did having good sources of information and examples help you make your point in a more convincing way? How does this help show the importance of using solid social scientific data to support an argument?

cohesion (e.g., How do the various parts of society work together?), some ask questions about problems in society (e.g., Why is there inequality?), and some ask questions about the ways we see ourselves in relation to others (e.g., How do our interactions with others influence how we see ourselves?). You will learn more about the most important theoretical perspectives that sociologists use in Chapter 2 and about topic-specific (middle-range) theories that fall under their respective umbrellas throughout the book.

The Scientific Research Process

To understand how society operates and to test our perspectives and theories about how society works, sociologists must collect and analyze data. We do so in systematic ways that we clearly describe and offer for critique from other social scientists and the general public. The purpose of sociological research is to constantly learn more about how society works. Doing so in open, systematic ways allows others to replicate our research process and to support our conclusions or reveal flaws in our data-gathering process and findings. Together, we gain a better, scientifically sound understanding of our society.

Sometimes, our findings are unexpected. For example, a sociologist who uses a theoretical lens that focuses on inequality and group conflict may be surprised to learn that a corporation she is

studying has a high level of camaraderie and evidence of strong teamwork among workers at all status levels. If our findings consistently diverge from our theoretical explanations, we need to adjust out theories accordingly. Sociologists are in the business of creating useful theories based on good generalizations.

Check Your Understanding

- What makes sociology a social science?

- How do sociologists use theoretical perspectives and theories?

- Why do sociologists collect data in open, systematic ways?

Differentiating between Good Generalizations and Stereotypes

Has anyone said to you that "you shouldn't generalize"? That was probably right after you said some disparaging remark about all the people from a particular town, all the movies starring a particular

Does this guy look like someone who just wants to crunch numbers all weekend? The movie *Harold and Kumar Go to White Castle* put a spotlight on some racial stereotypes about Asian Americans.

actor, or all roads in New Jersey. **Generalizations,** or statements used to describe groups of people or things in general terms, with the understanding that there can always be exceptions, tend to have a bad reputation among the general public. Sociologists, however, generalize all the time as they recognize and point out social patterns in society. We, however, aim to make good generalizations and avoid stereotyping.

Stereotypes

Predetermined ideas about particular groups of people (e.g., all Irish are drunks, all Asians are good at math) are called **stereotypes** and are passed on through hearsay or small samples and held regardless of evidence. Often, they are used to excuse discriminatory treatment. Stereotypes are bad generalizations. Some may be closer to the truth than others, but none is based on solid evidence.

Movies and television shows provide excellent examples of racial stereotypes. In one scene in the film *Harold and Kumar Go to White Castle,* the White, male boss hands Harold, a Korean American, a bunch of his work—so he can start his weekend early. The boss holds a stereotype of Asians that makes him think Harold (and all other Asians) "live for" crunching numbers. Of course, however, movie viewers know that work is the last thing Harold wants to do that weekend. More recently, in the television show *Awkward,* the only main Asian character, Ming, was relegated to stories about the sneaky, brilliant, and controlling "Asian mafia" at her high school and largely kept out of the rom-com scenes occupied by her White co-stars. After three seasons, both Ming and the Asian mafia were written out of the show— and seemingly not missed by any of the White characters!

Good Generalizations

Good generalizations, unlike stereotypes, are based on social scientific research. For example, one common stereotype is that women are "chatty Cathys" and talk incessantly. A good generalization, on the contrary, is that in mixed-sex conversations, men tend to talk and interrupt more than women. Women ask more questions than men and tend to work harder at fostering conversation, but it is men who tend to dominate verbal interactions (Gamble and Gamble 2015).

Did you notice how the generalizations in the paragraph above are phrased? Unlike the stereotype about "chatty Cathys," they describe what social scientists have found about speaking patterns without denigrating one sex or the other. Good generalizations are used to describe rather than judge groups of people.

Good generalizations also change or are discarded with new information. For example, the generalization that "most people in the United States oppose same-sex marriage" was once true but no longer qualifies as a good generalization. As our generalizations change with new data, so do our research questions. For example, we may now want to ask, What led to this change in attitudes toward same-sex marriage? And, will this acceptance of same-sex marriage also lead to national legislation to protect lesbian, gay, bisexual, and transgendered (LGBT) people from discrimination?

Check Your Understanding

- On what are stereotypes based?

- How do sociologists create good generalizations?

- How does new information affect (a) stereotypes and (b) good generalizations?

- For what purpose do sociologists use generalizations?

Stereotypes and Generalizations about College Students

In this exercise, you will examine the differences between good and bad generalizations.

1. Explain the difference between a stereotype and a generalization.

2. List three stereotypes you have heard about college students.

3. Now, do some research on college students (e.g., check out studies found at www.insidehighered.com/news/2013/04/25/new-study-links-student-motivations-going-college-their-success, http://blog.portfolium.com/7-trends-of-todays-college-students/, and www.bls.gov/tus/charts/students.htm).

4. Make three good generalizations about college students based on your research (be sure to cite your sources).

5. Describe how your good generalizations compare to the stereotypes you listed and how comparing them (and their sources) helps reveal the difference between stereotypes and good generalizations.

The Obligations of Sociology

The earliest sociologists used sociology to find ways to understand and to improve society. In 1896, Albion Small, the founder of the first accredited department of sociology in the United States, implored his fellow sociologists to do so with these words:

> I would have American scholars, especially in the social sciences, declare their independence of do-nothing traditions. I would have them repeal the law of custom which bars marriage of thought with action. I would have them become more profoundly and sympathetically scholarly by enriching the wisdom which comes from knowing with the larger wisdom which comes from doing. (Small 1896:564)

W. E. B. Du Bois, one of the key founders of sociology, whom many White sociologists of his era ignored due to their racism, needed no prodding. An African American, Harvard-trained scholar, Du Bois faced rejection when applying for tenured faculty positions at White colleges and universities due to his race. Undaunted, he spent his career leading research studies at Atlanta University, writing prolifically, and organizing civil rights efforts.

W. E. B. Du Bois, one of the founders of sociology, used sociological tools to show how society works and to fight racism.

Underwood Archives/Archive Photos/Getty Images

Throughout his long career, Du Bois carried out a combination of research and activism, achieving groundbreaking work in both areas. In the late nineteenth century, Du Bois conducted the first large-scale, empirical sociological research in the United States, with the clear goal of refuting racist ideas about African Americans (Morris 2015). Later, he helped found the National Association for the Advancement of Colored People (NAACP) and tirelessly promoted civil rights for African Americans. In the spirit of Du Bois and Small, Randall Collins (1998) has described two **core commitments** of sociology.

The Two Core Commitments

The first core commitment of sociology is *to use the sociological eye* to observe social patterns. The second requires noticing patterns of injustice and *taking action* to challenge those patterns. Collins and the sociologists who have authored this book believe that sociology should be used to make a positive impact on society. If you have developed a sociological eye, you are obligated to use it for the good of society. For example, if we perceive that in over half of the states in the United States, it is still legal to fire people based on their sexual orientation (in nonreligious institutions as well as in religious organizations), we should work to address that injustice.

Check Your Understanding

- For what purpose did the earliest sociologists use sociology?

- Why did W. E. B. Du Bois conduct large-scale empirical research in the United States?

- What are the two core commitments of sociology?

The Benefits of Sociology

Developing a sociological eye and gaining a sociological perspective will benefit both you and society. You will notice social patterns that many others cannot see. Even if these patterns are unpleasant (sexism, racism, ableism, etc.), noticing and understanding them will help you develop ways of dealing with them in your own life. Forewarned is forearmed. You can also see patterns that you can proactively use to your advantage (e.g., what careers will be most in demand soon, how to gain social

Consider This

Can you see yourself fulfilling the two core commitments of sociology in response to a particular issue? If yes, both or only one? Why? If not, why not? Do you think most of your peers would be able and willing to do so? Why?

capital useful in the job market, etc.). Through gaining a sociological perspective, you will learn how to act more effectively in groups and with members of different cultures. You will also gain the ability to collect, analyze, and explain information and to influence your society.

The last points concerning what you, personally, will gain from a sociological perspective relate to how sociology can help you contribute to society. Just knowing how society operates and how individuals are both shaped by and shapers of society can make you a more effective member of your community. You can learn how to work with others to improve your campus, workplace, neighborhood, and society. As seen in the following Sociologists in Action box, William Edmundson provides an excellent example of how sociology students can use sociological tools to benefit both individuals and society.

Sociology and Democracy

In democratic societies, it is particularly important for citizens who vote in elections to understand how society works and to develop the ability to notice social patterns. It is also vital that they be able to understand the difference between good information and fake news. Can you tell what news to trust? Checking to see if the data described in a news source were gained through the scientific research process and knowing how to tell the difference between good generalizations and stereotypes will help you discern real news from fake news.

Fake news became increasingly common during the 2016 presidential campaign. One piece "BREAKING: 'Tens of thousands' of fraudulent Clinton votes found in Ohio warehouse" was shared more than 6 million times on social media before the election. Cameron Harris, a recent college graduate,

The Clothesline Project

William Edmundson

In the fall semester of 2015, I helped lead the Clothesline Project on Virginia Wesleyan College's campus. I was able to do so through Dr. Alison Marganski's Family Violence: Causes, Consequences, and Responses course. The Clothesline Project is a community education campaign on the issue of violence against women—see www.clotheslineproject.info/ (note: our class also extended this to include other forms/types of family violence to be more inclusive of other victimization experiences).

Part of my contribution to the Clothesline Project were "Myth versus Facts" bookmarks; one focused on the victim while another focused on the abuser, and both displayed common myths with corresponding facts as well as local resources available both on and off campus. My classmates and I distributed them to students, staff, and faculty who stopped by the weeklong event to make a T-shirt to support the project. Through creating and distributing the bookmarks, I educated myself as well as others to recognize myths about domestic violence and to replace them with the facts they serve to mask.

Throughout our class, my classmates and I learned of the need for education with respect to family violence, including violence against women. The Clothesline Project enabled those directly affected by such violence to tell their stories through T-shirts they created and provided a form for the community to learn more about—and take a stand against—domestic violence. One victim both created a shirt and came into our class to share her story.

Additional course-related activities included advertising the event, running the T-shirt creation table, and displaying the created T-shirts at the end of the event.

Toward the end of the project, our class took all of the almost 100 T-shirts created during the weeklong event and hung them up across a walkway on campus. Hanging up the shirts served to both raise awareness and provide a medium for participants' voices to be heard. The strategic placement of these shirts allowed the entire campus community to gain exposure to the messages created by the participants.

My experience as a leader in the Clothesline Project taught me the extent of planning and networking required for such community outreach events. As a class, we were able to form connections with local organizations, such as the Samaritan House and the YWCA, whose members also distributed materials at the event. Hosting the Clothesline Project provided me with valuable organizing experience and helped me to create valuable networks with local organizations for potential volunteering positions, internships, or even jobs in the future. Perhaps the most important lesson I learned from the Clothesline Project was just how big of a role I could play in educating Virginia Wesleyan College about societal issues from a sociological perspective.

William Edmundson is a criminal justice major at Virginia Wesleyan College in Norfolk, Virginia.

created a fake news site, ChristianTimesNewspaper.com, and included a picture of some ballot boxes in a warehouse (no one could tell that the warehouse was in England, not Ohio) to make his story appear "real" to viewers who did not realize the need to look into the veracity of the news source or the information described in the story (Shane 2017). The completely fabricated story took off. It's hard to know how much this one story influenced the election, but it was far from the only fake news story sweeping across social media before Americans went to vote (you may remember "Pizzagate," one of the more famous of the fake news stories leading up the election) (Fisher, Cox, and Hermann 2016). Today, a

sociologically informed public is more necessary than ever for a democratic society.

> **Consider This**
> Give an example of how you can use sociology to understand how society works and to help shape society.

The Value of Sociology for All

In this exercise, you will write and deliver a brief statement explaining the value of sociology.

Imagine that you have been selected to represent all college students in the United States who have taken a sociology course. As part of your duties, you have been asked to present to the American Association of State Colleges and Universities a three- to five-paragraph statement on (a) how gaining a sociological perspective benefits both individuals and a democratic society and (b) why all public colleges and universities in the United States should make sociology a mandatory course for college students.

1. Write a draft and present it to a friend. Be sure to use information from this text (and feel free to find other good information about sociology, too). Cite your sources.

2. After the presentation, ask your friend for feedback and refine your statement.

3. Repeat this process twice more, so that you have presented and revised your statement three times.

4. Describe how and why your statement changed from the first draft to the last.

5. How convincing do you think your final draft is? Why?

Sociology and Careers

Finally, as noted earlier, sociological knowledge is useful in any career you can imagine—including teaching, business management, politics, human resources, medical administration, social work, nonprofit management, and marketing. For example, to be effective, social workers need to understand the populations they serve and the structural and cultural forces affecting them. A marketer must have the research skills to learn what appeals to different groups and how to advertise to each most persuasively. Managers need cultural competency to create a motivated and engaged workforce. From knowing what job to apply for, what skills you need to gain it, and how to conduct yourself in the workplace to advance, sociological skills can help you to succeed in the workforce. In each of the chapters that follow, take note of the sociological skills you gain and in what professions you might use them.

Check Your Understanding

- How can sociology benefit individuals?

- How can sociology benefit society, particularly democratic societies?

- How might you use sociology in your career?

Conclusion

In this introductory chapter, you learned that sociology, the scientific study of society, provides myriad benefits to both individuals and to society. We now turn to how sociologists make sense of how society operates by looking at the different major sociological perspectives. As you will see, each perspective views the world in distinct ways. As you read the chapter, think about which perspective(s) make the most sense to you.

⑤SAGE edge™

Want a better grade? Get the tools you need to sharpen your study skills. Access practice quizzes, eFlashcards, video and multimedia at **edge.sagepub.com/korgen**

Review

1.1 What is sociology?

Sociology is the scientific study of society, including how individuals both *shape* and *are shaped* by society.

1.2 What do the sociological eye and the sociological imagination allow you to do?

A sociological eye enables you to see what others may not notice. It allows you to peer beneath the surface of a situation and discern social patterns. The sociological imagination gives you the ability to connect what is happening in your own life and in the lives of others to social patterns in the larger society.

1.3 What key aspects of sociology make it a social *science*?

Sociologists use theories and the scientific research process to formulate research questions and collect and analyze data to better understand how society operates.

1.4 How can you tell the difference between a good generalization and a stereotype?

Good generalizations, unlike stereotypes, are based on social scientific research, used to describe rather than judge groups, and change or are discarded with new information.

1.5 What are the core commitments of sociology?

The first of the two core commitments is to use the sociological eye to observe social patterns. The second commitment requires us to notice patterns of injustice and take action to challenge those patterns. Sociology should be used to make a positive impact on society.

1.6 How can sociology benefit both individuals and society?

Through gaining a sociological perspective, you will learn to notice and deal with patterns others do not recognize; act more effectively in groups and with members of different cultures; collect, analyze, and explain information; and influence your society.

Sociological knowledge is useful in any career you can imagine.

In democratic societies, it is particularly important for citizens to develop the ability to notice social patterns and how to tell the difference between good generalizations and stereotypes.

Key Terms

- core commitments   12
- generalizations   10
- sociological eye   5
- sociological imagination   6
- sociology   3
- stereotypes   10

We all have perspectives or ways of seeing the world, but few of us are aware of alternative points of view.

Learning Questions

2.1 Why and how do sociologists use theoretical perspectives?

2.2 What is structural functionalism?

2.3 What is a conflict perspective?

2.4 What is symbolic interactionism?

2.5 How do structural functionalism, conflict perspectives, and symbolic interactionism work together to help us get a more complete view of reality?

Understanding Theory

Kathleen S. Lowney

What Is Theory?

Children often will try on another person's glasses. Sometimes they will see worse—things look out of focus and fuzzy—but other times, they will see better. Imagining theory as a pair of glasses that we put on to look at the social world can be a helpful metaphor. Theory can help us see some social patterns more clearly, while obscuring others.

Theories help us to notice and make sense of social patterns in society. Theories, therefore, are tools for understanding people's lives and how society works. A **theory** is created by one or a small number of sociologists working together; it attempts to explain a particular aspect of the social structure or a kind of social interaction between individuals.

When sociology was first created as a separate academic discipline in Western Europe, it primarily revolved around famous scholars, such as Émile Durkheim, Karl Marx, and Max Weber. In the mid-twentieth century, the focus shifted to the United States and to creating "families of theories." These "families" are what sociologists call **theoretical perspectives,** groups of theories that share certain common ways of "seeing" how society works. This chapter focuses on the three main theoretical perspectives in sociology—structural functionalism, conflict theory, and symbolic interaction—and how each of them "sees" or explains the social world.

Check Your Understanding

- What is theory?
- What is the difference between a theory and a theoretical perspective?

Understanding the Structural Functionalist Perspective

The view of modern societies as consisting of interdependent parts working together for the good of the whole is known as **structural functionalism.** Individuals work for the larger society's

Kathleen S. Lowney

I went to college knowing that I wanted to study religion. But then I took Introduction to Sociology—799 other students and I (yes, the course was 800 students!)—and I was hooked. Learning about structure, agency, and sociological theories gave me a language and intellectual framework to see the social world which I still use today. So the third day of that first quarter of college, I added sociology as another major. The questions that consume me still focus on the intersection of religion and sociology, be they about the new religion that I studied for my doctoral dissertation or for the last nineteen years when I have studied adolescent Satanism. I welcome each of you to the study of the academic discipline that I love.

interests, rather than their own, due to **social solidarity,** or the moral order of society. Families, religion, education, and other institutions teach individuals to help society function smoothly.

Consider This

Every theoretical perspective has been influenced by the life experiences of those who created the perspective. Think of how you make sense of your society. Do you believe anyone can "make it" in society if they just work hard enough? Or do some have more advantages than others? How have your life experiences influenced the "glasses" you use to see the world?

Durkheim and Types of Societies

Émile Durkheim, writing in the early 1900s, examined social solidarity throughout history. In smaller, preindustrial societies, social solidarity derived from the similarity of its members, what Durkheim referred to as **mechanical solidarity.** Most did similar types of labor (working the land) and had similar beliefs (based on religion).

As societies evolved and as science gained predominance over religion and jobs became differentiated during the industrial era, a different type of solidarity, an **organic solidarity,** formed. These societies operated more like a living organism, with various parts, each specializing in only certain tasks but dependent on

the others for survival (e.g., the circulatory system and the digestive system perform different functions, but if one does not do its job, the other will not survive). Durkheim argued that for a society based on organic solidarity to be "healthy" (i.e., in social harmony and in order), all the "parts" of the society had to be working well together, in an interconnected way, just as in a human body. Thus, sociologists who use this theoretical perspective tend to focus on **social harmony** and **social order.** They often overlook issues such as conflict and inequality. Instead, structural functionalists emphasize the role of the major social institutions and how they help to provide stability to society.

Social Institutions

What are **social institutions**? They are sets of statuses and roles focused around one central aspect of society (think of social institutions as similar to the different organ systems in a human body). A status is the position a person occupies in a particular institution. For example, you occupy the status position of college student. But you are also a son or daughter, a former high school student, and a member of many other groups. So, you have multiple status positions. A role is composed of the many behaviors that go into occupying a status. So part of your role as a college student is to come to class, on time, and be prepared.

These statuses that each individual occupies and the roles that they play come together to form the unique social structure of a group, an organization, an institution, or a society. Once the group becomes large enough, social institutions form around accomplishing the tasks central to the survival of the group. Thus, while social institutions are made up of individuals fulfilling their roles (what sociologists call the **micro level of analysis,** which focuses on either an individual or very small groups), social institutions are also much more than these individuals—they are societal (what sociologists refer to as the **macro level of analysis,** which focuses on the overall social structure

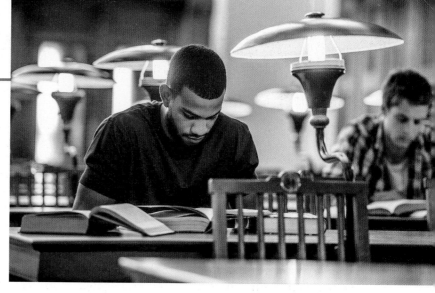

Studying is an important part of your role as a student.

©iStockphoto.com/vm

of society, and large-scale societal forces that affect groups of people) in nature.

Structural functionalists note that there are seven primary social institutions: family, religion, economy, education, government, health care, and media. These seven institutions cover nearly all the major aspects of a modern society. Each social institution fulfills tasks on behalf of society. Structural functionalism calls these tasks functions. There are two types of functions. Let's talk about one at a time.

Manifest Functions

The obvious, stated reasons that a social institution exists are known as **manifest functions.** Structural functionalists maintain that manifest functions of each institution fulfill necessary tasks in society. For example, let's look at the social institution of the family. One function the family performs is to encourage individuals to procreate—to have children. Otherwise, a society would likely die after one generation, wouldn't it? So a manifest function of the family institution in any society is reproduction. But institutions can have more than one manifest function. Families are also responsible for raising and instructing their children. In particular, families teach the children the cultural norms and values of their particular society, a process known as socialization.

Consider education as a social institution. What tasks does the education institution do for society? It teaches those in school the knowledge that society says is important to know in order to be a contributing adult member of that society. In the United States today, that includes grammar, spelling, mathematics, U.S. and world history, and many basic computer skills.

Latent Functions

Manifest functions are only the first type of function that structural functionalists use to examine the social world. They also use latent functions. **Latent functions** are good or useful things that a social institution does but are not the institution's reason for existing.

Let's return to the family institution for a moment. We know that its manifest function is to reproduce and then socialize children, so that the society can continue on indefinitely into the future. But family as a social institution supports the society in many other ways. Families help out the economic institution, for example, when they purchase food or school supplies or pay rent or buy a house. Helping the economy is a good thing, but it is not a family's core function.

> **Consider This**
> What might be some latent functions of the educational institution?

Latent functions almost always link to a second social institution (e.g., both family and education support the economic institution). These connections between one social institution and another build the social harmony that structural functionalists see when they look at society.

Sometimes behavioral patterns have unintended consequences, called **dysfunctions.** For example, the United States built the interstate highway system to move people and products more quickly from location to location, which helps the economic institution. But that good idea also led to an increase in air pollution (a dysfunction) because more people purchased cars and chose to drive, because locations were so much easier to get to and from.

Seeing the Social World Using Structural Functionalism

Structural functionalism is a macro-theoretical perspective. That means that its **unit of analysis,** the thing being examined, is society as a whole, rather than an individual or subculture. Imagine a sociologist

Manifest and Latent Functions of Institutions

*I*n this exercise, you will identify the manifest and latent functions of the seven social institutions.

Sociologists recognize seven key social institutions. Each institution has both manifest and latent functions. Think of at least one manifest and one latent function of each institution, then complete the following table.

Social Institution	Manifest Function(s)	Latent Function(s)
Economy		
Education		
Family		
Government		
Health care/medicine		
Media		
Religion		

standing at a distance and looking at how society is working. In this case, sociologists look for social order and harmony when they put on structural functionalism's glasses.

In looking at the big picture of society, functionalist sociologists focus less on discrete individuals and their daily lives and interactions with each other. Instead, they analyze social institutions and how they fit together to build social harmony and stability. So, for example, structural functionalists study the institution of the family, not individual families, to learn how social institutions function to meet societal needs. While particular families may not fulfill each of the functions, as a social institution, the family can and must carry out certain functions in order for society to function smoothly. By concentrating on social institutions, structural functionalism rises above the unique ways that millions of families go about their daily lives of cooking, taking out the garbage, cleaning up after each other, loving each other, raising children, and so on to focus on the vital role with which the institution of family is charged by society: to birth and then socialize children.

Using the structural functionalist lens, sociologists see that social institutions construct stability and order. In large part, this is because several institutions (e.g., family, religion, and education) have cooperated to socialize each of us into adhering to the same set of cultural norms and values. Thus, American drivers stay on the right side of the road, we stop at stop signs, we more or less follow the speed limit, and so on. We also don't rob banks or commit murder. Put differently, most citizens of a society are "good" people who follow the social norms.

Curbing Violations of Social Norms

But what about an individual who chooses to act against those shared cultural norms? How does structural functionalism see that person? First and foremost, that person—for whatever reason—is violating social norms. Perhaps he or she was not properly socialized by parents and thus did not learn the norms of society or may have learned them but do not see the norms as being acceptable (see Chapter 6). Or, perhaps the person might simply be selfish and putting her or his needs ahead of what is best for society.

So let's talk about a bank robber for a moment. He or she should have learned from family, teachers, and

Structural Functionalism in Newspapers

In this activity, you will find an example of structural functionalism in the media and write a brief explanation of your reasoning.

Find a newspaper article that uses the structural functionalist view of social problems. Think about how structural functionalists see society: social harmony, with a high degree of social order, and social institutions meeting their manifest and latent functions. Your article should illustrate at least one of those structural functionalist concepts.

1. Write one to two paragraphs explaining why the article you found represents this theoretical perspective.

2. Come to class prepared to share your article and your analysis with other students.

perhaps religious leaders that robbing a bank is not socially acceptable behavior. But despite those socializing messages, the person still chose to rob a bank. The person has stepped outside of the moral order of the community and must be punished (once caught, of course). But why? Why is punishment needed? Structural functionalist theorists believe that punishment is required for at least two reasons. First, accepting one's punishment is a step in the rehabilitation/resocialization process of the individual back into the community (if deemed possible). Second, structural functionalist theorists, building on the sociological work of Émile Durkheim, also worry that without punishment, "bad" behavior will spread like an epidemic in the community. If you were a customer in the bank and see the bank robber get a bunch of money and never get caught, then you might try to get away with something bad too. And then a third person might see you do that act of unpunished bad behavior and do something else . . . and so on. Soon, the social order will have broken down completely. So structural functionalists note the importance of punishing the deviant individual to "head off" future deviance acts—not only by that person but by others in the society who might use that person as a positive role model.

Social Change

Given this background, you can begin to predict how structural functionalist theorists view **social change.** What is social change? Sociologists see change happening when there are large-scale, macro, structural shifts in society or institutions within one or more societies. Functionalists, because they see harmony deriving from the stable functioning of institutions and cooperation among them, are not so sure that a lot of social change is necessarily a good thing. Change in one institution rips apart the social harmony and equilibrium between it and the other institutions and requires a long time for the other social institutions

We avoid accidents in traffic circles by following the norms for their use.

©iStockphoto.com/pro6x7

During World War II, women worked in formerly male-dominated jobs like these in the Douglas Aircraft factory in California.

to "catch up" and to reestablish social equilibrium. So theorists using a structural functionalist perspective would argue that, if change is needed at all, it should be done very slowly so as not to upset the equilibrium that undergirds the society and makes it strong.

What Doesn't Structural Functionalism See?

Can rapid social change and the disharmony that comes along with it ever be a good thing for society to experience? Structural functionalist theorists would argue that no, it wouldn't—indeed couldn't—be a good thing. But think about that more deeply and use your sociological imagination.

Imagine we could go back in time to America in the mid-1940s, just after World War II ended. Pick nearly any town in the United States; what was it like? Let's just focus on one social institution—economics. Most likely, many men were just returning from fighting overseas, and many women were still in the paid workforce. During the war, more women held jobs than they had before. As the war ended, many men came back home and wanted, even needed, their jobs back. Some women wanted to go back to primarily working only in the home, but others didn't. Of course, some—those widowed by the war, for instance—had to keep working to pay the family's bills. Some women were upset that they were urged to leave the labor force and return home to have babies and keep house. They resented the fact that their job opportunities were limited to so few fields, such as nursing and education.

How would a functionalist evaluate this situation? While they might not support the sex discrimination clearly evident in the labor force, they would want slow, incremental change to occur, because they could see how immediate gender equality in the workplace would create upheaval in the labor force. So they might have argued for the benefits of many women returning to unpaid labor while also advocating for public discussions and education about the possible merits of changing laws and regulations that discriminated against women in the workforce.

But another way of thinking about slow, gradual social change is that it would allow continued discrimination. Structural functionalism, by focusing on the need for social order and harmony, can overlook times in the life of the society where rapid social change—even if it may lead to some social chaos—is the just thing to do.

Using Structural Functionalism to Analyze the Case of the Meitiv Family

We will now make use of the structural functionalist perspective to examine an incident that hit the news in 2015: the case of Danielle and Alexander Meitiv; their two children, Rafi, age ten, and Dvora, age six; the Montgomery, Maryland, police; and the Child Protective Services of Maryland (for more about this case, including video, check out the sources at the end of the chapter). On December 20, 2014, the Meitiv children were at a local park at 5 p.m. and started to walk the one mile back to their house, alone. Three blocks from their destination, they were stopped by the police and taken to police headquarters. Later that night, they were placed in the custody of Child Protective Services (CPS). The Meitivs did get their children back later that evening but were told that they were under investigation by CPS. Asked why they let their children walk the one mile from the park to their home, they stated that "children learn self-reliance by being allowed to make choices, build independence and progressively experience the world on their own" (St. George 2015c, paragraph 16). Almost two months

Alexander Meitiv, right, prepares dinner with the help of his daughter, Dvora, and son, Rafi. The Meitivs' "free-range parenting" led to their facing charges of child neglect.

later, CPS completed its investigation, with a finding of "unsubstantiated child abuse" (St. George 2015c, paragraph 1). But the case was far from over.

Just a few months later, the parents dropped both children off at another park at 4 p.m. and told them to be home by 6 p.m. At 4:58 p.m., a man walking his dog called local police about two children who were unsupervised in the park. The man did not approach or talk with the children before placing the call. Police detained both children again, taking them immediately to CPS, where they were held without being allowed to contact their parents for a few days. Another CPS investigation was launched against their parents, questioning their ability to protect and parent their children correctly.

Why might the Meitiv parents allow their children to walk home alone? Are they just bad parents, too lazy to take proper care of them? No. The Meitivs practice what is called "free-range parenting," a parenting philosophy that encourages parents to allow children to grow up independently, with a minimum of adult supervision, appropriate to the age of the children. Free-range parents feel that American society prevents children from learning to be truly self-sufficient.

Let's analyze the situation at this point. From a structural functionalist perspective, the manifest functions of the family as a social institution are to reproduce and then socialize the children to accept and follow the prevailing values in society. Obviously, the Meitivs have children, so their family has met that first manifest function. Where this example gets murky is when we shift our attention to the second manifest function.

The United States as a society values individualism and independence, and therefore parents are expected to teach their children to be self-reliant and independent. The devil's in the details, though. *How* should they teach them independence and at *what* age? Are children aged six and ten too young to be walking alone on a moderately busy street? Is it abuse or neglect if a parent teaches this particular instance of self-reliance "too soon" (i.e., at a time when many in society feel it is inappropriate)? And should parents who do so be judged "bad parents" by authorities—in this case, law enforcement and Child Protective Services?

Here's the rest of the story. After the second instance of CPS and law enforcement involvement, the story was reported widely, and more and more individuals began to weigh in publicly, writing comments on online news articles and other social media. A social movement even sprang up after the first incident (St. George and Schulte 2015), which led, after the second incident, to a petition to change Maryland's laws, about allowing children to be outside alone without parental supervision. Other petitions were created and sent to county officials. For their part, the Meitivs filed a lawsuit against CPS and Montgomery County's law enforcement.

Consider This

If you were working in the Maryland Child Protective Services, tasked with helping children in need, how would you feel about the Meitivs' parenting style? Think especially about your judgment of the parents' choice to let their children walk home alone the *second* time.

This second investigation by CPS ended with "neglect 'ruled out'" (St. George 2015a, paragraphs 1, 7), and the case was closed. A spokesperson for Maryland's Department of Human Resources (to which CPS reports) added that "a child playing outside or walking unsupervised does not meet the criteria for a CPS response absent specific information supporting the conclusion that the child has been harmed or is at substantial risk of harm if they continue to be unsupervised" (St. George 2015a, paragraph 10).

Notice how this case shows the interrelatedness of social institutions (e.g., family and government), which is at the core of structural functionalism. Those using a structural functionalist perspective likely would leave unquestioned the assumption that family, law enforcement, and CPS all had a duty to be concerned about children in general and the Meitivs' two children in particular. Each agency's duty and, therefore, their employees' behavior were grounded in its manifest function.

Structural functionalists would likely argue that in a populous community like Montgomery County, Maryland, most parents would not allow a six-year-old to play unsupervised and walk back home at night, even in the company of a ten-year-old sibling. If this *is* the value consensus, then law enforcement and CPS's decisions to take the children into custody and investigate their home life could be easily justified as correct. CPS's initial review was meant to teach the Meitivs how to better parent their children and, simultaneously, to reinforce proper parenting behaviors to all who live in the county.

Consider This

Be a structural functionalist. What evidence in society can you find to illustrate that there is a consensus on how parents should raise children in the United States today?

Could other sociologists look at the story of what happened to the Meitiv family and reach different sociological conclusions? Let's turn next to the other macro-sociological theoretical perspective—conflict—and look at how sociologists using that perspective see social reality. Then we'll return to the Meitiv family as our example.

Check Your Understanding

- What do structural functionalists see as the cause of social problems? Why?
- Why do structural functionalists want social change to happen slowly?

- What social institutions were involved in the Meitiv incidents?
- Can you retell the story of the Meitiv family using the structural functionalist concepts of social institutions, manifest function, latent function, social harmony, and shared values?

Understanding the Conflict Theoretical Perspective

The second macro-theoretical perspective is **conflict theory.** The **conflict perspective** is rooted in the scholarship of Karl Marx, a nineteenth-century thinker. Marx studied history and economics to see how human societies grow and change. In doing so, he created a revolutionary theory of social change called economic determinism.

Karl Marx and Advanced Capitalism

Marx believed that there were ten stages of societal development but was most concerned with the last three stages. Given that, we'll start with stage 8, advanced capitalism. Marx held that advanced capitalism is an economic system based on profit and the pursuit of maximum profit. Capitalism divides people into two major categories and a third, smaller group. There are the **bourgeoisie,** the rich owners of the **means of production** (the technology and materials needed to produce products, such as factories), and the **proletariat,** the poor workers (in the factories, etc.). The perpetually unemployed comprise the third group, the **lumpenproletariat.**

The advanced capitalism of Marx's time was a far cry from what we know capitalism to be today in the United States. Since there were no labor laws and it was so much cheaper to hire children than adults, there were large numbers of children in the labor force. The bourgeoisie, eager to maximize profits, would hire children even if they could not completely manage the physical or intellectual tasks required on the job. There were no inspectors making sure that the workplace was safe, so many proletariat were injured. There was no worker's compensation insurance either, so injured proletariat faced a difficult choice: show up and work despite the injury (but face the wrath of the owner for working slower) or quit work to heal—and starve. Wages were incredibly low because the bourgeoisie could use the ever-growing pool of lumpenproletariat as a stick over any worker who dared ask for a raise. Such a worker would be fired, as it was very easy to find a member of the lumpenproletariat who would work for the original wage (or an even lower one).

False Consciousness

For Marx and like-minded individuals of the time period, the exploitation of the proletariat by the bourgeoisie was a bit puzzling at first. Why didn't the proletariat realize how economically exploited they were under advanced capitalism and, for instance, stop showing up for work? Surely that would bring down the capitalist system.

Marx theorized that the workers were in a state of **false consciousness.** They collectively and individually did not understand just how badly they were being treated; they were, he argued, misled. They believed that, if they just worked hard every day, they too might become a member of the bourgeoisie. The media of the day, the religious institution, and the political institution all promulgated this: a good worker, in time, could "strike it rich" and get in on the many advantages of capitalism. But that was not going to happen for most if not all proletariat, living on a subsistence wage while the factory owner was living in a huge home, profiting from the proletariat's hard work. Yet their false consciousness kept them from seeing the reality of their lives—as members of the proletariat, they were compelled to work on a factory floor, sewing button after button for sixteen hours a day, for the rest of their lives. Was this really what life should be, Marx asked?

Species Being and Alienation

No, it was not. The human race had what Marx called **species being**—the unique potential to imagine and then create what we imagine. Humans can sketch fantastically intricate designs and then make them become real in the world. No other animal can do that. But the proletariat were prevented from living up to their species being by the very nature of the capitalist exploitation they endured. They lived in a state of **alienation;** the proletariat were forced to give up on their creativity, their ability to imagine and then create. Instead, they were alienated from their true selves by having to work so hard for someone else, the bourgeoisie. The proletariat had no say in the structure of their workday or in the product that they created. Their monotonous jobs were small and repetitious; they often never even knew what the finished product of their labor looked like. Worse yet, they couldn't afford the products that they were making. Alienation was sapping the proletariat's species being and it was increasing.

Karl Marx and Socialism

Marx felt that, to move the proletariat from false consciousness to **true consciousness,** the proletariat had to come to grips with the depths of their exploitation by the bourgeoisie. He believed that his writing, along with others, would "wake them up" from their state of alienated false consciousness and lead them to bring about change in their society.

Marx believed that, when the proletarian revolution began, society would move from the eighth stage of societal development, advanced capitalism, into the ninth stage, socialism. This ninth stage was a sort of "working it out" stage of social change. Economically, things would be more just than under capitalism but not yet truly equal. In socialism, children would be off the factory floors and sent to free public schools while able-bodied adults would work. The state would take over the means of production from the bourgeoisie through imposing a heavy progressive income tax on all adult citizens. This tax would economically hurt only the bourgeoisie (although many in that group were expected to die in the revolution). A proletariat worker, with almost no income, would not have to pay much. This tax would ensure that rich families would no longer be able to pass money, property, and other expensive goods down to the next generation via the inheritance laws. After a bourgeoisie died, the socialist government would "inherit" the rest of their money and goods and redistribute it to the citizens.

Socialism, Marx predicted, would last a few generations. He felt that the values of capitalism, such as support for the accumulation of wealth in the hands of just a few, the acquisition of goods as a sign of high status, and so forth, would take a while to die out. It might take a generation or two with people who had grown up only under socialism as an economic system before society would be ready for the tenth stage of social development: communism.

Consider This

If you were alive when Marx was and you were a wealthy owner of a factory who'd been planning to pass down your wealth to your children, what would you think of Marx's new economic system called socialism? Why? And how would you feel as a member of the proletariat?

Karl Marx and Communism

Marx's vision of communism never became a reality, not even in nations that refer to themselves as communist. He believed that, after a few generations of socialism as an economic system, some of the key social institutions, such as the political and economic systems, would no longer be needed and would disappear. Under **communism,** all citizens would be equal and, at long last, able to fulfill their species being. Each person could contemplate and then go create. There would be no social classes under communism, because every person would make the same wage for work done.

All of these stages of social change are economic ones. Remember, Marx is often called an economic determinist. The social institution that was the base of the society, for him, was always the economy. He believed that, as the economy changed from advanced capitalism to socialism and ultimately to communism, the other six social institutions would necessarily change and adapt.

From Marx to the Conflict Perspective

It was in the 1960s, mostly in the United States, that Marx's theory became the intellectual foundation for our second macro-theoretical perspective: the conflict perspective. Conflict theorists hold on to some of his theoretical insights while modifying others.

At the root of Marx's theory is the idea that society is divided into competing classes: those who own the means of production and those who work for the owners. Conflict theorists today argue that Marx's analysis was too narrow. Oppression does not have to be only economic in nature. Rather, modern conflict theorists recognize many ways in which social rewards are unequally distributed (e.g., race, ethnicity, gender, sex, sexual orientation, citizenship status, age, ability/disability).

Since inequalities go beyond economic oppression, sociologists using the conflict perspective use different terms to reflect this social reality. They talk about the haves—those individuals and social institutions that gain access to more of society's scarce rewards—and the have-nots—those who are unable to get even their fair share of social rewards, due to their category membership. Noneconomic rewards include access to political power, education, and social status or prestige.

Seeing the Social World Using the Conflict Perspective

Again, conflict is a macro-theoretical perspective; it analyzes society as a whole. But while structural functionalist theorists examine society and see social order and harmony, conflict theorists see something completely different. They see oppression: the haves holding the have-nots back to maintain their own elevated status.

Conflict theorists note that the haves practice **value coercion,** wherein they use their power over the seven major institutions to force their values onto the have-nots, as part of their effort to maintain their higher status positions in society. The media, for example, rarely tell stories about the working class. When they do, the stories often make them appear deviant—buffoonish (think Homer Simpson) or overweight (think Mama June from *Toddlers and Tiaras* and *Here Comes Honey Boo Boo,* before she lost weight). Television news also participates in this value coercion, when they use racial terms to describe criminals of color but conveniently ignore race when the deviant is White (Mastro et al. 2009). Repeated over and over, these media messages socialize people into thinking that poor equals bad, or Black or Hispanic equals criminal. These messages support the skewed social structure that the haves created.

Conflict thinkers, unlike structural functionalists, do not see social problems as the result of the behavior of some "bad" individuals. Rather, they regard the inequitable distribution of resources and rewards as the cause of most social problems. Conflict theorists would ask what made the person so desperate as to commit a crime? What other opportunities to attain money do people from her social background have? Is this behavior part of a pattern due to one group in society oppressing another? For example, did the owner of the factory where she worked fire all the workers in town and ship jobs overseas?

Many conflict theorists aren't satisfied with merely recognizing such inequalities; they go that next step and suggest ways that they and others can reduce, if not completely eliminate, the oppression that they observe. Like Marx, sociologists who take a conflict perspective advocate social change to help the have-nots in society to gain more of society's rewards. And, unlike most structural functionalists, who want social change to be slow and gradual so as not to upset the social harmony between social institutions, conflict theorists believe that social change to alleviate social injustice should be done rapidly. For conflict thinkers, slow, gradual social change is merely another term for continued oppression. They want to help the have-nots—now.

What Doesn't Conflict See?

The conflict perspective is so laser focused on oppression and making life better for the have-nots that it can overlook moments when society is going along fairly well. By concerning itself primarily with injustices and oppression, conflict can overlook times of societal harmony and equilibrium. Moreover, conflict theorists do not always acknowledge how disruptive and harmful change can be—for the have-nots as well as the haves.

Subperspectives in Conflict Theory

The conflict perspective, while unified in the focus on oppression and efforts to combat it, has divided into subperspectives. For example, feminist conflict theorists argue that men as a category of people have greater access to social rewards than women (see Chapter 8 for more on this). Meanwhile, critical race theorists focus on the social construction of race and the White-dominated racial hierarchy (see Chapter 9). All conflict theorists, however, build on Marx's insight that some individuals and groups have more resources and rewards than others do, and this is unjust.

Disability scholars frequently use the conflict perspective to analyze how modern Western societies create the built environment (the architecture of public and private spaces) in ways that work for the able-bodied but not for those people living with disabilities. Why, for example, cannot every entrance to a building include a ramp? Often only one entrance is "made accessible." Notice that the language used implies that creating accessibility is an "extra," something that must be added to a structure rather than an organic part of every building. With that kind of a mind-set, it becomes easy to see that "normal bodies" are the standard against which all others are judged. Those of us with disabilities then are somehow lesser, deviant people and less deserving of access. As you can see, the fundamental assumption of the modern conflict theoretical perspective is still rooted in Marx's insight: the social rewards of society are not equally shared.

Using the Conflict Perspective to Understand the Meitiv Family

Now turn your attention back to the Meitiv family, who advocated free-range parenting, the way of parenting which encourages teaching children to be independent and autonomous from an early age. How might the conflict perspective analyze what happened to them? Recall the conflict perspective's basic assumption: different categories of people get different social rewards based on their location in the social structure. In the family's interactions with law enforcement and CPS, you can see a power imbalance right away.

An anonymous person placed a call to the police—without even talking to the children in question. Recall, an investigation had not yet occurred when the children first were detained by CPS. True, law enforcement and CPS workers were simply performing their jobs, but they represented the state and all of its power. The Meitiv parents, in contrast, had little or no power. Indeed, Alexander Meitiv had to listen to the police lecture him on the dangers of the modern world when the police finally did return the children after the first incident (St. George 2015a). Educated people (Alexander is a theoretical physicist, Danielle a climate-science consultant) discovered that they had not—at least in that moment—either the power or the freedom to decide how to raise their own offspring. And who had even less power in this situation? The children. Their feelings were ignored throughout the bureaucratic wrangling.

Now imagine the story playing out a bit differently. The family in question did not have an intact set of two parents but instead was led by a single parent. A poor, single parent. A poor, single parent of color who is working several jobs to make ends meet. Do you think that—at each step of the Meitivs' story—that this poor single parent of color would have been treated the same way as the Meitivs were? Would he or she have gotten the kids back the night of the first "walking alone" incident? Received a decision of "unsubstantiated child abuse" after the first incident? Still gotten the kids back after the second incident of them walking alone? Not had the children taken away, given the economic stress the

> **Consider This**
> What group(s) could be analyzed as the haves in the Meitivs' situation? Why?
>
> Who might be the have-nots? Why?

Nine-year-old Regina Harrell's mother was arrested and lost custody of Regina for almost three weeks because she allowed Regina to play in a park a block away from where she was working at a McDonald's.

AP Photo/Jeffrey Collins

family was under? Had enough money to sue CPS and law enforcement? In fact, might anyone have even placed the call to law enforcement at all had they seen two children of color walking alone? Or if there had been a call, might it have been less about concern for the children's *safety* and more about "what are those kids up to" (i.e., someone worried about what possible criminal behavior they might be about to do)?

Consider the 2014 South Carolina case involving Debra Harrell, a forty-six-year-old African American woman, and her nine-year-old daughter, Regina. Debra worked at a McDonald's and, lacking other childcare options, often had to bring her child with her. The girl would usually sit in the restaurant until her mother was done working, but on three days that summer, Debra allowed her child to play in a popular park nearby. On the third day, a parent of another child at the park asked Regina where her parents were. Alarmed when Regina told her that her mom was working, the parent called the police. Debra was then arrested on the charge of felony child neglect, and Regina was placed into foster care. Debra was released on $5,000.00 bail, but

Regina remained in foster care for seventeen days before being returned to her mother. Debra's arrest meant that she also lost her job (until media coverage pressured the local McDonald's to take her back) (CBS News 2014; Friedersdorf 2014; Reese 2014).

As tense as the Meitiv situation was, their race, education levels, and social class likely buffered them from the full power of CPS and the police, whereas families living in poor neighborhoods, who are people of color and who, like Debra Harrell, cannot afford to hire a private attorney, are often denied those opportunities to quickly "fix" the situation.

Check Your Understanding

- What are manifest functions of a social institution?

- According to Marx, why are the proletariat in a state of false consciousness in advanced capitalism?

- How does a society move from advanced capitalism to socialism, according to Marx?

- Can you explain what Marx meant by communism? Think about social classes, oppression, and so on.

- What are the conceptual differences between the terms *bourgeoisie* and *proletariat* and *haves* and *have-nots?* Can you correctly use these terms?

- According to conflict theorists, what is value coercion and how do the haves use it?

Consider This

U.S. society often states that "children are precious" and "children are so important," yet children have very few rights. Why do you think that is? How might a conflict theorist view this issue?

Understanding the Symbolic Interactionist Perspective

The macro-theoretical perspectives let sociologists see the big picture (the macro unit of analysis) of what is happening in the entire society, be it order and harmony (structural functionalism) or oppression (conflict). These theoretical lenses, however, miss something vital to the study of people in groups: interaction between individuals—the micro level. **Symbolic interactionism** provides that theoretical balance for sociology. As the micro-theoretical perspective, it asks questions macro perspectives do not. For example, we can use it to examine how any one person develops a sense of **self**—the knowledge that she or he is unique, separate from every other human, let alone from the furniture, a phone, the weather, or the book he or she is reading. It helps us study how meaning comes to be constructed and shared by a group of people. Symbolic interactionists view society as a social construction, continually constructed and reconstructed by individuals through their use of shared symbols.

The Social Construction of Reality

Interactionist theorists study how **culture**—the way of life of a particular group of people—comes to be created. Individuals come together around one or more shared purposes and begin to interact. This interaction, over time, becomes routinized in various ways. So, for example, when the individuals first interact, they may create a common greeting. That greeting gets repeated every time they meet and suddenly they have created a norm—an expectation about behavior. Now individuals *must* use this now-standardized greeting or else be judged by the group as deviant. These creators of the greeting continue to use it, further normalizing it for their group. They will then teach new members (either born into the group or converts to it) the greeting and pass it along to the next generation.

In effect, the group constructs its culture. Culture includes norms and the symbols through which we communicate (e.g., language, numbers, gestures, and the meaning we attach to objects such as a nation's flag, a swastika, and a cross). Culture also consists of values, what we believe to be good or bad, and material objects the group creates to make life easier and meaningful. All of these are social constructions. This raises a significant sociological question: how does this socially constructed content (i.e., culture)

get "inside" each person? Interactionists argue that happens through the process of socialization, the sharing of culture from generation to generation.

While socialization can happen at any time in a person's life, the most intense time for socialization is in childhood (what we often call **primary socialization**), so that will be our focus. George Herbert Mead and Charles Horton Cooley, the founders of the symbolic interactionist perspective, both emphasized the importance of the socialization process. You will learn more about Mead's work in Chapter 5. In this chapter, we will focus on Cooley's contributions. Through his "looking glass self" theory, he described how a child develops a sense of self in three steps.

The Looking Glass Self Theory

A child's first step in developing a sense of self is to imagine how she appears to relevant others—her parents, siblings, grandparents, and so on. Cooley argued that it isn't possible to receive direct information about how others think or feel; instead, the child tries to put herself in the shoes of the other person and then contemplates what that other person is feeling about her. So she might imagine, "I think I am loved by my parents."

In the second step, the child reacts to the feedback the parents and others give about their perceptions toward the child. That feedback could be verbal (e.g., "I love you") or nonverbal (e.g., holding hands, a quick hug, or a slap across the face). What is important in this step, Cooley argued, is that the child is responding to what she feels the feedback means about her. The child perceives who she is (to others—and thus to herself) via feedback from others. These others are the social mirror that the child uses to develop a sense of self.

Finally, in the third step, the child integrates the first two into a coherent and unique sense of self. Interaction with particular **primary groups** (small collections of people of which a person is a member, usually for life, and in which deep emotional ties develop, such as one's family of origin) shapes the child's sense of self. Others in effect become the "mirror" by which each person sees oneself.

While socialization in childhood is foundational, Cooley would argue that socialization continues throughout a person's life. A new employee receives feedback from the boss and peers and integrates that feedback into a sense of self as a worker, for example.

Dramaturgical Theory

Interactionism does not just focus on the construction of the self. Erving Goffman was a sociologist who analyzed interaction between small groups as if it was a play. So Goffman looked at the **social actors**

Using Dramaturgy Theory to Analyze a Social Event

In this activity, you will write a brief essay applying dramaturgical theory to a specific social event.

Dramaturgical theory can be helpful in examining all kinds of social interactions. Analyze a graduation ceremony or a wedding ceremony or a New Year's Eve party using this theory.

1. Write a short essay explaining Goffman's theory to a nonsociologist.

2. Pick a social gathering from the ones above to illustrate this theory, being sure to identify all the component parts that Goffman would use.

(the individuals involved in the interaction), the **social scripts** (the interactional rules) that people use to guide the interaction, and the **props** (material objects) that the social actors use to enhance their performances. Think about a first date. Who should ask whom out? What are typical things to do on a first date? Who should pay for the date? The fact that you and your friends would have similar answers shows that there is a social script at work.

Often the performance involves teams of individuals, not just two people, and interactions occur in particular settings. While Goffman (1959) discussed many settings (or regions), two of the key ones are the **front stage** (where the interaction actually takes place) and the **back stage** (where one prepares for the interaction). Getting ready in your apartment or residence hall would be back stage; front stage would be where the date actually unfolds (e.g., the car, a restaurant, a movie theater, etc.).

Let's say that an unexpected event occurs—the person who is supposed to pay forgot money (a prop). This forgetfulness immediately highlights the fact that there *is* a social script, which one social actor just violated. What would you do if you forgot your wallet in that situation? Maybe you would first talk to the waiter or the restaurant manager (bringing in a team member), to try to find a solution, without having to tell your date.

According to Goffman, we each try to control the vibe that we give off to others. Each of us uses **presentation of self** skills—shaping the physical, verbal, visual, and gestural messages that we give to others—to (try to) control their evaluations of us, what Goffman called impression management. So we know to dress nicely on a first date and try not to forget our wallets.

Goffman's dramaturgical analysis allows symbolic interactionism to move beyond the socialization

process (which primarily occurs within the family) to study a wide range of interactions. For example, Cahill (1999) wrote that mortuary science students (social actors) were ostracized by other students (other social actors); they were forced to eat alone in the school cafeteria (front stage) because they were perceived as symbolically tainted by death in the eyes of students seeking other degrees. Studying death and how to embalm a body made it difficult for mortuary science students to create a presentation of self that was "normal," no matter how much they tried.

What Doesn't Symbolic Interactionism See?

Recall that both macro-theoretical perspectives we have discussed allow us to examine the causes of social problems, how to solve them, and the rate of social change. But symbolic interactionism cannot think about those concepts.

Social problems and social change are macro-sociological concepts, but symbolic interactionism is a micro-level theoretical perspective. Interactionism calls the sociologist's attention to the dynamics of interaction between individuals and small groups. For example, it could be used to study the experience of a female cadet in a predominantly male military academy, but it would not focus on the institutional issues of gender inequality in the government, economy, and military that led to the academy being predominantly male. By focusing on how any individual becomes socialized into the norms and values of his or her social group and thereby shapes a sense of self, interactionism focuses on different questions than the two macro-theoretical perspectives.

Language and Social Construction

In this exercise, you will consider the ways in which language is socially constructed among people your age.

Language, both written and symbolic (think, for example, of our use of numerals in mathematics as a type of scientific language), is a social construction. It is different from place to place and group to group. Are your grandparents fluent in emoji? Do they know what a selfie is?

1. What are some elements of the language you use that are age specific? What words or symbols do you use that a member of an older generation is less likely to understand?

2. What does this tell you about the shared nature of language as a social construct?

Social Constructionism

Some sociologists, frustrated with symbolic interactionism's inability to study social problems, have combined it with conflict theory and created **social constructionism.** This theory begins with the social construction of reality, just as symbolic interactionism does: every society creates norms, values, objects, and symbols that it finds meaningful and useful. Along the way, though, different categories or groups of people in the society get different rewards, as conflict theory states. Some have more, some have less. Social constructionists argue that this stratification—while felt in the world by individuals—is ultimately created and sustained through social systems, which must be made more just.

So, constructionists would argue that it is more important to study the *idea* of poverty than individual poor people (Best 2012). They focus on the constructed nature of every stratification system (e.g., wealth/poverty, race, sex/gender, age, the digital divide, etc.). In turn, they see the possibilities for change embedded in social interactions that can persuade particular audiences (e.g., Congress, the mayor, the local press). So, for example, if poverty is constructed as "something that will always be with us"—if everyone believes that to be true—then policy makers do not have to focus their time, energy, or efforts on reducing poverty. However, if poverty is constructed as something that the richest country in the world can—and should—eliminate, then policy makers will feel more pressure to create policies that work to minimize, if not eradicate, poverty. So too, how the press covers policy makers will shift based on how poverty (or any other social problem) is socially constructed.

Using Symbolic Interactionism to Understand the Meitiv Family

We now return to the Meitiv family one last time, to examine their situation through the lens of symbolic interactionism. Danielle and Alexander Meitiv socialized their children by modeling appropriate behavior and incrementally giving them more responsibility. They then provided feedback to the children on their behavior. Part of that socialization process involved having the children walk together short distances. The parents followed behind the children, without their knowledge, to observe their behavior during these solo outings. What they saw led them to trust that their children could cope with any possibilities that might occur when they walked the mile home from school together. These successful outings boosted the children's self-concepts. Danielle described the reasoning behind their socialization methods, saying that "I think it's absolutely critical for their development—to learn responsibility, to experience the world, to gain confidence and competency" (St. George 2015b, paragraph 6).

> "We wouldn't have let them do it if we didn't think they were ready for it," Danielle said. She said her son and daughter have previously paired up for walks around the block, to a nearby 7-Eleven and to a library about three quarters of a mile away. "They have proven they are responsible," she said. "They've developed these skills." (St. George 2015b, paragraph 4)

But while the Meitiv parents felt that they were properly socializing their children, others did not see the children's behavior in the same way. They wondered if the children had enough life experience to cope with whatever might happen. When the children were reported to the police the first time, they did not have a card the family had created, which said that "I am not lost. I am a free-range kid" (St. George 2015b, paragraph 11). Without that prop—a symbolic piece of information—the police officers who responded had little information to go on about who the children were and why they were out alone and therefore took them into protective custody.

As the family became caught up in the Child Protective Services legal system, Danielle claimed that these authority figures were attempting to socialize her children to be fearful, in contrast to the parents' view that the world, overall, was a safe place for children:

> My son told us that the social worker who questioned him asked, "What would you do if someone grabbed you?" and suggested that he tell us that he doesn't want to go off on his own anymore because it's dangerous and that there are "bad guys waiting to grab you." This is how adults teach children to be afraid even when they are not in danger. (Meitiv 2015, paragraph 7)

When the Meitiv story became known via news stories in *The Washington Post,* it sparked controversy. Many parents weighed in—with many supportive but others opposed to their free-range parenting style. Their story showed that there are competing cultural understandings of what it means to be a child and to be a parent in U.S. culture.

The symbolic interactionist perspective can be used to understand how our interactions can lead to a variety of societal issues. In the Sociologists in Action, Chelsea Marty, an undergraduate at Valdosta State University, relates how she used symbolic interactionism to understand how the internalization of racism and racial stereotypes can lead to systematic oppression and institutionalized racism. Chelsea also describes the steps she is taking to confront and tackle these social problems.

Full Theoretical Circle

Each family creates, within reason, its own norms for how to raise children and implements those norms. But what do we mean by "within reason"? Society determines what is "reasonable"; it is socially constructed. Over time, certain behavioral patterns will become more commonplace in society and become

the institutionalized version (in this case, of the family institution).

And now we have come full circle: a small group creates its own norms. Over time, some of those norms get shared between more members of the society as people interact, which is what symbolic interaction studies. These norms end up constructing sets of statuses and roles around key aspects of how society operates and creates social institutions. Once social institutions become routinized, they shape society and how individuals react to those social institutions, which structural functionalism analyzes. And inevitably, power differentials are created between the haves and the have-nots in social institutions and in the broader society, which the conflict perspective then analyzes.

> **Consider This**
> Describe your hometown using one of the theoretical perspectives described here. Which one will you use? Why? Do you see social harmony or social oppression? Are you interested in how small groups in society construct and then implement their values?

The theoretical perspectives we have discussed give us ways to analyze human behavior. Each perspective (and the many theories it encompasses) offers the sociologist a unique viewpoint. None of them is the correct one; rather, each of the perspectives gives sociologists a particular lens with which to see human society. Structural functionalists focus on social order and institutions and agreement on the basic values that create and sustain that social order, but tend not to notice conflict and inequality. Conflict theorists do just the opposite; they see social problems caused by oppression and injustices but overlook moments of order and social harmony. Neither structural functionalists nor conflict theorists deal with the behavior of small groups, leaving that to symbolic interactionists who examine how culture is created and passed on to the next generation, but ignore macro issues of power and control, social harmony, and balance.

Most likely one or more of these perspectives make better sense to you, and that is fine. Practice using all three of them as you look around your social world, however. You will see how you can focus on different angles of society with each.

Sociologists in Action

Courageous Conversations about Race

Chelsea Marty

In the fall semester of 2015, I became involved with a speaker series titled *Courageous Conversations about Race* (*CCR*). This series grew out of an effort to address racial tension present on our college campus. We wanted students, faculty, and other members of the community to feel open and safe enough to discuss racial topics and concepts that otherwise go unexplored. In the process, we hoped to create a campus environment more inclusive and appreciative of diversity.

While working with *CCR*, I eventually became a member of the organizing and planning team. I, along with my research partner and friend Ashlie Prain, created a student-led *CCR* series in the spring semester of 2016. This series featured students who gave presentations, panels, and performances that focused on racial issues. Topics included White supremacy, colorism, intersectionality, police brutality, and race and politics.

During one *CCR*, I presented on the research project "The Path of Our Narratives," which I conducted with Ashlie Prain. Using narratives of racism encountered in childhoods, we discussed the early internalization of racism and racial stereotypes. We then connected the early socialization of such biases to systematic oppression and institutionalized racism.

My presentation and approach to constructing this series are closely related to the sociological perspective of symbolic interactionism. Symbolic interactionists focus on the social construction of reality and how interpretations and experiences shape our social structure. This is evident in my presentation as I point out how childhood experiences of racism can be linked to the institutionalization of racism itself.

For example, one narrative was of a young White girl being moved from a predominantly Black school to a predominantly White school. As a child, she was told this move was for her own good and that she would make better friends and have better opportunities. While this individual story may seem insignificant, it actually is indicative of the racial biases used to structure our school system. Such biases contribute to the segregation, underfunding, and lack of resources that severely damage the quality of education that marginalized groups in our society receive.

Additionally, the series as a whole reflected how social interpretations of race have influenced our actions, relationships, politics, and much more. Through an understanding of this major sociological perspective, we can collectively work to recognize and dismantle racial biases and stereotypes.

Perhaps the most encouraging aspect of *CCR* is that, in addition to sparking conversation and promoting education, it inspires action and encourages community involvement. Several individuals from the community have taken on the responsibility of planning more talks and campaigns that address racial issues within our community, and I look forward to being a part of those efforts.

Chelsea Marty is a student at Valdosta State University majoring in sociology and anthropology. She intends to earn her master's in sociology at Valdosta State and looks forward to eventually becoming a sociology professor and using sociological tools to work with others to improve our communities.

Check Your Understanding

- Why is symbolic interaction a micro-level theoretical perspective?
- What do sociologists mean by "the self"?
- According to interactionists, how is society socially constructed?
- How can different groups of individuals see the same social problem differently? Can you give an original example of this?

Conclusion

Theoretical perspectives frame the social world for sociologists. They highlight some parts of human behavior and blur others. Many sociologists use the lenses of multiple theoretical perspectives to compensate for the theoretical oversights of each perspective. The theoretical language you have learned in this chapter will reemerge in many future chapters, because these are the main ways sociologists see human behavior. Chapter 3 will add to your sociological skill set by showing you the varied ways that sociologists collect data about the social world—to which we then apply theoretical perspectives.

Review

2.1 Why and how do sociologists use theoretical perspectives?

The three theoretical perspectives—structural functionalism, conflict, and symbolic interactionism—help sociologists to examine the complexities of social life. Theories provide structure to the vast data that sociologists gather and allow us to find patterns in human behavior.

2.2 What is structural functionalism?

Structural functionalism is a macro-level theoretical perspective that help us analyze an entire society and how its parts work together. Structural functionalists tend to see social harmony and social equilibrium, based on the perceived smooth interactions of the seven social institutions. Structural functionalism is a "big-picture" way of viewing societies. Imagine a sociologist standing at a distance and looking at how society and its parts are working together.

2.3 What is a conflict perspective?

Conflict perspectives are macro-level perspectives that analyze entire societies. While structural functionalist theorists examine society and see social order and harmony, conflict theorists see something completely different. They see inequality—the haves holding the have-nots back to maintain their own elevated status. Conflict focuses on the oppression and injustice at work in society caused by the haves' excessive political, economic, and social power. Conflict thinkers advocate for rapid social change to give more social rewards to the have-nots.

2.4 What is symbolic interactionism?

Symbolic interactionism is a micro-level theoretical perspective that focuses on the individual or small groups rather than an entire society. Symbolic interactionists focus on how the self is constructed through socialization and how a group socially constructs norms and values that then govern the group's behaviors. Symbolic interactionism helps us to understand how individuals can shape, as well as be shaped by, society. It also helps us study how meaning comes to be constructed and shared by a group of people. Symbolic interactionists view society as a social construction, continually constructed and reconstructed by individuals through their use of shared symbols.

2.5 How do structural functionalism, conflict perspectives, and symbolic interactionism work together to help us get a more complete view of reality?

Each of the major theoretical perspectives provides a different view of society. Structural functionalists focus on how the social institutions of society can work together to create and sustain social order but tend to overlook inequality and conflict. Conflict theorists focus on inequality and conflict but tend to overlook social order and consensus in society. Neither of these macro perspectives focus on individuals and small groups in society. Symbolic interactionists use a micro lens to focus on how individuals and small groups work together to create and re-create society. In the process, they show how individuals develop a sense of self through socialization. Together, structural functionalism, conflict perspectives, and symbolic interactionism give us a more complete view and understanding of how society works.

Key Terms

- alienation   25
- back stage   30
- bourgeoisie   24
- communism   26
- conflict theory/conflict perspective   24
- culture   29
- dysfunctions   19
- false consciousness   25
- front stage   30
- latent functions   19
- lumpenproletariat   24
- macro level of analysis   18
- manifest functions   19
- means of production   24
- mechanical solidarity   18
- micro level of analysis   18
- organic solidarity   18
- presentation of self   30
- primary groups   29
- primary socialization   29
- proletariat   24
- props   30
- self   29
- social actors   29
- social change   21
- social constructionism   31
- social harmony   18
- social institutions   18
- social order   18
- social scripts   30
- social solidarity   18
- species being   25
- structural functionalism   17
- symbolic interactionism   29
- theoretical perspective   17
- theory   17
- true consciousness   25
- unit of analysis   19
- value coercion   26

Half of all Americans believe that immigrants increase crime in the United States, but in fact, immigrants are less likely to commit crimes than those born in the United States. Research allows us to distinguish fact from perception.

Learning Questions

3.1 Why do sociologists do research?

3.2 What are some of the different ways that sociologists collect data?

3.3 How do sociologists analyze data?

3.4 Think of a topic you might like to study. What would be the first steps in developing a research project on that topic?

3.5 Think of a hypothesis you'd like to test. What are the variables you would use to test it, and what type of sample would you use?

3.6 How do sociologists evaluate the quality of research?

3.7 How do sociologists evaluate news articles and graphical presentations that use survey data?

Using Research Methods

Mikaila Mariel Lemonik Arthur

According to a Pew poll, 50 percent of Americans believe that immigrants increase crime in the United States (Brown 2015), and this belief is commonly repeated by media commentators and political figures. But is it true? It is not (Ewing, Martínez, and Rumbaut 2015; Sampson 2008). Immigrants are less likely to commit crime than those born in the United States. One study found that people born outside the United States were 45 percent less likely than those whose families had been in the United States for at least three generations to commit violent crimes (Sampson 2008). Furthermore, while immigrants often live in high-crime neighborhoods, as the proportion of immigrants in a neighborhood goes up, the level of crime and violence actually declines (Sampson 2008). This means that increasing the immigrant population could actually *decrease* crime rates!

How do we know that this common perception that immigrants increase crime is incorrect? We know because researchers went out and systematically collected and analyzed data. Sometimes, research confirms what we expect to find, but in other cases, it shows that our assumptions were wrong. Correcting those misconceptions ensures that we better understand our world. It also helps us to make better policy, business, and life decisions. For example, consider how a small business owner might change his or her perceptions of where to locate a new store based on the research on immigration and crime.

What Is Research?

We can define **research** as *the systematic process of data collection for the purpose of producing knowledge*. This means that when we do research, we collect data according to a careful plan and use that data to figure out something new about the world. This definition of research might seem different from the research you have been asked to do in the past. In high school, for example, many students complete research projects based entirely on sources found in the library or online. When carrying out such a project, you were a consumer of knowledge, a person who finds knowledge that already exists and uses it enhance your understanding. But scientific research requires you to move beyond being only a consumer of knowledge and become a producer of knowledge. Producers of knowledge do research to find out things we did not know previously. Prior sources are indeed important to this research process—but for sociologists, the use of prior sources is only one step in the journey to new knowledge, and it is data collection that is most essential.

How I Got Active in Sociology

Mikaila Mariel Lemonik Arthur

As a high school student, I wanted to be a writer of fiction, and I began college planning to study creative writing. My favorite fiction were stories that helped to illuminate social dynamics—and I found that sociology provided a similar window into the social world. As I took more classes in sociology, I found that it provided me with better tools for investigating and writing about the social world than fiction. So I chose to major in sociology and go on to earn my PhD.

As a graduate student, I got the chance to teach various sociology courses and decided on a career in which I could do exciting sociological research *and* focus on teaching sociology to undergraduates. Today, I combine research and teaching while working in the Sociology Department at Rhode Island College, where I love introducing students to the process of sociological research and seeing them develop the skills to make new discoveries themselves and to bring the techniques they learn in college to their careers. I continue to use my sociological research and writing skills to illuminate the social institution of higher education and to contribute to debates about social policy.

Research must be **empirical** in nature. Empirical statements are statements that could hypothetically be proven true or false. In other words, they are statements of possible facts. These kinds of statements can be contrasted with **normative** statements, or statements where you are expressing an opinion. These include statements that have terms such as *should* in them, where you state that the world would be better in certain circumstances, or where you express a moral, ethical, or religious view. In other words, when we do research, we are trying to find out how the world actually is, not make an argument for how we wish the world would be. (Of course, once we do research and find out how the world is, we can use our findings to advocate for social change! But research itself is about the development of knowledge.)

The definition of research discussed above would apply to research in most physical, natural, and social science fields, but sociological research is distinct because it is social in nature. This means that sociological research is about groups, societies, and/or social interaction. In general, sociological research addresses patterns, comparisons, relationships, and meanings in social life. So, sociological research must involve people, organizations, or social systems. Where it involves people, it must involve aspects of those people's experiences that go beyond the biological or psychological. A simpler way to think about this is that sociological research must go beyond what is inside of people's heads.

Why Do We Do Research?

Sociologists Richard Arum and Josipa Roksa conducted a study of college students across the United States to determine how much students are learning in college and what factors tend to increase students'

likelihood of learning. Some of their results can be found in a book called *Academically Adrift* (Arum and Roksa 2011). In the course of their research, they asked these college students to report how much time they spend in a typical week "studying and preparing for classes." Before we go any further, take a moment to think about a few questions:

1. How much time do you, personally, spend studying and preparing for classes in a typical week?

2. How much time do you think that the average college student spends studying and preparing for classes in a typical week?

3. What do you think the relationship is between time spent studying and preparing for classes and learning?

In their study, which included 2,300 students at twenty-four colleges and universities, Arum and Roksa found that 37 percent of students spend less than five hours a week studying and preparing for classes. However, the average student spends twelve to fourteen hours a week studying and preparing for classes. Arum and Roksa note that even this figure represents a decline in time spent on academics in comparison with the past. In the mid-1900s, students averaged forty hours per week on studying and class time combined, while today that figure is more like twenty-seven hours per week (these figures represent only full-time students).

When considering how much students learn while they are in college, Arum and Roksa found that the typical student does not learn very much. However, those students who spent the most time studying and preparing for classes learned, on average, the most. In their conclusion, Arum and Roksa encourage colleges

In *Academically Adrift*, Richard Arum and Josipa Roksa document that students spend less time studying than they did in the past. Not surprisingly, they also found that those who spend more time studying learn more.

Used with the permission of the University of Chicago Press

and students who want to get the most out of their college experience will know what to do.

Using Research Skills outside the Classroom

While much of the research you will encounter as you continue your sociological education is conducted by academic researchers, the importance of research is not limited to the academic sphere. Indeed, an understanding of how to conduct and use research is a very marketable skill for college graduates looking for good jobs outside academia after they have completed their schooling. Research on students who complete college degrees in sociology finds that listing research-related skills on resumes helps students get jobs and that many students—even those working in fields that might seem unrelated to research—use their research skills at work (Spalter-Roth and Van Vooren 2008). As you will see in the following Sociologists in Action box, sociological research can lead to interesting careers that make a real difference in the world.

Research skills are useful outside the workplace as well. Understanding research makes us better citizens and more effective consumers. In the modern world, we are surrounded by data of all kinds, and knowing how to interpret, think critically about, and use these data helps us make better choices. Let's consider a few examples.

and college instructors to increase their expectations for students, because when students work harder in their classes, they are likely to learn more.

Do these findings surprise you? Or are they consistent with what you expected? Either way, we do research to find out if our expectations about how the world works are accurate. Before Arum and Roksa completed their research, most instructors, administrators, and students had their own views about how much time students spent on academics, whether that represented a decline in time spent on academics in comparison to the past, and how time spent on academics relates to learning. But only after *Academically Adrift* was published did instructors, administrators, and students have the opportunity to find out whether their views were accurate. Now that we have strong evidence to support the idea that spending more time studying and preparing for classes increases students' learning, instructors and administrators can make curricular decisions designed to promote learning,

Consider This

What do you think the differences might be between decisions made on the basis of research and those made without access to research? How might you make a decision both with and without access to research when considering whether to choose knee surgery or physical therapy to recover from knee pain? Or where to locate a new branch of your ice cream store chain? Or whether the state government should provide tuition-free college to students?

Understanding research can help people make better choices about the political candidates they support. Candidates and elected officials often put

Understanding How Americans Use Price Information in Health Care

David Schleifer

As part of a team, I worked on a project designed to understand whether, how, and why Americans seek and use price information in health care. This is an important question because individuals and families bear increasing responsibility for paying for their health care, not only due to growing insurance premiums but also due to increases in copayments, deductibles, and coinsurance.

To carry out this project, we first wrote a research proposal that included the study design and a budget. After it was funded by the Robert Wood Johnson Foundation, we carried out a multimethod data collection process, including interviews with experts working on health care price transparency, demographically diverse focus groups, and a nationally representative survey. We analyzed the interview notes and focus group transcripts, as well as the quantitative survey data, and wrote a full report, a shorter research brief, and a scholarly journal article.

Our research found that, as of 2014, about half of Americans have tried to find health care price information before getting care. Those who did seek price information used a variety of sources, such as calling their medical providers or insurance companies. However, only one in five compared prices across multiple providers. Among those who compared, the majority believe they saved money.

Our survey found that most Americans *do not* think price signals quality in health care. We also found that most Americans are not aware that health care providers' prices can vary, which suggests a need to help people understand the extent of health care price variation.

My organization, Public Agenda, has a communications team who ensured that our findings were covered in popular and trade media and shared our findings with policy makers and health care industry leaders. Our communications team also shared our findings via social media. In the first week after the release of our report in 2015, 18 percent of the report's page views on our website came from Twitter. Within the first month of its release, thousands of people had downloaded our report. When we published our scholarly journal article in 2016, the report and the article were subjects of additional media coverage. Later in 2016, with funding from the Robert Wood Johnson Foundation and New York State Health Foundation, we began fielding our survey again to explore changes over time and differences by state in people's use of and attitudes about price information.

Projects like this show how sociological research can contribute to knowledge and inform policy and practice. Many Americans bear significant out-of-pocket costs for health care. Many personal bankruptcies are related to health care expenses. Our findings have helped elevate and amplify public perspectives on health care prices, thereby helping policy makers and other leaders understand the urgency of Americans' interest in price information and the obstacles they face in understanding it. I hope that our research contributes to broader efforts to reduce the burden of health care costs on individuals and families.

David Schleifer is a senior research associate at Public Agenda, a nonprofit, nonpartisan organization in New York City. See www.publicagenda.org/pages/how-much-will-it-cost and http://www.healthaffairs.org/do/10.1377/hblog 20150326.045916/full/.

forward policy proposals of various kinds, and there is usually research available that assesses the likely cost and impact of these proposals. At the federal level, some of this research is conducted by the Congressional Budget Office (CBO); in other circumstances, academic or policy researchers have written articles and reports. For example, if your town wants to add parking meters to a busy commercial district, you might want to know whether this change would increase revenues to your town, if it would reduce spending at local businesses, and if it would increase the availability of parking as you consider whether to support or oppose such a change. Understanding research can also help you assess the results of political polls and surveys to determine if they are likely to be accurate reflections of public sentiment.

In terms of your role as a consumer, understanding research can help you make better decisions about products and services to use and buy. For example, if you visit the doctor with a medical complaint and are prescribed a particular medication, you might want to know whether this medication is likely to be effective, how common its side effects are, and whether there are equally effective alternatives that are safer or less expensive. Learning about research will give you the skills to understand the evidence about your medication so that you can decide for yourself whether you want to ask the doctor for a different option. Similarly, when you choose to buy a house or rent an apartment, your research skills will allow you to investigate the characteristics of the neighborhoods you are considering without relying on a real estate agent's perceptions and priorities.

Using Research

As the examples above suggest, we as a society use the results of research in many different ways. To understand some of the different ways in which we use research, let's consider the distinction between **basic research** and **applied research.** Basic research is research directed at gaining fundamental knowledge about some issue. In contrast, applied research is research designed to produce results that are immediately useful in relation to some real-world situation. The results of applied research help us solve specific problems. However, basic research is just as important, and it lays the foundation for applied research by enabling the development of key ideas necessary for applied research that will be undertaken later.

It may be easier to understand this distinction by considering an example from biomedical science. For most of human history, people had little idea what caused illnesses, often assuming that "bad air" or

spirits were responsible for disease. It was not until Antonie van Leeuwenhoek, an inventor who developed advanced microscopes, was first able to view a bacterium in 1676 that researchers had any chance of understanding how bacteria related to disease (Porter 1976). Note that van Leeuwenhoek's research was not designed to enhance our ability to treat illnesses; he just wanted to understand more about the world around him. Alexander Fleming, on the other hand, was conducting applied research when he discovered the *Penicillium* mold, the basis for the first effective antibiotic, penicillin (Bennett and Chung 2001). Fleming had been a doctor in the British military service, and his research was designed to seek treatments for the infected wounds that killed so many soldiers in World War I. Thus, van Leeuwenhoek was conducting basic research, while Fleming was conducting applied research. To use a more sociological example, a researcher interested in understanding the relationship between poverty and educational attainment would be conducting basic research, while a researcher testing new interventions to boost academic performance in disadvantaged schools would be conducting applied research.

Despite the importance of basic research to the later development of applied research, basic research is rarely economically profitable. Therefore, most basic research today is undertaken by academic researchers. Applied research can also take place in academic settings, but it is found in many other contexts, including nonprofit organizations, government agencies, market research firms, corporations developing new products and services, and many other entities. All of these types of organizations hire researchers, including

Sir Alexander Fleming discovered penicillin as he was trying to find treatments for infection. He was conducting applied research.

What Are Data and Where Do We Get Them?

So far, you have learned that research is fundamentally based on the collection of **data**. So what are data, then? Basically, data are pieces of information, including facts, statistics, quotes, images, or any other kind of information you can think of. Note that *data* is the plural; if you want to talk about only one piece of data, you would say *datum*. Sociological researchers collect data in many different ways.

Asking Questions

The most common forms of data collection in sociology involve asking people to answer questions. This is because, as sociologists, we are interested in the ways people think about and experience their worlds, and what better way to find out than to ask them! Data collection involving asking questions can be conducted either through **surveys** or through **interviews.**

In a survey, the researcher develops a set of prewritten questions and asks respondents to answer these questions. Survey questions are often multiple choice. For example, we might ask people to state their opinion about a particular political policy, product, or religious opinion by giving them a list of answer choices such as "strongly agree, agree, neither agree nor disagree, disagree, strongly disagree." Or, we might ask them to indicate the type of work they do by selecting from one of ten common categories, with the option of "other" for those who do not fit into any of the categories.

Surveys can also ask open-ended questions in which respondents provide a number for an answer (such as in a question asking how many children the respondent has) or a word or short phrase. Typically, however, surveys do not provide the respondent with the opportunity to explain their answers at length. While survey data can be collected in a variety of ways, typically respondents answer questions over the phone, on paper, or on a website.

Many researchers who rely on survey data do not go out and collect their own data. Some organizations conduct very large-scale surveys and make their data available to researchers for further analysis. For example, the General Social Survey (GSS) has been collecting data on social and political opinion among Americans every other year since 1972. The survey consists of hundreds of questions, and the data are freely available to researchers. Researchers also draw on data collected by government agencies such as the Census Bureau.

In contrast to surveys, interviews allow the researcher to develop a more nuanced and detailed

sociologists, to help develop suitable research projects, collect data, conduct data analysis, and interpret the results. Some of these positions are even suitable for recent bachelor's degree graduates!

Check Your Understanding

- What do sociologists mean when they talk about research?

- Why do sociologists do research?

- How can understanding research methods be useful in your nonschool life?

- What is the difference between applied and basic research?

understanding of what respondents think and believe. When conducting an interview, the researcher develops an interview guide, a list of questions to ask or topics to cover in the interview. The researcher then talks with each respondent, usually in person but sometimes over the phone or using a video chat app. Interviews are usually conducted with a single respondent at a time, but interviewers can interview multiple people at once by using a focus group. Respondents can speak at length in response to interview questions and can ask for clarification if they do not understand the question or think it does not apply to them. Researchers can also ask follow-up questions to flesh out each respondent's answers. When researchers conduct any type of interview, they must take detailed notes. Usually, they make audio recordings of the interviews and then transcribe the recordings to preserve an accurate written record of everything that was said.

Observing and Interacting

Not all research can be conducted by asking questions. Sometimes, we need to see how individuals actually behave in the real world. For example, imagine that you wanted to understand how individuals go about solving problems in groups. You could ask your respondents to answer questions about the last time they solved a problem in a group, but they may not remember what happened, and their answers may not reflect the experiences of other people in the same group. If instead you watched the group as they tried to solve the problem, you would probably get a much more accurate understanding of the group process and dynamics. Therefore, many sociologists turn to methods in which they can watch people act and interact in real life.

Sometimes, researchers who want to watch people act and interact do so through **observation,** where they simply observe as a spectator. More frequently, sociologists engage in **participant-observation,** where they observe action and interaction while participating as part of the social context they are studying. To consider this difference, think about a researcher who is studying friendship groups among first graders. A researcher conducting an observational study

would find a good spot in the classroom and simply watch and listen. In contrast, a researcher using participant-observation would interact with the students in the class. Perhaps he or she would take on the role of a teaching assistant, chatting with small groups working on class projects, monitoring recess, and performing other classroom tasks, allowing a closer and more personal understanding of the social dynamics of the classroom.

Participant-observation is particularly likely to be found in **ethnography,** research that systematically studies how groups of people live and make meaning by understanding the group from its own point of view. When researchers conduct observational or ethnographic studies, their data consist of field notes, or a written record of what the researcher saw, heard, and experienced as he or she conducted the research.

Another way in which researchers can get a clear picture of how people act is by conducting an **experiment.** Experimental research is the cornerstone of some fields, such as psychology and biomedical sciences, but is much less common in sociology. Still, sociologists can use experiments to find out how people are likely to act in particular circumstances.

Some experiments are conducted in a lab, where the researchers have control over the setting and interactions, so they can manipulate the conditions to test the effects of one particular circumstance. In a controlled laboratory experiment, researchers compare two groups, an experimental group that is exposed to some sort of treatment or manipulation, and a **control group** that does not experience the treatment or manipulation. By comparing the two groups, the researcher can see exactly what the impact of the treatment or manipulation was. Most sociologists who do

experiments, though, carry out **field experiments,** which are conducted outside the lab, in the real world. In both types of experiments, the researcher manipulates certain conditions so that he or she can find out what happens when these conditions are changed.

Consider an example of a field experiment. Sociologist Devah Pager wanted to find out how having a criminal record affected job applicants' job prospects. She could have just studied actual ex-cons after their release from prison, but it might be that aspects of these individuals' experiences, personalities, and backgrounds apart from their criminal record were shaping their job market experiences. Instead, she hired four young actors and trained them to present themselves in very similar ways. Two were Black and two were White. She then sent them out to apply for entry-level jobs, alternating which testers claimed to have a criminal record and which did not (all other elements of their background were kept the same). Pager found that having a criminal record made job candidates much less likely to get a call-back for a job interview, and she also found that Black job candidates were much less likely to get a call-back than were White job candidates (Pager 2003). Furthermore, Whites with a criminal record got called back at about the same rate as Blacks with no criminal record.

Looking at Documents

Sometimes, researchers use documents or other existing materials as the basis for their research. This type of research is particularly advantageous when researchers are interested in topics for which it would be very difficult to talk to people, such as questions about the past, or where researchers are interested in documents themselves, as in studies of the media.

When researchers look at documents from the past, we call this **comparative-historical research.** To conduct comparative-historical research, researchers typically visit archives, or repositories of historical documents; today, some such repositories can be found online. Researchers use these documents to develop an understanding of the events, context, and people they are studying. While such research might seem very much like the research done by historians, it is the different kinds of research questions—and the focus on social life—that makes comparative-historical research sociological. When comparative-historical research focuses on the more recent past, it may be coupled with interviews with those who remember the events in question.

Content analysis is another way researchers might use documents to collect data. When conducting content analysis, researchers use texts—which may be written or visual—and systematically categorize elements of those texts based on a set of rules. Content analysis can involve counting elements of a text (e.g., how many girls and boys show up in children's books) or can involve more interpretive and relational elements (e.g., the degree to which magazine advertisements are sexualized).

Research Ethics

When collecting data, researchers need to pay careful attention to their ethical responsibilities. Some of these ethical responsibilities might seem obvious—for instance, it is unethical to make up data or to plagiarize other people's work. Researchers also have special ethical duties to the human subjects who participate in their research: they must minimize any risks of harm to the participants, and they have to make sure to get **informed consent** from each participant. Informed consent requires that the participants be told the purpose of the research, what they will be asked to do, and any risks of harm prior to participating. Also, they must be given the chance to withdraw their participation at any time.

Any research receiving federal funding, almost all research conducted at colleges and universities, and most other research involving human subjects are reviewed by an **institutional review board** (IRB) to ensure the rights of human subjects are properly protected. The IRB's role is simply to protect human subjects, not to comment on the importance of the research or the research design.

Where the risks to human subjects are substantial or procedures for obtaining informed consent are not sufficient, IRBs will require changes in the research design to ensure the protection of human subjects. For example, an IRB might require a researcher to develop a protocol to ensure that the names of respondents remain confidential. Or it might require revisions to the consent form so that respondents clearly understand that they can drop out of a survey partway through if they are uncomfortable with the questions. The IRB engages in even more care when reviewing research involving special populations, including those younger than eighteen years and prisoners, who might be less able to exercise informed consent.

Check Your Understanding

- What are some of the different kinds of data sociologists use in their research?

- Why are the ethical obligations of a sociologists conducting research?

What Do We Do with Data?

Once researchers have collected their data, they need to analyze them. **Data analysis** refers to the process of reducing the mass of raw data researchers have collected to a set of findings that provide the basis for making conclusions. There are a wide variety of different types of data analysis techniques, but most can be classified as either **qualitative methods** or **quantitative methods.** Quantitative methods rely on numbers, while qualitative methods rely primarily on things other than numbers, such as words and images. To remember this distinction, you might find it helpful to think about the difference between quantity (counting) and quality (assessing deeper aspects of value). Some researchers use mixed methods, or approaches that include elements of both qualitative and quantitative methods.

There are a variety of approaches to qualitative analysis. Thick description is an approach in which the researcher crafts a detailed narrative so that readers can see for themselves what a social context is really like and assess whether the researcher's conclusions are supported by the data. For example, in Matthew Desmond's (2016) Pulitzer Prize–winning book *Evicted*, readers are taken along with Desmond as he spends time with tenants and landlords in poor urban neighborhoods at the height of the Great Recession, including observing evictions. The personal stories Desmond tells enable readers to understand the experiences of the people Desmond studied. Qualitative researchers also use qualitative **coding,** in which descriptive labels are applied to sections of text or images so that they can be classified into categories or themes. Other approaches to qualitative analysis involve developing maps, timelines, or other visual representations of the data.

Qualitative Data Analysis

In quantitative data analysis, the data are represented using numbers. This approach is typical for survey data. When a researcher conducts a survey, a numerical code is assigned to each possible answer choice for every question. It is these numerical codes that are recorded, not the actual words of the answer choice. If you are familiar with spreadsheet software such as Microsoft Excel or Google Sheets, you will have a sense of what these data would look like: each column would represent a particular survey question and each row a particular respondent. Once all the data are entered, they can be analyzed by using the tools available in various statistical software packages, including spreadsheet software like Microsoft Excel or Google Sheets but more frequently specialized software such as SPSS, SAS, STATA, or R.

Quantitative Data Analysis

Quantitative analysis techniques include both **descriptive statistics** and **explanatory statistics.** Descriptive statistics are those that describe the data, such

Understanding Basic Quantitative Analysis

In this activity, you will use a scatterplot graph to perform basic data analysis.

While most quantitative sociological research uses sophisticated computational and statistical techniques, at their most basic level, such techniques originate in the scatterplot, a kind of graph that allows analysts to see the relationship between different variables, as in Figure 3.1.

1. Looking at this graph, what do you think the relationship is

- Between health care spending and life expectancy?

- Between visits to the doctor and health care spending?

- Between life expectancy and visits to the doctor?

2. In this graph, the United States is what we call an outlier, or a data point that is far away from the rest of the data points. Why do you think the United States is such an outlier here?

FIGURE 3.1

Relationship between Health Care Spending, Doctor Visits, and Life Expectancy, by Country

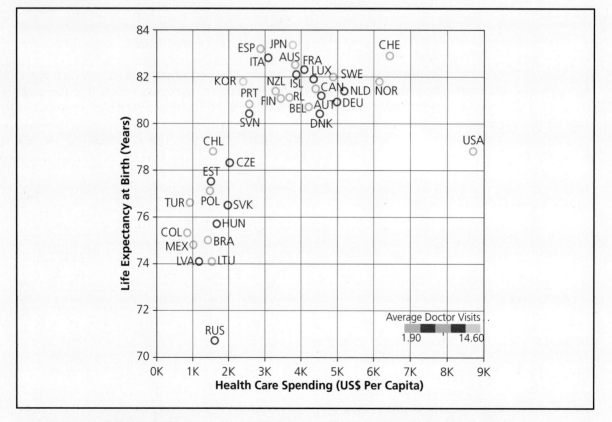

Sources: Most recent OECD data, 2010 to 2014 (Organisation for Economic Co-operation and Development 2016; Peltier 2009). A complete list of OECD country code abbreviations is available at http://www.oecd.org/migration/mig/34107835.xls.

Note: Key to country codes: AUS = Australia; AUT = Austria; BEL = Belgium; BRA = Brazil; CAN = Canada; CHE = Switzerland; CHL = Chile; COL = Colombia; CZE = Cyprus; DEU = Germany; DNK = Denmark; ESP = Spain; EST = Estonia; FIN = Finland; FRA = France; HUN = Hungary; IRL = Ireland; ISL = Iceland; ITA = Italy; JPN = Japan; KOR = Korea; LTU = Lithuania; LUX = Luxembourg; LVA = Latvia; MEX = Mexico; NLD = Netherlands; NOR = Norway; NZL = New Zealand; POL = Poland; PRT = Portugal; RUS = Romania; SVK = Slovakia; SVN = Slovenia; SWE = Sweden; TUR = Turkey; USA = United States; ZAF = South Africa.

as taking the average (or mean) of the answers to a particular question. Other common descriptive statistics include the mode, or most common answer choice; the median, or middle value when an array of data is lined up in order; and the standard deviation, which is a measure of the extent to which the data are spread out away from the mean. Descriptive statistics can also include graphs of the data.

Explanatory statistics are statistics designed to measure the relationship between different elements within the data. These include measures of the presence and strength of relationships. These sorts of quantitative analysis techniques also form the basis of the relatively new field of data science. Data science is an interdisciplinary field in which practitioners use various statistical and computational techniques to access, work with, and analyze large data sets in a variety of subject areas, including technology and social media, health care, finance, and government. Data scientists get advanced training in computer science, statistics, data analysis, and related fields and then apply this training to research questions, typically in applied research settings. Many analysts predict that data science will be a high-demand career field for years to come.

Check Your Understanding

- What is the difference between qualitative and quantitative data?

- How can understanding data analysis help you in your career?

- What is the difference between explanatory statistics and descriptive statistics?

Getting Started Doing Research

Now that you have a basic understanding of what sociological research is and how research projects in sociology are conducted, let's think about some of the details researchers must consider as they design and develop their research projects. Researchers must first decide what they will study. Then they must figure out what sort of data they hope to collect and how they will measure the concepts and ideas they are interested in studying. They must decide who they will include in their project and how they will find these respondents. And they must consider a variety of other issues important to ensuring that their project is conducted in a systematic and rigorous way consistent with the broadly held standards for sociological research.

Sociological research, like other scientific research, is conducting according to the **scientific method.** The scientific method is a systematic process of steps that takes researchers from the development of a research question through the collection and analysis of data. In the scientific method, researchers begin by defining a research question. Next, they find out what is already known about their research question by reading prior scholarly literature, a process we call the **literature review.** Based on this prior literature, the researcher must develop one or more **hypotheses,** or predictions about what they expect to find in their research. Then, the researcher develops a research design and collects data according to this design. Once data collection is completed, the researcher analyzes and interprets these data, as well as finally writes up and publishes the results of the research project. These results then become part of the prior literature to be used by the next researcher focused on this topic, making the scientific method a cyclical process.

Deductive and Inductive Research

The scientific method as discussed here is an example of **deductive research.** In deductive research, researchers begin with a general idea or prediction and then gather data to test this idea. However, sociologists can also engage in **inductive research,** where they gather data first and then use the data to generate new ideas and understandings.

In inductive research projects, researchers begin with a much broader research question. They use this question to shape their data collection, and once they have collected their data, they interpret and analyze these data. Based on the results of their analysis, they relate their results to prior research and develop conclusions and new ideas. Many inductive research projects move fluidly between these different stages, as new findings may encourage researchers to go back and collect more data or try another type of analysis. When they are finished, researchers then write up and publish their results.

For example, consider Matthew Desmond's research on evictions discussed above. If Desmond were to carry out a deductive research project about evictions, he would make a prediction about the sorts of factors that would be most likely to lead to a family getting evicted from their housing and what the consequences of the eviction would be for that family.

FIGURE 3.2

Deductive versus Inductive Research Processes

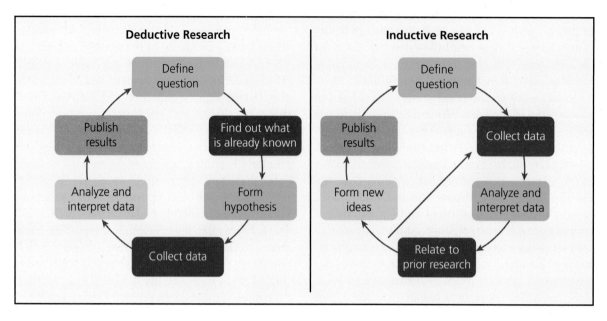

He would then gather data to test his prediction. In contrast, an inductive approach to this project would involve Desmond beginning to collect data without a clear prediction about what he might find. Instead, he would talk to people as they went through the eviction process to see what factors were shaping their lives before and after the eviction.

As you can see in Figure 3.2, the first step in the scientific method is to figure out what it is that the researcher is going to study. Researchers typically begin with **research questions,** or a clear question about what it is that the researcher plans to study. Researchers develop their research questions in various ways. Perhaps, as in many applied research projects, a supervisor or a client provides the research question. If the researcher gets to choose his or her own research question, this question might be developed based on personal interests or experiences important to the researcher or might stem from things the researcher has learned about in the course of taking sociology classes or conducting prior research.

Researching Theories

Researchers use their research questions to select or develop a **theory** (or more than one theory) guiding their research. Theories help sociologists to notice and understand social patterns in society. Researchers also make use of theory when figuring out what data to collect and how to make sense of the data once they have them. In the case of deductive research projects, theory development occurs early in the research process, before data have been

collected; in inductive research, theories are generated toward the end of the research process, as data analysis drives theory generation.

Researchers often conduct research to test theories, but they remain theories even after they have been tested many times. The idea that a theory is no longer considered a theory once it has been confirmed is a misunderstanding that lies at the root of several contemporary scientific controversies, for example, those about climate change and evolution. When nonscientists hear the phrases "the theory of evolution" or "the theory of global climate change," they assume these are untested ideas or speculation on the part of scientists. But to scientists, calling these ideas "theories" simply means that they are statements about relationships that explain patterns in data. Most scientists today agree that the evidence to support the existence of both evolution and climate change is very strong, but scientists still call these ideas theories.

Consider This

How are sociological research and sociological theory connected? What contributions does each one make to what we know and what we do in sociology, and how are those contributions strengthened when we consider them together?

In deductive research, researchers build on existing theories to develop hypotheses. As noted above, hypotheses are predictions about the expected findings of research, typically about the relationships between specific phenomena under study in the research project. A typical hypothesis is of the form "If x happens, then y is more likely to happen." It is important to note that a hypothesis must be testable. This means that it must be possible to imagine a way that one could carry out a research study to determine whether there is support for the hypothesis. It doesn't have to be possible to carry out the research study right away—for example, researchers have hypotheses about the impacts of widespread adoption of self-driving cars on the rate of traffic fatalities, the environment, and commuting behavior, but we cannot yet test these hypotheses because self-driving cars are still in the testing and development phase. While we cannot currently test these hypotheses, scientists expect that we will someday be able to do so. If we could *never* expect to be able to test them, as in the case of normative statements, then they are not hypotheses. So, if a researcher makes a prediction about the effects of self-driving cars on commuting behavior, that is a hypothesis; if the researcher says that self-driving cars are immoral because they remove personal responsibility from driving, that is a normative statement and thus not a hypothesis.

Once researchers have defined their research question(s) and/or hypotheses, they must begin to develop the specific details of how they will go about carrying out their study, including selecting one of the methods of data collection discussed above. Researchers then must determine if their research will follow a **cross-sectional** or **longitudinal** design. Cross-sectional studies are those that are carried out at one particular point in time and designed to explore and explain what is going on at that point in time. In contrast, longitudinal studies are carried out over a longer time period, with the researcher going back to collect more data—whether from the same respondents or different ones—at multiple points in time.

Check Your Understanding

- What is the scientific method?
- What is the difference between inductive and deductive research?
- What is the role of theory in developing a research project?
- In which kind of circumstances would you use cross-sectional versus longitudinal research designs?

Sampling and Measurement

Once researchers have figured out the basic parameters and design of their study, they must turn to the more detailed question of who and what they are collecting data about. **Sampling** refers to the process of selecting respondents for inclusion in the research project. This process of selection is needed because in most cases, researchers would be unable to talk to every single person who meets the criteria for participation in a study. For example, imagine that you were conducting a study of sophomores at your college or university. If you go to a very small college, perhaps it would be possible to interview every single sophomore. But if you attend Ohio State University, one of the largest in the country, you could not interview all of the more than 11,000 sophomores enrolled every year. Thus, you would need to select a sample of sophomores to participate in your study. Samples can be either **random** or nonrandom. In random samples, everyone who meets the criteria for participation in a study has an equal chance of being selected. For example, if you were conducting a study of sophomores at your college or university, all sophomores would have an equal chance of being selected; juniors, of course, would not. However, if you were conducting a random sample of students at your college or university, students in *all* class years would have an equal chance of being selected. Indeed, this is what "random" means to researchers: that everyone has an equal chance and there is no bias or other factor shaping who is included in the sample. This research-specific definition of *random* is quite different from the way the term is used in ordinary language, where it often means something like odd or unexpected.

Nonrandom samples are used when a random sample is impossible or extremely impractical to conduct. Since you need a list of potential respondents to conduct a random sample, nonrandom samples tend to be used where such a list does not exist. For example, if you wanted to conduct a study of sophomores at your college or university, the administration would be able to provide a list of all students meeting this definition. But if you wanted to conduct a study of students at your college or university who are currently dating someone living more than fifty miles away, you would not be able to get such a list.

As they begin thinking about the "what" of their study, researchers make a list of the important concepts in their research study. Concepts are abstract ideas: for example, "friendship" and "intelligence" are concepts. Once a researcher has figured out which concepts are important to his or her research project, he or she must **operationalize** these concepts. *Operationalize* is a big word, but all it really means is the process of turning an abstract concept into a concrete measure. In other words, when you operationalize, you develop a set of clear instructions for how to measure your concept in the context of your specific research project. For example, if you are collecting data about high school basketball players' athletic performance, you need to determine how you will measure athletic performance. The number of pounds the players can dead lift is probably not as important as how many free throws they can make in five minutes for this particular study, even though both are measures of athletic performance. And if you choose to measure free throws, you need to be clear about how you will measure that variable—how many minutes players will have to make their free throws is an important part of the instructions for measurement of this variable.

As they are operationalized, some concepts turn into **variables** and others turn into **constants.** Variables are factors that are likely to change (or vary) within the context of the study, while constants are those that stay the same for everyone in the study. For example, if you were conducting a study of the relationship between athletic performance and academic performance among high school basketball players, "athletic performance" and "academic performance" would both be variables, because different basketball players have different levels of each type of performance. On the other hand, whether or not someone is a high school basketball player would be a constant, because it is the same for everyone in the study. It is true, of course, that the individuals in the study will eventually leave high school, and many will stop playing basketball one day. But these changes are outside of the scope of the study—during the study, everyone remains a high school basketball player.

When we create variables to measure our concepts, we indicate precisely how we will measure those concepts. We might do this by writing a survey question, giving a respondent a test, or using any other specific measurement process. Think back to the concepts of "friendship" and "intelligence" noted above—how might we measure these? Well, if we were interested in friendship, we might ask survey respondents to indicate how many close friends they have. If we were

In this exercise, you will practice creating hypotheses and operationalizing variables for research questions.

1. How can introductory sociology courses be designed to improve students' learning of sociology?

2. What is the relationship between neighborhood disorder and crime rates?

3. What factors make working mothers most likely to continue breastfeeding their infants for at least six months?

4. How does exposure to fast-food advertising affect teenagers' eating habits?

5. How does the use of social media affect roommates' relationships?

Take the research questions above as a starting point. Develop hypotheses related to each research question.

Once you have developed these hypotheses, operationalize each variable in your hypotheses.

For example, consider the research question "How do hospital environments shape recovery times for patients?" You might write the hypothesis "Patients who have quieter hospital rooms will recover from abdominal surgery faster than those with noisy rooms." This hypothesis includes two variables: recovery time and loudness of hospital rooms. You might operationalize these variables by saying that recovery time is measured by counting the number of days from when the abdominal surgery occurred until patients say that they are able to go back to their normal activities. And you might operationalize loudness of hospital rooms by using a sound level meter to measure the number of decibels of noise in the hospital room at six specific times throughout the day, perhaps 9 a.m., 1 p.m., 5 p.m., 9 p.m., 1 a.m., and 5 a.m.

interested in intelligence, we might give respondents an IQ test. Sometimes, it can be much simpler—if we want to measure age, we can ask the respondent how old he or she is in years, and if we want to measure height, we can get a ruler and measure in inches. But note that even in these examples, the measurement instructions are precise and include the specific units of measurement we are using.

If we are doing research that is qualitative and open-ended in nature, such as interviews, once we figure out what kind of question to ask to measure our concept, we are done operationalizing. For example, if we are studying friendship, we might ask a respondent to tell us what makes someone a good friend. But if we are doing research that is quantitative and closed-ended in nature, we need to be even more specific, by plotting out all the potential answer choices to our variable. In the case of the variables like age or IQ, the answers will generally be provided as an actual number, but in many cases, we want to provide multiple-choice answer categories. We call these answer categories **attributes.** For example, if we ask a respondent whether she lives in a dorm, lives off-campus with her family, or lives off-campus away from family, each of those three options is an attribute.

Check Your Understanding

- Why do researchers use samples rather than simply studying everyone?

- How is the meaning of *random* different when discussing sampling in comparison to how you use it in regular conversation?

- What are concepts and how do researchers operationalize them?

- What are variables and constants?

What Makes Research Good?

When researchers carry out research projects, they strive to develop accurate and useful answers to their research questions. The decisions researchers make about research design can have important impacts on whether their projects ultimately meet these goals. In assessing the accuracy and usefulness of research projects, we assess whether the results and findings are generalizable, reliable, and valid. Research projects can achieve all of these goals, none of them, or any one or two, so they must be considered separately.

Generalizability refers to whether it is possible to assume that the patterns and relationships observed among the sample in the research study would also hold true for the broader population. In order for research to be generalizable, the participants must have been obtained via the use of a properly constructed random sample. This is because random samples give every member of the relevant population an equal chance to be selected into the sample, so there is nothing systematically different between those who participate and those who do not. However, research findings can only be generalized to the population from which the sample was drawn. For example, if you were to conduct a random-sample survey of student satisfaction among students living in the dorms at your college or university, and you designed your sampling strategy properly and carried out the project without

If a sociologist was studying the relationship between race and athletic performance among high school students, race and athletic performance would be variables and being a high school player would be a constant.

Distinguishing Concepts from Variables

In this activity, you will practice identifying variables and concepts.

For each of the phrases or words below, determine whether it is a concept or a variable. If it is a concept, operationalize it by coming up with a specific variable that would measure that concept. If it is a variable, determine what concept that variable is measuring.

1. Dollar amount of money in savings
2. Athletic skill
3. Food healthfulness
4. Hunger
5. Number of words per sentence in a book
6. Career success

bias, you could assume the results you find would be consistent with the degree of student satisfaction among all students living in the dorms at your college or university. These results could not be generalized to students living off campus or to students living in dorms at other colleges and universities, though, because the sample was not drawn from these populations.

Where random samples are not conducted, the results of research projects are not generalizable. However, researchers can still strive to ensure that their samples are **representative,** meaning that the people in their sample have characteristics typical of people in the broader population. While the results will not be automatically generalizable, if the sample is representative, the results can provide a good representation of the overall population studied.

Reliability refers to the extent to which research results are consistent. There are a variety of different types of reliability, but all involve the question of whether repeating research measurements will produce the same results each time. For instance, if you ask the same person the same question on multiple days, will he or she understand and respond to the question in the same way? If you give students an exam with similar questions on multiple days, will they get the same general score? Or if multiple observers view the same television advertisement, will they come to the same conclusion about whether the advertisement includes sexual imagery? This last case represents an example of a special, and important, type of reliability called **interrater reliability,** which is an assessment of the degree to which different people who are coding or rating the same data do so in the same ways.

In contrast, **validity** refers to whether the research results accurately reflect the phenomena being studied. There are a variety of types of validity, but all involve the question of whether the measures and findings of a research study make sense of the world in an accurate and reasonable way. For instance, if a researcher wanted to test your knowledge of sociology by asking you to sing your campus alma mater or fight song, this would not be valid. She or he would have to give you a properly designed sociology test instead. In some cases, research seeks to make predictions or diagnose problems, and when we check the validity of the research, we see if those predictions or diagnoses hold up going forward. Many factors can affect validity, such as poorly developed measures, researcher error or mistakes, and bias of various kinds, including the development of biased samples.

Roosevelt, Landon, and *Literary Digest*

An old story will illustrate the impact that sampling bias can have on validity. In 1936, during the height of the Great Depression, the magazine *Literary Digest* conducted a poll seeking to predict who would win that year's presidential election: Alfred Landon, then-governor of Kansas, or incumbent President Franklin Delano Roosevelt. The poll predicted that Landon would win easily, but if you remember your U.S. history, you'll know that Roosevelt won. Indeed, Landon ended up winning only two states, Vermont and Maine, while Roosevelt got the other forty-six (Alaska and Hawaii were not states yet in 1936).

Evaluating Reliability and Validity in Research

In this activity, you will examine research scenarios for potential reliability and validity problems.

Reliability and validity are different. As you think about the research scenarios below, determine if each one presents a reliability problem, a validity problem, or both kinds of problems.

1. We keep a thermometer right under a light bulb and use it to take your temperature every day.

2. We give students the answers to a test in advance and then use the test to measure how much they learned in class.

3. We ask several simulated jury panels to determine how much money to award in a fictional lawsuit and they come up with different amounts of money in damages.

4. We ask you how much you like your job, how satisfied you are with your work, and whether you look forward to going to work on most days, and you give different answers to the different questions.

5. We predict the likelihood that study participants will get married by using a magic-8 ball.

It turns out that the *Literary Digest* poll used a very biased sample. It selected its respondents using telephone directories, lists of subscribers to *Literary Digest,* and registered automobile owners. Remember, this was the Great Depression, and cars and phones were still new (and expensive) technologies, and not everyone could afford (or wanted) a subscription to *Literary Digest.* So, *Literary Digest* was only sampling well-off people, not those suffering the most from the Great Depression, who made up the majority of the population. It is easy to see how their results came to be so incorrect given this biased sample. Thus, one way to increase validity is to make sure the respondent pool is representative of the population the research seeks to make claims about.

Consider This

Assume that you were designing a poll like the *Literary Digest* presidential poll. What would you have to do to ensure that your sample was not biased? How might the method you use to contact potential respondents affect the extent to which your sample would be representative of the population?

Causation

Many researchers and consumers of research find that what they are really interested in is understanding **causation**—whether a change in one variable causes a change in another variable. It makes sense to be interested in causation. After all, if we could claim with certainty that a particular student behavior causes better grades, it would be easy for students to understand how to do better in classes! Alas, the real world is much too complicated for this. It turns out that it is almost impossible for researchers to demonstrate that a particular relationship is causal.

Demonstrating causation requires researchers to meet three specific conditions. First, they must demonstrate that the supposed cause is associated with the supposed effect. This means that if a change in the cause occurs, a related change should be observed in the effect. Second, they must demonstrate that the cause comes before the effect. After all, if the cause does not come first, it cannot very well be the cause, right? Finally—and this is the hard part—the researcher must be able to eliminate all other possible alternative explanations for the effect. There are hundreds or thousands of possible explanations for most social phenomena, though, and in most cases, it is impossible to study more than a handful of these explanations at a time. Thus, researchers are unable to show that a relationship is cause in most cases.

The only circumstances under which researchers can demonstrate causation is when they conduct a controlled laboratory experiment. Because researchers conducting controlled laboratory experiments have complete control over all aspects of the experimental context, they can ensure that the only difference between the experimental group and the control group is the one variable they are hoping to study. Thus, if a difference in results is observed between the two groups, it must be due to the manipulated variable and cannot be due to any other factor. Therefore, controlled laboratory experiments, when conducted carefully and properly, make it possible for researchers to assess causation.

Check Your Understanding

- Why is it important that research participants be representative of the broader population?

- Under which circumstances is it possible to generalize from research results?

- What is the difference between reliability and validity?

- Under which circumstances is it possible for researchers to demonstrate causal relationships in their research results?

Conclusion

This chapter has just been an introduction to sociological research, and there is so much more you can learn about collecting, analyzing, and using data and writing about the results. But even with this short introduction, you should now have a sense of how sociological research methods are used to find out new things about the world around us. Empirical research allows us to test our assumptions about the world and find out what is really going on. These results form the basis of the body of knowledge in the discipline of sociology. Sociological research can also inform decision making by helping nonprofits, government agencies, and companies understand the issues important to them and the likely consequences of different choices.

As noted above, sociological research skills can open the doors to many career opportunities, including those in academia, the corporate world, government, and nonprofits. People with training in sociological research can work as research assistants, project managers, data analysts, data scientists, and a variety of other positions drawing on these skills. The research tools you gain in sociological research are useful for other kinds of research as well, including—just to give a few examples—research in the health sciences, marketing, public policy, and fundraising. They can also help you in your personal life when you seek to make decisions about which political candidates and policy initiatives to support, where to live, what types of medical care to seek, and what products to buy.

If you think you might be interested in a research-related career or in further developing your research expertise, there are several things you can do during college to prepare. First of all, you will clearly want to take courses in research methods, but you will also want to take courses in the content areas you are interested in. After all, without content knowledge, you do not have any ideas where to start your research or what kinds of research questions are interesting and new in your field. Professional researchers continue to keep up on what is being studied in their fields by reading books and journals and going to conferences. Second, you will want to continue to be curious and creative. Researchers must want to know more about the world to continue to be excited about new findings, and creativity helps researchers develop new research questions and new approaches to designing research studies.

Finally, becoming a researcher requires lots of practice. Any set of skills, be they basketball, guitar, cooking, or sociological research, must be practiced over and over before someone can become really good at them. Research requires a lot of hard work, effort, and perseverance, and things often go wrong. Computer programs fail, potential respondents do not answer your phone calls, and results turn out differently than expected. But if you keep at it, you will develop more skills and do an even better job next time. As a college student interested in research, you can seek out research opportunities on campus, including opportunities to work with professors on their research projects as well as opportunities to develop and conduct your own research project. You can also look for internships and volunteer opportunities that draw on your growing research skills, such as helping a food pantry collect data on the people it serves or working with a government agency to clean up and use a data set on educational outcomes.

Research is the root of the discipline of sociology. As you continue reading this book and learning about sociology this term, everything you learn about—all the ideas, concepts, facts, and findings—have been developed and/or refined through the research process. When sociologists write about culture, socialization, deviant behavior, social inequality, social institutions, and social change (topics covered later in this book), they base their writing and their analysis on the finding from empirical research projects carried out according to the methods and procedures discussed in this chapter. Research is not just an important part of the process of doing sociology; it is actually part of what makes sociology *sociology*. Remember the definition of sociology from Chapter 1 ("Sociology is the scientific study of society . . .")? The word *scientific* in that definition refers to the fact that sociology requires careful, empirical, rigorous research to study its subject matter, society.

In this chapter, you learned how sociologists go about studying society. We now turn to an exploration of culture, an important factor shaping society and social experience. As you read the next chapter, as well as the others that follow, think about how sociological research methods have been used to develop the ideas and concepts you read about—and how you might use sociological research methods to find out more!

CHAPTER

3

⑤SAGE edge™

Want a better grade? Get the tools you need to sharpen your study skills. Access practice quizzes, eFlashcards, video and multimedia at **edge.sagepub.com/korgen**

Review

3.1 Why do sociologists do research?

Sociologists do research to understand how society works. Without research, all we would have to go on is our assumptions. While our assumptions sometimes turn out to be correct, in many cases, the real data tell a different story. Thus, research is essential for understanding social behavior and how society works. And this knowledge can also help us to make policy decisions, sell products, design solutions to social problems, and do other useful things.

Sociologists use research in a wide variety of career paths. For example, market researchers use interviewing, observation, and surveys to collect data about how people use products, what products they might be interested in buying, and which sorts of advertisements or promotions are most likely to encourage people to buy particular products. Law enforcement officers use interviewing and document analysis in the course of investigating crimes. They also collect quantitative data on crime rates in different areas of their city and at different times of day to develop better strategies for preventing and detecting crime and to schedule and organize patrol shifts. And health care researchers conduct survey and interview studies as part of their efforts to determine which kinds of treatments will most help individuals and communities improve their health.

3.2 What are some of the different ways that sociologists collect data?

Sociologists use a variety of techniques to collect data. Some of these methods involve talking to or interacting with people, including surveys, interviews, participant-observation, and experiments. Sociologists can also collect data through observation or by using existing documents. In many cases, sociologists combine multiple methods of data collection in one project. Regardless of the methods they use, sociologists must do their research in accordance with ethical standards.

3.3 How do sociologists analyze data?

Sociologists use qualitative, quantitative, or mixed-methods approaches to analyze data. Qualitative approaches rely on words, images, and ideas, while quantitative approaches rely on statistical, numerical techniques.

3.4 Think of a topic you might like to study. What would be the first steps in developing a research project on that topic?

When researchers begin a research project, they must first develop a research question. If their project is deductive, they complete a literature review and develop a theory, then design their research approach to test this theory. If their project is inductive, they design their research approach and begin collecting data while continuing to read prior literature and build theory as they work on the project.

3.5 Think of a hypothesis you'd like to test. What are the variables you would use to test it, and what type of sample would you use?

Consider the hypothesis, or research prediction, that "students who spend more time on social media earn, on average, lower grades in college courses." In this hypothesis, the independent variable would be time spent on social media, which we could measure by recording how many hours per day the student uses any social media site on any electronic device. The dependent variable would be grades, which we could measure by looking at the students' official grade point average. You would use a random sample of college students to test this hypothesis. Other hypotheses might require a nonrandom sample.

3.6 How do sociologists evaluate the quality of research?

Sociologists evaluating a research study expect to see a clear discussion of how the data were collected and analyzed. This discussion should accurately reflect whether or not the research is generalizable and whether it is able to demonstrate causation. In addition, sociologists are concerned with validity and reliability. Validity refers to the extent to which a study accurately reflects what is really going on in the world, while reliability refers to whether repeating the measurements used in a study produces the same results each time.

3.7 How do sociologists evaluate news articles and graphical presentations that use survey data?

When sociologists look at news articles that use survey data, they expect to see a clear discussion of who collected the data, how many people were surveyed, how they were contacted, what the **margin of error** was, and what questions were asked. When survey data are presented graphically, sociologists pay attention to the way variables are measured and what relationships between these variables are shown.

Key Terms

- applied research   41
- attributes   51
- basic research   41
- causation   53
- coding   45
- comparative-historical research   44
- constants   50
- content analysis   44
- control group   43
- cross-sectional   49
- data   42
- data analysis   45
- deductive research   47
- descriptive statistics   45
- empirical   38
- ethnography   43
- experiment   43
- explanatory statistics   45
- field experiment   44
- generalizability   51
- hypotheses   47
- inductive research   47
- informed consent   44

- institutional review board   45
- interrater reliability   52
- interviews   42
- literature review   47
- longitudinal   49
- margin of error   56
- normative   38
- observation   43
- operationalize   50
- participant-observation   43
- qualitative methods   45
- quantitative methods   45
- random   49
- reliability   52
- representative   52
- research   37
- research questions   48
- sampling   49
- scientific method   47
- surveys   42
- theory   48
- validity   52
- variables   50

What cultural traditions can be found in your culture? What makes your society unique?

Learning Questions

4.1 What is culture?

4.2 What are some ways that the different elements of culture influence everyday life?

4.3 How do societal types relate to variations in culture?

4.4 How do changes to our culture shape our behaviors and ways of viewing the world?

4.5 In what ways can you use cultural capital to help both yourself and society?

Recognizing Culture

David E. Rohall

Defining Culture

Here is a sociological riddle: what affects almost all of your thoughts, feelings, and behaviors but cannot be seen or touched in its entirety? The answer is culture! **Culture** refers to the characteristics of a group or society that make it distinct from other groups and societies. Technically, culture can take a physical form, but much of what we will be reviewing in this chapter emphasizes nontangible forms of culture. **Nonmaterial culture** includes concepts such as norms, values and beliefs, symbols, and language. **Material culture** consists of artifacts ranging from tools to products designed for leisure like flat-screen TVs or Xboxes. Material culture reflects the values and beliefs of the people who live in a culture.

Finding Culture

Take a few minutes to think about the physical items in your bedroom or living room. Note what these items are but also what they look like, the colors and placement of those items. What does this information say about you? Perhaps you only have a few items or you may have a room full of artifacts. Consider what other people can learn about you simply by observing the types of things that you own.

If you have a lot of sports memorabilia, it probably says something about your appreciation of sports. But these artifacts also represent the culture in which you live. For example, if you are in North America, you are much more likely to have baseball or (American) football-related items than someone in South America, where people play and watch soccer (football) rather than baseball or American football. Consider some other items. If you have a smartphone, a television, and a computer, these items reflect a way of life that did not exist 100 years ago and still does not exist in some places in the world today. While most places have started using some of these products, only some people—in some areas of the world—have access to the resources necessary to own and power all of them.

Let's go one step further: why do you own these items? You would probably say that you need these things, right? Smartphones keep us connected to other people and computers are for work—and everyone watches television! You can easily argue that you cannot live without them. The truth is that a good number of people live without one or more of them, even in the United States, but the belief that these things are necessary reflects an important dimension of the study of human culture: the social construction of reality, the ways that people give meaning to the world around them through interaction with other people (Berger and Luckmann 1966).

David E. Rohall

My first sociology textbook was coauthored by George Ritzer (famous for *The McDonaldization of Society,* among other books) at a much earlier stage in his career. It was from this book that I first learned about the sociological imagination. I started to see the ways that social structure affects my day-to-day life and to help understand the thoughts, feelings, and behaviors of the people around me. I continue to employ the sociological imagination as I study the nexus of the individual and society and how people develop their senses of self within the cultures they live. I view my textbook, *Social Psychology: Sociological Perspectives* (3rd ed., 2014), as a repository of theory and research on the ways that sociologists approach the study of social-psychological processes. My other research includes numerous projects that show how our membership in different subcultures affects how we think about the world. Together, I hope that this work reflects the importance of the sociological imagination for understanding our social world.

Consider This

Would you like to live and work in a country with a culture quite different from the one in which you were raised? Why?

Imagine you have a baseball you caught at a major league American baseball game. Even better, imagine this ball was caught during the World Series, the most important set of games of a given year. What would happen if that baseball was stolen? The absolute value of this baseball is probably around five American dollars. But its relative value, what you may be able to get by selling it on eBay, is much higher. Which one is the true value of the item? If you believe that it is worth a lot of money, its loss will cause you much more stress and concern than if you believe that it is only worth five dollars.

Things get more complicated when we consider how important the baseball is to you. You may never consider selling the ball because it has a lot of sentimental value, representing an important memory in your life. The loss of this baseball is likely to cause great stress and anxiety, not just because you lost a potential source of money but also because it symbolizes something important to you.

In any case, the ball has a lot of value because people give it value. You give it your own value as a cherished keepsake and the people around you value it for its association with an important baseball game. Once a value is established, once we come to believe that it is real, we think, feel, and behave based on that understanding rather than on any "objective" value that it has (e.g., on how much it costs to produce it).

Constructing Culture

Sociologists see culture as **socially constructed;** its meaning is created through interactions among people. For example, have you ever created a secret word or something that only you and a good friend or family member understood? Such a word may simply be a fun way of interacting with that person or a code to help you get out of a social situation. The key here is that this new language was created by you and the other person or persons (hence, socially constructed), and you use this new code to interact with each other in the future, as a way to convey what you mean to each other. The same process goes on in larger society, albeit on a much larger scale. Languages are taught at home and later in classrooms, but even then, languages change over time as we add and drop words over time (e.g., using the word *binge-watch* is new to the 2017 Merriam-Webster dictionary). These symbols are part of culture; they tell people something about us as a people. What do you think the term *binge-watch* says about American culture?

Our group affiliations and their respective cultures are brought into our sense of self, and other people identify us, in part, based on the cultures in which we were raised. Many people understand this idea in principle but fail to see it in their lives because their understanding of the social world is shaped by their cultural perspective. We tend not to even notice our culture and its influence on us until we find ourselves looking at it from a different cultural perspective, such as when we travel or read about another time or place. Any number of books and movies have been made about people who change their worldviews as a result of their personal experiences. The movie *Born on the Fourth of July* is about a Vietnam War veteran, played by Tom Cruise, who joins the Marines after a

Rings and the Social Construction of Reality

This exercise asks you to consider the message engagement rings send in American society and how that message is socially constructed.

In this chapter, you have just learned how members of a society give meaning to the objects around us. For example, consider how we view and make use of rings in our society.

Think about what comes to your mind when you see a ring with a diamond on it on the fourth finger of someone's left hand and then write your answers to the following questions:

1. What does the ring symbolize?

2. What was the gender of the person you imagined? Why?

3. What is it about our society that has led to that image?

4. Now, read the *New York Times* article "Men's Engagement Rings Proclaim, 'He's Taken'" (www.nytimes.com/2010/08/01/fashion/weddings/01FIELD.html) and answer question 3 again. Did the article influence your perspective on the topic? Why or why not?

5. How does this experience relate to the fact that we tend not to even notice our culture and its influence on us until we find ourselves looking at it from a different cultural perspective?

---

patriotic speech by John F. Kennedy. After some horrific experiences both overseas and recovering in a poorly equipped veterans' hospital in the United States after being wounded, the protagonist not only comes to view the war negatively but actively speaks out against it. Which view is the real one?

The view of life through our culturally tinted lens appears to be *the* rather than *a* version of reality (Berger and Luckmann 1966). This way of experiencing the world helps to keep us grounded. Imagine if you constantly thought that all your values were relative and that other values might be just as good and useful. It would make it very difficult to have a coherent sense of the world or to create stable relationships. The rest of this chapter will outline the contents of culture and how we use it in our everyday lives.

Check Your Understanding

- What is culture?

- What is the difference between material and nonmaterial culture?

- How do artifacts represent the culture in which we live?

- What do sociologists mean when they say society is socially constructed?

Identifying Elements of Culture

Groundhog Day is a funny film from the 1990s that portrays a television weather man who is stuck in time, repeating the same day over and over again. He does everything he can to break this cycle but he cannot seem to get out of this rut. Consider your own life. What do you normally do each day? What sorts of things do you own to help you in your routines? How do you feel when you are taken out of this routine?

Patterns of behavior may appear to be rather mundane or even boring at times, but they provide a framework for making decisions in our lives. If we follow these routines too closely, we may lose some sense of spontaneity, but without routines, it is very difficult to coordinate activities with other people. If, at your job, you must work in tandem with another person to complete a task, what happens if one of you decides not to go to work? What would happen to one of your courses if the professor just showed up whenever she felt like it? Or only a few of the students tended to go to class? This section reviews the basic ways that different cultures address the need to coordinate the lives of many different people. In doing so, we look at the various elements of nonmaterial culture: norms, values and beliefs, and symbols and language.

Imagine the chaos in this class if the students violated a classroom folkway and did not wait to be called on before speaking!

Social Norms

Norms refer to expectations about the appropriate thoughts, feelings, and behaviors of people in a variety of situations. The key to this definition is that it involves *expectations* about thoughts, feelings, and behaviors. We may not be actually thinking, feeling, or behaving in ways that follow the norms of society, but we tend to try to appear as though we are. For example, how are you supposed to feel at a funeral? Perhaps you are tired and feel nothing at all or you may even feel happy at the moment. You try to suppress those feelings so as not to offend the family of the deceased or simply to avoid the looks and sneers of people who believe that your feelings are inappropriate. You do not want to appear to be violating the norms of appropriate thoughts and behaviors at a funeral.

Consider almost anything you do in a given day and you can probably determine the appropriate norms that go with each behavior. On what side of the sidewalk do you walk? What do you say when someone sneezes? How do you greet someone you do not know very well? There are hundreds or even thousands of things that we do each day, and most of them have some sort of norm that goes along with them. How do we learn all of these norms? In many cases, we are instructed by our parents, teachers, and peers. In other cases, we simply learn the norm by observing how other people act.

We do not have to know each person we interact with before we have an idea of how to interact with them appropriately. Throughout our lives, we develop a collective knowledge of people that we bring to each situation. This concept is called the **generalized other,** our perceptions of the attitudes of the whole community (Mead 1934). You can recognize the generalized other whenever you or someone else uses expressions such as "most people think . . ." or "no one does that!" These expressions imply that we know what most people think or feel about something when we have never actually asked or observed *most* people behaving in a given situation. We learn from those with whom we have interacted and project those ideas onto the rest of society. For example, think about the past few times you were introduced to someone for the first time. You probably would not ask them how much money they earned, what political party they voted for, or how old they are. Chances are, in that first encounter, you each knew how to speak to each other without saying something that would surprise or insult the other person. Your sense of the generalized other helps you to navigate such interactions smoothly.

Do you do everything that you are told to do? Consider a time at work or home when a supervisor or parent told you to do something. Did you do what was asked? Perhaps you completed the work but did not put a lot of time and energy into it as a sign of disapproval. Or maybe you ignored the task altogether. It is important to note that you do not have to follow norms! You have probably violated norms many times in your life. People have **agency** or the ability to act and think independently of social constraints (Musolf 2003). Some norms are easier to ignore than others. **Mores** refer to widely held beliefs about what is considered moral and just behavior in society. In most cases, laws made by government entities would be considered mores, but many legal behaviors are also considered mores, such as publicly making racist or sexist comments or cheating on a partner. **Folkways** refer to rules of behavior for common and routine interactions. Common folkways in the United States and other cultures include waiting in line when buying something at a store or raising your hand if you want to ask a question or make a comment in class.

There are more sanctions associated with breaking mores than folkways; you can go to jail for violating some mores (stealing, causing a fire, etc.), but folkway violations (interrupting someone, belching in public, etc.) may only lead to a disapproving look. Someone, somewhere, is breaking a norm right now, even, perhaps, in the face of very stern sanctions. Murder is considered one of the worst norm violations, yet murders occur every day, even though people may face prison or death if they are found guilty

FIGURE 4.1

Teacher Status Index

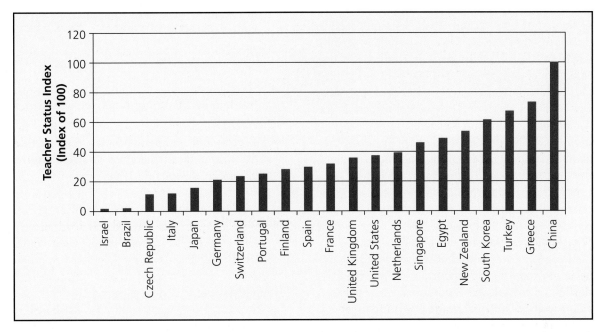

Source: Data from Varkey GEMS Foundation, *2013 Global Teacher Status Index*, Figure 1 (https://www.varkeyfoundation.org/sites/default/files/documents/2013GlobalTeacherStatusIndex.pdf).

of killing another person. The important thing to remember is that whether people decide to follow or go against the social norms that exist in society, they still serve as guideposts for our thoughts, feelings, and behaviors.

Status and Roles

In addition to norms, each society carries a number of statuses and roles. **Status** refers to our relative position in society while **roles** are the expectations about how people of a given status should think, feel, and behave. Status is about relative power and respect. Salaries reflect the value of positions most directly, with lawyers and doctors receiving more money for their time than, say, janitors. It is clear that roles of these three statuses also vary: doctors are expected to work with patients, lawyers with clients, and janitors clean. But statuses and roles can vary in each society. For example, consider the status position of teacher (see Figure 4.1). Teachers in China are considered on the same status level as doctors, while in France and Turkey, they are seen as on the same level as nurses (Varkey GEMS Foundation 2013). Therefore, how teachers think, feel, and behave also varies across these societies. For example, Chinese teachers, reflecting their relatively high status in society, tend to act toward their students in a very hierarchical way, expecting complete attention and obedience from their students.

Values and Beliefs

Values and beliefs are two other basic elements of culture. Sociologists define **values** as what a society holds to be as desirable, good, and important. **Beliefs** are what we deem to be true. The two ideas overlap in that we believe certain values to be true; one could say that all values are beliefs, but not all beliefs are values. We may believe that honesty is the most important thing in a relationship (a value), but the idea that the Kansas City Royals is the best baseball team of all time is a belief, not a value. People hold on to their values and beliefs and will find any number of ways to prove them to be true.

So, what is important to you? What do you believe? Is religion very important to you? Civil rights? Are you pro-life or pro-choice? Consider where and how you developed those beliefs. Studies regularly show that beliefs relate to the family in which you grow up; conservative adults typically come from conservative families, and liberal adults typically come from liberal families. In one study, for instance, researchers found the likelihood of people carrying out antiwar activities during the Persian Gulf War (1990–1991) was strongly related to having parents who participated in antiwar activities during the Vietnam War (1955–1975) (Duncan and Stewart 1995). Using this framework, whether you believe in evolution or that God created the world in seven days, your beliefs reflect the culture in which you were raised and may be traced to the social construction of reality.

People in each culture produce a set of values and beliefs from which to operate. Consider the fact that Americans typically say that they are Democrats or Republicans (even though there are actually dozens of smaller political parties in the United States) to describe their political affiliations and their political values and beliefs, while people in countries such as India can choose from over 1,000 political parties! Our culture provides both the content of our values and beliefs as well as a framework for them. If you come from a culture with a bilateral way of seeing politics, you will have to pick from one of those two sides and be judged by the people around you as being in one or the other camp. Conversely, places with additional frameworks provide other options to define one's values and beliefs. When it comes to culture, the society we grow up in provides "the box" when we use phrases such as "thinking outside of the box."

Using your generalized other, you will probably be able to come up with a short list of American values. While you may have a different set of personal values, you can still understand where the larger culture stands on any number of issues. Approximately fifty years ago, sociologist Robin Williams (1970) developed the following list of American values:

- Individualism: a focus on the person rather than the group

- Achievement and success: a concentration on hard work and economic well-being

- Activity and work: an emphasis on appearing busy and hard-working

- Science and technology: a reliance on technological know-how

- Progress and material comfort: the use of science and technology to produce items designed to make life easier

- Efficiency and practicality: an emphasis on getting things done without wasting time

- Equality: a desire for greater equality in the distribution of wealth and income in the United States

- Morality and humanitarianism: the prominence of moral issues in the United States

- Freedom and liberty: a focus on individual freedom and the right to pursue wealth and property

- Racism and group superiority: the fact that there is a racial hierarchy in which some groups are valued more than others

While these values may be relevant today, it is important to note that the list was published in 1970. Has American culture changed since then? What do you think?

Symbols and Language

A **symbol** refers to anything that has the same meaning for two or more people. Symbols can convey meaning to large numbers of people and instill both thoughts and emotions. Consider flags or national anthems. They can yield intense feelings of pride. For example, after terrorists attacked a soccer stadium in Paris in 2015, when the fans were finally allowed to leave the stadium, many sang the French national anthem to show their unity and bravery in the face of terrorism (see www.youtube .com/watch?v=4iQ2cHuZ0xE). Symbols can also produce negative feelings (e.g., the Nazi swastika). While any two people may create their own set of symbols, what is interesting about symbols in society is how many can affect such large numbers of people at the same time!

All U.S. presidents—no matter their political ideology—use the flag as a symbol of their patriotism.

Jeff Kravitz/FilmMagic, Inc/Getty Images

Saul Loeb/AFP/Getty Images

Exploring Norms and Symbols in Sports

In this exercise, you will examine the culture surrounding two sports.

There are norms and symbols associated with sports, both for players and for those watching the games. For example, baseball players regularly keep sunflower seeds in their mouths while they play (and spit them out!), and basketball fans try to distract opposing players attempting free throws by shaking things and making loud noises.

1. List as many norms and symbols associated with a sport or sports as you can.

2. Compare and contrast the norms and symbols for two different sports.

3. What are the norms associated with national flags and national anthems at sporting events?

4. What does it mean when norms associated with these national symbols are not observed?

Symbols are used by political leaders all the time. Consider the fact that both Republican and Democratic presidents—who have very different political ideologies—use the American flag when they give speeches in the United States. The flag is always placed on their right (your left as you look at them). They often start their speeches with "my fellow Americans" and end with something like, "God bless America." The use of these symbols gives presidents and other politicians the ability to invoke certain meanings and evoke certain sentiments among Americans. Those who hear these speeches feels a connection to the speaker because they share a common identity as Americans, a feeling that the speaker—like most Americans—is a religious person who respects God, the belief that God favors and blesses the United States. People from different cultures, however, would react differently to these same objects and phrases. They might feel indifference, puzzlement, or anger that Americans believe that God is on their side or bewilderment that someone would mention God in a political context. Each culture creates its own set of symbols.

Language refers to a series of symbols used to communicate meaning among people. Language can occur in the form of written letters and words but also in the form of body language. We learn both types of language in school, through reading, and from interacting with and listening to those around us. Language allows us to create levels of complexity in meaning that do not come from pictures or sounds alone because language, by definition, allows people to string together thoughts and feelings to create larger ideas with several dimensions. Consider some of the great works of literature

and philosophy, which may include hundreds of pages of ideas or stories that all work together to convey a central theme. It is language that provides the tools to create such complex sets of meaning.

Consider This

Write down a list of symbols that are important in American society today. What kinds of thoughts, emotions, and/or behaviors do these symbols tend to produce in Americans? How do they represent American culture?

The **Sapir-Whorf hypothesis,** also known as linguistic relativism, notes that language influences our understanding of reality above and beyond the meaning of its symbols (Sapir 1958). For example, a person from a culture with more words available to describe an object will be able to provide much more detail about it than someone from a culture with fewer words for the object. Consider wine tasting; there are many words that professional wine tasters use to describe a wine such as "full-bodied" or "full of tannins" or "acidic" or even that the wine has the flavor of a particular fruit such as cherries or strawberries or even chocolate. Not only do these words give people the ability to better describe people, objects, and experiences, but they also allow people to understand those things more fully. If you have ever been to a winery, you know that it is very common for the salesperson to encourage you to look for elements of the wine's flavor that you may not have been able to ascertain without being told.

Having access to words also gives people the ability to understand an object, person, or phenomenon in a much deeper way. Here is another way look at it: have you ever been speechless, lacking the words to describe your thoughts or feelings in a situation? In some cases, this experience may simply reflect your emotional shock or that you have not learned the language available to explain what you are feeling. In other cases, however, it may reflect your culture's lack of words to describe what is happening.

Symbols and language are a vital part of the social construction of reality. Language is used as a framework of meaning that two or more people use to make decisions in everyday life. However, we have the opportunity to modify meaning over time, adding new words or modifying the meaning of existing ones. For example, the word *wicked* usually means "evil," but in New England, it can be used to replace the words *very* or *really* (e.g., "It is wicked cold today!"). *Selfie* and *bestie* are two recently created words that have come into fashion throughout the United States. Often, technological inventions prompt the creation of new words. For example, you did not hear the word *sexting* before the invention of texting. In the next section, we will see the relationship between culture and societies at different stages of technological development.

Check Your Understanding

- How do patterns of behavior provide a framework for making decisions in our lives?

- How do we learn the norms that are appropriate for each of our behaviors?

- Why are there more sanctions associated with breaking mores than folkways?

- What is the relationship between status and roles?

- Describe how your values and beliefs relate to the family and society in which you were raised.

- How do symbols and language help us to socially construct reality?

Typology of Societies

Have you ever considered what you would be like if you were suddenly transplanted into a different country? If you are from Europe or the United States, you are more likely to find affiliation with the people in Japan and Germany simply because they share aspects of your lifestyle, including running water, electricity, smartphones, and so forth. These elements of material culture are a by-product, in part, of the level of technology in those societies and their economic development.

Gerhard Lenski (see Nolan and Lenski 2010) argued that technology is the driving force in the development of society and leads to different types of societies, from hunter-gatherer to postindustrial. Technological developments allow groups of people to increase in size. In turn, this population growth leads to cultural complexity and the development of subcultures that do not exist among groups with smaller populations. Let us look at the relationship between technology and culture among different types of societies.

Hunter-Gatherers

Groups defined as hunter-gatherers include people who use simple tools to gather available plants and to hunt animals. Some estimates say that these groups existed over 12,000 years ago, and a few groups of hunter-gatherers still exist today. These people are nomadic, and their food supply is limited to what is available to them at a given location.

Hunter-gatherers may be viewed as "presociety" in the sense that they lack the stability of place and time. That is, they must move from place to place to obtain the food and other supplies they need to live. As a result, they are unable to take many things with them. Imagine having to move every few months or years to a new location. How much could you take with you if you did not have access to cars and trucks to haul things? Perhaps you could load a few items on work animals, but these animals are quite expensive, and you probably would not have many of them, if any at all. The scope of your culture's artifacts is likely to be limited to those things that are portable and most useful to you. While each hunter-gatherer group develops its own culture, most of the roles and norms of these groups focus around food production. These societies tend to be more egalitarian than modern societies as a result of their comparatively simple means of existence.

Horticultural/Pastoral Societies

With the development of hand tools and domestication of animals around 10,000 years ago, people were able to maintain basic sustenance in one geographic location, in what we call horticultural/pastoral societies. A few such societies still exist today, including the Yanomami, a group of about 35,000 people who live in over 200 villages in the Amazon rainforest on the border of Venezuela and Brazil.

While people in this type of society do not have much if any excess food stores, they do grow their own food and, at least to some degree, rely completely on foraging. The result is that they are able to develop homes and common areas and better care for the sick, the very young, and the aged. These processes allow for populations to grow, and people can begin the processes of specialization, in which people split up the work of community life. Some may raise cattle while others farm grain or develop tools. Specialization is also associated with the growth of inequality as some skills become more valued and thus more highly rewarded than others.

Living in this type of society does not allow for a lot of free time because people still have to work hard to meet basic needs. People generally do not have access to more than what they need for survival; there are no video game consoles, televisions, Internet, or even lamps to read by! Each group does have a culture, but it focuses on the community and survival rather than personal development or technology.

Agrarian Societies

Agrarian societies are extensions of horticultural and pastoral societies except in the size and scope of farming. Like horticultural/pastoral societies, agrarian societies use tools to develop crops and domestic animals, but the scale of production is much higher among agrarian societies. There is no precise time or place where agrarian societies started to appear in the world, but a common example is the Fertile Crescent (modern-day Iraq, Lebanon, Cyprus, Jordan, Israel, and Egypt) over 8,000 years ago. Today, much of the world still lives in an agrarian-type society. According to the World Bank (2017), 46 percent of people live in a primarily rural area as of 2015. Many of the countries of South America and Africa, for instance, rely on agriculture to sustain their economies.

With the invention of more advanced tools to harvest crops and raise larger numbers of animals, agrarian societies were able to feed the larger number of people who come from greater access to food supplies. When societies gain more education and technology, they have better tools to grow and harvest food (e.g., irrigation systems and plows), which leads to the creation of more food than they need to eat. Those people with extra food can use it to trade for material goods; the possession of more material goods provides more money or capital to pay for other people to do work (i.e., workers or laborers), giving owners more time to devote to expanding their businesses, education, or even leisure activities.

The sport of polo, limited to those with access to horses and riding lessons, is a part of high culture. Baseball, which can be played by anyone with a little space, a stick, and a ball, is part of pop culture.

While every human society has rulers who may live a different lifestyle compared to average citizens, the agrarian world ushers in a level of distance between the upper classes (both political and economic elites) reflected in the concepts of **high culture,** the culture of elites, and **popular culture,** culture that exists among common people in a society. We see the development of music, poetry, and playwriting paid for and consumed by elites in agrarian societies since they do not labor in the fields but manage large estates farmed by both workers and slaves. Material culture goes viral as wealthy planters develop hobbies like traveling and art collecting, which require lots of time and money. They use their excess money to pay artisans to make things for them. As a result, the middle classes are formed by the excesses of the very wealthy. With this infusion of money from the truly wealthy classes, in this type of society, even the small middle classes can participate in high culture through education, although they do not have enough money to afford the lifestyles among the true elites (Bourdieu 1984). Lenski's typology of society, as illustrated in Table 4.1, demonstrates the ways that technological changes can affect the type of society that we live in.

Industrial and Postindustrial Societies

Industrial societies rely on the use of technology to produce goods as well as food. As in agrarian societies, excess food is produced, which can be sold and converted to capital (i.e., money). Some of this excess capital is spent on leisure activities among the wealthy, in support of personal development, but there is often more to spend. Many rich people invest their excess wealth in the production of material goods. In terms of culture, this is important because of the sheer number of objects that industrial processing can produce. As products like books, bicycles, and furniture become easier and cheaper to make, all classes have more access to these items, and the development of consumer cultures begins.

> **Consider This**
> Consider your upbringing. In what class would you say that you grew up? How might that class position affect the types of music with which you are familiar or the sports you play or follow? Why do we associate the appreciation of the fine arts (e.g., opera) with rich people?

Industrial societies continue the process in which very wealthy people invest in art and other forms of culture for the sake of art itself. Art among the masses tends to be functional in nature, serving both to bring pleasure and to serve a purpose, like cars or furniture, which can be both beautiful and useful at the same time (Bourdieu 1984). Meanwhile, among some classes, art can be enjoyed in its own right because this group has more than enough money to meet their day-to-day needs. They can buy objects that serve no purpose but to produce a sense of joy or happiness. This sparks the growth of more obscure art as artists experiment with new forms with the knowledge that there is a group of people who will have the desire—and the money—to purchase those art forms. Consider the invention of Jet Art, a form of painting invented in 1982 and created by a German prince by throwing gallons of paint in front of a jet engine onto a large canvas (Davies 2013). These paintings sell for up to $250,000! There is enough wealth in society that musicians and other artists become wealthy merely from their creative work while middle-class people participate in this process through education and enjoyment of some

TABLE 4.1

Lenski's Typology of Society

Society Type	Impacts on Lifestyle
Industrial	Very large populations, lots of diversity, growth of middle classes, and larger number of wealthy people
Agrarian	Larger, more diverse populations with excess food and resources among wealthier classes
Pastoral/ horticultural	Small, stable populations with adequate food supply
Hunter-gatherer	Small population, low diversity, less stable food supply

aspects of the art world online and through films, reprints or copies, and visiting libraries and museums, which cost considerably less than owning original works of art.

Check Your Understanding

- According to Gerhard Lenski, what is the driving force in the development of society?

- How does an excess of food affect societies?

- What is the difference between high culture and popular culture?

Considering Cultural Variations

A country's culture, much like one's own personality, changes over time as populations experience technological growth, interact with other cultures, and face large-scale events such as famines, economic depressions, wars, tsunamis, or earthquakes. Such experiences can change the way of life and perceptions of the world for large groups of people at the same time. The unique conglomeration of events reflects generational differences. Consider the Baby Boom Generation, people born between 1946 and 1964. What do they have in common? They all experienced the Vietnam War (and the protests associated with it), the Cold War and arms race, the sexual revolution, and the assassination of Martin Luther King Jr., among other things.

Historical events can have an impact a people's cultural heritage even if they do not have a direct impact on all of the people in a given society. For example, while the Great Depression is an important part of American history and led to great cultural changes, such as more trust in government and less in the marketplace and an emphasis on frugality, its direct impact on the day-to-day lives of families varied. The lives and lifestyles of many people (e.g., those who lost their jobs or significant savings or investments) changed dramatically, but people who did not experience any deprivation changed very little if at all as a result of the Depression. In either case, the Great Depression represents a major historical event that is associated with changes in American culture (Elder 1974/1999).

Think about events and inventions that have affected how members of your own generation act and view the world. How have terrorism, school shootings, global climate change, the invention of mobile phones, texting, and so on changed you and your peers? Consider a specific event like the 2016 mass shooting at a LGBT-friendly nightclub in Orlando, Florida, or the 2017 massacre in Las Vegas, two of the largest mass shootings in U.S. history (Lichtblau 2016). These horrific acts took the lives of many, wounded many more, and deeply affected people across the nation. A similar incident occurred in Australia in 1996 when twenty-eight-year-old Martin Bryant killed thirty-five people and wounded many more. This incident let to bipartisan support for stricter gun control laws in Australia.

Changes in law reflect changing norms and values as people try to put current conditions in context of large-standing cultural values. In the American case, the desire to stop massacres is in conflict with important cultural norms, specifically, some people's interpretation of the Second Amendment of U.S. Constitution, which states, "A well regulated militia being necessary to the security of a free state, the right of the people to keep and bear arms shall not be infringed."

Subcultures and Multiculturalism

As noted earlier, there can be many different cultures within a country, reflecting the diversity of its population and the different locations from which people come and when they are born.

If you live in a large city, you have probably interacted with people who are from another place (i.e., immigrants) or reflect a different lifestyle in their mannerisms or dress. **Subcultures** are simply cultural groups that exist within another, larger culture. Members of subcultures accept many of the values and beliefs of the larger culture while maintaining some unique ways of life. Some of these subcultures reflect immigration patterns, as people from another culture congregate into certain areas of a city, creating neighborhoods like Chinatown or Little Italy that reflect the different symbols, language, and material culture of the place from which they—or their ancestors—came. These neighborhoods take on elements of two different cultures, creating a new subculture. Other subcultures reflect

This 2017 picture of an Amish family in central Pennsylvania reveals some ways in which the Amish are part of a counterculture.

ideologies or lifestyles such as the "hip-hop" or youth cultures. Members may have unique slang and different styles of dress or appearance than other people in the area.

Consider This

To what subcultures do you belong? What are some of the rules, values, and artifacts that distinguish one of your subcultures? How do these aspects of your subculture give you a sense of belonging to this group and make your membership in it apparent to others?

How can subcultures exist if the role of culture is to build relationships among people, to give them a shared identity and help them relate to one another? The ideal of **multiculturalism** is that people respect differing cultures in a society and honor their unique contributions to a larger, "umbrella" culture that incorporates multiple subcultures. This ideal is often difficult to live out because differences in cultures often lead to conflict among groups. In cases where one group in a society espouses rules, values, or beliefs that conflict with the mainstream culture, they become a **counterculture.** Today, in U.S. society, the Westborough Baptist Church, the Nation of Islam, the Catholic Worker Movement, the American Indian Movement, the Aryan Brotherhood, and the Amish are all examples of countercultural groups. Each of these groups opposes one or more of the basic tenets of American culture outlined above. The Catholic Worker Movement, for instance, focuses on the ideals of communitarianism, a focus on the good of the community over the individual, which goes against the American emphasis on individualism. People in this movement have typically lived in group homes and give up their personal possessions for the good of the group.

While some countercultural groups exist peaceably within the larger society, as the Catholic Worker Movement does, others do not and threaten U.S. society in the form of domestic terrorism. The Federal Bureau of Investigation defines the Earth Liberation Front, for instance, as a domestic terrorist group because it espouses the destruction of private property as a way to stop businesses from exploiting the environment for profit.

Cultural Relativism and Global Culture

Franz Boas popularized the concept of **cultural relativism** in anthropology, the idea that cultures cannot be ranked as better or worse than others. He was writing in the nineteenth century, a time in which many social scientists believed that society was evolving much like species do. The model for this development included European countries as they transformed from agrarian to industrial societies. Boas's work initiated an intellectual movement to dispel the notion that hunter-gatherers or pastoral societies are less "advanced" than industrial nations; rather they are simply different. From this perspective, we cannot judge a people or their culture based on the type of society they live in, and we should look at each culture as unique.

While each society creates a unique culture, anthropologist George Murdock (1945) argued that there are some **cultural universals,** cultural practices that exist in most or all societies, such as social structures, tool making, art, song, dance, religious beliefs, rituals, families, a division of labor, and politics

(Brown 1991). The implication of this work is that people naturally develop certain elements of culture no matter their unique histories or backgrounds, that is, they are part of the human way of doing things. Under this schema, each human group does some of the same things but does them in different ways. Consider how visitors from another planet might view the whole human race; they would see many of the same types of things occurring in varying ways in every part of the world!

Cultural attributes can also spread throughout the world when some societies spread out and dominate others. The culture, both material and nonmaterial, of the nations that first became industrial and then postindustrial (the United States and those in Western Europe) has been introduced around the planet through colonization and the growth of capitalism. In the movie *The Gods Must Be Crazy,* an empty Coca-Cola bottle is dropped from an airplane onto the Kalahari Desert. The local people have very little contact with Western culture and try to understand the meaning of the event. At first, they view the event as a good thing but later decide that they must get rid of the bottle, leading to an adventure that serves as the basis for the rest of the movie. This comedy highlights the ways that Western countries can affect other parts of the world without consciously trying to do so. Of course, there are also conscious attempts to transmit around the world Western values, notably the importance of democracy and freedom, two American values that affect U.S. foreign policy decisions. Table 4.2 reveals some of the ways cultural traits can overlap and differ across societies.

The *Gods Must Be Crazy* is a comedy film about a man who is first exposed to Western culture from a Coke bottle dropped from an airplane.

Everett Collection, Inc./Alamy Stock Photo

TABLE 4.2

Similarities and Differences in World Values

	Germany (%)	India (%)	Iraq (%)	United States (%)
Importance of family (percent very or rather important)	95.5	93.7	99.3	98.2
Negative attitudes toward homosexuality[a] (percent who listed homosexuals as someone they would not like to have as a neighbor)	22.4	42.1	80.3	20.4
I see myself as a world citizen (percent who see themselves as a world citizen)	60.0	82.3	54.0	67.4

Source: World Values Survey, Wave 2010 to 2014 (http://www.worldvaluessurvey.org).

a. Percent of respondents who mentioned this as a response to the question: "On this list are various groups of people. Could you please mention any that you would **not** like to have as neighbors? Homosexuals" (emphasis added).

Check Your Understanding

- How can technological growth, interactions with other cultures, and severe events such as such as famine, economic depressions, war, tsunamis, or earthquakes change a country's culture?

- What is the ideal of multiculturalism?

- Explain the difference between a subculture and a counterculture.

- What are some cultural universals that exist in all societies?

- How has U.S. and Western European culture been introduced around the planet?

The Power of Culture

You have heard the expression that knowledge is power, right? In the case of culture, this is very true. Culture is a tool kit for us to use in our day-to-day life. Having the right cultural tools can help us interact with others effectively and gain what we seek (Swidler 1986). For example, before you go on a job interview, it makes sense to learn all you can about what your prospective employer expects of employees in terms of behavior, attitude, dress, and so on and display that culture during the interview. This cultural knowledge can help you to secure and advance in a professional position. Imagine what might happen if you showed up for an interview wearing jeans, only to be greeted by an interviewer in a suit? Chances are the interviewer will immediately judge you as not a good cultural fit for the company and you will lose out on the job!

Cultural Capital and Social Intelligence

You have also surely heard of the expression "it takes money to make money." An extension of this idea is that it takes capital to make capital. Capital refers to your assets, anything you own. Capital can take many forms, including fiscal capital (money) and intellectual capital, which can include skills or knowledge for which other people are willing to pay. **Cultural capital** is a type of capital related to education, style, appearance, and dress that promotes social mobility (Bourdieu and Passeron 1990).

Wealthier families with fiscal capital can provide their children with an elite education, travel, music lessons, fine dining, language immersion programs, and so forth so that they can develop cultural capital as they grow up. In turn, cultural capital can help us to gain employment and fiscal capital as we learn to interact effectively with powerful members of society (Mark 2003). Many businesses today need employees who speak multiple languages, can interact effectively with people of diverse cultures, and know what will sell (and how to sell it) in different areas of the world. We can use these forms of capital for both our own personal gain and in efforts to help shape society. Cultural capital provides the information people use when deciding if others are part of their group. In the case of elites, knowing how to tie a necktie properly or selecting appropriate clothing to wear at different events (e.g., polo or wine tasting) signals that a person belongs there (or not). It works the other way around as well; wealthy people trying to gain access to working-class environments face similar obstacles. The difference, here, is that wealthier people have access to more fiscal capital, hence access to personal and business loans and job markets, among other things. Being able to interact with people with high status has implications for our ability to grow wealth over time.

> **Consider This**
> List three ways we use culture in our everyday lives. Think about the types of clothing you wear in different social situations (e.g., work and home), the types of activities you engage in, and the material objects you have access to (e.g., automobiles vs. public transportation). How might you use this knowledge if you lived in a country with a culture quite different from the one in which you were raised?

The Differing Power of Imagery across Cultures

In this activity, you will consider the power of an image and compare its meaning across several cultures.

This is an image of the Twin Towers on September 11, 2001, when members of Al Qaeda hijacked four commercial airplanes and crashed two of them into upper floors of the Twin Towers of the World Trade Center. Write your answers to the following questions.

1. What does this image mean to you? What does it symbolize? What does it say about U.S. culture?

2. What do you think this image means to Al Qaeda?

3. What does it mean to members of other Western industrialized countries like Canada, Great Britain, Germany, and France?

Tammy KLEIN/Gamma-Rapho/Getty Images

Social Intelligence

Psychologist Daniel Goleman popularized the expression "social intelligence" in the 1990s (Goleman 2006). **Social intelligence** refers to our ability to understand social relationships and get along with others. This ability requires cultural capital. People with social intelligence know the appropriate cultural cues in their society (a sign of cultural capital) *and* can accurately read the cues given off by others. Those with high levels of social intelligence have great social skills and work well with others. They are able to read a room and know just what to say—and when.

An extreme example of the use of cultural and social intelligence comes from the literary classic *The Great Gatsby*. The main character, Jay Gatsby, uses his knowledge of how to interact effectively with wealthy people (and the fortune he earned illegally) to fake being a member of American elite society. He used fiscal capital to buy expensive things and host lavish parties, cultural capital to know and emulate how the wealthy live, and social intelligence to manipulate people's perception of him.

Culture and Identity

Cultural capital and social intelligence are housed in us through our social identities. **Social identities** are the unique set of statuses, roles, and traits that each of us has. As noted earlier, each society creates a unique set of statuses and roles to choose from; there are fathers, nurses, teachers, drifters, and children, each with their own relative power and prestige in a given society and each with a set of expectations about how to act in those positions that we have defined as roles. We develop our identities based on the statuses and roles available to us. It is important to know that individuals rarely accept all of the cultural expectations associated with a given role in a culture. Rather, as a person takes on new positions, he or she modifies the set of expectations, its role, by incorporating elements of culture with our own, individual way of doing things. A "good" college student in the United States may go to class, take notes, and do well on exams, but almost all students miss some classes during a semester because of a mix of decisions (e.g., caring for a sick family member or friend) and personal traits (e.g., difficulty getting up in the morning or a dislike for certain subject).

Assessing Cultural Capital and Social Intelligence

In this activity, you will use online quizzes to assess your own social intelligence and then consider how your skills may help or hurt you in your future career.

How well do you understand the cultural cues around you? We (often) unconsciously share our thoughts and feelings using cultural cues such as smiling to indicate happiness and raised eyebrows to represent shock or fear or surprise. It is possible to assess how well you "read" cultural cues, or the extent of your social intelligence.

Visit the following websites and take the quizzes provided, which will rate how well you are able read the people around you:

http://greatergood.berkeley.edu/ei_quiz/#15

http://socialintelligence.labinthewild.org/mite/

Write a one- to two-page essay describing some of your career goals and how the findings of either of the two tests may have an impact on those goals. For instance, if you plan to work in the areas of law or medicine, how might a high or low score affect that career? If you believe that a low score on the quizzes will have a negative impact, discuss ways that you might increase your abilities in these areas.

It is this synergy between our culture (expectations for being a good student in society) and individual traits (our unique personality or lifestyle) that makes our identity unique.

Social identity also gives us the power to change ourselves and society. If culture is part of our identity, we can change our identity by taking on new elements of culture and exposing ourselves to new culture. Living for a time in other countries exposes us to new ways of thinking about the world and teaches us new norms, symbols, and languages. We do not have to go to other countries to get this experience, however. Simply visiting a new neighborhood or volunteering at a local homeless shelter or organization for new immigrants can yield similar results. Spending time at the opera or other high-culture events can produce the same kind of personal change.

Consider This

Social identity includes the ways that we bring the cultures from our group affiliations into our sense of self.

How might this process be positive for individuals? How might it divide people in everyday interactions?

Understanding the dynamics of the self and society can help you to determine elements of society that you want to change. If there is a conflict between yourself, your identity, and the larger society, it will result in what psychologists call dissonance. **Dissonance** occurs when something is disordered and produces a negative feeling that we want to relieve in some way. Seeing homeless people in a wealthy neighborhood can create a sense of dissonance. Likewise, if your professional role in society gives you a sense of discomfort, you may want to change your profession—or change *the profession!* Dr. Paul Farmer, a medical doctor, believes that the role of the doctor should be to change the world; it should be less about personal wealth and prestige as it is in the Western world and more about serving other people. Farmer's life's work includes attempts to change the role of doctor in society to be more about helping the poorest of the poor through medicine (see Kidder 2009).

Another way to make decisions about what to change in society is to examine existing norms, symbols, or other elements of culture. Corey Dolgon, the sociologist featured in the following Sociologists in Action box, has spent his career doing so. Understanding how symbols affect culture can help us to make sense of social patterns—and to change them.

In 2015, a number of southern states in the United States decided to remove the Confederate

The Making of a Public Sociologist or the *Public* Part of Public Sociology

Corey Dolgon

My first job after earning my PhD was at the Friends World Program, a Quaker-based college program at Long Island University (LIU) in which students focused their studies on addressing the world's problems, while learning in various parts of the world. While there, I helped create the Southampton Coalition for Justice—a group of campus custodians, local activists, students, and staff who came together to challenge the LIU administration's decision to outsource janitors to a management company. Outsourcing meant that the custodians lost job security, seniority, tuition remission, and a host of other perks, but the action also exposed the inherent and institutional racism that had kept the predominately African American and Native American custodians from promotion and advancement for 30 years. Our work proved successful, and it formed a crucial framework for my first book, *The End of the Hamptons: Scenes from the Class Struggle in America's Paradise* (NYU Press 2005).

Over the past decade, my work has found a home in the burgeoning area of public sociology. I have continued to develop and teach courses at Worcester State University and now at Stonehill College that have community-based research and action projects at their core. My students have provided research to support Housing First movements in Worcester, Massachusetts, and youth organizing in Brockton, Massachusetts. I am co-chair of Brockton's Promise—an umbrella organization for youth service agencies—through which my students and I have built a network of school and community gardens, supported local homeless families in challenging unfit emergency shelters and forced state and local officials to change housing policies, and helped high school students protesting school-to-prison pipeline discipline procedures.

I have also written widely about community-based learning and current social problems. My latest book, *Kill It to Save It* (Policy Press 2017), documents and explains capitalism's triumph over democracy. My hope is that once we better analyze the root causes of social problems, we may address them more effectively as well.

For me, to be a public sociologist or a "sociologist in action" has always started from the theoretical framework of praxis: to study and learn while engaging community and its social problems, to research and write along with the people who know what questions to ask and how global forces affect their own communities. Public sociology conducts these efforts in such a collaborative and participatory way that suggest our goals must be, to paraphrase Marx, not just to interpret the world in various ways—but to change it.

Corey Dolgon is the first director of the new Office of Community-Based Learning at Stonehill College in Easton, Massachusetts, after serving ten years as professor and chair of Worcester State College's Sociology department as well as the director of its Center for Service Learning and Civic Engagement.

flag from courthouses. The civil war was fought largely over the Confederate states' defense of slavery, and hence the Confederate flag serves as a symbol to promote racism. Other people have contested these efforts to remove the flag from government buildings by putting Confederate flags on their cars and hanging them in or around their homes. Both sides realize the importance of this symbol in American culture. By removing it, government leaders sought to publicly distance themselves from a racist symbol, show their disapproval of racist views, and demonstrate their commitment to upholding civil rights laws in the United States. Changing culture is a powerful way to influence society!

Other efforts at changing culture can take place on more local levels. Student-led efforts to change high school dress codes (Baker 2012; Mazzola 2015) are one example. The "Free the Nipple" movement in Springfield, Missouri, is another. A group of women in Springfield have organized to challenge local ordinances that prohibit women from baring their breasts in public through public marches in the center of town, which included displays of nudity, a form of civil disobedience.

Check Your Understanding

- In what ways can the right cultural tools help you during a job interview?

- How is cultural capital related to social mobility?

- What is social intelligence and how does it relate to the development of cultural capital?

- What makes up our social identities?

- Describe how dissonance can lead to changes at the individual and societal levels.

- How might removing or displaying a cultural symbol change society?

Consider This
Are you now or can you see yourself becoming part of the Free the Nipple movement? How does/would your participation in such a movement relate (or not) to the various aspects of your social identity (your unique set of statuses, roles, and traits)?

Conclusion

Culture shapes our lives and our society. We may not be able to literally see or touch culture but, with a sociological eye, we can recognize it and learn to use it. In the next chapter, we examine socialization, the process through which we learn how we fit in society and how to interact with others. As you will see, the culture in which we live influences the socialization process and all the key actors in it. We cannot escape culture, but once we are aware of it, we can use it to influence our individual lives and our society.

CHAPTER
4

Want a better grade? Get the tools you need to sharpen your study skills. Access practice quizzes, eFlashcards, video and multimedia at **edge.sagepub.com/korgen**

Review

4.1 What is culture?

Culture refers to the characteristics of a group or society that make it distinct from other groups and societies. Nonmaterial culture includes concepts such as norms, values and beliefs, symbols, and language. Material culture consists of artifacts ranging from tools to products designed for leisure like flat-screen TVs and Xboxes. These things reflect the values and beliefs of the people who live in a culture.

4.2 What are some ways that the different elements of culture influence everyday life?

Patterns of behavior, guided by our culture, provide a framework for making decisions in our lives. The key elements of a culture—norms, values and beliefs, symbols, and language—help shape our everyday lives.

Norms (expectations about the appropriate thoughts, feelings, and behaviors of people in a variety of situations) guide our interactions. Our beliefs and values shape our understanding of the world and how we act in it. We communicate through the use of symbols, which can convey meaning to large numbers of people. The language we use refers to a series of symbols. The multicultural ideal respects differing cultures in a society and honors their unique contributions to the larger culture.

4.3 How do societal types relate to variations in culture?

Gerhard Lenski (see Nolan and Lenski 2010) argued that technology is the driving force in the development of society and leads to different types of societies and cultures. Technological developments allow groups of people to increase in size, and this population growth leads to cultural complexity that does not exist among groups with smaller populations. For example, with the invention of more advanced tools to harvest crops and raise more animals, agrarian societies were able to support larger numbers of people and to develop high culture (the culture of the elites).

4.4 How do changes to our culture shape our behaviors and ways of viewing the world?

A country's culture changes over time as its population experiences the impact of technological growth, interactions with other cultures, and severe events such as such as famine, economic depressions, war, tsunamis, or earthquakes. For example, school shootings and other acts of terrorism, global climate change, the invention of mobile phones, texting, and so on have affected the behaviors and perspectives of young adults today. These events also can create and influence subcultures, cultures that exist within another larger culture that accept many of the values and beliefs of the larger culture while maintaining some unique ways of life. They can also lead to the creation of countercultures, groups in a society that espouse rules, values, or beliefs that conflict with the larger umbrella culture of the society.

4.5 In what ways can you use cultural capital to help both yourself and society?

Culture is a tool kit for us to use in our day-to-day life. Having the right cultural tools can help us to interact with others effectively and gain what we seek. Cultural capital refers to knowledge related to education, style, appearance, and dress that promotes social mobility (Bourdieu and Passeron 1990). Cultural capital can help us to gain access to powerful arenas of society. We can use these connections and our cultural knowledge for both our own personal gain and in efforts to help shape society.

Key Terms

- agency   62
- beliefs   63
- counterculture   70
- cultural capital   72
- cultural relativism   70
- cultural universals   70
- culture   59
- dissonance   74
- folkways   62
- generalized other   62
- high culture   68
- language   65
- material culture   59
- mores   62

- multiculturalism   70
- nonmaterial culture   59
- norms   62
- popular culture   68
- roles   63
- Sapir-Whorf hypothesis   65
- social identities   73
- social intelligence   73
- socially constructed   60
- status   63
- subculture   69
- symbol   64
- values   63

How many of the ordinary things we do every day are taught to us by others?

Learning Questions

5.1 What is socialization?

5.2 According to George Herbert Mead, how does an individual develop a social self?

5.3 What are the key agents of socialization?

5.4 What is gender socialization?

5.5 What are status, social roles, and identity?

5.6 How do sociologists describe and analyze social interaction?

CHAPTER 5

Understanding Socialization

Amy Sodaro

What Is Socialization?

Think about what you did this morning. Probably you woke up to an alarm clock that you set last night to ensure that you would be on time for your classes or other obligations. When you got out of bed, you probably followed some kind of morning routine, such as taking a shower, brushing your teeth, getting dressed, and eating breakfast. For each of these activities, you may not have realized it, but you were following norms determined not by you but by your culture and society. You were not born knowing that you need to shower every day and brush your teeth to stay clean, or that you should wear clothes to go to class and eat cereal for breakfast. These are things that you learned through your interactions with others.

From the time you were an infant, your family, peers, and others have taught you what you need to know to live in your society, such as how to keep yourself clean, what kinds of foods are typically eaten for breakfast and how, and the importance of being on time for your classes and other obligations. Imagine that you were born in a village in the highlands of Peru or 200 years ago. Your morning routine would be quite different!

You know what to do to start your day because you have undergone the process of **socialization;** that is, you have learned, through social interaction, how to follow the social norms and expectations of your society. In Chapter 4, you learned about how culture structures our lives within society, establishing norms and social patterns that we are expected to adhere to, but we are not born knowing how to fit into our culture. Through the process of socialization, individuals become functioning members of their society.

Socialization is part of a larger process of **social reproduction,** in which a society's norms and values are passed on from generation to generation. Societies have continuity over time because individuals learn and internalize the values and norms of their society and pass them on to future generations. Values and norms of societies do change over time. Perhaps one of the first things that you did today was check your phone for social media updates, certainly not something your grandmother did as part of her daily routine! And 200 years ago, few people bathed daily. But many structural components of societies remain the same from one generation to the next—such as the organization of our days around family and work obligations and the expectation that you must get dressed to begin your day. These are some of the social norms that have been passed

How I Got Active in Sociology

Amy Sodaro

I was a latecomer to sociology. Astonishingly, although I had a lifelong interest in culture and society, I made it through my undergraduate degree with two majors—drama and classics—and not one sociology course. I was working in New York City as a costume designer when the terror attacks of September 11, 2001, occurred. Watching the towers fall convinced me that I didn't have a sufficient framework or vocabulary for understanding the complexity of contemporary society, so I enrolled in an interdisciplinary master's program at the New School for Social Research in New York. I took my first sociology course there and realized that sociology provides the conceptual framework I had been looking for to merge my interests in culture, politics, and society and make sense of the world around me. Both my PhD studies and my current research focus on the sociology of culture, with an emphasis on how societies remember and come to terms with violence. I currently teach sociology just a few blocks away from the World Trade Center site, at the Borough of Manhattan Community College, where I strive to demonstrate to students the value and importance of developing a sociological perspective.

down to you from your parents, grandparents, and great-grandparents.

Socialization begins the moment babies are born. Everything from the name they receive, to the blanket they snuggle in, to the hospital where they are born and the home where they reside is part of their socialization. It is a process that continues throughout the **life course,** or the various stages of one's life, from birth to death.

In different periods of life, individuals undergo new and different processes of socialization and **resocialization,** where they learn to adapt to new social norms and values. For example, when a young adult first moves out of her parents' home, she must learn how to perform a new social role: that of an adult living independently who must shop, cook, clean, manage money, and pay her own bills. This role requires learning new skills and new norms and disengaging from old norms that were appropriate when living as a dependent child. Becoming an adult involves learning a whole new role set and associated norms.

> ### Consider This
> Can you think of a resocialization process you have undergone?

Nature versus Nurture

Most of us cannot remember far enough back to recall when we first began to acquire the skills that we need to live in society. We learn things like language, how to walk and feed ourselves, and basic hygiene when we are very young children and internalize these skills to the point where they feel like a natural part of who we are. Occasionally, however, children are discovered

who did not undergo a "normal" process of socialization. They can help us to understand just how much we learn through our social interactions and how socialization cannot occur in social isolation.

In 1970, a young girl was found who had spent over ten years of her life in almost complete isolation. Genie, as she was called, is one of a handful of examples of feral—or wild—children. **Feral children** are raised in isolation and do not have the opportunity to interact with others and become socialized. Genie had spent most of her life alone in a locked room and did not know how to talk, use the toilet, or feed herself. She didn't know how to interact with others and in many ways behaved like an infant when she was found. Throughout history, there have been a handful of examples of children like Genie who were not socialized through regular human interaction. Their cases intrigue scientists looking to understand how much of who we are is shaped by **nature**—that is, biology, or how we were born—and how much is formed by **nurture** through our cultural and social learning. Sociologists are more interested in understanding the impact of culture and learning, or nurture, on individuals. Feral children remind us just how much of who we are is shaped by our social interactions with others in the process of socialization.

Check Your Understanding

- What is socialization?
- When does socialization occur?
- What is resocialization?
- What are social roles and how do we learn them through socialization?
- How do we know that social interaction is necessary for socialization?

Understanding Theories of Socialization

Sociologists have a deep interest in understanding why humans are the way we are. While sociologists are not interested in any one particular individual, they are interested in individuals as they are situated in and shaped by society. It is therefore important for sociologists to understand how, through socialization, individuals develop into social beings who are capable of navigating the many demands of social life.

Because socialization is focused on the individual, sociological understanding of it is shaped by the micro-level symbolic interactionist approach, particularly the work of its founder, George Herbert Mead (1863–1931). In Chapter 2, you learned about symbolic interactionism as a theoretical approach that focuses on the ways in which we construct meaning through our social interactions. Mead (1964) argued that it is through these symbolic interactions with others that we develop into social beings.

Mead's Theory of Childhood Development

As you read in Chapter 2, Mead was influenced by Charles Horton Cooley's concept of the looking glass self, which is a way of seeing oneself the way you think others see you. Cooley believed that we adjust our behavior and selves according to how we imagine others perceive and judge us. Think about taking a "selfie": when you snap a photo of yourself, you see yourself as others will see you, imagine their response, and adjust your appearance and expression accordingly. Taking a selfie is an example of your looking glass self. George Herbert Mead similarly saw the self as shaped by others through our social interactions.

Like Cooley, Mead believed that we are not born with a sense of self but rather learn **self-consciousness** through our social interactions. Self-consciousness is an individual's awareness of how others see her. The individual develops a sense of self through the reactions and attitudes of others. For example, babies are born completely unaware that they are individuals distinct from those individuals and things around them. This awareness is something that develops as babies grow into toddlers and interact with those around them. Mead was particularly interested in the role of play in the development of children's self-awareness. He maintained that children begin to develop into social beings who are aware of themselves as distinct individuals through what he termed **taking the role of the other**: that is, imitating those around them. Have you ever noticed a young child pushing a baby doll in a toy stroller? Or a toddler making mud "pies" in the sandbox? These children are imitating the grown-ups they see around them. As toddlers get older, they begin to put themselves in others' positions in imagined scenarios like playing doctor or school. While this may seem to be merely child's

Children imitate the adults they observe, especially those of the same gender.

©iStockphoto.com/tirc83

play, for Mead this is an extremely important step toward developing a social self. In taking the role of the other, children begin to see themselves the way others see them while also starting to understand that they are separate individuals distinct from those around them and capable of compelling particular reactions from others.

As children get older, their play becomes more sophisticated and they begin to play organized games. Mead uses the example of baseball to describe the importance of these games in the further development of the social self. Through imitation, children put themselves in the shoes of a specific and particular other and begin to see themselves the way others see them. In organized games like baseball, individuals must be able to imagine and anticipate the actions of *all* of the other players. A shortstop needs to understand the role of the pitcher and catcher, as well as the other fielders and the batter. Furthermore, there are rules that all players must follow for the game to work, and they all must agree upon the goal. What emerges in this kind of play is not the specific other of imitation but what Mead describes as the generalized other: an other that represents the whole community of players and ultimately of society. Just as young children develop an understanding of what it means to perform the role of a specific other, like a parent or teacher, older children engaged in organized games develop an understanding of the larger rules, norms, and values of the society in which they live. This leads to their each developing a self that responds not only to individual reactions but also to the norms and expectations of society.

What develops in these play and games stages is what Mead refers to as the **"me,"** which is to be distinguished from the **"I,"** the unsocialized response to the attitudes of others. The "I" is the self's impulses and

attitudes that respond to the reactions and attitudes of others in a way that is creative and active. But the "I" is often censored or held back by the "me," which is the part of the self that has internalized the generalized reactions and attitudes of other members of society (the generalized other). The "me" is the side of our self that follows the norms and expectations of society and works to control our behavior accordingly.

Consider This

How does a game like hide and seek teach children about the generalized other? What societal expectations does one learn in a game like hide and seek?

Check Your Understanding

- What is Cooley's looking glass self?
- According to Mead, how do children develop a social self?
- What is the generalized other?
- What does Mead mean by the "I" versus the "me"?

Agents of Socialization

People, groups, institutions, and social contexts that contribute to our socialization are known as **agents of socialization.** We encounter different agents of socialization as we move through the life course. **Primary socialization** occurs from the time we are born to when we start school. During this time, we learn things like language and other foundational skills

Families are the most influential agents of socialization regardless of the family's social class or structure. The sitcom *Modern Family* portrays evolving ideas of family structure.

Bob D'Amico/Disney ABC Television Group/Getty Images

for life in society; at this point, the family is the primary agent of socialization. However, as we age, we move through many different social groups and contexts that shape us, such as sports teams or clubs, schools, religious organizations, and neighborhoods. Some of us may join the military, a highly powerful agent of socialization that has its own distinct set of norms and expectations, and each of us will move through more than one workplace, in which we will encounter distinct processes of socialization and resocialization. Socialization is a lifelong process and central to our experiences as social beings.

Family

Because family is generally the first agent of socialization and interaction with family is so intense in the years from infancy to childhood, family is the most influential agent of socialization. While family structures vary widely in cultures and societies around the globe, most infants and children undergo significant socialization by their families.

In the Western world, the nuclear family predominates, meaning children are usually raised by a mother, father, and perhaps siblings. Throughout history and around the globe, extended families of grandparents, aunts, uncles, and cousins may be more typical family structures in which socialization occurs. And in today's world, family structures are rapidly changing, as is evidenced by the growth in single-parent households and same-sex couples (Vespa, Lewis and Kreider 2013); you'll learn more about the family in Chapter 10. No matter the family formation, family is an extremely important agent of socialization.

External social structures and forces influence socialization within families. Historically, the family one was born into determined an individual's position in life. While today there is more opportunity for social mobility, one's social class still greatly influences how families socialize children. Sociologist Annette Lareau conducted an ethnography of Black and White families of different social class statuses, the findings of which she published in her book *Unequal Childhoods: Class, Race and Family Life* (2002). She found that middle-class parents (of both races) engaged in what she termed "concerted cultivation," enrolling their children in extracurricular activities that structured their free time and encouraging them to be active, critical thinkers. Lower-income working-class and lower-class families, on the other hand, emphasized the "accomplishment of natural growth" and believed that their children would develop in schools and on their own. The children in these lower-income families had less structured free time and would "hang out," play, and watch television but did not have the same opportunities to develop the kinds of skills that would help them to later navigate college and the workforce. In Chapter 7, you will learn more about economic inequality, but from Lareau's study, we can begin to see how economic inequality shapes the process of socialization and is, in turn, reproduced through socialization.

We learn many essential things about our culture and society from our families, and their influence on us lasts a lifetime. Families teach us not only foundational skills like language and how to feed and dress ourselves but also the values, beliefs, and social norms that will shape us throughout our life course. We learn about gender roles and expectations by observing what our mothers and fathers, brothers and sisters do and how they behave (Chodorow 1978). For example, we might see our mothers cook, clean, and care for the children, while our fathers take out the trash, mow the lawn, and go off to work, reinforcing traditional expectations about gender roles, which we'll learn more about in Chapter 8. As individuals get older, they encounter different agents of socialization that may reinforce or challenge the things that they have learned from their families.

School

School is a significant agent of socialization; in America, most children begin school by the age of five, if not before, and spend much of the next thirteen years in school, with many then going on to college. In school, students not only learn academic content, such as reading, writing, mathematics, science, social studies, and so on, but also important norms and values. Through this "hidden curriculum," children learn how to interact with authority figures who are not their parents (teachers and administrators) and their **peers** (others in their age group). They also learn many rules and norms that are particular to the school context but can carry over into other settings, such as being quiet, raising one's hand to speak, following instructions, obeying authority figures, not cheating, and working with others (Jackson 1968). Schools also teach students about cultural values: For example, in this country, students often recite the Pledge of Allegiance each day before class, reinforcing their "allegiance" to American culture and values. In fact, many would argue that socialization is school's most important function in society (Parsons 1959; Karabel and Halsey 1978).

Various social factors influence children's experiences of socialization in schools. Educational psychologist Katherine Wentzel (2005), for example, found that students who are socially accepted and enjoy a "popular" status are more successful academically. Strong ties to peers from kindergarten through high school are linked to greater motivation in school and higher academic performance (Wentzel and Muenks 2016). This probably doesn't surprise you as you think about your own experience in elementary, middle, and high school, when fitting in with your peers was so very important. But other social factors, such as social class, race and ethnicity, skin color, and gender, also affect one's experience in school. For example, data from the Department of Education show that Black girls were suspended at a rate of 12 percent in 2011–2012 in comparison to a suspension rate of just 2 percent for White girls (Vega 2014). Another recent study showed that not only are Black students more likely to be suspended than White students, but Black students with darker skin tones were three times more likely to be suspended than their Black classmates with lighter skin tones (Hannon, DeFina, and Bruch 2013). Thus, the color of a child's skin may play a role in determining whether she learns to like school and feels a sense of safety and belonging in the classroom or views school as a place where she does not belong because she is perceived to be a troublemaker. In Chapter 9, you will learn about the impact of race on individuals and society and how racial inequalities are structured into social institutions like schools, affecting the experiences and socialization of students.

> **Consider This**
>
> What are some elements of your high school's "hidden curriculum"? Other than academics, what sorts of things did you learn in high school?

Peers

As children get older, they spend more time with their peers and less time with their families. Peers, then, become an increasingly important agent of socialization that can both reinforce and challenge what children have learned from the family. In school—and for many children today this can begin with preschool or daycare at age two or younger—children spend their days surrounded by other children of the same age, interacting with them both inside and outside the classroom. Peers become extremely powerful agents of socialization. You have, no doubt, heard the term **peer pressure.** Peers often expect conformity to a set of particular social norms relating to appearance, behavior, language, and so on. Accordingly, young people, surrounded by peers in school, often face pressure to conform to the norms accepted by their classmates.

Much of the sociological research on peers and socialization involves deviant behaviors, or behaviors that go against society's norms, which you will learn more about in Chapter 6. A recent study, for example, found that sixth- through twelfth-grade students were more likely to engage in cyberbullying if many of their friends were cyberbullying other students (Patchin and Hinduja 2013). Another recent study showed that students in the fifth through eighth grades were more likely to engage in homophobic

FIGURE 5.1

Growth in Media Consumption, 2008–2015

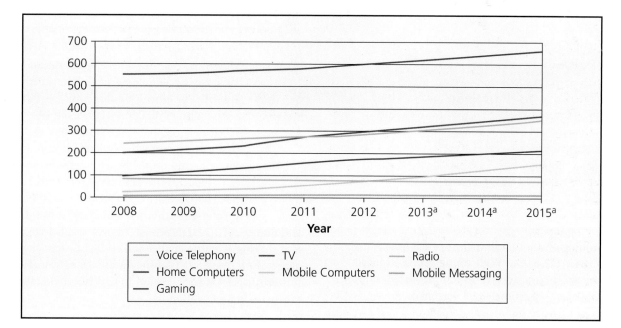

Source: From "American Media Consumption to Soar in 2015," November 5, 2013, *ZME Science*, http://www.zmescience.com/other/american-media-consumption-to-soar-in-2015.

Note: Values are presented in billions of hours.

a. Projected data.

name-calling if they saw their peers doing the same thing (Birkett and Espelage 2014).

Peers are critical agents of socialization at various stages in the life course and can challenge the kinds of norms and values learned from families, teachers, and administrators. With peers, we are exposed to new cultures, norms, values, and beliefs, some of which may manifest in deviant behaviors, but many of which develop individuals' understanding and experience of diversity and multiculturalism. For example, Pew Research has found that 71 percent of Millennials (the generation born after 1981) support same-sex marriage, a proportion much higher than Generation X (56 percent) and Baby Boomers (46 percent).

Media

Media are an increasingly influential agent of socialization. Books, radio, and television have long been influential social forces, but today we live in an "information age" in which we have unprecedented access to media, much of them conveniently and constantly accessible on our smartphones and tablets. A recent report from the University of Southern California estimated that Americans consume the equivalent of fifteen hours

of media a day (Short 2013); another report found that teens spend on average of nine hours per day consuming media that are not related to school work (Common Sense Media 2015). We live in a media-saturated society and are very much shaped by this constant stream of images and information. Every movie we watch, magazine we flip through, or text we read contains messages that contribute to the ongoing shaping of our values and norms.

The huge recent increase in media consumption (see Figure 5.1) has led to many questions about how it is influencing society, especially young people. Since long before the creation of the Internet and iPhones, studies have tried to determine the effect of media on children and young adults, especially violent media. For example, a 1956 study by Alberta Siegel found that four-year-olds who watched *Woody Woodpecker* cartoons, in which said woodpecker frequently violently pecks those around him, later behaved more aggressively than four-year-olds who had watched the relatively peaceful *Little Red Hen*. In 1968, communications scholar George Gerbner established the Cultural Indicators research project at the Annenberg School of Communication at the University of Pennsylvania to determine how television shapes viewers' perceptions of the world. The project's analysis of thousands of hours of television programming led Gerbner to argue that television creates "mean world syndrome,"

Video games are a socializing agent that, depending on the game, can have either positive or negative impacts on behavior.

©iStockphoto.com/dangrytsku

violent media and later aggression and violence (e.g., Anderson et al. 2003, 2010; Bushman and Huesmann 2012; Huesmann et al. 2003). However, most scholars agree that there is no one cause that can explain why someone becomes violent. And on the other side, scholars have found positive effects of some media like (nonviolent) video games, including greater empathy (Greitemeyer, Osswald, and Brauer 2010) and increased cooperation, helping, and sharing (Gentile et al. 2009). What all scholars agree on, however, is that media are an extremely powerful agent of socialization to which individuals are exposed more and more.

Agents of Socialization for Adults

While socialization may be most intense in our early years, we never stop being socialized. As individuals move into adulthood, they encounter new agents of socialization and have to unlearn some of their old norms and values. For example, for most people in cultures around the world, work is an important social context in which we spend much of our time. Before industrialization, most people did not work outside of their home; they farmed or had a trade in or very near their homes. Today that has changed, and most of us spend our work day in a different location, surrounded by people who are not our family and sometimes not even friends. Many Americans begin working when they are teenagers and continue to work for most of their lives.

Each new workplace one joins constitutes a new set of agents of socialization, including bosses, colleagues, clients or customers, and others. In the workplace, individuals are expected to perform particular social roles and adhere to a slightly different set of social norms and values than what they might follow at home or in other contexts. For example, someone with tattoos covering their arms may need to wear long sleeves to work. A gay man or woman might pretend to be straight to avoid discrimination in the workplace. As of 2016, only twenty-two states and Washington, D.C., had laws protecting employees from discrimination based on their sexual orientation (Bellis 2016).

leading people to believe the world is more dangerous than it actually is. With young people exposed to so much media today, much of them depicting violence—an estimated 90 percent of movies, 68 percent of video games, 60 percent of TV shows, and 15 percent of music videos include some violence (Wilson 2008)—these questions have become pressing, especially in the wake of mass violence committed by young people, such as mass shootings at Columbine High School; a movie theater in Aurora, Colorado; Sandy Hook Elementary School in Newtown, Connecticut; Emanuel African Methodist Episcopal Church in Charleston, South Carolina; and Pulse nightclub in Orlando, Florida.

Consider This

How have the media served as an agent of your socialization? Think, for example, of one of your favorite movies when you were younger. What did that movie teach you about social and cultural norms, values, and beliefs? Have any of those norms, values, and beliefs been challenged as you have grown older?

Recent studies have looked at new forms of media, especially video games, to try to determine whether and to what extent they are linked to violent real-life acts. Most studies find that there is a link between

The Netflix show *Orange Is the New Black* has taught many of us that a total institution, like a prison, has its own routines, values, and norms.

Pictorial Press Ltd/Alamy Stock Photo

Total Institutions

Many people will at some point find themselves in what is known as a **total institution,** an institution that is closed to external influences in which a group of people live together, following a strictly structured routine (Goffman 1961). In a total institution, our sleep, work, and play all occur within the confines of one institution—rather than in different locations—under a single authority that oversees and administers these activities.

Consider This

Describe how at least two different agents of socialization influenced your decision to attend college.

One example of a total institution is prison. According to U.S. Bureau of Justice Statistics, in 2013 (Carson 2014), a total of 1,574,700 adults were incarcerated in state and federal prisons. Each of these prisoners had to undergo resocialization upon entering prison, learning new norms to which they must adhere and new values. For example, prisoners must dress alike, eat, wake up, and sleep at the same time and follow the orders of prison guards. At the same time, they must stop following the norms that structure life as a free individual, like getting up when they want to, eating what and when they wish, and following their former daily routines. They also must give up old values, like autonomy and their relationship with family and friends, and embrace new values, like keeping to oneself, defending oneself when challenged, and not "snitching." Prisoners also learn a new language—prison slang—to communicate in this new social context.

Another total institution is the military, especially basic training or "boot camp." Military recruits live, eat, and train together, following a strict schedule and rules that guide practically every moment of their lives. They must wear uniforms and shave their heads, march in line and chant together, and leave behind civilian concerns in the face of an all-encompassing basic training experience. They are resocialized to follow the norms and expectations of this new and total institution, changing from a civilian to a soldier.

Check Your Understanding

- What are agents of socialization?
- What are some of the most important agents of socialization and what do we learn from each?
- Why are the media an increasingly powerful agent of socialization? What kinds of things do they teach individuals?
- What are total institutions? How do they resocialize adults?

Gender Socialization

Just as we learn the general norms and expectations of our society, we also learn the particular expectations of society when it comes to gender. Learning gender identity and roles through socialization is known as **gender socialization.** From birth—or arguably even as early as the sex of a baby is known—individuals are assigned gender roles and socialized through various socializing agents to perform these roles. From the way the nursery is decorated and the color of the birth announcements sent to

From Another Planet

In this exercise, you will analyze the messages about gender conveyed in a magazine.

Imagine that you are from another planet and know nothing about gender expectations in American society. Pick an American magazine and examine it for clues about what is required of women and men in this society. Spend some time looking at your magazine's depiction of men and women as a reference to learn your new culture, then answer the following questions:

1. What are men expected to be like in American society? How should they look, dress, behave, and so on?

2. What are women expected to be like in American society? How should they look, dress, behave, and so on?

family and friends, to how babies are dressed and how people interact with them, gender socialization is an ongoing process of learning the social expectations of males and females in one's society and culture.

In one classic study, new mothers were observed to behave differently with a baby depending on whether the child was presented to them as a boy or a girl. Although the women all reported that they did not treat their own babies differently based on their sex, they smiled more at the baby in the study if told it was a girl and held her closer to them. They were more likely to hold the boy away from them and offer him a toy train to play with, rather than a doll (Will, Self, and Datan 1976). Although the baby was only six months old, clear gendered patterns in interaction emerged among these mothers, although they were unaware of them.

These subtle differences in how boys and girls are treated as babies are reinforced through other social agents over the life course; you'll learn much more about gender socialization in Chapter 8. Throughout the process of socialization, gendered messages and expectations are all around us. Think, for example, about the kinds of toys that children play with. How do "girl" toys versus "boy" toys help to demonstrate what it means to be female or male in our society? Recall some of your favorite books or movies as a child: how did they help you to understand what it means to be a boy or girl or man or woman? Think about the media that you consume today. What music, sports, movie, or other icons do you follow and what do you learn from them about gender? Each different agent of socialization that we encounter teaches us something about the expectations of us regarding gender.

Consider This

Think back on your experience with gender socialization. How did it affect how you learned your gender role?

In Chapter 8, you will learn much more about gender and sexuality. Gender socialization affects all aspects of both men's and women's lives, sometimes in seemingly trivial ways that can actually have a big impact. For example, a group of sociology students at William Paterson University in New Jersey noticed that because individuals are socialized to believe that menstruation is a private issue that should not be publicly discussed, many low-income women do not have access to a fundamental necessity: feminine hygiene products. These Sociologists in Action decided to do something about this to help women have a "happy period."

Status, Social Roles, and Identity

Through the different agents of socialization, individuals learn the various social expectations of them in the different social statuses and social roles that they occupy throughout their lives. As you will recall from earlier chapters, status refers to one's position relative to others in society, while social roles refer to the expectations that others have of us in particular status positions in terms of how we act, behave, dress, and so on. Just as we perform distinct gender roles, as we move through our daily lives, we perform a range of social roles that hold social expectations of us in terms of the norms we follow, how we dress and appear, the language we use, and how we behave. For example, let's imagine a day in the life of an imaginary college student, Maria. Maria wakes up and is a roommate to the girls that she lives with. On her way to class, she stops and buys a coffee and muffin, and is a customer to the cashier. In class, she plays the role of student; after class, she meets a group of students to work on a project, performing the role of a classmate. She meets some friends for lunch, playing the role of friend. After lunch, she goes to her job in the campus bookstore and is an employee to her boss, colleague to her coworkers, and retail assistant to the customers. Later on, she calls her parents, playing the role of daughter, and perhaps after that she goes out dancing as a friend. In each of these roles, Maria faces different expectations: she would not behave in class the way she behaves around her friends, just as she would not talk to customers in the bookstore the

---

Sociologists in Action

"Helping Women Have a Happy Period"

Angelo R. Milordo, Shaney Lara, Peter Falcichio, and Cassandra Sundstrom-Smith

As part of our class requirement for our Public Sociology and Civic Engagement class, we were required to complete a total of 20 hours of volunteer work at Oasis, a "haven for women and children," in Paterson, New Jersey. Oasis provides low-income women and children with a variety of services, including GED, English as a second language, and job training courses; after-school and summer youth programs; meals; food bags; and clothing. While volunteering at Oasis, we used our sociological eye and observed that the women were receiving food, clothes, shoes, an education, and Pampers for their babies. However, we noticed a need that Oasis was unable to meet: feminine products for the low-income women the organization serves.

Every woman, regardless of race, social class, or any other social category, menstruates throughout much of her life. We tend, however, not to talk about it. Through our socialization process, most of us learn that menstruation is solely a women's issue and a matter not to be discussed in public—and certainly never with men. This contributes to many poor women having a difficult time gaining access to sanitary pads and tampons.

This relative silence around menstruation has also contributed to the taxation of such goods in most states and raising their price, even though they are necessary and not luxury items. One of YouTube's star interviewers, Ingrid Nilsen, asked President Barack Obama in a live YouTube interview, "Why are menstrual products being taxed?" Obama said that he had had no idea that this "tampon tax" was in place. However, he believes it exists "because men were making the laws when those taxes were passed." Even the president of the United States, who has two daughters and a wife, did not realize these products are taxed (see https://www.youtube.com/watch?v=8c2Ro54Alkk)!

In response to the need we noticed at Oasis, we decided to organize a drive called "Helping Women Have a Happy Period." The goal was to collect as many sanitary pads and tampons as possible for the women of Oasis. We created colorful boxes and fliers and collected the feminine products from everyone who was willing to donate on our campus. Throughout this process, we noticed that the women who donated were much more uncomfortable when approached by the men in our group than by the women. This is related to our socialization to treat menstrual cycles as private matters that women should only discuss among themselves. Women who donated quickly threw their pads and tampons into our donation box, embarrassed to be seen with these products in front of men. Shaney publicized our efforts on social media, and she is still receiving donations that she continues to give to Oasis. Through our efforts, we brought to light issues rarely discussed in public, collected hundreds of donations for the women of Oasis—and helped many women have happier periods!

Angelo R. Milordo, Shaney Lara, Peter Falcichio, and Cassandra Sundstrom-Smith are undergraduate students at William Paterson University in Wayne, New Jersey.

Working parents must constantly negotiate their social roles to minimize role conflict.

sister role; there is no way she can fulfill both roles at the same time. Although our roles have relatively clear expectations of us, this does not mean that they always fit together in a way that is comfortable, and we must constantly negotiate our social roles and statuses.

way she talks to her parents. At work, she might have to wear a uniform that she would not wear when she goes dancing with her friends. In each of these roles, Maria has a different status as well: when she is in the classroom as a student, she has a lower status than she has when she is with her friends and she dresses, speaks, and acts accordingly.

While it may sound exhausting (and sometimes is!) to perform so many social roles, each of us does this on a daily basis and usually moves seamlessly from one role and status to another. And while you might imagine that with your friends or family you are able to be your "true" self, you are still performing a role when you are with them. For each social context in which we find ourselves, there is a different set of social expectations of us in terms of our attitudes and behaviors.

Our social roles and statuses are not always compatible and comfortable. Sometimes we experience competing demands within a particular social role and status, or what is known as **role strain.** Maria may experience role strain in her role as a college student when she is required to do a sociology presentation on the same day that she has a physics exam. The demands of her role as a student to prepare for her presentation coincide with the expectations of her to study hard for her physics exam. These competing demands of her college student role result in a strain placed on Maria that is probably familiar to you!

Alternatively, when one's different social roles conflict with each other, we experience **role conflict.** Now imagine that Maria's younger sister is home sick from school and there is no one to stay home with her except Maria, who must miss class to do so. In this case, Maria's role of student is in conflict with her

> ## Consider This
> List five social roles you perform in your daily life. What are the expectations of you in these roles in terms of how you behave, the norms you follow, the language you use, the way you dress, and so on? Have you experienced role strain in any of these roles? What about role conflict between two or more of them?

Identity

Through the process of socialization, we learn about our culture and society but also develop our distinct identities. **Identity** generally refers to the characteristics by which we are known. Some of the key sources of identity are factors determined by society, such as gender, social class, race, ethnicity, and so forth. These are social categories to which we belong that shape our social identity, that is, the identity that others ascribe to us. Think of the many ways others might describe you: a student, an athlete, a woman, a man, a daughter, a son, a father, a mother, and so on. Each of us has multifaceted social identities that others assign to us. We also each have our own understanding of who we are—**self-identity**—that is shaped by our interactions with others. Through individual agency and

Stop and Hear the Music

In this activity, you will watch a video of a violinist in a train station and answer questions about status and roles of the people shown.

In 2007, the *Washington Post* asked Joshua Bell, one of the world's best violinists, to wear street clothes and play his instrument (valued at $3.5 million) in a D.C. Metro station during morning rush hour. Watch the YouTube video of what happened (http://www.youtube.com/watch?v=hnOPu0_YWhw) and answer the following questions:

1. What is going on in this video? What is the setting? What do you see people doing?

2. Why did hardly anyone stop to listen to Bell?

3. What social clues about status and social roles were people using to decide how to interact/behave in this situation?

4. How does this demonstrate the ways in which individuals define social situations and socially construct reality?

---

the social and symbolic world that individuals move through, identity is constantly shaped, reshaped, and negotiated through our interactions with others.

Check Your Understanding

- What are social roles?

- What is social status?

- How do role strain and role conflict differ? What are some examples of each?

- What is the difference between social identity and self-identity?

Social Interaction

"All the world's a stage, And all the men and women merely players; They have their exits and entrances, And one man in his time plays many parts." Well before sociologists began to analyze individuals' **social interactions,** or the way individuals behave and react in the presence of other people, Shakespeare penned this enduring description of the theatrical nature of human life. Almost four hundred years later, a Canadian American sociologist, Erving Goffman, built upon this insight and developed a dramaturgical approach to analyzing and explaining social interaction. As you learned in Chapter 2's discussion of the symbolic interactionist theoretical approach, Goffman used the metaphor of theater

to describe how our social lives are a kind of performance. We each play different roles as we move through out social lives, performing for different audiences on various "stages," just as Shakespeare suggested. Goffman is considered the pioneer of the study of social interaction in everyday contexts, or microsociology, and his work gives us tremendous insight into the sociological significance of our everyday behaviors and social interactions.

Social interaction is the basis for our lives within society. As we have seen, it is through social interaction that we develop a sense of self and undergo the socialization that allows us to live in society. Our everyday lives are made up of meaningful interactions with people we care about very much but also seemingly insignificant interactions: buying a cup of coffee, holding the door for someone, nodding at an acquaintance in passing, riding an elevator, and so on. Goffman believed that all moments in which we engage with others socially, no matter how fleeting, are fundamental to our lives as social beings.

Goffman argued that in social interactions, we use cues and clues from the individuals and objects around us to make meaning of what is going on, or to **define the situation.** As individuals, we become socialized into particular expectations about social interactions and use this knowledge to make sense of our social lives. In the way that we define the situation, we are also innovative and shape our own reality through the meanings we make of social interactions. Goffman focused much of his career on understanding why we act in the way that we do in everyday situations.

Performances and Impression Management

In his book *The Presentation of Self in Everyday Life*, Goffman (1959) developed his theatrical metaphor to describe how individuals' social lives consist of a series of performances of social roles for different observers, or audiences. Like Cooley and Mead, Goffman believed that individuals are very attuned to and concerned about how others see them. So, in their performance of different social roles, they work hard to make sure that others see them the way they want to be seen. Because we construct reality in our social interactions, it is very important that when we perform particular social roles, others believe that we are what we claim to be. For example, when you are performing the social role of student in the classroom, you are (hopefully!) working to make sure that your professor believes that you are, in fact, a good student: you come to class on time with your textbook, notebook, and pen or pencil; you raise your hand when you wish to speak; you make eye contact with your professor and nod along with what he or she is saying; and you take notes to show that you are following the class discussion (even if you are actually just doodling in your notebook!).

What you are doing when you perform this role of student is what Goffman termed *impression management*. As a student, there is a set of social expectations of your behavior and attitudes, and when you perform the role of student, you work hard to give off the right impression to your professor and classmates. As Goffman (1959:208) would say, you are "successfully staging a character." Impression management is a way of presenting oneself the way one wishes to be seen by others—it is the mechanism individuals use to convincingly perform their social roles.

In each performance, there is what Goffman (1959:22) referred to as the **front,** or the "expressive equipment" the individual uses to define the situation and convince others of the sincerity of their performance. The front consists of the setting, appearance, and manner of the context in which a particular performance occurs. To continue the example of the social role of student, the **setting** for the performance of student is generally a classroom, which is equipped with all of the necessary items for students' learning: desks, chairs, blackboards, screens and projectors, and the many "props" used by a student such as backpacks, notebooks, textbooks, pens and pencils, and so on. As has been noted before, these elements of setting are necessary for an individual to perform the role of student convincingly: a student who comes to class without a notebook and pen will likely be perceived by his or her professor and classmates as unprepared.

Appearance consists of everything from dress to age, sex, and race or ethnicity, to nonverbal forms of communication like body language and gestures. For example, a student who is wearing the school colors and sitting up straight and attentive in the front row of the classroom will convey a very different impression to those around her than one slumped in the back row with a baseball cap pulled low over her face. Appearance and setting work in conjunction with **manner,** or the attitude conveyed by an individual in his or her particular social role. And it is through this combined front that an individual seeks to influence the perception that others have of her.

> ### Consider This
> Have you ever interviewed for a job? How did you engage in impression management to try to get hired? What about using impression management on a first date? What are other some examples of how you use impression management in your everyday life?

Regions: Front Stage and Back Stage

Goffman's dramaturgical approach to describing our social lives goes further, to argue that there are also different regions in which we perform our interactions. The front stage is where we actively perform our roles, using impression management to compel a certain reaction from our audience. The back stage, on the other hand, is where we are "out of character" and no longer have to put on a performance. In performing your role as student, you are front stage when you are in class. You are acting out the role of student for your audience (your professor and classmates), raising your hand to answer questions, taking notes, and nodding along as the professor speaks. You are putting on a show to convince those around you that you are an excellent student who is fulfilling society's expectations of you as student. Perhaps, however, you pulled an all-nighter studying for your chemistry exam last night and did not prepare for class at all and are mostly trying to stay awake. As soon as you leave class, you might rush

Doing Sociology 5.4

Impression Management on Social Media

In this activity, you will conduct a content analysis of Facebook or Instagram to determine how users engage in impression management on social media.

Goffman formulated his theories of social interaction before the age of the Internet and social media. Social media sites like Facebook dramatically change the ways in which individuals are able to use impression management to ensure that people see them the way they want to be seen.

1. Select three people you follow on Instagram or are friends with on Facebook.

2. Analyze their profile photos by asking the following questions: What is the photo of? If it is a person, what is he or she doing? What is he or she wearing?

If it is not a person, what is it? Where? What impression of your friend does the photo create?

3. Next, review the last ten posts of each person. What are the posts about?

4. Create categories to help you classify the posts (e.g., politics, everyday life, accomplishments, vacations or other outings). If any posts are of photos, analyze the photo in the way that you did the profile picture.

5. Once you have coded the status updates, write a one- to two-page sociological analysis of how each individual uses impression management on Facebook.

home and fall into bed, texting a good friend that you just fudged your way through sociology class. This is your back stage region where you no longer have to put on a show.

It is important that we keep these regions separate in our social lives. For example, as a student, you might be embarrassed or your grade might be affected if it is clear that you are unprepared for class. It's often even more important in the workplace to keep front stage and back stage separate. For example, if you work in a restaurant or retail store, you are probably told that "the customer is always right." This means that you need to be polite even if the customer is nasty to you. You may wish to be rude back to him or her and you might vent your frustrations to colleagues, but if your back stage attitude toward the customer comes out when you are front stage, you may very well be fired.

Goffman constructed his theories on social interaction before the Internet and social media dramatically altered the ways in which we interact. While maintaining a separation between front stage and back stage in face-to-face interaction often seems very straightforward, it is more difficult to do in online interactions. For example, have you ever accidentally "replied all" on an email that you intended to send just to the sender? Or sent a text message to the wrong person?

New online forms of interaction often make it more difficult for us to keep track of which region we are in and for whom we are performing. For example, in 2015, a court clerk and two police officers in Ferguson, Missouri, were fired for sending and receiving racist emails, including several disparaging President Obama. Ferguson is well known today as the city where unarmed African American teenager Michael Brown was killed by a White police officer in August 2014, which led to protests that were the start of today's Black Lives Matter movement. The emails surfaced in a Department of Justice investigation that found that racism pervaded the Ferguson Police Department. The three individuals who were fired thought that they were joking with like-minded people but failed to realize that this "back stage" behavior becomes front stage when circulated through work email accounts.

Consider This
How do you maintain the distinction between front stage and back stage regions in your online social media interactions, such as on Facebook or Instagram?

Ethnomethodology

Harold Garfinkel was another sociologist who focused his work on seemingly unimportant everyday social interactions. He gave the most basic, trivial, everyday occurrences the kind of attention "usually accorded extraordinary events" (Garfinkel 1967:1). To do this, he created a field of study that he called **ethnomethodology,** the study of the "ethno" (meaning ordinary or everyday) methods people use to make sense of their social interactions.

Garfinkel's focus was on language and the simplistic small talk that makes up many of our basic interactions with others. He argued that language is not as simple as it may seem. Take, for example, the question "What's up?" If you are from this country, you probably know just what is meant by this question (something like "What is happening with you right now?") and what kind of response is expected (e.g., "not much"). However, for someone who is not from here and does not know the social context and background in which this question is being asked, this is a very confusing question, the answer to which is not at all clear: perhaps "the sky" or "the ceiling"?

Garfinkel conducted a series of experiments to help understand this complexity of language and the norms that dictate our everyday interactions through language. He enlisted his college students to carry out experiments with friends and acquaintances in which they would pretend to not understand the conventions of small talk and instead push their conversation partners to be more specific and precise in what they were asking. Here is one example of an experiment (Garfinkel 1967:44); S is the friend of E, the student experimenter:

S: How are you?

E: How am I in regard to what? My health, my finances, my school work, my peace of mind, my . . . ?

S: [Red in the face and suddenly out of control.] Look! I was just trying to be polite. Frankly I don't give a damn how you are.

Garfinkel and his students found that breaking the conventions of everyday small talk made people deeply uncomfortable and upset. We rely on others understanding our expectations when it comes to common verbal interactions, and it is unsettling and frustrating when these expectations are broken. Think of how annoying it is when you've politely asked someone "How are you?" as a form of small talk and you get their whole life story! Smooth navigation of such daily interactions requires shared cultural assumptions about how these interactions should proceed.

Check Your Understanding

- What is Goffman's dramaturgical approach?

- What is impression management and why do we use it?

- What is the difference between front stage and back stage?

- What is ethnomethodology? Why do people get upset when the rules of small talk are broken?

Conclusion

Through our interactions and the process of socialization, we learn how to act within our society and culture. This means we are very much shaped by the place and time in which we are born and raised. This should call to mind C. Wright Mills's concept of the sociological imagination and how individual lives are influenced by society and history.

Our social lives are structured by larger social and cultural patterns and norms that we learn through socialization. In each social context we find ourselves, we perform a different social role, based on the social expectations others have of us in that role. In these social interactions, we make meaning and construct the reality of our social lives. At the same time, however, there are limits to socialization and the social structures that pattern our behavior. Individuals, as you know, have free will and can make choices that breach or challenge social norms and expectations; you'll learn more about deviance, or breaking social norms, in the next chapter. For example, a half a century ago, homosexuality went very much against the norms of American society and was thought to be deviant and even criminal. A powerful gay rights movement began with a relatively small group of individuals who, through riots, protests, parades, and legal challenges of discriminatory laws, began to demand changes to the norms and values of American culture.

Over the course of about forty years, the gay rights movement changed attitudes of Americans toward gays and lesbians. For example, in 1996, only about 30 percent of the population approved of same-sex marriage; today, 56 percent of the population support same-sex marriage and, as you have seen, an even higher proportion of young Americans support it (Pew Research 2015). The movement also changed both informal norms and laws affecting them. The growing acceptance of equal rights for gays and lesbians became clear in 2015 when the Supreme Court overturned the Defense of Marriage Act, making same-sex marriage legal in all fifty states. This is but one example of how individuals can change the culture they live in, resisting the norms and values they were socialized to accept and instead creating social change. Thus, while socialization is a powerful phenomenon, you are not entirely a product of your culture but can also be an agent of change.

As Mills's concept of the sociological imagination tells us, individual lives are shaped by society and history, and understanding socialization gives us insight into just how much we are influenced by the norms, values, and beliefs of the culture that surrounds us. Everything from what you ate for breakfast this morning and how you sit in sociology class, to what you hold to be most important in your life, you have learned through socialization. But of course this does not mean that you are entirely a product of your society; learning never ends, and individuals have the free will and agency to also shape their own societies and culture.

CHAPTER

5

Want a better grade? Get the tools you need to sharpen your study skills. Access practice quizzes, eFlashcards, video and multimedia at **edge.sagepub.com/korgen**

Review

5.1 What is socialization?

Socialization is the social process through which individuals learn the norms of the culture and society that they live in. Through the process of socialization, individuals become functioning members of their society. It is a lifelong process that begins when we are born and continues through our many stages. As we age, we may undergo resocialization as we enter different social contexts and learn new sets of social norms and expectations. Socialization contributes to social reproduction, the continuation of a society's culture across generations.

5.2 According to George Herbert Mead, how does an individual develop a social self?

Mead's theory of child development was inspired by another social psychologist, Charles Cooley, who argued that individuals develop a sense of self, what he termed the looking glass self, by imagining how others see us. Mead similarly believed that individuals develop into social beings through their interactions with others. This begins when very young children engage in what Mead called taking the role of the other, or imitating those around them, putting themselves in someone else's shoes and seeing what kind of reaction they get. As they get older and engage in more organized games, like sports, they develop an understanding of the generalized other that represents society as a whole, with all of its norms and values.

5.3 What are the key agents of socialization?

Socialization occurs with individuals and within groups and social contexts, which are referred to as agents of socialization. Family is the primary agent of socialization, because it is generally the first group and sometimes only group an individual is exposed to in his or her earliest years. From our families, we learn many fundamental skills for life in society, such as language and how to feed and dress ourselves, as well as many other norms and values. As we age, we encounter different agents of socialization like peers, schools, the media, work, and so on, learning from each different norms and values. Some adults end up in total institutions where they must be resocialized into an entirely new culture and context.

5.4 What is gender socialization?

An extremely important aspect of socialization is learning gender roles and identity. Gender socialization begins the moment a baby is born (or that baby's sex is determined) when that individual is assigned a gender role and socialized to perform that role. Gender socialization is an ongoing process of learning the social expectations of males and females in one's society and culture.

5.5 What are status, social roles, and identity?

Throughout the process of socialization, individuals develop an individual identity and learn the various social expectations that come with the different social statuses and social roles that they occupy throughout their lives. Status refers to one's position relative to others in society, while social roles refer to the expectations that others have of us in particular statues and positions. Identity refers to the characteristics by which we are known. Through individual agency and the social and symbolic world that individuals move through, identity is constantly shaped, reshaped, and negotiated through our interactions with others.

5.6 How do sociologists describe and analyze social interaction?

Sociologists Erving Goffman and Harold Garfinkel both believed that our everyday interactions with others were important to analyze sociologically because this kind of microsociology gives us great insight into our experiences as social beings. Goffman used a dramaturgical approach to argue that individuals' social lives are a series of performances; we use impression management to perform our social roles in a way that compels others to see us the way we want to be seen. Garfinkel was especially concerned with how individuals make sense of what others say and do in everyday interactions. He created ethnomethodology as a field that could study how regular people make sense of the interactions that structure our social lives.

Key Terms

- agents of socialization   82
- appearance   92
- define the situation   91
- ethnomethodology   94
- feral children   80
- front   92
- gender socialization   87
- identity   90

- life course   80
- manner   92
- nature   80
- nurture   80
- peer pressure   84
- peers   84
- primary socialization   82
- resocialization   80

How do you know a deviant act when you see one? What can be deviant in one place and time can seem perfectly normal in another.

REUTERS/Susana Vera

Learning Questions

6.1 How do we define what is deviant?

6.2 What do sociological theories suggest about the causes of deviant behavior, including crime?

6.3 What are the social processes involved in creating social norms?

6.4 How does social location influence who and what is defined as deviant?

6.5 How do individuals manage deviant identities?

Identifying Deviant Behavior

Rena C. Zito

Defining Deviance

Think about and jot down five acts that you consider to be "deviant." Now rank those five acts from 1 (least deviant of the five acts) to 5 (most deviant of the five acts). What guided your rankings? Perhaps you considered how unusual the acts were (is this a typical behavior or something that rarely occurs?), the societal reactions to them (would onlookers call the police or simply laugh?), or the harm they produce (was anyone injured or were some people just offended?). You have just shown that you have your own sense of what makes a behavior deviant. But is your personal understanding of deviance reflected in sociological definitions? That depends. There are many approaches to the conceptualization of deviance. The word *conceptualization* refers to how we define a concept, like deviance, so that researchers can measure it. If we are interested in studying deviance from a sociological perspective, we must first figure out how to conceptualize deviance.

First we must consider what can be deviant. Sociologists argue that it is not just behaviors that can be deviant but also conditions and beliefs. For example, medical conditions, such as a facial disfigurement or having a feared disease like leprosy or AIDS, can be considered deviant. And subscribing to beliefs that are out of sync with the broader culture's belief system, such as believing that humans are alien life forms that will return to their home planet upon death, can also be considered deviant. But why are some behaviors, conditions, and beliefs considered deviant? The answer depends on the definition, or approach, used.

Approaches to Defining Deviance

The central question when conceptualizing deviance is, Deviance from what? There are statistical, legalistic, and normative approaches to defining deviance.

The Statistical Approach

If, when you ranked the five deviant acts you came up with, your rankings depended on how unusual the behaviors are, then you were using a **statistical approach** to the definition of

Rena C. Zito

As a young person, I saw adolescence as a kind of identity toy store where I could play with new, offbeat personas and see if I liked them, keeping the parts that felt right and discarding the rest. I also loved acting and improv, which was like wandering through the identity toy store in overdrive. Being able to manipulate how others perceived me, to create my own reality, felt like magic. This is probably why I fell in love with sociology while learning about symbolic interactionism at the University of Rhode Island. I'd found my intellectual home. I double majored in sociology and psychology and decided to pursue a PhD in sociology at North Carolina State University.

I have taught criminology, family sociology, and quantitative methods at Elon University and other institutions for a decade now, developing courses like Gender and Crime and heading our Criminal Justice Studies program. I still get just as excited about the learning process as I did when I was newly on the other side of it. But I'm still learning all the time, too, as I conduct research on families, adolescents, and criminal behavior.

deviance. Statistics are about probability and likelihood. Therefore, the statistical approach treats as deviant anything that is statistically unusual or anything that has a low probability or likelihood. It is about deviance from what is usual or common. When people defend their behavior by saying "everyone does it" (say, when "fudging" on their taxes or driving recklessly or drinking excessively), they are invoking a statistical conceptualization of deviance. But consider that the average twenty-year-old female in the United States is 5 foot, 4 inches, with fewer than 5 percent under 5 foot, 0 inches, and fewer than 5 percent over 5 foot, 9 inches (Centers for Disease Control and Prevention 2000). Using a statistical approach, we would say that a six-foot-tall twenty-year-old woman is deviant. But being tall does not meet the criteria most sociologists use to determine what is and isn't deviant. Instead, most approaches are about deviance from social norms.

Social Norms

As we discussed in Chapter 4, social norms are rules of behavior that tell us what is and isn't acceptable in a given culture. Sociologists identify three types of norms: folkways, mores, and laws (Sumner 1907). Folkways are the rules that guide everyday behavior, and responses to violation are mild. Think about the person who speaks too loudly in a library or uses a urinal directly next to another person when there are other options. They have violated folkways. Mores (pronounced *mor-ays*) are more serious rules that carry moral weight and, when violated, evoke harsher responses. Let's imagine that our rude library patron exposed himself or herself sexually to other library visitors. Laws, when violated, can result in formal punishments, as they are rules formalized by the state. Unsurprisingly, many mores (e.g., against killing, stealing, and exposing one's sexual organs in public spaces) are codified in law.

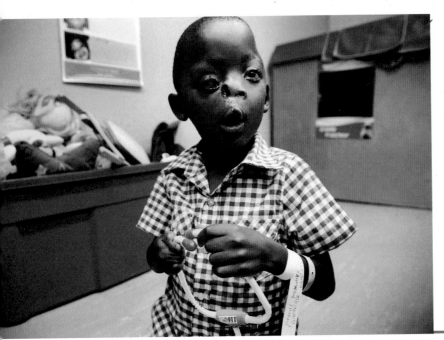

This boy, in Johannesburg, South Africa, is waiting to receive the first of two surgeries to repair his hare-lip and split pallet. Without the surgeries, he would face life with a deviant stigma, due to his facial deformity.

Mary-Ann Palmer/Foto24/Gallo Images/Getty Images

Deviance in the Ashley Madison Hack

In this exercise, you will consider the layers of potentially deviant behavior involved in identifying users of a website intended to facilitate extramarital affairs.

AshleyMadison.com was a dating website, but unlike other dating sites, this one was for married people seeking to have extramarital affairs. In July 2015, a group of hackers calling themselves "The Impact Team" stole the Ashley Madison user data and later released users' personally identifying information, including email addresses. Outcomes of the data breach included public shaming of users, extortion attempts, potentially serious legal consequences (e.g., 1,200 users had email addresses from Saudi Arabia, where infidelity can result in capital punishment), and even several suicides of publicly humiliated users.

The AshleyMadison.com data breach entailed multiple forms of so-called deviance: the theft and public release of the information by "The Impact Team," the marital infidelity (intended or actual) of the site's users, and the suicides that resulted.

Consider the following questions:

1. Which of these three do you consider the most deviant, and why?

2. Do you reject the label of "deviant" for any of these behaviors? Why or why not?

3. Considering both legal punishments and personal repercussions, who was likely punished most severely—the website operators, the website users, or the hackers? How would you match the severity of the punishment with the severity of the deviance? Explain.

The Legalistic Approach

If your rankings depended on whether the behavior was illegal, then you were using a **legalistic approach** to defining deviance. In this approach, any violation of the law is necessarily deviant. Therefore, shoplifting would be considered deviant but your professor wearing a Halloween costume to work (not on Halloween) would not, as the latter would be a violation of a folkway but not a law.

This approach requires us to distinguish between crime, sin, and poor taste (Smith and Pollack 1976). Crimes are violations of the law, such as assault, kidnapping, theft, or murder. Sins are deviant acts, conditions, or beliefs that violate religious or moral prohibitions, many of which are not subject to legal regulation, such as promiscuity or eating food deemed impure by one's religion. Sins are violations of mores, not folkways or laws. Behaviors, conditions, or beliefs in poor taste are violations of customs or etiquette, such as picking one's nose in public or wearing a bikini as classroom attire. Folkways indicate what is and is not in poor taste in a given culture. The legalistic approach considers only crime as deviant.

The Normative Approach

If, in your rankings, you considered what would evoke a disapproving response from others, then you were using a **normative approach.** Unlike the legalistic view of deviance, the normative approach considers violations of any norms—folkways, mores, or laws. And unlike in the statistical approach, behaviors, conditions, and beliefs need not be statistically unusual to be deviant in this perspective. Rather, the collective disapproving response, or sanctions, they garner is sufficient for making them deviant.

Sanctions

When people break rules they face **sanctions,** which are punishments or penalties. Sanctions can range from benign, informal penalties, such as being ignored or gossiped about, to serious, formal punishment, such as imprisonment or execution. Who is imposing the sanction determines whether the sanction is informal or formal. *Formal sanctions* are enacted by official agents of the state, such as local law enforcement, Child Protective Services, or the Drug Enforcement Administration. *Informal sanctions* come from nonofficial sources, including friends, family members, and strangers.

Applying Statistical, Legalistic, and Normative Approaches

In this exercise, you will compare and contrast statistical, legalistic, and normative approaches to understanding deviance.

In groups of three or four, think about and write down some behaviors, conditions, and beliefs that fit the following criteria:

- Deviant using a statistical approach but not a legalistic approach
- Deviant using a normative approach but not a statistical approach
- Deviant using all of the approaches

Now take a few minutes to write down your own responses to the following questions:

1. Which of the approaches best captures your own understanding of what constitutes deviance? Why do you think that approach is best?

2. Which of the deviant acts involved in the Ashley Madison hack (see Doing Sociology 6.1) meet the criteria for the statistical, legalistic, and normative approaches?

Assumptions about Social Reality and Perspectives on Deviance

Defining deviance requires that we make assumptions about social reality. What is good and acceptable in the social world (i.e., what we ought to do, value, and believe) is either the result of social interactions and the meanings we collectively decide upon or is objectively real, irrespective of the definitions we agree upon. Consider our offending library patron. Is sexually exposing oneself in a library deviant because we, as members of society, consider it to be unacceptable? If so, that would mean that in another cultural setting, such behavior could be nondeviant. Or is deviance part of the inherent character of the act, such that exposing oneself in public is deviant regardless of cultural circumstances? If you subscribe to the first perspective, as many sociologists do, then you are making relativist assumptions. The second perspective reflects absolutist assumptions.

Relativist Perspective

According to those who maintain a **relativist perspective,** behaviors, conditions, and beliefs are deviant only to the extent that cultures regard them as deviant. Deviance is not an inherent characteristic of an act but, rather, is the result of social construction. Social construction, as we saw in Chapter 4, refers to the creation of the social world through interaction and the shared understandings that emerge from interaction. For example, money (or gold or beads or whatever is used for trade in a society) has no inherent value. Instead, it becomes valuable because we define it as valuable in interaction with others. Behaviors (or conditions or beliefs), like money, have meaning because we ascribe meaning to them. Exposing oneself in a library or joining a dating website for married people are deviant acts to the extent that we collectively regard these acts as deviant and react to them with disapproval. Thus, in this view, deviance is subjective, or relative.

Absolutist Perspective

The **absolutist perspective,** in contrast, states that some behaviors, conditions, and beliefs are inherently, objectively deviant. Deviance is part of their nature. Even if we do not treat them as deviant, they remain deviant. For example, if we were to regard marriage among first cousins as inherently deviant and unacceptable, then the acceptance of such marriages in many societies throughout the world—about one in ten marriages worldwide are between first or second cousins— would not change the deviance of the act (Kershaw 2009). The definition of first-cousin marriage as deviant, in this example, is absolute rather than relative to the culture in which it develops (or fails to develop).

Research Approaches versus Individual Morality

Most deviance scholars employ a relativist lens when studying human behavior. That is, they put aside—or attempt to put aside—their own feelings and biases so that they can understand behaviors, conditions, and beliefs from the perspective of so-called deviants. For example, Philippe Bourgois and Jeff Schonberg (2009) lived among and studied homeless heroin addicts in San Francisco. They recounted the childhoods, work lives, crimes, relationships, medical conditions, and drug habits of the men and women they studied in their book *Righteous Dopefiend*. They did not pass judgment on their research participants or engage in ethnocentrism. Ethnocentrism occurs when people evaluate other cultures based on the standards of their own culture. Instead, Bourgois and Schonberg understood their participants from the perspective of the subculture in which they lived.

> **Consider This**
> Imagine a world without any deviance—what would that look like?

Using a relativist lens in research does not mean that sociologists do not have strong moral positions about the behaviors, conditions, and beliefs they study. For example, in the research for his book *The Stickup Kids,* about armed robbers and torturers, sociologist Randol Contreras (2012) employs a relativist lens while simultaneously recognizing his own moral opposition to his research participants' violent behaviors and racist and sexist attitudes. Taking an absolutist moral stance as an individual—for instance, by opposing gender inequality or violations of human rights—does not preclude using a relativist perspective in research.

Conflict/Critical Perspective

The **conflict perspective** (also known as the critical perspective) on deviance is a subtype of the relativist approach. Like all relativist perspectives, the conflict perspective regards deviance as socially constructed. It stands apart in that it emphasizes the role of social power in determining who and what is considered deviant. In this view, the label of "deviant" (and "criminal") is wielded as a weapon against the vulnerable in society and used to preserve and increase the social, economic, and political dominance of powerful groups. Conflict thinkers ask, Who benefits from this definition? For instance, in their now-classic text *The Rich Get Richer and the Poor Get Prison,* Jeffrey Reiman and Paul Leighton (2012) argue that the legal system operates as a carnival mirror that distorts the threats that face us, treating the minor deviance of the poor (e.g., illicit drug use and petty theft) as serious crimes and the harmful deviance of the wealthy (e.g., unsafe workplaces, environmental crimes, and corporate fraud) as minor wrongdoings. Theirs is a critical perspective.

"Nuts, Sluts, and Perverts" or "Deviant Heroes"?

What is in a name? The word *deviant* conjures up images of the outcast, the sexual psychopath, the persons and practices on the fringes of society. In 1972, sociologist Alexander Liazos argued forcefully against a "sociology of deviance." Attempting to humanize so-called deviants—Liazos used the phrase "nuts, sluts, and perverts" to identify those of greatest interest to sociologists at the time—and demonstrate that deviance and conformity are products of shared conditions, he argued that the creation of a sociology of deviance necessitates treating deviance as distinct from other behavior. Sociologists had, it seemed, created the very conditions they sought to abolish—stigmatizing those who do not conform to social norms. The solution? Liazos favored discontinuing the use of the term *deviant,* suggesting instead *victimization, persecution,* and *oppression,* which he believed better characterized the experiences of those on the fringes. What do you think? Should this chapter have a different title? If so, what should it be?

Sociologists have also argued that deviance is a requirement for social change (Wolf and Zuckerman 2012). Unjust and harmful social conditions will continue unless people challenge them by breaking the rules. Take, for instance, the Greensboro Four, a group of four African American college students who, in 1960, refused to leave a Woolworth's "Whites only" lunch counter until they were served. Their behavior was deviant in the Jim Crow South. Positive social change required their deviance. Can you think of any examples of "deviant heroes" today?

Check Your Understanding

- What are the three types of norms?
- What are the differences and similarities between the statistical, legalistic, and normative approaches to defining deviance?
- What are the differences between the relativist perspective, the absolutist perspective, and the conflict/critical perspective?
- Why is the "sociology of deviance" a controversial idea?

Understanding Theories of Deviance and Crime

Think about the last time you heard about a mass shooting, a bank robbery, or the suicide of a celebrity. Or perhaps think about the last time you saw a stranger dressed or acting unusually. You may have wondered, Why do some people violate norms? And why do other people conform to them? Sociologists develop theories to answer these questions.

Early Perspectives in the Sociology of Deviance and Crime

Many early theories focused on biological abnormalities as the root causes of crime and deviance. For instance, nineteenth-century criminologist Cesare Lombroso and his contemporaries believed some people were "born criminals," with innate criminal tendencies, a perspective that has been thoroughly discredited (Lombroso 1876). Émile Durkheim, often regarded as a founder of sociology, transformed the scientific study of deviance in the late nineteenth century. Unlike Lombroso, Durkheim offered a theory of deviance that sought to explain variation in rates of deviance across places, groups, and time periods. Rather than answer the question "Why do some individuals engage in deviance?" theorists like Durkheim seek to answer the question "Why do some places, groups, or time periods experience more deviance than others?"

Durkheim's Sociological Theory of Suicide

On August 11, 2014, comedian and actor Robin Williams committed suicide. In the weeks that followed, headlines proclaimed various possible causes of Williams's suicide, including depression and a recent diagnosis of a brain disease called Lewy body dementia. Like those headlines, most of us gravitate to individual-level explanations when we think about suicide. We consider the effects of a person's mental illness, health problems, money troubles, or relationship woes. Durkheim's (1951 [1897]) classic book, *Suicide,* in contrast, implores its readers to consider how the organization of societies gives rise to, or inhibits, suicide. He noted that some countries had consistently high rates of suicide and others had consistently low rates of suicide. This led Durkheim to conclude that characteristics of societies—namely, their ability to regulate behavior and foster social solidarity—mattered for deviance, including suicide.

Durkheim argued that norms become unclear and fail to constrain deviant behavior in the face of rapid social changes. He called this condition anomie. **Anomie** is a state in which a society's norms fail to regulate behavior. In anomic societies, the bond between the individual and the community breaks down, and society loses its moral force as personal and societal standards of behavior fail to align.

Now let's put Robin Williams's tragic suicide in sociological perspective. Williams, as a White, sixty-three-year-old man, was part of a demographic group with one of the highest rates of suicide in the United States. Examine Figure 6.1 and consider the following: How might Durkheim make sense of the high level of suicide among older White men in the United States? For instance, do older White men tend to be less connected to family life or religious institutions than younger White men or Black and Hispanic people?

Durkheim and the Normality of Crime

Durkheim's ideas about anomie were part of his larger structural functionalist perspective on human

FIGURE 6.1

Suicide Death Rates by Age, Sex, and Race/Ethnicity, 2014

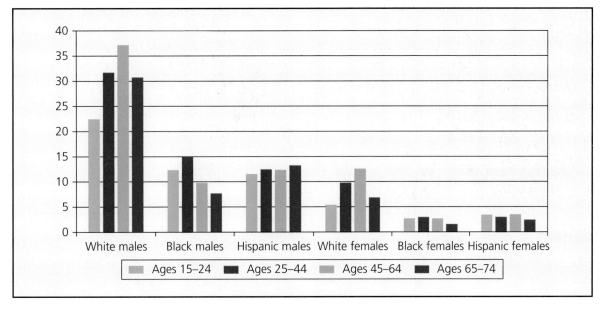

Source: Centers for Disease Control and Prevention, April 2016, https://www.cdc.gov/nchs/data/hestat/suicide/rates_1999_2014.pdf.

Note: Death rates per 100,000 resident population.

societies. Structural functionalism (also called functionalism) claims that all social activity, including crime and deviance, should be understood in terms of what it contributes to society, as we read about in Chapter 2. The very fact of its existence must mean, from the functionalist perspective, that it provides some necessary, positive function for society. Unsurprisingly, then, Durkheim argued that crime and deviance were normal and necessary aspects of human societies.

Durkheim points out that all societies, in all time periods, define some behaviors as deviant or criminal and that a society without crime is impossible. To understand this, Durkheim suggests we imagine a society of saints. Everyone is, by our standards, exceptionally well behaved. No one steals or fights or paints graffiti. But there will still be behaviors that are regarded and punished as crime. Crime might be raising one's voice or speaking out of turn. The definition of crime will look different from our standards, but there must be *something* that is criminal, because crime serves a necessary function for society. If it didn't, crime would not exist in all societies. The purpose of punishment, therefore, is not to reduce crime (we need it!). Instead, it is to assert our shared values.

Kai Erikson's (1966) book *Wayward Puritans* borrowed Durkheim's ideas to show that punishing deviants allows the members of society to come together to affirm their moral boundaries. In punishing the offender, they make a moral statement about what will and won't be accepted in their society. Erikson demonstrated this process by drawing on examples of "crime waves" in the seventeenth-century Massachusetts Bay Colony. These crime waves included challenges to the authority of church leaders, Quakerism, and witchcraft. The crimes of the colonists would, by contemporary standards, be considered noncriminal, yet they were punished with execution and banishment.

Consider This

By coming together to punish deviants, we make visible the moral boundaries of our community. In what ways might social media serve the same function as the public square did in the past for the control of deviants and the expression of collective anger? In what ways might it fail to make us aware of our moral boundaries?

According to Durkheim's functionalist view, when deviance increases, the bar for being defined as "deviant" rises. Once-deviant behaviors become normative or are at least no longer criminalized. Consider the contemporary example of cohabitation, or couples living together while unmarried. This formerly deviant and even sometimes criminal behavior—it was once illegal for unmarried couples to rent a room together in many states in the United States—is now, for many couples in the United States, a normal stage in romantic relationships. Or consider the legalization of recreational marijuana use in multiple U.S. states from Durkheim's perspective. Can you think of other examples of deviance being redefined?

Merton's Anomie Theory

Like Durkheim, Robert Merton (1938) believed that the ability of norms to regulate behavior was central to understanding rates of deviance. Unlike Durkheim, though, Merton conceptualized anomie specifically as a societal overemphasis on success goals and an underemphasis on the appropriate means to achieve that success. In the United States, Merton argued, making money is the primary measure of success. If you aspire to financial success, you can potentially achieve it through either legitimate means (e.g., working hard, inheriting it, or winning the lottery) or through illegitimate means (e.g., stealing, selling drugs, fraud, or embezzlement). An imbalance between cultural emphasis on goals and the appropriate means to achieve goals—or anomie—leads to a climate of "success at any cost" that produces high levels of crime, particularly when there is great inequality in access to legitimate means. According to Merton, "a cardinal American virtue, 'ambition,' causes a cardinal American vice, 'crime'" (Merton 1957:146). Thus, for Merton, deviance is not pathological. Instead, deviance is a product of the mainstream cultural and structural system.

Explaining Deviance and Crime Today

Some contemporary explanations of deviance focus on control, the factors that keep some individuals from engaging in deviance/crime and some places from having high rates of deviance/crime. Other explanations focus on motivation for engaging in deviance and crime, or the social factors that compel people to commit deviant/criminal acts.

Control Perspectives

Control can be a property of places. **Social disorganization** theorists argue that the reason some neighborhoods have more crime than others is that their structural conditions (e.g., high concentration of poverty and population turnover) make it difficult for the community members to achieve collective efficacy, the ability to work together to achieve their shared goals (Sampson, Raudenbush, and Earls 1997). Communities with low collective efficacy will be less effective at preventing, or controlling, deviance/crime, like keeping drug dealers off the corner or eliminating street-level prostitution. In contrast, a community with high collective efficacy might host local events where neighbors can share their concerns, organize a neighborhood watch, and contact and work with law enforcement to address the problems.

Control can also be a property of individuals. Imagine what would be (or was) at stake in your life if you were to be (or when you were) convicted of a serious crime. Perhaps you think about letting down your family members. Or perhaps you think about the impact it would (or did) have on your college career or future job prospects. If those concerns—about letting others down or jeopardizing your investments—keep you from deviance, then you are controlled by social bonds. Social bonds are one type of social control. **Social control** refers to the enforcement of conformity to norms through either the threat or experience of formal or informal sanctions. Social bonds are a source of informal social control that create "stakes in conformity" and include attachment to others, commitment to conventional activities, involvement in conventional activities, and belief in the moral validity of the law (Hirschi 1969:153).

Consider This

Merton argued that anomie produces high rates of crime, particularly crimes that yield economic gain, like robbery, drug dealing, or fraud. But what about noneconomic offenses, like rape/sexual assault, drunk driving, and hazing? How might we adapt Merton's anomie principle to help us make sense of a wider range of rule-violating behaviors?

Control can also come from within. **Self-control theory** claims that stable, lifelong traits such as impulsivity, risk seeking, preference for simple and physical tasks, and self-centeredness predispose some individuals toward engaging in "acts of force or fraud undertaken in pursuit of self-interest" (Gottfredson and Hirschi 1990:15). If caregivers fail to monitor, recognize, and punish self-interested deviant behavior in childhood, the theory suggests, children will fail to develop self-control, and this will be evident in persistent deviant behaviors throughout life.

Motivation Perspectives

Learning theories and strain theories are two contemporary theories that examine why some people are more likely than others to commit deviant acts. Both theories look at the forces that influence deviant behavior. Why are some individuals or groups more motivated than others to engage in deviance? **Learning theories** assert that deviant and criminal behaviors are no different from other social behaviors. Just as we learn from others what are acceptable table manners or acceptable ways of conducting ourselves in a classroom, we also learn whether it is acceptable to break the law or engage in other deviant acts. In other words, learning theories are about normative transmission, or the ways in which rules of behavior are spread socially through interaction. Analyses of deviant subcultures tend to rely on learning perspectives. For example, individuals initiated into prison gangs may learn that certain illegal behaviors are acceptable (e.g., using violence against members of rival gangs and participation in contraband markets) and other legitimate behaviors are not (e.g., forging cross-gang or interracial friendships).

Strain theories emphasize the role that stressful experiences and conditions play in motivating deviant and criminal behavior. Robert Agnew's (1992) **general strain theory** contends that three types of strain lead to deviance and crime: (1) failure to achieve positively valued goals (not getting what you want or need), (2) removal of positively valued stimuli (losing something you value), and (3) presentation of negatively valued stimuli (being treated negatively by others). Strains that produce anger are especially likely to lead to deviance, as anger readies us for "corrective action." Corrective action is any coping that seeks to address the strain itself or the negative emotions it produces. For instance, violent retaliation is one way of coping with strain, as is running away from a stressful home environment or using illicit drugs. For example, imagine a young person who is being bullied at school, a type of negative stimuli.

They become increasingly angry, leading them to lash out violently at the bullies or others, a form of corrective action.

Check Your Understanding

- What is the difference between individual-level and structural-level theories of deviance?

- What was Durkheim's perspective on suicide, and how did it differ from individual-level explanations of suicide?

- What is the functionalist perspective on crime and deviance?

- What were the main contributions of theorist Robert Merton?

- What are the differences among the contemporary perspectives on deviance and crime, including social control, self-control, learning, and strain perspectives?

Creating Deviance

Deviance is social. It cannot exist without a shared notion of what is deemed unacceptable or abnormal. The origins of those shared notions are the focus of this section: Just how do we come to define some behaviors, conditions, or beliefs as deviant? In other words, how is deviance socially constructed?

Moral Entrepreneurship

In some instances, individuals or groups, called **moral entrepreneurs**, actively seek to change norms to align with their own moral worldview (Becker 1973 [1963]), often while taking part in social movements, which are the focus of Chapter 14. It may help to think about the meaning of the word *entrepreneur*: an organizer or operator of a business enterprise who, through risk and initiative, seeks to make a profit. A moral entrepreneur is in the business of manufacturing public morality. The profit is the widespread change in norms and the enforcement of them. Consider, for example, the antialcohol crusaders of the pre-Prohibition era in the

United States. Temperance groups of the nineteenth and early twentieth centuries sought to change the norms surrounding drinking through religious and family-centered appeals as well as through the lobbying efforts that ultimately resulted in the Eighteenth Amendment, which prohibited the manufacture, transport, and sale of alcohol (ratified in 1920 and repealed in 1933). The Anti-Saloon League and the Women's Christian Temperance Union, antialcohol movements, were moral entrepreneurs.

Rule Creators and Rule Enforcers

Moral entrepreneurs comprise both rule creators and rule enforcers. Rule creators campaign to have their definition of deviance taken seriously. They seek to transform private troubles into public issues through the creation of new norms. Once new rules are created, rule enforcers seek to ensure that the rules are not violated. The role of enforcer is not limited to formal agents of control, such as police and judges. Anyone can be a rule enforcer. This can include parents, neighbors, teachers, employers, or anyone else who imposes sanctions on rule violators.

Creating Public Morality

Creating public morality requires two steps: generating awareness (or claims making) and moral conversion (Spector and Kitsuse 1977). To illustrate this social process, let's use an example: imagine you are a moral entrepreneur who is concerned with teenagers texting one another sexually explicit photographs of themselves (or "sexting").

Generating awareness involves multiple tasks. First, you need to provide danger messages: "Something must be done, and it must be done now! Your child could be next! And these images will haunt them for the rest of their lives!!" Danger messages like these move people to action.

Next, you will need testimonials from "experts" who support your position. Your experts might include child psychologists or high school teachers who have discovered sexts on students' phones. Then you will need to provide data in a compelling (and potentially misleading) way. For example, note that the rate of sexting has increased astronomically over the past ten years (but fail to mention that smartphone ownership and texting have also increased during that time period). Not all data provided by moral entrepreneurs are necessarily misleading, though. You may also note the percentage of teenagers who report sending or receiving sexts in national surveys. You will then need to highlight nonambiguous cases that evoke an emotional response and have no moral gray area. For example, you might highlight the case of a non–sexually active, honor roll student who was pressured into sending a sexually explicit photo that was then plastered all over the web, causing the student to commit suicide. Some claims making also includes the presentation of a syndrome, or the idea that the offending behavior is pathological, akin to a sickness in need of a cure. You could, for instance, present teenage sexting as an addiction requiring intervention.

Moral Conversion

Once the problem has been identified and awareness generated, moral entrepreneurs must convert people to their position. Moral conversion has three primary components. First, media attention must be sought. Public demonstrations, boycotts, and marches are useful for attracting coverage. Second, moral entrepreneurs must seek endorsements from respected public figures, typically nonexperts. Third, they must form coalitions, or partnerships, with powerful groups with shared interests, such as political organizations, religious groups, or professional associations. For your antisexting moral entrepreneurship, you might organize demonstrations at political events, obtain the support of a famous parent (such as an actress who plays a beloved sitcom mother and also has her own teenage children), and gain the support of the National Campaign to Prevent Teen Pregnancy and the organization Focus on the Family.

Moral Panic

Successful moral entrepreneurship can sometimes lead to a moral panic. A **moral panic** is an exaggerated, widespread fear regarding the collapse of public morality. Those blamed for the collapse and therefore treated as threats to the social order are called **folk devils** (Cohen 1972). Folk devils become the target of the public's anxieties about contemporary social life and the future, and they are blamed for a host of social problems. In a moral panic, the fear of a folk devil is out of proportion to its actual threat to society, even when the folk devil does, in some measure, contribute to some social problems.

In some cases, folk devils are falsely blamed or even entirely imaginary, such as in the 1980s moral panic about satanic ritual abuse at daycare centers. Accusations of satanic rituals involving child sexual abuse, largely based on the coached testimony of preschool-aged children, led to widespread hysteria that demonized daycare providers. The most famous case involved the trials of the operators of the McMartin

Moral entrepreneurs worked to establish the Eighteenth Amendment, which prohibited the manufacture and sale of alcohol in the United States until its repeal in 1933.

Preschool in Manhattan Beach, California, who had been accused of conducting satanic rituals involving sexual activity with animals, travel through underground tunnels, and other bizarre allegations. Like other investigations of such claims, this six-year series of trials revealed the moral panic to be based on nothing more than overactive imaginations. Sociologists note that the hysteria took hold due to widespread anxieties about women's large-scale entry into the labor force and the growing reliance on childcare providers (de Young 1997).

Examining drug scares, or moral panics focused on substances (e.g., alcohol, marijuana, cocaine), Craig Reinarman (1994) identifies what he calls "key ingredients" of any full-scale scare. Although his focus was on drugs, we can observe how these ingredients comprise many other kinds of moral panics. For example, the crack cocaine drug scare of the 1980s included many of the ingredients listed in Table 6.1 on the next page: people were using crack cocaine (kernel of truth); there was a great deal of media attention given to the "crack epidemic," particularly focusing on so-called crack babies born to addicted women (media magnification); politicians focused their attention on crack, passing legislation that provided harsh penalties for even low levels of possession (politico-moral entrepreneurs); crack was portrayed as a drug solely of the Black urban underclass despite use across demographic groups (linking to a "dangerous class"); and crack markets and crack use were blamed for entrenched urban poverty rather than seen as the result of poverty (scapegoating for public problems).

Contemporary Folk Devils

Contemporary folk devils have included crack addicts (particularly crack-addicted pregnant women), undocumented immigrants, alleged Satanists, and, according to Abigail Saguy (2013), obese people. In her book *What's Wrong with Fat?* Saguy describes how obesity has been transformed from a personal health concern to a public issue in need of immediate intervention, with obese people's supposed lack of self-control blamed for a breakdown in society's

TABLE 6.1

Reinarman's Key Ingredients in a Drug Scare

Ingredient	Description
Kernel of truth	Drug use is occurring, providing some foundation for claims that the behavior is problematic.
Media magnification	Sensationalized media accounts create "routinization of caricature" wherein extreme cases are presented as typical.
Politico-moral entrepreneurs	Individuals or groups, often including political elites, take on the cause of changing behavior and laws.
Professional interest groups	Professional groups (e.g., the American Medical Association, law enforcement agencies) vie for "ownership" of the drug problem so that they may get to define its solution.
Historical context of conflict	Social context must be fertile for a scare, with mounting anxieties (e.g., about the economy, culture, politics) making the public receptive to defining certain people as "problems."
Linking to a "dangerous class"	The scare is not about the drug itself but, rather, the persons said to use the drug. Drug use will be defined as a "problem" (and a moral panic ensues) to the extent that it is associated with a group perceived as threatening.
Scapegoating for an array of public problems	The drug is blamed for a host of social problems that already existed and that are often only indirectly related to drug use.

collective well-being. Playing on Cohen's term *folk devil*, Saguy claims that the moral panic regarding the so-called obesity epidemic in the United States produces a "fat-devil."

Medicalization of Deviance

The modern era has seen a transformation in the social construction of deviance. Many behaviors, conditions, and beliefs once attributed to the deviant's evil character, or "badness," are now constructed as due to pathology of the mind, or "madness." The transition from badness to madness is also referred to as the **medicalization of deviance.** What was once evidence of sin is now evidence of sickness, and sickness can be treated. This can be seen in the growth of the American Psychological Association's fifth edition of the *Diagnostic and Statistical Manual of Mental Disorders* (*DSM-5*). The most recent edition contains over 300 disorders, described in the 947-page text, including "exhibitionistic disorder" (exposing one's genitals to others to gain sexual satisfaction), "kleptomania" (compulsive stealing), and "female sexual interest/arousal disorder" (inability to attain or maintain sexual arousal). In contrast, the first edition of the *DSM*, published in 1952, was under 150 pages in length and contained just 106 disorders. Although the growth in the *DSM* may simply reflect a more nuanced understanding of mental health conditions, it is clear that many human experiences that differ from the norm are now diagnosable.

Consider This

What do you think led to the medicalization of deviance and the movement away from a "badness" orientation and toward a "madness" orientation? What are the social consequences—good and bad—of the medicalization of deviance?

Labeling Perspective

So far, this section has addressed how behaviors, conditions, and beliefs are socially constructed as deviant. This next portion will describe how certain individuals (or groups) come to be regarded as deviant through a process of **labeling.** The labeling perspective has its roots in symbolic interactionism.

As seen in earlier chapters, symbolic interactionism posits that human action is driven by the meanings that individuals ascribe to people, objects, and interactions. The meanings themselves are the result of social interaction and are subject to change. Consider, for example, a young man standing outside of a convenience store. He is there to register

What's Wrong with Fat?

In this activity, you will listen to a podcast episode focusing on the idea that the "obesity epidemic" is a moral panic and then write a brief paper applying the concepts in this chapter.

Listen to the *Office Hours* podcast interview with Abigail Saguy on her research for her book *What's Wrong with Fat?* (http://thesocietypages.org/officehours/2013/09/30/abigail-saguy-on-whats-wrong-with-fat/).

Then, in a one-page paper, answer the following questions:

1. What is "framing" and how does it help us to understand moral entrepreneurship?

2. What elements of claims making and moral conversion (or "key ingredients" identified by Reinarman) seem to be present in the construction of the obesity epidemic, as described by Saguy?

3. Has listening to her interview challenged any of your ideas about fatness as a public issue? Why or why not?

---

voters. But a passerby, seeing the young man's well-worn clothing and unkempt appearance, assumes that he is there to panhandle and averts her eyes and picks up her pace to avoid interaction. Her behavior is driven by the meaning she has ascribed to his appearance. His behavior, in response, will result from the meaning he attaches to her avoidance behavior. Symbolic interactionists argue that sociologists should examine how people experience the social world, including how their interactions create—and are the result of—interpretations that are attached to symbols (i.e., people, objects, and interactions).

Labeling theory emphasizes the power of definitions. Who is defined, or labeled, as deviant is the result of a social process in which others react as though the person is deviant. Although deviant labeling may be related to rule-violating behavior, it is the *reaction* rather than the behavior itself that produces the label of deviant. Following this logic, no actual rule-violating behavior is necessary for the deviant label to be applied. The man outside the convenience store is a deviant because of the woman's reaction, not because of any behavior or belief he may hold. Moreover, labels have the power to transform people. He who is treated as deviant becomes deviant.

The Thomas Theorem

Labeling theory relies on the logic of the Thomas theorem: "If men define situations as real, they are real in their consequences" (Thomas and Thomas 1928:572). Franklin Tannenbaum (1938), an early

labeling theorist, referred to this as the "dramatization of evil." Tannenbaum's focus was on youth behavior. He argued that police reactions to the ordinary rule-breaking behaviors of adolescents construct them as deviant or "bad." The social interplay of the adolescent and the police (the drama) is what creates the "evil," not the act itself. For instance, imagine two friends who get into an argument at school that leads to shoving and then punches being thrown. Are these just teenagers blowing off steam or are they criminals committing assault? It depends on whether they end up in the principal's office or the backseat of a police cruiser. And where they end up depends on how school authorities and the police already view them—"good kids" get the principal's office, "bad kids" get the police cruiser. Deviant labeling, thus, operates as a kind of self-fulfilling prophecy wherein it "sets in motion several mechanisms which conspire to shape the person in the image people have of him" (Becker 1973 [1963]). The definition makes it so.

Primary and Secondary Deviance

Edwin Lemert (1951) elaborated on Tannenbaum's ideas, discerning between primary and secondary deviance. **Primary deviance** is rule breaking that individuals engage in in the absence of a deviant label. They do not regard themselves as deviant, nor—so far—do others. A great deal of primary deviance goes undetected. But sometimes it is identified and reacted to as deviant. Further rule-breaking behavior that occurs as a result of a deviant label is called **secondary deviance.**

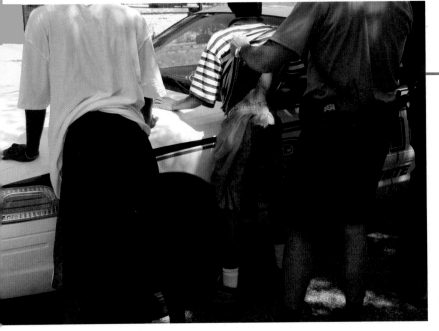

coworkers, or neighbors. Both official and informal labels are stigmatizing. **Stigma** is a mark of disgrace and interactions that communicate that one is disgraced, dishonorable, or otherwise deviant.

The stigmatizing reactions of both official authorities and everyday people matter for secondary deviance because they can lead to role engulfment. **Role engulfment** occurs when the deviant role takes over people's other social roles due to others relating to them in response to their "spoiled identity" (Goffman 1963).

For example, if a person has a felony record, like person B in the DUI example above, then others may, to the extent that they know about the spoiled identity, relate to them based on their felon status, including landlords who won't rent to them, employers who won't hire them, and men and women who won't date them. In some instances, the deviant label—or spoiled identity—becomes a **master status,** or the primary status by which others interact with a person. Labels such as "sex offender" or "murderer" are particularly likely to become master statuses because of the extent of the stigma assigned to them.

Although early labeling theorists focused primarily on the impact of stigma on a person's view of himself or herself, contemporary theorists note that there are other reasons that stigmatizing labeling matters, including the creation of structural barriers to conventional life (e.g., the inability to get a job) and involvement in a deviant subculture that celebrates or at least tolerates spoiled identities.

To illustrate, let's imagine there are two people attending a party. Both get behind the wheel after drinking too much. Both cause an accident involving another driver who is badly injured. Person A drives away from the scene and is not caught. Person B cannot drive away from the scene because his car was badly damaged in the collision. Person B is arrested and ultimately pleads guilty to felony DUI with injury. As a result, person B is sentenced to twelve months in state prison and now has a felony record. The drunk driving that led to the label of "felon" for person B (and didn't for person A) was primary deviance. According to the labeling perspective, the "felon" label will increase the risk that person B will go on to engage in other criminal acts, or secondary deviance. Person A, in comparison, avoided a deviant label that would increase her likelihood of future rule breaking.

Official and Informal Labels and Stigmas

The label of "felon" in the example above is an official label. *Official labels* are labels applied by an authority, such as the state (e.g., felon, delinquent, sex offender), the military (e.g., dishonorably discharged), a school (e.g., truant), or a hospital (e.g., mentally ill, HIV positive). Official labels, because they are documented by recognized authorities, are difficult to shed and have important consequences for obtaining resources, such as jobs and housing. *Informal labels,* in contrast, occur when a person has been deemed deviant by family members, teachers,

Social Position and Labeling

Social location—where one resides in a system of social stratification—is central in the labeling perspective. The power to define others as deviant and to resist having the label applied to oneself is linked to social position. Those with greater power—for example, politicians, professionals, and other members of the upper-middle and upper classes—are better able to resist deviant labeling, even when their behavior does not differ from that of the

Sociologists in Action

Creating a More Just Society for All

Sarah Shannon

I sometimes like to tell students that the best job I ever got with my sociology degree was cleaning toilets. Usually there's some nervous laughter while they wait for the punchline. My first job after my BA was at a home health agency where my main task was supervising child protective visits between parents and their children in foster care, but I also filled out my hours doing housekeeping for other agency clients. This brought me into daily contact with some of society's most stigmatized people—parents accused of abusing or neglecting their children and people with serious mental health challenges. This job was the beginning of "sociology in action" for me.

Later I worked for an employment services agency helping people with criminal records find jobs. My clients' records ranged from minor drug offenses to more serious convictions, such as sex offenses. I was floored by the seemingly insurmountable obstacles put in front of people who were earnestly trying to reintegrate into society. Even my clients with very minor records could not get an interview, much less a job. Once I returned to graduate school, initially for a Masters of Social Work (MSW) and ultimately a PhD in sociology, there was no doubt that I wanted to study these kinds of issues and help improve public policy and reduce stigma.

Along with collaborators similarly dedicated to doing research that is relevant and accessible to the public, I have worked on a range of projects focused on how the criminal justice and social welfare systems affect social inequality. For example, despite the fact that you can easily find out anyone's criminal history with a few keystrokes on Google, we don't know exactly how many people in the United States have a criminal record. One of my collaborative projects has been to estimate the number of people that have ever been to prison (about 7.6 million) and that have ever been convicted of a felony (nearly 20 million). We regularly receive requests from the media and policy makers asking for these numbers, especially as they relate to employment and voting (in some states, you cannot vote if you have a felony conviction).

I am also studying how young adults navigate reentering their communities after spending time away in various institutions, including prison but also other places like mental health treatment and the military. This qualitative study reveals in depth just how hard these transitions can be and how individuals struggle to form identities and forge "successes" for themselves despite the stigma and barriers they face. In another project, I am working with collaborators in seven other states to uncover how states use monetary sanctions (fines, fees, etc.) to fund their criminal justice systems, often at the expense of their poorest citizens. Taken together, these research projects allow me to make an impact by creating knowledge that students, academics, and the broader public can use to make sense of our social systems and, hopefully, create a more just society for us all.

Sarah Shannon is an assistant professor of sociology at the University of Georgia.

---

less-powerful "deviant." This can be seen clearly by comparing the results of two sociological works.

In his book *Punished,* Victor Rios (2012) describes the "youth control complex" that characterizes the daily lives of low-income Black and Latino teenage boys in Oakland, California. In the boys' social world, the mundane misbehavior of adolescence (e.g., fighting, talking back to teachers) is treated as serious crime in need of criminal justice intervention. The boys are viewed by teachers, police, and business owners as potential criminals who must be managed, and there are few second chances for boys caught breaking the rules. The boys—marginalized economically, educationally, and racially and ethnically—were defined as a problem as soon as puberty hit and sometimes even before.

Scott Jacques and Richard Wright's (2015) *Code of the Suburb* examines a different group of teenage boys: White, middle-class drug dealers in a suburb of Atlanta, Georgia. Unlike the boys in *Punished,* the boys in *Code of the Suburb* are largely ignored by law enforcement, are regarded as upstanding young men, and experience few negative consequences of their lawbreaking behavior. Their privileges of wealth, race, and place enable them to resist detection and, when detected, stigmatizing labeling. In this chapter's

Applying Labeling Theory to a Village of Registered Sex Offenders

In this exercise, you will practice applying labeling theory and answer questions about the effects of labeling.

Watch this short documentary from the *New York Times* about a "sex offender village" in Florida at www .nytimes.com/2013/05/22/opinion/sex-offender-village .html?_r=0.

With the emergence of sex offender registries and city ordinances that limit where registered sex offenders can reside, many have begun to live together in tent cities, under highway overpasses (such as the Julia Tuttle Causeway in Florida), and in communities like Miracle Village.

Apply labeling theory concepts to what you saw in the documentary.

1. According to a labeling perspective, what is the likely outcome of being "labeled for life"? Explain your response.

2. Why do you think the stigma assigned to sex offenders far exceeds the stigma assigned to other offenders, including violent offenders?

3. How might social location affect—or fail to affect—the labeling of sex offenders?

Sociologists in Action, Sarah Shannon similarly studies the impact of stigmatizing labels on marginalized groups.

Howard Becker's Typology of Deviance

Howard Becker (1973 [1963]) refers to those labeled as deviant or criminal despite the absence of any actual deviant or criminal behavior as the "falsely accused." Marginalized, or relatively powerless, members of society are at greatest risk of being falsely accused, although certainly it can happen to others, such as the operators of the McMartin Preschool accused of satanic ritual abuse.

As Table 6.2 notes, Becker described those who engage in deviance or crime as "pure deviants," as the label is a true reflection of their actions. The drug dealers in the *Code of the Suburb* were what Becker called "secret deviants," because they avoided detection and labeling. Conformists, in contrast, do not engage in deviance behavior and are not labeled (we might also conceive of conformists as "pure nondeviants").

Check Your Understanding

- What is moral entrepreneurship, and how do moral entrepreneurs generate awareness and convert others to their cause?

- Why do moral panics occur and what are folk devils?

- What are the central claims of labeling theory (including symbolic interactionist assumptions, primary vs. secondary deviance, role engulfment, and master statuses)?

TABLE 6.2

Becker's Typology of Deviance

	Deviant Behavior	Conforming Behavior
Labeled deviant	Pure deviant	Falsely accused
Not labeled deviant	Secret deviant	Conformist

Managing Deviant Identities

Have you ever done something that violated your own code of ethics, such as stealing, cheating on a partner, or cheating on a test? If you have, then you have probably also sought to minimize the deviance of your act, either for yourself or for others. Perhaps you convinced yourself that you had no other choice, that you only did it because you had been drinking, or that it wasn't that big of a deal. You may have sought to justify or excuse your behavior.

Justifications are accounts of behavior that take full responsibility for an action but deny the wrongfulness of the act. An example of a justification would be an embezzler (one who steals money with which he or she has been entrusted, such as an employee stealing funds from a work account) claiming that she deserved the money because her employer underpaid her. Excuses accept the wrongfulness of an act while denying full responsibility. For example, another embezzler might claim that his coworkers pressured him to steal the money or that he needed the money to pay off debts. Both justifications and excuses are ways that those with deviant—or potentially deviant—identities can maintain and project a positive self-concept.

Techniques of Neutralization

Justifications and excuses allow rule violators to minimize, or neutralize, their deviance. Sykes and

Matza (1957), in researching delinquents, found that lawbreaking adolescents often felt guilt and shame about their actions. To do "bad" while maintaining a sense of one's self as a "good" person, they must neutralize, or minimize, their deviance. The strategies deviants use to maintain a positive self-concept or **techniques of neutralization** include the following:

1. **Denial of responsibility.** Offenders claim they are not to blame. They may claim to be victims of circumstance or that the act was accidental or that they were subject to pressures beyond their control (e.g., alcohol or peer pressure). Denial of responsibility redefines the deviant as not culpable, reducing both social stigma and the feeling that one has failed oneself morally.

2. **Denial of injury.** Offenders say they have not done anything wrong because either the act produced little or no harm or their intentions were not to inflict harm. This is a typical neutralization technique among those who engage in "victimless" offenses, such as drug use, as well as among those who can frame their behavior as victimless, even if another person is affected (e.g., auto thieves who use cars to "joyride," later returning them).

3. **Denial of victim.** Offenders acknowledge that their actions are harmful but refuse to acknowledge a legitimate victim. This can happen in two ways: either the offender claims that the victim deserved what happened, such as in cases of retaliatory violence, or the victim is unknown, abstract, or otherwise absent, such as in cases of fraud in which offenders never interact with and may not even know the names of their victims. In the former, the victim is denied status as a victim (i.e., "they had it coming"). In the latter, the victim is not visible and therefore is less of a burden on the offender's conscience.

4. **Condemning the condemners.** Offenders direct attention to those who judge them rather than their own behavior, claiming that those who condemn their actions have no right to do so because they are "hypocrites, deviants in disguise, or impelled by personal spite" (Sykes and Matza 1957:668).

5. **Appeal to higher loyalties.** Offenders claim that the act was necessary to meet the moral obligations of a group even if it means violating

another set of rules, such as laws. There are multiple, competing loyalties in the offender's life—to obey the law, to help friends, to assist coworkers, and so on. In this claim, the offender states that the loyalties to one group (e.g., to one's fraternity or to one's children) are more important—or higher—than the duty to obey the law or some other set of rules (e.g., religious prohibitions).

In their book *Identity Thieves,* Copes and Vieraitis (2012) describe the ways that incarcerated identity thieves manage their spoiled identities. These offenders ranged from small-scale credit card thieves to mortgage fraudsters netting millions in illegal profits. They excused and justified their actions by denying injury, denying the victim, and appealing to higher loyalties. Examine the following quotes from the identity thieves they interviewed and see if you can identify the techniques of neutralization.

Danny: "I mean, like, real identity theft, man I can't do that. Intentionally screw someone over—it's not right to me. So I couldn't do that. But corporations, banks, police departments, the government? Oh, yeah, let's go get 'em. Because that's the way they treat you, you know what I'm saying. If they done screwed me over, screw them!" (p. 50).

Abbey: "I did it for my son. I thought if I had money and I was able to live, have a nice place to live, and not have to worry about a car payment, I could just start a new life and that life is for him . . . I just wanted my son to be happy and loved" (p. 52).

Dustin: "With credit cards if you notify them that your credit cards were missing then [victims are] not liable. . . . The bank is gonna be insured, so the bank is gonna get their money back. The consumer is not gonna be hurt. Nobody really loses but the insurance companies. It's not taking for an individual per se, like a burglary" (p. 48).

Stigma Management

Techniques of neutralization allow individuals to minimize the deviance of their acts and maintain a positive self-concept, thereby avoiding a deviant identity. Once an identity has become spoiled, people can employ strategies to reduce the stigma they receive as a result of their deviant condition, such as having an official deviant label, an unusual physical appearance, a physical or mental health condition, or uncommon gender or sexual identity. Stigma management strategies, or methods of reducing deviant stigma and maintaining a positive identity, differ depending on whether the stigma experienced is visible or invisible. Visible stigmas are those that are immediately apparent in face-to-face interaction (e.g., facial disfigurement or physical disabilities), whereas invisible stigmas can be hidden (e.g., sexual orientation, religious identities, or mental illness).

Managing Visible Stigmas

Managing visible stigmas involves **compensatory strategies,** in which individuals attempt to offset the deviance that is ascribed to them or make others more comfortable with their stigma. Compensatory strategies include acknowledgment, individuating information, and increased positivity. *Acknowledgment* occurs when a stigmatized person directly addresses his or her stigma in an attempt to relieve the tension in interaction. *Individuating information* involves revealing information about oneself to diminish the likelihood that the person with whom they are interacting will rely on stereotypical ideas about their status. *Increased positivity* is a kind of emotion work—or management of feelings, typically to preserve relationships—in which a stigmatized person intentionally tries to become more likeable to counter the negative impact of stigma.

> **Consider This**
> Think of a time that you attempted to manage stigma, either visible or invisible. Did you use compensatory strategies, passing, or revealing? If so, were your efforts successful? Why or why not?

Managing Invisible Stigmas

Those whose identities may be spoiled as a result of invisible stigma have more options for managing their deviant identities, falling into two broad categories: passing and revealing. Passing involves attempts at presenting oneself as a member of a nonstigmatized group. Sociologists describe several forms of passing, including fabrication and concealment. *Fabrication* involves the presentation of a false identity. For example, in time periods, regions, and subcultural groups in which gay men, lesbians, and bisexuals are stigmatized and labeled deviant, fabrication may take the form of crafting a false heterosexual social identity at work. Unlike fabrication, *concealment* does not involve deception; rather, it involves taking steps to keep one's stigmatized identity hidden. For instance, in a study of homeless adolescents, Roschelle and Kaufmann (2004) describe the code words that the teenagers used to hide their homelessness from their classmates. For instance, rather than referring to the person "sleeping three cots down" (at the shelter), they used the language "lives three houses down." This enabled the adolescents to hide their stigmatized status and fit in with peers who did not know they were homeless.

Revealing is a stigma management technique that intentionally and strategically makes the invisible stigma visible, including signaling, normalizing, and differentiating. *Signaling* is a revealing strategy that does not involve direct disclosure but instead relies on subtle or cryptic indications of one's deviant status. For instance, mentioning needing to pick up one's Prozac refill is a subtle signal of one's mental health status. Others seek to directly disclose their stigma but frame it for others as normal, called *normalizing*. An example would be a person who discusses his or her HIV status as though it were no different from any other nonstigmatized medical condition. *Differentiating* involves direct disclosure with the goal of differentiating oneself from the nonstigmatized group. In emphasizing differences, the revealer challenges others' perceptions and rejects stigmatizing labeling. It is a reclamation of one's identity. An example would be a transgender man who, while able to pass as biologically male from birth, chooses instead to identify as transgender in the workplace in the hope that the institution will become more inclusive of transgender workers and clients.

Consider This
Think back to how you imagined the world would look without any deviance. How would you answer that question now?

Check Your Understanding

- What is the difference between justifications and excuses?

- What are the distinctions among the five techniques of neutralization, and what do they accomplish for individuals with deviant identities?

- What are some stigma management strategies, and how do they differ for visible versus invisible stigmas?

Conclusion

Sociologists regard deviance as any behaviors, conditions, or beliefs that violate norms (i.e., folkways, mores, and laws) and/or are penalized with stigmatizing sanctions, consistent with a relativistic, social constructionist view of the social world. Sociological theories of deviance and crime focus on how the organization of societies (i.e., social structure) and individuals' relative positions within their societies shape control and motivation, ultimately influencing the likelihood of deviant behavior. In addition, sociologists detail the processes whereby behaviors, conditions, beliefs, and individuals come to be defined as deviant, as well as the strategies used by individuals seeking to reduce deviant stigma and reclaim a nondeviant identity. The next chapter will continue to explore how the social world can constrain behavior and shape life outcomes, with a focus on economic inequality.

CHAPTER

6

$SAGE edge™

Want a better grade? Get the tools you need to sharpen your study skills. Access practice quizzes, eFlashcards, video and multimedia at **edge.sagepub.com/korgen**

Review

6.1 How do we define what is deviant?

Deviance includes behaviors, conditions, or beliefs that violate norms and/or incur stigmatizing sanctions. Sociologists distinguish between statistical, legalistic, and normative approaches. The approach used depends on one's assumptions about the nature of deviance, including absolutist assumptions, relativist/social constructionist assumptions, and conflict/critical assumptions.

6.2 What do sociological theories suggest about the causes of deviant behavior, including crime?

Sociological theories seek to explain either why some individuals engage in more deviance and crime than others (individual-level theories) or why rates of deviance are higher in some regions, in some time periods, or for some groups than others (structural-level theories). Their explanations focus on either control (e.g., social bonds, self-control, or community control) or motivation for engaging in deviance and crime (e.g., anomie, personal strains, or learning deviant norms).

6.3 What are the social processes involved in creating social norms?

Moral entrepreneurs create norms (and deviance) by actively campaigning for social change. Some moral entrepreneur campaigns produce moral panics in which the public regards the newly deviant behavior, condition, or belief as a threat to public morality. Those deemed responsible become folk devils. Social norms are then maintained by stigmatizing rule violators and labeling them as deviant.

6.4 How does social location influence who and what is defined as deviant?

Individuals and groups with relatively little social power have less ability to resist the label of "deviant" or "criminal." Powerful individual and groups, in contrast, are less likely to be falsely accused of being deviant, are more likely to avoid detection and stigma if they do engage in deviance, and have greater power to determine what will be defined as deviant through moral entrepreneurship and the imposition of deviant labels on others.

6.5 How do individuals manage deviant identities?

Those who are labeled deviant or risk being labeled deviant engage in techniques of neutralization that enable them to maintain and project a positive self-concept. Those who have stigmatized statuses manage stigma in interaction with others through compensatory strategies (with visible stigmas) and passing or reveal strategies (with invisible stigmas).

Key Terms

- absolutist perspective   102
- anomie   104
- compensatory strategies   116
- conflict perspective   103
- folk devils   108
- general strain theory   107
- labeling   110
- learning theories   107
- legalistic approach   101
- master status   112
- medicalization of deviance   110
- moral entrepreneurs   107
- moral panic   108

- normative approach   101
- primary deviance   111
- relativist perspective   102
- role engulfment   112
- sanctions   101
- secondary deviance   111
- self-control theory   107
- social control   106
- social disorganization   106
- statistical approach   99
- stigma   112
- techniques of neutralization   115

Why do some jobs pay so much more than others? Does everyone who works full-time deserve a living wage?

Marjorie Kamys Cotera/Bob Daemmrich Photography/Alamy Stock Photo

Learning Questions

7.1 What is the difference between income and wealth?

7.2 How do major sociological theories explain income inequality?

7.3 What is social stratification and how does it work in society?

7.4 How has social mobility changed in the United States?

7.5 What are the impacts of class position on education, health, and other social outcomes?

7.6 What programs might address income inequality?

CHAPTER

7

Confronting Economic Inequality

Sandra Enos

What Is Economic Inequality?

The lifestyles that people in a society can afford, the cars they drive and houses they live in, the schools they attend, the respect they command, and their access to power differ according-ing to their place on the economic ladder of society. This unequal distribution of economic resources (e.g., income and wealth) is known as **economic inequality**.

Economic inequality exists in every society. The extent and reasons for that inequality vary from society to society, however. Sociologists look at the reasons why. Why do some people seem to reap great benefits from work while others struggle to make ends meet? Are these differences the result of differences in talent or hard work or luck? Are men and women, White people and people of color, native-born and immigrant members, equally represented among the rich and the middle class and the poor? Or do we see some other patterns here?

While we focus on economic inequality in this chapter, as you know from discussions of intersectionality in previous chapters, economic inequality relates to and is influenced by other forms of inequality, such as those based on gender, race, sexual orientation, and disability. Sociology gives us the tools to question why these patterns occur. After reading this chapter, you will have a better understanding of how these patterns relate to your life and your economic position in society.

> **Consider This**
> Based on your own experience and observations, is family income, the schools one attended, or individual motivation and determination most important to success in school and later life? Which is least important? Why?

Measuring Inequality

When we talk about economic inequality, we usually are discussing income and wealth. While the two terms are sometimes used interchangeably, they refer to two different sources of resources.

Sandra Enos

I often joke that I have wanted to be a sociologist since I was five years old, and that statement is mainly true. As the first student in my family to graduate from high school, I was deeply aware early on in my life that life chances were not equally distributed in our society. My small town's population was made up of a diverse group of immigrants and their children—Italians, French Canadians, Poles, Portuguese, Germans, and others. I was intrigued by the cultural differences among these groups. I didn't discover sociology until my junior year, but it was love at first reading. It lit up my curiosity and opened up my world.

After earning a BA in sociology, I spent a year as a VISTA volunteer in rural Alabama, then went on to Brown University for a master's in sociology. I subsequently made a career in public service, working in child welfare, corrections, policy work, and higher education reform. After a nearly twenty-five-year break in my education, I earned a PhD in sociology and have been teaching for eighteen years. My long career applying sociology to real-world problems helps me make sociology real and important for students.

Economic inequality is represented, in part, by the houses we live in and whether or not we can afford to own our home.

MBI/Alamy Stock Photo

Income refers to earnings, whether those come from employment, government programs, investments, or inheritances. Money received from a paycheck, stock return, or Social Security benefits counts as income. **Wealth,** on the other hand, refers to assets one owns, like savings accounts, houses, cars, and investment portfolios holding stocks and bonds minus debts.

Income Inequality

Researchers asked people in forty countries how much more chief executive officers (CEOs) should earn than the unskilled workers employed by them.

U.S. respondents said CEOs ought to make 6.7 times as much money as their employees. Worldwide, the answers ranged from 3.6 in Israel to 8.3 in Australia. They were also asked to estimate the real earnings disparities. In the United States, those taking the survey estimated that CEOs earned 30 times what unskilled workers earned when, in fact, the ratio of earnings between CEOs in the United States and their unskilled workers was 354 to 1, the highest of all industrialized nations (Kiatpongsan and Norton 2014). Since that survey was conducted, in 2014, low-wage workers have seen their earnings increase a little (by 3.1 percent), thanks in large part to increases in the minimum wage in many states (Morath and Jargon 2016).

> **Consider This**
> Why do Americans and citizens of other nations underestimate the ratio of the earnings of CEOs and those of low-paid workers?

Since most people underestimate the magnitude of the differences between CEO salaries and those of average workers, relatively few citizens have demanded a reduction in these gaps (Gavett 2014). Kiatpongsan and Norton (2014) calculated what workers should be paid on average if respondents' ideal ratio of CEO salaries to workers' salaries was put into place. As Table 7.1 reveals, given the average American CEO's compensation of more than $12 million, if we raised the salaries of workers to achieve the ideal pay ratio described by survey respondents, the average American worker would earn nearly $2 million.

Wealth Inequality

To really understand economic inequality, we need to look at wealth. It stands to reason that one cannot accumulate great assets without a good income. After all, if you have meager earnings, there is little chance that you will have money left over to save for a house or to invest in the stock market. When individuals and families have assets that they inherit or that their parents can share with them, they have an advantage over families with little household wealth. Wealth can be passed down from one generation to the next, which further concentrates wealth, unless these assets are taxed at high rates or given away as charitable gifts.

A recent report from the Pew Research Center (DeSilver 2015) examined three different ways to measure economic inequality. These include measures of income, wealth, and consumption. As Figure 7.1 indicates, the top richest 20 percent of U.S. families own 89 percent of all wealth, 62 percent of all income, and account for 38 percent of all expenditures in the nation.

Some people believe the more income and wealth entrepreneurs retain, the more they will invest in the economy. They maintain that business leaders who create jobs should be amply rewarded for their contributions, with taxes kept low. Such an economy rewards risk taking and creativity and entrepreneurship.

Consider This

What would it be like to live in a society with no inequality at all compared to one where there are sharp differences between the rich and the poor?

Other policy analysts argue that the concentration of great wealth has important negative implications for the economy and for society as a whole. For one, the concentration of wealth at the top of the income pyramid has led to fewer resources for the rest of the population. If the rich were getting richer and the middle class were thriving as well, that would be a good thing. If the rich were getting richer and the living standards of the poor were improving, that would also be a positive development. In fact, the bottom 60 percent of the population is poorer than they were just a few decades ago. Moreover, although business leaders like Bill Gates, founder of Microsoft, and Mark Zuckerberg, founder of Facebook, have pledged large parts of their fortunes to charitable giving, generally speaking, lower- and middle-income households donate higher percentages of their income to charity than do wealthier people (Daniels 2014).

TABLE 7.1

What Average Workers Should Be Paid

Nation	Actual Ratio	Ideal Ratio	CEO Average Compensation	Worker Average Compensation	Worker Compensation at Ideal Ratio
Australia	93	9.3	$4,183,419	$44,983	$502,012
France	107	6.7	$3,965,312	$38,132	$594,794
United Kingdom	84	5.3	$3,758,412	$44,743	$704,707
Poland	28	5.0	$561,932	$20,069	$112,386
United States	354	6.7	$12,259,894	$34,645	$1,838,975
Germany	147	6.3	$5,912,781	$40,223	$946,045

Source: Data from Kiatpongsan, Sorapop, and Michael I Norton. "How Much (More) Should CEOs Make? A Universal Desire For More Equal Pay." *Perspectives on Psychological Science* 9, no. 6 (2014): 587–93.

FIGURE 7.1

The View from the Top: Wealth, Income, and Consumption

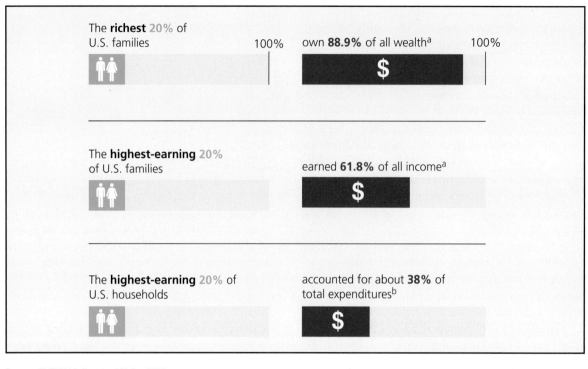

The **richest** 20% of U.S. families — 100% — own **88.9%** of all wealth[a] — 100%

The **highest-earning** 20% of U.S. families — earned **61.8%** of all income[a]

The **highest-earning** 20% of U.S. households — accounted for about **38%** of total expenditures[b]

Sources: Wolff (2014); Hasset and Mathur (2012).

a. 2013.

b. 2010.

How Income Is Distributed: Race, Gender, and Other Factors

As we compare incomes and wealth across demographic variables, we can see some distinct patterns. What variables have played a role in whether or not you are living in poverty now? Sociologists Mark Rank and Thomas A. Hirschl have created a tool that predicts our future chances of falling into poverty. Their economic risk calculator (http://riskcalculator.org/) considers race, education, and marital status to predict the likelihood that individuals will experience poverty in the next five, ten, or fifteen years. If you play with the calculator, you can readily see how much difference these three factors make in our risk for poverty (Rank and Hirschl 2016).

As seen in Figure 7.2, the Pew Research Center shows that the wealth gaps between Whites and ethnic and racial minorities have grown even wider since the Great Recession (Kochar and Fry 2014). Before the recession, wealth held by White families was ten times greater than that held by Black families and eight times greater than that held by Hispanic households. After the recession, those numbers climbed to thirteen and ten times as much wealth, respectively.

Check Your Understanding

- Why are sociologists interested in inequality?

- How can we measure income inequality?

- What is the difference between wealth and income?

- Is income or wealth more concentrated?

- What race/ethnic-based differences do we see in wealth attainment?

The Impact on Income and Wealth of Race, Ethnicity, and Gender

In this activity, you will read an article about family assets and wealth and answer questions about wealth and social mobility.

How do the effects of race, ethnicity, and gender affect the distribution of income and wealth? Read the report published in the *Washington Monthly* that examines the impact of family assets in determining the wealth of American households (www.washingtonmonthly.com/magazine/novemberdecember_2015/features/the_second_racial_wealth_gap058468.php?curator=Media REDEF&page=2).

In two paragraphs, combine the lessons from Figure 7.2 and your reading of the essay in the *Washington Monthly* to answer the following questions:

1. What is the role of gifts between family members in determining wealth? Think about the difference in economic prospects for two individuals—one whose parents can pay for his college education and can help him with a down payment for a first house and another whose parents cannot afford either. How are the futures of these children different?

2. How do these differences affect individuals' ability to move up in social class?

3. What is the impact of these differences in the long and short run for different demographic groups?

FIGURE 7.2

Racial, Ethnic Wealth Gaps since the Great Recession

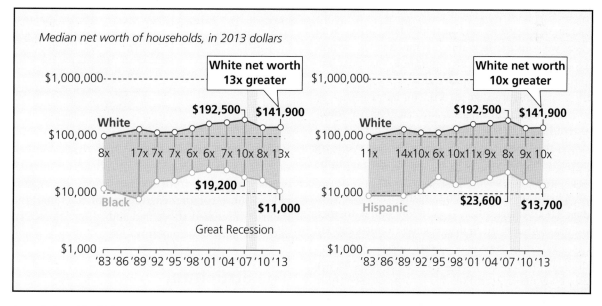

Source: Kochar and Fry (2014).

Notes: Blacks and Whites include only non-Hispanics. Hispanics are of any race. Chart scale is logarithmic; each gridline is ten times greater than tha gridline below it. The Great Recession began Dec. '07 and ended June '09.

Why Is There Economic Inequality?

Where does economic inequality come from? Does economic inequality reflect differences in abilities and talents among us? What would be the right balance between enough inequality to reward those differences yet not so much that we perceive the system as unjust and unworkable? The two macro-theoretical perspectives we have discussed here have answers to these questions.

Some philosophers, like Jean-Jacques Rousseau (Rousseau and Cress 1983), wrote that private property is the source of social ills since it leads to competition, unfair advantages, and the domination of some individuals and groups over others. On the other hand, other theorists like Thomas Malthus (Malthus 1951) argued that private property improves social conditions as it leads to the distribution of resources to the wealthy and the culling out of poor populations through starvation or disease. According to Malthus, private property provides incentives for ambitious individuals to organize enterprises and to create wealth. This creates jobs, enhances social organization, and improves the standard of living for all who survive.

Max Weber (Weber, Gerth, and Mills 1958) saw class quite differently. For Weber, class is not just about whether or not you own capital but also about your own "human capital" (skill sets) and social status. Weber suggested that three traits determined **socioeconomic status** or social standing: class, status (or prestige), and power. In this understanding of social class, we consider how much someone may earn in a job, the esteem in which others hold that position, and the power that position exerts. In some cases, all these elements are aligned. A doctor may earn a large salary, is held in high regard, and can exert her power and influence over others. On the other hand, a drug dealer may earn lots of money and may be quite a powerful figure to those who work for him, but he may have little prestige in general society.

When Harris, the polling organization, surveyed over 2,500 Americans in 2014, it found that doctors, military officers, firefighters, and scientists topped the list of most prestigious occupations. At bottom of the list were stockbrokers, union leaders, and real estate agents (Harris Poll 2014). You can see those and more results of the Harris Poll in Table 7.2.

What value do you bring to the economy? If you have an education and valuable skills, your labor will be more highly valued than that of those with less to offer and you can demand a higher salary and better working conditions. Another element of class,

TABLE 7.2

Public Perceptions of Prestige Based on Career

Career	Percent of respondents who say the career . . .	
	has prestige	is not at all prestigious
Doctor	88	12
Military officer	78	22
Firefighter	76	24
Scientist	76	24
Nurse	70	30
Engineer	69	31
Police officer	66	34
Priest/minister/clergy	62	38
Architect	62	38
Athlete	60	40
Stockbroker	38	21
Union leader	35	27
Real estate agent	27	24
Actor	55	45
Entertainer	53	47
Member of Congress	52	48

Source: Harris Poll (2014).

Weber argued, is **status,** the prestige that we assign each other. The higher our status, the more respect we may command from others. Weber's theory provides a more comprehensive view of class than the theories discussed above and adds dimensions that allow for more class mobility.

The Structural Functionalist Perspective

Few of us would argue that we should all earn the same income no matter what we do or how we contribute (or not) to the economy. Most would suggest that some inequality is essential and productive for

One of America's most cherished myths is that anyone who works hard can become economically successful.

Blend Images/Alamy Stock Photo

a society like ours. People who study hard, earn a degree, and work at demanding jobs should earn more than those who choose to slack off. Following this line of reasoning, as we discussed in Chapter 2, structural functionalists suggest that inequality is functional for society (Davis and Moore 1945). Our economic system should recognize and reward those who are talented and do the work that a society needs.

From the structural functionalist perspective, inequality is necessary to get the work of that society done. If everyone earned the same amount of money, we may not get people to do the work that is required. We need to make certain that the positions in a society that fulfill that society's needs—health, education, cleaning the streets, managing companies, ensuring public safety, and much more—are filled. To achieve this, we have an unequal distribution of rewards. According to structural functionalism, the positions that garner the greatest rewards in terms of income and prestige are those most important to the functioning of that society. Such a society relies on a meritocracy.

A **meritocracy** is a society in which those with the most talent rise to the top and are appropriately rewarded for their contributions. In some societies, advancement comes through inherited offices or corruption, but meritocracies reward excellence rather than family relations or other influences. In meritocracies, income reflects the contribution of the social role to the larger society. For example, in a meritocracy, doctors earn more than nurses because they have more responsibility and have invested more years in their education. Likewise, teachers earn more than custodians because they have more training and because they fulfill important roles related to educating children. In a meritocracy, those with the ability to become key contributors to society, like doctors and teachers, should be guided toward those careers and given the training they need to succeed in them.

There are several critiques of the meritocracy theory. When we look at the way income is distributed, can we really imagine that hard work is equally rewarded whether you are a janitor or a CEO? If hard work and merit determine rewards, how do we explain the fact that women earn 80 cents on the

Consider This

Is the United States a meritocracy? Do all children in U.S. society have an equal chance to develop their skills and talents? Do leaders always recognize merit and reward it accordingly?

dollar for what men make in comparable jobs? Also, a child may work very hard and excel in his public school, but if that school is of low quality and his interests and talents are not developed, that child's effort may not be rewarded in the same way as that of a child who has the advantage of having college-educated parents, enrichment activities, and other advantages. This theory of meritocracy assumes a level playing field (McNamee and Miller 2004).

The Conflict Perspective

As we learned in Chapter 2, Karl Marx (Marx, Engels, and Bender 1988), the founder of the conflict perspective, saw things very differently from structural functionalists. He argued that social order is organized around social classes—not merit. Marx pointed out that throughout history, there have always been two classes—the owners of the means of production (bourgeoisie) and those who work for them (proletariat).

Grade Distributions and Inequality in Educational Motivation

In this activity, you will assess the impact of inequality across various grade distribution patterns.

How much inequality is good for teaching and learning? Suppose there are twenty-five students in a class. Imagine that you could know ahead of time what the grade distributions were going to be in a class before you took it. Which of these six options would you choose?

Grades	Option 1	Option 2	Option 3	Option 4	Option 5	Option 6
A	1	5	5	5	2	
B	2	5	20	5	3	
C	3	5			15	25
D	7	5		10	3	
F	12	5		5	2	

In a two-page paper, answer the following questions:

1. Which distribution would most encourage you to work hard? Why?

2. Which distribution seems the worst to you? Why?

3. If you had to design your ideal distribution system, what would it look like? Describe the merits and potential downsides of your system and why you think it would be the best possible system of distributing grades.

According to Marx, control of the means of production—how the economy creates goods and services for consumption and trade—is key to wealth. Economic inequality is a consequence of the fact that the interests of the bourgeoisie (to make profit by lowering costs and keeping wages low) and the interests of the proletariat (to make a good living) are incompatible. The bourgeoisie make a profit by employing the proletariat at wages lower than the true value of their labor. Marx predicted that the proletariat would eventually rise up against the bourgeoisie in a revolution.

Marx also wrote, however, that the proletariat may be fooled by the bourgeoisie into accepting a high level of economic inequality. If the wealthy control the media and cultural messages, they may be able to convince the workers that the economic system is just and that the wealthy and the poor deserve their fates. A powerful **ideology**, or set of beliefs, about how wealth is created may convince the workers to support policies that benefit the bourgeoisie. For example, if they are convinced that the wealthy deserve their riches (and that if they work hard enough, they can be wealthy, too), they might support policies that would lower taxes on the wealthy and cut programs that benefit low-income households. When members of a class embrace values that work against their own interests, they have developed what Marx called a false consciousness.

How Much Inequality Should a Society Have?

Should a society have inequality to motivate people to work hard? How do we avoid having so much inequality that some people simply give up and don't work at all? Should we try to ensure that everyone in society has an equal opportunity to gain from and contribute to society? You can debate these issues and help create public policies that support the goals you think are most important for our society.

In India, the Dalit, or the "untouchables," are on the lowest rung of the Hindu caste system of stratification.

Bloomberg/Bloomberg/Getty Images

Check Your Understanding

- How did Rousseau and Malthus view private property?

- According to Weber, what is the basis of economic inequality?

- How does structural functionalism explain economic inequality?

- How does Marx's theory explain economic inequality?

- Why might the proletariat support policies that support the bourgeoisie at their own expense?

Understanding Social Stratification

It is hard to imagine a gathering of humans not organized according to some hierarchy, whether based on physical strength, birthright, or some other variable. Stratification systems are not just a matter of personal preference. These social standings are the result of **structured inequalities,** advantages and disadvantages built into social institutions, such as racial segregation and public schools funded by property taxes, which means that students from wealthier families will have access to better schools than children from poorer backgrounds. The way valuable goods and desired intangibles (like social status and prestige) are distributed in society is known as **social stratification** and is determined by social institutions and social attributes.

Systems of Stratification

Various systems of stratification exist, from the most rigid and severe to those that allow some movement across divisions. The most rigid form of stratification is **slavery,** where individuals own other individuals as property and have the legal right to dispense with that property as they wish. Slavery is now against the law in every nation but still exists in many areas of the world (e.g., children sold to pay off family debts, women forced into the sex trafficking trade) (http://www.freetheslaves.net).

In an **estate** system, there is very limited social mobility, but those with the least standing, the serfs or peasantry, have more freedom than slaves. In this system, laws distribute power and rights based on social standing. For example, the right to vote might be restricted to those holding property. Certain rights and privileges would be granted to members of the clergy, the nobility, and commoners—each person would have his place in the social order and would generally assume the social position held by his parents. These systems were prevalent in Europe and in Asia until the 1800s.

Unlike the estate system, **caste** systems are rigid systems that confine individuals to a social group for their lifetimes, assigning to them specific roles in a society with tight rules over the relationships among castes. Examples of caste systems exist in South Asia, in nations like India, where four main castes are in place. Members of lowest caste, the Dalits, are restricted from occupations that require purity and are confined to jobs like cremating corpses and dealing with human waste. In **class-based** systems, like the United States, members of a given social class share common economic statuses and lifestyles. For example, members of the middle class can afford to live in moderately priced houses, take annual vacations, and send their children to college. Unlike in slavery or caste systems, individuals in a class-based system may move up or down the economic ladder.

Those living in the United States are all members of a social class. Social class serves as an identity for us, as do race, ethnicity, gender, place of birth, and other social markers. During our lives, the fortunes of our families may rise or fall, and there may be social movements or dislocations that improve or damage our position in society.

Understanding the Social Positions of Others

One challenge in thinking sociologically is to imagine ourselves in the social position of others. It can be hard to put ourselves in the shoes of someone with very different circumstances from our own. Philosopher John Rawls (1971) proposes a theory of justice that would require us to create rules for society from behind a **veil of ignorance**. By this, Rawls means that we would craft these rules without knowing our own social position. We would have no idea what social class we would be born into or whether we would be male or female, White or a member of a minority group, gay or straight, native-born or immigrant. So, the rules we make should not carry with them any class, race, gender, or nativity bias, or we might be creating rules that put us and others in our social position at a disadvantage!

> ### Consider This
>
> How can we better understand how members of other social classes live? Do the media help us to understand these situations? Do the images that we tend to receive in the media confirm stereotypes we may have about social class or do they challenge those images? Can you think of a recent movie, television show, or a YouTube video that presents an accurate portrayal of social class?

It is nearly impossible for those with economic advantages to imagine the lives of those with fewer advantages (Hale 2012). They see the world through a **veil of opulence**, which means they misunderstand the struggles faced by those who don't have the privileges of attending a great school or being a member of group that is well connected to opportunities for success. They assume that others also have resources to lift themselves by their own bootstraps. For example, an individual who has been born to a wealthy family may not recognize the advantages she enjoys because her parents are college educated, she attended a highly regarded public school, and she had opportunities for extracurricular experiences that enhanced her application to an Ivy League university. She may underestimate how hard it is for students from disadvantaged backgrounds whose parents did not graduate from high school and who attend poorly funded schools to do as well academically as she does. She may believe that the difference in, let's say, SAT scores between herself and a poorer student is due to effort or talent, not the structural advantages and disadvantages built into the system of social stratification.

Check Your Understanding

- What is social stratification?
- How do class- and caste-based systems of stratification differ from each other?
- What is the veil of ignorance?
- What is the veil of opulence?

Examining the Class System

Social class refers to distinctions among groups of people in terms of income, lifestyles, and values. As discussed above, we typically divide classes based on income, occupation, and education. Most scholars have settled upon five distinct social classes: the upper, upper middle, middle, lower, and lowest. We will focus on three of those classes in this chapter—the upper class, the middle class, and the working class. These constitute quintiles (one-fifths) that allow us to examine how much wealth each fifth of the population possesses and to categorize each class in terms of income, wealth, and life chances (opportunities for class advancement).

As Table 7.3 shows, the U.S. Census (2014a, 2014b) breaks down the five quintiles by household income.

In 2015, the richest 20 percent of households earned annual incomes of $117,000 or more, equal to 51.1 percent of the nation's income, while the

TABLE 7.3

Income by Quintile

	Percent of Total U.S. Income	Median Income	Income Range
Highest quintile	51.1	$202,366	More than $117,002
Fourth quintile	23.2	$92,031	$72,001 to $117,002
Third quintile	14.3	$56,832	$43,512 to $72,001
Second quintile	8.2	$32,631	$22,800 to $43,511
Lowest quintile	3.1	$12,457	Less than $22,800

Source: Proctor, Semega, and Kollar (2016).

poorest 40 percent took home 11.3 percent of the nation's income (Proctor, Semega, and Kollar 2016).

When we look at wealth across the social classes, we see another, even more extreme, picture. As this map of the United States shows, relatively few Americans have much wealth. Almost all of us survive financially through our incomes. As Marx would describe it, the overwhelming majority of the population are members of the proletariat, rather than the bourgeoisie.

This concentration of wealth at the top of the income pyramid has grown significantly since the 1970s (Saez 2013; Zucman 2016). Wealth has been concentrated in hands of the richest 1 percent, but it has been further concentrated in the top .1 percent of the population. That small sliver of the population holds as much wealth *as the bottom 90 percent* (Saez and Zucman 2014).

The Upper Class

Among the **upper class,** tools to maintain social status include residential enclaves, exclusive private schools, and clubs with invitation-only admission policies. This creates a bubble where children are not exposed to members of other social classes but instead provided a well-supervised and carefully monitored socialization experience solely among their peers. Expensive vacations, education, and leisure activities guarantee that children will be exposed only to children like themselves. These families give their children extraordinary advantages, investing in high-quality childcare, enrichment activities, private tutoring, and other supports. Together, this comprises the **social class reproduction** process, through which members of the upper class ensure that their children maintain their status. Children from lower-income groups receive far fewer supports and their families have less political power to advocate for changes to policies that would enhance their opportunities.

At the top of the class ladder are the **power elite,** members of the corporate community that dominate politics in Washington. These individuals share membership in the same closed clubs, circulate among luxury resorts, and attend the same elite schools. The power elite supports a range of institutions, like foundations and think tanks, that advance their ideas and influence policy makers and voters. They have power and influence over government decisions affecting every facet of U.S. life, including health care, education, the minimum wage, and efforts to bolster the rights of workers and to improve workplace conditions (Domhoff 2000).

This picture, taken in New York City, helps capture economic inequality in the United States today. Note that the women seem to completely ignore the homeless person right next to them as they talk to each other.

Ulrich Baumgarten via Getty Images

Bill and Melinda Gates and Charles and David Koch (pictured with the opera singer, Samuel Ramey) are members of the power elite.

fotopress/Getty Images   PATRICK MCMULLAN/Patrick McMullan via Getty Images

Social Class and Ethics

In an interesting set of experiments, researchers examined the impact of social class on decision making that involves ethics, law breaking, game playing, and other behaviors (Kraus et al. 2012). Trained observers stood at busy intersections and observed drivers' behavior and the make and model of their cars. The results revealed that individuals driving luxury vehicles were more likely to break turn-taking norms at busy intersections and less likely to yield for pedestrians in an intersection than were drivers of lower-status vehicles. Upper-income individuals displayed less ethical behavior in other test situations, as well, such as taking advantage of others in negotiations and reporting positive attitudes and orientations toward greed.

Consider This

When we explain lawbreaking, we often rely on explanations that suggest that the poorer you are, the more likely you are to commit a crime because you are desperate and lack legitimate means to get what it takes to survive and advance in society. How do we explain why those with more resources may be more likely to break the law or violate social norms?

The researchers explained the class-based differences by suggesting that higher-status individuals have fewer structural constraints on their behavior. They are accustomed to self-governance and perceive less risk in breaking rules than do lower-status individuals. They may also believe that if they break rules, they will have the resources to deal with the consequences, whether that is a fine or other penalty. Finally, they may also base their behavior on other upper-status individuals whom they perceive would act as they do. This set of orientations promotes values of greed and self-interest (Piff et al. 2012).

The Middle Class

Among American core beliefs is the strong assertion that the middle class serves as the center of the nation's economic power and prestige. Being a member of the middle class means that your family can take a vacation, you can help your children with their college expenses, and you can afford a house and a car. A strong middle class provides opportunities for class mobility and provides enough wealth to fuel consumption, savings, and investments in housing and education. For long periods in our history, most Americans (among a wide range of incomes) identified as members of the middle class. More recently, there has been concern that the middle class is growing smaller and may even disappear as the wealthy increase their fortunes and as the economic prospects of others continue to fall.

The Wealth Gap and *The One-Percent*

In this exercise, you will write a short paper responding to questions about the extreme wealth concentration in America.

In 2006, Jamie Johnson, an heir to the Johnson & Johnson fortune, produced an 80-minute documentary on the wealth gap and the ways the richest families in America get richer. As an insider, Johnson has a unique perspective on how the very richest see their place in the American social structure. While we may look at those individuals with envy and respect, we can also consider whether some of the income under their control should be distributed to others through higher taxes or other means.

The documentary, titled *The One-Percent*, can be found at www.youtube.com/watch?v=HmlX3fLQrEc.

Watch the documentary and take notes on the arguments individuals make regarding wealth and the economy. In a one- to two-page paper, respond to the following questions:

1. Should there ever be any limits on the amount of wealth that individuals can accumulate? Why?

2. What impact does a lack of limits on wealth accumulation have on lower classes? What implications does such a policy have for how well others live and survive?

3. What sacrifices do the poor, working class, and middle class make for the concentration of wealth at the top of the economic ladder?

4. If you were an elected official at the national or state level, what kind of legislation could you propose that could address the concentration of wealth? Would you do so? Why?

A family of four must earn between $48,000 and $145,000 to be considered middle class by social scientists. If we refer to Table 7.3, this puts the middle class in the third and fourth income quintiles, using median income as a measure. Given the very different lifestyles of those at the lower and upper ends of the middle-class income spectrum, some divide the middle class into the lower middle class and the upper middle class. Overall, half of American adults today live in middle-class households, down from 61 percent in 1971. Twenty-one percent reside in upper-income households, up from 14 percent, and 29 percent are in lower-income households, compared to 25 percent in 1971 (Pew Research Center 2015).

The Working Class, the Poor, and the Deep Poor

About 20 percent of households are classified as **working class,** those who work at manual, low-skilled jobs, in so-called blue-collar occupations with annual incomes between $20,000 and $38,000. The economic challenges faced by the working class mean that parents must devote long hours to work at low wages. Children in these families may join the workforce early so they can contribute to household income.

Another 20 percent of the population is **lower class** or poor, with household incomes of less than $17,000 a year. These individuals typically have only part-time employment or do not work at all. Low-wage workers make up the largest sector of employees in industries such as retail and fast food.

Poverty levels take into account the size of households and all the income that household receives (U.S. Department of Health and Human Services 2016). According to the federal government, as of 2015, individuals earning less than $11,770 a year or families of three earning less than $20,090 were living in poverty. The poverty level is used to assess need and determine eligibility for programs like TANF (Temporary Assistance to Needy Families), food stamps, and school lunch programs.

Absolute poverty is when a household or an individual fails to have the income required to meet the basic human needs of subsistence, including food, shelter, and clothing. **Relative poverty** considers how a household compares to others. You can have little money but if everyone you know has less, you may not feel the pain of being poor as much as you would if you lived among those who had much more money than you do.

Consider This

How we feel about our economic situations is affected by those around us. Why might an upper-middle-class person be more focused on how much poorer she is than her rich neighbors, rather than on how advantaged she is compared to those who have less? Would a middle-class person feel relatively wealthy or relatively poor at your school? Why?

Realities and Perceptions of Poor People

When we think about poor people, many of us divide the population into two groups: the **deserving** and the **undeserving poor.** Into the first group, we place those who are poor but who we believe are hardworking. The deserving poor are those who warrant our help because they are poor through no fault of their own. On the other hand, we characterize the underserving poor as those who are lazy and fail to try to lift themselves up by their own bootstraps. We reject support for the undeserving poor because we believe that their poverty is of their own making.

Culture of Poverty Theories and Policies toward the Poor

Oscar Lewis coined the term the **culture of poverty** in 1959 to describe the beliefs, attitudes, and values that characterize those living in poverty. Conditions of poverty and deprivation created cultural responses geared to survival in these harsh living arrangements. He suggested that this culture distinguished the poor from the more productive members of society. The poor find themselves in networks of mutual support and obligation with other poor people, which allow them to survive under severe economic constraints but also make it nearly impossible to move out of poverty. The culture of poverty thesis would suggest that the poor are to blame for their poverty.

Other theorists suggested that the poor, unlike the middle class, are focused on the present, not on the future (Moynihan 1965). The poor, becoming reliant on welfare, lose their incentive to move out of poverty. An orientation toward the present because of the need to survive day to day means that the poor don't plan for the future. Once again, this suggests that unlike other social classes, the poor reject the value of hard work as a means to get ahead. Such theories influenced the welfare reforms of the 1990s that created time limits for welfare assistance.

Due to welfare reform, fewer of America's poor can rely on welfare checks, and increasing numbers of Americans are falling into **deep poverty**, meaning they subsist on incomes of less than half the poverty level (Edelman 2012). Today, more than 10 percent of American children under the age of six live in families experiencing deep poverty (Cuddy, Venator, and Reeves 2015).

Reflecting the influence of the theories about a culture of poverty, many people still believe that generous welfare programs create dependency and are not good investments of government funds (Krogstad and Parker 2014). In a 2014 poll, 51 percent of Americans said the "government couldn't afford to do much more to help the needy." A sizable minority disagrees, however. In the same poll, 43 percent said that the government should do more to help the needy even if the government must take on debt to do so.

The Most Economically Disadvantaged

The most severely economically disadvantaged people tend to be single adults without children (Fox et al. 2015). Welfare reform in the 1990s frayed the safety net for this population. There are few benefits available to adults who don't have dependent children. In some states, these individuals may lose even their eligibility for SNAP (Supplemental Nutrition Assistance Program, previously known as food stamps) after being on the program just a few months. This population is also disadvantaged in that they are isolated from many social service programs that focus more on families with children.

Check Your Understanding

- What is social class?
- How do we distinguish the upper, middle, and lower classes from each other?
- What is the difference between absolute and relative poverty?
- How have theories on the culture of poverty influenced policies toward the poor?
- What is deep poverty?
- What demographic groups tend to be among the most economically disadvantaged today?

Mobility within and across Generations

Mobility refers to the movement between social classes in a society. Individuals may experience **upward mobility,** when they climb up the economic ladder, or **downward mobility,** when they lose class position. An individual may start out as a member of a working-class family, earn a college education, and secure a place in the middle class. We would refer to that as upward mobility. This would also be an instance of **intergenerational mobility** if she has children who have a different social class position than she had as a child. Intragenerational mobility refers to a change in social class during one's lifetime. For example, a recent college graduate may take a low-paying job in a company to get a foot in the door in the industry. As time passes, she is promoted and finds herself in an executive position after twenty years of working in this firm, moving from working class to the middle class.

Changes in the Economy

Changes in the economy can affect individuals' places in the social structure. For example, imagine you entered the workforce with a well-paying job as a machinist. If that sort of work is automated or shipped offshore, you will lose not only your job but also your social class position and way of life. **Structural mobility** occurs when changes in the economy create or destroy jobs for workers. As globalization has led to U.S. workers competing for jobs with workers in low-wage nations, unions have lost power, automation has increased, and downward mobility is increasingly a factor in the American economy. Among members of the middle class, to attain a lifestyle similar to that of their parents, children must go to school longer, continually acquire new skills, and, in many cases, take on debt to stay afloat.

Survey results reported by the Brookings Institution found that Americans are more optimistic than the residents of other nations about their prospects of doing well in the economy if they work hard. In these surveys, Americans were also less likely to believe that the income gap between the rich and the poor was too large or that the government should implement social policies to address income inequality (Isaacs 2007). Despite public opinion, some research indicates that the chance of moving up the economic ladder from one generation to the next is not as good in the United States as it is in other nations. Studies by Corak (2006) and Jantti et al.

(2006) found that there was less mobility in the United States than in Canada, Norway, Finland, and Denmark and that there was more "stickiness" among the wealthiest and poorest social classes than the middle classes. In other words, in the United States, children born to these social classes were less likely to move into other social classes than those born into other classes.

Emerging trends, like the rise of **contingent employment** in the new gig economy, may not be good news for workers. Contingent employment allows employers to hire nonpermanent workers at will as demands change. These workers, who are part-time, temporary employees without standard workweeks and no guarantee of continued employment, now make up almost 16 percent of the workforce, up from 10 percent in 2005—an increase of 9.4 million workers (Katz and Krueger 2016). Contingent workers can be found working for retail stores that have seasonal fluctuations. Temporary employment agencies also employ contingent workers in catering, light assembly, and other assignments. The drivers who work for Uber, Lyft, and Postmates are contingent workers, as well.

Contingent workers don't earn sick or vacation time. They can have unpredictable work schedules with lots of hours some weeks and no work the next. With erratic work schedules and paychecks that change from week to week, families find it hard to budget for monthly expenses and to plan for childcare and other arrangements. While some members of the gig or contingent economy are managing quite well, vast numbers of contingent workers are poorly paid and have few employee protections. The rise of these working arrangements benefits employers and contingent worker employment agencies but affords few pluses for the contingent workforce (U.S. Government Accountability Office 2015).

Check Your Understanding

- What is mobility?

- What is structural mobility and how does it affect individual mobility?

- How has the rise of the contingent economy affected the economic prospects of individual workers?

- What is the difference between intergenerational and intragenerational mobility?

Consequences of Inequality

Economic inequality relates to other forms of social inequality. For example, economic inequality influences (and is influenced by) the type of education you received and where you live. Economic inequality can even affect how long you live!

Education

If you ask most Americans about the best way to get ahead, they will say that getting a good

Consider This

Think about the high school you attended. What percentage of the students graduated? How many dropped out? Did everyone go to college? Could you observe rankings within your high school by social class? If you compare your high school to those attended by the students enrolled in this class with you, what do you find? Were there differences in teacher quality, academic quality, technology and equipment, curricular and extracurricular activities, instructional styles, or other areas?

education is the surest ticket to a good job. We know, however, that there is an achievement gap between wealthy students and those at the bottom of the economic pyramid. Test scores for wealthy students are better than those of middle-class students, which are higher than those of students from low-income families.

As you will see in Chapter 11, children who live in higher-income communities tend to go to more well-resourced schools. But not all the advantages that wealthier students have come from the schools they attend. For example, poor children who have significant gains in learning during the school year lose ground during the summer months (Alexander, Olson, and Entwistle 2007). Therefore, the achievement gap between wealthy students and poorer can also be traced to differences in learning *outside* classrooms. While wealthier parents use the summer months to involve children in enrichment activities, poorer children tend to manage their own time and activities (Alexander, Olson, and Enwistle 2007). This results in disadvantages that accumulate over the years that children spend in school, with poorer children falling farther and farther behind. Some researchers propose that poor children be enrolled in schools with longer school years and longer school days to make up for the learning advantages that wealthier students have outside of school (Alexander, Olson, and Entwistle 2007). As we read in Chapter 4 and will discuss later in Chapter 11, it is important to account for differences in cultural capital across social classes when considering educational inequality. Cultural capital includes the material aspects of consumption, the cultural knowledge that people have, and the connections and affiliations they have to social institutions. A wealthy family has the advantage of cultural capital in education: they have books in the home, they know how to navigate social systems for success, and they have access to prestigious colleges and internship opportunities for their children.

Figure 7.3 shows the relationship between parents' income and the SAT scores earned by their children (Pink 2012). As we see, the wealthier the parents, the higher the test scores of their children.

FIGURE 7.3

SAT Scores and Parental Earnings

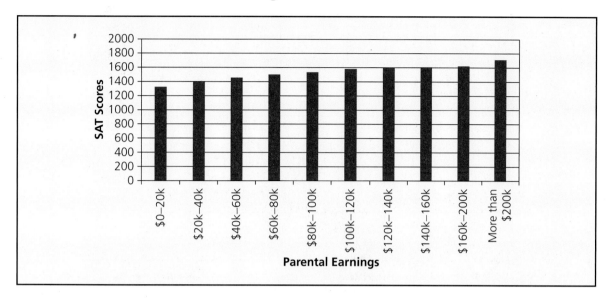

Source: Pink, Dan. "How to Predict a Student's SAT Score: Look at the Parent's Tax Return." Dan Pink. February 2012. Reprinted with permission from Dan Pink.

Class and College

There has been a strong push to get every American to go to college so they can participate in a globalized economy that demands advanced skills for good wages. As we know, getting a college degree is expensive, even at less costly schools. But *not* going to college can be even more expensive. The average lifetime earnings of an individual with a bachelor's degree is $2.8 million, nearly twice that of someone with only a high school diploma (Carnevale, Rose, and Cheah 2014).

If we look at Figure 7.4, we can see that the difference in real wages earned by men with varying levels of education over the period 1963 to 2012. A clear pattern emerges. Wages of all workers, no matter what education level they possessed, were much more similar in earlier decades. Earning at least a

Doing Sociology 7.4
Surviving in the Economy

In this activity, you will play an online game, *Spent*, that simulates living in poverty and answer questions about the experience.

Many Americans face severe hardship at the bottom of the income ladder. They encounter low-wage jobs, high rents, poor nutrition, lack of access to health care, and other challenges. Play the game *Spent* (http://play spent.org) to see how long you can survive on the proceeds of a low-wage job. How soon will your expenses exceed your income? *Spent* will ask you to make a series of decisions and report the consequences back to you.

Play this game at least three times and answer the following questions:

1. What strategies did you use to make your money last through the month?

2. How did you feel as you followed your strategy? For example, did denying a request for help from a family member feel like the right thing to do? Did going to work even though your child was sick seem like the best choice that you had?

3. What lessons did you derive from this exercise about living on the income earned from a low-wage job?

FIGURE 7.4

Changes in Real Wage Levels of Full-Time U.S. Male Workers by Education, 1963–2012

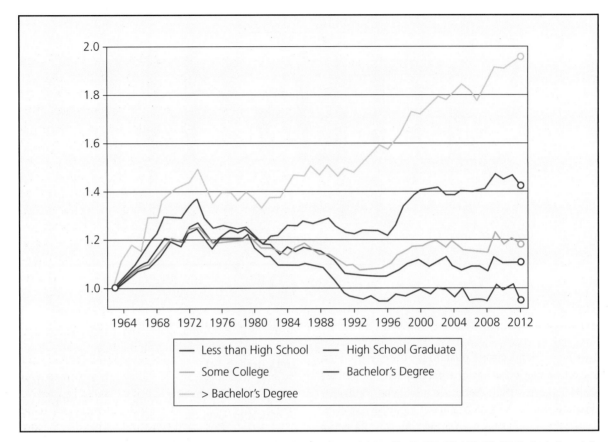

Source: David H. Autor, "Skills, education, and the rise of earnings inequality among the other 99 percent," *Science*, May 23, 2014; 344, 6186: 843–851. Reprinted with permission from AAAS.

Summer enrichment activities, like these girls are experiencing, are common among members of high-income families but relatively rare among children from families with low incomes.

bachelor's degree is without question more important than ever.

An equally important problem is that many college students fail to complete their studies. Getting into college (as high a hurdle as that seems) may be easier than persisting through to graduation. The major reasons why students fail to graduate from college include the high costs of attending college; the stresses of managing work, family obligations, and academic demands; and lack of adequate preparation for college-level academic work (Carlozo 2012). Forty-five million Americans have outstanding student loans totaling $1.3 trillion. Approximately 30 percent of students who take out a college loan fail to complete their degrees, which means that these students carry debt for attending college but do not benefit from the added earnings that come with a college degree (Steele and Williams 2016). The National Center on Educational Statistics conducted a study following high school sophomores into their late twenties. The students represented four income groups from the lowest to highest incomes. The students completed a series of tests, which measured academic preparation, to examine the relationships between income, high math achievement, and graduation. As shown in Figure 7.5, high-scoring poor students are as likely to graduate from college as high-income students with mediocre scores (Dynarski 2015).

Health

Why would health be related to social class? When we think about living a long life, we often consider what we eat, whether we get enough exercise, how much stress we endure, and whether we avoid harmful practices (like smoking and drinking too much alcohol)—and we try to make good decisions based on those factors. Sociologists who look at social class and health outcomes, however, also examine social, cultural, and environmental factors. In addition to our personal choices, social factors also affect our health. Among the factors that affect health in a population include access to health care, the stresses in jobs and living conditions, exposure to environmental toxins like lead and dirty air, public safety, and the level of services and programs in communities (Office of Disease Prevention and Health Promotion n.d.).

Life expectancy refers to the average number of years an individual is expected to live.

For the past century, we have seen steady increases in life expectancy for all social groups—men and women, Whites, Blacks, Hispanic, Asians, and Native Americans. We have also seen steady increases in life expectancy across social classes (National Academy of Sciences 2015). More recently, however, we have begun to see a growing gap in the life expectancy for the rich and the poor. As Figure 7.6 indicates, this gap in life expectancy has grown as income inequality has increased in the United States.

FIGURE 7.5

The Advantage of Wealth in College

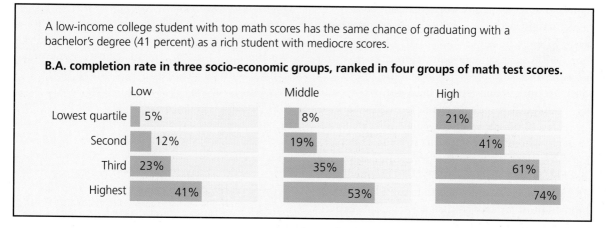

A low-income college student with top math scores has the same chance of graduating with a bachelor's degree (41 percent) as a rich student with mediocre scores.

B.A. completion rate in three socio-economic groups, ranked in four groups of math test scores.

	Low	Middle	High
Lowest quartile	5%	8%	21%
Second	12%	19%	41%
Third	23%	35%	61%
Highest	41%	53%	74%

Source: Department of Education, Education Longitudinal Study.

FIGURE 7.6

Inequality in Life Expectancy for Men

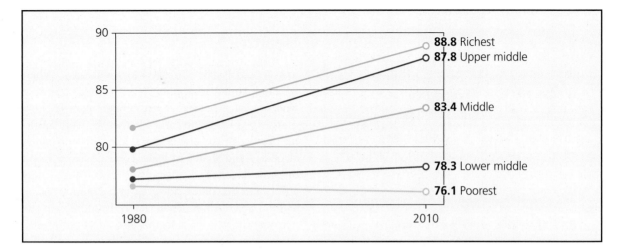

Source: National Academy of Sciences (2015).

Note: Data show life expectancy for fifty-year-olds in a given year, by quintile of income over the previous ten years.

Between 1999 and 2013, the life expectancy of middle-aged (forty-five- to fifty-four-year-old) White men in the United States declined—with a sharp increase in mortality in this group caused by suicide, drug overdoses, alcohol poisoning, and cirrhosis of the liver. Men with low educational levels experienced the greatest losses—equal to half a million deaths (Case and Deaton 2015).

The United States is also seeing a rise in deaths among all Whites between twenty-four and thirty-four years old, with the largest increase among those with the least education (Kolata and Cohen 2016). Causes for this decline in life expectancy include the availability of prescription painkillers and heroin, the impact of the Great Recession, the decline in the number of well-paid blue-collar jobs, and the overall strain of living in an increasingly unequal society where educational credentials have become more important than ever to attain decent wages (Cherlin 2016).

Sociologist Andrew Cherlin applies **reference group theory** to explain why Whites, particularly White men, without a college education are suffering increases in health problems and higher morbidity rates. To understand human behavior, we need to comprehend how people evaluate their own lives compared to others: when I evaluate how well I am doing, to whom am I comparing myself? That comparison group is a reference group. In comparing themselves with their parents, White men with low educational levels may see that they have fewer opportunities for success than their parents experienced. Many feel abandoned by a government that they perceive as working to increase opportunities

Consider This

How does this increase in death rates in the White less-educated population illustrate the connection between social factors and life expectancy? How do you think it should be addressed?

for racial minorities, including immigrants, and women (through civil rights legislation, affirmative action programs, immigration reform, etc.) but doing little to save them from the repercussions of globalization and automation (Cherlin 2016; Hochschild 2016). Marx would call this false consciousness and an inability to see the influence of the power elite over government, but the result has been despair, anger, and resentment against the prevailing status quo in government. No doubt, it also influenced the results of the presidential election of 2016, with Donald Trump, an individual with no military or governmental experience, winning the highest electoral office of the United States.

Housing and Location

It is no surprise that resentment against the political status quo has grown, considering the cost of

housing in the United States today—and that evictions are a profit-making business for some. Many poor people spend more than 50 percent of their small incomes on rent; 20 percent devote 70 percent of their incomes to housing. In 2013, because families were squeezed between high costs for housing and declining wages, one in eight could not pay their full rent and faced eviction (Desmond 2015).

Harvard sociologist Matthew Desmond spent eight years studying evictions in America and discovered that the challenge of finding and keeping a roof over their heads often leads families into poverty. As Desmond documents, falling wages and rising housing costs have put poor and working-class people in an untenable situation. Eviction can be caused by the loss of a job, a complaint from a neighbor, a complaint about the apartment itself, incarceration, or many other reasons. When families are evicted, not only do they lose a roof over their heads, but there is also loss of stability in employment, schooling, social services, and other resources. Eviction means that a difficult situation will grow worse, putting the family in crisis and landing them in deeper poverty. They may lose a security deposit attached to their old lease and incur expenses as they find temporary housing and find a new place to live. High rates of eviction in a neighborhood also mean higher rates of violent crime for the residents left behind as vacancies create more instability in the community (Desmond 2016).

It should be understood, as well, that there is considerable amount of profit to be made in the eviction business. Landlords can take tenants' security deposits, confiscate their household goods, charge excessive rents, and fail to maintain decent and safe housing for residents.

Location, Social Mobility, and Life Expectancy

Where you live also has important impacts on your life expectancy and social mobility. Poor

people live longer when they reside in cities with better social and health services and in the states that imposed higher taxes on cigarettes. For example, among New Yorkers and Detroit residents at the bottom 25 percent of the U.S. income ladder, New Yorkers have a life expectancy of 81.8 years compared to 77.7 years for those living in Detroit. When communities extended health care to the poor and when there were higher levels of government spending, life expectancy increased for the poor (Chetty et al. 2016).

Likewise, when children grow up in better neighborhoods and out of concentrated poverty, their social class outcomes are much better as adults. They earn higher incomes than those children who remained in poorer neighborhoods (Chetty and Hendren 2015). Another study tracked children who left public housing because their units were demolished and compared them to children who remained in public housing. Those who were pushed out of public housing and moved to new neighborhoods were 9 percent more likely to be employed as adults and their earnings were 16 percent higher than those who remained in public housing and surrounded by poverty. Being forced to leave public housing added approximately $45,000 to lifetime earnings for these children, even more if they moved when they were younger (Chyn 2016).

Other Outcomes of Income Inequality

It is important to remember that class is a family affair. We are born into families who occupy a social

Consider This

Does poverty lead to homelessness or does homelessness lead to poverty? How are these related to each other?

class, and we tend to marry within our social class. Sociologists call this **assortative mating** or **homogamy.** While we are increasingly marrying people outside of our religious, racial, and ethnic groups, research shows that we are less likely to marry someone outside of our class group. Greenwood and his colleagues examined the educational levels of husbands and wives who married over the period from 1960 to 2005 and found that the educational gap between them declined over this time. The connection between homogamy and income inequality is an important one. In fact, one-third of the increase in income inequality between 1960 and 2005 can be traced to the fact that more individuals are marrying within their social class (Greenwood et al. 2014).

With the growing pattern of two-earner families and increased educational attainment by women, assortative mating has become a powerful factor influencing economic inequality (Cowen 2015). When college graduates marry each other, they greatly increase their household income compared to their less educated peers who married their high school educated sweethearts (Bruze 2015). In fact, marriage is increasingly becoming a middle-class luxury. As more people wait to get married until they gain an education and a well-paying job that can support a family, the marriage rate has dropped. Working-class men and women are less likely to get married, less likely to stay married, and less likely to have children within married families. And the poor are even less likely to marry (Silva 2013).

Global and Local Inequality: The United States and Other Nations

If we look at the nations of the world, do we see a social class hierarchy among them like we observe in the United States? Looking at data compiled by the World Bank for 2015, important differences among high-income (like the United States), middle-income (like Mexico and Brazil), and low-income (like Nepal, Bangladesh, and Haiti) countries are apparent. High-income nations have average annual incomes over $40,000 per person, compared to $567 for the low-income nations (World Bank 2015). Similarly, life expectancy reaches eighty years at the top and fifty-nine at the bottom. Among 1,000 births, five babies will not survive until their first birthday in the rich countries compared to sixty-three babies in the poor nations.

A recent report by Oxfam (2016) found the world's eight richest people now hold as much wealth as half of the world and that between 2010 and 2015, a half-trillion dollars of wealth flowed to the wealthiest while the poor lost that much wealth. It appears from the report that no matter what the stage of development a nation falls, benefits from the growth of the global economy have been absorbed by the wealthy, not distributed to other social classes. For example, the CEO of India's largest tobacco company earned 439 times as much as the company's average worker. In Nigeria, Africa's largest exporter of oil, billions of dollars in profits are funneled to a small number of elites with state support. These funds could have greatly benefited the people of this developing nation (Hardoon 2017).

This growing inequality has strong effects on the lives of individuals (Wilkinson and Pickett 2009). The more inequality in a nation, the higher its rates of incarceration, homicide, mental illness, and out-of-wedlock births and the lower its degree of social trust and educational achievement. The same relationship is seen for the fifty states in the United States: the more income inequality in a state, the higher the level of social problems. So, not only is income inequality a problem for those who are at the bottom of the economic pyramid, but a high degree of income inequality also creates problems for society as a whole—including the well off!

Figures 7.7, 7.8, and 7.9 show the relationship between income inequality and social outcomes—health, incarceration, and life expectancy—across the globe and in the United States. As Figure 7.7 shows, the greater the inequality in U.S. states, the worse the health and social problems. Furthermore, the more inequality within a nation, the higher the rates of imprisonment. In Figure 7.8, the United States stands as the nation with the highest rate of imprisonment and a high degree of inequality. Figure 7.9 compares life expectancy in the world's richest countries and shows that life expectancy is positively related to the level of equality in a society.

Check Your Understanding

- What is the relationship between income and educational achievement?

- How are poverty and homelessness related?

FIGURE 7.7

Health and Social Problems Are Worse in More Unequal U.S. States

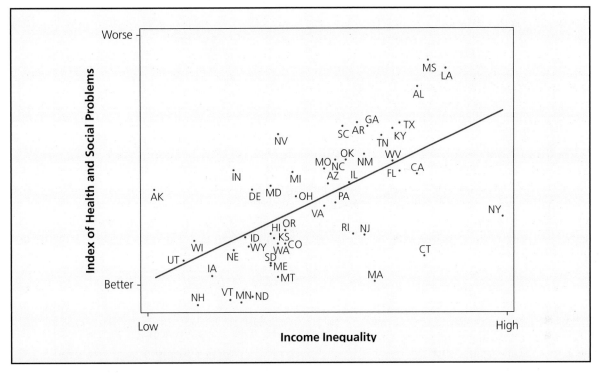

Source: *The Spirit Level: Why Greater Equality Makes Stronger Societies* by Richard Wilkinson and Kate Pickett. Copyright © 2009, 2010 by Richard Wilkinson and Kate Pickett. Reprinted with permission from Bloomsbury Press, an imprint of Bloomsbury Publishing Inc.

FIGURE 7.8

Rates of Imprisonment Are Higher in More Unequal Countries

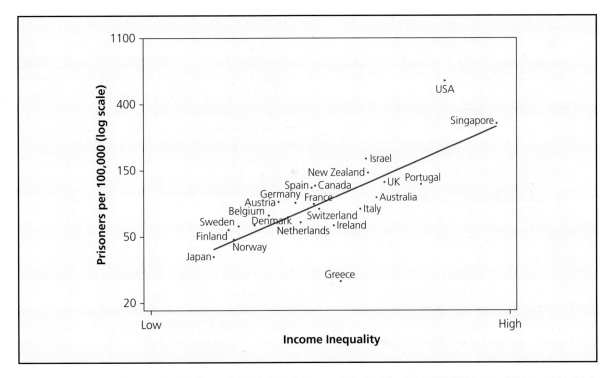

Source: *The Spirit Level: Why Greater Equality Makes Stronger Societies* by Richard Wilkinson and Kate Pickett. Copyright © 2009, 2010 by Richard Wilkinson and Kate Pickett. Reprinted with permission from Bloomsbury Press, an imprint of Bloomsbury Publishing Inc.

FIGURE 7.9

Life Expectancy Is Longer in More Equal Rich Countries

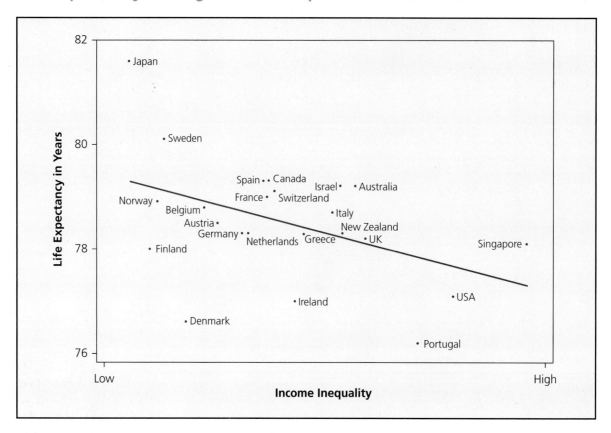

Source: *The Spirit Level: Why Greater Equality Makes Stronger Societies* by Richard Wilkinson and Kate Pickett. Copyright © 2009, 2010 by Richard Wilkinson and Kate Pickett. Reprinted with permission from Bloomsbury Press, an imprint of Bloomsbury Publishing Inc.

- What is the relationship between educational inequality and economic inequality?

- How is where you live related to your chances of success?

- How is social class related to our choice of life partner?

- How can economic inequality, globally and in the United States, affect everyone?

Addressing Inequality

Did you know that nearly three out of four poor people receiving public assistance work? Over 60 percent of those families receiving Medicaid and over a third of those receiving SNAP have jobs. One of every two fast-food workers, four in ten child-care workers, and one in four instructors serving as part-time or adjunct faculty members are eligible for and receive some public assistance (Jacobs, Perry, and MacGillvary 2015).

It is important to understand here that not only are many workers struggling to meet their living expenses but also that taxpayers are bearing the cost of their low wages. For example, in 2014, workers at Walmart received more than $6 billion in taxpayer-funded programs because of the low wages paid to the company's 2.2 million employees (Americans for Tax Fairness 2014). In other words, because Walmart workers earn so little, they qualify for tax-supported programs like Medicaid, public assistance, and food stamps. In effect, these public benefits subsidize the work that the employees do at this company. And Walmart is not alone. The comparable bill to taxpayers for the more than 2 million workers employed by the largest fast-food companies in the United States is an estimated $3.8 billion per year (National Employment Law Project 2015).

A June 18, 2017, snapshot of a slum in Kolkata, India. More than one in four people across the world live on less than $2 a day.

Debajyoti Chakraborty/NurPhoto/Getty Images

Why Don't the Oppressed Rise Up?

Over the past five years, we have seen more attention in the United States and globally to economic inequality. Bernie Sanders, a long-serving U.S. senator, garnered 43 percent of the votes in the Democratic primary with a campaign message that focused on the concentration of wealth in the upper classes (Silver 2016). A majority of Americans, however, are not now interested in establishing higher taxes on the wealthy and providing more governmental support for the needy like food stamps and welfare. Although Americans may see that wealth is concentrated at the top of the income distribution, they do not think that the government is competent enough to put polices in place to fix this problem (Kuziemko et al. 2015). As misinformed as Americans are about the disparity in wealth concentration and in the ratio between CEO pay and those of workers, the population also overestimates the extent of upward mobility in our society (Davidai and Gilovich 2015). Most Americans still believe that they, too, can become wealthy, a good example of the idea of false consciousness that we discussed earlier in this chapter.

Meanwhile, big businesses and some states have taken some steps to address the demands for higher wages for those at the lowest rungs of the economic ladder. Thirty-one states and the District of Columbia expanded Medicaid coverage under the Affordable Care Act, providing health insurance to 15 million Americans (FamiliesUSA 2017). In 2017, nineteen states raised their minimum wages, and major cities, including Los Angeles, San Francisco, and Seattle, have passed legislation for $15 minimum wages (Khalid 2016; Morath 2016).

Facing increased public pressure to raise their wages and increased competition for workers, given the dropping unemployment rate, in 2015 Walmart pledged to pay all of its workers a minimum of $9 an hour and increased that to $10 an hour in 2016 (Irwin 2015). That is well above the federal minimum wage of $7.25 but less than the $15 an hour that many advocates are proposing. Starbucks, another large employer, with nearly 200,000 workers, provides health care for its workers and offers no-cost online education for employees who work twenty hours a week (Starbucks 2015).

What Can We Do to Narrow the Wealth Gap?

When we think about the global disparities in wealth, we must come to grips with the fact that more than 2.7 billion people, or more than one in four individuals, live on less than $2 a day. How do we lift so many people out of poverty? What strategies really work? Although some approaches like micro-lending to the very poor so they can start their own businesses make sense for some, it is not feasible to turn every poor person into an entrepreneur. Major improvements that affect individuals across society—better schools, more opportunities for girls, better roads and infrastructure, improved access to basic health care—need to be carried out. Programs that successfully lift people out of poverty are typically those that focus on lifting up the community, not just individuals (Desai 2007). Many sociologists, including Brad Rose, featured in the following Sociologists in Action box, focus on just these issues.

Universal Basic Incomes

Some scholars have suggested that everyone should be provided a basic level of income, without the stigma that comes with welfare. This would provide a true safety net without all the rules and requirements now attached to welfare and public benefits. Universal basic incomes would be especially helpful for women who generally provide lots of unpaid labor associated with bearing and raising children and caring for others. Since all citizens would receive this benefit, there may be less resistance to this program

Marchers demand an increase in the minimum wage to $15 an hour in Chicago on April 14, 2016. The governor vetoed this bill. The minimum wage in Chicago is set to raise from $11 to $13 in 2019.

Scott Olson/Getty Images News/Getty Images

nations where citizens enjoy better social outcomes in health, education, and other areas (Stiglitz 2013). Reformers interested in reducing income inequality also advocate closing the many tax loopholes to which the rich, unlike most other people, have access.

than there is to welfare and similar programs, which many perceive as encouraging freeloading.

Establishing universal benefits would be expensive. They could, though, be somewhat offset by eliminating welfare and other public benefits along with the bureaucracy that manages these programs at the federal, state, and local levels. Such a system would, however, also require most Americans to change the way they view the relationships among work, income, caretaking, and the well-being of society (Shulevitz 2016).

Increasing the Minimum Wage and Worker Benefits

As discussed above, a movement to increase the minimum wage to $15 an hour has gained support recently. Although $15 an hour would help workers to move out of poverty, it is hardly a cure-all. Some economists fear raising the minimum wage so dramatically would cause job losses, as some businesses might be unable to afford more expensive labor costs. Perhaps more important, there are also other problems associated with low-wage work, like lack of health insurance or a retirement plan, limited sick and vacation leave, and lack of worker protections that unions afford. Increasing the minimum wage will also accelerate the ongoing transfer of many jobs from humans to computers.

Increasing Taxes on the Wealthy

Finally, other scholars have proposed increasing the tax rate on the wealthiest Americans so that public funds can be used to strengthen infrastructure and public education and provide more social supports. Wealthy citizens in the United States pay far less in taxes than they did during most of the twentieth century and much less than those in other developed

Consider This

Now, having read this chapter, again consider whether family income, the schools one attended, or individual motivation and determination are most important to success in school and later life. Which is least important? Why? Did your answers change from those you gave when answering this question at the beginning of the chapter? Why?

Check Your Understanding

- What percentage of Americans receiving public assistance also work?

- Why don't the oppressed rise up?

- What are some suggestions scholars and policy advocates have made to reduce inequality?

Conclusion

Although social class serves as a key determinant of life chances and identity, class doesn't explain all aspects of inequality. The life chances of racial and

Sociologists in Action

Making the World Better through Program Evaluation

Brad Rose

Sociologists conduct program evaluations to determine the merit, worth, and effects of a program or initiative. They conduct applied, "real-world" research to answer questions such as the following: Is the program or initiative carried out effectively? What is the impact of the program? Should the program be continued or expanded? Should it be duplicated?

As an applied sociologist who conducts evaluations of a wide range of programs—from those serving homeless people to those assisting college and university faculty—my sociological education has helped me design and carry out evaluation research to determine the effectiveness of programs, initiatives, and policies. During the course of my career as an applied sociologist, I have evaluated

- the effectiveness of job training programs for homeless women;

- a professional development program designed to prepare preservice and in-service K–12 teachers so that they are better prepared to meet the needs of special needs students;

- a statewide AmeriCorps program that seeks to enhance the capacity of nonprofit organizations to serve their constituencies;

- a federally funded national center's efforts to deliver technical assistance and training to state departments of education so that these departments are optimally positioned to meet the learning needs of their states' deaf, blind, and otherwise disabled students;

- a program that addresses the needs of first-generation, primarily minority, college students as they enter their freshman year of university;

- a multisite after-school program for elementary school-aged students staffed by college and university students; and

- a college's Urban Resource Institute, which mobilizes campus resources to support the urban development of one of Massachusetts's small cities.

I have also conducted an evaluation of a national foundation's multicollege/university initiative to increase the number of minority students earning a PhD and pursuing an academic career in the arts and sciences. For this project and the others, my sociological training allowed me to design an effective evaluation strategy, collect appropriate information, analyze data, and provide critical analyses that helped my clients to strengthen their programs and initiatives.

During the minority PhD initiative evaluation, I gathered information that documented the program's achievements and challenges. For example, we looked at how many students the program has successfully shepherded through the PhD process and the difficulties involved in efforts to increase that number. Based on my findings, I made suggestions that could strengthen their ability to help more minority students earn a PhD.

My sociological understanding of organizations, the impact of social structure on opportunities, economic inequality and poverty, race, and gender allows me, in all my evaluation work, to view the systemic rather than merely personal dimensions of the issues the programs and initiatives seek to address. Moreover, my sociological training gives me the tools to design effective evaluation strategies, collect appropriate information, analyze data, and provide critical analyses to help each of my clients to strengthen their programs and initiatives.

Ultimately, my sociological skills enable me to assist clients as they, in turn, attempt to address many of the social challenges—from homelessness to the underrepresentation of minorities in higher education—that confront contemporary American society.

Brad Rose is an applied sociologist and president of Brad Rose Consulting, Inc. (www.bradroseconsulting.com), a program evaluation firm based in Boston.

---

ethnic minority group members are typically worse than those of Whites in the same social class. Also, women still tend to earn less than their male colleagues, and they suffer the effects of poverty to a greater degree than males because of discrimination and gendered family responsibilities. We will see in the following chapter how gender and sexuality play out in organizing social relationships.

CHAPTER

7

 **SAGE edge**™

Want a better grade? Get the tools you need to sharpen your study skills. Access practice quizzes, eFlashcards, video and multimedia at **edge.sagepub.com/korgen**

Review

7.1 What is the difference between income and wealth?

Income refers to earnings from employment, government programs, investments, or inheritances. Money received from a paycheck, stock return, or Social Security benefits counts as income. Wealth, on the other hand, refers to assets one owns, like savings accounts, houses, cars, and investment portfolios holding stocks and bonds.

7.2 How do major sociological theories explain income inequality?

Structural functionalism posits that merit works to distribute good and services so that social stratification mirrors the contributions individuals make to society. In contrast, conflict theory contends that the powerful manage the economy to benefit themselves, exploiting workers so that they can maximize profits.

7.3 What is social stratification and how does it work in society?

Social stratification refers to the ways in which valuable goods and desired intangibles like social status and prestige are distributed in society, determined by social institutions and social attributes.

7.4 How has social mobility changed in the United States?

According to some research, the United States may not be the country where the chances of social mobility are the greatest. Structural changes have transformed the labor force, making workers more contingent, depressing wages, and narrowing the paths of mobility for more citizens.

7.5 What are the impacts of class position on education, health, and other social outcomes?

Those at the top of the social structure will enjoy better health, longer lives, better schools, higher educational achievement, safer neighborhoods, and more opportunities for mobility. Furthermore, they are able to pass along these advantages to their children.

7.6 What programs might address income inequality?

Programs for universal basic income and others that benefit a broad range of social programs would help to address income inequality. Policies and programs that enhance the wages and working conditions of low-wage workers and provide stronger support for education and opportunity for those at the bottom and middle of the income ladder are also promising approaches to reducing income inequality. In addition, raising taxes on the wealthiest Americans would reduce inequality and increase support for education, health, and other social supports.

Key Terms

- absolute poverty   133
- assortive mating   142
- caste   129
- class based   129
- contingent employment   135
- culture of poverty   134
- deep poverty   134
- deserving poor   134
- downward mobility   135
- economic inequality   121
- estates   129
- homogamy   142
- ideology   128
- income   122
- intergenerational mobility   135
- life expectancy   139
- lower class   133
- meritocracy   127
- power elite   131
- reference group theory   140
- relative poverty   133
- slavery   129
- social class   130
- social class reproduction   131
- social stratification   129
- socioeconomic status   126
- status   126
- structural mobility   135
- structured inequalities   129
- undeserving poor   134
- upper class   131
- upward mobility   135
- veil of ignorance   130
- veil of opulence   130
- wealth   122
- working class   133

How did you select the toys you played with when you were a child? Toys and childhood games are part of the gender socialization process.

Learning Questions

8.1 What are the sociological definitions of sex, gender, intersex, and transgender?

8.2 How do the four major theoretical perspectives help sociologists understand gender?

8.3 How do we learn and create our gender?

8.4 How does gender affect workforce experiences?

8.5 How do women's and men's experiences in intimate relationships differ?

Constructing Gender, Sex, and Sexuality

Maxine P. Atkinson

Defining Sex, Gender, Intersex, and Transgender

Asking someone who is old enough to be in college to define sex and gender may seem like a silly thing to do. After all, if there is anything a college student knows, it is the difference between sex and gender, right? Let's see. If someone asked you if you had ever had sex, you might answer "no" or "yes" or something like, "it depends on what you mean." But, if you were asked to designate your sex on a form, you would know what you were being asked—right? So, is sex a verb or a noun, an activity or a person? Not only is there a difference between sex and gender, the term *sex* is often used in at least two different ways.

How about gender? When we think about our gender, do we all equate our gender with our sex? Do all males see themselves as men? Do all females think of themselves as women? The terms *male* and *female* and *women* and *men* are crucial here because they designate the differences between sex and gender. **Sex** is a biological construct and is defined by our external genitalia, chromosomes, and internal reproductive organs. When we are born, someone, usually a physician or midwife, looks at our genitals and declares "it is a girl!" or "it is a boy!" They are announcing our sex, clearly declaring that we are either female or male. Most of us fit into one of these two categories, but as many as 1 of every 1,500 babies are born **intersex** (American Psychological Association n.d.), meaning they are not clearly biologically male or female. Sometimes these biological characteristics result in ambiguous genitals, but other times, intersex conditions are only evident later in life (American Psychological Association n.d.). Parents are often very uncomfortable if their child is intersex, and some use surgery to assign their child to one sex or the other. It is easier to assign an intersex person to being a female, and that is the most common practice (Fausto-Sterling 2000). Intersex is not to be confused with transgender. Transgender concerns identity and is thus a social construct. **Transgender** people see themselves as a gender other than the one assigned to them at birth. They may or may not choose to have surgery but do not typically present themselves in a way that is traditional for their assigned sex. Hair and clothing styles are used to socially construct gender and are easily changed.

Maxine P. Atkinson

I graduated from a large state university where I was happily memorizing my way through college and finding it pretty easy, especially in the STEM courses. Then, I took a sociology course at the suggestion of one of my friends. I was introduced to how poverty and privilege are reproduced and how deviance is socially created. Suddenly I understood the "way the world worked" and was no longer content to simply play the game of racking up A's because I could.

I am passionate about undergraduate education because I believe that higher education can be a mechanism for addressing issues of social justice and creating opportunities for social mobility rather than simply a mechanism for the privileged to pass on their advantage. My research focuses on methods of effective teaching and learning principles of sociology. I teach introductory classes, sociology of family and gender classes, and a graduate class titled "Teaching Sociology." I focus a lot of my time and energy working with graduate students to advance their teaching skills, believing that we can harness the power of "doing sociology" to make a difference.

In this chapter, we focus on the importance of gender, how we learn our genders, and the impact of gender on our lives. Our **gender,** unlike sex, is a social concept and must be taught to us and continually created by us through interactions with others. This process varies across time and cultures as our assumptions about men and women change, but gender and gender identity, or the way we define ourselves as women or men, exist in some form or another in every society.

Of all the demographic groups to which we belong, perhaps none is more important than our gender. Gender has a tremendous impact on who we are, how others interact with us, and the opportunities we are granted or denied. That is a strong statement to make. How do we know that gender has that great an influence on us? How is gender reflected in our everyday lives? What impact does gender have on our life chances? These are all questions we will address in this chapter.

Check Your Understanding

- How do sociologists define sex, gender, intersex, and transgender?

- Sex, gender, intersex, and transgender—which are social concepts and which are biological?

Major Perspectives Used to Understand Gender

In this section, we review four major theoretical perspectives used to explain gender: structural functionalism, conflict theories, symbolic interactionism,

and gender as a social structure. Gender is about who we are as individuals, but it is also about the expectations others have of us and the social institutions that are a part of our societies. As our society changes, so do our understandings of gender. So, for example, structural functionalism, which was dominant in the 1950s, appears out of date today.

Structural Functionalist Perspectives

Structural functionalists typically equate sex and gender and see men and women as essentially different and complementary. Men play instrumental roles in society, being leaders and breadwinners, and women play expressive roles supporting men and providing nurturance for children and the elderly. Men are seen as natural leaders in all societal institutions, including the family, politics, business, and religion. In this view, it is only "natural" that only men would be authority figures in the family, presidents, governors, chief executive officers, priests, ministers, and rabbis. Women are seen as best suited to housework, taking care of children, and, if they work outside their homes, being nurses, teachers, and secretaries. Structural functionalists assume that these complementary roles contribute to order and stability in society and ignore the unfairness and inequalities inherent in this perspective. Very few sociologists now use this explanation of gender, but it was the dominant perspective from the 1940s into the 1960s.

Conflict Perspectives

Conflict theorists, like structural functionalists, focus on macro-level social structures that are a part of every society but see these social structures

Some religions, such as Greek Orthodox, still allow only men to hold leadership positions. This custom has worked to create and reinforce the notion of male superiority and inequality between men and women.

REUTERS/Eliana Aponte

and their effect on us in very different ways than structural functionalists. Conflict theorists who study gender are referred to as feminist theorists and examine the seven institutions discussed in Chapter 2—family, religion, economy, education, government, health care, and media—and how they influence our lives through their unequal distribution of resources to each gender, the roles they assign to girls and boys and women and men, and the messages they convey.

We can see examples of the influence of institutions on gender and the inequalities created within them by looking at the family and religion. Every society has expectations for how men and women will behave as family members. In the United States, many husbands and fathers are still expected to be breadwinners and women are still expected to take responsibility for work in the home, including childcare. While men have increased their time doing housework and childcare, women still do the bulk of household work. For example, women spend about twelve hours a week doing childcare and men spend about six hours. Women do about sixteen hours per week doing housework, while men spend about ten (Bureau of Labor Statistics 2016; see Chapter 10). Fathers represent about 16 percent of all stay-at-home parents but about a third of those say that the main reason they are home is because they cannot find a job or they are physically unable to work (Livingston 2014).

Some religions allow only men to be clergy, the most powerful roles in any religion. The Roman Catholic Church is a good example of a religious institution with carefully scripted and differentiated roles for women and men. Women are not allowed to be priests, and women are certainly not considered when it is time to choose a pope! Likewise, Orthodox Jewish synagogues have only male rabbis, and some evangelical Protestant religions also prevent women from attaining leadership positions. As noted in Chapter 12, most religious leaders throughout history have been men. Conflict theorists who study inequality between men and women focus on how male dominance affects the unequal allocation of resources to women and men.

Symbolic Interactionist Perspectives

Socialization is a process emphasized by symbolic interactionists who focus on the gender lessons we learn as children, that is, how we define and present ourselves as boys and girls and, later in life, as men and women. Sociologists who study socialization see gender as socially created rather than biologically based but assume that gender is difficult to modify once we have learned it. This chapter presents several examples of gender socialization.

Symbolic interactionists who place emphasis on the ways that we actively create our genders are referred to as social constructionists. These theorists argue that we create or "do" gender based on what we think is appropriate for our "chosen" gender in a given context (West and Zimmerman 1987). For example, those of us who identify as being women create and re-create ourselves as women every day by the clothes we wear, our hairstyles, and, for many, makeup. Those who identify as men, likewise, create their gender identity by choice of clothing, hairstyle, and, usually, lack of makeup. We also create our gender by the way we talk, walk, carry our bodies, and use space.

These symbolic interactionists assume that gender is social, fluid, and, to some extent, chosen by individuals—but that choice is constrained by cultural norms. It is very hard not to follow the gender norms of our society because the penalties can be harsh if we violate our culture's rules about the definitions of masculinity and femininity. "Sissy" boys pay a high price, and girls who refuse to be soft and sweet are also penalized. Bullying often keeps children in their gendered place, and adults can be just as hard on other adults who violate gender norms. "Sissy" men

Why are female breasts obscene and male breasts are not? Are there other body parts that are seen differently if they belong to men and women?

Scott Metzger/Cartoonstock www.CartoonStock.com

Consider This

How would you explain this cartoon? Explain your reasoning.

are seen as weak and as cowards, and they are often thought to be gay. Strong women are often referred to as "bitches."

Despite the costs of not following traditional gender norms, we can move toward gender equality by "undoing gender" (Deutsch 2007). That is, we can create social structures and practice interactional patterns that emphasize everyone's humanity. For example, we can create social policies that require employers to provide family leave for both men and women so that fathers and mothers can choose to share childrearing. The social policies are examples of social structure, and the choice fathers and mothers make to actually share childrearing is an example of social interaction.

A More Inclusive Perspective: Gender as Social Structure

A recently developed perspective provides us with an inclusive and overall view of how gender operates in our lives. Barbara Risman (2004) argues that gender should be studied as a social structure itself, just as we would study race or social class. She (Risman and Davis 2012) explains that, instead of choosing one perspective on gender over another, we should make use of all of them as we seek to understand gendered behavior. Her **gender as social structure** perspective emphasizes that gender incorporates socialization, social interactions, and organizational structures and that these are all dimensions of every society's gender structure. Gender is not only taught to us when we are children but also re-created as we interact with others over our lifetimes—resulting in structural (institutionalized) disadvantages for women.

This chapter provides many examples of how we learn our gender from our parents, the books we read, and the films we see. We also create our genders as we interact with our family members, teachers, and, very importantly, with our peers. Institutions are structured in ways that limit women's opportunities and advantage men. Occupations, schools, and even intimate relationships are settings that create unequal access to valued resources. In short, Risman reminds us that gender is not just about who we are as individuals but also about the societies in which we live. This chapter helps us understand gender as a social force created and reinforced through our individual interactions and through social organizations and institutions.

Check Your Understanding

- How does structural functionalism view gender?

- How does conflict theory view gender?

- What does social constructionism emphasize?

- How does the idea of gender as a social structure use the other theoretical perspectives to understand gender?

Gender Lessons Learned in Childhood

In this activity, you will think about how you were taught to express your gender as a child.

Socialization is an important part of childhood. Our parents, peers, and teachers, not to mention the media we consume, communicate to us in countless ways how to behave properly as a boy or a girl.

If you were raised as a girl, make a list of the kind of lessons you have been taught about how a polite or good young woman should act. If you were raised as a boy, make a list of the kind of lessons you have been taught about how a polite or good young man should behave. Think back to your childhood/youth and answer the following questions with as many examples as you can:

1. "When I was a child, I was taught that a polite young man or young woman should _____." If you were raised as a boy, you might report examples like "never hit a girl." If you were raised as a girl, you might remember examples like "be sure to cross your legs at the ankle."

2. "When I was a child, I wanted to be like _____ because _____." You might relate that you wanted to be like Batman or Miss America.

3. What can you do to change this socialization process to create more equality between men and women?

Learning and Creating Gender

As you learned in Chapter 5, socialization is the process by which we learn to follow the norms and expectations of our society. **Gender socialization** is the process by which we learn to be a man or a woman in our particular place and time.

Starting Gender Socialization at Birth

We can see the importance that society places on gender in a number of different ways. For example, from the moment we are born, others begin to construct our gender for us and teach us how to behave appropriately. Given ultrasound technology, couples must decide if they want to know the sex of their unborn child and if they will share that information with others before the birth. No doubt, they will be asked, again and again, if they know the sex of their child. Once they learn the sex, some expectant parents throw a "gender reveal" party to announce it and the assumed gender of their child. Why do you think people are so eager to know the sex of the baby? How are their images of and expectations for the child influenced by the words "It's a boy!" or "It's a girl!"? Why?

Imagine how you might feel if a person mistook your baby boy for a girl or vice versa. Does it matter? Have you seen people respond when someone assumes their child is a boy when she is a girl or vice versa? Most new parents make the sex of their baby very clear through how they dress their baby. We put bows on little girls' heads even if they do not yet have hair—just to make sure it is clear to everyone that she is a girl. Or have you ever encountered a baby dressed neutrally, perhaps in a simple green outfit? What would you assume? How would you speak about the child to the parents?

Anyone who has ever tried to buy gender-neutral clothing will tell you how difficult it is. Boys' clothing almost always comes in primary or vibrant colors and may have images of objects associated with masculinity such as trucks or some masculine but cute male character like Mickey Mouse—never Minnie Mouse! Girls' clothing is usually pastel and more likely to have images of Bambi or dancers or some other soft and sweet image. Baby boys' and girls' booties are likely to have a bow for girls and a teddy bear for boys.

Recall that in Chapter 5, you read that parents not only dress their children differently, based on their sex, but also treat them differently. Parents perceive much greater differences between male and female babies than actually exist and help create the differences that we see later in childhood and on into

adulthood. Both social scientists and neuroscientists document the differences in the ways we perceive and treat our boy and girl babies and the effects of such treatments. For example, one study looked at the ability of girl and boy babies to crawl on a sloped, carpeted surface. Both sets of babies were equally good at crawling and equally willing to attempt to crawl on sloped surfaces. However, parents of girl babies assumed that the girls were not as physically capable as the parents of boy babies assumed their male babies were. Even at this young age, girls were overprotected and discouraged from challenging themselves physically (Eliot 2009).

Consider This

Can you remember a time when you witnessed a male child or a teenager being ridiculed for "acting like a girl"? What had he done to prompt this ridicule? What were the consequences of this ridicule—how did it make the boy react? In your experience, are girls as likely to be ridiculed for "acting like a boy"? Why?

Gender Socialization through Children's Media

Our gender socialization does not end in infancy. We continue to get feedback throughout childhood (and beyond!) from our environment that defines gender expectations for us. Think about the gender ideas the media teach us on a daily basis. Advertisements, television and radio news, talk shows, magazines, and movies all instruct us on what a woman and a man should be and the consequences of not living up to these ideals (Gill 2007).

Children's books communicate to girls and boys how they should behave and what they can expect to become. For example, in Hans Christian Anderson's (1844) classic story *The Ugly Duckling,* the only female character is the mother duck, who sits on the eggs until they hatch. The ugly duckling is a male who overcomes obstacles and ultimately turns into a swan or, in other words, an accomplished adult. *Where the Wild Things Are* (Sendak 1963), another children's classic, is a great example of what men and women are expected to do and be. Max is the main character and he gets angry, has a temper tantrum, and goes on an adventure. The female character is again a mother, a nurturing woman who brings Max his supper, even though he's been naughty. What lessons do these books teach?

The majority of characters in children's books are males, even among those awarded the prestigious Caldecott Medal for best picture book. Girls and women simply are less likely to exist than boys and men; they are invisible. Even the animal characters in children's books are much more likely to be male than female. *The Very Hungry Caterpillar* is a male, all the characters in *Winnie the Pooh* are male except for Kanga, and in *Good Night Moon,* the bunny who needs to be calmed before bed is a male and the female character is a serene maternal figure. This gives children the message that men are more important than women (DeLoache, Cassidy, and Carpenter 1987; McCabe et al. 2011).

Children's fairytales also send messages about appropriate ways males and females should behave and be judged. Central female characters in children's fairytales tend to be beautiful and rewarded for being beautiful; less worthy female characters tend to bear descriptions of "ugly" (e.g., the stepsisters in *Cinderella,* the Red Queen in *Alice in Wonderland*). Girls learn that beauty is necessary and highly valued. Should it surprise us that women spend so much money on cosmetics? While male characters are sometimes described as handsome, their physical appearance is not as important, nor is it as commonly mentioned as it is for female characters (Baker-Sperry and Grauerholz 2003). Notice that we even use different words for attractiveness for girls and women than for boys and men. Women are beautiful or lovely; men are handsome.

Children's films are also gendered. Only about 33 percent of speaking characters and about 20 percent of narrators in G-rated films are female. The female characters that do appear are very attractive or sexy and often passive while the male characters tend to be athletic and brave. The popularity of Disney films, especially the Disney Princess line (e.g., Snow White, Cinderella, The Little Mermaid, etc.), have made children's films powerful instructors of what it means to be a woman or a man for young children.

Learning Gender in School

Part of the hidden curriculum or the latent functions (see Chapter 2) of our schools are the gender lessons we pass along to our children. The hidden curriculum consists of the attitudes, behaviors, and values the educational system transmits outside the formal curriculum (see Chapter 11). In elementary school, when girls and boys are asked to line up separately or encouraged to compete against one another in classroom contests, the lesson is clear. Boys and girls are different. Boys are often taught to be "gentlemen" and girls are taught to be "ladies." Boys and girls may also be encouraged to engage in different activities during outside play. On some older school buildings, you may even see signs indicating what were once separate school entrances for boys and girls!

In schools, children learn that women nurture and that men are in charge. Most kindergarten and elementary school teachers are women. If there are men present in elementary schools, they tend to be in either leadership positions (e.g., the principal) or traditionally masculine occupations (e.g., physical education teacher or custodian) (Bureau of Labor Statistics 2015). Women comprise 64 percent of primary school principals but only 42 percent of principals in public middle schools and only 30 percent in public high schools (http://dpeaflcio.org/wp-content/uploads/School-Administrators-Fact-Sheet-2016.pdf, accessed June 12, 2017).

This pattern continues throughout most of our experiences with formal education. The higher up the prestige ladder in teaching, the more likely the position will be filled by a man; the majority of college professors are men.

Peers, Gender Socialization, and Masculinities

Gender socialization continues during high school. Our peers are powerful agents of socialization, and we spend many hours a day with them from pre-school through high school. The consequences of not sticking to our **gender scripts**, or expectations for behavior appropriate for our assigned genders, can be harsh. This is especially the case for boys. C. J. Pascoe's (2007) powerful book, *Dude, You're a Fag: Masculinity and Sexuality in High School,* documents ways in which adolescents enforce gender and sexuality stereotyping. **Sexuality** refers to our emotional and physical attraction to a particular sex. The categories for sexualities include heterosexual/straight (attracted to a different sex), homosexual/gay/lesbian (attracted to members of our own sex), bisexual (attracted to both sexes), and asexual (not attracted to either sex).

Pascoe found that high school boys must adhere to a strict gender script and reject any stereotypical feminine behavior. Boys who dare to violate their gender scripts can pay a high social price. They must be stoic at all costs, hide any emotion other than anger, and be very careful to never show any physical affection for other men. If they violate this script, they will likely be tarred with the label of a "fag." While the term *fag* has been used to ridicule gay boys and men, Pascoe finds that it embodies far more than homosexuality and reaches to the core of what being a "man" is. Her research helps reveal the relationship between homophobia and the construction of masculinity. To be a "real man," you must be heterosexual. Homophobia is a key element of socially constructing masculinity (Connell 1995; Kimmell 1994).

Fathers in particular tend to be concerned with the social construction of masculinity and the relationship between masculinity and heterosexuality for their sons, even for their very young sons. One father is quoted by Pascoe as saying, "I don't want him to be a little 'quiffy' thing, you know. . . . It's probably my own selfish feeling of like 'no way, no way my kids, my boys, are going to be like that'" (Kane 2006: 166). Fathers of adolescent sons see interest in girls as signs that their son is reaching adulthood, and some are adamant about their sons' heterosexuality. In response to a question asking if he had talked with his sons about sexuality, one father replied, "Oh yeah. Definitely. Yeah, we want them to be as heterosexual as possible" (Solebello and Elliott 2011:301). Parents tend not to be as concerned about their daughters' sexuality.

Creating Gender by Designing Candles

*I*n this exercise, you will suggest designs for candles especially for men. Answering the accompanying questions will help you practice identifying the social construction of gender.

In 2012, the Yankee Candle Company introduced a special series of "Man Candles," that is, candles marketed to men. The candles were scented with fragrances like "Riding Mower," "First Down," "On Tap," and "Man Town."

1. In pairs, using a full sheet of paper, draw two candles that represent different images for gender, including shape, color, and size. Suggest an appropriate fragrance for each candle.

2. Write a paragraph explaining how and why your candles represent gender.

3. How is this exercise similar to or different from how people create their gender?

4. Imagine that you owned Yankee Candle and wanted to help people understand that strictly defining gender could be potentially harmful. What company policies would you create for the artists who work for your company?

Dude, You're a Fag takes intersectionality into account. That is, it considers variations due to race, class, gender, and sexualities and does not take for granted that everyone's experiences are the same. Race influences perceptions of appropriate behavior for high school boys. Pascoe reports that the White high school males she observed were not allowed to touch each other except in jokingly violent ways and faced negative sanctions if they behaved in "feminine" ways by dressing or dancing too well. Black males, on the other hand, were rewarded for dressing and dancing well and were perceived as more masculine for doing so. Meanwhile, the gender scripts for the female high school students Pascoe observed were not as strict. For example, being athletic, a traditionally male trait, could raise their status among their peers.

The Media and Gender, Sex, and Sexuality

As children grow older, media become an even more important part of their lives. Keeping up with the latest trends in music, apps, movies, and so on helps teens fit in with their classmates and gives them a sense of belonging with their peer group. It also teaches them how to create gender and sexual identities.

Music

Music plays a big role in the life of teens and young adults and provides potent gender lessons. Male performers display their masculinity by playing instruments in an aggressive manner, engage in displays of force, and sing about sexual conquests real or imagined (e.g., Kanye West's lyrics about Taylor Swift, which she publicly declared to be misogynistic: "I feel like me and Taylor might still have sex/I made that bitch famous" [Kreps 2016, para. 1]). Female performers are more likely to touch their hair and delicately touch their bodies. They give the audience sultry looks and dance suggestively (Wallis 2011). These messages do not go unnoticed. Exposed, often daily, to this form of media, men can't help but notice that they are expected to be aggressive and assertive while women absorb the message that they should act out their gender through delicacy and sexual suggestion.

News and Advertisements

Music is only one form of the media that teaches gender lessons. Indeed, it would be difficult to find any media source that does not teach gender. For example, men are much more likely to be newscasters than women, and news stories are much more likely to feature men than women. If you

Beyoncé provides lessons on how to be sexually alluring in this perfume ad for "Heat."

Jemal Countess/Getty Images Entertainment/Getty Images

turn on a news show on the major networks, (ABC, NBC, and CBS), you are three times as likely to see a man than a woman reporting the news (Women's Media Center 2017). The message is clear. Men are knowledgeable leaders to whom we should listen (Gill 2007). When the news takes a break, we see advertisements. While there are exceptions, men are usually portrayed in ads as independent, in-charge, aggressive beings. Women are presented as very concerned about getting clothes clean and taking care of others. They are thin and beautiful.

Advertisers are well known for selling products by presenting idealized images of women that are impossible for most to obtain. The implicit—and sometime explicit—message is that if you use a particular product you, too, will look like the gorgeous woman depicted in the ads (Gill 2007; Wood 1994). Perfume ads give us good examples. Beyoncé stars in a sultry ad for the perfume "Heat" wearing a very low-cut red dress suggesting that if you use this perfume, you too will generate sexual "heat." The sexual imagery in these ads teaches sex roles for women and men, as well as portrays sexual behavior and sexuality as crucial aspects of life that men and women must master to advance in society.

Challenging Stereotypes

Advertisers, however, may also challenge existing gender- and sexuality-related stereotypes. The American Association of Women notes that women now make up almost 45 percent of football fans and that advertisers seem to be more aware that women have significant purchasing power. For example, at the 2015 Super Bowl, Always launched its "Like a Girl" ad campaign, which challenged the message that running, throwing, and fighting like a girl should be an insult and featured girls and women of many different races. During the 2016 Super Bowl, Mini Cooper ran an ad in which Serena Williams and Abby Wambach, among others, described the stereotypical view of the car and exhorted viewers to "defy labels" (AAUW 2016).

Doing Sociology 8.3
Influential Characters in the Media

In this exercise, you will discuss characters in the media and how they help teach gender expectations.
   Your teacher will assign you to a group.

1. As a group, spend three minutes coming up with a list of the most significant/important characters you

can think of in film or television. When you suggest a character to your group, be sure to explain why you think this character is important—and make sure you all agree.

2. What do we learn about expectations for women and men based on the characters you chose?

Changing Attitudes toward Same-Sex Marriage

In this exercise, you will write a brief paper analyzing changing views, by age and over time, of same-sex marriage.

These bar graphs illustrate opinions about the acceptability of same-sex marriage among a representative sample of U.S. adults surveyed in 2003 and another sample surveyed in 2013. Assume that the survey was correctly administered in both years and that any differences in the samples do not account for differences in the data.

Okay for Gays to Marry, 2003

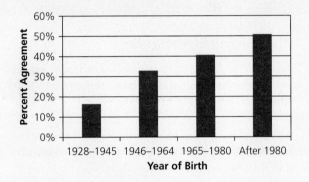

Source: Pew Research Center (2013).

Okay for Gays to Marry, 2013

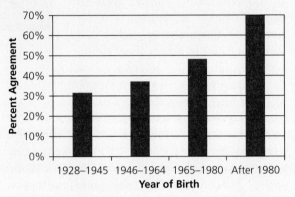

Write a short paper of 250 to 500 words responding to the following prompts:

1. Summarize the information presented in these two bar graphs.

2. Some make the argument that older U.S. adults will never approve of marriage between same-sex partners. To what extent do these data support that argument? Explain.

3. Recall that the *Obergefell v. Hodges* Supreme Court decision in 2015 made same-sex marriage legal in the United States, and thirty-seven states had already legalized same-sex marriage by then. Would you have predicted that outcome based on the data presented above? Explain.

We have experienced some progress toward gender equality, and the Super Bowl ads provide good examples. The more we see women portrayed as powerful, the more likely we are to encourage them to be so. But, notice that the Super Bowl ads have not focused on men being nurturing or exhibiting other characteristics we are taught that women should have.

The Media, Sexuality, and Backlash

Other media forms have influenced attitudes toward members of the lesbian, gay, bisexual, and transgender (LGBT) community. Television shows like *Glee, Modern Family, Gravity Falls, Orange Is the New Black,* and *Transparent* have helped shape many people's feelings toward LGBT people. In the 2016–2017 season, 4.8 percent of regular characters on television shows were identified as gay, lesbian, transgender, and queer—a record high (GLAAD 2016). Laverne Cox, a transgender woman who stars in *Orange Is the New Black,* is a civil rights advocate for transgender people and a leader in the transgender movement. She has told of being bullied in school, including being beaten up with drumsticks by members of the band (Steinmetz 2014). Shows that feature gay, bisexual, and transgender characters in a positive light help build empathy for transgender people. The media coverage of Caitlyn Jenner's (formerly Bruce Jenner, the 1976 Olympic Decathlon winner) gender identify transformation may also have affected people's level of exposure to and thoughts about transgender people.

The percentage of people in the United States characterizing themselves as LGBT increased from 3.5 percent in 2012 to 4.1 percent in 2016, with more than 10 million people now claiming that label (Gates 2017). Younger people (those born between 1980 and 1998) are about twice as likely to identify as LGBT as those from their parents' and grandparents' generations. As the numbers of people who identify as LGBT have increased, attitudes regarding gay rights, including around same-sex marriage, have changed (Bridges 2017).

On the other hand, we have also seen significant backlash and increased hate crimes committed against LGBT people. In 2014, LGBT adults were more likely to be the targets of hate crimes than any other group, including Jews, Muslims, African Americans, Asians, and Hispanics (Park and Mykhyalyshyn 2016), despite the fact that the number of hate crimes decreased overall since 2005. The legal status of LGBT people is also an indicator of the extent to which they are accepted; it remains legal to discriminate against LGBT people in many states.

In over half of the states in the United States, an employer can fire workers because of their sexual or gender identity. Even going to the bathroom can be an ordeal for some LGBT people. North Carolina has become famous for its so-called bathroom law, which required everyone to use bathrooms consistent with the sex on their birth certificate even if they were transgender. In March 2017, the bill was

Laverne Cox is a role model for transgender people and has helped make *Orange Is the New Black* highly successful.

Jason LeVeris/FilmMagic/Getty Images

repealed, but the bill that took its place did not include protections for LGBT people (Segal 2017). The United States is not the only place where discrimination is legal. In eight countries, having a same-sex relationship is punishable *by death* (Associated Press and Bertrand 2015; Cameron and Berkowitz 2016). Figure 8.2 reveals the status of rights for gay people around the world.

FIGURE 8.1

Hate Crimes per One Million Adults

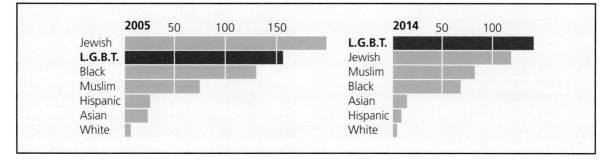

FIGURE 8.2

Lesbian and Gay Rights around the World, 2017

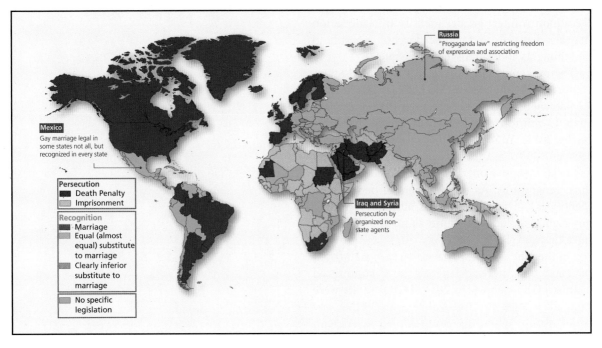

Source: International Lesbian, Gay, Bisexual, Trans and Intersex Association, May 2017, http://ilga.org/downloads/2017/ILGA_WorldMap_ENGLISH_Overview_2017.pdf.

Check Your Understanding

- How do we tend to treat girl and boy babies differently?

- Where do we get our ideas about how we should behave as boys and girls?

- What are some of the ways we learn gender at school and from our peers?

- What do the media teach us about gender? How have the media influenced attitudes toward LGBT people?

Gender, Sexuality, and Work

As Figure 8.3 indicates, the majority of women now work outside the home. Approximately 57 percent of women and 69 percent of men hold jobs in the paid labor force. While they comprise almost half of all workers, women still face many inequalities based on their gender.

Gender Segregation in the Labor Force

The U.S. labor force continues to be segregated by gender. **Gender segregation** is the extent to which women and men are separated into different jobs. More than 40 percent of employees still work in occupations where 75 percent of employees are members of their own sex. For example, 95.6 percent of all secretaries are women and 97.6 percent of all construction laborers are men. Other jobs are also highly gender segregated. Ninety-six percent of truck drivers are men and 78 percent of chief executives are men, whereas 90 percent of registered nurses and 88 percent of all bookkeepers and accountants are women. The only occupation among the nation's largest twenty-five occupations that comes close to gender parity is financial managers. Men comprise 47 percent of these managers and women make up 53 percent (Cohen 2013). To reach occupational integration, 40 percent of all men and women would have to change jobs (Cha 2013).

FIGURE 8.3

Labor Force Participation by Gender, 1972–2016

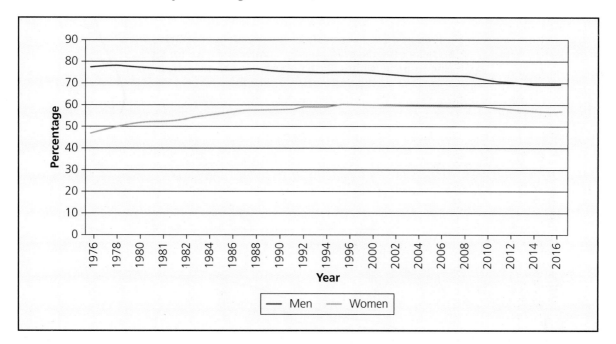

Source: Bureau of Labor Statistics (2017).

Male-dominated professions tend to pay better than female-dominated professions. During the 1970s and 1980s, occupations became less segregated, but there has been little change since 1996 (Hegewisch et al. 2010).

Consider This

Would you prefer to work in an occupation segregated by gender? If so, would you want to work in an occupation with more people of your own gender or one dominated by another gender? Explain the reason for your choice.

Do differences in education or training explain why men and women are segregated in different professions? Figure 8.4 shows how many people had, by the age of twenty-eight, attained a bachelor's degree, by birth cohort, sex, and race. Notice that White women are most likely to have completed at least an undergraduate degree and that has been

the case since the birth cohorts of the mid-1960s. Figure 8.5 reveals that, more recently, women have also surpassed men in earning PhDs and professional degrees.

What type of degrees do males and females earn? For example, how many women major in science, technology, engineering, or math (STEM) and subsequently pursue careers that require this background—and tend to pay more than other professions? As seen in Figure 8.6, the percentage of female biological scientists and chemists and material scientists has increased recently. Women now make up 50 percent of biological scientists and almost 40 percent of chemists and material scientists. On the other hand, the percentage of women in computer and mathematical occupations has decreased since 1990, from 35 percent to just 26 percent from 1990 to 2013. Meanwhile, the sex ratio of engineers has remained virtually the same, rising just 3 points, from 9 percent to 12 percent, between 1990 and 2013.

Gender socialization leads men into and women away from STEM fields. Women face stereotypes, a form of gender bias, that they are not as competent as men in these areas. While many sociological studies spell out this bias in nuanced ways (England 2010), a study of faculty who work in scientific fields and reported in the *Proceedings from the National Academy of Sciences* (Moss-Racusina et al. 2012) is

FIGURE 8.4

Educational Attainment

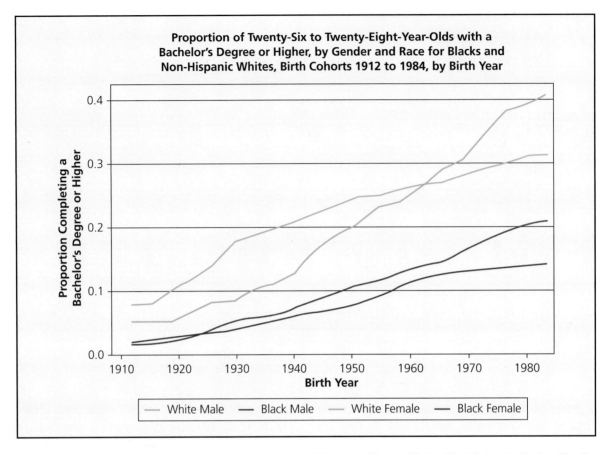

Proportion of Twenty-Six to Twenty-Eight-Year-Olds with a Bachelor's Degree or Higher, by Gender and Race for Blacks and Non-Hispanic Whites, Birth Cohorts 1912 to 1984, by Birth Year

— White Male   — Black Male   — White Female   — Black Female

Source: "Gender Disparities in Educational Attainment in the New Century: Trends, Causes, and Consequences," Thomas A. DiPrete and Claudia Buchmann in *Diversity and Disparities*, John R. Logan, editor, Russell Sage Foundation, 2014. Reprinted with permission.

particularly telling. Professors at six major research universities were asked to evaluate applications for the position of laboratory manager. The applications were created by the researchers, who described identical skills and research backgrounds on every application. They then split the applications into two groups—one with the applicant's name listed as John and the other listed as Jennifer. When the professors were asked to evaluate the applications, John was rated more highly than Jennifer. When asked to name a starting salary appropriate for the applicant, the professors were willing to offer John an average of $30,328.00 but were only willing to offer Jennifer $26,508.00. The bias against the female applicant was obvious and apparent among both women and men professors.

Ironically, the researchers' rationale for doing the study arose from scientists' claim that they are not biased because they have been trained to be objective and analytical in their work. But the researchers found that even trained scientists have gender bias!

Scientists, like all people, are raised in societies with gender roles that work to confine men and women to certain behaviors and professions and result in gender inequality.

Consider This

Does it surprise you that women's educational achievement is now higher than men's? Why do you think this has not resulted in women and men being more equally distributed in various occupations?

Gender segregation prevents some people from doing work that they would be good at and that they

FIGURE 8.5

Doctoral and Professional Degrees by Gender

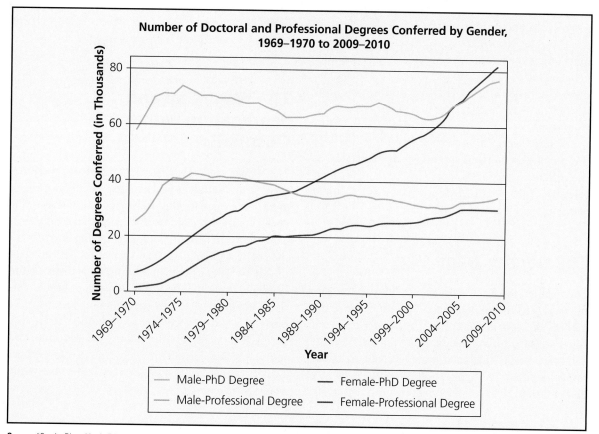

Number of Doctoral and Professional Degrees Conferred by Gender, 1969–1970 to 2009–2010

Source: "Gender Disparities in Educational Attainment in the New Century: Trends, Causes, and Consequences," Thomas A. DiPrete and Claudia Buchmann in *Diversity and Disparities*, John R. Logan, editor, Russell Sage Foundation, 2014. Reprinted with permission.

FIGURE 8.6

Women in Selected STEM Occupations, 1990–2013

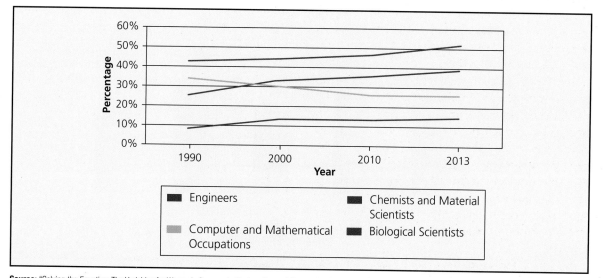

Source: "Solving the Equation: The Variables for Women's Success in Engineering and Computing." Reprinted with permission from The American Association of University Women.

Note: Postsecondary teachers are not included. For biological scientists in the 1980 and 1990 Censuses, data include life scientists as well as biological scientists. For chemical and material scientists in the 1960 and 1970 Censuses, the category was titled "chemists"; in the 1980 and 1990 Censuses, the category was titled "chemists except biochemists." For computer and mathematical occupations in the 1960 Census, no category for computer scientists was included; in the 1970 Census, the category was titled "mathematicians and computer specialists"; and in the 1980, 1990, and 2000 Censuses, the category was titled "mathematical and computer scientists."

would enjoy. That hurts individuals, but there is also a cost to society as a whole. When we keep talented people out of particular types of jobs, we all lose. We are all more productive and creative if we enjoy the work we do, and productivity is diminished if this is not the case. In order for our economy to be the most efficient and effective, we need the best match between talent, skills, and the work that needs to be done (Davos-Klosters 2014). By limiting the jobs women have, we restrict over half of our population from some of the most important work in our country. Gender segregation in the labor force is one of the main reasons for the gender wage gap, that is, the difference between wages of men and women (Hegewisch et al. 2010). Gender segregation limits women's wage-earning ability.

The Gender Wage Gap

Like gender segregation in the workforce, the **gender wage gap** has not decreased very much since the 1990s. As seen in Figure 8.7, women who work full-time earn on average between 80 and 83 cents for every dollar that men earn (Bureau of Labor Statistics 2016). The gender wage gap varies by race and ethnicity, with Asian women earning 78 percent of what Asian men make and White women earning 82 percent of the wages of White men. The wage gap between Black women and Black men and Hispanic women and Hispanic men is somewhat smaller (with the women earning, respectively, 90 percent and 89 percent of the men's wages).

The Wage Gap and Segregation within Occupations

The wage gap also results from occupational segregation within as well as across occupations. The gender wage gap for physicians, for example, is influenced by the specialty women and men choose. In general, women are in the lowest paying and men in the highest paying medical specialties. In the class of 2013–2014, women made up 58 percent of the residents in family medicine, 75 percent of the residents in pediatrics, and 85 percent of the residents in obstetrics and gynecology. Men dominated in surgery (59 percent), anesthesiology (63 percent), and radiology (73 percent). Family practice physicians earned on average just under $200,000 a year while many surgeons earned about $500,000 per year

FIGURE 8.7

Median Weekly Earning, by Gender and Race/Ethnicity

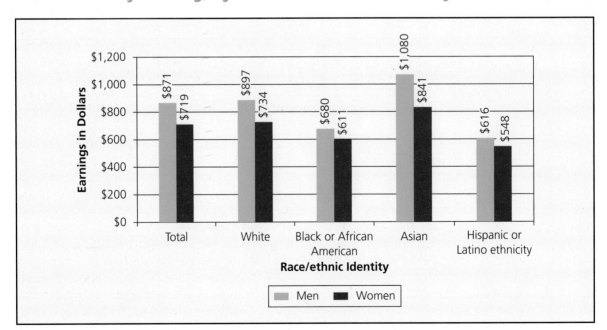

Source: Bureau of Labor Statistics (2016).

Note: People of Hispanic or Latino ethnicity may be of any race. Estimates for the race groups shown (White, Black or African American, and Asian) include Hispanics.

(Dill 2015). Over their careers, the average male physician makes $794,560 more than the typical female physician (Vassar 2015).

The specialization choices that male and female physicians make relate directly to male and female gender roles in society—and work to support them. Women are more likely to specialize in areas that allow them flexible hours and a family life, while men are more likely to have wives (with flexible hours) who can take care of them and their families (see Chapter 10).

The availability of mentors and the gender climate of specialty areas also affect the wage gap. Women have become doctors and surgeons more recently than men, so there are fewer senior women mentors. Finding mentors, therefore, may be more difficult for women, and male physicians may be less accepting of female mentees. Dr. Yoshimi Anzai, vice president of the American Association for Women Radiologists says, "I have had to work harder than my male colleagues to be recognized as a competent radiologist and to move into leadership. I hope that is changing" (Darves 2012).

Likewise, there are relatively few licensed female lawyers today. Women make up only 36 percent of the field (up from 28 percent in 2000) (American Bar Association 2016). Perhaps the most powerful explanation for difference in salaries for attorneys, who tend to charge clients an hourly rate for their work, is the amount of time women and men tend to spend in childcare, which takes away from the hours they can spend at work (Dau-Schmidt et al. 2008). While fathers today have increased the time they spend on childcare from an average of only 2.5 hours a week in 1965 to 7 hours a week in 2008, mothers who work outside the home still spend about twice as much time caring for children as do fathers (Bianchi 2011; Parker and Wang 2013). Men may be paid more because they are more able to work long hours and be available to work whenever their company needs them (Goldin 2014).

Some companies, such as the accounting firm Ernst and Young, have created flexible work programs to retain women employees. They found that women were leaving their firm at a rate 10 to 15 percent higher than men just as they were becoming eligible for promotions. The costs of replacing employees such as these are 150 percent to 175 percent of the employee's salary (Boushey and Glynn 2012). Thus, an attorney who makes $100,000 would cost $150,000 to replace. Their women employees could not both take care of their families and work in an inflexible job (Bernard 2014, para. 20). Their new flexible hours have stemmed this movement of women out of the firm. However, only 20 percent of companies offer most of their workers the opportunity to work a flexible schedule (Sweet et al. 2014).

Discrimination and the Wage Gap

While gender segregation contributes to the wage gap, it is not the sole cause of it. Sometimes employees simply pay men more than they pay women—even when they are doing the same job, with the same credentials. Although doing so is against the law, thanks to the Equal Pay Act of 1963, such discrimination persists. For example, in 2015, men who taught elementary and middle school earned $1,077 a week while women who taught at the same level earned $957.

From the moment our parents know our sex, we are perceived differently, and as we grow up, we learn from advertisements, movies, and music that women are nurturing and soft, and men are strong and resilient. Men are expected to be leaders and breadwinners, and women are more likely to be expected to be nurturers. Our peers treat us differently if we are men or women, and the majority of the leaders in all of our institutions, from schools to churches, are men. The lessons we learn are that men are simply more competent than women.

Research on transgender men allows us a unique perspective on gender inequality in the workplace that reinforces the advantages of being a man. Kristen Schilt (2006) studied transgender men (men who transitioned from being women to being men) and the consequences of this gender change. The respondents began their jobs as women and then transitioned to men. Most reported gaining authority and prestige at work even when they remained in the same job. For example, an attorney reported that his boss was congratulated for firing "Susan" and hiring "the new guy." But, the new guy was Susan—he had just changed his name to Stephen! After they had transitioned, these transgender men could clearly see that men succeed at higher rates than do women not because they are more skilled but because our culture perceives men as more competent than women. One of Schilt's respondents put it this way: "I swear they let guys get away with so much stuff! Lazy ass bastards get away with so much stuff and the women who are working hard, they just get ignored." The job requirements did not change; the only thing that changed was the gender of the person doing the job, clearly indicating the advantages that come from simply being male. The social construction of gender is clear (Schilt 2006:473).

The Glass Ceiling

Many women experience a phenomenon known as the "glass ceiling." The **glass ceiling** is the unofficial barrier that women and minorities face when trying to advance to the upper levels of an organization. In 2016, Hillary Rodham Clinton broke a political glass ceiling when she became the first woman nominated as a presidential candidate by one of the two major political parties. The glass ceiling is called "glass" because it is invisible and not openly acknowledged. There are no formal rules that say that women cannot advance. However, when you bump up against it, it is as real as wood and plaster. And you can see it if you use your sociological eye. For example, if you were looking for evidence of a glass ceiling in a group of corporations, you would notice that the gap between the percentage of men and women increases from the managerial to vice-presidential to CEO levels.

The glass ceiling becomes a "maternal wall" when women have children (Williams 2013). Young women (ages twenty-five to thirty-four), on average, earn 90 cents for every dollar earned by men, but parenthood increases the gender wage gap. Thirty-nine percent of women compared to 24 percent of men take significant time off from work to care for a child or other family member. Slightly more than a

quarter (27 percent) of women leave paid work completely to take care of their family (Brown and Patten 2017). Some would argue that mothers cannot even enter the room with the glass ceiling!

The glass ceiling (and the maternal wall) is more pronounced in some professions than in others. It is a particularly powerful impediment for women in *Fortune* 500 companies, where few women have been able to break through. In 2014, just 5.2 percent of all CEOs of *Fortune* 500 companies were women.

> **Consider This**
>
> Who benefits from the existence of a glass ceiling? Who is hurt by the glass ceiling? Do married men benefit if their wives experience a glass ceiling? When mothers experience a glass ceiling, do their sons benefit from or pay a price for the glass ceiling?

FIGURE 8.8

Women CEOs in *Fortune* 500 Companies, 1995–2017

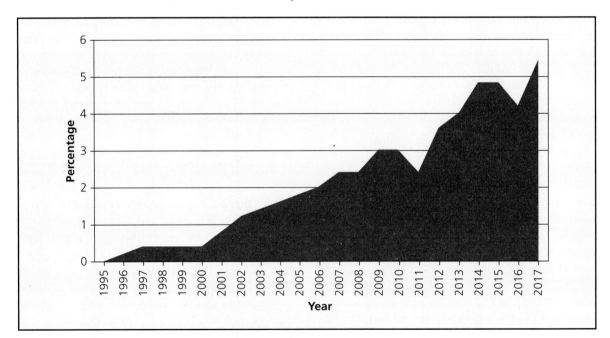

Source: *Fortune* 500 and Catalyst, via Pew Research Center. http://www.pewsocialtrends.org/chart/women-ceos-in-fortune-500-companies-1995-2014/.

Note: Prior to 2017, based on the percentage of women CEOs at the time of the annual published *Fortune* 500 list. For 2017, share is as of the end of the first quarter.

Women in Leadership Positions

In this exercise, you will look at data on leaders in politics, business, and education and propose a college curriculum to close the gender gap.

Look at the data on women in leadership positions in politics, business, and education presented by the Pew Research Center's Data on Women Leaders: http://www.pewsocialtrends.org/2015/01/14/the-data-on-women-leaders/.

1. Find one graph that most surprises you. Jot down questions you have about the graph.

2. Pair up with another student, compare your choices, and propose a college curriculum that would help bridge the gap between men and women in at least one of the graphs. What classes would be required? What skills would need to be taught? Would it be important for women to be the professors in these classes? Who would take the class? Would you assume that women would need to increase their skills or would socializing men be more helpful?

The Impact of Breaking the Glass Ceiling

While it is easy to see the glass ceiling can have a substantial negative impact on the careers and salaries of women, what happens when some women do break through? Do women in lower-level positions fare better when there are women at the top of an organization? Yes! And the more women in the highest positions, the better for women throughout the organization. When women occupy leadership positions at the lower end of the management hierarchy, the gender wage gap may decrease somewhat. However, the wage gap in an organization tends to decrease significantly when women serve in upper-level management positions (Cohen and Huffman 2007).

The Glass Escalator

While women may be held back by the glass ceiling, some men experience a glass escalator. Men who work in female-dominated occupations, like nursing, social work, library science, and elementary school education, are often given a ride on a glass escalator. The **glass escalator** is the unfair advantage that men who work in female-dominated occupations can receive over women in the same job. Just being male becomes a valued asset. As noted earlier, men in predominantly female occupations tend to earn more than their female counterparts. They also tend to gain promotions more easily than women in the same jobs (Williams 2013). The fact that most school principals are men, despite the fact that most teachers are women, is an example of the glass escalator at work.

However, the glass escalator does not work the same for all men. Men of color, gay men, and working-class men do not enjoy the same privileges that their White, heterosexual, middle-class counterparts enjoy. For example, while White male nurses may be seen as out of place, they are also often mistaken for doctors or administrators and given a lot of respect by their female colleagues and patients. They tend to be seen as qualified for more prestigious work and promoted to positions of leadership or encouraged to enter higher-status nursing specialties. Black male nurses, on the other hand, are likely to be mistaken for people in lower-status positions, such as janitors or other service workers. Rather than being viewed as competent professionals providing care, they are seen as being there to clean up (Harvey Wingfield 2009).

Consider This

If you were the CEO of an organization—and had just read this chapter—what would you do to address the glass ceiling/glass escalator in your organization? How would you get your managers to buy into your ideas and put them into practice?

Few women break through the glass ceiling in their professions and, if they have children, women employees are likely to face a "maternal wall."

©iStockphoto.com/hudiemm

Intimate Relationships

Our most intimate relationships are also gendered. That is, women and men's behavior in relationships and our attitudes toward our intimate lives differ by gender. Gender influences our private lives in everything from who does what around the house to how we conduct our romantic relationships.

Family Work

Married women do more housework than the men to whom they are married, right? Everybody knows this! And, it turns out that the research supports this notion. Although the differences have declined over time, women still do more housework than men (Bianchi et al. 2012).

Gender ideology—our ideas about gender—influences who does what around the house. One might think that men do less housework because they work more hours and earn more money. That would make perfect sense. However, that is not the case. *Even when women work more hours and earn more money,* they still tend to do more housework than men (Greenstein 2000; Bianchi et al. 2012).

Social constructionists point out that one of the ways that men construct their gender and assert their masculinity is by avoiding housework. Employed women, on the other hand, may make up for the fact that they are enacting a traditional masculine role by doing more housework and affirming their femininity and their husbands' masculinity. Married mothers still do about twice as much housework as married fathers (Bianchi et al. 2012). Childcare follows a similar pattern. While

today's fathers spend more time with their children than those in previous generations, mothers still spend more time doing childcare work (see Figure 10.4, p. 216).

Sinkka Elliott, the Sociologist in Action for this chapter, works on a project studying nutrition, gender, and the family. She notes that women are largely responsible for making sure that family members are fed. Women, more than men, shop for groceries, prepare meals, and try to make sure that their children eat well or at least as well as the family can provide for them. Women may even skip meals themselves to feed their children.

Intimate Partner Violence

Violence between partners who are involved in a romantic or sexual relationship or were involved in such a relationship in the past is known as **intimate partner violence** (IPV). By some estimates, about one in four women and one in nine men have been the victim of sexual abuse, physical abuse, or stalking by an intimate partner that resulted in some injury. Even more have been the victim of minor violence. Men as well as women are victims of IPV but not at nearly so high a rate (Smith et al. 2017).

Sexual Assault on Campus

For college students and their parents, one of the biggest concerns about IPV is sexual assault on campus. **Sexual assault** can be defined as "nonconsensual sexual contact," including "sexual penetration and sexual touching or kissing" through physical force or incapacitation (Cantor et al. 2015). Awareness and concern about sexual assault on campus is not limited to students and parents of those currently in college but rather is recognized as a national issue and addressed by the Violence Against Women Act of 2014. The Violence Against Women Act enacts several changes to the Crime Awareness and Campus Security Act of 1990, popularly known as the Clery Act, which includes requirements that campuses report sexual assault and that they provide education programming to help prevent sexual assault.

Increasing Access to Healthy Food and Places to Be Active

Sinikka Elliott

With a group of dedicated and talented colleagues and community members, I am involved in a five-year project that aims to increase access to healthy food and places to be active in three North Carolina communities—two communities are in rural areas and one is in an urban city. All three communities have a high proportion of residents who are low income, and many are food insecure—meaning they do not have enough food for an active, healthy life. Food insecurity is more prevalent in households with children, especially female-headed households, and is related to the feminization and juvenilization of poverty. Mothers in food-insecure households make personal sacrifices to try to make sure that their children have enough to eat, such as skipping meals themselves.

We wanted our efforts to improve access to healthy food and places to be active to be community driven, so we drew on our relationships with local organizations in each of the three communities to recruit research participants to be a part of a five-year study of food and families.

All participants are low-income mothers or grandmothers of small children from diverse backgrounds, approximately mirroring the racial/ethnic composition of the communities. We focused on women because they are still largely responsible for the work of feeding the family. Along with interviewing participants about their experiences feeding a family, we conducted ethnographic observations of families' food-work inside and outside of their homes (e.g., grocery shopping, going to food pantries, preparing meals, enticing children to eat) to situate food experiences and practices within everyday life.

On the basis of our research findings, we have engaged in a variety of community outreach efforts. Specifically, we have worked to encourage partnerships that make it easier for local farmers to donate excess produce to food pantries. We have also helped to create several community gardens that enable low-income residents to grow seasonal food. Walking trails, Zumba classes, mobile food trucks, and fresh produce at convenience stores are some other initiatives we've supported in the three communities.

Listening and learning about each community's unique context and existing resources have helped to ensure that our efforts are community led and collaborative. For example, we have emphasized throughout how the participants' voices are stimulating community change (in fact, the project is called *Voices into Action: The Family, Food, and Health Project*). We have shared the research and community outreach with participants through monthly newsletters, social media, and community festivals and held community workshops to strategize ways to build on local resources. We have also drawn broader attention to the often-invisible work of feeding families by writing in accessible venues and being interviewed on radio programs.

These types of collaborative research efforts are rewarding for both researchers and participants. Ultimately, it is care, compassion, and connecting with others that inspire and nurture us all as we strive to make the world a better place.

Sinikka Elliott is an associate professor of sociology at North Carolina State University.

About 23 percent of undergraduate heterosexual women and about 6 percent of undergraduate heterosexual men report sexual assault. It is important that we also consider the experiences of students who do not identify as heterosexual. About 24 percent of undergraduate TGQN students (transgender, genderqueer, or nonconforming, questioning) report being sexually assaulted (Cantor et al. 2015). Black women, bisexual women, and sorority women are at a higher risk of being assaulted than others (Worthen

and Wallace 2017). There are reasons to believe that the rates of sexual assault may actually be higher and that some students who are assaulted may not report assaults to authorities.

One powerful reason that women fail to report assaults is concern that they will not be believed, due to the inaccurate idea that women lie about sexual assault and blame innocent men. This belief is a rape myth, or a widely held but false belief about rape, that justifies this violence and distrusts women's account

FIGURE 8.9

Percentage of College Students Who Reported Sexual Contact Involving Physical Force or Incapacitation

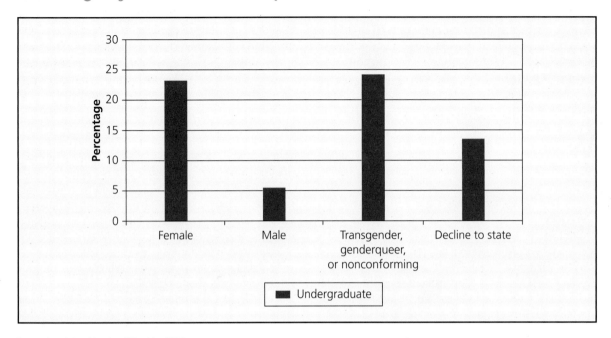

Source: Association of American Universities (2015).

of their experience. Less than 10 percent of reports of sexual assault are false reports, but even police officers often fail to believe victims of sexual assault. Women know that they are likely to be doubted, which makes it more difficult to report an assault. Perpetrators of sexual assault on campus are rarely arrested, charged, or convicted (Weiser 2017).

Domestic Violence

Violence between married or cohabiting partners, or **domestic violence,** is also a common occurrence with an estimate of 12 percent to 18 percent of women reporting at least one incident of IPV during the past year. Violence may be physical, sexual, or psychological. Violent marriages usually end in divorce, and 30 percent of divorced couples report violence in their marriages (Johnson, Leone, and Xu 2014).

There are two primary types of domestic violence. **Situational couple violence** (SCV) is violence that results when arguments escalate. This type of violence occurs in both same-sex and heterosexual relationships. Both men and women are the victims and the perpetrators of situational couple violence. Examples of situational couple violence include throwing objects, shoving, or slapping. However, both the meaning and the outcome of such violent outbursts

differ by gender (Johnson 2008; Johnson, Leone, and Xu 2014). Men's violence can be perceived as necessary, justified, and powerful while women's violence is seen as irrational and ineffective. Men may even react with laughter at women's violent acts while women are more likely to feel humiliated and fearful (Anderson 2010).

The second primary type of domestic violence is **intimate terrorism** (IT) (Johnson 2008) or physical violence and other tactics that are used for overall control of a partner. Men in heterosexual relationships are the predominant perpetrators of intimate terrorism. Acts of intimate terrorism may not be more frequent than situational couple violence. One act of physical abuse may be sufficient to scare a partner enough to allow the perpetrator to control that partner with nonphysical tactics such as threatening to harm children, threatening to leave the partner, or controlling the family income.

Again, it is important to consider both the outcomes and meanings of domestic violence. Intimate terrorism is more likely than common situational violence to escalate over time and causes more fear and severe injury than situational couple violence (Anderson 2010). This type of violence is often seen among women who flee to women's shelters. Violence of both types is a way of demonstrating and socially creating masculinity. For example, men are more likely to be violent if their wives have higher income and if the male partner believes in traditional gender roles (Atkinson, Greenstein, and Lang 2005). Violence substitutes for the assumed "natural" place of men as breadwinner.

One of the most common questions raised about wife abuse is why women stay in abusive relationships. Women who are economically dependent, have negative self-images, and have no place else to go are likely to feel as though they do not have the option to leave. Family and friends may be judgmental of an abused woman, seeing the decision to stay in simplistic terms rather than the complicated choice it is (Yamawaki et al. 2012).

Romantic Relationships: From Bundling to Hooking Up

We might think of our ancestors' romantic relationships as being sexually inhibited and rigidly defined by their genders. We tend to think of ourselves as being free to create our intimate relationships independent of gender norms and see ourselves as much more sexually liberated. While the social structures under which we live our most private lives have changed, our romantic relationships are remarkably gendered, and our ancestors were more sexually active than we might assume.

The Colonial Era

Heterosexual romantic relationships have traditionally been gendered. Men and women's experiences in these relationships differ in both meaning and behavior. That was true during the Colonial era and remains true today. Our ancestors were also sexually active outside of marriage, despite contemporary perceptions. By the last half of the 1700s, bed courting or bundling was common. The unmarried couple could spend the night together in a bed with a board between them or in a bundling sack, something like a sleeping bag with a seam up the middle. Ostensibly, bundling provided an opportunity for couples to get to know each other, even in the winter when days were short and distances between homes could be long. Bundling took place in the woman's home, and in theory, the couple did not engage in physical intimacy (Gardner 2007; Godbeer 2004). However, the bridal pregnancy rate was about 33 percent (Godbeer 2004).

Marriage changed men's lives more than it did women's in this era. Laws and custom bound men who were not married to live in another man's household. However, once he was married, he was the head of his own household, and everyone in the household and all their property were his to control. Young women's lives were not so markedly changed. While marriage symbolized their passage from youth to adulthood, they still only moved from one man's household to another's. The man to whom they answered was their husband, rather than their father or some other family member, but still, they answered to some man. Men were often more anxious to get married than were women (Eustace 2001).

The Victorian Age

By the 1830s and 1840s, the Victorian age emerged and, along with it, a different gendered division of labor and new norms and behaviors for courting. As our agrarian economy gave way to a more industrial economy, middle-class men often worked outside the home in professional and managerial jobs and middle-class women were reassigned from working alongside their husbands, as they did during the Colonial era, to domestic work and childrearing (Coontz 1992). This is perhaps why women were often not as anxious to get married as were men (Rothman 1984).

The norms that defined what it was to be a woman (for White women in the middle and upper classes) during most of the 1800s were called the "Cult of True Womanhood." Women were judged by their adherence to "piety, purity, submissiveness and domesticity," and young men were told to first look for piety as the most important virtue in a wife. Young girls were taught that religion would soothe their "longings" and that being pure was a requirement for marriage, but men were more likely to be excused from purity because of their more "sensual" nature (Welter 1966). Regardless of what was taught, there is evidence that although "bundling" was no longer practiced, courting couples often did engage in sexual behavior, and love was seen as a requirement for marriage, unlike expectations during the Colonial period (Rothman 1984).

The "Cult of True Womanhood" was a part of the middle-class definition of gender and included a set of ideals that working-class women were unlikely to be able to meet. Working-class girls and poor women often did housecleaning and cooking for wealthier families, working-class men and boys worked in coalmines, Black women and children picked cotton, and Jewish or Italian girls worked in sweatshops and textile miles (Coontz 1992). However, the economic changes that created jobs for young women in urban factories and department stores also allowed them a measure of freedom that was difficult to manage for middle-class girls during the nineteenth century.

Middle-class girls were kept at home and thus could be more carefully monitored by their families. Living in boardinghouses and furnished rooms may have had its disadvantages, but it also afforded freedom from family's oversight and thus more independence (Bailey 2004).

The city streets and dance halls created a place for leisure that was organized around sexuality. Men were expected to "treat" women to drinks, tickets to entertainment events, and other favors. In exchange, women provided sexual favors. While middle-class couples courted in the family's parlor, working-class couples courted in public places and stole private moments wherever they could (Peiss 2004).

The Twentieth Century

"One day, the 1920s story goes, a young man came to call on a city girl. When he arrived she had her hat on" (Bailey 2004:23). He was shocked. He expected to court in the parlor, perhaps to listen to her sing or play the piano and be served a snack. But he had missed that "dating," which had emerged from working-class urban culture, had replaced "calling." The young woman expected to be entertained.

While the norms for calling stipulated that women invited men to "call" on them, men asked women for dates to accompany them on some kind of outing, a social event, movies, and so on. Men planned the outing, paying for any expenses and driving them, or otherwise organizing transportation to wherever they were going. The opportunity for sexual intimacy increased because couples were now away from the protective environment of the girl's home, and the question became what a girl owed in return for the money that was spent on her. Thus, women's access to enjoyment of their sexuality improved, but their power in the courtship market decreased. The 1920s have been labeled the "first sexual revolution" (Coontz 1992).

By the 1950s, many couples were "going steady," or dating only each other. Men usually gave their steady date some form of visible token such as a class ring or an identification bracelet, and more sexual intimacy was expected than with simply dating. However, this exclusive form of courtship was not necessarily tied to marriage (Coontz 1992).

By the 1960s, the notion of dating was giving way to what many called the second sexual revolution (Bailey 2004; Coontz 1992). During the decade of the 1950s, 70 percent of women and 60 percent of men reported being virgins at age eighteen, but by the 1980s, only about 50 percent of both women and men reported being virgins at age eighteen. The decade of most rapid change was the 1960s, when the

birth control pill was first widely available (Schwartz and Rutter 1998). It is important to note that it was women's behavior that changed the most.

During the 1970s, a gay movement also arose that demanded sexual freedom for themselves as well as heterosexuals. Many social changes contributed to the sexual revolution of the last four decades of the twentieth century, including an intensified interest in political activity on behalf of the Baby Boomers who were coming of age, women's growing autonomy, and the enhanced educational opportunities that were available to women (Coontz 1992).

Hooking Up

Do college students on your campus date or just hook up? Several sociologists have examined the hookup culture on today's college campuses. In the most extensive study, over 20,000 college students from twenty-one public and private colleges and universities provided researchers with information about their hookup behavior and attitudes in an online survey. These students were recruited primarily from sociology courses like the one you are in right now. The Online College Survey was conducted between 2005 and 2011 (England 2015).

Hooking up generally means getting together at the end of an evening that has been spent at a party or at a bar for the purposes of an intimate, no-strings-attached encounter. Either the man or the woman can begin the hookup. The encounter might simply be kissing or could extend to sexual intercourse. Although not a rule, alcohol is often central to the hookup experience, with many students reporting that they would not be able to engage in hookups that include sex without drinking. It is primarily White students who hook up. Working-class, Black, and gay students tend to be left out of the college party scene where hooking up occurs (Wade 2017).

Hooking up is a common experience on today's college campuses, with 71 percent of senior men and 70 percent of senior women reporting that they had hooked up at least once while in college (England 2015). Does this mean that college students now accept casual sex as being OK? To some extent, the answer is "yes," but there are limits. There are norms or social rules for hooking up just as there were, and still are, for dating. Hooking up "a lot" is not seen in a positive light, and about half of college students lose respect for those who have casual sex frequently (Allison and Risman 2013).

Not surprisingly, there is a double standard based on gender. Men still control the sexual experience, and women who engage in casual sex are viewed more negatively than men. Perhaps because of this fact, women are less likely to say that they are interested in casual sex (England and Bearak 2014; Allison and Risman 2013). Other research indicates that in a hookup culture, women pay a bigger emotional price than do men. Showing sentiment for a hookup partner is viewed as being especially problematic for women (Wade 2017).

Hookup culture has not led to the death of dating on campuses. Among college seniors surveyed, 74 percent of college women and 66 percent of college men had a dating relationship during college and, on average, at least two relationships that lasted six months or more (Ford, England, and Bearak 2015). Nor are young people today having sex at a younger age, or more often, than their parents. In fact, data show just the opposite.

Women born between 1979 and 1984 were less likely to have sex before age twenty than those born before them (Armstrong, Hamilton, and England 2010). Between 2011 and 2013, 44 percent of unmarried teens said they had had sex compared to 51 percent of the same age group in 1988 (Martinez and Abma 2015).

Finally, most college students do not hook up all that often. The great majority (80 percent) of those who have hooked up only do so once a semester or less, and hooking up with strangers is relatively uncommon. Most hookup partners know each other. When asked about their latest hookups, only about a third reported sexual intercourse. Twenty percent of college seniors had never had intercourse (Armstrong, Hamilton, and England 2010).

Check Your Understanding

- Do men tend to do more housework than their wives if their wives work more hours and earn more money?

- Has the amount of housework and childcare men do increased over time?

- What are the different types of intimate partner violence and who is most likely to experience each type?

- Trace the history of courtship over time.

- What is hooking up?

- How common is hooking up on college campuses today?

- Are unmarried teens today more or less likely to have had sex than those in other periods of our history?

Conclusion

Gender is a socially constructed characteristic that is usually, but not always, consistent with the biological sex we are assigned at birth. The penalties for not abiding by the gender roles we learn in our homes, in our schools, and from our peers can be quite dramatic. Gender affects every part of our lives, including our opportunities in the labor force and our most intimate relationships. Knowing that it is a social construction gives us the ability to promote change in gender roles and to work for gender equality.

Race, another social construction that affects every aspect of our lives, is the focus of the next chapter. Like gender, it has become increasingly fluid over the past several years. Nonetheless, it remains a powerful force of inequality in society. As it does with gender, sociology gives us the tools to recognize and address societal issues related to race and ethnicity.

$SAGE edge™

Review

8.1 What are the sociological definitions of sex, gender, intersex, and transgender?

Sex is a biological construct that is defined by our external genitalia, chromosomes, and internal reproductive organs. On the basis of our external genitalia, someone, usually a physician or a midwife, declares that we are a boy or a girl when we are born. From that moment on, we are treated differently depending on our biological sex. Our gender, however, is a social concept, and we learn to be a woman or a man from interacting with others. These lessons are both subtle and direct and are taught to us throughout our lifetimes.

Intersex people are not clearly biologically male or female. In our culture, we are often very uncomfortable if our child is intersex, and some parents use surgery to assign their child to one sex or the other, usually to being female. Transgender is not a biological characteristic but rather an identity, a social construct. Transgender people see themselves as a gender other than the one assigned to them at birth and may or may not choose to have surgery.

8.2 How do the four major theoretical perspectives help sociologists understand gender?

The four major theoretical perspectives are structural functionalism, conflict theory, symbolic interactionism, and gender as a social structure.

Structural functionalists typically equate sex and gender and see men and women as essentially different and complementary. Men play instrumental roles in society, being leaders and breadwinners, and women play expressive roles, supporting men and providing nurturance for children and the elderly. This perspective ignores that assigning these roles results in gender inequity. Conflict theorists focus on the unequal distribution of resources between men and women and the inequality that results. Symbolic interactionists emphasize the mechanisms we use to teach expectations for gendered behavior. Symbolic interactionists who emphasize social construction point out that gender is fluid and not simply learned as children but rather that we create and re-create our genders throughout our lifetimes. Gender as social structure reminds us that to understand gender, we should not simply pick and choose perspectives; rather, we must understand socialization, social interactions, and inequalities embedded within organizational structures. Gender reflects all of these dimensions of social life.

8.3 How do we learn and create our gender?

We learn our gender from the environment around us as we interact with others. We learn from the clothes we are given to wear, the toys that are chosen for us, the lessons taught by our teachers, our peers, and the media representations of men and women we see and hear. Gender socialization is the process by which we learn to be a man or a woman in our particular place and time. Gender scripts are the expectations for behavior that are assigned to genders. Boys and men tend to have more narrowly defined gender scripts and face harsher reactions when they violate them. The meaning and consequence of gender vary depending on a number of other attributes such as race and sexuality.

8.4 How does gender affect workforce experiences?

Being a man or a woman affects our work lives in powerful ways. Gender segregation is the separation of men and women into different types of occupations. The gender wage gap is the difference between men's and women's wages. Men and women are often paid different salaries for the same job, and men generally have more opportunities for advancement than do women. Women often face a glass ceiling or a maternal wall while men sometimes benefit from a glass escalator. The glass ceiling is the barrier that women face in moving up in a work organization and earning the equivalent of men in the same position. A maternal wall is the barrier mothers face, which is an even greater disadvantage than the glass ceiling. The glass escalator is the unfair advantage that men who work in female-dominated occupations can receive over women in the same job.

8.5 How do women's and men's experiences in intimate relationships differ?

Our family lives are structured by gender. Gender ideology, our ideas about gender, influences who does what around the house. Although there has been some recent change, women still tend to do more housework and more childcare than men—even if they work more hours and earn more money.

Our romantic lives are also affected by our gender. Men tend to have more freedom to be sexually active than women, and this has been true historically. Intimate partner violence is not uncommon and occurs on campus as well as within partnered couples. Hooking up is now a common experience among college students, but women are less likely to be respected than men if they hook up often. Dating relationships (having a boyfriend/girlfriend relationship) still exist on college campuses. Like hooking up, they are structured by gender. Among college students, more women than men have dating relationships. While the practice of hooking up has made many older adults think college students are having more casual sex than they had when they were younger, this tends not to be the case.

Key Terms

- domestic violence   172
- gender   152
- gender scripts   157
- gender segregation   162
- gender socialization   155
- gender as social structure   154
- gender wage gap   166
- glass ceiling   168
- glass escalator   169

- hooking up   174
- intersex   151
- intimate partner violence   170
- intimate terrorism   172
- sex   151
- sexual assault   170
- sexuality   157
- situational couple violence   172
- transgender   151

> If you want to understand society, you have to acknowledge race and ethnicity—and the impact of these social constructions.

Learning Questions

9.1 What are race and ethnicity?

9.2 What is the difference between prejudice and discrimination?

9.3 How has racism influenced social policies throughout U.S. history?

9.4 How can you show that racism and ethnocentrism are key social issues in the United States—and across the world—today?

9.5 How can you work to diminish racism and racial discrimination?

Recognizing the Importance of Race

Kathleen Odell Korgen

Defining Race and Ethnicity

Ask a sociologist to define race and ethnicity, and you will probably want to pull up a chair. It may well take a while, but the time will be well spent. Understanding race and ethnicity will help you understand society—and your experience in it.

Ethnicity can be explained much more easily than race. Members of a particular **ethnic group** share the same cultural heritage (e.g., language, nation of origin, and religion). There are various ethnic groups in the United States today, including African Americans, Jamaican Americans, Cuban Americans, Italian Americans, Irish Americans, and Chinese Americans. Diverse ethnic groups, with very different cultures, can fall under the same racial label (e.g., both Korean and Japanese Americans are considered Asian in the United States). Definitions of racial groups and how we group people into different racial groups have changed over the years.

Once thought of as based on biological or genetic differences among humans, race is now widely recognized as a social construction that varies over time and from society to society. Today, sociologists define a **race** as a group of people *perceived* to be distinct on the basis of physical appearance (not genetic makeup). We tend to categorize people we meet into racial groups based on their skin tone and facial features (Black, American Indian or Alaskan Native, Asian or Pacific Islander, or White).

How people identify *themselves* racially may not match the perceptions of others, however. Rapidly increasing numbers of Americans identify with more than one race. According to a U.S. Census study that included Hispanics as a racial group, 7 percent of the population now identifies as multiracial (Frey 2014). Today, how Americans of multiracial heritage identify racially relates to a variety of social and minor genetic factors, including appearance (e.g., skin tone, facial features), ancestry, social class, location (where they live), the place they answer the question (e.g., school or home), and socialization (e.g., how their parents racially identify them) (Ignatiev 1995; Khanna 2013; Korgen 2010, 2016; Rockquemore and Brunsma 2008).

Distinguishing between race and ethnicity becomes complicated when dealing with Hispanic Americans—officially an ethnic group on the U.S. Census. While Hispanic Americans comprise an umbrella ethnic group and can be of any race, they tend to be treated as a distinct racial group.

How I Got Active in Sociology

Kathleen Odell Korgen

When I neared the midpoint in my PhD program and needed to identify a dissertation topic, my brother announced I was soon to be an aunt. He, a White man, had married a Black woman, and they were going to have a baby boy! I started thinking about how my nephew's racial background would impact his life. To my dismay, I found that the existing research indicated that he would face all sorts of racial discrimination and live as a marginalized person, not fully accepted by either White or Black people. I had a sense, and certainly a hope, society had changed and the research needed updating—I had found my dissertation topic.

It turns out that I was right. My nephew—and other members of his generation of mixed-race people—was not doomed to face a life of marginalization. That is not to say, however, that race no longer matters—it does. Race, a social construction, continues to affect our society and every institution and person in it. Recognizing that reality is the focus of this chapter.

A combination of skin color, accent, and Spanish or English speech (characteristics that vary widely among the Hispanic population) largely determines the extent to which they face discrimination in the United States (Rodriguez 2000).

Realizing that many Americans are confused by the terms *race, ethnicity,* and *country of origin,* the U.S. Census may drop the *race* and *origin* terms on the 2020 Census and, instead, ask people to check off "categories" (asking what "categories" rather than race or ethnicity describe people, but still including the racial and ethnic options of White; Hispanic, Latino, or Spanish; Black or African American; Asian, American Indian, or Alaska Native; Native Hawaiian or Other Pacific Islander) (Cohn 2017). As was the case under the 2010 Census, respondents will be able to select all categories that apply to them. Also under consideration is a new Middle East/North Africa (MENA) classification. Now, despite the racial and ethnic prejudice and discrimination many Arab Americans face, they are officially considered White. This makes it more difficult to track and address discrimination aimed at this group.

Despite how individuals, institutions, and governments classify people, biologically speaking, the old saying, "there is only one race—the human race," is true. We now know, thanks to the Human Genome Project, that there are more genetic differences *within* than between racial groups. All humans share common ancestors and 99.9 percent of the same genetic makeup. Differences in "racial" appearance result from adaptations to different environmental conditions as humans spread across the world from their common origin in Africa (Jorde and Wooding 2004; Rutherford 2015; Smithsonian Institute 2016; see Figure 9.1).

The Social Construction of Race

To see how racial categories are socially rather than biologically constructed, one need only look at the U.S. Census. For example, in the 1930 U.S. Census, Mexican Americans were included under the category "Mexican." However, in 1940, they were placed under "White," "unless they appeared to census interviewers to be 'definitely Indian or of other Nonwhite races' (U.S. Bureau of the Census, 1943:3)" (Rodriguez 2000:84). Today, they are asked to choose a racial category listed on the Census and indicate that they are ethnically Hispanic/Mexican.

Susie Guillory Phillips and the "One-Drop Rule"

As noted earlier, today most people in the United States place people into particular racial categories based on physical appearance, such as skin tone and facial features. In the past, however, your heritage

> ### Consider This
> Leading up to and during World War II, President Roosevelt turned back thousands of Jewish refugees seeking to enter the United States, due to fear that some of them were Nazi spies. It turns out that this fear was largely unfounded (Gross 2015, paragraph 5). Many of those rejected by the United States were put to death by the Nazis. What do you think you would have done, if you were president at the time? Why?

FIGURE 9.1

Human Migration from Africa

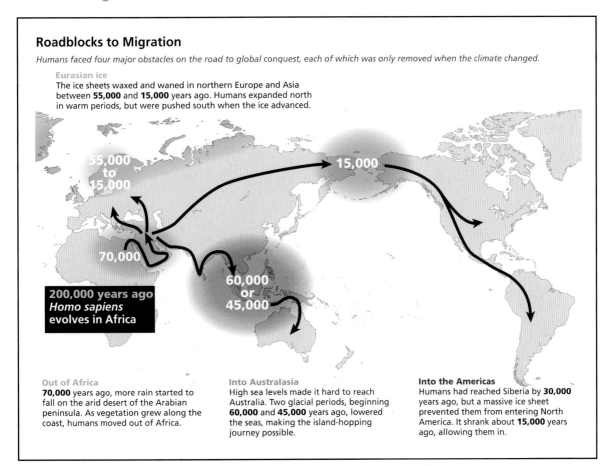

Roadblocks to Migration

Humans faced four major obstacles on the road to global conquest, each of which was only removed when the climate changed.

Eurasian ice
The ice sheets waxed and waned in northern Europe and Asia between **55,000** and **15,000** years ago. Humans expanded north in warm periods, but were pushed south when the ice advanced.

55,000 to 15,000

15,000

70,000

200,000 years ago
Homo sapiens evolves in Africa

60,000 or 45,000

Out of Africa
70,000 years ago, more rain started to fall on the arid desert of the Arabian peninsula. As vegetation grew along the coast, humans moved out of Africa.

Into Australasia
High sea levels made it hard to reach Australia. Two glacial periods, beginning **60,000** and **45,000** years ago, lowered the seas, making the island-hopping journey possible.

Into the Americas
Humans had reached Siberia by **30,000** years ago, but a massive ice sheet prevented them from entering North America. It shrank about **15,000** years ago, allowing them in.

Source: Map based on Michael Marshall, "Climate Change Determined Humanity's Global Conquest," *New Scientist,* September 19, 2012. © 2012 New Scientist Ltd. All rights reserved. Distributed by Tribune Content Agency, LLC.

Doing Sociology 9.1
Sorting People by Race

In this exercise, you will attempt to place people into racial categories based on their appearance.

As part of a documentary series, *RACE—The Power of an Illusion*, PBS created an online tool that allows you to sort a series of photographs of people by race and then check your answers against what those people marked on the U.S. Census form.

Visit http://www.pbs.org/race/002_SortingPeople/ 002_00-home.htm and click "Begin Sorting" to get started. Once you have completed the activity, answer the following questions:

1. Was it easy or difficult for you to place the people into the categories they selected on the U.S. Census. Why?

2. Which of the people pictured might face racial discrimination in the United States today? Why?

3. Describe at least two things this exercise teaches us about racial and ethnic categorizations in the United States today.

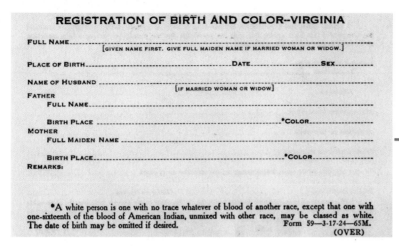

REGISTRATION OF BIRTH AND COLOR—VIRGINIA

FULL NAME
[GIVEN NAME FIRST. GIVE FULL MAIDEN NAME IF MARRIED WOMAN OR WIDOW.]

PLACE OF BIRTH   DATE   SEX

NAME OF HUSBAND
[IF MARRIED WOMAN OR WIDOW]

FATHER
    FULL NAME

    BIRTH PLACE   *COLOR
MOTHER
    FULL MAIDEN NAME

    BIRTH PLACE   *COLOR
REMARKS:

*A white person is one with no trace whatever of blood of another race, except that one with one-sixteenth of the blood of American Indian, unmixed with other race, may be classed as white. The date of birth may be omitted if desired.   Form 59—3-17-24—65M.
(OVER)

After passage of the "Act to Preserve Racial Integrity" in 1924, all residents of Virginia were required to complete this form. Acts like these worked to uphold the "one-drop rule." The Census 2000 was the first U.S. Census to allow respondents to identify with more than one race.

Library of Virginia

defined your race. In the early twentieth century, as states began to codify practices of segregating the races, many states began to distinguish Whites and Blacks using the "one-drop rule," meaning that if you had any trace of Black racial heritage, you were Black. Starting with the 1930 U.S. Census, census workers were instructed to categorize anyone with any "Negro" blood as Negro, and they continued to do so until individuals began to categorize themselves in 1970. The influence of the one-drop rule can be seen most powerfully in that 1970 Census, when there was not a noticeable drop-off in the number of people counted as Black even after individual heads of households, rather than census workers, began to identify themselves and their families racially. People of all races had been socialized to identify anyone, with any trace of Black heritage, as Black.

The state of Louisiana officially modified its one-drop rule, albeit just slightly, in 1970, when it passed a law that declared that anyone 1/32 or more Black (meaning they had one Black great-great-great-grandparent) was Black (Harris 1983). The state had done so as a compromise during a closed session of the state legislature after a New Orleans lawyer had lobbied on behalf of a client with 1/32 Black lineage who wanted to be legally identified as White (Harris 1983). The rigidity of that 1970 law and of the "one-drop rule," in general, made headlines in the 1980s with the case of Susie Guillory Phipps.

In 1977, Phipps, a seemingly White homemaker married to a wealthy White man, applied for a passport for an upcoming trip her husband had planned. To her horror, she was told that she would not be granted the passport because she had indicated her race was different from that listed on her birth certificate. Phipps learned that she had been classified as "colored" on her birth certificate. Frightened at the thought of what his reaction might be if he found out her birth certificate identified her as colored, Phipps told her husband she couldn't travel because she was ill. She then proceeded (secretly at first, using her "wife allowance" and writing cashier's checks) to sue the state, asking it to change her race on her birth certificate. When she finally did tell her husband—after five years—he supported her efforts, arguing that she was White and that her birth certificate should indicate it.

Ultimately, Phipps lost. The state traced her lineage back 222 years and discovered that her great-great-great-great-grandmother was a Black slave and some more recent ancestors had some Black ancestry. The court determined that she was 3/32 Black and ruled against her request to change her official race on her birth certificate (Jaynes 1982; Harris 1983). Although the state of Louisiana repealed the 1/32 law in 1983, Phipps never won the right to change the race on her birth certificate. When the case landed before the Supreme Court in 1986, the Court refused to hear it, leaving the ruling against her in place.

Check Your Understanding

- What is race?
- What are ethnicity and ethnocentrism?
- What is the "one-drop rule"?
- How does Susie Guillory Phipps illustrate the social construction of race?

The Repercussions of Race

Just because race is a social construction does not mean that the repercussions of separating humans into racial groups are not real. When Phipps discovered that her "official" race was Black, she became physically ill and so scared about her husband's reaction at the news that she did not tell him for *five years!* This case proceeded during the late 1970s and early 1980s, after the successes of the civil rights movement.

Inequality in school funding remains a persistent problem in public education in the United States. Wealthier communities have more resources and better school facilities.

Cynthia Lindow/Alamy Stock Photo   AP Photo/Kamil Krzaczynski

Even today, race still matters. Interracial marriages are on the rise (as we discuss below), but racial prejudice and discrimination remain issues in the United States and beyond. The racial group into which you are categorized by people in your society has profound implications on your life—and your life chances.

Prejudice, Stereotypes, and Discrimination

Members both of racial and ethnic minority groups and of dominant groups face prejudicial attitudes and biased behavior that affect every aspect of their lives—from the neighborhoods in which they reside to how long they can expect to live. **Prejudice,** irrational feelings toward members of a particular group, can lead to **discrimination,** unfair treatment of groups of people. As you will recall from Chapter 1, prejudice can stem from **stereotypes,** predetermined ideas about particular groups of people (e.g., all Irish are drunks, all Asians are good at math). Stereotypes are bad generalizations, passed on through hearsay or small samples and held regardless of evidence.

Racism is a belief in the superiority of one or more racial groups that creates and maintains a racial hierarchy. While people of all races can hold stereotypes and prejudice about members of other racial groups, only members of dominant racial groups can be racist. Racism requires prejudice *and* power. The very idea of race was an invention of White people designed to

lend support to the notion that Whites are inherently superior to and should be granted more power and privilege than people of color (Crenshaw et al. 1995).

As social interactionists note, we help shape our society (and its racial hierarchy) through our daily interactions with one another. Through socialization, we learn stereotypes about different racial and ethnic groups in our society that influence our interactions. Again, people of all races can hold negative stereotypes about members of other races. And everyone can practice individual acts of racial discrimination. Only a dominant racial group, however, can move from racial prejudice and individual acts of racial discrimination to shaping and defending a racial hierarchy in society.

Institutional Discrimination

Sometimes discrimination can occur without prejudice—or even intent. **Institutional discrimination,**

> **Consider This**
> Imagine you were born into a different racial group (or groups) than the one (or ones) into which you were born. What aspects of your life would be different now? Why?

which happens as a result of how institutions operate, can exist even if the people who run them do not feel negatively toward the group(s) hurt. For example, school funding that relies on local taxes may be based on the desire for community control of schools. The result, however, is that schools in poor communities, which are disproportionately attended by students of color, receive less funding than wealthier schools with more White students. The intent to discriminate many not be present; nonetheless, the discrimination (more money for wealthier and Whiter schools) and its negative repercussions exist.

Check Your Understanding

- Why does race matter—even if it is a social, rather than a biological, construction?

- What is a stereotype?

- Describe the difference between prejudice and discrimination.

- Give an example of how institutional racial discrimination can take place even without intent or racial prejudice.

Discrimination by the U.S. Government

Often, however, racial discrimination comes with conscious intent. The history of the United States is full of examples of blatant racial prejudice and discrimination at both the individual and institutional levels. Indeed, it can be found in the nation's founding documents as well as in legislation and court decisions throughout U.S. history.

The Constitution, the Compromise of 1877, and *Plessy v. Ferguson*

The Constitution of the United States acknowledged and supported slavery in the new nation. The **Three-Fifths Compromise,** which treated slaves as three-fifths of a person for purposes of representation in the House of Representatives and taxation, is perhaps best known, but the Constitution also explicitly barred Congress from restricting the international slave trade until 1808. The so-called Fugitive Slave Clause guaranteed that slaves who escaped to the North, if caught, would be returned to their masters in the South.

Slavery was finally abolished in 1865, after the Civil War, with the Thirteenth Amendment, but the federal government's efforts to protect the rights of Black people in the South were stopped with the **Hayes-Tilden Compromise of 1877.** The 1876 presidential election between Rutherford B. Hayes, the Republican (Northern) presidential candidate, and Samuel J. Tilden, the Democratic (Southern) presidential candidate, was deadlocked, with Tilden receiving more of the popular vote but neither receiving enough electoral votes to win the presidency. A committee in Congress assigned to break the impasse—the day before the new president was to take office—voted narrowly to give the election to Hayes. The Democrats agreed to go along with the decision if Hayes promised to withdraw federal troops from the former Confederacy and allow Whites to once again dominate political power in the South. Hayes agreed, and Southern states began to establish Jim Crow laws that legally established a racially segregated society. The Supreme Court upheld these measures with the *Plessy v. Ferguson* decision in 1896, which ruled that "separate but equal" facilities were constitutional (King 2012).

Immigration Legislation

Racism also influenced immigration legislation throughout the history of the United States. For example, Chinese and Japanese immigration were halted, respectively, through the **Chinese Exclusion Acts of 1882 and 1892** and the **Gentlemen's Agreement of 1907.** Then, a series of laws curtailed immigration

FIGURE 9.2

Shifts in Immigrant Origins, 1960 and 2013

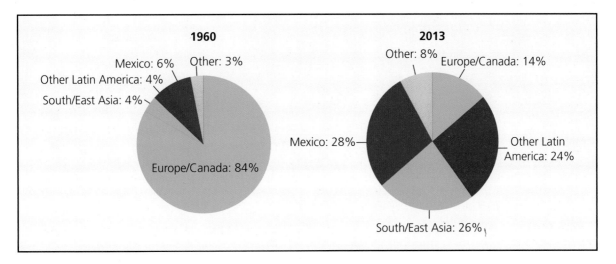

Source: http://www.pewhispanic.org/2015/09/28/chapter-5-u-s-foreign-born-population-trends/.

of Southern and Eastern Europeans (at the time, they were considered "less than White"), culminating in the **Immigration Act of 1924**, which established 2 percent immigration quotas per nation, based on the 1890 U.S. Census (when relatively few Southern and Eastern Europeans were in the United States). So, for example, if there were 100,000 Italians residing in the United States in 1890, only 2,000 new migrants from Italy would be granted entry that year. A provision in the 1924 act limited immigration to those eligible for citizenship. As Asian immigrants were not eligible for citizenship, it totally cut off immigration from Asia. (The Walter-McCarran Act in 1952 finally gave Asian Americans the right to citizenship. Prior to that, Asian immigrants in America could not vote and lacked access to other rights restricted to citizens.[1])

Japanese immigrants and their descendants faced the harshest discrimination. In the late 1800s and early 1900s, Washington State and California passed

laws aimed at Asian immigrants that prohibited non-citizens from owning land. In 1941, after Japan attacked Pearl Harbor, Hawaii, and the United States joined World War II, over 100,000 Japanese Americans who lived on the West Coast were forced to give up their businesses and most of their belongings and move to internment camps in the interior of the United States until the camps were shut down in 1944 and 1945 (Spickard 2009; Torimoto 2017).

It was not until 1965, at the height of the civil rights movement and in the midst of worldwide pressure to address racial discrimination in the United States, that the racist immigration quotas fell. The **Immigration Act of 1965** abolished national quotas (replacing them with quotas for the Eastern and Western Hemispheres) and did much to increase immigration and alter the racial makeup of the United States. The foreign-born population rose from 5.4 percent in 1970 (Gibson and Lennon 1999) to 13.1 percent in 2013 (Pew Research Center 2015b). Figure 9.2 shows the dramatic shift in the makeup of the foreign born before the 1965 Immigration Act and today (Pew Research Center 2015b).

---

1. There were some exceptions to Asian exclusion before 1952. In 1943, as China fought with the United States during World War II, President Roosevelt signed the Magnuson Act, which repealed the Chinese Exclusion Act; established an annual quota that allowed 105 Chinese immigrants to come to the United States per year; and granted Chinese immigrants the right to apply for citizenship. In 1946, the Luke-Cellar Act established a quota of 100 immigrants per year from India and the Philippines and allowed immigrants from those nations to apply for citizenship. And from 1924 to 1934, Filipinos were under the rule of the United States, so they were eligible to immigrate to the United States and become naturalized citizens.

Why Do People Immigrate and What Happens Once They Do?

What would make you leave family members, friends, your neighborhood, and your country? You probably would not do that lightly, would you? People tend not to leave their homes and move to another country without very compelling reasons.

The Statue of Liberty portrays one image of U.S. immigration policy while history and current policies reveal another. The second picture shows a 2017 protest against President Trump's executive order to halt immigration from many predominantly Muslim nations.

D Dipasupil/Getty Images Entertainment/Getty Images   REUTERS/Brian Snyder

A variety of "push" and "pull" factors drive immigration. Push forces include war, ethnic or political persecution, economic depression, climate change, and so on. Receiving nations can pull immigrants to them with jobs, freedom, and safety. Immigration policies tend to be relatively open in peaceful and economic boom times and more restrictive during wars and economic downturns.

Consider This

If you visit the Statue of Liberty in New York Harbor, you can read these words by the poet Emma Lazarus:

Give me your tired, your poor,

Your huddled masses yearning to breathe free,

The wretched refuse of your teeming shore.

Send these, the homeless, tempest-tost to me,

I lift my lamp beside the golden door!

What is your reaction when you read these words? Why? How closely do you think these words reflect the history of U.S. immigration—and current U.S. immigration policy? Why?

Assimilation and Conflict Perspectives

The first sociological theories that tried to explain what happens after immigrants reach a new land described a process of assimilation wherein the new arrivals (and their descendants) would gradually become a part of the dominant group. Robert Park's work in the early twentieth century described a four-step assimilation process:

1. Contact (when the groups meet)

2. Conflict (they compete for goods and power)

3. Accommodation (one group establishes dominance)

4. Assimilation (the minority groups embrace the ways of the dominant group and become accepted into it) (Desmond and Emirbayer 2009)

While this describes the experience of some European immigrant groups, it does not apply to all racialized minority groups in the United States (e.g., Black Americans and American Indians). Although Irish, Italians, and other Europeans were eventually able to "become White" and assimilate into the dominant culture and structure of U.S. society, others were not (Ignatiev 1995).

W. E. B. Du Bois, a conflict theorist and contemporary of Park's, rejected Park's theory of assimilation, noting it did not explain the experience of African Americans. A prolific writer, activist, and sociologist, Du Bois spent much of his life proving, through sociological studies, that the key factor behind the relatively low socioeconomic level of Black Americans was the discrimination they faced. Like Marx, he looked at the economic basis for racial hierarchies. In doing so, he described how capitalism produces a dominant group exploiting minority groups for private profit. Assimilation is not possible when the dominant institution sets groups against one another. Instead, the only solution to such group conflict and exploitation is to overthrow the oppressive system, replacing it with one establishing public ownership of all resources and capital (Du Bois 1948, 1961).

Other conflict theorists describe the experience of American Indians, African Americans, and Hispanic Americans as **internal colonialism,** resulting from one ethnic or racial group (White Americans) subordinating and exploiting the resources of other racial and ethnic groups (Blauner 1972). As European powers established colonial empires across the world, taking the land and exploiting the labor of the local peoples, in the United States, both government and business leaders worked to take the land of Mexicans and American Indians and the labor of African Americans. These leaders worked in tandem to create a capitalist society with a White-dominated racial hierarchy by moving American Indians off their land, enslaving Africans, and annexing much of Mexico after the Mexican War.

Check Your Understanding

- How can you show that racial discrimination is evident through the founding documents of our nation and legislation and immigration policies throughout our history?

- Why do people immigrate?

- According to sociologists using Park's assimilation theory, what happens once two racial groups confront one another?

- Why did W. E. B. Du Bois disagree with Park's assimilation theory?

- According to conflict theorists, how is the historical experience of American Indians, African Americans, and Hispanic Americans an example of internal colonialism?

Racial and Ethnic Inequality Today

We can see the impact of historical and present-day racism in the United States by looking at how different racial groups are currently situated in some of the major social institutions in the United States— housing, the economy, education, the criminal justice system, health care, and government. While much progress has been made in race and ethnic relations in the United States, racial and ethnic inequality persists.

Housing

Have you ever tried to find an apartment to rent or a house to buy? Your experience may well depend on your race. Prior to passage of the Fair Housing Act of 1968, the reality of housing discrimination was much worse—and far more blatant. The Fair Housing Act prohibited discrimination by landlords, property owners, and financial institutions on the basis of race and national origin (except "owner-occupied buildings with no more than four units, single family housing sold or rented without the use of a broker, and housing operated by organizations and private clubs that limit occupancy to members") (FindLaw .com 2016, paragraph 3). Before 1968, racial discrimination in housing was commonplace—and backed by the federal government. In fact, the government used maps displaying "perceived investment risk," with affluent, White neighborhoods in green and Black neighborhoods in red, to determine what mortgages it would insure (or not). This "redlining," among other forms of housing discrimination, prevented Black people from benefiting, as White people did, from the explosion in home ownership after World War II (Swarns 2015). As you saw in Chapter 7, low historical rates of homeownership among Blacks are one of the drivers of wealth inequality. Furthermore, unofficial redlining practices persist today, even though they are now prohibited by law.

Today, while not explicitly refusing to give loans to racial minorities, many banks simply do not offer services in areas with high percentages of minorities— resulting in relatively few home loans for people of color. Banks have also driven Black and Latino applicants to mortgages with higher rates. For example, in 2017, the city of Philadelphia sued Wells Fargo, accusing it of discriminating against Black and Hispanic people seeking home mortgages. The suit says that African Americans were twice as likely and Hispanics 1.7 times as likely as *equally qualified* Whites to be offered only high-cost mortgage loans. This is part of

FIGURE 9.3

Average Yearly Income by Race and Ethnicity, 2013

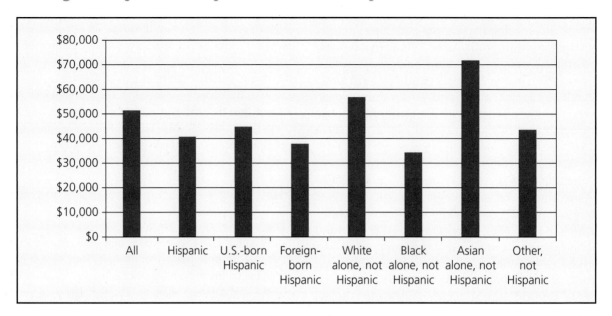

Source: http://www.pewhispanic.org/2016/04/19/statistical-portrait-of-hispanics-in-the-united-states/ph_2015-03_statistical-portrait-of-hispanics-in-the-united-states-2013_current-31/.

a pattern. In 2012, Wells Fargo paid $175 million to settle a lawsuit brought by the Department of Justice that claimed the bank offered loans to Blacks and Latinos at higher interest rates than the loans they gave to White applicants with similar qualifications. So, if Black and Latino home buyers are able to secure loans at all, they tend to have to pay more for them than similar White applicants (Marte 2017; Swarns 2015).

The Department of Housing and Urban Development, which is responsible for enforcing the Fair Housing Act, reports that housing discrimination by landlords and housing owners also persists. Paired testers, consisting of two equally qualified buyers/renters, one White and the other a person of color, revealed patterns of racial discrimination in twenty-eight different municipalities across the United States. When renting, Blacks, Hispanics, and Asians were respectively informed by real estate agents about 11.4, 12.5, and 9.8 percent fewer units than prospective White renters. When buying, Hispanics were told about an approximately equal number of homes for sale, but Blacks and Asians were, respectively, told about 17 and 15.5 percent fewer homes than White prospective buyers. They were also offered less help with financing and asked more questions about their income and wealth (U.S. Department of Housing and Urban Development 2013). Home ownership is one of the primary means of attaining wealth in the United States, and racial and ethnic minorities consequently lag far behind White Americans in household wealth.

The Economy

The differences found in wealth attainment by race and ethnicity in the United States are large—and larger than most people surmise. As described in Chapter 9, White Americans hold, respectively, ten and thirteen times the wealth of Hispanic and Black Americans. We described how racial discrimination in both the past and present influences people's abilities to obtain a home (and the wealth equity that comes with it). Income also plays a role in home ownership, as one must have an income to purchase a home. As Figure 9.3 indicates, income varies according to race and ethnicity.

Except for the very wealthy, income usually comes in the form of a job. The unemployment rate varies considerably by race and ethnicity. For instance, in the second quarter of 2017, the unemployment rate was 3.7 percent for Whites, 4.7 percent for Hispanics, and a notably higher rate at 7.3 percent for Blacks (Bureau of Labor Statistics 2017). Moreover, as Figure 9.4 shows, this gap has been consistent since the Bureau of Labor Statistics began to collect such data in 1954 (Desilver 2013).

We know these differences in employment relate to both past and *current* practices of racial discrimination. For example, in research using paired testers, similar to the one described above conducted by HUD, Whites were more likely to receive job interviews than either Blacks or Hispanics. In fact, White

FIGURE 9.4

Unemployment Rates by Race, 1954–2013

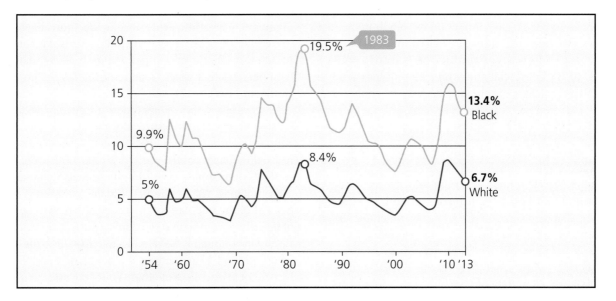

Source: Drew Desilver, "Black Unemployment Rate Is Consistently Twice That of Whites," Pew Research Center, August 21, 2013, http://www.pewresearch.org/fact-tank/2013/08/21/through-good-times-and-bad-black-unemployment-is-consistently-double-that-of-whites/.

Note: Seasonally adjusted. "Black and other," 1954 to 1971; "Black or African American" thereafter. 2013 average is January to July.

FIGURE 9.5

Education Completion Rates by Race and Ethnicity, 2014–2015

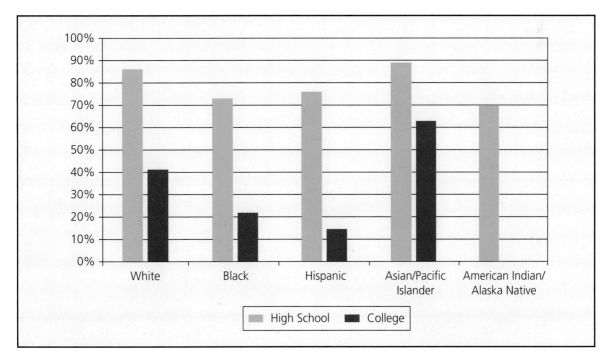

Sources: High school data from National Center for Education Statistics (2017); college data from Krogstad (2016).

Note: Whites, Blacks, and Asians include only non-Hispanics. Hispanics are of any race. College graduation rates for American Indian/Alaska Native not available.

applicants with a criminal record were more likely to receive an interview than Black applicants without criminal records (Pager, Western, and Sugie 2009). You can see a layperson's experiment with this type of employment discrimination by watching the José vs. Joe video that has been viewed millions of times (https://www.youtube.com/watch?v=PR7S G2C7IVU). Racial and ethnic stereotypes tend to hurt applicants of color and help White applicants.

Education

Good jobs also usually require at least a college education. Educational experiences tend to vary widely along racial, ethnic, and class lines. These different school experiences (which you will learn more about in Chapter 11) play a role in racial and ethnic differences in high school and college graduation rates (as seen in Figure 9.5). Racial differences can even be seen as early as preschool. For example, Black children make up 18 percent of preschoolers but 50 percent of suspended preschoolers. Among all age groups, Black students are three times as likely as White students to be suspended. American Indians make up 1 percent of the public school population but 2 percent of those suspended. Harsh punishments, like suspensions and expulsions, are given to students of colors more often than White students, even when students commit the same rule-breaking actions (NPR 2014).

Criminal Justice System

Racial disparities are also evident in the criminal justice system—from arrests to sentencing and even selections of jury pools. Blacks are more likely to be imprisoned on drug convictions than Whites, even though Whites are as likely to use and sell drugs (National Research Council 2014; Rothwell 2014). Figures 9.6 illustrates that Blacks are more likely to receive plea deals that include imprisonment. In addition, Blacks are 20 percent more likely than members of other races to be removed from a jury (Kahn and Kirk 2015).

A recent *New York Times* report uncovered "wide racial differences in measure after measure of police conduct" (LaFraniere and Lehren 2015). These race-based differences contribute to disproportionate percentages of prisoners of color in the United States, as seen in Figure 9.7. While Black males represent 13 percent of the population, they comprise 37 percent of the prisoners in state and federal prisons. The trend is similar, although less dramatic, for Hispanic males, who represent 17 percent of the population and 22 percent of prisoners. Note that Whites are underrepresented in the prison population, making up 32 percent of prisoners but 62 percent of the population. A prison sentence has life-changing implications, with the formerly incarcerated facing discrimination in employment and housing and, in some states, denial of the right to vote (Flake 2015; Domonoske 2016; National Conference of State Legislatures 2016).

The results of this discrimination in the criminal justice system lead to disproportionate numbers of Black families with absent and unemployed parents. Even after serving sentences, people with criminal records face further punishment, particularly in employment. People, particularly people of color,

FIGURE 9.6

Plea Offer Types for Felonies

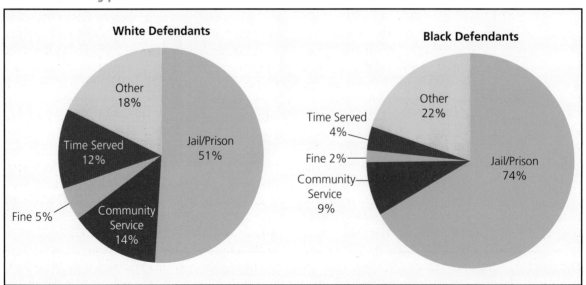

Source: Adapted with data from Besiki Luka Kutateladze and Nancy R. Andiloro. January 31, 2014. Prosecution and Racial Justice in New York County.

FIGURE 9.7

Male Population in State and Federal Prison by Race and Ethnicity, 2014

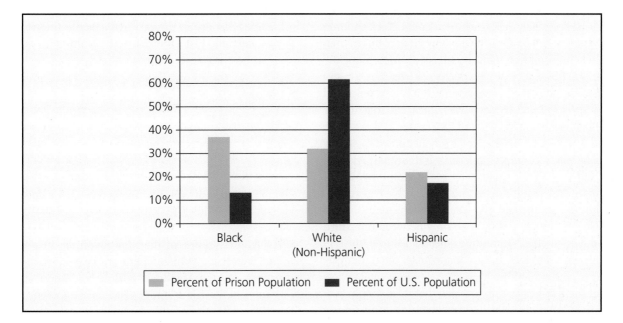

Sources: Bureau of Justice Statistics, http://www.bjs.gov/content/pub/pdf/p14.pdf; U.S. Census Bureau, https://www.census.gov/content/dam/Census/library/publications/2015/demo/p25-1143.pdf.

with prison records tend to have a much harder time finding jobs than those who have not been convicted of a crime (National Research Council 2014). Approximately 60 percent of formerly incarcerated people are still without a job a year after leaving prison. In a recent survey of former prisoners, 76 percent said that trying to find a job was "very difficult or nearly impossible" (deVuono-Powell et al. 2015).

Health Care

Based on what you just read, you may not be surprised that a recent study of White, Hispanic, Black, and Asian American adolescents that asked them how certain they were to live to at least age thirty-five revealed startling ethnic and racial differences. White adolescents were most likely to believe they would live until thirty-five. Those from racial, ethnic, and immigrant minority groups were less likely to believe they would reach that age (with the exception of Cuban Americans, who had rates similar to White adolescents). Foreign-born Mexican adolescents were the least likely to believe they would live until thirty-five. The lead author explains, "Whites are not subject to the racism and discrimination, at institutional and individual levels, experienced by immigrants and U.S.-born racial and ethnic minorities that undermine

health, well-being, and real and/or perceived life chances. . . . Such experiences—including fear of victimization and/or deportation—can be a source of chronic stress for racial and ethnic minorities, as well as immigrants, that further undermines well-being, even among youth" (Warner, as quoted in ScienceDaily 2015, paragraph 1).

Racial minority groups also face discrimination in health care. White patients tend to receive better care than patients of color (Pearson 2015). They are also less likely to receive a misdiagnosis of a severe mental illnesses. Even when they have the same symptoms, Hispanics are three times as likely and African Americans are four times as likely as Whites to be diagnosed with schizophrenia (Schwartz and Blankenship 2014). This follows a pattern in which mental health clinicians are more likely to diagnose African Americans than Whites with severe disruptive disorders. Being misdiagnosed with a severe mental illness, like schizophrenia, can adversely disrupt people's lives, preventing them from receiving proper treatment and, perhaps, even leading to unnecessary hospitalization and confinement (Feisthamel and Schwartz 2009). In addition, despite the success of the Affordable Care Act (also known as Obamacare) in decreasing the percentage of Americans without health insurance, Whites and Asians are more likely to have health insurance coverage than Black and Hispanics (National Center for Health Statistics 2015).

Whites are also more likely than Blacks to receive treatment for pain by doctors—in and out of emergency rooms (Singhal, Tien, and Hsia 2016). Even among children in the hospital for appendicitis, this disparity in pain relief treatment holds. Black children receive opioid pain relievers only 20 percent as often as White children (Goyal et al. 2015). Also, while the gap in life expectancy has decreased over the past several decades, the life expectancy for White males and females (76.5 and 81.2) is still higher than that of their Black counterparts (72 and 78.1).

In 1978, the federal government agreed to supply federally recognized American Indians and Alaskan Natives with free health care. Today, almost two out of three American Indians and Alaskan Natives receive health care through the federal government's Indian Health Service (IHS). With only between one-third and one-half of the funding it needs, however, the IHS provides services that are inadequate, often "dangerous," and sometimes "deadly." A congressional review of the IHS health care revealed that it "is simply horrifying and completely unacceptable," according to Senator John Barrasso (R-Wy.), chair of the Senate Committee on Indian Affairs (Dovey 2016, para. 1 and 3). One deadly example comes from the treatment of Debra Free, who died in 2011 while in a Winnebago hospital in Nebraska. She was overmedicated and then left unattended by improperly trained staff. She died of a heart attack, on the floor, after falling out of her bed. American Indians and Alaskan Natives can expect to live 4.4 years less than the average life expectancy of all other races combined (73.7 years compared to 78.1 years) (Indian Health Service 2016).

Government

You may be asking yourself, at this point, "Why hasn't our government done more to address racial and ethnic inequality?" One way of answering this question is to look at the racial and ethnic makeup of the U.S. government. Just as we saw in Chapter 8 that conditions for women employees improve when women are in high levels of management, our government tends to do more for racial minorities when there are more racial minority legislators in office. For example, increases in minority representation in state legislatures tend to lead to greater funding for districts with high minority enrollments. Other research indicates that Black and Hispanic legislators are more likely than White legislators to advocate for policies supported by many Blacks and Hispanics (Ueda 2008; Griffin 2014).

As Figure 9.8 reveals, the U.S. electorate is more diverse that ever.

Relatively few people of color are elected to political office, however. Reasons include

- racial gerrymandering—creating district lines that group the vast majority of minority voters into just a few districts, resulting in few minorities elected to office;

- a lack of the time and money needed to run for office, which restricts access to such endeavors to wealthier people (who tend to be White);

- the self-perpetuating lack of access to power and money that comes from not having ties to people already in political office; and

- low rates of voting among Hispanics and Asians (Wiltz 2015; Krogstad and Lopez 2017).

Today, forty-seven of the fifty governors in the United States are White. There are two Hispanic governors (Susana Martinez, NM; Brian Sandoval, NV) and one Pacific Islander (Hawaiian) governor (David Ige, HI). None is Black. As Figure 9.9 shows, the U.S. Congress is also disproportionately Whites. Figure 9.10 reveals the relatively low voting rate among Hispanic and Asian citizens.

FIGURE 9.8

Eligible Voters by Race and Ethnicity, 2016

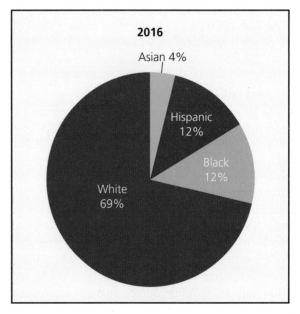

Source: Data from Krogstad (2016). http://www.pewresearch.org/fact-tank/2016/02/03/2016-electorate-will-be-the-most-diverse-in-u-s-history.

Note: Eligible voters are U.S. citizens ages 18 and older. White, Black, and Asian include only non-Hispanics. Hispanics are of any race. American Indians, Native Hawaiian/Pacific Islanders, and multirace Americans not shown.

FIGURE 9.9

Whites in Congress versus Overall U.S. Population

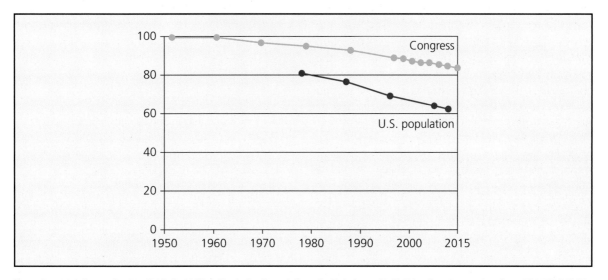

Source: From 115 Congress Sets New High for Racial, Ethnic Diversity, Pew Research Center Fact Tank, January 24, 2017, http://www.pewresearch.org/fact-tank/2017/01/24/115th-congress-sets-new-high-for-racial-ethnic-diversity/ft_17-01-20_minoritiesincongress_line-2/.

Note: Nonvoting delegates or commissioners excluded. Makeup of Congress reflects composition on session's first day. For 1980, 1990 population figures, Whites include only non-Hispanics. For 2000 and later, Whites include only non-Hispanics who reported a single race.

FIGURE 9.10

Voting Rates among U.S. Citizens by Race and Ethnicity

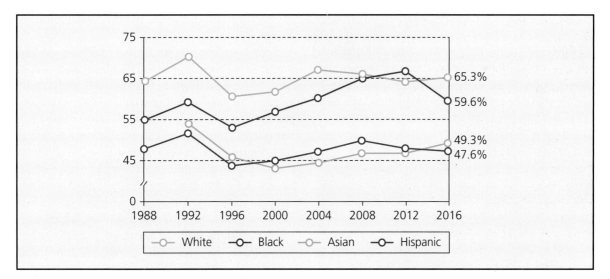

Source: From Black Voter Turnout Fell in 2016, Even as a Record Number of Americans Cast Ballots, Pew Research Center, May 11, 2017, http://www.pewresearch.org/fact-tank/2017/05/12/black-voter-turnout-fell-in-2016-even-as-a-record-number-of-americans-cast-ballots/ft_17-05-10_voter-turnout/.

Note: Eligible voters are U.S. citizens ages 18 and older. Whites, Blacks, and Asians include only non-Hispanics. Hispanics are of any race. Data for non-Hispanic Asians were not available in 1988.

Of course, justice for racial and ethnic minority groups need not require equitable representation across racial and ethnic groups in Congress. For example, there were no Black senators and only six Black representatives in Congress when that body passed—and a White president signed—the Voting Rights Act of 1965. As you will learn in Chapter 14, social movements can work outside institutions to create social change. Massive pressure from the civil rights movement and international politics effectively pushed White leaders to pass laws to address racial discrimination.

How Diverse Is Your State Legislature?

In this activity, you will compare the demographics of your state legislature with the state's population.

Across the country, minority groups are underrepresented in elected office. The Pew Charitable Trusts has created a tool to compare the racial and ethnic makeup of each state's legislature to the state's overall population. Go to "Legislative Boundaries, Lack of Connections Lead to Few Minority Lawmakers" at http://www.pewtrusts.org/en/research-and-analysis/blogs/stateline/2015/12/09/legislative-boundaries-lack-of-connections-lead-to-few-minority-lawmakers and complete the following exercise:

1. Find the map tool on the website and click on your state.
2. Compare the demographics of the state's population and its legislature.

3. Find the contact information for your elected officials at http://act.commoncause.org/site/PageServer?pagename=sunlight_advocacy_list_page.

4. Email your state legislator and ask him or her to explain how your legislature creates legislative districts and the discrepancy between the demographic makeup of so many state legislatures and their state populations (specify your own, if you notice a discrepancy in your own state).

5. In a one- to two-page paper, explain how the information you gathered from your state legislator relates to what you learned in this chapter. Be sure to use and cite your text.

The civil rights movement was only necessary, however, because there were so few representatives of oppressed groups within the institutions that create and oversee the implementation of laws in the United States. These leaders had to made aware both of the injustice of racial discrimination and the cost of perpetuating that injustice. As the great abolitionist Frederick Douglass (1857) said, "Power concedes nothing without a demand."

Consider This

How aware were you of the extent of racial and ethnic inequality before reading this chapter? Why? What happens when a majority of people in a nation are unaware of the inequality that exists within it?

The Asian Exception?

As we have seen, as a group, Asian Americans tend to have lower unemployment rates and higher levels of education and income than other racial minority groups. Why?

Let's compare the situation of Hispanic and Asian Americans. Both Hispanic and Asian American populations in the United States include people who have been in the United States for many generations, alongside first- and second-generation immigrant families. Both also contain many different subgroups with very different socioeconomic statuses. For example, third-generation Cuban Americans and first-generation Mexican Americans both fall under the Hispanic umbrella, but the former group includes more high salaried, highly educated, and light-skinned members than the latter. This means that their socioeconomic status and experiences with racial and ethnic inequality differ markedly.

Likewise, the experience of Asian subgroups also varies widely. The majority of Asians who immigrated to the United States over the past few decades brought with them high levels of education and entered the United States legally to find greater economic opportunities than exist in their nations of origin. However, some Southeast Asian immigrants (such as war refugees from Vietnam, Cambodia, and Laos) came to the United States with little money or education. Today, other vulnerable Asians (such as young women from

This picture shows Syrian refugees trying to cross the border into Greece on March 14, 2016. Three refugees had drowned while trying to cross that morning, but more kept trying, fearing the danger behind them more than the river or the ethnocentrism they might face in a new society.

REUTERS/Stoyan Nenov

poor areas) are smuggled into the United States to work as indentured servants.

Despite these variations across subgroups, Asian immigrants to the United States, as a whole, tend to have more education than Hispanics. Among foreign-born workers in 2012, 43.6 percent of Hispanics had less than a high school diploma and only 12.6 percent had a college degree. On the other hand, 58.1 percent of Asian foreign-born workers were college graduates.

Indeed, Asian Americans, as an umbrella group, regularly outperform all other racial groups in terms of educational success. A recent study shows that Asian American students from families who immigrated to the United States within one or two generations (the differences decline after families have been in the United States for three generations) have more pressure from their parents to do well and are more likely to believe that academic abilities can grow with hard work than White students (Hsin and Xie 2014). Refuting the stereotype that all Asians are gifted academically, this study indicates that cultural factors, like parental pressure and the belief that hard work leads to success, help explain the relatively high levels of education of Asian Americans (Hsin and Xie 2014).

One result of the disparity in education levels of the various immigrant groups is the difference in the positions they achieve in the U.S. workforce and in their subsequent socioeconomic status. Obtaining a college degree tends to lead to greater income, and foreign-born Asian workers make almost double what Hispanic foreign-born workers earn per week (Bureau of Labor Statistics 2017). Even highly educated Asians in high salaried professional positions face discrimination, however. Many experience a glass ceiling that prevents them from advancing into management and CEO positions. For example, "while Asians are well-represented—even overrepresented—at the staff and professional levels, they are underrepresented in the management pipeline and barely seen at the executive levels" in Silicon Valley companies (Poyhonen 2015, paragraph 8). In Silicon Valley, White men and women

are, respectively, 149 percent and 260 percent more likely than Asian men and women to be executives (Poyhonen 2015).

Check Your Understanding

- How can you show that racial and ethnic inequality exists in housing, the economy, and education institutions in the United States today?

- How can you show that racial and ethnic inequality exists in the criminal justice system and health care?

- How does the demographic makeup of elected officials reflect and help perpetuate racial and ethnic inequality in the United States?

- What are some reasons Asian Americans, as an umbrella racial group, have higher incomes than Hispanic Americans?

Racism and Ethnocentrism Globally

Far from being a problem only in the United States, racism and ethnocentrism exist around the world. **Ethnocentrism** refers to the belief that one's own culture is superior to others. Europe's reaction to refugees from Syria provides a powerful example. Syria is a diverse nation, but most Syrians are ethnically Arab and Sunni Muslims. As of July 2016, approximately 5 million Syrians had fled the war-torn nation as refugees. The United States, during the Obama administration, agreed to take in just 110,000 Syrian refugees—but even that small number was met with a strong political backlash, and President Trump has called for a ban on all Syrian refugees from entering the United States (Bradner and Barrett 2015; Valverde 2017). Most of these refugees are now in countries near Syria (Lebanon, Jordan, Turkey, Egypt, and Iraq), but over a million have sought asylum status in Europe.

A backlash against the influx of refugees led some European nations to close their borders for the first time since agreeing in 1985 to allow people in the European Union (EU) to travel freely within union states (Syrianrefugees.eu 2016; Davis 2016). In June 2016, Britain voted to leave the EU, a referendum that was largely seen as a vote against the relatively open EU immigration policies (Zucchino 2016). Far-right, anti-immigrant parties have gained a greater share of the electorate in increasing numbers of European nations. A 2016 poll by the Pew Research Center found that more than 60 percent of people in Hungary, Italy, Poland, and Greece and at least 25 percent in every other EU country say that they have unfavorable opinions about Muslims in their nation. This negative reaction aimed at Muslim immigrants tends to arise from a form of ethnic prejudice that associates all Muslims with terrorism, particularly after recent ISIS-led terrorist attacks in Europe. It also stems from resentment at the governmental assistance refugees receive (during a period of high unemployment throughout the EU) and a belief that Muslim immigrants refuse to adapt to the dominant culture of their adopted nations (Wike, Stokes, and Simmons 2016; Zucchino 2016).

For people in many European nations, the recent influx of immigrants is their first experience of cultural diversity. For example, the native-born population in Denmark dropped from 97 percent in 1980 to 88 percent today. The reactions to these demographic changes include a dramatic reduction in assistance for immigrants, a sharp rise in hate speech against Muslim immigrants, and rising support for far-right, anti-immigrant political parties. As of 2016, the anti-immigrant Danish People's Party held the second highest number of seats in Parliament (Zucchino 2016). In nations across Europe, most people do not see diversity as a net positive experience for their society (Wike et al. 2016).

Animosity to racial and ethnic diversity exists far beyond Europe. A recent study analyzed data from sixty-one nations (including the United States) using respondents' answers to the following two questions:

TABLE 9.1

Racism around the World

	Country	Percent Who Don't Want Neighbors of Another Race	Percent Who Witnessed Racist Behavior
1	India	43.6	64.3
2	Lebanon	36.3	64.4
3	Bahrain	31.1	85.7
4	Libya	54.0	33.5
5	Egypt	NA	39.7
6	Philippines	30.6	49.1
7	Kuwait	28.1	37.9
8	Palestine	44.0	32.0
9	South Africa	19.6	61.8
10	South Korea	29.6	36.5
11	Malaysia	31.3	34.4
12	Nigeria	21.0	42.5
13	Iraq	27.7	37.8
14	Kyrgyzstan	28.1	35.9
15	Ecuador	34.5	32.0
16	Algeria	19.8	41.0
17	Pakistan	14.5	48.8
18	Yemen	34.0	31.2
19	Hong Kong	18.8	40.4
20	Russia	17.0	38.5
21	Thailand	39.8	19.0
22	Cyprus	26.7	26.1
23	Turkey	33.8	19.1
24	Morocco	13.8	35.6
25	Japan	22.3	29.7

Source: http://businesstech.co.za/news/lifestyle/116644/the-most-racist-countries. Reprinted with permission from BusinessTech.

Note: NA = not available.

Many of the largest corporations in the United States support affirmative action programs in higher education, knowing that a diverse workforce is necessary in an increasingly multiracial and ethnic United States and in the global marketplace.

Mark Wilson/Getty Images News/Getty Images

(1) whether they would like having people from another race as neighbors and (2) how frequently racist behavior occurs in their neighborhood. Table 9.1 shows the twenty-five nations that scored highest in this measure of racism (based on their average ranking after combining their rankings for each variable).

The Dangers of External Inequality and the Benefits of Diversity

Racial and ethnic discrimination has negative consequences for all members of a society. As discussed in earlier chapters, functionalists point out the interdependence of various parts of society. Durkheim stressed that individuals need to be socialized to work for the benefit of society rather than just their own individual interests. For society to function at its most effective, people must be allowed to do what they do best for the good of society. If, for example, one group of people are forced to work only as menial laborers, despite the fact that some of them might be valuable to society as engineers or teachers, this can harm *all* of society. What if one of those menial laborers could have found a cure for cancer, if given the opportunity to gain the education and lab experience needed to do so?

Durkheim (1997 [1892]) divided social inequalities into *internal* (based on people's natural abilities) and *external* (those forced upon people). He argued that the existence of *external inequality* in an industrial society indicates that its institutions are not functioning properly. Because an industrial society needs all its members doing what they do best to function most effectively, external inequality—like racial discrimination—that prevents some people from using their innate talents damages all of society.

The same reasoning holds true for postindustrial societies. That is one reason many business leaders support affirmative action programs in higher education. Writing to the Supreme Court in support of such programs, more than sixty *Fortune* 500 member companies pointed out that

the individuals who run and staff [our] corporations must be able to understand, learn from, collaborate with, and design products and services for clientele and associates from diverse racial, ethnic, and cultural backgrounds. American multinational corporations . . . are especially attuned to this concern because they serve not only the increasingly diverse population of the United States, but racially and ethnically diverse populations around the world. (Botsford et al. 2000, paragraph 14)

Reducing racial and ethnic inequality and promoting diversity efforts is not only the just thing to do—it also makes good business sense.

Check Your Understanding

- What are some of the causes of the animosity of many Europeans (and Americans) toward Muslim refugees?

- Explain the difference between external and internal inequality, as described by Durkheim.

- How is racial discrimination an example of external inequality? Why is it harmful for society?

- Why do many business leaders support affirmative action programs on college campuses?

Race Relations as Seen on Television

In this exercise, you will watch a clip of the show Black-ish *and answer questions about its perspective on race relations.*

Black-ish, a hit television show on ABC, has projected race-related issues into living rooms across America. Watch this brief clip from a 2016 episode at https://sojo .net/articles/less-two-minutes-clip-blackish-explains-why-racism-america-isn-t-over (from the Sojourners article "In Less Than Two Minutes, This Clip From 'Black-ish' Explains Why Racism in America Isn't Over") and answer the following questions:

1. What issues discussed in this chapter does this clip raise?

2. Is the male character's perspective on race relations today positive or negative? Why?

3. Do you agree with his perspective? Why?

4. How do your own racial background and racial experiences influence your answer to question 3?

5. Do you agree with the title given to the clip by the authors of the article in which it is embedded that "everyone should see" this clip? Why or why not?

Responding (or Not) to Racism and Ethnocentrism Today

As you will learn in more detail in Chapter 14, social movements that achieve their goals tend to face a backlash as those who lost power because of the success of the movement try to gain it back. This can be seen in reactions to the women's movement, the gay and lesbian movement, and the civil rights movement. After the successes of the civil rights movement, many people began to argue that racial discrimination was no longer a problem. This "colorblind" way of thinking gained further traction after the election of President Barack Obama, our first president of Black descent (Sacks and Thiel 1996; Ford 2008; McWhorter 2008).

The Colorblind Ideology and Racism Evasiveness

Young adults today grew up and were socialized in an era when the colorblind perspective on racial issues had tremendous influence over how people in the United States talked about (or avoided) issues of race. People who follow the **colorblind ideology,** or way of viewing race, maintain that if we ignore race and racial issues, racism will not exist. In reality, however, the colorblind ideology has worked to support,

rather than reduce, racial inequality. Eduardo Bonilla-Silva describes four themes, or frames, of the colorblind perspective on race. He argues that each is used to justify or support the racial hierarchy in the United States today.

- *Abstract liberalism:* agreeing that everyone should have equal rights but opposing policies that will help achieve equality

- *Minimization:* believing that race does not matter anymore and that racism is no longer a problem

- *Naturalization:* maintaining that racist practices like segregation and opposition to interracial marriage are simply natural and part of human nature rather than based on racism

- *Culturalization:* arguing that it is their inferior culture that has hurt Black people rather than racism

Today, it is clear that the widespread use of the minimization frame has led to major changes in racial interactions in the United States. Since the *Loving v. Virginia* Supreme Court decision in 1967 that struck down state laws banning interracial marriage, such unions have become increasingly common. Among couples married in 2010, 9 percent of Whites, 17 percent of Blacks, 26 percent of Hispanics, and 28 percent of Asians married someone of a different race. Ten percent of babies born in 2013 had parents of different races (Pew Research Center 2015a), and this

The Black Lives Matter movement has helped publicize and challenge racial discrimination in the criminal justice system.

REUTERS/Eric Miller

group has a growth rate three times that the rest of the population (U.S. Census Bureau 2012; Frey 2014; Pew Research Center 2015a).

The spread of the minimization frame has also had negative consequences. In fact, it has diminished efforts to address, or even discuss, racial discrimination. Americans (including Americans of color, to some degree) raised in the colorblind era grew up with the pervasive message that they should avoid talking about racial issues. Even noting someone's race could result in a negative sanction—maybe even an accusation of being racist for doing so. Does this sound familiar to you?

Ironically, these colorblind ways of thinking led not to the decline of racism but to **racism evasiveness**—ignoring issues of racism. Not talking about race does not reduce racism in a society with an established racial hierarchy but lets it operate without a check. In reality, "what people are ultimately avoiding when they say they do not see color, when they overlook differences in power, or avoid 'race words' is racism" (Beeman 2015:131).

The Era of Black Lives Matter and the Presidential Election of 2016

Thanks to viral videos of police killing unarmed Black men and the Black Lives Matter movement that rose up to highlight and address these acts of racial injustice, the colorblind ideology has been challenged. It is much harder to minimize and evade racism when you can see it before your eyes in the form of a video. Thanks to social scientific research, we can show that these horrifying videos are but extreme examples of present-day racial discrimination. As former President Jimmy Carter describes it, the now widely known information about current discrimination against Black people has "reawakened" the country to the fact that racism still exists and must be addressed (Goodstein 2016, paragraph 8).

Meanwhile, as noted in Chapter 7, the presidential election of 2016 brought racial resentments to the forefront, as economic frustration among less educated White people led to a desire for radical change and a backlash against minority groups (racial and ethnic, as well as sex and gender minorities) seen as gaining more rights and greater acceptance in recent decades. President Trump ran for office promising to "make America great again" by deregulating big business, tearing up major trade agreements with other nations, banning Muslims from entering the United States, forcing Mexico to pay for a wall to stop the flow of "rapists" and "criminals" into the United States, and bringing more stop-and-frisk policies to urban minority neighborhoods (Ye Hee Lee 2015; Alcindor 2016; DelReal 2016). Racial and ethnic hate crimes spiked after the election as some people felt that it was suddenly acceptable to publicly vent their anger on minority group members (Levin 2017).

Teaching White Students about Racism

Meghan Burke

often encounter raised eyebrows when I tell people that I co-developed and direct a diversity program that is only for White students.

I was raised in a small town in Michigan, which at the time consisted mostly of White people, like my family. I never questioned why our community looked the way it did or why some families struggled more than others. If anything, I thought it was a simple matter of hard work and having the right values, like most of the people I knew. I was colorblind.

It was not until college that I learned how so much of our history, along with the many barriers or privileges that stifle or elevate us on otherwise arbitrary categories like race or gender, remains largely hidden from view. I had developed a sociological imagination and a passion for social justice, and I wanted to help others see what had been invisible to me for so long. This is why I became a professor, but I still wanted to do more.

I was in my first year working at my university when a colleague, Kira Banks, approached me with an idea that she had: many U.S. colleges and universities have preorientation (or, as we call them, Pre-O) programs for international students and students of color, so that they can assemble a support network and tools for survival on predominantly White campuses. But weren't we missing a key demographic? We realized that if we really want to shift the climate on predominantly White campuses like ours, we have to be intentional in our work with White students, so that they can develop the capacity to work for social and racial justice.

The "Pre-O" that Kira and I developed, and which I continue to direct, brings a voluntary group of about thirty White students onto campus early, creating an intentional space for these students to process hard questions about race and privilege. It's not a totally separate program. We do lots of fun activities and deep discussions with the other Pre-O programs, so that students can form friendships and support networks across the color and culture line. That's crucial. But we also do some caucus work on our own, diving deeply into the dynamics of racial inequality and White privilege—that stuff of the sociological imagination that I wasn't able to fully see until I started taking sociology courses.

And it works. Students who go through this program show decreased levels of colorblindness and a heightened awareness of, and ability to challenge, social and racial inequalities in both the short and long term. Efforts like this should always center on the voices and experiences of people of color. But, as a White person, I also think that part of my work is to reach out to other White folks, to help us see what too often remains hidden. After all, before we can confront systems of power, we must recognize them. Programs like ours allow White students to recognize a system of racial inequality—and to take steps to challenge it.

Megan Burke is an associate professor of sociology at Illinois Wesleyan University.

Ways to Address Racism and Ethnic Discrimination

The good news is that more Americans are now aware that racism is a problem, and the minimization frame of the colorblind perspective has begun to crumble. A *Washington Post*–ABS News poll taken in July 2016, after the widely publicized shootings of two Black men in Baton Rouge, Louisiana, and St. Paul, Minnesota, by police officers and of Dallas police officers by a man who said he was enraged by those killings, indicates that almost two out of three Americans (63 percent) now believe that race relations in the United States are generally bad. This is the highest rate recorded since the race riots in Los Angeles after the Rodney King verdict in 1992. The increase is "primarily driven by white Republicans and independents, some of whom long have been skeptical of seeing racial discrimination as a national problem" (Thompson and Clement 2016, paragraph 5). The racial discrimination outlined earlier did not just spring up during the season of the 2016 presidential election, but now more Americans—of all races—recognize its existence.

So, what can you do to address racial and ethnic discrimination? Here are some ways:

- Use your sociological eye to notice patterns of racial inequality around you and in the larger society—and hold the leaders in your community and the larger society accountable for addressing them.

- Make an effort to interact with people of races and ethnicities other than your own. Research shows that such interactions on a level playing field (e.g., among students on campus, coworkers of the same rank, campmates) can reduce racial and ethnic prejudice (Pettigrew and Tropp 2008).

- Call out racism and ethnocentrism when you see or hear it. **Microaggressions**, everyday slights aimed (intentionally or not) at racial and ethnic minority groups, can cause real damage. When you hear one, say something.

- Advocate for and participate in efforts on your campus to recognize systemic racial inequality—and to take steps to dismantle it.

Check Your Understanding

- What led to the creation of the colorblind perspective on race?

- How has the minimization frame contributed to the increase in interracial marriages?

- How does the minimization frame of the colorblind perspective led to racism evasiveness?

- How have the viral videos of police killing unarmed Black men and the Black Lives Matter movement affected the minimization frame of the colorblind perspective?

- What are some ways that you can address racial and ethnic discrimination?

Doing Sociology 9.4

A Refugee Integration Plan for Your Campus

In this activity, you will draft a plan, using the information you have learned about race and racism, to help a group of refugees newly arrived at your school.

Imagine your college or university has agreed to accept a number of refugees from another nation and asked you to design a program to help them adjust to campus life and to ensure that they will be accepted by and integrated into the campus population. You can assume that they all want to come and that their academic abilities match the typical student at your school.

Choose one of the following refugee groups:

- Fifty students from a college in Dublin, Ireland, that burned to the ground

- One hundred students from a Christian college in Nigeria closed after an attack by a terrorist group

- Twenty students from a Syrian college destroyed by the Syrian government

Now complete the exercise below, being sure to use information and terms (e.g., stereotypes, prejudice, discrimination, ethnocentrism) from your text in your answers:

1. In two to three pages, draft an outline of a plan.
2. How was your plan shaped by the refugees' nation of origin, race, religion, language, the number of refugees, and the demographic makeup of students at your school?
3. What challenges might you face in carrying out this plan? Why?
4. How would you overcome those challenges?
5. Which groups on campus would you turn to for help? Why?
6. What do you think are the chances your plan will be successful? Why?
7. Now, using your answers to the questions above, revise and improve your plan and describe what you think are your chances of success (and why).

Consider This

President Trump wants to ban all Syrian refugees from entering the United States for fear that some may be terrorists. Do you support the creation of such a ban? Why? How does this compare to what President Roosevelt did leading up to World War II? Do you think the results would be the same for Muslims as it was for Jews?

with more people able to fully contribute to them. It can also help individuals succeed in virtually any profession. For example, teachers and social workers need to understand the racial and ethnic-based perspectives and experiences of their students and clients. Medical professionals must understand how the social realities of their patients can affect their health. Business managers have to recruit and manage diverse workforces to succeed in an increasingly diverse marketplace. Those who hope to succeed in business or the nonprofit world must learn to work effectively with people from other racial and ethnic backgrounds.

Addressing racial and ethnic inequality also connects deeply with the core mission of sociology—to understand how society works and to use that knowledge to improve it. Increasing numbers of Americans now recognize that racial inequality exists. Now *you* know how sociological tools can help address it.

To fully address racial and ethnic inequality, we must reform our institutions, as well as our attitudes and behavior on the individual level. In the following chapters, you will learn more about some of the key social institutions in our society: the family, education, and religion. We will look first at the family.

Conclusion

Learning about race and ethnicity and addressing racism and ethnocentrism can benefit every member of society—and society as a whole. It can make society and the organizations within it stronger,

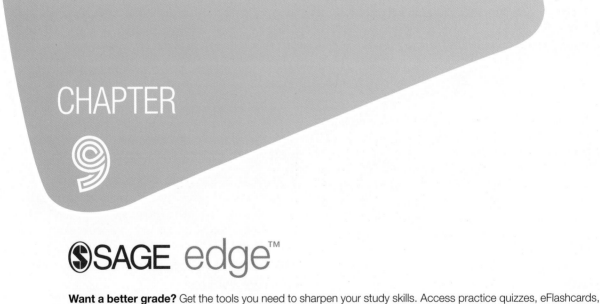

CHAPTER 9

$circledS$ SAGE edge™

Want a better grade? Get the tools you need to sharpen your study skills. Access practice quizzes, eFlashcards, video and multimedia at **edge.sagepub.com/korgen**

Review

9.1 What are race and ethnicity?

Once thought of as based on biological or genetic differences among humans, race is now widely recognized as a social construction that varies over time and from society to society. Today, sociologists define a race as a group of people *perceived* to be distinct on the basis of physical appearance (not genetic makeup). We tend to categorize people we meet into racial groups based on their skin tone and facial features (Black, American Indian or Alaskan Native, Asian or Pacific Islander, or White).

Members of a particular ethnic group share the same cultural heritage (e.g., language, nation of origin, and religion). There are various ethnic groups in the United States today, including African Americans, Jamaican Americans, Cuban Americans, Italian Americans, Irish Americans, and Chinese Americans.

9.2 What is the difference between prejudice and discrimination?

Prejudice is irrational feelings toward members of a particular group, while discrimination is unfair treatment of people based on their (perceived) group membership. Prejudice can stem from stereotypes, predetermined ideas of particular groups of people (e.g., all Irish are drunks, all Asians are good at math). Discrimination can occur with or without prejudice or intent.

9.3 How has racism influenced social policies throughout U.S. history?

The history of the United States is full of examples of blatant racial prejudice and discrimination at both the individual and institutional levels. Indeed, it can be found in the nation's founding documents as well as in legislation and court decisions throughout U.S. history (e.g., the Constitution, the Compromise of 1877, and *Plessy v. Ferguson*).

Racism also influenced immigration legislation throughout the history of the United States, with complete bans on Chinese and Japanese immigration and restrictions on migration from Southern and Eastern Europe. It was not until 1965, at the height of the civil rights movement and in the midst of worldwide pressure to address racial discrimination in the United States, that racist immigration quotas were finally eliminated.

9.4 How can you show that racism and ethnocentrism are key social issues in the United States—and across the world—today?

We can see the impact of historical and present-day racism in the United States by looking at how different racial groups are currently situated in some of the major social institutions in the United States—housing, the economy, education, the criminal justice system, health care, and government. While much progress has been made in race and ethnic relations in the United States, racial and ethnic inequality persists.

Far from being a problem only in the United States, racism and ethnocentrism exist around the world. Europe's reaction to predominantly Arab and Muslim refugees from Syria provides a powerful example. For people in many European nations, the recent influx of immigrants is their first experience of cultural diversity. In nations across Europe, most people do not see diversity as a net positive experience for their society (Wike, Stokes, and Simmons 2016).

9.5 How can you work to diminish racism and racial discrimination?

Use your sociological eye to notice patterns of racial inequality around you and in the larger society—and hold the leaders in your community and the larger society accountable for addressing them. Make an effort to interact with people of races and ethnicities other than your own. Become aware of the racial and ethnic stereotypes you have and learn to dismiss them (as such) as they arise. Call out racism and ethnocentrism when you see or hear it. Advocate for and participate in efforts on your campus to address racism and promote racial and ethnic diversity.

Key Terms

- Chinese Exclusion Acts of 1882 and 1892   184
- colorblind ideology   198
- discrimination   183
- ethnic group   179
- ethnocentrism   195
- Gentlemen's Agreement of 1907   184
- Hayes-Tilden Compromise of 1877   184
- Immigration Act of 1924   185
- Immigration Act of 1965   185

- institutional discrimination   183
- internal colonialism   187
- microaggressions   201
- prejudice   183
- race   179
- racism   183
- racism evasiveness   199
- stereotypes   183
- Three-Fifths Compromise   184

Families are perhaps the most cherished social institution in our society, but they vary more than most of us understand.

Learning Questions

10.1 What are families? In what ways are families the by-product of the social world?

10.2 How have families changed over time? What has caused these changes?

10.3 How do different theoretical perspectives help sociologists understand families?

10.4 Who does the caretaking?

10.5 What challenges do families face?

10.6 How do work and social policies influence family life?

CHAPTER 10

Understanding Institutions

Family

Carissa Froyum

What Shapes Families?

Imagine a time machine has allowed you to share a holiday dinner with your great-great-grandparents. The conversation turns to courtship and marriage. They tell you how they met and courted, how many children they had and when, what expectations they faced, what challenges threatened family life, and how they divided work, child-care, and caring for the household. Then, the conversation turns to you and your life, particularly your own dating, marital status, and fertility history. How are your experiences similar? How are they different? What economic, technological, and cultural changes have happened across those generations to shape your experiences? For example, how have cellphones shaped dating? How has birth control changed the timing of having children? How have immigration and urbanization influenced how many children people have and the role children play in families?

Consider This
How can a sociological, rather than an individualistic, perspective on families benefit you and society?

In their most basic form, a **family** is a group of people who take responsibility for meeting each other's needs. Whom we consider family, the basis for our bonds, and the needs families meet, however, change over time in response to the social environment. Do you think you define family in the same way your great-great-grandparents did? Biological connections, living together, economic responsibility for each other, and the law probably featured prominently in your great-great-grandparents' understanding of family. Their definition even may have emphasized **nuclear family:** parents and their children. Does yours?

You may consider close friends to be family, even though you are not legally tied to them, because they provide you support and are there for you when you need them. Your definition likely emphasizes emotional bonds and the desire to decide who your family is. And yet, if you

Carissa Froyum

Like many of the boys in my small town growing up, my two older brothers played football when they entered fifth grade. I had grown up watching football—the Vikings—alongside my dad and brothers, from whom I absorbed the intricacies of I-formations and cross-blocking. But as my brothers grew older and developed more in the game, the family devotion to football became more intense. My dad coached so we talked football nonstop and watched game-day tape. My mom knew all the plays and cheered so loudly I could pick out her voice on the videos my family reviewed every week. Football was always central to what it meant to be a "Froyum." When I entered fifth grade, I remember thinking, "Girls don't get to play football? Well, that's not fair! How can I be a Froyum without playing football?"

By the time I found sociology in college at Concordia College in Moorhead, Minnesota, issues of fairness, justice, and belonging occupied many of my thoughts. I wanted to know why the world was the way it was, and couldn't we make it better for those left behind? Sociology was an entrée to grappling with those questions.

In 1996, President Bill Clinton signed DOMA, the Defense of Marriage Act, which defined marriages as between one man and one woman and allowed states not to recognize same-sex marriages. The Supreme Court ruling *Obergefell v. Hodges* overturned DOMA in 2015.

AP Photo/J. Scott Applewhite

are not legally connected to them, your chosen family members cannot make medical decisions for you. They have no legal economic responsibility for you (or you for them). They cannot declare you as a dependent on taxes, you do not report their income when applying for financial aid for college, and you cannot sue them for support. Policy makers and government agencies still hold onto a definition of family that may better resemble families of generations past than your own. According to the U.S. Census, "a family consists of a householder and one or more other people living in the same household who are related to the householder by birth, marriage or adoption" (Pemberton 2015).

Socially Constructing Families

As society changes, so do our families and our understanding of what makes a family. A social construction approach suggests we think of family as a verb—we *do* or *accomplish family* in interaction with each other. Our socially constructed definitions and the needs families meet in society are **institutionalized**, or encoded in laws, policies, and widely accepted practices that organize our family life. These laws, policies, and practices can change over time, as seen in the legal and popular support for same-sex marriage over the past decade.

Our sociological imaginations push us to consider who most influences and benefits from specific ways of doing family. In 1996, for example, President Clinton signed the Defense of Marriage Act (DOMA). DOMA defined marriage as between one man and one woman, and it allowed states not to recognize same-sex marriages granted by each other. Despite the desire of some same-sex couples to marry, the social legitimacy and benefits afforded to family—visiting each other in the hospital, inheriting property after death, and others—were restricted to heterosexual couples.

As described in Chapter 8, in 2015 the definition of marriage expanded, conferring the benefits of official recognition to families headed by same-sex partners. In the landmark case *Obergefell v. Hodges,* the Supreme Court ruled states must issue marriage licenses to same-sex couples and recognize same-sex marriages from other states. The shift to gender-neutral marriage is the most recent in a long line of legal and moral contests over who should and should not be considered family. In 1967, *Loving v. Virginia* overturned bans on interracial marriages, while 1987's *Turner v. Safley* upheld the right for inmates to marry. These changes help show us that marriage is a social construct that changes over time and place.

Consider This

How would you convince someone who has never taken a sociology class that families are socially constructed? Would it be hard or difficult? Why?

Check Your Understanding

- What shapes families?

- In their most basic form, what are families?

- What is a nuclear family?

- How can you show that family is a social construction?

The Changing Family across History

We can use our sociological imaginations to understand the origins of family and how and why families have changed across time. Looking across history, it is possible to see how changes in the political and economic institutions of societies influenced the construction and purpose of families.

Early Families

According to Stephanie Coontz's *Marriage, A History* (Coontz 2005:40), families and family life changed as human societies changed. In the earliest years of human life, hunting and gathering groups developed marriage and kinship systems as a way to forge bonds and encourage cooperation with each other. "Bands needed to establish friendly relations with others so they could travel more freely and safely in pursuit of game, fish, plants, and water holes or move as the seasons changed" (40). Marriage expanded the group's social network into a group of "in laws," which facilitated goodwill and access to resources.

With the development of settled agriculture about 12,000 years ago, and later as European cultural influences spread, groups became more concerned about owning land, controlling surplus goods, and maintaining their social status. Accordingly, marriage and lineage systems became increasingly strategic, exclusive, and political (Coontz 2005). Marrying the right person from the right background allowed you to attain or secure wealth and social standing.

Preindustrial U.S. Families

During the sixteenth and seventeenth centuries, "North American native societies used family ties to organize nearly all their political, military, and economic transactions" (Coontz 2010:33).

Doing Sociology 10.1

What Is a Family?

*I*n this activity, you will consider what constitutes a family and draw a representative picture.

What makes someone family? What differentiates "family" from "friend"?

1. Provide a definition of a family.

2. Draw a picture or a diagram that illustrates your definition.

Putting Inclusive Definitions of Family into Action

In this exercise, you will examine some of the ways traditional families are still considered typical, to the exclusion of other varieties.

Pretend for a moment that your university or college has a new diversity officer who is responsible for making the school more welcoming and inclusive for all people. One of the officer's first actions is to assemble a task force to examine how inclusive the university is for students with all types of families. You are serving as a student member of the committee. The task force has two charges: (1) to uncover any areas of college life that assume students come from, or are currently part of, a traditional middle-class, nuclear family and (2) to suggest specific changes that will make the school more inclusive of all family types.

The task force must present a report to the diversity officer outlining its findings in relation to the two charges above. As a key member of the task force, your job is to write about one problem and one change in the report.

1. Describe at least one area of campus life that assumes students come from or are currently part of a traditional middle-class, nuclear family.

2. Describe one or more changes you would recommend to address this area of campus life and make the campus more inclusive of other family types.

Native American societies did not have other social institutions, such as police or courts, to resolve conflicts. Nor did they consider land or property to be something that could or should be owned by individual people. Instead, kinship groups administered justice and organized how resources were gathered and shared.

Among European preindustrial families in the colonial United States, there was a "family economy." Families created the goods they consumed (Cherlin 1983), such as food and clothing, rather than buying them at a supermarket or retail store. In a time of short life spans, families also provided ways of passing along land and status to the next generation and forging connections to others. While there was much religious diversity within the American colonies, most fell under the Calvinist Protestant umbrella, which emphasized individualism, the importance of marriage, and male headship of families. This set the stage for **coverture,** the legal doctrine in which wives' standing was subsumed into their husbands'. Only men could own property and sign contracts (Cherlin 2009). Although men were heads of households, both women and men carried out essential work and depended on each other to survive.

Slavery and Families

Families were of central importance to slaves, who established and maintained kinship ties, even as slave owners intervened in them. Slaves could not enter legally binding contracts, and slave owners could allow or disrupt informal marriages at their whim. The sale of children and other loved ones regularly ripped apart families (Staples and Johnson 1993).

In 1662, Act XII of Virginia law declared, "All children borne in this country shall be held bond or free only according to the condition of the mother." In other words, whether a child was free or a slave depended on whether his or her mother was free or a slave. This act ensured lifetime servitude based on the mother-child relationship and transformed family relationships into a means of reproducing the labor force. White men increased their own slave holdings by raping Black slave women, who bore legally Black slave children owned by their own White fathers. Nonetheless, slaves coupled, developed broad kinship units for support, searched for sold-off loved ones, and socialized their children to survive the horrors of slavery (Dill 1988).

Consider This

How would you describe a "typical" family in the United States?

One of the most brutal practices of slavery was selling family members to different owners, including separating mothers from children.

Industrial U.S. Families

Families are the site of **reproduction,** where people create and raise members of the next generation. Prior to industrialization, reproductive labor (creating and raising a family) and productive labor (the creation of goods to trade or sell) took place in the same location—at home. With industrialization during the late 1700s and 1800s, however, families increasingly moved off of farms and into cities, where they worked outside the home, in factories, setting the stage for a "family wage economy" (Cherlin 1983).

Work and family life, for many, separated into public and private spheres, with women specializing in domesticity (**private sphere**) and men in breadwinning (**public sphere**) (Dill 1988). Concentrating on maintaining a home and raising children was possible only for well-off White women, however. They could rely on their husbands' earning capacity and focus on demonstrating their purity and piety through domesticity (Dill 1988). Many poor immigrant and Black women worked in factories or as domestic workers (Kamo and Cohen 1998).

By the mid-1800s, as activists for women's rights gained victories, new laws allowed married women to own property, take legal action, and gain custody of children following divorce (Cherlin 2009:57). Children became an economic liability for the urban poor and working classes, and use of early forms of birth control spread.

On farms, children were still considered small adults and expected to do their fair share of farm labor. But off farms, childhood for the middle and upper classes came to occupy a special time marked by innocence and protection (Mintz 2004). More people divorced, although divorce was still uncommon. Affection and emotional intimacy grew in importance (Cherlin 1983). Across the century, family sizes shrank and private life concentrated on the nuclear family. By 1900, these changes gave rise to **companionate marriage,** or a partnership based on romantic love.

The 1900s and Emotion-Based U.S. Families

Emotion-based marriage dominated the 1900s. New technologies, such as the automobile and later the birth control pill, brought couples freedom to date outside of the home and experience sexuality for the sake of intimacy and enjoyment without fear

The 1950s nuclear family has been romanticized as an ideal family type but is based more on nostalgia than reality.

many economic opportunities. Domestic violence and economic stress were commonplace, albeit hidden from view. Our image of 1950s families is based more on nostalgia than reality.

Diversifying U.S. Families

The 1960s and 1970s were times of social upheaval and rapid change. The feminist, civil rights, and sexual revolution movements drove ideological change, affirming the values, rights, and independence of women, people of color, and gay and lesbian individuals. A wave of civil rights legislation prohibited workplace and housing discrimination based on sex and race, and the Equal Employment Opportunity Commission (EEOC) was created to ensure fair hiring practices. Policies, like affirmative action programs, were enacted to help more Americans of color gain a foothold in the middle class.

During the 1970s and 1980s, however, the U.S. economy deindustrialized, destroying the family wage and pushing many more women into the paid workforce. Manufacturing work shifted out of central cities to the suburbs and then later overseas. Service industries, such as insurance, travel, and retail, grew, creating lower-paying, nonunion, less stable jobs.

During these turbulent 1960s and 1970s, family life upended, too. Couples waited to marry until they were older, and rates of premarital sex increased. Divorce rates also rose, as families experienced the **stalled revolution.** Women expected men to more fully share household responsibilities such as cooking and cleaning, while men valued the traditional family where women were responsible for private life. But as women increasingly worked for pay, few men picked up the slack at home. Many families found themselves overstretched and conflict ridden over who should do what. Stepfamilies and single motherhood became increasingly common, and same-sex couples began to come out of the closet in greater numbers. The idea of the traditional nuclear family as the norm started to become a remnant of the past.

of pregnancy. During World War II, young couples hurriedly married before men left for war, while many women, some for the first time, worked in factories to support the war effort. Divorce rates spiked as men returned changed by war and women were displaced from workplaces.

The end of World War II brought greater economic prosperity and veterans benefits for Whites (e.g., the GI Bill and VA home loans), which fed suburbanization for White families and a national baby boom. The post–World War II economic boom produced a **family wage,** meaning that many men (particularly White men in unions) earned enough to support an entire family, permitting their wives to remain at home. In turn, this supported the separation of the public and private sphere for both White middle- and working-class families during the 1950s. Americans idealized the traditional 1950s nuclear family with a breadwinning husband and homemaking wife (Coontz 1992).

Within the collective U.S. imagination, families of the 1950s occupy a special, overly nostalgic, space. Oftentimes, we imagine 1950s families as perfectly ordered and harmonious, a place of refuge and happiness. Dad supposedly went to work every day and returned to a happy homemaking wife and a well-kept house, filled with the smell of freshly baked cookies. In the decades to follow, many in the United States, especially White, heterosexual, middle-class individuals, looked back to the 1950s as if they were the "good old days." But for many others, the "perfect" family of the 1950s represents, as Stephanie Coontz (1992) shows us, "the way we never were." Same-sex couples were in the closet, and families of color were denied equal rights and

Making Way for Families of Today

Today, more and more adults in the United States remain single or live with but do not marry their partners. Figure 10.1 shows that the percentage of Americans living alone climbed from 8.6 percent in 1970 to 14.4 percent in 2015. Over the same time period, the number of **cohabitating couples**—those living together but unmarried—rose dramatically from just 0.5 percent to 7.5 percent. Meanwhile, the proportion of married Americans plummeted from 70 percent to 51.4 percent.

Marriage has become a class luxury. More and more young adults view marriage as too risky unless they are financially stable, which is too often not possible for poor or working-class couples and increasingly difficult for those in the middle class. Single parenthood—especially single *motherhood*—has become socially accepted, especially for working-class and poor families who value having children but are cautious about the possibilities of divorce (Edin and Kefalas 2005). Today, 40 percent of all babies born in the United States have unmarried mothers. As you can see in Figure 10.2, the rate varies by race and ethnicity as well as social class. The racial and ethnic groups with higher income levels (White and Asian

Americans) have fewer births outside of marriage than other groups.

Over the past couple of decades, divorce rates—although still high—have dropped, in part because people delay marriage until they are older and more economically secure. Higher-income, better-educated families have less stress, can deal with unexpected expenses more readily, and can afford counseling if things go awry. Figure 10.3 shows us the divorce rate among women. As you can see, after rising dramatically in the 1970s, it has declined in recent years. In 2015, the divorce rate was at a forty-year low.

FIGURE 10.1

With Whom Do Adults Live? Living Arrangements of Adults, 1970–2016

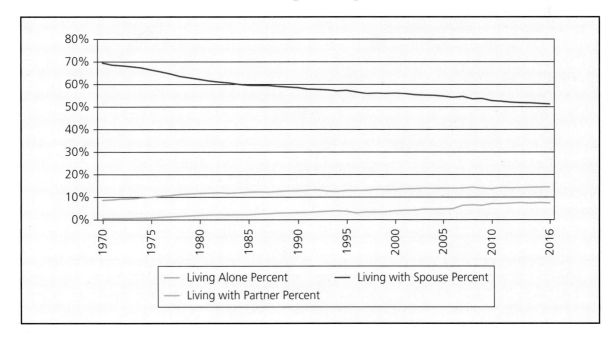

Source: U.S. Census Bureau. 2016. "Living Arrangements of Adults, 18 and over, 1967 to Present." https://www.census.gov/data/tables/time-series/demo/families/adults.html (Table AD-3).

FIGURE 10.2

Percentage of All Births That Were to Unmarried Women, by Race and Hispanic Origin, 1960–2014

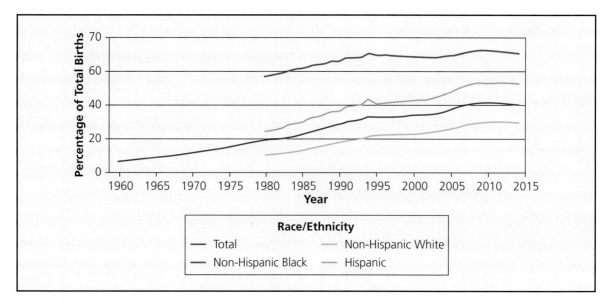

Source: Adapted from https://www.childtrends.org/wp-content/uploads/2015/03/75_Births_to_Unmarried_Women.pdf.

FIGURE 10.3

Women's Divorce Rate, 1970–2015

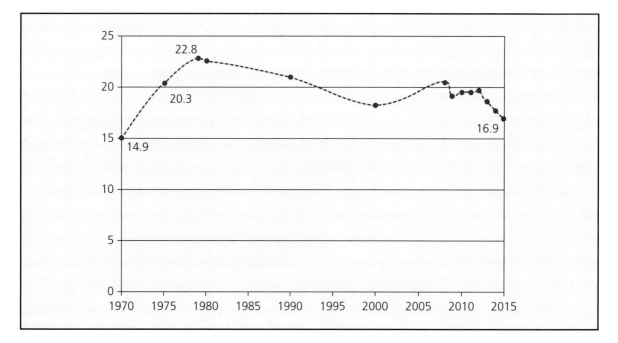

Source: Divorce Rate in the U.S. Geographic Variation, 2015. Lydia R. Anderson. FP-16–21. http://www.bgsu.edu/ncfmr/resources/data/family-profiles/anderson-divorce-rate-us-geo-2015-fp-16-21.html. Reprinted with permission from The National Center for Family & Marriage Research, Bowling Green State University.

Check Your Understanding

- Why do we live in families?

- What social, political, and financial needs did early U.S. families meet? Industrial families? Families in the 1900s and 2000s?

- What social, political, and technological changes have influenced families over the course of U.S. history?

- What role has the economy played in supporting (or not) particular ways of doing family?

- Describe how and why rates of marriage, births to unmarried mothers, and divorce rates have changed over recent decades.

Understanding Families through Theory

As you have seen in earlier chapters, theoretical perspectives provide us with ways to make sense of how society and its institutions operate. We now look at how structural functionalism, feminist theory, intersectionality, and social exchange theory offer different ways of thinking about and understanding families. As you will see, each gives us a unique angle through which to view families.

Structural Functionalism

Recall from Chapter 2 that structural functionalists are primarily concerned with how various social institutions, such as families, create stability in social life and social harmony. This approach to understanding families emphasizes how families serve as a socialization agent that allows society to move, without disruption, from one generation to the next. Functionalists also focus on the structure of families and which types of family arrangements provide the most stability, especially for children. For example, structural functionalists often worry that replacing traditional nuclear families with other family types creates problems for children and the broader society. Functionalists argue that families are important because they regulate sexual behavior, legitimize childbirth, and establish a division of labor.

Functionalists view marriage much like a puzzle: distinct and complementary individual parts that come together to form a stable whole. For example, in the 1950s, structural functionalist Talcott Parsons viewed women and men as having different biological natures and, hence, different roles in the family. He described women as expressive (emotion oriented) and men as instrumental (task oriented). Women were expected to act out their expressive natures by doing housework and care work, while men were supposed to act out their instrumental natures by being the heads of the house and the primary earners (Parsons and Bales 1956).

While many people may consider functionalist approaches to families old-fashioned, they have played an important role in social policies aimed at family life. In 1996, President Clinton's welfare reform legislation included "promoting marriage" among poor families as an explicit goal (Hays 1996). George W. Bush's administration implemented marriage promotion programs as a way to reduce poverty, and Supreme Court Justice Antonin Scalia cited research conducted in the functionalist tradition in his dissent in the Supreme Court case that legalized same-sex marriage (Pear and Kirkpatrick 2004; Supreme Court of the United States 2014).

Conflict Perspective

Conflict theories have shifted the paradigm within family research away from an emphasis on maintaining family stability through traditional nuclear families and toward understanding families as a site of inequality. Conflict theorists emphasize two things in family research. First, social inequalities affect family life. For example, poor families and families of color have less access to affordable housing, creating strain on family life. Our nostalgia for traditional nuclear families often ignores these realities. Second, family life is an arena for acting out inequalities, particularly gender inequalities.

Feminist Perspective

Sociologists who use a feminist perspective illustrate how families tend to create and reinforce gender inequality. Feminists view families as a gender factory (Berk 1985). They argue that family relationships are inherently gendered because we expect individuals to learn and act out gendered expectations around caring for others and breadwinning through family life. Many families provide girls and boys with gendered toys that teach girls (through dolls, dress-up, play houses) to care take and boys (through sports, weapons, superheroes) to dominate.

While, as seen in Chapter 8, gendered roles and expectations have begun to change somewhat, with parents of both genders expected to play parenting roles in the family, traditional gender ideologies still maintain a strong influence on family life. In adulthood, women face expectations that they focus on caring for children, spouses, and parents. We also expect them to run an efficient and clean household. These expectations are true even for career-oriented high-earning women (Schneider 2011) and busy single mothers (Elliott, Powell, and Brenton 2015). Many men, on the other hand, now feel pressure to be involved parents but also to reveal their manhood by being the breadwinner, disciplinarian, and "man of the house." Despite all of the social and economic changes of the past 150 years, traditional gender ideologies still influence families and promote gender inequality.

Intersectionality

As you have seen in previous chapters, intersectionality is a conflict perspective that pushes sociologists to look at multiple forms of inequality, such as sexuality *and* class *and* gender, at the same time (Collins 2000). Intersectionality has encouraged family researchers to ask, for example, if gender expectations shape LGBTQ families differently from straight ones. Perhaps surprisingly, these families face many of the same pressures to perform gender roles that straight families do (Biblarz and Savci 2010; Carrington 1999; Moore 2011). Intersectionality researchers also examine such issues as how parenthood varies across social classes (Hill 2012; Shows and Gerstel 2009), the challenges of single motherhood in the most fragile families (Edin and Kefalas 2005), and how poverty and racism interact to create hardships for fathers (Edin and Nelson 2013).

Social Exchange Theory

Individual family members are treated as rational actors in **social exchange theory.** It presumes they make decisions by weighing the benefits and costs of various actions and then pick the action or arrangement that brings the biggest reward (or least cost). Social exchange theorists note that when contemplating divorce, each marriage partner analyzes the rewards of his or her current arrangement in relation to (1) other marriages and (2) other relationship types. If he or she views either one to be more rewarding than his or her current relationship, marriage satisfaction decreases and motivation for separation increases. The person may still not pursue a divorce, however, if the costs of divorce, such as social disapproval or alimony, seem too high.

The Norm of Reciprocity

Exchange theorists use the **norm of reciprocity,** or the expectation that we give and take with others in relatively equal ways, to help explain how we think and feel about our relationships. The norm of reciprocity is evident when someone does something nice for you and you feel compelled to repay him or her in a relatively commensurate way. For example, if a stranger offers you assistance on the side of the road when your car breaks down, you may offer him or her some money in return or feel compelled to "pay it forward" by performing a similar act of kindness. In relationships, the norm of reciprocity dictates that partners support each other in relatively equal ways, even if the type of support is different, to maintain relationship happiness.

Check Your Understanding

- What are the functions of families, according to structural functionalists? How do functionalists view women and men's roles in families? Why?

- How do feminist theory and intersectionality challenge the approach of structural functionalists?

- What makes family members content, according to social exchange theorists? What makes them discontent?

Families Caring for Each Other

One of the primary tasks of families is to meet the needs of family members, especially children. Raising children involves making sure they are safe, well fed, housed, healthy, educated, and loved. The ways we think about childhood and how we meet children's needs, however, have changed dramatically over the past several centuries. As noted earlier, until industrialization, the expansion of the middle class, and the rise in sentimentality during the 1800s, childhood as we know it now did not exist (Mintz 2004).

During the early 1900s, as compulsory public education spread throughout the United States, more children spent much of their time with their peers in school, developing unique peer cultures (Corsaro 2005). Adults considered children to be malleable and believed they required moral training and education to develop their full character.

The socialization of children has varied greatly across historical periods and social classes.

©iStockphoto.com/kali9

Mothers and teachers turned to science to guide them in proper childrearing techniques (Mintz 2004).

Psychology turned an unprecedented critical eye onto childhood, characterizing stages of development and interrogating the nature of children's relationships with their mothers and siblings (Mintz 2001). The result was **intensive mothering** (Hays 1996), an exhausting child-centered style of parenting that requires women to copiously devote emotions, money, and time to raising children.

Intensive mothering is still the standard we measure mothers against today. Intensive mothers (and, increasingly, intensive fathers) research—reading advice books and blogs—how best to parent to ensure their children's development—even before their children are born or adopted. They keep an eye on their children at all times. They sign up their children for lessons to ensure they have every opportunity. Intensive parents focus on spending quality time *and* an abundant quantity of time with children. Today, even single parents who lack the financial or time resources to parent intensively feel pressured to do so (Elliott, Powell, and Brenton 2015).

Discipline and Social Class

While some financially struggling parents may feel pressure to parent intensively, inspired by images of intensive parenting in television and other media, most working-class families follow child-raising techniques that differ from those of wealthier families. These differences arise because of how they themselves were raised, their occupations, and the stresses working-class families face juggling work and family. Middle-class families tend to adopt a **concerted cultivation** approach to interaction and discipline through which they proactively engage with and guide their children (Lareau 2002). They reason and negotiate with their children, exploring their children's feelings and motivations for their behavior. They provide them with various structured, extracurricular experiences and teach them how to interact effectively with teachers, coaches, and other authority figures (Bernstein 2003). Through their experiences in these families, middle-class kids learn to negotiate with authority.

Working-class and poor parents, on the other hand, tend to be more authoritarian, using directives, obedience, and discipline, sometimes including physical punishment, to guide children (Kohn 1977). The parents' status as adults establishes their authority over their children. Neither reasoning nor negotiating with their children, they simply tell them what to do and demand compliance (Bernstein 2003). Children raised in these families gain an "emerging sense of constraint," which orients them to do as they are told. In other words, working-class kids learn to defer to authority for obedience's sake (Lareau 2002).

Caretaking and Changing Gendered Roles

Historically, fathers' most important roles have been as breadwinners and disciplinarians. But with high levels of divorce, women's mass employment, and shifting gender attitudes, men increasingly assume caretaking roles, as well. As shown in Figure 10.4, over the past three decades, fathers have tripled the number of hours per week they spend doing childcare. As discussed in Chapter 8, fathers, as well as mothers, desire time with their children—and most wish they had more of it!

Consider This
Look back at how you described a "typical" family in the United States earlier in the chapter. If asked the same question now, how would you respond?

FIGURE 10.4

Who Does Childcare? Hours per Week Doing Childcare, 1965–2008

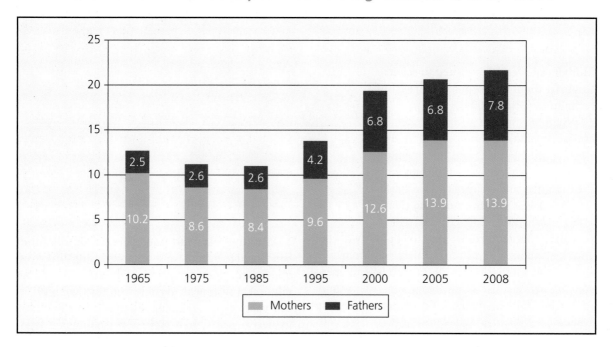

Source: Bianchi (2011).

The Sandwich Generation

The **sandwich generation** has double caretaking duties. These midlife adults are raising children and caring for aging parents at the same time. Whereas families have always been responsible for caring for aging relatives, especially those who lived with them, extended life spans, working away from home, medical bureaucracies, and diminished social supports often leave the sandwich generation squeezed by competing responsibilities. Working families of today coordinate doctors' appointments and complex medical treatments while juggling daily caregiving duties for both parents and children and the demands of a job. Dealing with the prospect of a parent dying is emotionally difficult, especially if the parent is uncomfortable planning for death. Because families have fewer children and live farther apart from each other than in the past, caretaking of a parent may fall to one adult child, creating extra strain.

Check Your Understanding

- How has childhood changed over time?
- How does parenting vary by social class?

- Describe some factors that have led fathers to take on more caretaking in the family.
- What are some challenges the sandwich generation faces?

Family Problems

While most families provide stability, safety, and nurturance in their members' lives, sometimes family life becomes conflict ridden (Turner et al. 2012). For example, the stress of work may bleed over into the home, or worries about money may cause partners to argue. Partners can have different expectations about who should contribute how much financially, who should do what housework, when to have sex, or how to make family decisions. Or the burdens of dealing with racism or sexism in public life may lead to discord at home (Hill 2005).

Violence and Victimization

Some families become sites of violence. **Family violence,** or when someone in a family hurts or controls someone else, takes on many different forms: sexual abuse, financial abuse, emotional mistreatment, and physical violence.

Children are more often victims of family violence than adults. Moreover, those victimized often experience multiple forms of abuse and maltreatment, the negative effects of which accumulate (Finkelhor 2008). Abused children are more likely to become depressed, anxious, and angry (Finkelhor, Ormrod, and Turner 2007; Turner et al. 2012). Inconsistent and hostile parenting, emotional mistreatment, witnessing family violence, and parental conflict are especially hard on children (Finkelhor, Ormrod, and Turner 2007). In two-parent and single-parent families, about 38 percent of children experience victimization by a family member; victimization is even more common in stepfamilies, where 63 percent of children have experienced it (Turner, Finkelhor, and Ormrod 2007). Each year, approximately 10 percent of children witness a family member being assaulted, and one in five see this during their childhood (Finkelhor et al. 2009).

Breaking Apart and Staying Together

Today, about half of married couples will eventually divorce or separate (Amato 2010). As with other aspects of social life, families draw on the resources available to them to create stability and deal with problems when they arise. What may become a crisis leading to stress and conflict in some families may be more readily absorbed in families with more financial and social resources. Take the case of a broken-down car or a health scare such as finding an unexpected lump under an armpit. Families with savings in the bank and quality health insurance with low copays, for example, may quickly address the problems by taking the car to a repair shop and setting up a doctor's appointment to address the lump. Families without these resources, though, may have to take unpaid time off work to take the car to a friend who knows about cars or choose between paying the doctor's copay or going grocery shopping. What seems like small problems in the first family become big, compounding problems in the second.

Research on divorce shows that couples with fewer resources are more at risk of divorcing than others. Marrying young, growing up in a divorced family, being poor, and losing a job, for example, are key risk factors for divorce (Amato and Hohmann-Marriott 2007; Amato 2010). Education especially brings stability to family life because it opens up resources and opportunities to couples: more secure jobs with benefits, financial resources to deal with life challenges, neighborhoods with quality schools and little violence, and social ties with other well-educated people who can help navigate life's difficulties. College-educated couples are more likely to stay together than their non-college-educated peers, and as more couples have gotten college degrees over the past several decades, we have seen the divorce rate drop (Amato 2010).

Effects of Instability on Children

Sociologists have historically been very concerned about the potential effects of family instability on children. Family separation or the loss of a parent can be hard on children. On the extreme end, for example, children who have had a parent die perform worse academically, internalize their problems (e.g., experience anxiety and loneliness), and struggle to maintain self-control more than other children (Amato and Anthony 2014). Children with divorced parents also tend to have poorer academic performance, lower self-esteem, and more mental health and disciplinary problems than children from intact families (Amato and Anthony 2014).

However, the effects of these events tend to be modest because children are remarkably resilient, especially when they have family and economic resources to help them work through tough times. Some children actually fare better after their parents divorce. Research shows *most* children experience no negative effects from divorce (Amato and Anthony 2014). About a quarter of children experience negative effects, such as decreased school performance or externalizing problems (Amato and Anthony 2014). About 15 percent experience *positive* effects following divorce because the conflict in their family decreases (Amato and Anthony 2014). However, sociologists see multiple family transitions (e.g., repeated divorces, a divorce and moving the family to a new city) as more detrimental than a single event.

Other separations are also challenging for families, especially military deployment, migration, or incarceration of a parent (Creighton, Park, and Teruel 2009; Gorman, Eide, and Hisle-Gorman 2009; Turney, Schnittker, and Wildeman 2012). Each physically separates partners from each other and children from their parents, leading to the loss of a caretaker in the household and possibly lost wages (particularly in the case of incarceration). Families also experience added stress as members miss their loved ones, fear they may be hurt or killed, or even deal with the stigma that comes with single parenthood or incarceration. Children, especially, are at risk of negative consequences, such as dropping out of school (Creighton, Park, and Teruel 2009; Gorman, Eide, and Hisle-Gorman 2009).

Supporting Children

Parents can mediate the challenges posed by family disruption. For example, when families experience stressful events, parents can seek couples or family therapy to learn how to help their children cope. Divorced parents can cooperatively coparent by working together to prioritize the needs of their children and help children maintain healthy relationships with both parents. Parents can attempt to minimize other transitions, such as switching schools, to add stability. Finally, parents can seek support from teachers, school counselors, friends, neighbors, and extended family. Accessing community resources and cooperating improve children's resiliency in the face of transitions.

Check Your Understanding

- What are some typical causes of stress in families?

- Describe the backgrounds of people most likely and least likely to get divorced.

- What are some life experiences that are particularly challenging for children? How can parents mitigate their effects on children?

How Work and Policy Shape Families

In *The Second Shift,* originally published in 1989, Arlie Hochschild describes how one married couple, Nancy and Evan Holt, tried to balance work and home responsibilities. Nancy, a social worker, expected her husband, who did not work as much as she did, to contribute to the routine work of the household, such as cooking, cleaning, washing, shopping, and caring for their young child. Despite his promises to do his share of the housework, however, Evan failed to do his share. He resisted doing what he considered women's work around the house. This left Nancy having to do the mundane and time-consuming housework and childcare—after she came home from work, working what Hochschild dubbed **the second shift**. Over time, the marriage became increasingly conflict ridden (Hochschild and Machung 2012).

Nancy and Evan's struggles show how closely family life is tied to the economy. Evan could not adjust to an economy that required two earners in a household and consequent gender role adjustment at home. The result was a resentful, exhausted Nancy—and marital conflict.

> **Consider This**
> If you could pick your ideal arrangement, how many hours per week would you work for pay and how many hours would you spend doing housework, cooking, and childcare? How would you deal with your competing obligations if you lived alone? How would you deal with your competing obligations if you lived with a partner who didn't want to contribute to housework or childcare?

Addressing Work and Family Challenges Today

Whereas a majority of U.S. households were headed by male breadwinners in 1970, a majority are now headed by dual-earner couples (Jacobs and Gerson 2004). The number of single mothers heading households has also grown substantially. As a result, not only do U.S. families *depend* on the earnings of women to make their families work, but many U.S. families are also **overworked**, or devoting more time to paid work than ever, leaving less time for leisure and home life. In addition, a growing number of dual-earner couples work extremely long hours: research shows that 14.5 percent of dual-earner married couples together work more than 100 hours a week for pay, an increase from 8.7 percent in 1970 (Jacobs and Gerson 2004:43). These work environments, paired with intensive parenting standards and responsibility for caring for the elderly or sick, leave many families stressed and overwhelmed.

Work-family strain experienced by families in the United States is exacerbated by the dearth of workplace policies accommodating family life. Childcare is perhaps the most important benefit workplaces or government agencies could offer, but few employers

Comparing Paid and Unpaid Leave in Twenty-One Countries

In this activity, you will analyze a graph showing leave policies in various countries.

Figure 10.5 presents the number of weeks of leave, both paid and unpaid, available to workers in the United States and those in other countries. Examine the graph and then answer the questions below.

FIGURE 10.5

Family Leave: How Does the United States Compare? Paid and Unpaid Leave for Two-Parent Families by Country

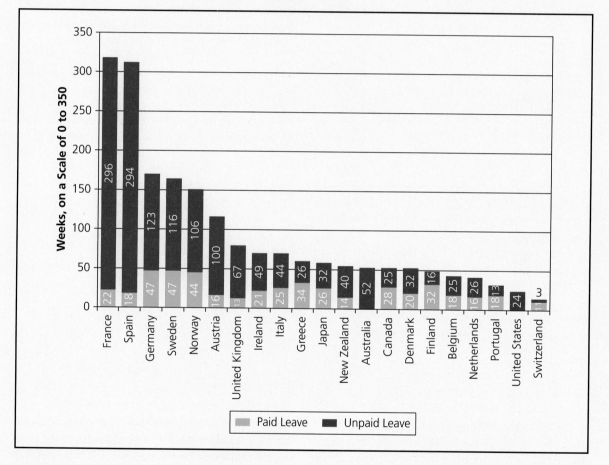

Source: Ray, Gornick, and Schmitt (2009).

1. How many weeks of paid leave does the United States guarantee its employees who become ill or need to care for someone else? What about unpaid leave for illness or to care for someone?

2. Which countries provide the largest number of weeks of total leave? Which countries provide the most paid leave?

3. Where, in relation to the other nations, does the United States stand?

4. Assume that you are running for political office. Would you make guaranteed time off from work a part of your political platform? Why or why not? If you would campaign for guaranteed leave, would you emphasize paid or unpaid leave? Why?

Sociologists in Action

Public Sociologist

Barbara Risman

I **was** part of the women liberation movements in the 1970s as an undergraduate at Northwestern University. When the Equal Rights Amendment—a constitutional amendment passed by Congress in 1972—failed to be ratified by the states, I couldn't believe so many women voted against their own self-interest, against their own equality. I had to figure that out.

Sociology allowed me to put my two major commitments together: political activism and understanding why and how people do what they do.

The way I now combine my activism and scholarship is through public sociology, communicating sociological findings to the public. I have concentrated my efforts on building the Council of Contemporary Families (CCF), a group that brings research and clinical expertise on families into the public realm. CCF was started by a group of psychologists and sociologists two decades ago. In the beginning, we focused on getting accurate information about families to the press. We scholars started putting out white papers and briefing papers answering questions such as the following: What do we know about how to support different types of families? What can we do to help children whose parents go through divorce?

Today, we communicate with journalists and policy makers about information social scientists and clinicians have but the rest of the world does not yet know. For example, for the fiftieth anniversary of the *Moynihan Report,* we held a symposium on how policy has not addressed poverty in minority communities. Such symposia report what we as researchers have discovered and let us hold public debates about issues on which we disagree. We scholars don't always find the same results from our research. For example, our findings about whether or not hooking up is empowering are inconsistent. CCF points out the complexities of the issues.

My public sociology contributions include having served as president of CCF, and my edited book, *Families as They Really Are,* is a compilation of writings by CCF experts on the most pressing family issues of the day. Recently, I published a commentary in the *Chicago Tribune* based on my interviews with millennials, entitled "Are Millennials Feminists?" I address an observation that shocked me: why young women seem to be less excited than older feminists about the prospect of a female president. My research shows that millennial women have grown up believing they can be anything they want to be; they experience gender as a personal attribute rather than as a social identity that would influence their voting for women. On the other hand, millennial men experience teasing and bullying when they fail to "man up." Men feel resentful because they don't have the choices that young women now think they have. This is one example of how my research brings insight to the social issues of our day.

Spreading information from our research is really important. It is up to us as activist-scholars to make sure what we know that might be useful for decision makers gets into their hands.

Barbara Risman is professor of sociology at the University of Illinois Chicago. Her latest book is on gender and partnering among millennials.

in the United States do so and the government does not either. Nor does the United States have a federal *paid* family leave policy allowing workers to care for a newly born or adopted baby, sick parent, ill child, injured spouse, or personal illness. The federal Family and Medical Leave Act, passed in 1993, entitles eligible workers up to twelve weeks of *unpaid*, job-protected leave—and only applies in workplaces with fifty or more employees. California, New Jersey, and Rhode Island have created their own, modest, state-based paid family leave programs to help fill the gap, but most U.S. workers face great financial hardship if they must take an unpaid leave, if they even qualify for leave. The United States lags far beyond other industrialized countries in this regard (Ray, Gornick, and Schmitt 2009; Bartel et al. 2014).

Other workplace policies, such as paid vacation, bereavement leave, sick leave, flextime scheduling, or flexible work locations, ease pressure on workers and increase productivity but are not available to some or most workers (Council of Economic Advisers 2014; Bloom and Van Reenen 2006). For example, only 12 percent of workers have employers who offer paid family leave (U.S. Department of Labor 2015). Workers, furthermore, often fear they will be looked down upon or fired for asking about or using flexible workplace policies. San Francisco and Vermont have adopted "right to request" laws, which protect workers from retaliation from their employers if they request a flexible work arrangement (Council of Economic Advisers 2014). Sociologists, such as Barbara Risman, featured in the above Sociologists in Action box, use their research and clinical expertise to help policy makers and business professionals understand and respond to the challenges families face today.

Using Sociology to Address Family Issues

Being a professional researcher who studies families is just one way to use sociology to support families. Sociology offers many other career opportunities to make life better for families. In the nonprofit sector, for example, family sociologists work as volunteer coordinators in domestic violence shelters, case managers in child-advocacy organizations, and patient advocates at hospitals. If you are interested in public sector work, family sociology can help you better support families whether you work as a case manager in a Department of Human Services, an advocate with Child Protective Services, a parole officer, a school administrator, or a policy maker. You can also support families through work in the private sector as a business owner, manager, or human resources officer by advocating family-friendly leave policies. Even if your job does not put you directly in charge of some dimension of family life, understanding the role of families in our society will help you better serve your clients and coworkers.

Check Your Understanding

- Who are the overworked and the underworked?
- How does the United States compare to European nations in terms of workplace family policies?
- What is the Family and Medical Leave Act of 1993?
- How can sociological knowledge of the family help professionals in a variety of fields?

Conclusion

Families are a central part of social life. As an institution, the family is flexible and adaptive to changing social conditions. The needs families meet and how they meet them have changed over time. Industrialization, the decline of the family wage, shifting ideologies about gender and sexuality, and technological innovations have transformed families from sites of economic production and political connection building to those of emotional comfort. How we parent has also changed over time and depends on our own socialization and the resources we bring to the task.

Families are where we deal with the stress and strain of life at work and in the public realm. Economic, social, and policy resources affect the well-being and stability of families. Despite all of the changes families have undergone, they remain as vital to our lives as ever. Understanding families in a sociological way leads us to wonder about what new needs families will meet in the next fifty years and what families will look like then.

⑤SAGE edge™

Want a better grade? Get the tools you need to sharpen your study skills. Access practice quizzes, eFlashcards, video and multimedia at **edge.sagepub.com/korgen**

Review

10.1 What are families? In what ways are families by-products of the social world?

Families are groups of people who take responsibility for meeting each other's needs. What needs families meet has changed over time; families were once sites of economic production and political connection building but now offer emotional comfort. Our definitions of family are institutionalized through social policy, law, and our shared beliefs.

10.2 How have families changed over time? What has caused these changes?

Our sociological imaginations help us identify social factors that influence family life. Some of the key social factors include slavery, industrialization, social class, technological innovations (such as the car, birth control, and mobile phones), social movements, and gender roles. Since the 1970s, social factors such as deindustrialization, the decline of the family wage, and several social movements have led to change in norms around marriage, cohabitation, and births outside of marriage. Same-sex marriages are now recognized but the overall marriage rate has declined, while cohabitation and births to unmarried mothers have increased.

10.3 How do different theoretical perspectives help sociologists understand families?

Different theories allow us to view families from various angles. Structural functionalists emphasize the socialization functions of families and the structure of families. Conflict theorists focus on how social inequalities affect family life and how families provide an arena for acting out inequalities. Sociologists who use a feminist perspective show how families tend to create and reinforce gender inequality. Those who use intersectionality look at multiple forms of inequality, such as sexuality *and* class *and* gender, at the same time within families. Social exchange theorists maintain that people contemplate costs and rewards when making decisions, such as whether to stay married.

10.4 Who does the caretaking?

Families are tasked with taking care of their own, especially children. Intensive parenting invests copious time and resources into raising children and is practiced by middle-class and wealthier families. Mothers still spend more time caretaking, but over the past few decades, fathers have increased the time they spend caring for their children. Many adults take care of their aging parents, as well, as part of the sandwich generation.

10.5 What challenges do families face?

While families often are places of comfort and security, sometimes they become stressful, distressful, or abusive. Children are especially susceptible to family abuse. Family violence, when someone in a family hurts or controls someone else, takes on many different forms: sexual abuse, financial abuse, emotional mistreatment, and physical violence.

Families may break apart when their members are unhappy and conflictual or have little commitment to each other. While most kids fare well after divorce, about a quarter of children of divorced parents experience academic or behavioral problems and about 15 percent of kids actually benefit from divorce. Families that experience discrimination have to deal with additional stressors.

10.6 How do work and social policies influence families?

Family members balance the demands of work life with those of home life. Work (too much or too little) can cause families stress and strain. The lack of family-friendly workplace policies in the United States leaves most families overburdened. Most other postindustrial nations have far more policies in place to help their citizens balance work and family life.

Key Terms

- cohabiting couples   211
- companionate marriage   209
- concerted cultivation   215
- coverture   208
- family   205
- family violence   216
- family wage   210
- institutionalized   206
- intensive mothering   215
- norm of reciprocity   214

- nuclear family   205
- overworked   218
- private sphere   209
- public sphere   209
- reproduction   209
- sandwich generation   216
- second shift   218
- social exchange theory   214
- stalled revolution   210

Education plays a major role in all societies. It can train its members to be productive citizens, workers, and family members. It can also pass along privilege and inequality from one generation to the next.

Learning Questions

11.1 What does it mean to look at education as a social institution?

11.2 How do historical moment, the social structure, and changing systems of production shape the functions of education over time and across place?

11.3 How do functionalism, conflict theory, and symbolic interaction approach and explain education as an institution?

11.4 How does education reproduce social inequality?

11.5 What are the central issues facing global education today?

11.6 How do policy debates surrounding pre-K, K–12, and higher education all revolve around the tension between public education and individual choice and responsibility for accessing opportunities and achieving success?

Understanding Institutions

Education

Melissa S. Fry

What Is Education as an Institution?

Kadijah Williams, a young woman from California, spent her childhood moving from shelter to shelter, sometimes sleeping on the street or in a bus station. In high school, her evening study sessions were often cut short by "lights out" at the homeless shelter, but she never gave up. From tenth to twelfth grades, she woke at 4:30 a.m., took several buses, and spent two hours each morning commuting to keep herself from having to switch schools for a thirteenth time. She was determined to graduate from Jefferson High, which was a consistent touch point for her (OWN Videos 2013).

The instability of her homeless life affected Kadijah's ability to make friends and perform well in school. She described her experience this way: "Though school was my salvation, my test scores suffered as a result of missing so much school and having no place to study" (Kristof 2016). Still, Kadijah worked hard and applied to Harvard University. Harvard accepted her on a full scholarship. Her university dorm room provided a needed home.

Kadijah credits her mother's high expectations and access to the Los Angeles Public Library for helping her to remain focused and envision a different life (OWN Videos 2013; Oprah's Lifeclass 2009). Kadijah graduated from Harvard with a sociology degree and now works for the Washington, D.C. city government helping homeless kids. Kadijah combines her personal experiences with the sociological perspective to understand and address the issue of homelessness.

Kadijah's story is one that many Americans embrace as evidence that the United States is a meritocracy, a society where one's status, income, and place in the social structure are determined by hard work and ability. In reality, Kadijah's story is a rare exception. Most Americans grow up to have earnings similar to their parents' and occupy the same socio-economic status as their parents (Jonsson et al. 2011; Pfeffer and Hertel 2015; Hertel and Groh-Samberg 2014). The myth of meritocracy in America reflects the **dominant ideology** (a widely held set of beliefs embedded in the culture of a society and acting to inhibit the development of radical political dissent).

How I Got Active in Sociology

Melissa S. Fry

I started college as a life sciences and Spanish double major with clear plans for medical school and a future serving the health needs of underserved Latino communities. Then Rodney King was beaten. On video. The four officers that we watched beat him on the video were acquitted by an all-White jury. Los Angeles erupted in flames and violence. The irrationality of racism got under my skin, and all I wanted to do was learn about how and why our society divided itself along the lines of race and ethnicity. I wanted to know how the "justice" system could produce such an outcome in a country that embraced ideals of equality.

That was the spring of my first year of college. I enrolled in an urban sociology course the following fall and fell in love with the discipline. I could not read enough, never had trouble writing papers, loved attending classes—my whole approach to learning changed. My interest in race and social movements evolved into an interest in political institutions and public policy. Race fundamentally shapes education policy, as well as the institutions and organizations that comprise our public education system, in ways that reproduce social inequality. The need to understand the social dynamics that produce and reinforce this feedback loop and others like it are what hooked me on sociology.

Education is essential to upward mobility, movement up the class and status structure. This chapter explores education, its functions, the power dynamics that shape education, and the ways that education relates to upward mobility and social inequality. It also examines education's role in socialization and cultural reproduction, as well as current issues in global and domestic education policy and practice.

Institutionalizing Education

Education is the process through which a society transmits its culture and history, as well as teaches social, intellectual, and specific work skills that result in productive workers and citizens. Like the family, education has been institutionalized, encoded in laws, policies, and common practices that organize schools and their support systems. Institutionalization is important to stability. Roles, rules, and routines limit how much individual personalities shape an organization's operation. This allows for smooth transitions when people are hired or depart, and it ensures that different organizations within an institution are comparable. Have you ever switched schools? If so, you know that some things were different, but you could also count on many things being basically the same. With a pretty good understanding of how "school" works, kids can readily adapt to a new setting.

Institutions reflect the time in which they exist. In preindustrial societies, adults passed knowledge and skills through modeling and oral tradition. The rise of manufacturing in the industrial age moved parents' work away from the home and family, and it required skills that many parents could not teach. For example, building a needed piece of equipment or spinning wool at home was different from running a machine responsible for a particular step of production or operating large textile production machines in a factory. Society thus needed a system to prepare workers for the labor force. In addition to particular work skills, the industrial era required a workforce that could be on time, follow directions, conform to a structured work environment, and accept the authority of management. A compulsory public education system emerged to meet these needs.

Institutions are also **durable,** meaning they are slow to change. Institutions resist change because people like routines and because some people benefit from keeping things as they are. Major changes may be perceived as illegitimate and resisted or rejected. For example, segregation in public schools was legal for nearly 100 years after the Fourteenth Amendment, until the *Brown v. Board of Education of Topeka* Supreme Court decision in 1954. Today, more than seventy years later, schools still tend to be segregated by race and ethnicity.

Check Your Understanding

- From a sociological perspective, why is it important to recognize that Kadijah's story is exceptional?

- What does it mean to see education as a social institution?

- What does it mean to say that institutions are durable? In what ways is institutional durability functional? Dysfunctional?

Education and Modes of Production

As societies change, so do their institutions. Education prepares people to fill different roles in relation to the means of production (the methods for producing goods). If the means of production change, education must adapt to reflect those changes.

Preindustrial Societies

In preindustrial societies, school as we know it did not exist. Peasants didn't need formal education to fulfill their role in the production system. Only the wealthy and religious leaders went to school, where classes focused on philosophy, sacred texts, and the arts.

Most children in preindustrial societies worked alongside their parents, who taught them work skills, life lessons, and values. In agrarian societies, where farming was the means of production, land ownership was the primary source of economic and social power, and it transferred to the next generation through inheritance. The aristocracy held the land and the peasants worked it with simple tools that did not require education outside of the family.

Industrial Manufacturing and Large-Scale Agriculture

Industrialization altered the division of labor and resulted in mass migration to industrial centers and in changes to education (Rauscher 2015). Industrialization created a need for mechanics, welders, factory workers, newspaper writers, bookkeepers, and other skilled workers. The demand for skills like reading, writing, and calculating laid the foundation for a compulsory educational system.

The U.S. government developed a land-grant program (with the Morrill Acts of 1862 and 1890) to establish institutions of higher education that would train people in advanced agriculture techniques, science, and engineering to propel industrial and agricultural development. This mission contrasted with established colleges and universities where the young and privileged explored philosophy, literature, and the arts. At the same time, the government also established "normal schools," which trained students to become teachers in the growing public school system. Education at land-grant and normal schools prepared citizens for positions in the newly created middle class, between the laboring class and the elites who owned the means of production.

Doing Sociology 11.1

How the Intersection of Biography and History Shapes Educational Experiences

In this exercise, you will look at how your educational experience is shaped by the time in which you live and your personal biography.

The fundamental insight of the sociological imagination is that an individual's reality is the product of the intersection of biography and history. Take a few moments to consider how your own experience and understanding of education are shaped by the intersection of your individual biography with the historical moment in which you live and answer the following questions:

1. What year were you born? What year did you begin formal schooling? What year did you graduate from high school?

2. List three to five specific things related to schooling and your education that you think are different for you than they were for your parents or grandparents.

3. What historical changes might be responsible for differences between your experiences and opportunities and your parents' or grandparents'? These may be social, cultural, technological, or political changes. Be specific.

4. If you could implement one policy in all public schools, what would it be? Why?

Examining the Local School Board as an Institution

In this activity, you will use the website of a local school board to examine the policies and processes that make it an institution.

Using a web browser of your choice, search for a local school board website. Explore the site and answer the following questions:

1. What are the vision and mission of the school board? If they do not have both, note what they do have.

2. What is the stated function of the school board? This may be listed as objectives or goals.

3. If agendas and minutes are posted on the website, review a few of their recent meeting agendas and minutes and describe the routines for these meetings. Is there a regular order and pattern of activity? Describe that pattern in two to four sentences.

4. Based on posted agendas and minutes, list three recent topics addressed.

5. Are there any rules for school board membership or for attending meetings? If so, what are they?

6. Why is it important for the school system to have a board with clear roles, rules, and routines that govern their action? Why might meetings be organized the same way (or nearly the same way) every time?

7. Imagine you are a parent of a child in the school district. What is a policy you would like to see the school board change or implement? Based on looking at the agendas, describe how you could use the institutional structure of the school board to bring your idea up for discussion and consideration.

The Postindustrial Knowledge and Service Economy

In the late 1970s and early 1980s, U.S. manufacturing started to decline as companies moved their factories to places with cheaper labor. At the same time, higher levels of education coupled with new computing technology expanded knowledge-based work. The mid-century baby boom produced the largest and most highly educated generation in U.S. history. They created more demand for goods and services, and they made innovation itself a valued commodity.

Since the late 1970s, the numbers of both professional and service jobs have grown dramatically. At the high end, new jobs require much higher levels of education. On the low end, low-wage service work in retail and food service has replaced many U.S. manufacturing jobs. Securing higher-paid work requires more education, while throughout the labor market, work increasingly demands strong social skills.

The highest rewards in the new economy go to creativity and innovation. Today's Silicon Valley companies now operate in a context where rapid innovation, creativity, and adaptability are essential (Saxenian 1996 [1994]). Teaching children to show up on time, conform to a rigid structure, and yield to authority fails to develop either the creativity or knowledge needed to succeed in the current economy. These skills may still be important, but alone they cannot ensure social mobility.

Public Education and the Postindustrial Economy

The education system in the United States today reflects the industrial age more than it does the information era that it now serves (Robertson 2005). Vocational programs continue to operate on the assumption that a technically focused high school diploma will be enough to secure one of the remaining manufacturing jobs, which require more technological knowledge and training than most high schools offer. Schools are also not adequately developing the knowledge, critical thinking, and creativity that most professions demand.

Check Your Understanding

- How have changing systems of production shaped education historically?

- What factors led to the emergence of compulsory public education?

- How are the labor needs of the postindustrial service and knowledge economy different from those of the industrial era?

Theorizing Education

Sociological theories help us examine the structure, functions, power dynamics, and interactions within and among institutions through different lenses. Functionalists point to the ways that a compulsory education system contributes to socialization and economic development. Conflict theorists view those same functions as working to create and justify inequality. Symbolic interactionists examine the explicit and implicit curriculum of values and behaviors transmitted through social interactions in schools. All of these perspectives will help you to notice and understand both the obvious and obscured aspects of education.

The Social Functions of Education

Functionalists point out that the institution of education provides a structure that teaches students about our shared

As economic changes create the need for different skills, education must adapt to help workers prepare for changing job requirements.

©iStockphoto.com/FatCamera

culture and socializes workers and citizens. It trains and sorts workers by strengths and interests, and it provides access to various parts of the labor market while leveling the playing field with universal access. And it protects democracy by teaching citizens the importance of civic engagement.

As noted in earlier chapters, in addition to these manifest functions, a mandatory education system has latent (hidden) functions like providing child care for working parents and regulating entry into the labor force. The **hidden curriculum** is also responsible for reinforcing elements of social status and order, such as ideas about gender-appropriate roles and behaviors and race and class hierarchies. These messages are delivered through substantive choices in the curriculum and often through the social structure and functioning of the school itself.

Socialization: Cohesion and Control

While families are the site of primary socialization, functionalists note that schools are essential to **secondary socialization**—teaching us how to behave appropriately in small groups and structured situations. Schooling, for example, teaches children to be punctual, follow rules and directions, obey authority figures, and complete assigned tasks. Whenever you listen quietly to a presentation at work or raise your hand to speak, you are expressing the values and norms you learned in the classroom.

Labor Force Preparation

Public schools, from the perspective of functionalists, give everyone an opportunity to succeed in and contribute to society. Education holds out the

promise of being a great equalizer in a society where all children have access to it. In fact, compulsory schooling emerged as part of a modern era where merit, talent, and effort were expected to replace privilege and inheritance as determinants of status and mobility (Sadovnik 2007:xiii). Indeed, education does, in some cases, allow people to move up the social class ladder, like Kadijah Williams.

Public schools benefit both individuals and society by helping children develop essential skills while sorting these future workers into appropriate positions in the labor market. From a functionalist perspective, success in the classroom leads to higher-level courses and acceptance into highly competitive and elite colleges and graduate schools. Those with the highest abilities receive the most advanced training, earn the highest credentials, and enter the most challenging fields. Likewise, those with less ability receive less training, earn lower-level credentials, and enter less demanding (and less lucrative) areas of work (Davis and Moore 1945).

Building an Educated Citizenry

Ever wonder why all schools teach history and civics? Early proponents of public education argued that democratic societies require an educated citizenry capable of making informed and responsible decisions about who will govern them (Hurn 1993, as cited in Sadovnik 2007:5). This reasoning, along with the need for a skilled workforce, was one of the driving forces behind establishing public education in the United States.

Consider This

How has your education prepared you to be a knowledgeable voter and active citizen? Now imagine if every other student had a similar experience. What are the ramifications for our democracy?

The National Assessment of Educational Progress is the "largest assessment of what America's students know" (National Center for Education Statistics 2014). *The Nation's Report Card* regularly reports and updates the study's findings. The 2014 edition of *The Nation's Report Card* showed that only 18 percent of American eighth graders scored proficient or above in U.S. history, 27 percent in geography, and 23 percent in civics (*The Nation's Report Card* 2016). These scores revealed a slight improvement from the first year of the study (1994). If a key function of public education is to develop an informed citizenry ready to engage and understand democracy and the historical context for public policies, our schools are not functioning as they should.

Conflict, Power, and Education

While functionalists contend that education promotes **social cohesion** and stability, conflict theorists argue that the power dynamics of society shape schools and student outcomes. Differences in school experiences range from teacher quality and the physical state of school facilities (Kozol 1991) to classroom interactions and school discipline (Curtis 2014; Glock, Krolak-Schwerdt, and Pit-ten Cate 2015; Rudd 2014). These differences are not distributed randomly.

Consider This

How do your grade school and high school experiences reflect patterns based on race, class, or gender?

Social Class and School Experiences

In his landmark book, *Savage Inequalities,* Jonathan Kozol (1991) takes readers into the very different worlds of America's poorest and richest schools. In America's poorest schools, burned-out teachers struggle to teach and children struggle to focus in overcrowded classrooms with leaky ceilings, poor heating, and inadequate school supplies. In contrast, wealthy schools filled with new technology, well-trained and energized teachers, and abundant extracurricular opportunities provide a clear picture of the benefits of wealth in U.S. society. Kozol's work sounded the alarm and posed the question, "Do American schools provide equal opportunities for children?" His answer—they do not.

Beyond the physical aspects of the school environment, sociologists recognize that even within a single classroom, children may have very different experiences based on social characteristics, including race, class, and gender. Research in the 1970s and 1980s indicated that boys' voices, even when they were wrong, were more highly valued and sought in the classroom than were girls' (Cherry 1975; BenTsvi-Myer, Hertz-Lazarowitz, and Safir 1989).

In the spotlight today are the ways that racial bias in school discipline may be criminalizing young Black boys in ways that may become self-fulfilling prophecies (Fabelo et al. 2011; Curtis 2014). Current studies indicate that Black boys are more likely than other students to face criminal consequences for disciplinary infractions in school (Rudd 2014). Some argue this "criminalization" of child and adolescent behavior facilitates the so-called school-to-prison pipeline (Amurao 2013).

> **Consider This**
> What functions do you think your experience of education served? Think about this both at the individual level and at the larger societal level.

The Curriculum, Ideology, and Inequality

Conflict theorists argue that the school curriculum, the courses and material taught in school, reinforces dominant ideologies and the status quo by presenting only the perspective of those in power (Loewen 2007 [1995]; Zinn 2003 [1980]). This version of our history tends to minimize or ignore inequality based on race, class, gender, and other social characteristics. For example, our historic celebrations of Columbus Day ignore the genocide of millions of Native Americans. The way most high school history courses jump from the Emancipation Proclamation to celebrating the civil rights movement, without explicitly acknowledging the more than 4,000 Blacks who were lynched in between, provides another example of how school curricula can shade and ignore racial abuse or make inequality seem like a justified reflection of historical contributions (Equal Justice Initiative 2017; Loewen 2007 [1995];

> **Consider This**
> Can you think of at least two ways that your social class influenced your school experience? How might your school experience be different if you were a member of a much higher or lower social class? Why?

Zinn 2003 [1980]). Marx would point out that the school curriculum helps create a false consciousness among students from poor and working-class families, as it encourages them to support, rather than challenge, the political and economic structures of the nation.

Tracking and Inequality

Conflict theorists also maintain that schools reproduce social stratification by tracking students toward occupations consistent with their social class. Students' vocabulary, ways of interacting, and communication skills are all shaped by their home environments and experiences. Teachers and administrators interpret these behavior patterns, and their education is tracked accordingly (Gamoran 2001; Oakes 1994a, 1994b; Glock, Krolak-Schwerdt, and Pit-ten Cate 2015). Children who show up to school less attuned to the social rules around sitting still, quietly awaiting instruction, raising their hands, and taking turns speaking may be seen as less intelligent or less able to manage more challenging work and will be funneled into lower tracks. Students who arrive at school with reading time etiquette, listening skills, deference to a teacher's authority, and understanding of hand raising and taking turns may be perceived as more intelligent and will be tracked into higher-level reading groups that will consistently prepare them for more challenging work throughout their school experience.

> **Consider This**
> Do you agree with conflict theorists that public schools are designed to create a false consciousness among students? Why? If yes, how do they do this?

Symbolic Interaction, Socialization, and Cultural Production in Schools

While functionalists acknowledge that schools socialize individuals into citizenship and worker roles and conflict theorists focus on how education reproduces social inequality, symbolic interactionists examine how social interactions create and reproduce meaning. Because

Applying Sociological Theory to Educational Issues

In this exercise, you will take on the role of a school principal to analyze and respond to community concerns about your school.

Imagine you are a high school principal. Your teacher will assign you one of the following challenges:

- You receive a series of parent complaints that their daughters have noticed that the high school biology teacher never presents any examples of, or research from, female research scientists.

- An area newspaper publishes an investigative report documenting that students of color at your school are more likely to be placed in lower tracks and appear to have lower average test scores than otherwise similar White students.

- You attend a community meeting where local employers complain that the last three years of high school graduates have noticeably lower skills in answering phones and interacting in a professional manner with customers. Employers are concerned they may need to look elsewhere for qualified workers.

Prepare responses to the following questions:

1. Why is the issue raised by the parent, reporter, or employer a concern to the person who raised it and/or the students directly affected?

2. Why is it a social problem? How does it affect society, rather than just individuals? Consider the three theoretical perspectives we have discussed.

3. Which theoretical perspective do you find most useful in explaining why the issue is a social problem? Why?

4. Based on your analysis of the problem through the lens of your chosen theory, describe two policies you would enact to address the issue.

traditional schools structure classrooms based on age, most social exchanges are with other kids who are the same age. Peer interactions teach kids the norms and values of youth culture, ingroup/outgroup boundaries and meanings, and ultimately their definition of self.

Imagine a high school freshman who enjoys playing chess when he arrives on campus and is happy to hear that the school has a chess club. He soon hears his new peers making jokes about kids who play chess and now has to contend with a new self-definition placing him outside his peer ingroup. To manage impressions and retain his ingroup status, he decides not to join the chess club.

Interactions with teachers and administrators teach kids about trust in and submission to nonparental authority as these adults try to socialize students to adult group behavior. A close relationship with a teacher may also provide important mentoring on what it takes to be successful in life. Think about how your teachers influenced your sense of your own competence as a student and your ability to succeed in college and a career.

Socialization and Socioeconomic Status

The roles and rules that structure educational settings sort students based on how well they demonstrate the social skills and behavioral expectations of a system designed by people with high levels of education working in a professional setting (Bourdieu and Passeron 1977). Students who come from these social class positions will have an easier time adopting the school's norms than students who come from blue-collar families with less education.

Consider This
Among the three theoretical perspectives described above, which would you use to make sense of your own K–12 educational experience? Explain your choice.

The children of parents with higher levels of education will also tend to have greater exposure to books and other reading materials and to be socialized to sit through the reading and discussion of books from an early age. They are more likely to participate in structured leisure activities like organized sports, music lessons, cultural events, or concerts where they learn the norms for such activities (Podesta 2014; Lareau 2003:276–77). Children from blue-collar families do more of their early learning through less structured experiences like free outdoor play with other children, which requires less restrictive behavior (Podesta 2014; Lareau 2003:276–77). Kindergarten may be the first time they are expected to conform to a more structured environment. Children who have trouble conforming can be labeled as troublemakers, face disciplinary action, and ultimately have to deal with the label's effect on their self-concept and future interactions.

Check Your Understanding

- What are the functions of compulsory education in the United States?

- According to conflict theorists, how do schools reproduce inequality?

- From the perspective of symbolic interactionists, how do peers and teachers influence students?

- How can socialization within families affect children's success in school?

Education and Social Inequality in the United States

Universal access to education is supposed to provide the opportunity for individuals to build their **human capital** (knowledge, skills, habits, and attributes necessary to succeed in work and in life) and realize their full potential. In this way, education produces economic mobility and, ideally, sorts the most talented individuals into the most challenging roles. But is this really how it works? This section uses a sociological lens to explore how American education is both a product and producer of social inequality in the United States.

Class and Family Background

A significant body of research suggests that educational institutions reproduce relations of power and social inequality rather than leveling the playing field. The strongest predictors of educational success are parents' education and income (Jonsson et al. 2011; Teachman 1987; Featherman and Hauser 1978; Blau and Duncan 1967; Coleman et al. 1966). Children tend to follow their parents' path in school.

In 1966, the U.S. Department of Education released *Equality of Educational Opportunity* (Coleman et al. 1966). Lead researcher James Coleman, a sociologist, found that the quality of schools and teachers had some impact on student outcomes, but the strongest determinant was the students' socioeconomic status. Parents' education and income begin shaping children's educational readiness, school performance, outcomes, and access to opportunity from birth (Teachman 1987; Featherman and Hauser 1978; Blau and Duncan 1967; Coleman et al. 1966).

> **Consider This**
> If the best predictors of educational success are parents' income and education (shaped by class), can education be an equalizer?

Leveling the Playing Field with Early Education

The research on early childhood brain development suggests that providing quality care and education from birth to age five can reduce child poverty and increase labor force participation. Quality preschool programs improve nutrition and stimulate brain development, closing the gap between poor and privileged children before they ever walk into a kindergarten classroom. These structured programs also prepare children to interact effectively in school settings (Heckman 2006; Hillemeier et al. 2013). Unfortunately, today less than two-thirds (64.8 percent) of three- to five-year-olds are enrolled in pre-K programs.

During World War II, the U.S. government provided childcare to support women entering the labor force as part of the war effort (Stoltzfus 2000). This was a notable exception, however. Early education and care in the United States have traditionally been the responsibility of individual families. Our culture

embraces the notion that a stay-at-home mom provides the best care for any child. This, however, was and is a largely higher-class privilege. Poor and working-class families have always juggled the need to earn income to support their families with the need to care for their young.

Since the early 1970s, women's labor force participation has increased dramatically across class lines, and the portion of households headed by women with no other earner present also increased (Stokes and Chevan 1996). Today, roughly 65 percent of U.S. women with children under the age of six work in the paid labor force (Bureau of Labor Statistics 2017). Early education, however, has yet to catch up with the reality of single-parent and dual-earner working families.

Low-income and even many middle-income families struggle to access affordable, quality education and care for preschool-age children (Moodie-Dyer 2011; Liu 2015). The federal government recommends that families spend no more than 10 percent of income on childcare. Yet, the average cost of quality childcare ranges from $4,800 to more than $21,000 per year per child depending on location and age of child ("Map" 2014). A family with two $10 per hour full-time jobs earns a net income of less than $40,000 per year. Even the cheapest child care will cost that family 12 percent of their income for a single child.

Race and Ethnicity

Imagine two five-year-old girls in the Chicago suburbs, Julie, a White child on the north side in Winnetka, and Denise, an African American child on the south side in Chicago Heights. By age five, the two girls have had very different experiences as a result of their social class positions, and this, in turn, has affected brain development (Hanson et al. 2013; Center on the Developing Child 2016). Both girls can take advantage of a free public education, which should be an opportunity to eliminate any differences arising from family resources. In reality, it does not.

Julie will enter a nearly all-White school with the children of educated parents who read to them at home, engage them in stimulating play, and take them to the zoo on a regular basis. Denise will enter a school where a large percentage of the children come from low-income single-parent households where a working mother with a high school education has little time or energy to read, play games, or make trips to the zoo. These very different experiences represent the extremes of the U.S. class hierarchy—wealth with racial and class privilege for Julie and poverty with racial and class barriers for Denise.

Even if the two schools are able to spend their unrestricted state funding (i.e., funding not tied to the school's poverty rate, portion of students who do not speak English, or portion who require special education) the same way, Julie's will be enhanced by the portion of the school's funds (about 45 percent in Illinois) that come from local taxes, given the high property values in her district (see "School Funding and Inequality" below, for more information), and will attract more highly educated teachers. Denise's school will have a smaller tax base from which to supplement state funds and will struggle to attract and keep quality teachers because of the challenging school environment. Denise's school will receive additional state funding for special populations but will spend that money on special education to compensate for what kids did not gain in those precious first five years, on maintaining an aging and decrepit building, and on security to prevent street violence from entering the school. Julie's school will spend their locally enhanced resources on enrichment opportunities, academic and social clubs, the arts, and gifted programs. Denise's school will be less likely to offer a full range of math and science courses and more likely to use expulsion and suspension as disciplinary tools (Government

This 1978 picture shows schoolchildren boarding a bus in Seattle, the first major city in the United States to desegregate using a voluntary busing program.

AP Photo/Barry Sweet

Accountability Office 2016; Brown 2007). These girls' stories are not determined by the individuals in their families but by education systems that reproduce the existing class structure rather than providing a vehicle for class mobility.

The Supreme Court decision in *Brown v. Board of Education of Topeka* declared school segregation unconstitutional in 1954. In the 1970s, when it was obvious that many states had not moved to integrate their schools, mandatory **busing** programs were enacted in highly segregated school districts (Harper and Reskin 2005:361). Busing overcame residential segregation by transporting Black students to predominately White schools and, in some cases, White students to Black schools. Busing was not a popular public policy, and protests erupted in many cities where it was mandated.

Some school districts created high-quality and often specialized programs in the arts or science and technology at schools in Black urban areas. These programs were supposed to be "magnets" that attracted White students. Magnet schools were the original school choice program. They were quite effective for a time and remain so in some places. Over the years, however, and especially during the second Bush administration, the integrative mission lagged and schools focused more on academic achievement and innovation without attention to diversity (Siegel-Hawley and Frankenberg 2012).

More than sixty years after *Brown* ended legal racial segregation, the public school landscape has largely resegregated. Federally mandated desegregation—and most busing programs—ended in the 1990s, and since then, school segregation has returned to pre-*Brown* levels (Harper and Reskin 2005; Farkas 2003:128–29; Orfield 2001:32, Table 9, as cited in Harper and Reskin 2005:362; Kozol 2005). The percentage of K–12 public schools in the United States with 75 to 100 percent of students who are poor and Black or Hispanic nearly doubled between 2000 and 2014 (Government Accountability Office 2016).

Affirmative Action in College Admissions

Higher education officials recognized the value of diversity and the barriers that many minority students faced competing on a "level" admissions playing field. Race-neutral efforts (meaning actions that do not allow schools to consider race) were insufficient for anything beyond token integration (Harper and Reskin 2005:362). In the 1960s and 1970s, selective public and private colleges and universities voluntarily engaged in affirmative action practices to recruit minority students and examine student applications in a more holistic way to identify and admit promising students from underrepresented minority groups (Harper and Reskin 2005:362). These policies produced more minority college graduates and increased minority representation in graduate and professional programs.

In 1996, California passed a referendum that barred racial preference in admissions. Within a few years, Washington, Florida, Michigan, Nebraska, Arizona, and Oklahoma passed similar legislation. Minority enrollments declined. A series of court decisions determined that it is only constitutional to consider race as part of individualized assessments of each applicant (largely impossible for large schools that receive tens of thousands of applicants each year). Schools have used a number of strategies to remain within these rulings while pursuing diversity. Some tried class-based affirmative action strategies. Income-based policies promote social class diversity but do not achieve strong minority representation (Harper and Reskin 2005:363; Wilson 1999:97, 99).

Table 11.1 shows that Whites and Asians continue to enjoy far higher levels of educational attainment than do Blacks and Hispanics. Considering associate's degrees and higher, 39 percent of Whites and 51 percent of Asians earn a degree, compared to 29 percent of Blacks and only 20 percent of Hispanics.

TABLE 11.1

Educational Attainment by Race and Hispanic Origin

	Less Than High School (%)	High School Graduate (%)	Some College but No Degree (%)	Associate's Degree	Bachelor's Degree	Graduate or Professional Degree
Total population	12.3	29.6	19.4	9.4	18.9	10.4
White	11.9	29.6	19.1	9.6	19.2	10.6
Asian	1.2	10.4	20.1	14.7	6.6	29.4
Black	15.0	33.8	22.5	9.2	13.0	6.5
Hispanic	31.9	30.3	17.4	7.2	9.4	3.8

Source: U.S. Census Bureau (2015).

A "Model Minority" in Education

Asian American students, an ethnically diverse group with varied histories and experiences, are often assumed to be academically gifted. While this is true for some, those who struggle are often overlooked as the result of the "model minority" stereotype (Wing 2007; Wexler and Pyle 2012). As noted in Chapter 9, the diverse ethnic groups that comprise the Asian population in the United States include a full range of economic and social experiences that, as with all other groups, affect school experiences, performance, access to higher education, and overall attainment.

For example, a second-generation Japanese American whose father immigrated for a job in computing during the rise of the tech industry is likely to experience all of the benefits of at-home support for education and well-resourced schools serving the children of highly educated professionals. Meanwhile, a first-generation Hmong refugee from Vietnam may come from a home with two low-wage working parents with little time, energy, or resources for enriching activities with their kids. This child may live in a crowded apartment in an insular enclave of other immigrants. The community may be strong and supportive, but with parents who may still be learning English and whose work schedules leave little time for homework help, the Hmong child may struggle more than the Japanese child.

Gender and Education

Historically, higher education has been the domain of men. As illustrated in Figure 11.1, it was not until the second wave of the women's movement in the 1960s and 1970s that women began entering higher education in significantly larger numbers.

At the same time that women's opportunities and ideas about their own futures opened up, overall wages stagnated and more women were compelled to work to help support their families (Szafran 2002). While demand for higher levels of education grew, two incomes became necessary for families to maintain middle-class standing. Women turned away from traditional gender roles that kept them in the private sphere

Affirmative action is a mechanism used to ensure greater racial and ethnic diversity in higher education.

FIGURE 11.1

Percent of Population with Four Years or More of Higher Education by Gender, 1940–2015

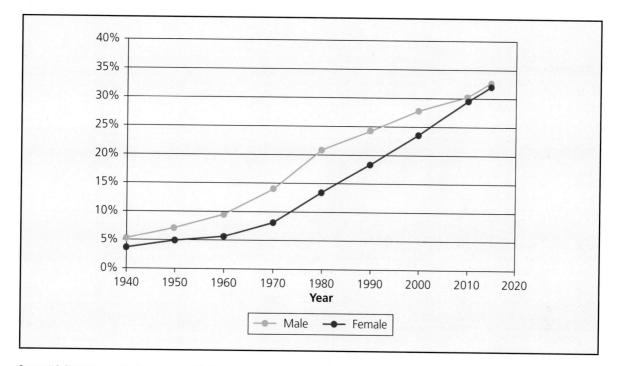

Source: U.S. Census Bureau, https://www.census.gov/hhes/socdemo/education/data/cps/historical/.

of home and family and moved toward higher education and careers (Alwin, Baun, and Scott 1992).

Women's Lower Returns for Education

Despite the fact that today more women than men attend college and complete undergraduate and graduate degrees, women do not experience the same financial benefits from education as men. Figure 11.2 shows that at all levels of education, a higher proportion of women than men are poor.

As noted in Chapter 8, men continue to hold an advantage in the labor market and earn higher salaries, even when they hold the same positions (Gamoran 2001). Figure 11.3 illustrates the difference in median earnings for men and women overall and at each level of education. Men see a greater return on education than do women.

School Funding and Inequality

Public schools in the United States receive funding through a combination of local, state, and federal funds. The portion that comes from each level of government is determined by school funding formulas that vary by state (on average, 45 percent comes from the state, 45 percent from local property taxes, and 10 percent from the federal government). Local funding for schools is often tied to property tax revenues. In areas with higher property values, communities have more local funding for public schools. In areas with lower property values, communities have less local school funding (Turner et al. 2016). As you can see in Figure 11.4, funding levels vary widely between states.

How do these funding disparities affect education's capacity to level the playing field? Without resources, it is very difficult for low-income schools to be effective in making up differences in kids' school preparedness that are related to parents' income and education levels.

Resources also affect teachers' experiences in schools. Teachers in schools where support services for students are readily available, books are up to date, and the physical space is in good repair can devote their energy to developing engaging classroom experiences. Moreover, school funding differences affect teacher pay. Desirable teaching jobs, in terms of the school atmosphere and salary, attract quality teachers. In many well-resourced schools, for example, the majority of teachers hold advanced degrees.

FIGURE 11.2

Poverty Rates by Educational Attainment for Men and Women, 2010–2014

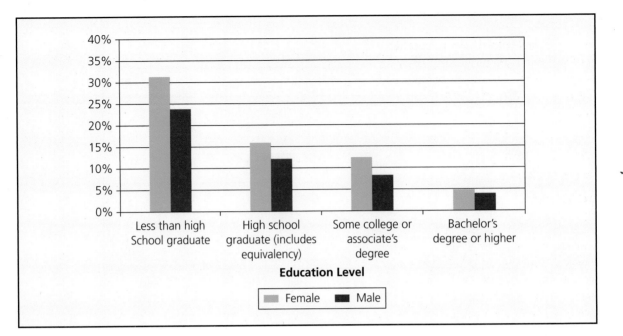

Source: U.S. Census Bureau (2015a).

FIGURE 11.3

Median Income for Women and Men by Educational Attainment

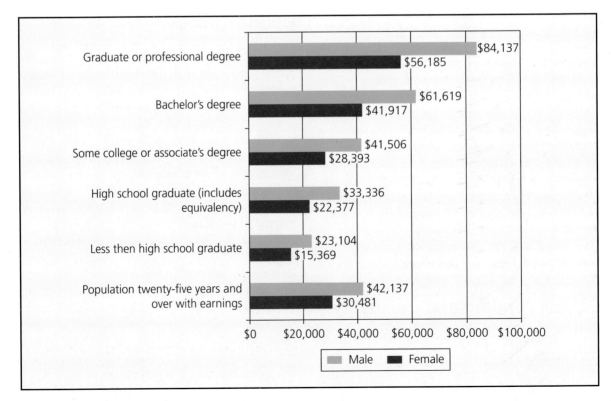

Source: U.S. Census Bureau (2015a).

Schools also vary in terms of parental engagement, which can affect funding and support for extracurricular activities. Parents in professional occupations have more flexibility in their work schedules and can more easily participate in school activities. Engaged and supportive parents can enhance school offerings through volunteer work and fundraising.

Reproducing Inequality within Schools

Race and class segregation can be created within as well as among schools. The practice of **tracking** involves placing students in classes based on "ability," often measured by classroom behavior, academic performance, and academic aspiration (i.e., college bound or vocational). High school courses, for example, might be offered at Advanced Placement (AP), honors, regular, and remedial levels. Tracking seems like a logical way to make teaching and learning more efficient. Tracking, however, privileges the education of some students over others and determines future education and career paths from an early age.

Higher-class White and Asian students are overrepresented in college preparatory tracks while lower-class Black and Hispanic students are overrepresented in vocational tracks, suggesting that factors other than ability shape placement (Worthy 2010; Oakes 1994a, 1994b). As noted earlier, kids who arrive at school with cultural capital may attract more positive attention from teachers regardless of their intellectual ability. This positive attention may feed positive outcomes. Similarly, teachers may conclude that students who lack cultural capital also lack intellectual ability (Worthy 2010; Palardy, Rumberger, and Butler 2015). Parental involvement also affects student tracking. Educated parents who understand the college application process are far more likely to push to place their children into the advanced tracks that look better on college applications. They are also more likely to recognize that challenging high school courses prepare their children for

FIGURE 11.4

Per Pupil Expenditures by State, 2013

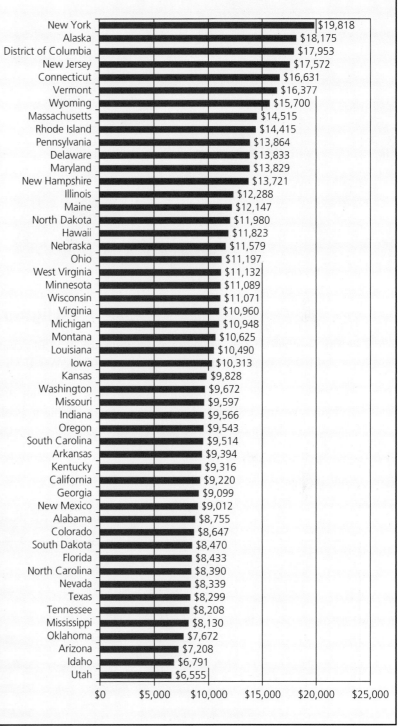

State	Expenditure
New York	$19,818
Alaska	$18,175
District of Columbia	$17,953
New Jersey	$17,572
Connecticut	$16,631
Vermont	$16,377
Wyoming	$15,700
Massachusetts	$14,515
Rhode Island	$14,415
Pennsylvania	$13,864
Delaware	$13,833
Maryland	$13,829
New Hampshire	$13,721
Illinois	$12,288
Maine	$12,147
North Dakota	$11,980
Hawaii	$11,823
Nebraska	$11,579
Ohio	$11,197
West Virginia	$11,132
Minnesota	$11,089
Wisconsin	$11,071
Virginia	$10,960
Michigan	$10,948
Montana	$10,625
Louisiana	$10,490
Iowa	$10,313
Kansas	$9,828
Washington	$9,672
Missouri	$9,597
Indiana	$9,566
Oregon	$9,543
South Carolina	$9,514
Arkansas	$9,394
Kentucky	$9,316
California	$9,220
Georgia	$9,099
New Mexico	$9,012
Alabama	$8,755
Colorado	$8,647
South Dakota	$8,470
Florida	$8,433
North Carolina	$8,390
Nevada	$8,339
Texas	$8,299
Tennessee	$8,208
Mississippi	$8,130
Oklahoma	$7,672
Arizona	$7,208
Idaho	$6,791
Utah	$6,555

Source: U.S. Census Bureau (2015b).

their own perceptions of what they can or cannot achieve.

Which college or university students attend and whether they graduate directly affects their adult position in the social structure (Bowles and Gintis 1976). Figure 11.5 shows that education is strongly related to unemployment and earnings. Students who neither gain skills for trades nor preparation for college will face tough futures, with lower earnings and higher levels of unemployment.

success in college (Gamoran 2001; Worthy 2010; Oakes 1994a, 1994b).

The unintended consequences of tracking are not limited to teacher perceptions and parental engagement. Tracking labels some students as "academic" and others as "vocational," which in turn structures the students' interactions. These interactions in turn determine students' self-concept and

Higher Education

While controversial at the time, the post–World War II GI Bill changed the face of higher education. Previously accessible only to the wealthy, the GI Bill democratized higher education by making it available to returning soldiers regardless of their parents' social class. By 1947, 49 percent of

FIGURE 11.5

Earnings and Unemployment Rates by Educational Attainment

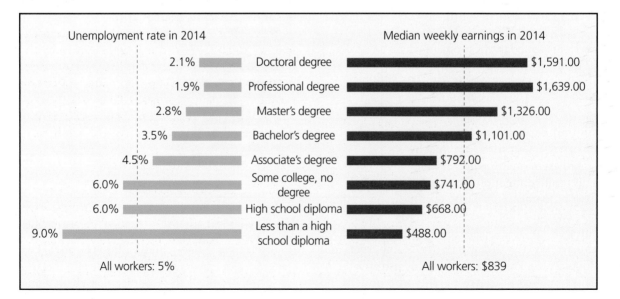

Unemployment rate in 2014		Median weekly earnings in 2014
2.1%	Doctoral degree	$1,591.00
1.9%	Professional degree	$1,639.00
2.8%	Master's degree	$1,326.00
3.5%	Bachelor's degree	$1,101.00
4.5%	Associate's degree	$792.00
6.0%	Some college, no degree	$741.00
6.0%	High school diploma	$668.00
9.0%	Less than a high school diploma	$488.00
All workers: 5%		All workers: $839

Source: U.S. Bureau of Labor Statistics, 2014, Current Population Survey, www.bls.gov.

all college students were veterans, and by the time that GI Bill ended in 1956, 7.8 million World War II veterans had used the bill to fund their educations and job training (U.S. Department of Veterans Affairs 2013). One consequence of the GI Bill was to demonstrate that students from across the social structure could find success and reap the rewards of higher education.

The GI Bill's success in democratizing higher education and the increasing labor market demand for higher levels of education contributed to a "college for all" (CFA) approach made possible by a community college system with open enrollment policies (Rosenbaum 2001, 2007). As a result, more low-income students enroll in college now than they did in the 1970s. However, they are less likely than their middle-class peers to graduate (Douthat 2005). In fact, "through boom and recession, war and peace, the proportion of the poorest Americans obtaining college degrees by age twenty-four has remained around six percent" (Douthat 2005).

Despite having better access to postsecondary education, lower socioeconomic status or "SES" (for students, this is determined by parents' income, occupational status, and educational attainment) students face significant nonacademic barriers to completion. First-generation college students and low-income students often lack full support from their families. They may have to work to pay bills while in school, reducing available study time and creating scheduling conflicts. When faced with a conflict between keeping their job and succeeding in coursework, they often choose the job. Over time, this role strain takes a toll and many drop out.

Types of Colleges, Student Success, and Tracking

Tracking in the K–12 system, a biased process, affects what type of college a student will attend. AP and honors classes generally funnel students into the elite universities and liberal arts colleges (Bowles and Gintis 1976). These schools teach students to be creative leaders and innovators. Students receive the message that they will occupy top leadership positions that will shape the future. These schools offer access to social networks of people with higher SES, and their degrees confer prestige that moves graduates' résumés to the top of the pile (Rivera 2011).

AP and honors students who go to public universities are more likely to go to one of the flagship institutions where they will find research assistantships and enrichment opportunities that give them an edge, from social networks and experience, upon graduation.

President Bill Clinton takes part in a ceremony in 1994 marking the 50th anniversary of the signing of the GI Bill. The GI Bill made it possible for many working-class men to attend college.

AP Photo/Greg Gibson

The next level in higher education is state (nonflagship) universities. These universities prepare students for roles in local leadership positions and mid-level management. Community colleges may help people access white-collar work or management of low-wage work, such as retail.

To the extent that tracking, which may start as early as third grade and is largely shaped by the class markers students arrive with in kindergarten, determines which type of postsecondary education students are likely to pursue (Elman and O'Rand 2007), a student's future class status may be largely determined before they even reach high school.

Funding for Higher Education

Higher education was once viewed as a public good that was well funded by state governments. States now give far less support to their public universities and colleges, which must therefore rely more on student tuition for funding. As Figure 11.6 indicates, on average, state funding for public higher education has declined by 18 percent since 2008 (Mitchell, Leachman, and Masterson 2016).

FIGURE 11.6

Percent Change in State Spending per Student, Inflation Adjusted, 2008–2016

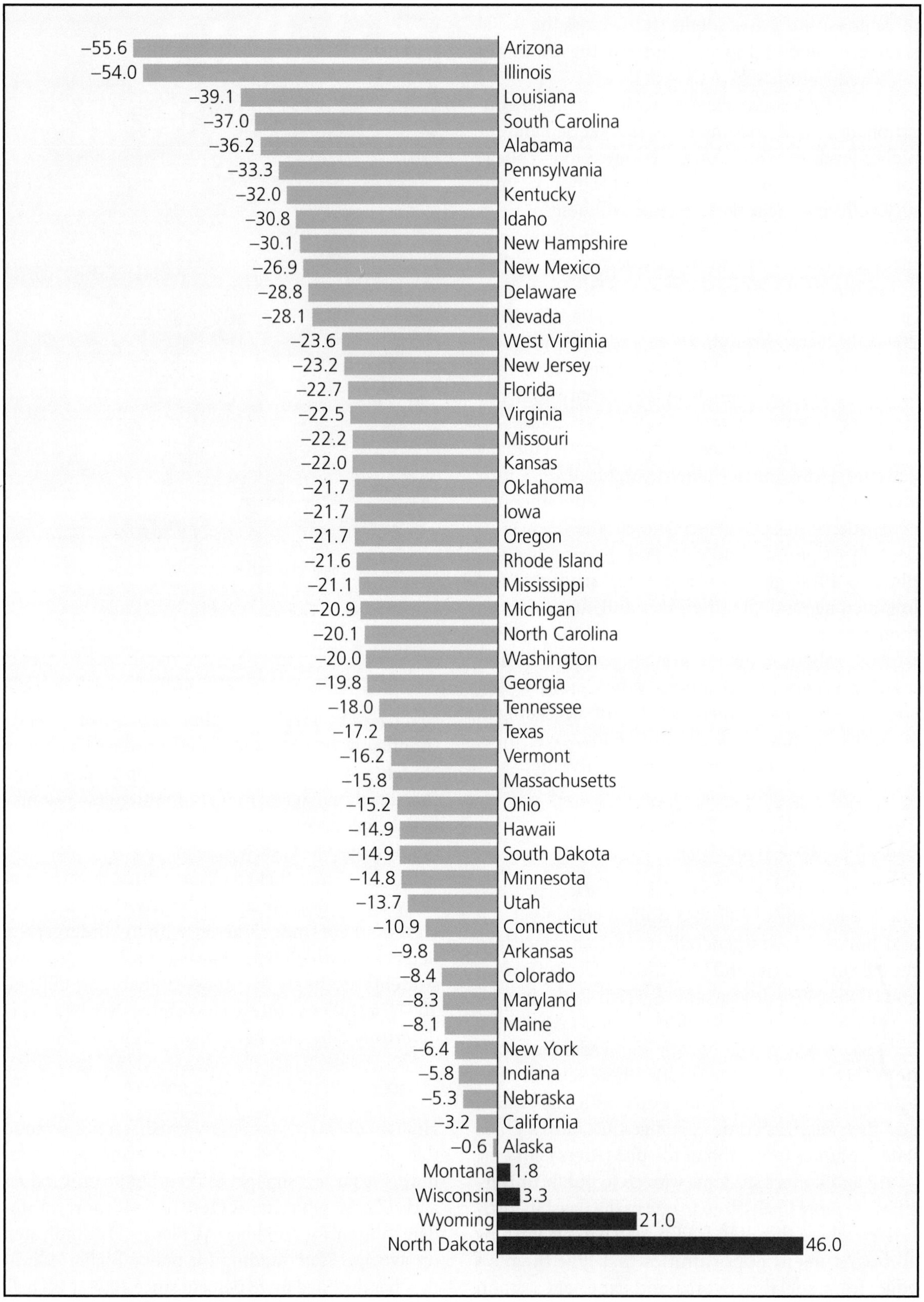

−55.6	Arizona
−54.0	Illinois
−39.1	Louisiana
−37.0	South Carolina
−36.2	Alabama
−33.3	Pennsylvania
−32.0	Kentucky
−30.8	Idaho
−30.1	New Hampshire
−26.9	New Mexico
−28.8	Delaware
−28.1	Nevada
−23.6	West Virginia
−23.2	New Jersey
−22.7	Florida
−22.5	Virginia
−22.2	Missouri
−22.0	Kansas
−21.7	Oklahoma
−21.7	Iowa
−21.7	Oregon
−21.6	Rhode Island
−21.1	Mississippi
−20.9	Michigan
−20.1	North Carolina
−20.0	Washington
−19.8	Georgia
−18.0	Tennessee
−17.2	Texas
−16.2	Vermont
−15.8	Massachusetts
−15.2	Ohio
−14.9	Hawaii
−14.9	South Dakota
−14.8	Minnesota
−13.7	Utah
−10.9	Connecticut
−9.8	Arkansas
−8.4	Colorado
−8.3	Maryland
−8.1	Maine
−6.4	New York
−5.8	Indiana
−5.3	Nebraska
−3.2	California
−0.6	Alaska
Montana	1.8
Wisconsin	3.3
Wyoming	21.0
North Dakota	46.0

Source: Center on Budget and Policy Priorities, "A Lost Decade in Higher Education Funding State Cuts Have Driven Up Tuition and Reduced Quality," Michael Mitchell, Michael Leachman, and Kathleen Masterson, August 23, 2017. Reprinted with permission.

FIGURE 11.7

Bachelor's Degree Attainment by Age Twenty-Four by Family Income Quartile, 1970–2013

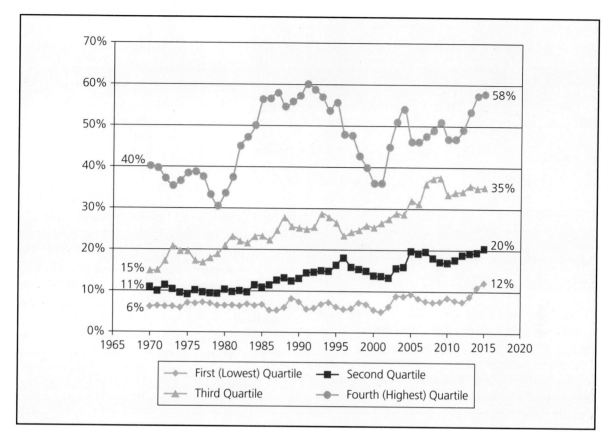

Source: *Indicators of High Education Equity in the United States, 2017 Historical Trend Report.* http://www.pellinstitute.org/downloads/publications- Indicators_of_Higher_Education_Equity_in_the_US_45_Year_Trend_Report.pdf (p. 77). Reprinted with permission from The Pell Institute.

What was once a public good is now a private good paid for by individuals. This shift is placing higher education out of reach for many high school graduates at a time when the labor market demands higher levels of education to secure a living wage (Carnevale, Jayasundera, and Gulish 2015). Figure 11.7 shows difference in college completion based on class background over time. The gap between attainment in the top income quintile and the rest has widened since 1980, the same period during which public funding has declined.

Consider This

How did your parents' education and income shape your educational opportunities?

Check Your Understanding

- How do schools reflect inequality across communities?

- In what ways does tracking within schools reproduce inequality?

- In what ways do the tiers of higher education reflect the class structure?

- Is college accessible to all today? Explain how decreases in public funding for higher education affect inequality.

- Is education leveling the playing field?

Developing nations are often not able to provide education to all of their children, widening global inequality.

Global Education and Global Inequality

Today, both individuals and nations compete in a global economy. And educational systems must prepare citizens to work in a global marketplace. To do this, educational institutions must continually adapt to changing economic forces and teach students how to interact effectively with people from other countries and cultures.

Giving U.S. Students a Global Perspective

A global economy demands international knowledge and experience. In 2015, the Student Exchange Visitor Program (SEVP) reported 1.2 million foreign students studying in the United States (U.S. Immigration and Customs Reinforcement 2016). By contrast, only 1.5 percent of all U.S. students currently enrolled in institutions of higher education studied abroad and just 10 percent of all U.S. college graduates had study-abroad experience (NAFSA 2015).

A 2013 study reported that "almost 40% of companies surveyed missed international business opportunities because of a lack of internationally competent personnel" (NAFSA 2015; Daniel, Xie, and Kedia 2014). This means that our economy would grow faster if we had a more internationally culturally competent workforce. Individual workers, companies, and the nation would benefit from more study-abroad experiences for college students.

Global Literacy and Education

Like domestic inequality, global inequality affects and is affected by educational attainment. Education and health are essential precursors to economic development and the basis for addressing all other social concerns (Rosling 2007). In 2000, at the World Education Forum in Dakar, Senegal, 164 governments agreed on a plan for meeting some key education goals by 2015. The international effort yielded positive results. They reduced the number of children and adolescents out of school by half, increased school attendance dramatically, and achieved greater gender parity, particularly in primary education. Still, significant gaps remain: 58 million children remain out of school globally, around 100 million do not complete primary education, and many leave primary education without basic skills (Global Monitoring Report 2015).

Security concerns keep many children out of school, and funding for education remains a problem worldwide (Global Monitoring Report 2015: i–ii). Lower-income children are less likely to attend school than higher-income children. Gender disparities in primary education declined significantly between 2000 and 2015, but progress has been slower in secondary schools (Global Monitoring Report 2015).

Finland: Global Leader in Quality Education

Finland stands out as a top-performing country on standardized tests of secondary students. Most notable is the consistency of performance across schools and among students within schools (Organization for Economic Cooperation and Development [OECD] 2010:118). The gap between the highest performing and lowest performing schools and students is quite small (118).

The Finnish system is relatively new and is the result of a national effort to establish a single compulsory system that educates all children without

Supporting Life Chances for Our Most Vulnerable Populations

Gabriella C. Gonzalez

As a sociologist of education and immigration, I learned all about Marx, Weber, and Durkheim; about **social capital** and the strength of weak ties; about inequality and its effects on children's life chances; and about social stratification and how schools act as organizations to either reproduce the status quo or propel change. I felt empowered by how statistical analysis of large data sets could find objective truth: relationships and correlations that otherwise would be obscured by political rhetoric. I was enraptured by how ethnography and qualitative methods could unearth the meaning and feelings of populations we studied and answer the question of "why is that?"

But I wanted more. I wanted to roll up my sleeves in schools, with students, with teaching professionals. I wanted to make a difference.

In 2002, I joined a nonpartisan think tank, RAND Corporation, which enabled me to make a difference through policy-based research. Rather than examining social problems from the sidelines, I now spend my days on interdisciplinary team-based projects (often with psychologists, anthropologists, economists, or political scientists) working directly with countries and school districts to enact change and make a direct impact on the lives of the children in most need of support.

From 2003 through 2007, I helped the country of Qatar develop curriculum standards and assessments for their schoolchildren—using sociologically based understandings of how language, ethnicity, and identity formation could affect students' approach to learning. I am now in the United States applying my sociological training to work in urban school districts. I've worked closely with district officials, principals, and teachers in Pittsburgh, Baltimore, New Haven, and Jackson, Mississippi, to evaluate the effectiveness of new education reform efforts, the rebuilding of school facilities, and programs to improve school climate and safety on students'

social and emotional well-being and on their academic achievement and college going. For example, I have a three-year grant from the National Institute of Justice to evaluate a program, Tools for Life, which provides children in grade 3 through grade 8 with nonviolent conflict resolution skills in schools in Jackson Public Schools in Mississippi. I am leading a multidisciplinary research team of an adolescent psychologist, a statistician, an education policy researcher, and two research assistants. I am also monitoring the implementation of the program, meeting with district officials and program designers each week. We just started the project in January 2016 and will follow students who were exposed to the program over time, comparing them to sociodemographically similar students who were not exposed. We will be looking at whether the two groups differ through time in academic and social outcomes as well as in reported feelings of safety in their schools. The best part of this project is working hand-in-hand with my partners at Jackson Public Schools and Tools for Life, making a difference for the students.

Each project I lead brings a sociological lens to ensure that the interplay of social structures, family background, peer networks, race, class, and gender is not lost in how school districts develop and implement policies and practices to improve schooling.

What have I learned? Without considering the social context and struggles in which our students live, no policy or practice will make a dent. Without getting full buy-in and support from families and teachers, the shiniest, most innovative, and potentially effective effort will fail . . . miserably. Not because it wasn't a good idea, but because it wasn't implemented to its full potential. Or worse, no one thought it mattered.

Gabriella C. Gonzalez is a RAND Corporation senior sociologist with a PhD in sociology from Harvard University.

---

tracking (OECD 2010:118–21). The upper grades offer a vocational path, but that path also prepares students for higher education in technological fields and is no less rigorous than the academic track (120). The system is learner centered and emphasizes happiness and well-being. These approaches require highly qualified and engaged teachers. All teachers must hold a master's degree, and they are generally drawn from the pool of high academic performers (121). This system has led to

Finland's top rankings on international standardized assessments across schools and students, resulting in significant economic growth tied to a highly qualified and innovative workforce.

Finland is a society that has seen its investments in education pay off. While the United States is larger and more diverse, there are lessons in the Finnish experience (e.g., in teacher recruitment and training). Many sociologists, such as Gabriella Gonzalez, featured in the Sociologists in Action box, work to improve the lives of children through designing education policies and curricula.

Check Your Understanding

- Why do U.S. workers need to be internationally competent?

- List three key issues the World Education Forum seeks to address.

- In what ways is Finland's school system different from what you have learned about the U.S. education system? How might this example inform U.S. discussions of school reform?

Leveling the Playing Field: Public Policy and Education

Recent policy debates about public education in the United States center on a desire to improve the quality and competitiveness of the system. Some argue that market-based models are the best way to achieve these goals (Chubb and Moe 1990; Finn, Manno, and Vanourek 2000). Others argue that directing greater attention to equalizing quality within and across schools is the best way to improve educational outcomes and global competitiveness (Ravitch 2010; Ripley 2014). The following sections explore policy debates and options for American education from birth through college.

Pre-K Education

Proponents of the value of quality early education and care argue for universal access from birth to age five and rigorous education and training for pre-K teachers. Ninety percent of the brain's architecture develops by age five (U.S. Department of Education 2013; California Newsreel 2014). This means that the experiences of children from birth through age five are vital to later outcomes (Center on the Developing Child 2016). Research suggests that public investments in quality pre-K education and care can reduce public spending on special education, juvenile justice, criminal justice, and social welfare programs (Warner 2009). When families have access to affordable quality care, more parents work (Gould and Cooke 2015; California Newsreel 2014; Warner 2009). The rise in employment reduces child poverty and increases tax revenue to help pay for the public provision of care (California Newsreel 2014; Warner 2009).

The Abecedarian Project

The Abecedarian project examined the long-term impacts of quality pre-K education and care. Researchers randomly selected children born between 1972 and 1977 and assigned them to the intervention group or a control group. The intervention group received full-time, high-quality education and child care from infancy through age five. Educational games and activities supported social, emotional, and cognitive development. Researchers followed up with both groups at ages twelve, fifteen, twenty-one, thirty, and thirty-five, and the results were encouraging: kids enrolled in the Abecedarian pre-K program were four times more likely to attend college than kids in the control group (California Newsreel 2014; Temple and Reynolds 2007).

K–12 Education

In 1983, the National Commission on Excellence in Education released *A Nation at Risk: The Imperative for Educational Reform*. The report found U.S. schools underperformed and failed to produce a globally competitive workforce (National Commission on Excellence in Education 1983; Ravitch 2010). Concerns about the failure of U.S. schools gave rise to market-based models for improving quality, lowering costs, and increasing accountability (Ravitch 2010). The *Nation at Risk* report led to major reform efforts that culminated in the 2001 No Child Left Behind Act (NCLB).

NCLB increased standardized assessments, raised penalties for low performance, expanded school choice through charter schools and vouchers, monitored teacher quality through student performance, enacted a "reading first" approach aimed at ensuring that all children read at grade level by the end of third grade, and consolidated bilingual and immigrant education programs (U.S. House of Representatives 2001). The most apparent results of this reform were a dramatic increase in class time spent preparing for

The purpose of "No Child Left Behind" was to improve the quality of education for all children but also resulted in increased time spent taking standardized exams.

and administering standardized tests, an increase in **school choice** options, and the rapid growth of charter schools and the use of vouchers. School choice options vary by location but can include the ability to attend the public school of the family's choosing, attend a charter school, or use a voucher to subsidize attendance at a private school.

Charter Schools and Vouchers

Supporters of market models argue that when individuals are free to choose and to maximize their own benefit, the cumulative enterprise also benefits. When consumers choose their own cable television provider, the companies in the market must compete, luring customers with lower prices and better service. Advocates of this movement argue that, if a school falls short in providing services, consumer-citizens can opt for alternatives, support higher-quality options, and generate a virtuous cycle of improvement.

The two primary mechanisms for creating a market in public primary and secondary education are charter schools and vouchers. Beginning in the 1990s, states began passing laws authorizing **charter schools,** publicly funded schools, established under a charter, and governed by parents, educators, community groups, or private organizations. The "charter" details the school's mission, curriculum or philosophy, students to be served, performance goals, evaluation plans, and commitments. Depending on state law, charter status may free these schools from some of the legal and bureaucratic constraints of the traditional public school structure and thus allow for greater innovation. After more than two decades, however, the effects of charter schools on student achievement appear to be mixed. Overall, charter school students do not necessarily perform better than other public school students on tests such as the SAT or ACT, but more go on to college (Berends 2015).

School voucher programs also began in the 1990s. **Vouchers** are certificates of government funding that make each pupil's state funds portable, allowing parents to choose to use their child's funds at a public or private school of their choice. Proponents argue that every student is entitled to their state funding

allotment, and where they choose to use it should be up to them. Others argue that states are not funding individuals but a system. When vouchers are used to pay for private education, needed funds are removed from the public schools.

The market approach assumes that consumers are knowledgeable and engaged. Students whose parents research and discern the best options will benefit from market models, while the children of parents who lack the time, ability, or interest in researching options will be disadvantaged by the market model and left in failing schools. Critics argue that increased use of vouchers will further segregate schools by class as better educated and well-resourced parents will use vouchers to send their children to the best schools, diminishing the resources of the public schools they leave behind and filling those public schools with students whose parents likely have less education and lower incomes. This creates a feedback loop going the wrong direction. Detractors argue that segregating students in this way will exacerbate existing problems in the public school system and further separate the haves from the have-nots.

Fifteen years after the implementation of NCLB, concerns about the quality and competitiveness of American schools remain (Porter and Rivkin 2012). Test scores have not improved for disadvantaged groups (Strauss 2015). The emphasis on high-stakes testing has come under fire as physical education, arts, and humanities courses have been cut back to funnel resources to test preparation (Ravitch 2010; Layton 2015; Supovitz 2016).

Responding to this criticism, Congress passed the Every Student Succeeds Act (ESSA) in 2015, in an effort to address some of the unintended negative consequences of NCLB. Notably, the ESSA deemphasized punitive responses, such as schools losing funding or being closed down, for persistent poor student performance, and emphasized the use of incentives to improve school and teacher quality (U.S. House of Representatives 2015). The act reduces onerous testing requirements while maintaining a focus on accountability (White House 2015). With the election of President Donald Trump and his appointment of school choice advocate Betsy DeVos as secretary of education, we can expect a greater emphasis on market-based approaches to school reform.

Consider This

How do you think the United States could change the public education system to level the playing field and produce better outcomes? Be specific about policies, practices, or approaches that could make a difference.

The Future of Public Higher Education

As noted earlier, state governments across the country have cut funding to institutions of higher education. They also have done little to provide opportunities for rigorous high-tech training and higher education outside of the traditional college setting to build a qualified workforce for new manufacturing jobs.

At the forefront of discussion in the coming years will be the question of whether higher education is a public good or a private expense. When education is a private good, only those with the most resources can afford it. Looking at education from a sociological perspective, however, it is clear that everyone benefits from a country with more educated workers and citizens. Education lays the foundation for progress, economic success, democracy, and quality of life. Given that everyone benefits from an educated citizenry, it follows that the cost of education should be shared by all.

Consider This

Should higher education be publicly supported and accessible to all qualified students? Why?

Check Your Understanding

- What are the arguments in favor of market models (charters and vouchers) for improving public education?

- What are some unintended negative consequences of applying market models to public education?

- Explain the arguments for and against publicly funded childcare, public K–12 schools, and higher education.

Conclusion

Education is an essential institution in society. It provides the foundation for development and innovation, and it is the centerpiece of the American belief in meritocratic success. Educated people can shape their lives and their society.

Schools provide sites of secondary socialization that teach children, adolescents, and young adults about the unwritten rules for social interaction. They also work to ensure that the citizenry knows the history of the country, its key figures, and major events. These aspects of socialization prepare students for adult roles as workers, citizens, community and economic leaders, parents, and spouses. International education can bridge geographic and cultural distance and create economic growth. But education is also an institution that reflects, and even reproduces, dominant ideologies and systems of inequality in the United States and around the world.

A sociological perspective can help us understand and shape the educational institution to more fully reflect the meritocratic values it serves. Approaching education with a sociological lens brings attention to the functions and power dynamics in systems of education and in school-level interactions. This critical perspective can help societies build education systems that create opportunity for all.

Sociology provides a similar opportunity to examine religion as an institution. Religion serves some of the same functions as education but also additional cultural and explanatory functions. A closer look reveals the ways religion produces and reinforces inequality and informs cultural practices, values, and beliefs. The next chapter will explore the functions, power dynamics, and cultural impacts of religion.

⑤SAGE edge™

Want a better grade? Get the tools you need to sharpen your study skills. Access practice quizzes, eFlashcards, video and multimedia at **edge.sagepub.com/korgen**

Review

11.1 What does it mean to look at education as a social institution?

Education comprises roles, rules, and routines that provide consistency across time and place and are slow to change. These patterns help individuals—students, staff, and parents—move from one organization to another within the institution and limit the influence of individual personalities on the functioning of organizations.

11.2 How do historical moment, the social structure, and changing systems of production shape the functions of education over time and across place?

Education reflects the mode of production across time and place. In preindustrial societies, parents had their children work alongside them, learning the skills and modeling the behaviors necessary to meet basic needs.

Formal schooling emerged with the industrial system of manufacturing that separated workers from their homes and required new skills to meet the needs of a growing and diverse economic system. Production required basic reading, writing, and math skills and benefited from a system that socialized workers to show up on time and conform to authority. Compulsory public schooling emerged to meet these needs.

In a service and knowledge economy, soft skills, including communication, depth of knowledge, and problem solving, are essential. Today's economy requires strong critical thinking, collaborative work habits, and creative innovation. As a durable institution, education has not made the shift from rote memorization to effective development of adaptability and creativity.

11.3 How do functionalism, conflict theory, and symbolic interaction approach and explain education as an institution?

Functionalists note that education provides children with secondary socialization, which helps young people learn to interact within organizations, with peers, and in nonfamily group settings. Schools play an important role developing a national identity, a qualified workforce, and an educated citizenry. Schools also serve latent functions of providing universal childcare for children ages five to eighteen years and regulating entry into the labor force.

Conflict theorists point out that in the United States, school structures, resources, and the content of the curriculum all reflect larger systems of social inequality. Schools tend to favor middle-class norms and values. Educators perceive and treat children based on elements of behavior that are largely reflective of parents' income and education. From physical structures and course offerings to tracking and discipline, education systems favor those with more power and higher status.

Symbolic interactionists focus on interactions within schools and how they lead to cultural reproduction. Schools transmit a hidden curriculum of cultural values and beliefs. The hidden curriculum supports and promotes dominant ideologies about the economy and system of governance but may also reflect inequalities embedded in stereotypes tied to race, class, gender, and other social characteristics. These messages shape their perceptions of others, their self-esteem, and their behaviors and thus produce outcomes that reflect the social norms, rules, and stereotypes of the culture.

11.4 How does education reproduce social inequality?

School systems reflect the inequalities of the labor market and race and class segregation in housing. This affects physical aspects of schools, the curriculum offered, parent engagement, and the learning readiness and educational focus of the student population. Schools assess student potential and ability based on measures of performance and behavior that favor children from educated middle-class backgrounds. Schools track students based on these assessments and provide different levels of challenge and rigor, preparing students for distinct education and career paths. More often than not, the system funnels children into the same relative class status as their parents.

11.5 What are the central issues facing global education today?

In an increasingly globalized world, cultural and international competency is essential, making international education more important than ever. Low literacy and school attendance rates in many poor and war-torn nations and neglect for the education of girls leave many areas of the world unable to develop and progress. Meanwhile, among developed nations, Finland provides some of the best education in the world by focusing on equal quality education for all citizens, hiring only highly qualified teachers, and offering a holistic approach that focuses on child happiness and well-being.

11.6 How do policy debates surrounding pre-K, K–12, and higher education all revolve around the tension between public education and individual choice and responsibility for accessing opportunities and achieving success?

Childcare and preschool, a high-quality public school system for all, and publicly supported higher education all work to provide equal opportunity to all citizens. Market-based approaches, such as charter schools and vouchers, rely on citizens to be actively engaged critical consumers, which may leave students with fewer resources behind. Current approaches to pre-K and higher education place quality programs out of reach for many. Current policy debate revolves around how to pay for and hold accountable an education system that needs to meet the changing needs of a diverse population in a knowledge-based economy.

Key Terms

- busing   235
- charter schools   247
- dominant ideology   225
- durable   226
- education   226
- hidden curriculum   229
- human capital   233

- school choice   247
- secondary socialization   229
- social capital   245
- social cohesion   230
- tracking   239
- vouchers   247

The concept of the sacred is a powerful social idea that guides the lives of millions of people.

REUTERS/Tarmizy Harva

Learning Questions

12.1 How do sociologists define religion, religiosity, and spirituality?

12.2 What are pluralism and secularization?

12.3 What is fundamentalism?

12.4 What are the current trends in religious affiliation and participation in the United States?

12.5 How does the process of global diffusion apply to religion?

12.6 How do each of the major theoretical paradigms in sociology explain religion?

12.7 What are some recent examples of how religion has fostered social change efforts?

CHAPTER 12

Understanding Institutions

Religion

Andrea N. Hunt

Defining Religion Sociologically

In *The Elementary Forms of Religious Life* (1995 [1912]), Émile Durkheim distinguished between the **profane,** a sphere of everyday life, and the **sacred,** that which inspires reverence and devotion. While it may be difficult to distinguish between the sacred and profane within some religions (such as Hinduism), the notion of the sacred serves as the basis for most *general* definitions of religion.

Sociologists define **religion** as a social institution that involves the beliefs and practices of what has been socially constructed as sacred in a given society. Religion is a social institution that bonds communities through a shared meaning system; a set of beliefs, practices, and symbols that reflect the shared meaning system; a sense of belonging; ethics that guide the lives of the members; and routinized social expectations (Roberts and Yamane 2016:21).

> **Consider This**
> How can we determine how religious people are or to what extent they practice their religion?

These elements do not describe a certain religious affiliation but rather capture the broad characteristics of religion in general. These characteristics can be seen in different religious traditions such as Islam, Christianity, Buddhism, Confucianism, Hinduism, Buddhism, Judaism, and many others. Despite some very general similarities, each of these religions has unique beliefs and practices that differentiate them from each other.

We can measure religiousness or **religiosity** through looking at a range of religious beliefs, activities, and practices in which people participate. People are often considered religious when they engage in behaviors seen as sacred in a particular society. This might include the set of beliefs or ideology that people hold true and the rituals that they practice. For some people, participation in religious ceremonies and church, temple, or synagogue attendance are a way to celebrate and practice faith as a member of a larger community. Their attendance at a religious ceremony is a reflection of their belief system. For others, attending a religious ceremony might just be a public

Andrea N. Hunt

I was originally a psychology major and planned to pursue marriage and family therapy for a career. I didn't have an engaging experience in introduction to sociology so my first real ah-ha moment came in a course on juvenile delinquency. I was fascinated by the role of the family in shaping the life course of youth and was even more intrigued by juvenile programming. This led to a research assistantship during my master's program, evaluating juvenile aftercare programs, and to the beginning of a life as a public sociologist. As a doctoral student, I discovered the scholarship of teaching and learning and came to more fully understand the importance of the introduction to sociology course as the key to bringing students into the discipline. Today, I regularly teach introduction to sociology. Another of my favorite topics to teach about is religion. It's a great way to show students how to apply the major theoretical perspectives in sociology, understand how inequality is reproduced in our society, and assess how positive social change occurs.

display of adherence to a religion while their actions in everyday life do not reflect faith-based practices. A reliance on rituals and practices alone as a measure of religiosity can be problematic.

What is the difference between religion and spirituality? **Spirituality** is the search for the sacred, which involves finding meaning or purpose in your life and trusting in some higher power. This implies more of a journey or process rather than being defined by the boundaries of specific religions (Roberts and Yamane 2016; Stanczak 2006). Spirituality is fluid rather than a constant with clearly defined practices, which means that it is not always compatible with organized religions. Some people consider themselves spiritual but not religious and may reject organized religion while embracing more individualized forms of spiritual practice such as prayer, meditation, and yoga. However, spirituality does not stand in direct opposition to organized religion since both include practices orientated toward the sacred (Stanczak 2006; Roberts and Yamane 2016).

Consider This

How are religion and spirituality related and how are they different? Some people say they are spiritual but not religious, but is it also possible to be religious but not spiritual?

Religion Is More Than a Private Matter

Our sociological imagination gives us the ability to see how outside forces affect our individual lives and the connections among different parts of society. For example, we can see how religion operates as an individual belief system but also as a social institution that creates a shared meaning system and defines acceptable behavior for a group of people. The sociological imagination also allows us to see how religion intersects with other major social institutions such as the family and the educational system. Recall the discussion in Chapter 10 of how Calvinist religious beliefs about marriage shaped legal doctrine around who was able to own property and who was seen as the head of households. For many people, wedding ceremonies are both a civil contract that join two people legally and a religious rite that includes religious symbols, practices, and rituals. At one time, interracial marriage in the United States was prohibited. The U.S. Supreme Court struck down individual state laws prohibiting interracial marriage in the landmark case *Loving v. Virginia* (1967). The Virginia judge who originally heard the case cited biblical passages justifying racial segregation in his decision. Prayer in school continues to be debated today even after the U.S. Supreme Court prohibited school- or state-sanctioned prayer in 1962. Some schools have adopted "moments of silence" to reflect the level of religious pluralism in the United States today.

Check Your Understanding

- How do sociologists define religion?

- What is the difference between religion and spirituality?

- How do you know if someone is religious?

- How is religion more than a private matter?

Thinking Critically about Religion

In this activity, you will use the SEE-I method to think critically about religion.

Religion can seem like a difficult concept to describe in the abstract, although it touches many of our lives in profound and intimate ways. Use the SEE-I (State, Elaborate, Exemplify, Illustrate) critical thinking method (Nosich 2009:33–38) to clarify and understand the concept of religion.

1. *State* a basic definition of religion in one sentence.

2. *Elaborate* on the concept of religion in your own words and describe the difference between sacred and profane.

3. *Exemplify* the concept of religion by giving concrete examples of the different components of the definition of religion provided in the text.

4. *Illustrate* the concept of religion with a picture or diagram that shows the difference between religion and spirituality.

Religious Pluralism and Secularization

Religiosity can be affected by social changes in society, including changes in the economic system, political and social movements, and immigration. Current trends in the United States show more diversity in religious affiliation and participation than in previous decades.

Changing Demographics and Pluralism

Due in large part to changing demographics of new immigrants, we have seen increases in non-Christian faiths in the United States (Chaves 2011). Figure 12.1 shows that from 1992 to 2012, the percentage of immigrants identifying with non-Christian religions increased by 6 percent. In Figure 12.2,

FIGURE 12.1

Growing Share of Legal Immigrants Belong to Religious Minorities

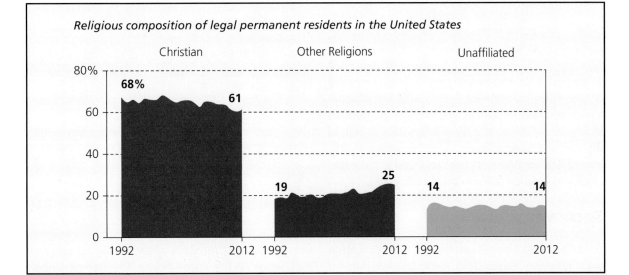

Source: "The Religious Affiliation of U.S. Immigrants: Majority Christian, Rising Share of Other Faiths," Pew Research Center, May 17, 2013, http://www.pewforum.org/2013/05/17/the-religious-affiliation-of-us-immigrants.

FIGURE 12.2

Growing Share of Muslim and Hindu Immigrants

Religious composition of legal permanent residents in the United States belonging to non-Christian faiths

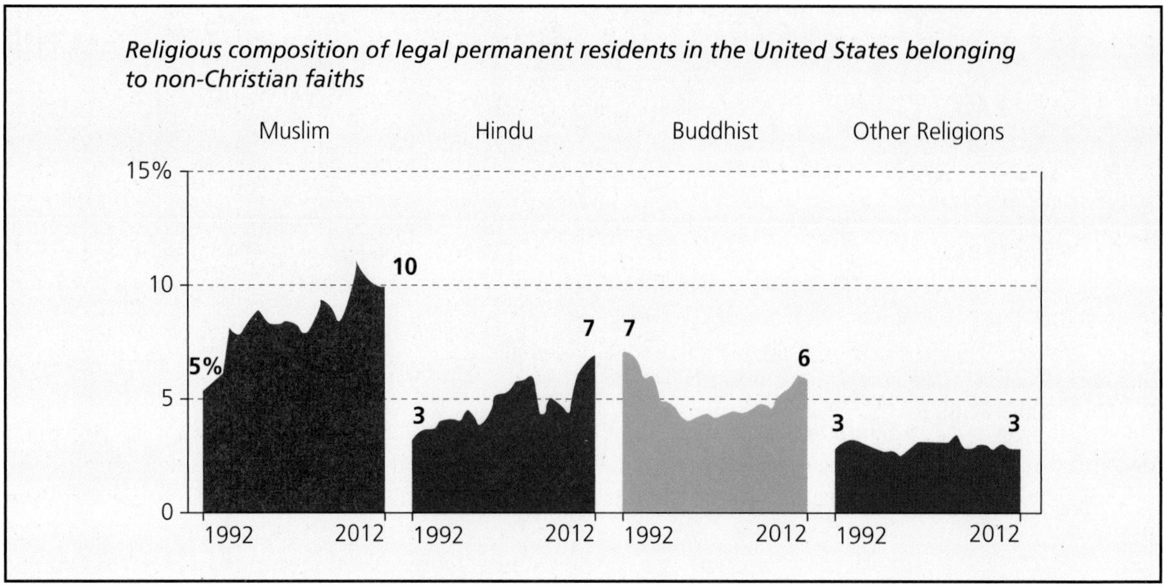

Source: "The Religious Affiliation of U.S. Immigrants: Majority Christian, Rising Share of Other Faiths," Pew Research Center, May 17, 2013, http://www.pewforum.org/2013/05/17/the-religious-affiliation-of-us-immigrants.

you can see an increase in Muslim and Hindu immigrants. Historically, immigrants to the United States originated primarily from European countries and brought with them Christian (mostly Roman Catholic) and Jewish religious traditions. Today, there are still many immigrants to the United States who identify as Christian, and they tend to arrive from Central and South America. However, there are also an increasing number of immigrants from Asian and African countries who are more likely to be Muslim, Hindu, or Buddhist.

Religious pluralism arises when different religious belief systems coexist within a society. Immigration can lead to more religious diversity and, in some cases, create a religiously pluralistic society with increasing numbers of interreligious marriages. The Pew Research Center's (2015b) Religious Landscape Study shows that 39 percent of Americans who have married since 2010 report marrying someone from a different religion. This is up from 19 percent of those who got married before 1960. While pluralism suggests a degree of diversity and more religious and spiritual choices, religious pluralism does not necessarily lead to more religious participation (Chaves and Gorski 2001).

Secularization

A society's movement away from identification with religious values and institutions is known as **secularization.** Data in Table 12.1 from the Pew Research Center's (2015b) Religious Landscape

TABLE 12.1

Unaffiliated Makeup Growing Share across Generations: Percentage of Each Generation That Identifies Current Religion as Atheist, Agnostic, or Nothing in Particular

	2007	2014	Change
Silent generation (b. 1928–1945)	9	11	+2
Baby Boomers (b. 1946–1964)	14	17	+3
Generation X (b. 1965–1980)	19	23	+4
Older Millennials (b. 1981–1989)	25	34	+9
Younger Millennials (b. 1990–1996)	NA	36	NA

Source: America's Changing Religious Landscape, Pew Research Center, May 12, 2015, http://www.pewforum.org/2015/05/12/americas-changing-religious-landscape/.

Note: NA = not applicable.

Study indicate an increase in the percentage of people in the United States indicating no religious affiliation. While many people who are religiously unaffiliated still have a belief in a God, a rising number of people do not share in this belief. This

Today, many more Americans marry someone from a different religion than in the past, reflecting the religious pluralism of our society.

Paul Quayle/Alamy Stock Photo

includes those who may identify as **athe-ists,** who do not believe in a God, and those who are **agnostic,** maintaining that nothing is known or can be known about God(s). Agnosticism is different from atheism in that agnostics do not disbelieve in a God, but they also do not claim a particular faith-based belief system. Some humanists can be included in both groups. **Secular humanists** believe that humans have the capability of being moral and just without religion or a divine God.

There are several possible explanations for this increase in people who identify as religiously unaffiliated. There has been a longstanding relationship between religion and politics, with religious ideologies influencing governmental practices. However, the influence of religion in governmental matters declines with urbanization, migration, developments in science and technology, and mass participation in the political process. Even with these changes, though, there are still connections between some religious affiliations and conservative political

ideologies (Chaves 2011). For example, Mormons and Evangelical Protestants are more likely to identify as both religiously and politically conservative and agree that religion is an essential part of the political process (Pew Research Center 2015b). For others, there is less adherence to dominant religious and political ideologies. The connection between religion and politics may affect some people's perceptions of organized religion and their likelihood of identifying with a particular, or any, religious affiliation. As Figure 12.3 illustrates, just as fewer people in the United States are identifying with a religion, fewer are also identifying with a political party.

FIGURE 12.3

U.S. Party Identification, Yearly Averages, Gallup Polls, 1988–2015

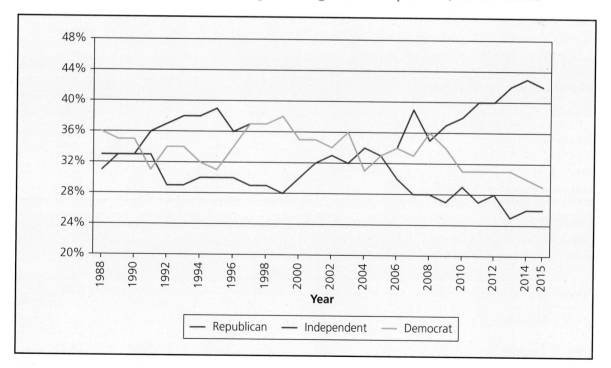

Source: Adapted from Democratic, Republican Identification Near Historical Lows, January 11, 2016, Gallup. http://www.gallup.com/poll/188096/democratic-republican-identification-near-historical-lows.aspx.

Live-streaming worship services provide ways to participate in religion in an informal way.

Ed Simons/Alamy Stock Photo

Growing numbers of Americans, particularly younger Americans, are rejecting both traditional political parties and organized religions.

Second, there are more ways for people to express their faith today outside of organized religion and in more informal contexts and venues (Cadge, Levitt, and Smilde 2011). This can be seen in the growing number of online communities of faith (Campbell 2013), televised or live-streaming worship services, and informal fellowship opportunities on many college campuses today (i.e., campus ministries) (Mankowski and Thomas 2000). Third, religious involvement in youth is one of the best predictors of involvement in adulthood. Recent cohorts are more likely to be born into nonreligious households, which creates a cohort effect in religious affiliation. As Table 12.2 shows, Millennials are less likely to report a Christian affiliation and more likely to say they are unaffiliated with any religion compared to previous generations. This means, in turn, that their children are less likely to be born into a religiously affiliated household than they were.

Last, **secularization theory** (Berger 1992) suggests that modernization encourages the demystifying of the world and undermines the influence of religion. **Modernization** happens as countries undergo the process of industrialization, and decisions begin to be based more on reason and logic than tradition. As a

TABLE 12.2

Generational Replacement Helping Drive Growth of Unaffiliated, Decline of Mainline Protestantism and Catholicism

	Silent Generation (b. 1928–1945)	Baby Boomers (b. 1946–1964) (%)	Generation X (b. 1965–1980) (%)	Older Millennials (b. 1981–1989) (%)	Younger Millennials (b. 1990–1996) (%)
Christian	85	78	70	57	56
Protestant	57	52	45	38	36
Evangelical	30	28	25	22	19
Mainline	22	17	13	10	11
Historically Black	5	7	7	6	6
Catholic	24	23	21	16	16
Other Christian groups	3	3	4	3	3
Other faiths	4	5	6	8	8
Unaffiliated	11	17	23	34	36
Don't know/refused	a	1	1	1	1

Source: America's Changing Religious Landscape, Pew Research Center, May 12, 2015, http://www.pewforum.org/2015/05/12/americas-changing-religious-landscape/.

a. No one in this column (Silent Generation) responded with "don't know" or refused to answer.

result of this, organized religion takes on a less significant role in people's lives, faith becomes more individualized, and the prominence of religion as a social institution decreases.

Critics of secularization theory suggest that modernization brings about religious pluralism and could lead to more religions, not fewer (Berger 2008). For example, even as the percentage of Americans who identify as unaffiliated is growing, the United States is considered a religiously pluralistic nation because of the diversity of religions practiced within its borders. Singapore, a majority Buddhist nation, has similar rates of religiously unaffiliated as the United States but also has more religious pluralism than most countries—with people practicing Buddhism, Christianity, Islam, Hinduism, and other religions (Pew Research Center 2012). In contrast, Vatican City, which is home of the Catholic Church, has one of the lowest levels of religious pluralism, with over 99 percent of the population identifying as Christian.

Sects, Cults, and New Religious Movements

Some people are not satisfied with current established religions and form counterreligious movements that reject the beliefs and practices of dominant religions. These include sects, cults, and new religious movements. **Sects** are subgroups of larger religions and have some of their own distinct beliefs and practices. They are branches or offshoots of larger religions and are often closed off to outsiders. Sects are common among all religions. For example, Sthavira nikāya is one of the earliest schools of Buddhist thought and consists of eleven different sects. Likewise, the Community of the Lady of All Nations is one of the many sects within Catholicism.

What comes to mind when you hear the word *cult*? You may think about groups that have charismatic leaders that use force or conversion methods such as brainwashing to keep members, such as the Charles Manson family, Heaven's Gate, the Branch Davidians, and Jonestown. In each of these cases, the religious leaders had total control over their members to the extent that followers harmed others or themselves in the name of their beliefs. All of these cases have also received a lot of media coverage, which has shaped the way that the public thinks about cults. But **cults** are simply unorthodox sects, and violence is not a necessary component. In sociology, cults are also called newly formed religious movements (NRMs). At one point in time, every established religion (including Catholicism, Calvinism, and Islam) was an NRM. Sects want to preserve traditional beliefs, whereas cults or NRMs are creating different religions. Many NRMs are countercultural and are founded by charismatic leaders who develop their own rituals, beliefs, and practices. For example, the Church of Scientology was founded in 1953 by L. Ron Hubbard and has followers around the world.

Consider This

Do you see religious pluralism or secularization in your hometown or college campus? What factors in your hometown or college campus contribute to this? Do you agree with secularization theory or its critics? Why?

Check Your Understanding

- How can religious pluralism affect religious participation?

- What are some explanations offered for the increase in secularization in the United States?

- How are secularization and modernization related?

- What do sociologists refer to when they use the word *cult*?

Religious Fundamentalism

Fundamentalism does not exist without modernization and secularization (Emerson and Hartman 2006). **Fundamentalists** resist such societal changes and hold on to idealized, conservative, traditional religious practices. Table 12.3 provides a list of ideological and organizational characteristics that can be found within fundamentalist groups and movements regardless of their religious affiliation. As you will see, strict ideological and organizational guidelines for followers control most aspects of their lives.

While fundamentalism was originally associated with conservative Protestants beginning in the late

TABLE 12.3

Characteristics of Fundamentalist Groups and Movements

Ideological Characteristics (Roberts and Yamane 2016)	
Radicalism	Focused on returning to an idealized cultural version of the past
Scripturalism	The belief that the scriptures are the literal word of their deity
Traditionalism	Traditions of the past are still relevant and applicable to today
Oppositionism	Hostility to modernization or secularization
Totalism	Religion regulates all aspects of life without any possible compromises
Puritanism	The search for internal purity and militant opposition to an impure world

Organizational Characteristics (Emerson and Hartman 2006:134)	
Chosen	Members see themselves as selected to defend religious tradition
Sharp Boundaries	Either you are a believer or not, a defender of religious tradition or not
Authoritarian	Typically have charismatic leaders who are seen as chosen by their deity
Behavioral Restrictions	Regulate speech, dress, sexuality, drinking, eating, family, children, etc.

1800s, it is now a global phenomenon (Emerson and Hartman 2006). Fundamentalist groups have strong ideological and organizational beliefs and practices that shape their worldview. They believe that their religion is the one true religion and is without flaws (Altemeyer and Hunsberger 2004). Fundamentalism is often associated with groups that use their beliefs to justify harmful and violent actions toward others. For example, the 9/11 attacks in 2001 or the ISIS attacks at the Ariana Grande concert in Manchester in 2017 are both examples of the type of violence that is perpetrated by some fundamentalist groups who practice religious extremism, strict conformity to religious scriptures, and believe that they have the absolute truth. Domestic hate groups within the United States such as neo-Confederates and the Ku Klux Klan also intertwine religious beliefs with political ideologies. Both of these groups identify as Christian organizations and use Christianity to support their beliefs and actions.

It is important to note that not all fundamentalist groups use violence or force, and some groups that do use violence are not considered fundamentalists. The Fundamentalist Church of Jesus Christ of the Latter-Day Saints is one of the largest Mormon fundamentalist religions today. They have strong core religious beliefs and practices around marriage, dress, schooling, and property ownership that members must adhere to. The Westboro Baptist Church is another modern fundamentalist group. They are well known for their anti-LGBTQ beliefs and protests at the funerals of U.S. soldiers killed in action. Both the Fundamentalist Church of Jesus Christ of the Latter-day Saints and the Westboro Baptist Church have the ideological and organizational characteristics described in Table 12.3 and are examples of nonviolent fundamentalist groups. Moreover, responses and solutions to terrorist attacks and hate crimes also often draw upon religious teachings and traditions. Religion not only defines the sacred but also serves as a lens through which people view the world and make decisions within their everyday lives—including about how they should act toward those who hold different religious beliefs.

Extreme and Violent Fundamentalism

If we know that not all fundamentalist groups are violent, then what factors can lead some of these religious groups to violence? First, fundamentalists may be threatened by pluralism and use violence to as a way to keep groups segregated. Second, fundamentalists may use violence in reaction to the fear of economic dependence on different, alien others and a desire to retain autonomy from those deemed as impure (Roberts and Yamane 2016). Last, fundamentalists may resort to violence as a reaction against modernization, a separation of social institutions from religion, and religious reforms. Religious groups that turn to violence also tend to be influenced by patriarchy, ethnocentrism, nationalism, and homophobia (Roberts and Yamane 2016; Zwissler 2012). In sum, some fundamentalists use violence as a means to protect a certain way of life, as seen in the 9/11 terrorist attacks by Al Qaeda. More recently, the attacks in Beirut, Baghdad, Paris, Istanbul, and Manchester by the Islamic State in Iraq and Syria (ISIS) have brought attention to fundamentalism and violence. After the 9/11 terrorist attacks, news media portrayals of Muslims and Arabs increased, and they were often framed as violent fundamentalists, which contributes to **Islamophobia** or the fear or dislike of all or most Muslims and shapes the way we think about violence, religions, and fundamentalism.

Check Your Understanding

- What is fundamentalism?

- What are some of the characteristics of fundamentalist movements?

- What factors may lead to the use of violence among some religious fundamentalist groups?

Consider This

In what types of societies might fundamentalist religions gain the most followers? Why?

Changing Religious Life in the United States

Many factors affect religious affiliation and participation in the United States, including race, ethnicity, gender, and sexual orientation. There are signs of increased racial and ethnic diversity among U.S. congregations, and more women now hold leadership roles within congregations. In the United States and globally, there is also growing acceptance of lesbian, gay, bisexual, and transgender (LGBT) clergy, and more religious organizations now sanction same-sex marriages.

Religious Affiliation and Race

Standing on the steps of the National Cathedral in Washington, D.C., on March 31, 1968, Dr. Martin Luther King Jr. said that Sunday at 11 a.m. was the most segregated hour in America. He was referring to the widespread racial segregation in American churches. Today, many people still worship in racially segregated congregations. However, research suggests a growing trend toward greater racial and ethnic diversity within Christian religions in the United States (Chaves 2011) (see Figure 12.4). This change can be attributed to the growing racial and ethnic diversity in the United States and the increasing number of immigrants today who have strong Christian affiliations. As secularization increases, churches become more dependent on new immigrants to keep their congregations going. Many Catholic, mainline Protestant, and Episcopal leaders have publicly criticized restrictive immigration policies. This public support of immigrants may be a part of what is drawing members of color to their congregations.

FIGURE 12.4

Increasing Racial and Ethnic Diversity within Christianity in the United States

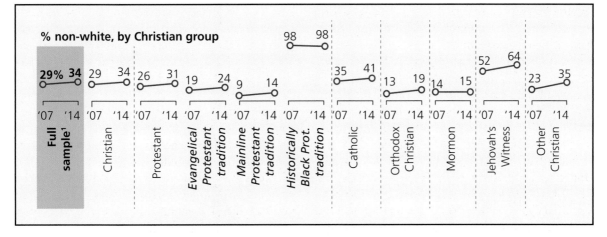

Source: America's Changing Religious Landscape, Pew Research Center, May 12, 2015, http://www.pewforum.org/2015/05/12/americas-changing-religious-landscape/.

Fundamentalists believe that their belief system is the only legitimate religion.

Al Drago/CQ-Roll Call Group/Getty Images

Religious Affiliation and Gender

Religion and gender have a complicated relationship. Feminist theorists draw attention to how social institutions, such as religion, and the practices associated with those institutions promote social inequality, patriarchy, and gender stratification. Most of the dominant religious figures throughout history have been men such as Jesus of Nazareth, the Prophet Mohammad, Confucius, and the Dalai Lama. Many religious groups, such as Roman Catholics, Orthodox Jews, and some evangelical Protestant denominations, still only allow men to serve as clergy. Many of the major world religions have supported patriarchy through their teachings, and many holy texts define what are appropriate gender roles for their followers. Many religious teachings reinforce women's subordinate status to men and include guidelines for women's dress and behaviors. Yet, women, especially Christian women, are more likely to report a religious affiliation (Chaves 2011) and engage in worship services than men (Pew Research Center 2016). Among Muslims and Orthodox Jews, on the other hand, men are more likely to attend religious services than women because of the strong cultural norms and traditions that emphasize male religious attendance (Sullins 2006). Religion is often the basis for debates regarding female veiling, birth control, abortion, and same-sex relationships. It has been used to sanction violence against women, such as honor killings, female genital cutting, and dowry murders (Zwissler 2012), all of which reinforce the idea that women are subordinate to men. Yet, many religions have worked toward greater gender equality and now have women clergy. Feminists, including Muslim, Christian, and Jewish feminists, have worked for greater human rights for women and argued that gender equality should be at the center of religion and faith.

Doing Sociology 12.2

Personal Conceptions of God

In this exercise, you will consider the physical appearance you ascribe to God and the consequences for society of that image.

The way we imagine God to look varies dramatically, depending on the religion of the people doing the imagining and their personal beliefs. Consider what image appears in your head when you think of God and answer the following questions:

1. Write a paragraph describing your image of God. What does God look like? In your image, is God a masculine or feminine figure? Old or young? Large or small?

2. How did you come to have this kind of image of God? Think of all the socializing agents that encouraged you to view God this way.

3. How does this image of God affect our understanding of gender?

4. How might our society change if most people had a different vision of God?

While most religions continue to oppose same-sex marriage, more and more Christian denominations and branches of Judaism have started to support marriage equality. The reluctance of some religions to accept same-sex marriage may help explain why fewer young people attend religious services today.

Marc Piscotty/Getty Images News/Getty Images

Religious Affiliation and Sexual Orientation

Many LGBT individuals continue to seek a "church home" and want to remain active in religious communities after they come out, despite the stigma and marginalization they face (Roberts and Yamane 2016). Over half of the LGBT sample surveyed in the Religious Landscape Study reported religious affiliation, with 48 percent identifying as Christian (see Figure 12.5).

Homosexuality and religion remains a frequent topic of debate, with people on both sides holding strong convictions. Most religious institutions continue to oppose same-sex marriage, citing scripture as the basis for definitions of sexual contact and

marriage. However, over the past two decades, more Christian denominations and some branches of Judaism (see Table 12.4 for a more complete list) have begun to support marriage equality and equal rights for LGBT members of society (Pew Research Center 2015b). These congregations often signify their support by identifying as "open and affirming." Growing acceptance of homosexuality can also be

FIGURE 12.5

Religious Composition by Self-Reported Sexual Identity

Among those who identify as . . .

Gay, lesbian or bisexual (Sample size 1,604)

Christian: 48%

Non-Christian faiths: 11%

Unaffiliated: 41%

Protestant: 29%

| 13% | 11 | 5 | 17 | 2 | | 8 | 9 | 24 |

Evangelical — Mainline — Historically Black Prot. — Catholic — Other Christian* — Atheist — Agnostic — Nothing in particular

Straight (Sample size 32,439)

Christian: 72%

Non-Christian faiths: 6%

Unaffiliated: 22%

Protestant: 48%

Agnostic

| 26% | 15 | 7 | 21 | 3 | | 3 | 4 | 15 |

Evangelical — Mainline — Historically Blact Prot. — Catholic — Other Christian* — Atheist — Nothing in particular

Source: Lesbian, Gay and Bisexual Americans Differ from General Public in Their Religious Affiliations, Pew Research, May 26, 2015, http://www.pewresearch.org/fact-tank/2015/05/26/lesbian-gay-and-bisexual-americans-differ-from-general-public-in-their-religious-affiliations/.

* Other Christian groups include Orthodox Christians, Mormons, Jehovah's Witnesses, and a number of smaller Christian Groups. Don't know/refused answers are omitted.

TABLE 12.4

Where Major Religions Stand on Same-Sex Marriage

Sanctions Same-Sex Marriage	Prohibits Same-Sex Marriage	No Clear Position
Conservative Jewish Movement	American Baptist Churches	Buddhism
Episcopal Church	Assemblies of God	Hinduism
Evangelical Lutheran Church in America	Church of Jesus Christ of Latter-day Saints (Mormon)	
Presbyterian Church (USA)	Islam	
Reform Jewish Movement	Lutheran Church – Missouri Synod	
Society of Friends (Quaker)	National Baptist Convention	
Unitarian Universalist Association of Churches	Orthodox Jewish Movement	
United Church of Christ	Roman Catholic Church	
	Southern Baptist Convention	
	United Methodist Church	

Source: David Masci and Michael Lipka, Where Christian Churches, Other Religions Stand on Gay Marriage, Pew Research Center, December 21, 2015, http://www.pewresearch.org/fact-tank/2015/12/21/where-christian-churches-stand-on-gay-marriage.

seen in the numerous denominations that now ordain LGBT clergy such as the United Church of Christ, the Evangelical Lutheran Church in America, the Presbyterian Church (USA), and the Episcopal Church.

Check Your Understanding

- How has Christianity in the United States become more racially and ethnically diverse?

- How are religious affiliation and religious activities related to gender?

- How are some congregations changing to become more inclusive of sexual orientation?

Global Diffusion of Religion

Globally, the most common religions today are Christianity, Islam, Buddhism, Hinduism, Judaism, and folk religions (African traditional religions, Chinese folk religions, Native American religions, and Australian Aboriginal religions). Other religions are practiced worldwide, such as Bahá'í and Sikhism, but they are not as common as the others. As shown in Figure 12.6, Christianity is currently the most widely practiced religion and can be found almost everywhere in the world. Islam is the second most common religion, with most Muslims living in the Asia-Pacific region, the Middle East, and northern Africa. Most Buddhists, Hindus, and followers of folk religions are found in the Asia-Pacific region while the vast majority of Jews live in either Israel or the United States.

The Pew Research Center (2015a) projects that the distribution of people following the major world religions will remain steady over the next several decades, with the exception of Buddhists losing and Muslims gaining adherents. The Muslim population is expected to reach parity with the Christian population by 2050 (see Figure 12.7). While religious conversion (e.g., unaffiliated converting to Islam) explains some of this trend, the projected change is largely due to the age of followers and fertility rates. Muslims are predominantly younger in age compared to Christians and have more children.

Cultural Diffusion

Cultural attributes, like religion, can spread throughout the world through a process known as **cultural diffusion.** The global diffusion of religion is

FIGURE 12.6

Largest Religious Group, by Country

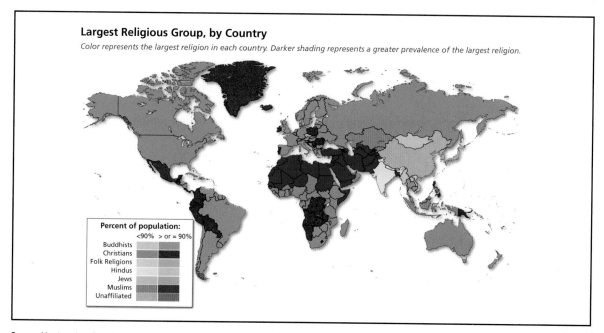

Largest Religious Group, by Country

Color represents the largest religion in each country. Darker shading represents a greater prevalence of the largest religion.

Percent of population:
<90%   > or = 90%

Buddhists
Christians
Folk Religions
Hindus
Jews
Muslims
Unaffiliated

Source: Map based on Conrad Hackett and Timmy Huynh, What Is Each Country's Second-Largest Religious Group? Pew Research Center Fact Tank, June 22, 2015, http://www.pewresearch.org/fact-tank/2015/06/22/what-is-each-countrys-second-largest-religious-group.

Note: Estimates for the year 2010. Followers of other religions do not make up the largest religion in any country.

FIGURE 12.7

Projected Change in Global Population

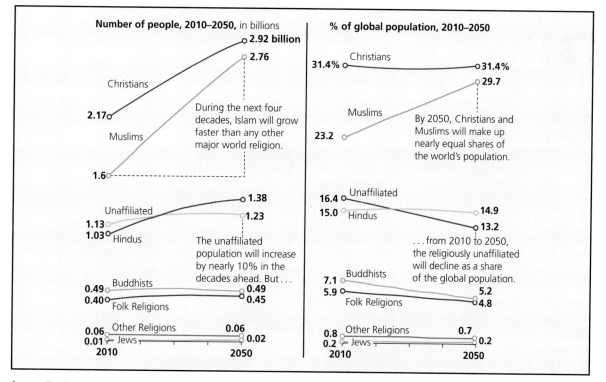

Number of people, 2010–2050, in billions

Christians   2.92 billion
2.76
2.17
Muslims
1.6

During the next four decades, Islam will grow faster than any other major world religion.

Unaffiliated   1.38
1.13   1.23
1.03   Hindus

The unaffiliated population will increase by nearly 10% in the decades ahead. But . . .

0.49   Buddhists   0.49
0.40   0.45
Folk Religions

0.06   Other Religions   0.06
0.01   Jews   0.02
2010   2050

% of global population, 2010–2050

Christians
31.4%   31.4%
29.7
Muslims
23.2

By 2050, Christians and Muslims will make up nearly equal shares of the world's population.

16.4   Unaffiliated
15.0   Hindus   14.9
13.2

. . . from 2010 to 2050, the religiously unaffiliated will decline as a share of the global population.

7.1   Buddhists
5.9   5.2
Folk Religions   4.8

0.8   Other Religions   0.7
0.2   Jews   0.2
2010   2050

Source: *The Future of World Religions: Population Growth Projections, 2010–2050,* Pew Research Center, April 2, 2015, http://www.pewforum.org/2015/04/02/religious-projections-2010-2050/.

Participant Observation of a Religious Service

In this activity, you will attend and observe a religious service outside your own faith.

You are going to learn outside of the classroom by attending a religious service in your community. If you are not religious, this is a great opportunity to examine a religious service. If you are religious, this will allow you to visit with a religious faith other than your own or to analyze (and not just participate in) a service in your own religious organization.

In Chapter 3, you learned about *participant observations* where you observe, interact, and participate in the social context that you are studying. You will conduct a participant observation of a religious service. Before conducting your research, you need to think about the ethical and methodological issues of doing participant observations. You do not want to present yourself as someone else. If you are asked about yourself, you can say, "I am a student at [*school*]. My professor gave us an assignment to visit a religious service and I am interested in learning more about your religion." You must be respectful of the religious practices and rituals while also paying attention to what you see around you. You can take mental notes or, if appropriate, take notes on a small pad of paper. As soon as you leave the service, you should take further notes so that you remember what you observed. Pay careful attention to the following:

1. What was the gender and approximate age of the person leading the worship service?

2. What was the demographic makeup of the people attending the worship service? Was it racially and ethnically diverse? Were there more women than men? Were there mostly older people in attendance? Did children attend the same worship service?

3. Was the worship service formal or informal? What kinds of rituals and practices contributed to this?

4. Was technology involved in the worship service? How so?

5. Were there contradictions between the message conveyed during the service and your observations noted above? For example, what did the service say about women and what did you observe women doing?

part of a larger globalization process (Roberts and Yamane 2016). As elements of one culture spread to another through modernization and migration, two other processes emerge: pluralism and assimilation. In a pluralistic society, smaller groups within a larger society maintain their unique cultural and religious identities, and their values and practices are accepted by others. When smaller groups adopt the cultural and religious practices of the dominant group, we call it assimilation.

While some immigrants assimilate to the dominant religious practices in their new countries, others maintain the cultural and religious practices of their countries of origin. The fact that some people maintain traditional religious practices after moving to another nation results in transnational religious connections where religion spans societal borders (Wuthnow and Offutt 2008). It can also help lead to the formation of ethnic enclaves in new countries with a strong religious commitment among recent immigrants. Ethnic enclaves help immigrants maintain a shared identity and a sense of belonging. While ethnic and religious identities are intertwined for recent immigrants, second-generation immigrants may

Consider This

Imagine you just told your neighbors that you are Catholic. How do you think they would respond? How would their own immigration status, ethnicity, race, economic status, religious affiliation, sexual orientation, and so on influence their response? Now, imagine you just told your neighbors that you are Muslim. How do you think they would respond? Why?

practice their parents' religion but without the same ethnic elements. Second-generation immigrants often weave together religious traditions of parents and family while incorporating practices from the dominant religious practices within their home country. This results in a fusion of religious practices that draws from multiple religions (Levitt, Lucken, and Barnett 2011).

Check Your Understanding

- What changes are projected in religious affiliation in the global population?

- How does the process of cultural diffusion apply to religion?

- How can ethnic enclaves and religious practices support immigrants and affect religious pluralism?

Applying Sociological Theory to Religion

Theoretical perspectives are frameworks that help us make sense of the world around us. When applying the major sociological theories to religion, we can see the role of religion in our larger society and how religion shapes individual lives.

Structural Functionalism

As you recall from Chapter 2, structural functionalism assumes that all parts of society work together to promote solidarity and stability. According to structural functionalists, social institutions such as religion have a specific function or purpose in our society. Religion works with other major social institutions to create norms, customs, and practices that maintain social order. Faith-based organizations also provide many social services, addressing social problems such as poverty and homelessness. For example, the Episcopal Church has over 600 ministries in the United States that specifically address poverty and community development. On a global scale, thirty leaders from major world religions along with the World Bank Group issued a call for action in 2015,

"Ending Extreme Poverty: A Moral and Spiritual Imperative," to end poverty by 2030. The statement acknowledges that all faith leaders and communities have a collective role in ending poverty and should assist in those efforts.

For Durkheim and other structural functionalists, religion provides a strong common morality that guides and constrains our actions. This can be seen in religious teachings, doctrines, and the rules that prescribe certain behaviors. Religion also creates a sense of social order and social cohesion through shared symbolism and rituals. Last, it provides people with a sense of purpose and meaning even in times of despair. In his research on suicide, Durkheim (1951 [1897]) found that lower suicide rates were connected to integration within a social group and the guidance they offered. Close-knit religious groups were found to have lower levels of suicide. Durkheim pointed out that religion provided these strong integration functions, which lowered suicide rates; however, he also cautioned that religion can create an extreme amount of social integration and conformity that can also result in suicide, for instance, mass suicide or religious suicide bombers. In such cases, the religious groups that support these actions have many of the ideological and organizational characteristics of fundamentalism. Mass suicide and suicide bombing then become an act of totalism where religion dictates all aspects of life even to extent of who lives and who dies.

> ### Consider This
> What functions does religion serve in U.S. society? How does your answer compare to what a structural functionalist would say?

Conflict Theory

While structural functionalists focus on the interrelatedness of social institutions, conflict theorists highlight how the economic, societal, religious, and political systems create a system of social stratification. Conflict theorists note that power and resources are unequally distributed across society. Those with more power and prestige are invested in maintaining the status quo and use religion to oppress and exploit subordinate groups.

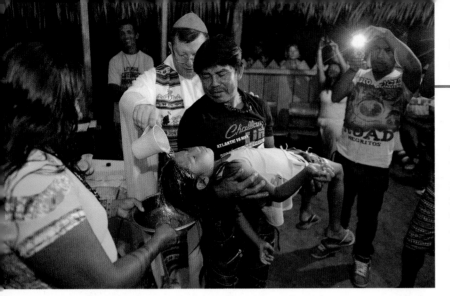

Rituals are center pieces of all religions.

imageBROKER/Alamy Stock Photo

technology and other aspects of their business—the perfect recipe for capitalism. Those who did not succeed financially were clearly deserving of their poverty, as they were destined to go to hell. Together, predestination and rationalization created the "Protestant work ethic."

Karl Marx

Karl Marx (1970 [1843]) referred to religion as the opiate of the people. He believed that the people in power (those who own the means of production) use religion to distract the workers. He argued that religious leaders, whose salaries tend to be based on donations from the wealthy, encourage workers to focus on gaining rewards in the afterlife rather than on demanding present-day justice and overthrowing the capitalist system.

Consider This

Do you agree with Marx that religion is the "opiate of the masses"? Why or why not?

Max Weber

Max Weber spent much of his life studying religion. In *The Protestant Ethic and the Spirit of Capitalism,* Weber (1958 [1904]) connected the system of ideas present in organized religion with the rise of a capitalist economic system. He maintained that the Protestant Reformation and the rise of Calvinism encouraged industrial capitalism. Calvinists believe in predestination, the idea that people are destined for heaven or hell from birth. Financial success became seen as evidence that one was preordained to go to heaven. This, combined with the Calvinist emphasis on simple lifestyles, encouraged people to work hard and to rationally invest their money into new

Symbolic Interactionism

Structural functionalists and conflict theorists provide a macro-analysis of religion while symbolic interactionists focus on the micro-aspects. From a symbolic interactionist perspective, religion is characterized by having a set of symbols, **rituals** (or ceremonial behaviors), and a shared understanding of people within a particular group. Individuals actively create religions as they construct their social environments based on the meanings they attribute to their actions and interactions (Blumer 1969).

Some symbols, such as the pentagram, are used by different religions to mean different things.

©iStockphoto.com/zager

Religion consists of socially constructed sets of practices based on what has been defined and accepted as sacred. For example, fasting rituals associated with the Islamic Ramadan, Jewish Yom Kippur, and Christian Lenten Season all have meaning to those who take part in these practices. Likewise, some practices serve symbolic purposes such as the Catholic ceremony of the Eucharist where bread and wine become sacred as they are transformed, in the eyes of believers, into the literal body and blood of Christ.

Religious practices and the meaning of religious symbols can change over time. We can also see how religions alter their gender-related practices as the societies around them change. The acceptance of the ordination of women in many Western Christian congregations provides a prime example of how religions can adjust to changing gender roles. As societies change, so do their institutions—including religion.

Symbols mean something when groups ascribe a meaning to them. For example, the pentagram, a five-pointed star, is a symbol that is used across religions with different meanings attached to it. In Christianity, the pentagram is a symbol of the five wounds of Jesus. The pentagram is also used to refer to ancient Greek and Chinese elements. The pentagram has meaning within the Bahá'í faith, which is a new religious movement and means "temple" in Arabic. The pentagram is also a Wiccan symbol for the goddess Morgan and refers to the five elements of life.

Table 12.5 summarizes how each of the major sociological perspectives contributes to our understanding of religion.

Consider This

What are some examples of religious symbols and rituals?

Check Your Understanding

- What are the major functions of religion?
- Why did Marx call religion the "opiate" of the people?
- How did Calvinism help create capitalism?
- What is the relationship between religion and gender inequality?
- What role do rituals play in religious practice?

TABLE 12.5

Applying Sociological Theory to Religion

	Structural Functionalist Perspective	Conflict Perspective	Symbolic Interactionist Perspective
Level of analysis	Macro-level	Macro-level	Micro-level
Contributions to understanding religion	Establishes cohesion and social solidarity Provides a sense of purpose and meaning	Connected to the growth of industrial capitalism Used to oppress and exploit subordinate groups	Socially constructed set of practices Contains symbols, rituals, and shared understanding of the sacred

Religion, Social Issues, and Social Change

While religions must adjust to changes in society, they can also influence followers' perspectives on social issues and help create social change. Throughout history, many of the roots of both violence and positive social change can be found in religion. Religions have been used to enforce hierarchies and to mobilize efforts to dismantle such oppressive structures.

Religious Affiliation and Attitudes toward Social Issues

The **subcultural identity theory** (Smith et al. 1998) is particularly helpful in explaining the relationship between religious affiliation and attitudes toward social issues. This theory suggests that individuals seek a collective identity that helps provide them with a strong moral code. The group identity becomes stronger when there is an ingroup/outgroup distinction. Religious groups and organizations strive to create a moral commitment on the behalf of followers, which leads to complying with the larger group norms and values. This includes defining what is sacred and what behavior is sinful. Observance of these beliefs signifies ingroup membership and loyalty to the religious organization.

One of the ways members demonstrate being a member of a specific religious group is through their

Malala Yousafzai was the youngest person to ever receive the Nobel Prize. She is helping establish the right to education for all girls, in defiance of the Taliban.

charitable giving and volunteer service. In the United States, people who identify as highly religious are more likely to volunteer than others. Not surprisingly, they tend to volunteer primarily in religious settings versus **secular** (nonreligious) settings (Taniguchi and Thomas 2011). Many religious organizations provide ample opportunities for their members to volunteer and act out their faith through good works.

Consider This

On your campus, do you think volunteerism is affected by religious affiliation? On what would you base that opinion? What other factors encourage volunteerism on your campus?

Religion and Social Change

While the KKK used Christianity to justify their violence, African American churches fostered and became symbols of the civil rights movement. Religious leaders such as Dr. Martin Luther King Jr. and many others played a large role in the leadership of the civil rights movement. Dr. King's "I Have a Dream Speech" remains a powerful symbol of racial equality. Recall that Dr. King was a Baptist minister who saw Christianity as a powerful force in creating social change. Black clergy became spokespersons and strategists. Church auxiliaries, mostly run by women, provided food and help to those in need while laity organized protests and carpools during the bus boycotts.

The Taliban, an Islamic terrorist group, that now controls territory in Afghanistan and Pakistan has forbidden girls from attending schools. Taliban leaders claim that they cannot allow cross-gender contact between boys and girls. Malala Yousafzai also uses her Islamic faith, but to counter the ways that the Taliban uses Islam. Along with her father, Malala promotes education for girls while showing how some groups, like the Taliban, misuse religion to pursue their own agendas (https://www.malala.org/). She defied the Taliban by writing blogs about the treatment of girls in Pakistan and by attending a school for girls that was founded by her father. As a result, Malala and her family had received threats, even in the newspaper. On October 9, 2012, as she was heading to school, a gunman boarded her school bus and shot her in the head (also wounding two of her friends). Malala was fifteen years old at the time of her shooting. Her message about faith and social change had become a threat to the Taliban. The attempt on her life was intended to silence her forever, but the shooting (and miraculous survival) led to widespread fame and helped her spread her message of girls' access to education across the globe. Soon after, Pakistan passed its Right to Education Bill, guaranteeing (at least on paper) the right to a free education for all children ages five to sixteen. In 2014, Malala became the youngest person to ever receive the Nobel Prize.

Meanwhile, Pope Francis has called for a rethinking of the world's problems as human problems and urged all people—of all religions—to help each member of the human family. Pope Francis has challenged European leaders and advocated on the behalf of refugees. He has urged leaders to not think of refugees as numbers but as people with names and stories. In his speech to the people of Lesbos, Greece, to where many Middle Eastern, African, and Asian refugees fled, Pope Francis said, "Europe is the homeland of human rights, and whoever sets foot on European soil ought to sense this, and thus become more aware of the duty to respect and defend those rights. You, the residents of Lesbos, show that in these lands, the cradle of civilization, the heart of humanity continues to beat" (Vatican Press Office 2016:3). He urged people to think about religion as a force for good that can heal the wounds of human tragedy. The American civil rights movement, Malala Yousafzai, and Pope Francis are all examples of how religion continues to inspire global social change.

Sociologists in Action

Religion and Democratic Life

Richard L. Wood

I am a professor of sociology, trained in a model of "public sociology" deeply rooted in research and intellectual work.

My public sociology takes three forms: first, in my teaching, I ask the students in my university classroom to reflect critically and appreciatively on American culture and institutions, across their distinct viewpoints rooted in remarkably diverse backgrounds. Many of my students are first-generation college students while others come from highly educated families. They come from rural, urban, and suburban areas (most are from New Mexico but some are from other states or even nations) and have various social class and racial and ethnic backgrounds (mostly Latino, but also White, Native American, and African American).

Second, I advise the American Catholic bishops who oversee one of the largest antipoverty and poor people's empowerment efforts in the United States, the Catholic Campaign for Human Development (CCHD). In that role, I have helped the bishops respond to attacks from those objecting to empowerment of poor people as part of the Church's mission—in part by encouraging them to defend community organizing as a practical embodiment of Catholic social teaching. I also help them understand recent transformations in the field of community organizing, including its embrace of racial equity work. Conversations about personal experiences of racism and White privilege now happen across racial lines in many community organizing groups.

Third, my research on faith-based community organizing has given me a role in advising many different local organizations and national or regional community organizing networks that work across faith traditions to empower poor and middle-class communities (such as the Gamaliel Network, the DART Network, the Industrial Areas Foundation, and the PICO National Network). I have spoken at retreats for organizers, pastors, and lay leaders from various community organizing organizations. I recently joined the national board of the PICO National Network (http://www.piconetwork.org/) as that organization strives to build a state-of-the-art organizing structure capable of shifting American culture, politics, and public policy in more democratic directions. I serve as a "thought partner" with PICO as it redesigns its organizing infrastructure and works on campaigns that include increasing voter turnout among people of color and White working families, ending the mass incarceration of people of color, creating a path to citizenship for unauthorized immigrants, and outlawing predatory lending.

In all these roles, I draw on sociological and theological insight into social movements, religion, organizations, social ethics, and democracy to help CCHD, PICO, and faith-based organizing generally act more successfully to build a faith that does justice in the world.

Richard L. Wood is professor of sociology at the University of New Mexico. His most recent book is A Shared Future: Faith-Based Organizing for Racial Equity and Ethical Democracy *(University of Chicago, 2015; coauthored with Brad Fulton), and he is the author of* Faith in Action *(University of Chicago, 2002), which was recognized as best book of 2002 by the American Sociological Association's religion section.*

Consider This

Consider again the question from the beginning of the chapter: how can we determine how religious people are or to what extent they practice their religion? Has your answer changed after reading this chapter?

Check Your Understanding

- How does religious affiliation affect attitudes toward social issues?
- What role did religion play in the civil rights movement?
- How is Malala Yousafzai using her religion to advocate for girls and women?
- According to Pope Francis, how does religion help us take action when displaced groups need assistance?

Consider This

How has religion been used in your own hometown to address social problems? Are there any faith-based organizations that work toward ending poverty and feeding the hungry? Are any churches in your hometown involved in advocacy for different populations?

Conclusion

Even with changing religious affiliation and participation, faith-based practices remain an integral part of U.S. society and many people's individual identities. Using the sociological imagination, we are able to see how religion can both contribute to and counter patriarchy, racism, homophobia, nationalism, ethnocentrism, and violence. An understanding of the sociology of religion is helpful in any job that requires interacting with others, particularly for those in volunteer or outreach coordinator positions, religiously affiliated nonprofit organizations, campus ministry, childcare, bereavement, adoption, and foster care settings.

In the next chapter, you will learn how culture and social status affect perceptions of environmental issues and learn about environmental justice. You might consider how human and environmental systems interact and the role of religion in understanding environmental issues. Indigenous religions, such as those practiced by Native Americans, have long stressed the importance of the spiritual relationship between the Earth and its inhabitants. Religious environmentalism is a growing area of interest that refers to the environmental actions of religious leaders and communities within organized religion as well as more general environmentalism grounded in spirituality (Jenkins and Chapple 2011). Pope Francis has made combatting climate change and environmental degradation one of the primary foci of his papacy, and many other religious leaders—from across the religious spectrum—are leaders in proenvironmental efforts. The environment and sustainability connects people across religious affiliations to solve one of the most pressing social issues of today.

CHAPTER

12

$SAGE edge™

Want a better grade? Get the tools you need to sharpen your study skills. Access practice quizzes, eFlashcards, video and multimedia at **edge.sagepub.com/korgen**

Review

12.1 How do sociologists define religion, religiosity, and spirituality?

Religion is a social institution that involves the beliefs and practices of what has been socially constructed as sacred in a given society. Religiosity is the level of religiousness of an individual and includes religious activities, practices, and beliefs. Spirituality is the search for the sacred that may occur outside of doctrinal boundaries.

12.2 What are pluralism and secularization?

Pluralism refers to a diversity and coexistence of different religions. Secularization refers to a society's movement away from identification with religious values and institutions and can be seen in the growing number of people who identify as nonreligious.

12.3 What is fundamentalism?

Fundamentalism is a response to modernization and secularization. Fundamentalists resist such societal changes by holding onto idealized, conservative, traditional religious practices; strict conformity to religious scriptures; and a belief in one true religion.

12.4 What are the current trends in religious affiliation and participation in the United States?

The current trends in religious participation in the Unites States suggest an increase in non-Christian faiths, which can be attributed to changing demographics and more acceptance of religious diversity. As the percentage of nonreligiously affiliated Americans continues to increase, many religious groups have become more racially and ethnically diverse, more accepting of female leadership, and more supportive of LGBT people and same-sex marriage.

12.5 How does the process of global diffusion apply to religion?

The Pew Research Center (2015a) provides the contemporary global trends in religion and projects that Christian affiliation will decline while adherents of Islam will grow, resulting in equal shares of Christians and Muslims among the world population. The expansion of religion across spatial boundaries is part of the globalization process and the global diffusion of religion. Globalization also affects the spread of secularization and fundamentalism.

12.6 How do each of the major theoretical paradigms in sociology explain religion?

From a structural-functional perspective, religion works with other major social institutions to create norms and practices that maintain stability and social order. The functions that religion serves in a given society include establishing social cohesion, creating social integration, promoting social control, and providing people with a sense of purpose and meaning. Conflict theory focuses on the unequal distribution of power and resources across society. From this perspective, those with more power and prestige are invested in maintaining the status quo and use religion to oppress and exploit subordinate groups. Symbolic interactionists see individuals as actively constructing their social environments as they interact. They use symbols, practices, and shared understanding to create religions. Like other parts of society, most religions change over time, as they respond to social forces within and outside their organizations.

12.7 What are some recent examples of how religion has fostered social change efforts?

While religion has been used as the basis for violence throughout history, it is also a driving force in positive social change. The American civil rights movement shows how churches can become a safe haven from violence. Malala Yousafzai demonstrates how young people today are using their faith to counter messages of hatred. Pope Francis is an example of the role of religious leaders in advocating for displaced and disadvantaged groups.

Key Terms

- agnostic   257
- atheists   257
- cults   259
- cultural diffusion   264
- fundamentalists   259
- Islamophobia   261
- modernization   258
- profane   253
- religion   253
- religiosity   253

- religious pluralism   256
- ritual   268
- sacred   253
- secular   270
- secular humanists   257
- secularization   256
- secularization theory   258
- sects   259
- spirituality   254
- subcultural identity theory   269

Environmental problems are social problems.

AP Photo/Erik McGregor

Learning Questions

13.1 Why are environmental problems social problems?

13.2 How do sociologists study environmental issues?

13.3 How would eco-Marxists and ecological modernization theorists define and discuss environmental problems and their solutions?

13.4 What are the promises and constraints of green consumption?

13.5 What is environmental justice?

13.6 What are social solutions to environmental problems?

CHAPTER 13

Saving the Environment

John Chung-En Liu

Facing Our Environmental Challenges

We now face serious environmental challenges. Air and water pollution, soil erosion, ocean acidification, biodiversity loss, species extinction, cancer villages, food safety, and so on—this unnerving list can go on. And there is global warming. The year 2015 overtook 2014 to become the hottest year in recent human history. And 2016 broke the record again. The changing climate is leading to rises in sea levels, ecosystem disruptions, increased numbers of epidemics, and displacement of many vulnerable communities. Some scholars argue that we have entered the "Anthropocene" period—a new geological era characterized by human impacts on the planet (National Centers for Environmental Information 2016).

As citizens of the Earth, what should we do? Some students respond to this question by emphasizing the importance of technological development:

"Install solar panels!"

"Drive electric cars!"

"How about we try geoengineering or carbon storage and capture?"

Others talk about the small steps that everyone can do in their everyday lives:

"I always make sure that I recycle diligently."

"Turn off lights when you leave the room."

"Bike or take public transportation, minimize driving your car!"

Indeed, technology can be our friend—solar panels, in most cases, are more environmentally friendly than burning coal. We probably will rely heavily on various technological breakthroughs in our pursuit for a cleaner future. In addition, individual actions are certainly laudable—we all want to do something to help save the planet, right? When asked, however, "Do you really believe we can solve all the environmental problems by developing new technologies, recycling,

John Chung-En Liu

I was a latecomer to sociology. In college, I was a chemical engineering major; in my master's program, I focused on economics and environmental policy. My intellectual journey made me realize that environmental problems—the challenges that I've been seeking to address—are ultimately social problems.

That was the moment that I found my love in sociology. At the University of Wisconsin, I was nurtured by a tradition that specifically focuses on communities and environment. The training allowed me to rigorously examine the origins of environmental problems and, at the same time, boldly imagine solutions. In my own work, I use sociology to come up with policy insights that can contribute to solving urgent environmental issues such as climate change. Recently, my work on climate change skepticism was featured in *Foreign Policy* and Public Radio International.

Besides research, I also have a passion in teaching sociology. I especially like to use various hand-on projects to connect sociological knowledge with our everyday lives. My goal is to help students create a sense of sociology imagination with ecological consciousness.

planting trees, and riding bikes?" a few students are optimistic, but many more are uncertain.

As you will learn from this chapter, sociologists go beyond the common technocratic and individualistic framework when examining environmental problems. Sociologists, first and foremost, consider environmental problems as *social* problems. Environmental problems are problems *for* society, threatening our current forms of social organization. In other words, the environment is not something to be "saved" by us—we're really saving ourselves by addressing environmental degradation.

Environmental problems are also problems *of* society. This means that the problems are not the result of bad intentions or ineffective leaders; instead, they are the consequences of larger social forces and social organizations. To fundamentally deal with environmental problems, we need to address the ways we collectively structure our lives (Bell and Ashwood 2015). With this sociological perspective in mind, let's turn to the physical reality of environmental problems. Are things really as bad as many environmental activists claim?

Consider This

Think of all the things we can do to help save the environment. Which do you think are the most important?

The Physical Reality of Environmental Problems

When looking at the state of the environment, it is useful to start with the concept of **sustainability.** A sustainable social-economic system can function within the Earth's ecological constraint. In 1987, the United Nations Commission on Environment and Development published *Our Common Future* (also known as the Brundtland Report), in which it defined **sustainable development** as "[the] development that meets the needs of the present without compromising the ability of future generations to meet their own needs" (chap. 2, para. 1). How we achieve this ideal remains a subject for heated discussions. How can we continue to live the way we have been living indefinitely? Sociology, especially its subfield of **environmental sociology,** which focuses on the interaction between the social and the natural systems, provides many useful insights to guide us toward sustainability.

Some researchers developed the **ecological footprint** indicator as a yardstick to sustainability (Wackernagel and Rees 1998). The ecological footprint represents the productive area—expressed in number of "planet Earths"—required to provide the resources humanity is using and to absorb its waste. According to the calculation, based on our food consumption, energy use, transportation, and so on, we need 1.5 Earths to sustain our current consumption level. Moreover, if everybody lived like an average U.S. resident, we would need five planets. Obviously, one is all we have! Footprint analysis scholars argue that we are in an unsustainable **overshoot** situation—using resources at a pace more than the Earth's regenerative capacity.

Based on the concept of the ecological footprint, others have developed similar measures such as "carbon footprint" or "water footprint" to illustrate our environmental impacts. These indicators certainly are not without their flaws. The data sources are not perfect, and the calculation is often difficult; more important, they do not directly tell us who or what are driving these environmental impacts. Yet, the central take-home message is clear: we cannot continue consuming resources at our current pace forever!

Footprint analysis has shown another important result: individual consumption is only a small part of overall resource use. A major portion of our economic activities happens in the "background"—infrastructure, power generation, agriculture—the things usually beyond individual control. No matter how "green" you try to be, there are activities at the collective level that you, alone, cannot control. We are all in this unsustainable system together, willingly or reluctantly. This lesson illustrates the need to think and act sociologically to respond to environmental problems. The quest toward sustainability is a team sport. It is not enough to confine our thinking to individual attitudes and behaviors. We need to be thinking about larger social forces that shape environmental outcomes and facilitating changes in our communities (on our campus, city, state, nation, and world), as well as changing our individual behavior.

Check Your Understanding

- What is sustainability?

- What is an ecological footprint? What does it measure?

- What do scientists mean when they say we are in an ecological overshoot?

- On what does the subfield of environmental sociology focus?

- Why must we think and act sociologically to respond to environmental problems?

How Do Sociologists Study Environmental Issues?

Before sociologists tackle environmental degradation, we step back to reflect deeply, sometimes even philosophically, on our understanding of

---

Doing Sociology 13.1

Calculate Your Own Ecological Footprint

In this activity, you will use an online tool to calculate the ecological footprint of your lifestyle.

Ecological footprint analysis is one approach to gauging our environmental impacts on the planet. Use the online tool developed by the Global Footprint Network to calculate your own ecological footprint (http://www.footprintnetwork.org/en/index.php/GFN/page/calculators/) and then answer the following questions:

1. How much is your ecological footprint? How many planets would we need to support humanity if everyone maintained your lifestyle?

2. What factors are the largest contributors to your footprint? Food? Shelter? Services?

3. What are some possible steps you could take to decrease your footprint?

4. How would your footprint change if you changed your dietary habits or transportation modes in the tool?

5. Now, answer the questions in the tool again as if you lived in a different country. What do you see as the cause of any difference in the size of ecological footprint?

6. Imagine you are an urban planner working for a city council. What would you recommend the city council do to reduce residents' ecological footprints?

environmental issues. We ask questions such as the following:

- What is nature?

- Where does our environmental knowledge come from?

- What shapes our understanding of a particular environmental issue?

- Does everyone perceive environmental problems in the same way? If not, what explains the variation?

Answering these questions helps ensure that our actions are sociologically grounded and not biased by individualistic or ethnocentric perspectives. In this section, we look at the social construction of nature and environmental problems.

Social Construction of Nature

To protect the environment, conventional wisdom is that we should use "natural" products instead of artificial ones. Sounds great, right? But, what exactly do we mean when we say something is "natural"? What about germs, viruses, and diseases? They are part of "nature," too. Also, are humans part of nature? If yes, what makes artificial things "unnatural" if humans make them? The more you think about this, the more you'll see the difficulty in drawing a clear boundary between the "artificial" and the "natural" components. This conundrum gets to the concept of what sociologists called social construction—an idea you have already encountered in other chapters of this book. It means that a category (e.g., natural or artificial) or a phenomenon (e.g., climate change or biodiversity loss) is understood to have certain characteristics because we agree they do.

American Wilderness

A **constructivist analysis of the environment** focuses on the role of ideology and knowledge in understanding our environmental conditions. For example, environmental historian Bill Cronon has famously traced the concept of **"wilderness."** We tend to think of wilderness as the highest ideal of nature: pristine, pure, and untouched by humans. Cronon demonstrates that the concept of wilderness is a product of America's frontier mentality, in which people romanticized the vast and supposedly untrammeled landscape (Cronon 1996). Such an understanding of nature is a social construction and a product of North American cultural and historical contexts.

Outside of the Western world, most cultures do not distinguish the "wild" from the "nonwild" environment. In some cases, they do not even have an equivalent term for wilderness or pristine nature in their languages! For example, in classical Chinese, the closest word to "nature" is *tiandi* (meaning heaven and earth) or *wanwu* (literally, ten thousand things), neither of which applies to the categorical distinction between humans and their environment (Weller 2006).

So what? You might wonder. We care about the social construction process because it often leads to tangible political and social implications. For example, seeing "wilderness" as the truest exemplar of nature, the United States and many countries following its lead have established national parks to protect nature from human development. The process sometimes has led to forced removal of local people from their homes, strangled the ecological relationships between indigenous communities and wildlife, and distracted us from attending to the mundane nonpristine environments around us. The creation of national parks is a human intervention based on a very particular cultural construct of nature.

China's Great Leap Forward

Another example of the social construction of nature can be found in the environmental disasters during revolutionary China in the mid-1900s. Threatened by Western powers and driven by Marxist ideology, Chinese leader Mao Zedong took an adversarial and extreme stance toward the natural world. He viewed humans as distinctly separated from nature. In his

"Backyard furnaces" in China led to large-scale environmental disasters as people chopped down trees to provide fuel for them.

words, humans must "conquer" and "defeat" nature to achieve the modernist ideal. This philosophy represented a sharp break from the traditional Chinese emphasis on harmony between humans and nature and moderation in resource consumption. The consequence was large-scale environmental and social disasters (Shapiro 2001).

During the Great Leap Forward—a political, economic, and social campaign to catch up with the West—Mao encouraged every commune or neighborhood to build small furnaces in their backyards to produce steel. Finding fuel to work these backyard furnaces led to massive deforestation. Mao also championed unscientific agricultural practices, including eradicating sparrows—birds that eat grains—and overusing fertilizers, resulting in the largest famine in human history and irreversible ecological damage to Chinese soil (Shapiro 2001).

As you can see from these examples, the social construction of nature has material consequences. How we think about nature influences how we act toward it. To think sociologically is to be mindful of how our thoughts about nature can influence our actions and, in the process, our society.

Constructing Environmental Problems

A social constructivist approach also examines how we come to perceive and define certain issues—such as air pollution, the ozone hole, and climate change—as environmental problems. You must have heard of the "ozone hole," but have you wondered what kind of "hole" it is? It turns out the hole is not an area with zero ozone in the atmosphere—just that the ozone layer is a lot thinner there. The more scientific term for ozone hole would be *ozone thinning* or *ozone depletion*.

The hole metaphor is a particular (and powerful) representation of the problem—that hydrofluorocarbons from aerosol sprays, refrigerants, and so on were severely thinning the ozone layer that protects us from the sun's harmful ultraviolet rays. "Ozone hole" caught many people's attention and led to the establishment of the Montreal Protocol to limit ozone-depleting substances. The Montreal Protocol, subsequently, was widely recognized as the most successful international environmental agreement and effectively phased out the ozone-depleting substances.

Under the 2015 United Nations (UN) Paris Agreement on climate change, nations across the globe have agreed to work to limit further warming of the world to within 2 degrees Celsius. (President Trump pulled the United States out of the agreement in 2017.) Why 2 degrees? Why not 1.5 to make it safer? How about 3, 4, or 5? We collectively, under the guidance of scientists, construct the extent of change (in this case, global warming) that we deem alarming.

While the idea of social construction we've discussed in other chapters (of gender, for instance) appears to happen organically or unconsciously, the social construction of an environmental problem—defining the problem and its solutions—can be quite direct and contentious. By now, you have probably figured out that environmental problems relate to people's interests. Different groups can try to shape them for their own benefit. For example, as efforts to address climate change threaten the fossil fuel industry, some fossil fuel companies have used misinformation campaigns to create confusion among the public about the realities of climate change (McCright and

Dunlap 2003; Jacques, Dunlap, and Freeman 2008). Scholars call them the "Merchants of Doubts" that delay critical actions through attacking the social construction that climate change is happening and/or is a problem that threatens the well-being of humans (Oreskes and Conway 2010).

To be clear, saying that climate change is socially constructed does not negate the physical reality that the world is warming. It does, however, help us to see how our views toward it are shaped by social forces. It enables us to recognize where our environmental knowledge comes from, how environmental concerns evolve over time, and why some problems are prioritized over others.

Environmental Awareness and Concern

Why are some of your friends tree-huggers while others couldn't care less about the environment? Our interactions with the environment depend on social experiences. Nature is often a symbolic environment for humans to confer meanings. For example, Émile Durkheim, one of sociology's founding figures, found that some aboriginal people worship particular types of plants or animals—the totem—as part of a ritual that increases social solidarity (Jerolmack and Tavory 2014). A study of male Turkish immigrants in Berlin, Germany, revealed that they experience a connection to their homeland and express their ethnic identity through keeping domestic pigeons, as they had in Turkey (Jerolmack 2007). In England, rural villagers who self-identify as "country people" believe that they live a more authentic and wholesome life than city dwellers—whom they see as removed from nature. Villagers believe that their proximity to nature offers them an escape from urban societal ills such as greed and alienation (Bell 1994).

To make sense of the rise of contemporary environmental concern, sociologists Riley Dunlap, William Catton, and their colleagues have come up with the **paradigm shift theory** (Catton and Dunlap 1978). They distinguish two sets of worldviews—the old "human exemptionalist paradigm" (HEP) and the "new environmental paradigm" (NEP). The former reflects an anthropocentric, or human-centered, relationship with the environment. Nature is to be mastered by humans. Humans are meant to dominate the Earth, without concern for their impact on it. The new ecological paradigm views humans as only part of the complex ecosystem and subject to ecological limits. The paradigm shift theory suggests that environmental concerns arise as people gradually adopt a more environmentally aware worldview—shifting from the HEP to the NEP.

Our likelihood to make the shift from HEP to NEP relates to our social positions. Environmental issues, contrary to the stereotype, tend not to be an elite concern. Women and minority groups rate environmental problems a higher concern than other demographic groups (McCright and Dunlap 2011). People in more dominant positions tend to have better resources to protect themselves from environmental risk and, thus, may care less about the environment.

Environmental concern is also influenced by **risk perception**—the tendency to evaluate the danger of a situation in not purely rational terms but through the lens of individual biases and cultures. For example, the physical risks from traveling in cars far outweigh the risks from flying in airplanes. According to the National Transportation Safety Board, the probability of some kind of airplane accident is 1 in 1.2 million, while the odds for one to be killed in a car crash is 1 in 5,000. But people usually fear flying more than driving. Similarly, the chance of dying from terrorist attacks is negligible in the United States, roughly equal to the chance of being killed by unstable furniture or televisions at home. It is hard to avoid hearing about the threat of terrorism. When is the last time you heard someone speak about being afraid of their furniture or their TV?

Social scientists using the **cultural theory of risks** note that risks not only are about material threats but also relate to our cultures. They categorize cultural values into two dimensions—from individualist to communitarian (the group) and from egalitarian to hierarchical (the grid). People who fall in each of the four quadrants (see Figure 13.1) have a

Consider This

The Intergovernmental Panel on Climate Change has reached the consensus that climate change is caused by human activities, and 97 percent of all climate scientists agree (Anderegg et al. 2010). Who decides what you should know and how you know it? Whom do you trust, and why?

FIGURE 13.1

Worldviews and Conceptualizations of Nature

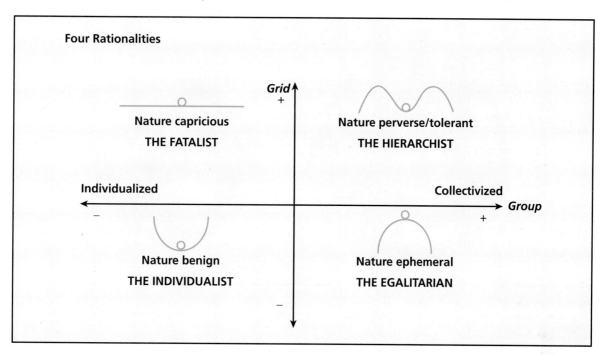

Four Rationalities

THE FATALIST — Nature capricious

THE HIERARCHIST — Nature perverse/tolerant

Individualized / Collectivized — Group

THE INDIVIDUALIST — Nature benign

THE EGALITARIAN — Nature ephemeral

different conceptualization of nature. People who hold more communitarian and egalitarian worldviews—meaning they are concerned with the well-being of the community and value equal rights for all—tend to see nature as fragile and perceive higher environmental risks (Kahan et al. 2007; Douglas and Wildavsky 1983).

Recognizing environmental risks is based on more than having the best information and exercising rational calculations. Values also matter. As our values often come from the communities in which we live, group identities also come into play in our concerns regarding the environment. The debate about climate change in the United States provides a good example. Research has shown that the persistent disagreement over its existence and the danger it poses to humans is, to a large extent, driven by political polarization. As a result, climate change has become an us-versus-them issue rather than primarily a scientific matter. As Figure 13.2 reveals, among Americans "who care a great deal" about climate issues, 72 percent are Democrats and 24 percent are Republicans (Funk and Kennedy 2016).

We often assume that if we only let people *know* about the importance of saving the environment,

things will improve. But this idea that inaction is caused by a lack of information is wrong or at least incomplete. Environmental education is certainly useful, without a doubt. And awareness raising is among the most common missions of environmental organizations. Yet, it is essential to understand that it is not only lack of awareness or scientific knowledge that keeps people from taking environmental action.

Maybe you are too busy to recycle; maybe you do not have the financial resources to shop green—even if you know you should for the environment. The **attitude-behavior split,** when we think one way and act another, does not mean that we are hypocrites. It does, though, reveal that we live in a society and do not have complete control over the everyday choices we are offered. Many environmentally significant decisions, such as fuel economy standards, food safety regulations, and city planning, happen at the societal level. As individuals, we can only control a small part of our environmental impacts. Responding to environmental challenges is also about reflecting on how we should live as a society and designing a more sustainable social system.

FIGURE 13.2

Americans Who Care about Climate Change

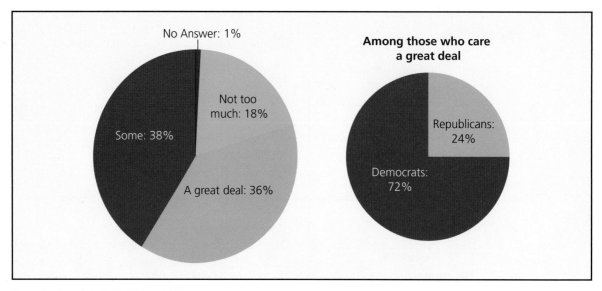

No Answer: 1%

Not too much: 18%

Some: 38%

A great deal: 36%

Among those who care a great deal

Republicans: 24%

Democrats: 72%

Source: Pew Research Center, May 10–June 6, 2016.

Note: Republicans and Democrats include independents and other nonpartisans who "lean" toward the parties. Respondents who do not lean toward a political party are not shown.

Doing Sociology 13.2

Climate Change Campaigner for a Day

In this activity, you will consider the ways in which you would tailor a message promoting efforts to combat climate change depending on your audience.

Suppose you are trying to persuade people to take action on climate change. As we have learned, values matter in how people understand and respond to environmental problems. Brainstorm different ways to present climate change that will resonate with different individuals or groups of people.

Write a few sentences explaining how you would make the case for climate change actions to each of the following people:

1. The president of the United States

2. The president of China

3. Executives in oil companies

4. Low-income households in an inner-city neighborhood

5. Regular churchgoers

6. Your local Parent-Teacher Association (PTA)

Check Your Understanding

- How do people in the United States describe the concept "wilderness"? Why do sociologists say it is socially constructed, and what are the consequences?

- What do we mean when we say the ozone hole problem is socially constructed?

- Explain the cultural theory of risks. What determines our risk perception in this framework?

How Did We Mess Up? Theories of Environmental Change

So far, we have discussed how our current levels of economic development and consumption are not sustainable. We also learned how we form our understanding of environmental issues. For sociologists, the next big issue is to diagnose the drivers of environmental destruction and ways to address them.

Population and the Environment

Are there just too many people on the planet? Linking population with environmental degradation is not a new argument. We can trace this school of thought all the way back to *An Essay on the Principle of Population,* published by English philosopher Thomas Robert Malthus in 1798. Malthus noted that populations tend to grow *exponentially*—that is, more and more rapidly—while food supply only increases *linearly*—that is, at a steady rate. If population growth is left unchecked, he predicted that society will end up with misery, starvation, and resource scarcity. This is the so-called "Malthusian catastrophe."

Malthus's prediction was proven largely incorrect. Yet, his ideas never faded away completely. As the ecological economist Herman Daly said, "Malthus has been buried many times . . . anyone who has been buried so often cannot be entirely dead" (Daly 1991:43). Modern-day neo-Malthusian works, such as Paul Ehrlich's (1968) *Population Bomb* and the Club of Rome's *The Limits to Growth* (Meadows et al. 1972) still argue that overpopulation is the main driver of environmental degradation, despite the absence of the large-scale famine and food shortages that their theories would predict.

What's wrong with Malthus's prophecy? The blind spot of Malthusianism lies in its overly deterministic view on population and the environment. Human interaction with the environment is mediated through technologies that change constantly. Malthus failed to foresee the tremendous productivity growth in agriculture that supports an ever-growing number of people. Also, linking famine to the food supply is too simplistic. The problem lies in the *access* to food, not the *availability* of food. For example, Amartya Sen—a Nobel Prize–winning economist and philosopher—examined four major famines and discovered that there was enough food for everyone, but the food did

FIGURE 13.3

Demographic Transitions Associated with Modernization

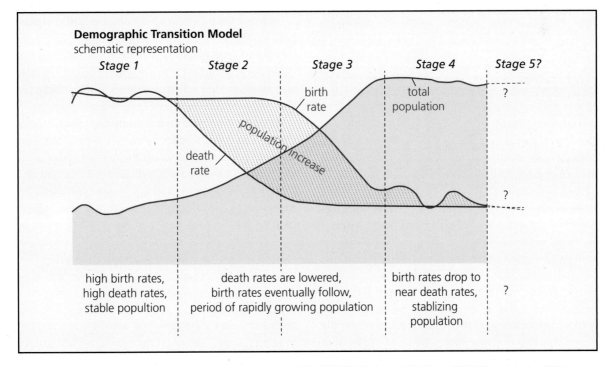

Source: *One Small Planet, Seven Billion People by Year's End and 10.1 Billion by Century's End.* UNEP Global Environmental Alert Service (GEAS). With permission from UN Environment.

not reach the people who needed it (Sen 1981). Famines typically happen when systems of food distribution, rather than production, break down.

Malthus's argument that population growth causes poverty is also off base. Experiences from many developing countries tell us that the causal effect works the other way around. People in poverty tend to have more, rather than fewer, children. Children are economic assets in agrarian societies, as they can help with farm work. High death rates due to poverty, therefore, lead poor agricultural households to have more children, not less.

Finally, Malthusians overlook the **demographic transition** associated with modernization (see Figure 13.3). Looking at population growth trends, demographers have noticed that, in traditional societies, the **birth rate** (number of births per 1,000 people per year) and **death rate** (number of deaths per 1,000 people per year) are both high, causing the population to stay in a stable state. As the societies go through industrialization, the death rate tends to drop before the birth rate due to improvements in health and increases in food supply. Since the birth rate is higher than the death rate, the population increases. In the last stage of economic development, social norms finally catch up with the improved standard of living, causing the birth rate to drop to a level similar to the death rate. The population thus stabilizes again. Some scholars optimistically predict that the global population will cease growing by 2050.

The demographic transition theory is a simplified model. We have seen countries follow somewhat different paths through the transition. The process very often involves frantic political projects—sometimes violent ones—such as China's One Child Policy (which came to an end in 2015) and India's sterilization campaign in the 1970s. One lesson is particularly worth mentioning: scholars consistently find that the status of women is the best predictor of the fertility rate. The more power women have in society, the fewer children they tend to have. Therefore, women's empowerment is not only a gender issue but also an environmental issue.

Just because Malthus's predictions did not come to pass does not mean that population does not affect the environment. More people on the planet requires more food on the table and affects our ecological footprint. Calculations of that footprint, covered earlier in this chapter, take population into account in the analysis. Yet, having more people living in McMansions has a much larger environmental impact than an increase in the number of people struggling to stay above the poverty line. We need to consider a population's production and consumption of resources rather than merely its size.

Production and the Environment

To sociologists, environmental degradation is not a result of too many people in the world, nor is it due to individuals' bad intentions or technological failures. Instead, it is a product of our unsustainable economic system.

What leads to an unsustainable economic system? Understanding **externalities** is the key to answering this question. Externalities are all the side effects—things that people fail to incorporate in their decision making—of economic activities. Externalities can be both positive and negative, and, by definition, they affect a party that does not choose to incur the cost or benefit (that's why they are "external").

An example of *positive* externalities would be the flowers in your front yard: maybe you plant them to decorate your house, but everyone in the neighborhood benefits from them. They are beautiful to look at and give the impression of a well-cared for home and neighborhood, increasing property values for all. Pollution, on the other hand, is a classic example of *negative* externalities. Industries produce goods we all use and need, but when they emit pollutants as by-products, the dirty air or water harms plants, animals, and people not involved in the production or consumption of the goods being created. In modern societies, economic exchanges are rarely, if ever, strictly between buyers and sellers. They also affect other parties. Thus, both positive and negative externalities are common features in our economy.

Many scholars are quick to point out that **capitalism,** defined by private properties, markets, and profits, has an ecologically destructive tendency. In the capitalist system, firms do not simply produce goods and services; they try to maximize profits. To do so, they have incentives to externalize the costs.

Imagine that you own a company. Your profits come from the difference between the price that you sell your merchandise for on the market (your revenue) and what you paid to produce it, including raw materials, labor costs, and environmental management (your cost). Under intense competition, which required you to set your prices low, your company barely made any profit last year. Your instinct tells you to cut costs to increase profits. Earlier this week, your best employee enthusiastically proposed buying a new device to install at the end of your smokestacks to control pollution. Seeing the balance sheet, you decide to postpone buying the new devices. You try to justify your decision: "Dirty air won't kill people immediately." And you can't remember the last time your local government sent someone to audit the

"The Story of Stuff"

In this activity, you will watch a brief video exploring where consumer goods come from and end up, then answer questions about the environmental impact of this system.

This 2007 video about the life cycle of consumer products was an instant sensation in YouTube's early days. The producer, Annie Leonard, provides a sharp critique of our production and consumption system.

Watch the video (https://youtu.be/9GorqroigqM) and summarize Leonard's view on the causes of the environmental crisis in our society by answering the following questions:

1. What is the linear production-consumption system?

2. In Leonard's view, what is the relationship between corporations and the government? How does that matter to the environment?

3. What are some marketing and design strategies that exacerbate environmental degradation?

4. Are marginalized communities represented in this video?

5. Do you agree with Leonard's assessment?

6. Are there statements or assertions that make you uncomfortable? If so, which ones? Why?

7. Now watch "The Story of Solutions" (https://youtu.be/cpkRvc-sOKk). What are the solutions provided by the producers of this video? What are some other solutions you can think of?

---

pollution numbers—you're not going to get caught anyway.

Now imagine a year has gone by and you find yourself in the same situation, no profit, company barely surviving. You now consider sourcing raw materials from a new Chinese company, whose price is 30 percent cheaper than the partner you've worked with for twenty years. Maybe the Chinese company has very low labor and environmental protocol, but that is really the last thing you can worry about now. And the cycle goes on. . . .

Eco-Marxists and the Treadmill of Production Theory

The scenario above reflects the Marxist-inspired conflict theory of the **"treadmill of production"** (Schnaiberg 1980; Schnaiberg and Gould 2000). On the capitalist treadmill, firms have to use and degrade natural resources to sustain their profits. Because of the constant pressure to expand profits, they are forced to compete with others by running faster and faster, producing more and more, and drawing ever more resources. If they don't, they will go bankrupt and "fall off the treadmill." In this process, firms face no choice but to externalize environmental and social costs or lose out to firms that do.

Many other schools of Marxist-inspired analysis have reached the same overall conclusion—capitalism is the ultimate cause of our ecological crisis.

According to capitalist logic, the system must continue to grow, seeking to secure raw materials, cheap labor, and new markets. The mantra of growth and accumulation inevitably will run into the physical limit of finite natural resources (Magdoff and Foster 2011). Eco-Marxists (Marxists who focus on the environment) argue that if we do not steer our societies toward an alternative economic system, they will collapse. Their solution is a massive radical movement toward a system that focuses on communal needs and the balance between human and nature.

The eco-Marxist analysis of the roots of our environmental problems paints a very grim picture. Indeed, the challenge is daunting. But is overthrowing capitalism our only way out? Some people disagree.

Ecological Modernization Theory

The idea that material conditions—the challenges of sustainability—have led us to reshape our social institutions and to adapt to environmental changes is known as **ecological modernization** theory. Societies have the potential to develop "ecological rationality"—decision making that incorporates ecological concerns—to replace the old model of modernization, which only focuses on economic growth and industrial development. The proponents of ecological modernization argue that humans are smart enough to internalize the negative externalities—to shoulder the costs of conducting their business in ecologically friendly ways—through new technologies, social innovations, and better management. Researchers found that some European countries, such as Germany and the Netherlands, have successfully achieved economic growth while lowering environmental impact through better product design, clean technology, and government incentives for innovation. For example, there is a regulation in the European Union requiring car manufacturers to take back vehicles that have reached the end of their product life span, resulting in a reduction of hazardous substances and better reuse of car components. Ecological modernization proponents argue that a different modernization is possible for the United States and the rest of the world (Spaargaren and Mol 1992; Mol, Spaargaren, and Sonnenfeld 2014).

Consider This

Eco-Marxists and ecological modernization theorists see the world through a drastically different lens. Which do you think is most helpful? Why?

Check Your Understanding

- What is the Malthusians' view on population and the environment? What is the weakness of this theory?
- What are positive and negative externalities?
- According to eco-Marxists, what is the root of environmental problems?
- How do ecological modernization theorists view environmental issues?

Consumption and the Environment

The previous section mainly considers environmental degradation as a result of production. What about the other side of the coin—consumption? After all, people have to buy things to complete the economic transaction.

Consumption does not happen in a vacuum. There are many factors going into *what* you buy, *why* you buy, and *how* you buy. For sociologists, the central tenet is that consumption is not an individual but a social process. This perspective traces back to Thorstein Veblen's book *The Theory of the Leisure Class,* published in 1899. Veblen came up with the concept of **conspicuous consumption**: buying luxury goods to publicly display one's power (Veblen 1899).

The items that symbolize social status change over time and place. For example, not long ago, in all parts of the world, any kind of smartphone was considered a piece of conspicuous consumption. Today, in many communities, only the latest version of the iPhone— and only in the first days of its release—elevates a person's status. Even though status objects may change constantly, the bottom line remains the same: we always have other people's reactions on our mind when buying stuff!

Conspicuous consumption has ecological implications. To be conspicuous, you have to do better than the community average. The process is inherently competitive. This creates momentum to constantly elevate the consumption level, leading to increasing environmental degradation. Every time people buy a new smartphone, they necessitate the production of that phone, with all the ecological impacts that implies. They also usually get rid of an older phone, which had similar environmental costs to produce and now must be thrown into a landfill or broken down into its component parts in another environmentally costly process.

Green Consumption

You might be wondering by now whether all consumption is bad. What about organic, local, and fair-trade goods? Those created through renewable energy?

Indeed, we have seen in recent years a growing trend of green consumption. **Green consumption** allows consumers to "vote with their pockets" and to engage in social change through the marketplace. Its logic goes like this: if you care about the environment, you should shop accordingly.

Producers use various **ecolabels** to indicate the superior environmental standards for their particular product (Hatanaka, Bain, and Busch 2005; Bartley 2007). Nowadays, you can find sustainability certification for a wide variety of foods and material goods. For example, you can purchase organic bananas, fair-trade coffee, Marine Stewardship Council certified salmon, paper towels that contain paper certified by the Forest Stewardship Council, and a brand-new flat-screen TV with an Energy Star label on it.

Weddings provide an opportunity for conspicuous consumption during which families can display their wealth.

Ecolabels sound like a good idea. Some people, however, say the green certification process privileges larger producers. If you run an organic family farm, the cost associated with being certified as "organic" can become a real financial burden.

Another important problem lies in credibility. According to the Ecolabel Index, a global clearinghouse of green labeling, as of late 2016, there were 465 ecolabels in 199 countries and 25 industry sectors. There are almost always multiple labels within one product sector. Who oversees their claims?

For consumers, labeling does not always provide useful information but sometimes gives us an illusion that we're choosing something environmentally friendly. Do you know the difference between *Rainforest Alliance Certified* and *USDA Organic*? Even worse, the standard may be so loose that the ecolabel does not mean anything. Ecolabels might become a tool for **greenwashing**—a green PR campaign that promotes an environmentally friendly, positive image of an organization, while its environmental practices are not in line with the image (Laufer 2003). Smart consumers should use caution when using ecolabels to determine their purchases.

Inverted Quarantines

Focusing our environmental efforts on our purchases can also distract us from addressing the causes of environmental degradation (Maniates 2001). In his book, *Shopping Our Way to Safety: How We Changed from Protecting the Environment to Protecting Ourselves,* Andrew Szasz (2007) uses the term **inverted quarantine** to illustrate this idea. Normally, we quarantine bad things from our clean environment, but as our environment is increasingly polluted, many of us have started to quarantine ourselves from the unsafe environment. For example, people worried about the chemicals in the municipal water supply protect themselves from it by buying bottled water.

Szasz argues that such individual efforts distract us from carrying out necessary political actions (not to mention that some bottled water is just tap water put into bottles or the environmental harm created through producing, packaging, and distributing bottled water). He points out that we could be using our resources more effectively by pressuring elected officials to pass legislation to improve the quality and infrastructure of public water supply systems. People ought to question and address why the water is contaminated and unsafe to drink in the first place!

Check Your Understanding

- What is conspicuous consumption? How does it relate to the environment?
- What is green consumption?
- How can ecolabels promote "greenwashing"?
- In what ways do people carry out environmental inverted quarantines? What are the negative effects?

Who Suffers Most from Environmental Problems?

Flint, Michigan, is a predominantly African American and low-income community. In mid-2014, the city switched its municipal water source from the Detroit water system to the Flint River. Before long, local citizens started to complain about the strange color and foul smell coming from the tap water. A few months later, people began to report rashes, hair loss, and vision problems. It turns out the water is seriously contaminated with lead—a persistent pollutant that can accumulate in the body over time and have devastating effects. The Environmental Protection Agency (EPA) has set a goal to eliminate lead in drinking water and takes action if it is detected at levels higher than 15 parts per billion (ppb). In some homes in Flint, the lead level was as high as 10,000 ppb.

Government officials did not, at first, take the concerns of the Flint residents seriously. They allowed Flint residents to continue to drink lead-tainted water. It was not until researchers from outside the community verified the lead poisoning—and held a news conference about it—that government officials began to acknowledge and address the issue (Hohn 2016). Finally, in early January 2016, the state of Michigan declared a state of emergency to address the crisis, and the federal government followed suit a week later, freeing up $5 million in federal relief.

Would the drinking water problem in Flint have been handled differently if it had taken place in a White suburb of Detroit? The answer seems to be "yes." The Flint Water Advisory Task Force commissioned by the state government of Michigan found that

> the facts of the Flint water crisis lead us to the inescapable conclusion that this is a case of environmental injustice. Flint residents, who are majority Black or African American and among the most impoverished of any metropolitan area in the United States, did not enjoy the same degree of protection from environmental and health hazards as that provided to other communities. . . . Flint residents were not provided equal access to, and meaningful involvement in, the government decision-making process. (Flint Water Advisory Task Force 2016:54)

Environmental Racism

Flint is no isolated case. Across the United States and the world, low-income and minority communities do not receive the same level of environmental protection as Whiter, wealthier communities. As in the case of Flint, Michigan, they often bear disproportionate burdens of environmental harm. Sociologists have come to use the term **environmental justice** to document the social inequality in the environmental realm (Mohai, Pellow, and Roberts 2009).

Sociological research on environmental justice issues was sparked by recognition of **environmental racism**—when environmental hazards are disproportionally borne by racial and ethnic minority groups (Bullard 1990, 1993). In the early 1980s, the U.S. General Accountability Office (GAO) found that four major landfill sites in the South were situated near a disproportionately high percentage of African American communities. In 1987, the United Church of Christ (UCC) published a landmark study, *Toxic Wastes and Race in the United States* (United Church of Christ 1987), showing that African Americans are two to three times more likely than Whites to live close to a hazardous landfill. A third classic study, by Robert Bullard, found that twenty-one of Houston's twenty-five waste facilities were located in African American neighborhoods. These cases show that, rather than the ordinary "Not in My Backyard" (NIMBY) politics, many waste-siting decisions follow the route of "Put in Blacks' Backyard" (PIBBY). Sociologist Bullard (1990) explains that governments and private industries seek the "path of least resistance" to distribute pollutants. Since African American and other minority groups are less represented in the political processes and have less power to defend themselves, they are more likely to end up with these pollutants near their homes.

The Environmental Justice Movement

This research on environmental racism helped to create a vibrant **environmental justice movement,** with the goal of ending the practice of using poor and racial and ethnic minority areas as dumping grounds for environmental hazards. In the fall of 1982, a group of roughly 500 people participated in a six-week protest to stop the placement of 32,000 cubic yards of PCB-contaminated soil in a mostly African American rural community in Warren County, North Carolina. The protest did not achieve its goal, and the landfill was completed. Yet, as one of the first fights against environmental racism that gained national attention, the Warren County protest became a

E-waste is more likely to be disposed in China than anywhere else in the world. Guivy, in southeast China, is a major hub for e-waste disposal where hundreds of thousands of laborers work to dismantle electronic junk, endangering their health and their community in the process.

AP Photo/Stringer

transformative event. Many other communities also formed organizations and coalitions to fight for environmental justice (McGurty 2000).

The environmental justice movement is a reminder of how our social status and experiences shape our interaction with the environment. When an upper-middle class White man tries to preserve a natural habitat for his birding interest, the local minority community might be going through a fight against groundwater contamination poisoning their drinking water. Same environment, but very different interests and experiences. As a result, the environmental justice movement, since its inception, has had an uneasy relationship with the mainstream environmental movement— predominantly represented by Whites and the middle class (Taylor 2000; Martinez-Alier 2003). The environmental justice activists have criticized the mainstream environmental organizations as "lost in the woods" and focusing too much on preserving nature—often in the form of wilderness we discussed early in this chapter—rather than fighting environmental injustice.

Consider This

Think back to how you answered the first Consider This question in this chapter. Given what you have learned, would you change your list of the most important things we can do to save our environment? Why?

The environmental justice movement has made substantial and positive impacts. For example, the federal government officially recognized the principle of environmental justice in 1994. Executive Order 12898, signed by President Bill Clinton, mandates "fair treatment and meaningful involvement of all people regardless of race, color, national origin, or income with respect to the development, implementation, and enforcement of environmental laws." The recognition of environmental justice issues has led mainstream environmental groups to make greater efforts to diversify their membership and goals.

Meanwhile, environmental justice scholars and activists have broadened their efforts from their initial focus on racism to include issues of social class, as well. There has been a long-lasting debate on whether race or class better predicts the distribution of environmental harms (Ringquist 2005; Mohai et al. 2009). There are also ongoing efforts to tease out the causes of environmental injustice—whether it is a product of intentional political targeting or the result of economic sorting whereby disadvantaged groups move closer to pollution because of lower housing prices. These are complicated questions to answer. In general, we have learned about the importance of looking beyond the simple perpetrator-victim framework to pay more attention to history and local contexts that produce the inequality (Pellow 2000).

Sacrifice Zones

In recent years, environmental justice has increasingly become a global concern and a global movement (Pellow 2007). In many cases, when a company appears to make progress in its environmental practices in developed countries, it just moves the dirty parts to developing countries, where the costs of pollution are cheaper. These **sacrifice zones** are defined by more than race and class; they also relate to countries of origin.

A village named Guiyu in Guangdong province in China is one sacrifice zone. A town of 150,000 people, it contains thousands of factories, many of them illegal, processing electronic waste from around the world. Workers strip down discarded electronic devices to recover the lead, gold, copper, and other metals they contain. During the process, they are exposed to many

Creating Engaged Climate Justice Scholarship

Timmons Roberts

I founded the Climate and Development Lab (CDL) when I came to Brown in 2010. The CDL is an experiment in engaged learning and scholarship, whose mission is to contribute timely, accessible, and impactful research that informs more just and effective climate policy. The lab has two very different groups running under very different models—one working on international climate justice and the other on local and state issues and legislation.

Since 2010, the international part of the CDL has brought over fifty Brown students to the annual UN climate change negotiations, in Cancun, Durban, Warsaw, Lima, Bonn, and Paris. That group's research focuses on how equity, justice, and finance have an impact on the UN climate change negotiations. We focus on providing research support to the Least Developed Countries group—the world's forty-eight poorest nations through collaborating with leading international research institutes, environmental nongovernmental organizations (NGOs), and negotiating groups.

My students and I provide "capacity" to the neediest countries and to the most effective civil society organizations in the UN climate negotiations by conducting research that meets their interest to which they would otherwise not have access. We usually seek to first publish streamlined core research findings as policy briefing papers, whose impact is tied to their originality and their timeliness. We release those widely and target them to climate experts. These experts and participants in the tussle of climate politics provide immediate feedback, help publicize our findings, and use them in social policy change efforts. We also put our research on our websites (www.climatedevlab.brown.edu and AdaptationWatch.org), as well as write blogs and tweet about them and many other timely issues of climate and equity. We then sometimes turn our research findings into peer-reviewed scholarly articles and incorporate the findings into our books.

In a fall semester seminar on "Engaged Climate Policy," students first receive "boot camp" training of the essential parts of global climate governance. They participate in small team-based climate policy research groups, preparing briefing papers with experts around the world. Students are then "embedded" with organizations prior to and during the UN climate change talks, which allows them to develop and use their academic knowledge of global climate governance in practical and meaningful ways. During this time, students prepare op-eds, blogs, and individual presentations on key areas of climate policy.

The domestic part of CDL has focused on climate change legislation in Rhode Island and in Providence. In talking to local officials, we learned we could work with state legislators to develop and help introduce bills. The first bill we worked on created a permanent standing committee to study the issue of climate change. In 2014, we helped draft the first state legislation addressing adaptation to climate change that included targets for reducing emissions by 80 percent by 2050. Most recently, we have been working on carbon pricing legislation.

Timmons Roberts is Ittleson Professor of Environmental Studies and Sociology at Brown University.

toxic substances. As a result, the children in Guiyu suffer from an extremely high rate of lead poisoning (Economy 2011). You can find places like Guiyu in India, Malaysia, Ghana, and Nigeria. The high costs of end-of-life treatment of electronic products are invisible to consumers in Global North nations.

Climate Justice

Climate change can also be viewed through an environmental justice lens. To sociologists, **climate justice** highlights the fact that climate change relates to global inequality, in its creation and its impact (Roberts and Parks 2006, 2009). Countries have made vastly different contributions to the problem. The per capita carbon emission of the average person in the United States is about ten times that of the average Indian! Furthermore, if we look at the greenhouse gases in the atmosphere, most were released by Western countries over the history of industrialization, while the contribution from most developing countries is negligible.

The inequality in climate change also lies in the fact that the people who contributed the least to it suffer the most from it. Many citizens in low-lying Bangladesh and in island countries are facing an existential threat. Current research predicts that much of their homeland will be under water well within this century. And they have no way to turn the tides, literally. Using the environmental/climate justice framework, researchers now use the concept of "climate debt" or "development rights" to describe the disproportionate atmospheric space developed countries have taken and demand they take stronger actions to mitigate the impact of climate change and to help developing nations to prepare for it (Rice 2007). Sociologists, such as Professor Timmons Robert in the Sociologists in Action box, have made contributions to climate justice through capacity building, action research, and policy advisement.

Consider This

Look at the electronic gadgets you own. Think about the whole "chain" between the birth and death of a product—from mining, to manufacturing, to waste disposal. What are some of the environmental impacts these devices create? Who bears the burden of these gadgets?

Check Your Understanding

- What is environmental racism?
- Why is there a tension between the environmental justice movement and mainstream environmentalism?
- How is environmental justice a global issue?
- What does the term *climate justice* highlight?

Social Solutions to Environmental Problems

The environment does not exist outside of our social life. Sociology is concerned with the social consequences of environmental issues, as well as the social causes of them. Environmental problems are intertwined with social inequality.

Social problems require collective solutions. It is not enough to put bottled water containers into the recycling bin correctly. It may give you a warm moral glow, but it, alone, does little to lower the environmental impact of bottled water. A more sociological approach is to think about how bottled water becomes an acceptable commodity and the actors involved in the process. Why don't we install more drinking water fountains so that people don't need to buy bottled water? Or, more radically, how about simply banning the sales of bottled water like the city of San Francisco does on its city-owned properties?

The term **virtual environmentalism** characterizes the second approach (Bell and Ashwood 2015). Virtual environmentalism seeks to create social conditions that lead people to help preserve the environment without thinking much about it. Examples include building a public transportation system that becomes the most convenient and affordable way to move around, creating bike lanes so that biking is safe and enjoyable, and revamping agricultural regulations so that the food always comes from sustainable farms. There are many more examples. Rather than focusing on enlightening individuals, virtual environmentalism aims to cultivate sustainable communities.

Creating sustainable communities is a team effort. It requires us to be active citizens. It demands that we build social capital and work with others to achieve our goals. It also reminds us to be always conscious of the environmental consequences of our consumption. The good news is that such change is already happening. People have started to realize the negative impacts, both socially and environmentally, of fast food, fast fashion, and the throw-away society. The burgeoning sharing economy, maker culture, local food movement, and

Creating safe conditions for bikers would encourage more people to bike and reduce car emissions.

©iStockphoto.com/olaser

open-source models all point to the potential to slow down the economic treadmill and connect more with others in our communities. While we create a more enjoyable and connected society, we will also slow down pollution and reduce climate change (Schor 2011).

Check Your Understanding

- Why is individual action not enough to solve environmental problems?
- What is virtual environmentalism?

Conclusion

In this chapter, we learned that environmental problems are social problems and require social solutions. Sociology, through social constructivist analysis, offers us sharp insights on how environmental problems are defined and understood by the public, as well as how individuals may perceive the environment differently based on their social locations. Sociology also highlights that environmental degradation is mainly a systematic problem of our unsustainable production and consumption system. In addition, negative environmental impacts often fall unequally onto low-income and minority groups. Environmental issues are social justice issues, too.

We can all agree that society cannot exist without the environment. If you care about society, you have to care about the environment. The environmental movement has become one of the most vibrant realms of social activism today. You can learn more about it and what it takes to create a successful social movement in the next chapter.

CHAPTER
13

$SAGE edge™

Want a better grade? Get the tools you need to sharpen your study skills. Access practice quizzes, eFlashcards, video and multimedia at **edge.sagepub.com/korgen**

Review

13.1 Why are environmental problems social problems?

Environmental problems are problems *for* society, as they threaten our current social order; they are also problems *of* society, as they are the results of our current unsustainable social practices. To address these problems and search for sustainability, we need to use our sociological imagination to think beyond individual behaviors (e.g., recycling, changing light bulbs, turning off lights) and focus on the social constraints that shape our everyday choices.

13.2 How do sociologists study environmental issues?

Before sociologists tackle environmental degradation, we ask questions such as the following: What is nature? Where does our environmental knowledge come from? What shapes our understanding of a particular environmental issue? Does everyone perceive environmental problems in the same way? If not, what explains the variation? Sociologists view both nature and environmental problems as social constructions with social solutions.

13.3 How would eco-Marxists and ecological modernization theorists define and discuss environmental problems and their solutions?

Eco-Marxists believe that environmental problems are based in the roots of capitalism. On the capitalist "treadmill," businesses have to use and degrade natural resources to sustain their profits. In this process, firms face no choice but to externalize environmental and social costs. Their solution is a radical transformation to a new economic system.

Ecological modernization theorists argue that the challenges of sustainability can lead us to reshape our social institutions to adapt to environmental changes. Societies have the potential to incorporate *ecological rationality*—considering environmental consequences in decision making—to replace the old model of modernization. Humans are smart enough to internalize the negative externalities through new technologies, social innovations, and better management. Their solution is reformist, focusing on technological development and innovations in existing institutions.

13.4 What are the promises and constraints of green consumption?

Green consumption allows consumers to protect the environment through buying environmentally friendly products marked with "green" labels. These labels are not always accurate, however, and consumers should use them with caution. Ecolabels might become a tool for greenwashing—a green PR campaign that promotes an environmentally friendly, positive image of an organization that does not accurately reflect its practices.

13.5 What is environmental justice?

Sociologists have come to use the term *environmental justice* to document the social inequality in the environmental realm. Across the United States and the world, low-income and minority communities do not receive the same level of environmental protection as Whiter, wealthier communities. As in the case of Flint, Michigan, they often bear disproportionate burdens of environmental harm.

The environmental justice movement seeks to equalize the exposure of environmental problems, as well as involve disadvantaged communities in the decision-making processes.

13.6 What are social solutions to environmental problems?

Social problems, like climate change and other environmental problems, require collective solutions. Individual behavior, alone, cannot adequately address them. Virtual environmentalism aims to cultivate sustainable communities rather than focusing on changing individuals. For example, rather than just encouraging people to recycle their water bottles, we can work to create policies requiring drinking fountains in public buildings or banning the sales of bottled water. Creating social solutions to environmental problems is a team effort that requires us to work with others to develop sustainable communities.

Key Terms

- attitude-behavior split   281
- birth rate   284
- capitalism   284
- climate justice   290
- conspicuous consumption   286
- constructivist   278
- cultural theory of risks   280
- death rate   284
- demographic transition   284
- ecolabel   286
- ecological footprint   276
- ecological modernization   285
- environmental justice   288
- environmental justice movement   288
- environmental racism   288

- environmental sociology   276
- externalities   284
- green consumption   286
- greenwashing   287
- inverted quarantine   287
- overshoot   276
- paradigm shift theory   280
- risk perception   280
- sacrifice zones   289
- sustainability   276
- sustainable development   276
- treadmill of production   285
- virtual environmentalism   291
- wilderness   278

AP Photo/Anonymous

Social movements work to promote social change. In January 2017, an estimated 600,000 people joined the Women's March in Washington, D.C., and millions more gathered across the United States and the world to protest the policies of President Donald Trump.

Learning Questions

14.1   What is a social movement?

14.2   Why do people participate in social movements?

14.3   What are the different types of social movements?

14.4   How would you use a sociological theory to explain a social movement?

14.5   What are the steps a social movement must take to become successful?

14.6   What tactics do social movements use to achieve their goals, and what kind of backlash do they face?

14.7   How can we create social change?

CHAPTER 14

Changing Society through Social Movements

Wendy M. Christensen

What Is a Social Movement?

Five people are gathered outside city hall after a city council meeting. Each had attended the meeting to demand that the city address the rapidly multiplying feral cat population. Each was involved in helping reduce the feral cat population on their own, spending their own time and money to trap and spay/neuter cats. Noting the dangers faced by the cats and the smell and noise of the growing feral cat population, these five residents came to the meeting to press the city council to adopt what is known as a TNR program (trap-neuter-return). A coordinated, citywide program could reduce the population and would get cats fixed and adopted.

Despite the impassioned pleas of the five concerned residents, the council members did not promise to address the feral cat problem. The five are agitated as they talk about the council's disinterested response to their requests. One suggests that they join together to form a new organization, "Friends of Cats," to raise awareness and push the city council to act. They exchange numbers and promises to find each other on Facebook before heading home.

Two days later, the fledgling social movement has a Facebook page with over 100 followers. Soon after, membership grows from the original five to fifteen individuals. Meeting at a local coffee shop to plan their next steps, they decide to make informational flyers to distribute around town and start a petition demanding the city council adopt their proposed policies.

The next time the city council meets, Friends of Cats has thirty-five people in attendance, all with signs demanding the council take action. They present a petition with 1,500 signatures of local residents and introduce experts on TNR policy from the Animal Protection League to speak to the council. At that meeting, the council agrees to form a committee with Friends of Cats members on animal control. A few months later, it drafts and passes a TNR policy for the city.

Components of a Social Movement

The formation of the social movement organization "Friends of Cats" is typical for social movements. A **social movement** forms when people who want social change create an organization that is collective, organized, and sustained and challenges authorities, powerholders, or cultural beliefs and practices in noninstitutional ways.

Wendy M. Christensen

I often joke that I began thinking sociologically when I listened to Pink Floyd's album *Animals* nonstop as a teenager (*Animals* is a rock album about economic inequality, borrowing from George Orwell's *Animal Farm*). But, I was a sociologist long before that. From the time I could read, I devoured books that focused on women's rights, racism, and social inequality.

I started college as a technical theater major. I took a sociology course as part of my general requirements. I enjoyed the material, and the professor suggested I switch majors. But it took a couple years, including transferring and taking a year off, to finally switch to sociology. For the first time, I loved my college courses. I wrote an undergrad thesis on masculinity and school shootings. My advisors encouraged me to apply to graduate school.

Since earning my PhD, I feel like I have the best job possible. I study what interests me, which right now is community-based political activism. My favorite courses to teach are Social Movements and Social Stratification. My work allows me to be active in my community and contribute to social justice movements. I love teaching social activism in nonacademic settings to carry the lessons of past movements into today's social movement community.

Friends of Cats is a *collective,* made up of a group of people cooperating as they work toward a shared goal. Its members discovered they cared about the same issue (feral cats) and had the same goal as the city council (humanely reducing the feral cat population). They decided that joining forces and working with city council members would make them more powerful.

Consider This

When you think of a social movement or protest, what comes to mind? Have you ever participated in a protest? Why?

Friends of Cats is also *organized;* the members coordinate their efforts. They started organizing through email, Facebook, and face-to-face planning meetings soon after they met. As with many social movements today, social media tools facilitated their organizing efforts.

The movement members *sustained* their efforts until their goals were met. Their sustained efforts included passing around a petition, distributing literature, recruiting experts to research and present their case, attending city council meetings, and making themselves visible at those meetings. Their close work with the council led to the council turning to them when they selected people to place on the city's Animal Control Committee.

Friends of Cats mobilized through *noninstitutional* means. They organized *outside* established institutions like city government. Their noninstitutional protest strategies and activism got them noticed by government institutions, specifically the city council. Eventually, after their noninstitutional mobilizing efforts, members became part of city government by working on the Animal Control Committee.

Together, the Friends of Cats members challenged powerholders with the goal of changing city policy. To be successful, social movements must target the institution or authority figure with the power to make the changes they seek. Such target institutions or figures could be a city council, a mayor, a member of Congress, a school principal, or any other group or individual in a position of power.

Protests: The Most Visible Part of Social Movements

When you think of a social movement, what images come to mind? You might picture groups of individuals demonstrating out in the street with signs, yelling; individuals sitting with their arms linked, blocking the access to a building; or tens of thousands of people flooding a public space, singing and chanting for social change. These are all examples of a **protest**, an individual or group act of challenging, resisting, or making demands toward social change. Protests are often the most visible part of social movements, while the behind-the-scenes work of organizing and mobilizing is often unnoticed but will be covered in this chapter.

Some movements use **civil disobedience** in their protests, purposely breaking social customs or laws to make their point. Lunch counter sit-ins during the 1960s civil rights movement are an example of civil disobedience. The 1999 protests against the World

Trade Organization (WTO) in Seattle, Washington, provide another example. Protestors disrupted the 1999 WTO meeting by taking over street intersections and preventing delegates from getting to their hotels.

Check Your Understanding

- What is a social movement?
- Why is organization important for a social movement?
- Why do social movements work outside institutions?
- Who are some of the powerholders that social movements might target for social change?
- How do sociologists define a protest?

Participating in Social Movements

Social movement organizing takes considerable time and resources. Not everyone has time to spend passing out petitions, marching in demonstrations, and organizing meetings and protests. Individuals who participate in social movements may face other costs, as well. If a demonstration becomes heated or disrupts the routines of others (by blocking traffic etc.), demonstrators risk confrontations with non-participants and police, as well as possibly arrest.

So, why do individuals become involved in social movements? Members of the Friends of Cats organization are all individuals committed to improving the lives of feral cats. They have volunteered their own time and often their own money to rescue feral cats. As individuals, they stand to benefit if the city adopts a TNR program. Their individual efforts and expenses will be replaced by the city's animal control department. These members are **beneficiary constituents,** people who stand to benefit directly from the social change being sought. Other individuals who are not involved in animal rescue may join the social movement organization because they believe the city would benefit from helping animals. These members would be **conscience constituents,** people who care about the cause but do not benefit directly from the changes.

Power and Inequality Issues in Social Movements

While there are social movements focused on animal rights, many social movements fight for people's rights. In the Black Lives Matter movement, Black Americans experiencing discrimination are the beneficiaries of the movement. But consider for a minute the role White people play in the Black Lives Matter movement. They are not beneficiary constituents who stand to directly benefit from the movement's efforts but instead join as allies, morally committed to the cause as conscience constituents.

The roles conscience constituents take in social movements raise issues of power and inequality in social movement organizations. Some social movement organizers argue that the voices of the marginalized—those the movement is fighting for—must be centered in the movement. If the voices of the marginalized are not centered, the movement risks forming goals or mobilizing actions that do not actually help the individuals they want to help. For example, members of an impoverished community may need better access to affordable grocery stores, instead of another food pantry. White people can be strong allies in civil rights movements, but

In this picture, MoveOn.org leaders present petitions calling for a ban on assault weapons. Through this effort, they hope to gain the attention and support of members of Congress.

Jim Watson/AFP/Getty Images

addressing racism requires listening to the experiences of people of color who confront racism on a daily basis. By the same token, men can be important allies in the feminist movement, but women must be the ones to decide how the movement addresses sexism. Participating in a social movement can be empowering for community members when they are encouraged to take part in their own mobilization.

Socioeconomic Status and Ability

Participation in social movements can be limited by socioeconomic status and ability. Demonstrations, protests, and marches require physical stamina, leaving some less able-bodied individuals out. Not every student has the financial support to take off a summer from work and volunteer, as some students did during the Freedom Summer campaign to register Black voters in Mississippi in 1964. Attending meetings and demonstrations can be difficult for lower-income workers who often have multiple jobs, inflexible hours, and no childcare. Participating in a social movement can be empowering, but not everyone has the economic or social security required to take some of the risks associated with participation. The potential for confrontation with powerholders or with the police is also not a gamble everyone can take. Many individuals cannot risk their jobs, children, public assistance, or education with an arrest record.

Mobilizing and Organizing

The process of mobilizing begins with **emergence** (Blumer 1995). During this stage, people who share the same grievance get together and find others who support their goals. This means spreading the word and bringing people together to support the goal of the social movement. The Internet, particularly social media, makes social movement participation easier for a wider variety of people. Online communication also makes **mobilizing** a social movement easier. Mobilizing efforts can be facilitated by social networking sites like Facebook and Twitter.

The next stage of social movement mobilizing is **organizing** or **coalescence,** when people come together more formally toward a shared goal (Blumer 1995). Organizing includes coordinating the regular operations of the social movement, which is another key part of social movements. Successful social change efforts require both. Social media campaigns can be very powerful for organizing, like the 2014 hashtag #BringBackOurGirls, which over 6 million people tweeted to demand the release of Nigerian schoolgirls kidnapped by Boko Haram. But, the campaign was criticized as "slacktivism" as the hashtag itself did

nothing to further the release of the schoolgirls. Other hashtag campaigns have successfully mobilized activists on and offline. The hashtag #whyImarch worked to mobilize individuals' participation in the Women's March on Washington the day after the 2017 inauguration of President Trump and fueled the political activism of those marchers after the demonstration itself was over.

Community-Based Organizing

Social movements can grow nationally or internationally, around an issue that affects people's lives at any level. Amnesty International, for example, is an organization focused on issues of human rights around the world. Other social movements are located and organized within communities. Through **community-based organizing,** individual activists become involved in a movement because of an issue directly affecting their community. Friends of Cats is an example of a community-based organization.

The Industrial Areas Foundation (IAF) is one of the oldest national community organizations in the United States. Founded in 1940, the IAF was developed to foster and support community-based groups, by training local-level leaders and organizers so they can make change in their local communities. Some of the organization's achievements include passing health care reform in Massachusetts, creating green jobs in Seattle, and successfully lobbying for school reform in Texas (IAF 2017). The IAF often works through local religious organizations, as does People Improving Communities through Organizing (PICO), a national network of faith-based community organizations.

Some sociologists also work with organizations to make social change. See, for example, sociologist Professor Alicia Swords's activism against poverty in her community described in the following Sociologists in Action box.

Check Your Understanding

- What are beneficiary constituents?
- What are conscience constituents?
- How can someone's economic status affect his or her ability to participate in a social movement?
- What is the difference between mobilizing and organizing?
- What is community-based organizing?

Sociologists in Action

Participating in the Movement to End Poverty

Alicia Swords

My teaching and scholarship are grounded in the experiences and knowledge of the people most affected by the inequalities I study. For years I've been mentored by leaders of the University of the Poor, a national network of poor people's organizations committed to building a movement to end poverty. They helped me answer questions like the following: Why are people poor in a land of plenty? What can be done to unite people across racial and religious lines? Their answers resonated with what I knew and with the sociologists I was studying. They challenged me to ask questions that deeply matter and develop my accountability as a scholar and a sociologist with the tools to help change society.

My involvement in the University of the Poor gives me evidence of the realities of poverty that I share with my students at Ithaca College. When we study the history of the organized poor in the United States, students in my classes often say, "Why did I never learn about this before?" We analyze "projects of survival"—homeless people organizing tent cities and housing takeovers in Philadelphia, low-wage workers uniting for decent pay in Baltimore, and rural people resisting mountaintop removal mining in West Virginia. My students take part in immersion programs where they learn firsthand from those engaged in struggles against hydro fracking and mountaintop removal. They also participate in action research by interviewing people who get food from food pantries and pantry volunteers to learn about their experiences and explanations for poverty and hunger.

There are enough resources in the world to end poverty, but it will take political will—a massive social movement—to change the fundamentals of our economic system and make it happen. Today it's clear such a movement to end poverty has to be global. I was part of a University of the Poor delegation of homeless people that met with the Landless Workers movement in Brazil. It was remarkable to realize the common struggles of the poor around the world and the power of connecting the poor transnationally.

Willie Baptist, an organizer, scholar, and formerly homeless father, has been a key part of building this global movement. He has traveled tirelessly, meeting and cultivating local leaders, listening to their stories, and helping them see they aren't alone and their struggles are interconnected. Baptist insists that solving the problem of poverty requires combining poor people's life experiences with rigorous study. "Never in the history of the world has a dumb force risen up and overthrown a smart force," he says. That's one place where the work of sociologists is so important! We can bring perspectives from history and from all over the world to efforts for social change. Although the movement to end poverty will have to be led by the poor, it also requires engaged intellectuals, young people, students, and people from all segments of society. I love getting to be a part of this effort every day through my teaching and sociological research.

Alicia Swords is associate professor of sociology at Ithaca College. She conducts research with social movements in the United States and Latin America and enjoys supporting student engagement with grassroots efforts for social change.

Types of Social Movements

Many people think of social movements as progressive, but in fact, they are active all over the ideological map. Some of the most extreme conservative social movements are racist hate organizations like neo-Nazi groups and the Ku Klux Klan. While some social movements push for massive social change, others press for limited changes to society. There are four different types of movements: alternative, redemptive, reformative, and revolutionary.

Alternative social movements advocate for limited societal change but do not ask individuals to change their personal beliefs. They often target a narrow group of people and focus on a single concern. Friends of Cats is an example of an alternative social movement. Their goal was to change animal control policy in their city. The DREAMers movement, for example, advocates for a pathway to citizenship for children of undocumented immigrants. Many environmental movements—like the antifracking

The Use and Effectiveness of "Slacktivism"

In this activity, you will find and examine the effectiveness of examples of "slacktivism."

Slacktivism is a term used to describe activism that requires very little time or effort. Usually slacktivism is online (changing a profile picture, posting a link or a tweet) but could also be offline (signing a petition, wearing a T-shirt).

1. Go online and find at least five examples of slacktivism. Where did you search and what search terms did you use to find these examples?

2. Describe the kinds of images and words these examples use. What do they have in common?

3. Have you ever changed your Facebook or Twitter picture to make a political statement? Does this count as social activism?

4. Can online protest actions like "slacktivism" be effective? When and how?

---

movement—are examples of alternative social movements. Mothers Against Drunk Driving (MADD) or Mothers for Gun Control are both examples of movements advocating for change to specific policies and laws. MADD advocates for harsher laws against drunk driving, and Mothers for Gun Control lobbies for stricter gun control laws and gun safety.

Some social movements can fall into multiple categories. MADD is also an example of a **redemptive social movement** as they ask individuals to change their behavior and not drive while intoxicated. Redemptive social movements seek radical change in individual behavior. For example, the Temperance Movement in the 1800s advocated for individuals to stop drinking alcohol. While People for the Ethical Treatment of Animals (PETA) is an alternative social movement in that they advocate against animal abuse, they are also a redemptive movement with the goal of convincing individuals to adopt a vegan diet and lifestyle.

While alternative social movements are focused on social change for a narrow portion of society, **reformative social movements** work for specific change across society. In working for an end to racism and racial injustice, the civil rights movement and the more recent Black Lives Matter movement fit this type of movement. The marriage equality movement is another example of a reformative social movement; it aimed to change one aspect of society—the ability for same-sex couples to marry. Reformative social movements can also be conservative, aiming to restore traditional ways of behavior or maintain the status quo. For example, conservative movements like the anti–marriage equality movement try to keep traditional gendered family roles. Another movement, the Minutemen Militia, patrol the border of the United States and Mexico to stop illegal immigration and may be driven, in part, by fear and status anxiety (Weeber and Rodeheaver 2004). Illegal immigration spurs fear that immigrants will monopolize limited employment opportunities and take advantage of welfare resources (Stein 2001).

> ## Consider This
> What type of social movement would be the easiest to organize, one that focuses on a changing a limited part of society or one that seeks broader social change?

The goal of **revolutionary social movements** is a radical reorganization of society. The American Revolution is an example of a revolutionary social movement. The Communist Party in the United States and around the world challenges capitalism and government policies that exploit workers. It advocates for environmental protection, living wages for workers, the rights of labor unions, and shared ownership of resources. U.S. militia organizations (like the Militia of Montana) are paramilitary groups that seek to end the federal government's power in areas like the economy, trade, and business, in favor of individual and business rights.

Check Your Understanding

- Describe and give examples of the different kinds of social movements.

- Which type of social movement seeks the most limited kind of change?

- Which type of social movement advocates for the most radical social change?

Social Movement Theory

Sociological theories help us understand how social movements form, how they act, and whether or not they are successful. Theories about social movements highlight the different aspects of social movement mobilization, from how they function to the symbolism they use. Social movement theories follow the main theoretical approaches in sociology: structural functional theory, conflict theory, and symbolic interactionism.

Structural Functional Theories

As discussed in earlier chapters, the functionalist perspective focuses on how all the pieces of society function together. In looking at social movements, functionalists emphasize how social movements are formed through dysfunction, or a need for social change, and mobilization to create social change (Smelser 1962). For example, a social movement may organize in response to widespread pollution in a community and the lack of government regulation of the polluting industries. The goal of cleaning up the environment ties the movement together, forming the basis for action.

Collective behavior theory is a classic functionalist theory used to understand social movements. According to this theory, social movements begin during times of crisis, when there is social disruption (Oliver 1993). For example, during the Vietnam War (1955–1975), young people protested the war and the draft lottery where young men were selected to go to war, whether willing or not. When people experience a crisis or drastic social change—such as a war and a draft—they are more likely to act collectively in protest. However, this theory tends to assume people behave rationally (Snow and Benford 1988) and have collective needs and ideas that they can act on. During the Vietnam War, for example, not all Americans who were against the war identified with young protesters, who were criticized for appearing to not support service members (Beamish, Molotch, and Flacks 1995; Lembcke 1998). Often people in the same social movements have contrasting needs and ideas, and those differences can be a source of conflict during mobilization (Porta and Diani 2008).

Mass society theory also falls under the functionalist umbrella and understands social movement collective action as a response to social isolation. Mass society theorists maintain that feelings of isolation

Pastor Thirkel Freeman wears a hoodie and carries bags of Skittles, two symbols used to counter the image of Treyvon Martin and other young Black men as dangerous, at a memorial for Martin in Washington, D.C., on March 23, 2012.

Keith Lane/Tribune News Service/Getty Images

and alienation lead people to join a social movement. Mass society theory could be used to explain the 2015 protests in Baltimore in response to the police killing of Freddie Gray. When Gray's death was ruled a homicide, the Black community protested for nearly a month. According to mass society theory, these protests would be a response to not only Gray's death but also the social isolation of the community. This theory has been largely discredited, however, as research shows individuals who have strong connections to others are more likely to join a social movement than those who do not (Gusfield 2009). In Baltimore, the protests centered on the strong feeling of community, not social isolation.

Conflict Theories

Conflict theorists focus on how social movements develop out of systematic inequality. According to conflict theorists, social movements arise when goods and services are distributed unevenly. Two of the most well-known conflict theories used in the arena of social movements are resource mobilization and relative deprivation.

Resource mobilization theory focuses on the resources needed to mobilize and sustain a social movement. The presence of resources—followers, money, political connections, and so on—predicts whether or not a movement will be successful. Resource mobilization theorists believe all social movements need resources to mobilize, and without these resources, mobilization is much more difficult, if not impossible (McCarthy and Zald 1977). However, focusing on resources does not help us understand how individuals and groups with little to no resources (poor people, marginalized people) form a successful social movement (Cress and Snow 1996). For example, undocumented migrant farm workers have relatively

little power to protest their working conditions. They do not have access to typical resources like money, politicians, the media, or food distribution companies. However, even without these resources, migrant workers ran a five-year strike against Delano grapes and, by withholding their labor, gained the media coverage needed to spark a consumer boycott. Despite their relative powerlessness, the farm workers were successful in improving their working conditions and pay.

According to **relative deprivation theory,** people join social movements when they feel dissatisfied with their current position in society (Gurney and Tierney 1982). When individuals see that others have rights they do not have, they feel deprived and are likely to join a movement advocating for those rights. This theory explains why, for instance, gays and lesbians started and joined the marriage equality movement—others had marriage rights that they, too, wanted. But relative deprivation theory does not explain the presence of conscience constituents who do not benefit directly benefit from a movement's goal.

Symbolic Interactionist Theories

As you know, symbolic interactionists focus on how people interactively construct meaning through shared symbols and language. The peace sign, for example, is a shared social movement symbol calling for an end to war. Symbolic interactionists theorize that collective behavior develops when established institutions no longer provide meaning that aligns with the views of a majority of its constituents (Benford and Hunt 1992). For example, if the state defines *marriage* as an institution only male-female couples can participate in but society is largely open and accepting of same-sex couples, a social movement will organize to redefine the meaning of *marriage* to include same-sex couples.

Symbolic interactionists look at how people create meaning, goals, and shared culture within their collective action. The powerful use of symbols during the collective actions carried out after Trayvon

In this exercise, you will apply the idea of framing to slogans associated with the gay rights movement over the past several decades.

Go online and find images from the gay rights movement (1970s to current). Look for images of signs, buttons, and T-shirts that activists use to advocate for equality. If you are not working on your computer in class, print at least three of these images and bring them to class.

Working with a group of other students, compare framing in early slogans like "Come out," "We're here, we're queer, get used to it," and "queer pride," with more recent slogans like "love is love," and "freedom to marry," and "love makes a family."

1. What master frames are being used?

2. What do these changing frames tell you about shifts in the strategy of the gay rights movement?

3. How did this framing shift lead to marriage equality in 2015?

Martin, a seventeen-year-old African American male, was killed in 2012 in Sanford, Florida, by neighborhood watchman George Zimmerman provides an example. Martin was walking home from a local convenience store, but Zimmerman was suspicious of what the teen was doing in the neighborhood and followed him. Zimmerman and Martin got into an altercation, and Martin was shot. Zimmerman claimed self-defense, but Martin was unarmed (Blow 2012). The killing started nationwide protests against racism and the perception that young Black men are dangerous.

When Zimmerman confronted him, Martin was wearing a hoodie and carrying Skittles candy and an Arizona iced tea. These items became symbols of Martin's innocence at the time of the shooting, and the innocence of all young Black men stereotyped as dangerous. To make this point at antiracism demonstrations, protesters held up Skittles and iced tea. Protesters wore hoodies to mock the idea that a hoodie makes a Black teenager look dangerous.

Consider This

What symbols, objects, and phrases can you think of that have helped mobilize people for social action? Why do you think they were so powerful?

Social Movement Framing

The framing approach is another way to understand social movements under the symbolic interactionist umbrella. Sociologists who use the framing approach focus on how social movements use images and language to frame their causes. Through **framing,** leaders influence how people think about an issue by highlighting certain facts and themes, while making others invisible (Snow et al. 1986). For example, when making their pitch to the city council, the Friends of Cats organization would frame the issue around how the city can save money with a TNR program. In their meeting with other organization members, however, they would use the frame of love for animals to make a case for TNR policy. Context matters for framing. The same frame that works in one context will not necessarily be successful in another.

In U.S. culture, there are frames that appeal nearly universally. These **master frames** include ideas like "freedom," "democracy," "love," and "choice" and can be used by movements with different goals. Think about both sides of the abortion rights debate. The "pro-life" movement chose that name to center the issue on a master frame everyone values: life. The "pro-choice" movement similarly framed their movement around the universally valued idea of choice. But on bumper stickers, the "pro-life" movement evokes the same master frame to declare "fetuses don't have a choice." This is an example of **frame competition,** when organizations use another group's frames to discredit or ridicule their position (Oliver and Johnston 2000).

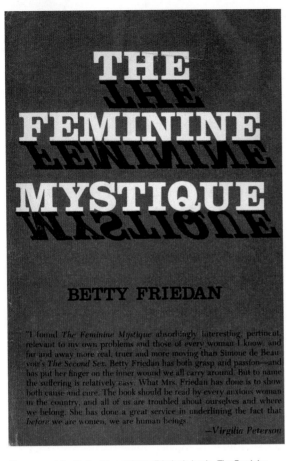

The cover of the first edition of Betty Friedan's book, *The Feminine Mystique* (1963), that helped spark the second wave of the women's movement.

When Betty Friedan's book *The Feminine Mystique* came out in 1963, it helped start this new women's movement in the United States. But her book spoke largely to middle-class, straight, White women and excluded low-income women, lesbian and bisexual women, and women of color. Concerned the movement would be perceived as "anti-male" and that lesbian women would threaten the image of feminists, Friedan described lesbian women within the movement as the "Lavender Menace." While the term was meant to be derogatory, lesbians in the movement made "Lavender Menace" T-shirts and wore them to a protest—which showed just how many lesbians were a part of the movement.

> **Consider This**
> Is it possible to mobilize around a shared identity and also be inclusive of differences?

Check Your Understanding

- How do functionalist theorists understand the origins of social movements?

- According to conflict theorists, why do social movements arise?

- What do symbolic interactionists tend to focus on when studying social movements?

- What is a master frame? Provide an example of a master frame.

- What does it mean to organize around a shared identity?

New Social Movement Theory

Before the 1950s, social movements tended to focus on economic concerns and workers' rights. New social movements (NSMs), however, tend to mobilize around issues of rights and collective social identities. For example, the civil rights movement organized around a shared racial identity and experience. The **women's movement** brought women together *as women* to fight for rights and equality. **New social movement theory** aims to explain this phenomenon.

Organizing around a shared identity can be empowering for movement members, especially when that identity has been marginalized. But, collective mobilization around a shared identity can also exclude individuals who do not fully fit that identity. For example, the women's movement of the 1960s and 1970s is often criticized for mobilizing around the collective identity of White, heterosexual, middle-class women, whose experiences of oppression are not the same as those of other women.

The Six Steps of Social Movement Success

Social movements tend to be successful when they can identify a goal they can rally others around, form a group, create an effective strategy, mobilize enough resources, organize effective actions, and build power. Those that can't do all of these will not reach their goals. Much also depends on the social

The first wave of the women's movement focused on attaining the right to vote for women. It began in 1848 and culminated with the ratification of the Nineteenth Amendment in 1920.

and historical context and the forces that muster for or against the movement. Social movements are more likely to develop in political climates where people have the freedom to organize and mobilize for their cause.

Social movements occur in every country all over the world. This section covers primarily U.S.-based social movements, with an emphasis on activism and organizing in the twentieth- and twenty-first-century civil rights and women's movements.

Identify an Issue

The first task of any social movement is to identify an issue that needs to be addressed. This could be a widespread change in culture or a specific change to policy or an institutional practice. The goal must be described as necessary to improve people's lives or make the world and/or community a better place. The context leading up to a social movement matters a great deal.

The Women's Movement

Identifying an issue to organize around also means making a case for why change should occur. The women's movement in the United States follows four distinct waves of collective action—1848 to 1920, the 1960s and 1970s, the 1990s, and from 2000 on. Each wave had its own goals. The first wave, the suffrage movement, focused on women gaining the right to vote. In arguing for this right, suffragists asserted that women were fundamentally different from men and would bring their unique qualities to government if they could participate. This argument of **difference feminism** used images of women as caring, nurturing mothers to argue that women would bring an end to war and poverty if they could vote and serve in office (Fox-Genovese 1994).

The antisuffrage movement also emphasized gender differences by arguing that women would be taking on men's roles in public, at the expense of taking care of the household. Antisuffrage postcards depicted women in pants, demonstrating on street

National Rally for Equal Rights

corners, while husbands suffered at home trying to take care of crying children. Despite opposition, the suffrage movement won women the right to vote throughout the United States with the ratification of the Nineteenth Amendment in 1920.

The second wave of the feminist movement started in the 1960s and peaked in the 1970s. After working in factories during World War II, women were expected to go back to being full-time wives and mothers once the war ended. During this time, women had few rights and were expected to become wives, mothers, and full-time homemakers. In 1963, Betty Friedan released her book *The Feminine Mystique,* in which she criticized the 1950s image of the modern, suburban housewife. The book recognizing the discontent housewives felt and became widely popular as a result, sparking the second wave of the feminist movement, which advocated for an end to gender discrimination in the workplace and reproductive rights for women. Some feminist leaders established the National Organization for Women (NOW) to lobby Congress for women's rights.

Form a Group

The next step in a successful social movement is to form an organization of both beneficiary and consciousness constituents who will work toward the movement's goals. Beneficiary constituents and consciousness constituents must believe the change is necessary.

The Civil Rights Movement

The civil rights movement consisted of individuals joining together to fight racial injustice. You have probably heard of the importance of Black churches during the civil rights movement, but did you know that students played an important role in the civil rights movement? From participating in the Student Nonviolent Coordinating Committee to planning large-scale actions like Freedom Summer in 1964, students were essential to the movement's success. During that summer of 1964, college students and other young people—Black and White—from all over the United States volunteered to join groups traveling to Mississippi to register Black voters. Because of various means of racial discrimination, only 7 percent of the state's eligible Black voters were registered. While many participants were beneficiary constituents, White students participated as consciousness constituents. Partly because some of these students were White, they were able to gain national media attention as they traveled through the South (McAdam 1990).

The Women's Movement

By title, it would seem the women's movement comprises entirely women. But movement membership has varied over the years. When you think of a feminist, what kind of person comes to mind? Do you think of a young woman burning her bra in the 1970s, demanding equal pay for equal work? A radical lesbian, refusing to shave her legs and screaming against the patriarchy? A member of a men's anti-rape group? A college woman marching in a Take Back the Night event on her campus, advocating for women's safety?

A **feminist** is someone who is committed to gender equality. A **feminist organization** is an organization working to end women's oppression.

As noted earlier, the women's movement has not always been inclusive of all women. The needs of poor women and women of color were largely excluded from the second wave of the movement as activists focused on issues such as professional

Who Counts as a Feminist?

In this activity, you will consider the impact of public figures' statements on mainstream views of feminism.

Celebrities, particularly women, are often asked if they consider themselves feminists. Some agree that they are, some say they are not, and others try to redefine the term. Using an Internet search, find recent examples of public figures (celebrities, politicians, etc.) who have identified as feminist and answer the following questions:

1. Do you think celebrities or politicians influence how individuals perceive the cause of feminism? Why or why not?

2. Based on the information you have read in this text, do you think feminism is still necessary? Why or why not?

---

opportunities and salary equity—and largely ignored issues related to classism and racism (hooks 1984). During the 1980s, feminists faced a backlash, with headlines like the *Time Magazine* cover asking "Is feminism dead?" (Faludi 1994).

By the 1990s, however, a new, third wave of feminism was well under way. Instead of assuming all women experienced oppression in the same ways as White, middle-class women, the third wave focused on inclusiveness and intersectionality. Third-wave feminists drew from a diverse group of women to advocate around various issues, including sexual violence, gay rights, and reproductive justice. One of the most visible groups in third-wave feminism were the Riotgrrrls. The Riotgrrrl movement developed out of the feminist hardcore punk music scene, and activists published and sold self-made 'zines (magazines) on feminist issues. Activists, musicians, and writers in the movement covered everything from body-positive messages to surviving sexual violence. 'Zines used images and commentary to empower young women to feel good about themselves and speak up against patriarchy (Rosenberg and Garofalo 1998).

Challenges to Forming a Group

Convincing beneficiary constituents and consciousness constituents to join a group is not without challenges, however. Beneficiary constituents must believe their situations will improve based on their participation. Consciousness constituents must be willing to see something as a problem even when it does not directly affect them. Social movements also face issues such as keeping participants engaged over long periods of time, especially when there are stretches without clear victories. Social movement organizations must keep beneficiary and consciousness constituents engaged by fostering a shared sense of purpose and achievable small goals.

Marginalization of Members

Social movements can limit participation by marginalizing some members within the organization. For example, despite playing important roles in civil rights efforts, women were marginalized in the civil rights movement (Barnett 1993). Women in organizations like the National Association for the Advancement of Colored People (NAACP), Student Non-Violent Coordinating Committee (SNCC), and the Southern Christian Leadership Conference (SCLC) found they were often assigned clerical work instead of on-the-ground organizing work. While male leaders placed themselves on the front lines of demonstrations and marches, women like Diane Nash and Ella Baker did much of the backstage work of organizing.

Cultural Differences

Organizing becomes more difficult when social movements are global and cross-cultural. The women's movement, for example, ran into a problem trying to alleviate the perceived oppression of women in other countries (Rupp 1997). The 1984 U.S. book *Sisterhood Is Global: The International Women's Movement Anthology* by Robin Morgan is an example of how some movements can have a culturally biased perspective. The phrase "sisterhood is global" implies all women experience oppression in the same way, and they are equal to one another

Joan Jett plays with singer Kathleen Hanna and drummer Tobi Vailfrom of Bikini Kill at Irving Plaza in New York on 14th July 1994. Jetts' collaboration with Bikini Kill helped bring the punk extension of the third wave, Riot Grrrl, into the mainstream media.

Ebet Roberts/Redferns/Getty Images

in oppression, as sisters. The book was criticized for glossing over the different ways women are oppressed and for not addressing how oppression and empowerment may mean different things in different contexts. For example, wearing a hijab might seem like oppression from a Western perspective, when in fact a woman may see her hijab as a personally empowering choice to honor her religion (Read and Bartkowski 2000).

The idea that "sisterhood is global" also ignores inequalities among women. Now global feminist movement organizations strive to understand that not all women face the same types and extent of oppression and that some women (poor women, women of color) are more vulnerable than others. These organizations must consider how oppression and empowerment look different across contexts as they strive to create groups that can work together effectively.

Create a Strategy

To be successful, social movements must identify a strategy for making social change. Doing this requires consulting with experts and with the affected community to find solutions to the problem. Often the best strategies for social change are the result of careful research into what the problems are and what the best solutions might be. While creating a strategy, social movements must also identify the powerholders they need to target. These powerholders are people, institutions, voters, or lawmakers who have the power to enact the change the movement members want to see happen.

The Civil Rights Movement

Strategic research and planning was a key part of the civil rights movement. For example, before

they began sit-ins at lunch counters in Nashville, Tennessee, activists collected data on how the lunch counters were run and how customers and employees responded to incidents of integration. Using this information, civil rights organizer James Lawson trained student activists to use nonviolent responses to the open aggression and hostility they expected to receive. They carefully rehearsed and prepared for their actions. In 1960, after their four-month campaign, Nashville became the first city to desegregate department store lunch counters (Morris 1981). This successful campaign to desegregate lunch counters through sit-ins became a model, and activists in many other the cities carried out similar actions.

Mobilize Resources

A successful social movement needs resources. Constituents are every social movement's most important resource. Other resources include money, access to media, and supplies. Organizations must assess what resources they have and organize to gain those they need.

The Women's Movement

Women are a key resource for the women's movement. To mobilize women to join, women's organizations during the second wave of the women's movement in the 1960s and 1970s held consciousness-raising circles where women could share their experiences of oppression in a safe space. This helped connect more women to the movement.

As noted earlier, third-wave feminists used 'zines and music as resources to distribute their message. The Internet is a vital resource for the fourth wave of the women's movement (post-2000). Today, feminists use blogging and social media (Facebook and Twitter) to organize protests and rallies, as well as raise awareness about issues of rape culture, consumerism, beauty standards, and sexuality. Hashtag campaigns like "#EverydaySexism" and "#RapeCultureIsWhen" spread across the globe, generating conversations about key feminist issues (Clark 2014).

Organize Actions

Social action is the lifeblood of social movements. Specific actions, or tactics, might include protesting, marching, boycotting, and so on. Goals of actions include raising awareness, building constituents, and/or directly asking for change. As symbolic interactionists argue, shared cultural symbols and language are powerful parts of social movement action and used by movement leaders to organize and inspire followers. It is also important to remember that actions, no matter how well planned, organized, or eloquently inspired, come with risks.

The Civil Rights Movement

Before going to Mississippi in 1964, the Freedom Summer activists were taught how to talk to people about voting and how to register voters. They planned summer-long Freedom Schools to educate Black Mississippians on voting, politics, Black history, and other topics. All their preparation could not always keep them safe, however. When they went to Mississippi, the activists were threatened and lived with families who faced hostility for hosting the volunteers. One of their buses was burned, and many endured beatings and jail time. Three activists were abducted and brutally killed in Neshoba County, Mississippi. The murders of James Earl Chaney, Andrew Goodman, and Michael Schwerner symbolized the connection between brutality and racism and brought national attention to Freedom Summer (McAdam 1990).

Not everyone in the civil rights movement agreed on which tactics were best for the movement. We frequently learn about peaceful civil rights protests and marches but do not learn that some participants in the movement broke the law (through civil disobedience) and used violence to fight for civil rights. The Black Panther Party, for example, rejected the nonviolence of Martin Luther King's followers, believing instead that Black people needed to defend themselves against state-sanctioned violence (Bloom and Martin 2013). They often went to protests and events openly armed, to symbolize the seriousness of their intent to defend their community.

Gaining Power and Success

Every social movement must gain power to be successful. If they successfully complete the steps above, movements will gain power and the subsequent ability to achieve their goals. Both the civil rights movement and the women's movement were able to reach many of their key goals. Movement success arrives when the problem is solved or the goal achieved.

Consider This
Under what conditions is violence (against property or people) ever justifiable in a social movement? If never, why not?

every state (including on many college campuses), and a strong lobbying presence in Washington, D.C.

Why Social Movements Fail

Social movements may fail to reach their goal for a variety of reasons. Failure may come from organizational issues (disagreements and infighting), a lack of resources, or an inability to mobilize supporters. Social movements may also be repressed. **Repression** takes place when people and/ or institutions with power use that power to control or destroy a movement. Countries that ban any form of public protest include Russia, the Ukraine, and Egypt. Making a social movement's activities— like distributing flyers—illegal is another example of repression. During the Arab Spring in 2011, the Egyptian government shut down the Internet to impede the ability of activists to coordinate their efforts and broadcast their protests to the world.

Social movements can also be co-opted. **Co-optation** can happen when the leadership of the movement begins to identify with the targets of social change and starts to work more for them than for the original movement goals. Social movements can also end up taking on the values and actions they are trying to change. For example, the environmental movement seeking corporate responsibility in growing and selling coffee found their language of "fair trade" co-opted by some coffee sellers to appeal to a high-end niche consumer, without much concern about whether or not the coffee was actually fairly traded. Social movement goals—like fair-trade coffee—may become watered down or changed to accommodate the corporation's needs.

The Civil Rights Movement

The successes of the civil rights movement included the following:

- Civil Rights Act of 1964, which forbids discrimination based on race, color, religion, sex, or national origin;

- Voting Rights Act of 1965, which made it illegal for states and local governments to block individuals from voting and created a system to monitor counties with low voter turnout among minorities; and

- Civil Rights Act of 1968, which prohibits discrimination in renting, selling, or financing housing based on race, color, religion, sex, or national origin.

Thanks to the civil rights movement, the United States largely dismantled Jim Crow legislation that enforced racial segregation and other forms of discrimination (such as in employment and housing) and prevented millions of Black Americans from voting.

The Women's Movement

The women's movement won victories like the Equal Pay Act of 1963 and the 1973 Supreme Court decision in *Roe v. Wade,* granting women legal access to abortion. The women's movement also became an influential part of mainstream political institutions. Started as an organization targeting politicians for social change, the National Organization for Women now has hundreds of thousands of members, chapters in

Check Your Understanding

- List the steps social movements must take to become successful.

- What kinds of strategies did the civil rights movement use in planning actions?

- What is a feminist?

- What is the most important resource for all social movements?

- What are some of the key achievements of the civil rights movement and the women's movement?

Success Can Bring Backlash: The Marriage Equality Movement

The marriage equality movement is one of the most successful movements in recent history. As Figure 14.1 indicates, public approval for same-sex marriage rose dramatically in a single decade, with 35 percent supporting it in 2006 compared to 55 percent in favor in 2016 (a year after the Supreme Court ruling legalizing it).

Successful Tactics of the Marriage Equality Movement

The movement used a variety of tactics to achieve marriage equality, including increasing numbers of gay and lesbian public figures coming out. By the late 1990s, there were openly gay and lesbian main characters on primetime television shows like *Ellen*, starring Ellen DeGeneres. Today, television shows with gay characters and gay married couples are commonplace. This changed public perception of gays and lesbians and of same-sex couples, paving the way for marriage equality (Fetner 2016).

Direct action and protests were other tactics that helped the movement become successful. The gay rights movement in the United States, of which the marriage equality movement was an offshoot, began with the Stonewall riots on June 28, 1969. During the 1950s and 1960s, it was illegal for bars to serve gays and lesbians, and they could lose their liquor licenses for letting gay people congregate. The riots broke out in the Stonewall Inn, a bar in New York City frequented by gay men and lesbians. Police raids on known gay and lesbian bars were

FIGURE 14.1

Percent of Opposition and Support for Same-Sex Marriage, 2006–2016

Source: Hannah Fingerhut, Support Steady for Same-sex Marriage and Acceptance of Homosexuality, Pew Research Center, May 12, 2016, http://www.pewresearch.org/fact-tank/2016/05/12/support-steady-for-same-sex-marriage-and-acceptance-of-homosexuality.

commonplace, but when police raided the Stonewall Inn, patrons decided they had enough and fought back (Carter 2005). The riots served to galvanize the gay and lesbian community to organize into activist groups and push for equal treatment. The following year, to commemorate the anniversary of the riots, gay and lesbian rights activists held a march in New York City running from the Village up Fifth Avenue to Central Park. This was the first Pride March, now an annual event held on the last Sunday of June in New York.

Beginning in 2000, the marriage equality movement turned to the court system to advocate for equality, strategically suing states for the right of same-sex couples to marry. In 2004, they enjoyed their first major victory. As the result of a discrimination case brought to the Massachusetts Supreme Court, gay and lesbian couples won the right to marry in Massachusetts.

After Massachusetts, individual states passed either marriage equality laws or "marriage protection" laws (defining marriage between a man and a woman). Each state presented a challenge for activists. For example, in early 2009, Maine's legislature passed a marriage equality law. People around the state then organized against marriage equality and were able to get the issue on the ballot. In November 2009, Mainers voted to keep marriage "between one man and one woman." In response, the marriage equality movement changed its organizing strategy. Activists surveyed people around the state, particularly in rural areas, to discuss the importance of marriage and family. When marriage equality was put on Maine's ballot again in 2012, activists went door-to-door explaining that gays and lesbians in Maine wanted the same things everyone else did—lifelong love and commitment. Commercials by organizations like Maine Equality depicted very few actual gay individuals, instead depicting families and loved ones who believed love and marriage should be accessible to everyone. In 2012, marriage equality won in Maine.

By 2015, all but fourteen states had marriage equality laws. Then, the Supreme Court decided that the Fourteenth Amendment requires states to issue marriage licenses to couples, regardless of sex. Marriage equality became the law of the land. Individuals and institutions used social media to show their support of the ruling. Facebook made it possible for people to superimpose a rainbow flag over their profile picture—some 26 million users showed their support (Dewey 2015).

With Success Comes Backlash

Sometimes successful movements face backlash. As support for a movement grows, fear and resentment of this change among those most ardently opposed to the movement also grow. This can lead to increased acts of discrimination. Same-sex couples seeking marriage licenses after the *Obergefell v. Hodges* (2015) decision have sometimes faced local officials who refuse to follow the law. Interracial couples trying to get married shortly after the *Loving v. Virginia* (1967) decision, which made interracial marriages legal, faced similar obstacles. Also, as noted in Chapter 8, in a majority of states in the United States, employers still have the legal right to fire employees simply for being gay, lesbian, or transgender. Most horrifyingly, LGBT people have also faced violent attacks. When gay and lesbian people gain equality through policies, social acceptance increases and hate crimes also decrease overall. But we also see an increase in the more extreme and violent hate crimes (Levy and Levy 2017).

On June 12, 2016, Omar Mateen opened fire at Pulse, a gay night club in Orlando, Florida. He killed forty-nine people and himself. It was the deadliest shooting the United States has seen up until that time and drew national mourning and outrage. As a result of the shooting, the gay and lesbian movement has joined forces with the gun control movement. It remains to be seen what these two movements can accomplish now that they are working together (Carlson and Pettinicchio 2016).

Check Your Understanding

- What were the tactics of the marriage equality movement?
- Why can successful movements face backlash?
- What are some examples of discrimination the LGBTQ community still faces?

How Can We Create Social Change?

The success of a social movement depends on everything from the number and commitment of activists, the kinds of actions planned, the resources available to the movement, to the symbolic power of the movement to grab media and public attention. Money certainly makes it easier to exert influence. But civil rights protesters who changed Jim Crow laws did not have large amounts of money behind them. Instead, they had large numbers of people and careful planning. Their power came from organizing effectively and successfully mobilizing people and influencing public opinion through their carefully planned actions.

Francis Fox Piven's (2006) concept of **interdependent power** helps explain how social change can come from the organized efforts of relatively poor and powerless individuals due to the ties that bind institutions and individuals together. Individuals are connected to one another through institutions that organize our lives. Teachers rely on having students in their classrooms, just as students rely on access to a teacher for their educations. These same institutions depend on the actions of their members—teaching, learning—to survive. Take, for example, the growing problem of student loan debt. Individuals who owe student loans can do little alone to change the system of financing higher education. They relied on the loan company to pay for school, and the loan company relies on them to pay that loan back. As individuals, they would face negative consequences for not paying their student loans back. But, as part of a large group (40 million Americans), they have power. If all 40 million people stopped paying their loans, they would be exercising interdependent power and affecting all the players. That kind of mass action would be difficult to organize, but the concept of interdependent power does explain some of the ways social change can happen from below.

Participatory Action Research

Sociological research skills can help foster social change and organize social movements effectively. **Participatory action research** (PAR) starts with the idea that people are the experts in their own lives and can participate in the research process. Instead of the typical model of a researcher coming into a community to study it, the people who live in that community participate in the research process and help produce the knowledge collectively (Greenwood and Levin 2006).

PAR is an especially useful technique in disadvantaged communities where members may not trust outsider researchers and are more likely to talk to one another. Take, for example, the Friends of Cats organization described in the beginning of this chapter. If Friends of Cats found the community was reluctant to support outside solutions for the feral cat problem, PAR could be a solution. Using PAR, sociology researchers might work with Friends of

The White House on June 26, 2015, following the U.S. Supreme Court ruling in favor of same-sex marriage.

AP Photo/Drew Angerer

Books and Documentaries about Social Movement

Books about Social Movements

Poor People's Movements: Why They Succeed, How They Fail by Frances Fox Piven

Social Movements 1768–2004 by Charles Tilly

Bringing the War Home: The Weather Underground, the Red Army Faction, and Revolutionary Violence in the Sixties and Seventies by Jeremy Varon

The Autobiography of Malcolm X by Malcolm X

The Next American Revolution: Sustainable Activism for the Twenty-First Century by Grace Lee Boggs

Democracy in the Making: How Activist Groups Form by Kathleen Blee

The World Split Open: How the Modern Women's Movement Changed America by Ruth Rosen

Social Movement Documentaries

Eyes on the Prize (PBS, 1987)

Berkeley in the Sixties (Kitchell Films, 1990)

Freedom on My Mind (Clarity Films, 1994)

This Is What Democracy Looks Like (Big Noise Films, 2000)

Brother Outsider: The Life of Bayard Rustin (PBS, 2003)

This Black Soil: A Story of Resistance and Rebirth (Bullfrog Films, 2004)

The Billionaire's Tea Party (Larrikin Films, 2011)

The Black Power Mixtape 1967–1975 (Story AB, 2011)

How to Survive a Plague (Independent Lens, 2012)

American Revolutionary: Grace Lee Boggs (PBS, 2013)

Disruption: Climate Change (PF Pictures, 2014)

She's Beautiful When She's Angry (Music Box Films, 2014)

Stay Woke: The Black Lives Matter Movement (BET, 2016)

Cats and community leaders to better understand the community members' views on the issue. They would design a research plan together. They might distribute a survey they created together. With the information they gathered, they would be able to construct an animal control policy likely to gain the support of the community. In PAR, the act of gathering information is community building and can lead to meaningful social action.

Empowerment, Responsibility, and Making Social Change

Being a part of a social movement can be very empowering. Social movements bring individuals together in a kind of **collective solidarity,** or sense of social bonding, that strengthens our ties to one another (Oliver 1993). When social movements bring victories—no matter how small—members are empowered to see they can take part in social change. For this reason, individuals who take part in social movements are more likely to take part in other protests and to be politically active.

Being a part of collective efforts for social change is also a responsibility. Many of the social movements you have read about in this chapter have struggled with issues of inclusion. Organizing around a shared identity can be a powerful experience but can leave others out. Feminist organizations committed to intersectionality work to make sure that all voices within the organization are heard, especially the voices and needs of those women who are most vulnerable.

Men in the feminist movement and White people in the Black Lives Matter movement have also raised questions of how to be a good ally. An **ally** is a conscience constituent who is committed to the cause (Porta and Diani 2008). While allies can be important parts of a movement, they need to make sure they do not speak for those they are fighting for or take advantage of their own privilege by being in the spotlight or taking credit for activism. Being a good ally means listening to the needs of beneficiaries and working together to plan a course of action that will bring about change.

How You Can Help Bring about Social Change

- Be aware of inequalities and oppression. Find out which groups are the most marginalized in our society and why. Learn about their marginalization from their perspective.

- Learn the history of social movements. There are fantastic books and documentaries about social movements. Find causes that matter to you and learn the history of that movement.

- Examine inequality and oppression from an intersectional perspective. Race, class, gender, sexuality, age, and ethnicity are all intertwined. Consider how your activism may include some while excluding others.

- Raise awareness. Share links and news on Facebook and Twitter. Follow social movements you care about online. Sign online petitions. Engage in discussions with friends and family. But do not stop at "slacktivism." Think about how you can become a more active activist.

- Engage in the political process. Learn who your representatives are and communicate with them through letter writing and social media. Follow political campaigns at the local, state and national levels. Vote.

- Go to a local political meeting. Attend city council or school board meetings in your community. Find out what issues matter and what decisions are being made.

- Work to not make assumptions about oppression and privilege. What might look like oppression to you may mean freedom to someone else. Listen to people's experiences and goals.

- Speak out about issues that matter to you. Sometimes speaking out means taking risks, and only you can decide what risks you are comfortable with.

- Work with others who share your concerns. Organized people have more power.

Consider This

What social or political issue are you concerned about? How would sociology and sociological theory help you to understand this issue? Brainstorm some ways you could become involved in addressing this issue.

Check Your Understanding

- What is interdependent power and how can it help individuals without much power alone effect change?

- What is participatory action research?

- What can you do to help bring about social change?

- Why should you work with others when seeking social change?

Conclusion

Studying social movements helps us understand what matters in our society and where we might be heading. Sociological tools can also help social movements work more effectively. For example, being able to conduct surveys and interviews with community members about their needs and goals is an essential skill for mobilizing and organizing people. Understanding how to gain power and effect change are invaluable assets for social movement leaders.

Knowledge of social movements can also come in handy in a variety of careers. Knowing how to mobilize people to action can help anyone who works with people—in any field. Professionals in fields from community organizing to nonprofit management to education to marketing use these skills. Think of how you can use them in your chosen career.

As we have seen in this chapter, social change can come from the top (from people with resources and influence) or from the bottom (from community action and exercising interdependent power). Social change can also come through education—informing people about activism, equality, and independence. While social movements usually begin outside of established institutions, participating in the political process (by voting, campaigning, etc.) can also bring about social change. Individuals, like you, can use all these avenues to help create social change and make an impact on society.

CHAPTER 14

Want a better grade? Get the tools you need to sharpen your study skills. Access practice quizzes, eFlashcards, video and multimedia at **edge.sagepub.com/korgen**

Review

14.1 What is a social movement?

A social movement is a collective, organized, sustained effort to make noninstitutional social change.

14.2 Why do people participate in social movements?

People participate in social movements when they feel passionately about an issue. They may participate as beneficiary constituents, who will directly benefit from the goals of the social movement (i.e., same-sex couples who would like marriage equality). Or, they may participate as contentious participants, who will not benefit directly but feel strongly about the cause.

14.3 What are the different types of social movements?

While some social movements push for massive social change, others press for limited changes to society. There are four different types of movements: alternative, redemptive, reformative, and revolutionary. Alternative social movements advocate for limited societal change. Redemptive social movements seek more radical change in individual behavior. Reformative social movements work for specific change across society. The goal of revolutionary social movements is a radical reorganization of society.

14.4 How would you use sociological theory to explain a social movement?

Sociologists use theories to understand different aspects of how social movements work. Structural functionalist theories focus on how people come together during a time of crisis to accomplish an agreed-upon goal. Conflict theorists look at how social movements develop from inequality. When a group of people feels deprived of something they believe they should have access to (rights, money, power, etc.), they will protest. Symbolic interactionists are interested in the shared language and symbolism—like the peace sign—that hold social movements together and help spread their message.

14.5 What are the steps a social movement must take to become successful?

Social movements that succeed follow the following steps:

1. Identify a social change goal

2. Form a group of likeminded people committed to the goal

3. Create a strategy (a plan of action to achieve the goal)

4. Mobilize resources

5. Organize actions

6. Build power

Movement success arrives when the problem is solved or the goal achieved.

14.6 What tactics do social movements use to achieve their goals, and what kind of backlash do they face?

Some organizations stay within the limits of the law, protesting with permits and cooperating with police and officials. Other organizations may decide to participate in civil disobedience—blocking roads or buildings—to make their point heard. Other more radical organizations might break into buildings, destroy property, and further disrupt people's lives. Each of these tactics has positive and negative aspects the movement must consider. Organizations often do research and work with communities to find the best tactics for social change. Effective tactics build support for a movement, but this growth in support can inspire fear and resentment of change among those most ardently opposed to the movement. This can lead to increased acts of discrimination.

14.7 How can we create social change?

Social change can come from the top or the bottom, but it requires getting involved. Examine inequality and discrimination from an intersectional perspective. Raise awareness about the things that matter to you and engage in the political process. Speak up when you disagree with what you see around you, but be sure to listen to people with other perspectives and consider their views.

Key Terms

- ally   314
- alternative social movements   299
- beneficiary constituents   297
- civil disobedience   296
- collective solidarity   314
- co-optation   310
- coalescence   298
- collective behavior theory   301
- community-based organizing   298
- conscience constituents   297
- difference feminism   305
- emergence   298
- feminist   306
- feminist organization   306
- frame competition   303
- framing   303

- interdependent power   313
- mass society theory   301
- master frames   303
- mobilizing   298
- new social movement theory   304
- organizing   298
- participatory action research   313
- protest   296
- redemptive social movements   300
- reformative social movements   300
- relative deprivation theory   302
- repression   310
- resource mobilization theory   302
- revolutionary social movements   300
- social movement   295
- women's movement   304

Glossary

Absolute poverty: when a household or an individual fails to have the income required to meet the basic human needs of subsistence, including food, shelter, and clothing.

Absolutist perspective: states that some behaviors, conditions, and beliefs are inherently, objectively deviant.

Agency: the ability to act and think independently of social constraints.

Agents of socialization: people, groups, institutions, and social contexts that contribute to our socialization.

Agnostic: maintain that nothing is known or can be known about God(s).

Alienation: theoretical concept to describe isolating, dehumanizing, and disenchanting effects of working within a capitalist system of production.

Ally: a conscience constituent who is committed to the cause.

Alternative social movements: advocate for limited societal change but do not ask individuals to change their personal beliefs. They often target a narrow group of people and focus on a single concern.

Anomie: a state in which a society's norms fail to regulate behavior.

Appearance: consists of everything from dress to age, sex, and race to ethnicity, to nonverbal forms of communication like body language and gestures.

Applied research: research designed to produce results that are immediately useful in relation to some real-world situation.

Assortative mating: marrying within your social class.

Atheists: do not believe in a God.

Attitude-behavior split: when we think one way and act another.

Attributes: answer categories.

Back stage: where one prepares for an interaction.

Basic research: research directed at gaining fundamental knowledge about some issue.

Beliefs: what we deem to be true.

Beneficiary constituents: people who stand to benefit directly from the social change being sought.

Birth rate: number of births per 1,000 people per year.

Bourgeoisie: the rich owners of the means of production.

Busing: transporting Black students to predominately White schools and, in some cases, White students to Black schools to push toward integration.

Capitalism: characterized by private properties, markets, and profits, with externalized costs.

Caste: rigid systems that confine individuals to a social group for their lifetimes, assigning them specific roles in a society with tight rules over the relationships among castes.

Causation: whether a change in one variable causes a change in another variable.

Charter schools: publicly funded schools, established under a charter, and governed by parents, educators, community groups, or private organizations. The charter details the school's mission, curriculum, or philosophy; students to be served; performance goals; evaluation plans; and commitments.

Chinese Exclusion Acts of 1882 and 1892: halted Chinese immigration.

Civil disobedience: purposely breaking social customs or laws to make a point about a cause.

Class based: in these systems, members of a given social class share common economic statuses and lifestyles and have social mobility.

Climate justice: highlights the fact that climate change relates to global inequality, in its creation and its impact.

Coalescence: or organizing, when people come together more formally toward a shared goal.

Coding: description labels are applied to section of text or images so they can be classified into categories or themes.

Cohabitating couples: couples living together without being married to each other.

Collective behavior theory: this theory holds that social movements begin during times of crisis, when there is social disruption. Holds that people behave rationally, which may not always be the case.

Collective solidarity: sense of social bonding that strengthens our ties to one another.

Colorblind ideology: way of viewing race that maintains that if we ignore race and racial issues, racism will not exist.

Communism: under Karl Marx's conceptualization of communism, all citizens would be equal and able to fulfill their species being.

Community-based organizing: individual activists become involved in a movement because of an issue directly affecting their community.

Companionate marriage: partnership based on romantic love.

Comparative-historical research: when researchers look at documents from the past.

Compensatory strategies: when individuals attempt to offset the deviance that is ascribed to them or make others more comfortable with their stigma.

Concerted cultivation: an approach to interaction and discipline through which the parents proactively engage with and guide their children.

Conflict theory/conflict perspective: tensions and conflicts arise when resources, status, and power are not distributed equitably; these conflicts then become the driving force for social change.

Conscience constituents: people who care about the cause but do not benefit directly from the changes.

Conspicuous consumption: buying luxury goods to publicly display one's power.

Constants: variables that stay the same for everyone in a study.

Constructivist analysis of the environment: focuses on the role of ideology and knowledge in understanding our environmental conditions.

Content analysis: when researchers use texts and systematically categorize elements of those texts based on a set of rules.

Contingent employment: allows employers to hire nonpermanent workers at will as demands change.

Control group: group that does not experience the treatment or manipulation in a study.

Co-optation: happens when the leadership of the movement begins to identify with the targets of social change and starts to work more for them than for the original movement goals.

Core commitments: The first core commitment of sociology is *to use the sociological eye* to observe social patterns. The second requires noticing patterns of injustice and *taking action* to challenge those patterns.

Counterculture: cases where one group in a society espouses rules, values, or beliefs that conflict with the mainstream culture.

Coverture: the legal doctrine in which wives' standing was subsumed into their husbands'.

Cross-sectional: studies carried out at one particular point in time and designed to explore and explain what is going on at that point in time.

Cults: unorthodox sects; violence are not necessary components. Cults are also called newly formed religious movements.

Cultural capital: type of capital related to education, style, appearance, and dress that promotes social mobility.

Cultural diffusion: how cultural attributes can spread throughout the world.

Cultural relativism: the idea that cultures cannot be ranked as better or worse than others.

Cultural theory of risks: maintains that our reaction to risks relate not just to material threats but also to our cultures. They categorize cultural values into two dimensions—from individualist to communitarian (the group) and from egalitarian to hierarchical (the grid).

Cultural universals: cultural practices that exist in most or all societies, such as social structures, tool making, art, song, dance, religious beliefs, rituals, families, a division of labor, and politics.

Culture: the characteristics of a group or society that make it distinct from other groups and society or the way of life of a particular group of people.

Culture of poverty: describe the beliefs, attitudes, and values that characterize those living in poverty; the poor are blamed for their poverty.

Data: pieces of information, including facts, statistics, quotes, images, or any other kind of information.

Data analysis: the process of reducing the mass of raw data researchers have collected to a set of findings that provide the basis for making conclusions.

Death rate: number of deaths per 1,000 people per year.

Deductive research: researchers begin with a general idea or prediction and then gather data to test this idea.

Deep poverty: those who subsist on incomes of less than half the poverty level.

Define the situation: making meaning of what is going on by using cues and clues from the individuals and objects around us.

Demographic transition: when societies begin to have lower birth and death rates after industrialization.

Descriptive statistics: measures that are used to characterize the data.

Deserving poor: those who warrant our help because they are poor through no fault of their own; they are hardworking.

Difference feminism: holds that men and woman are different but no value judgment can be placed on these differences.

Discrimination: unfair treatment of groups of people.

Dissonance: occurs when something is disordered and produces a negative feeling that we want to relieve in some way.

Domestic violence: violence between married or cohabiting partners.

Dominant ideology: widely held set of beliefs embedded in the culture of a society and acting to inhibit the development of radical political dissent.

Downward mobility: when one loses a class position.

Durable: slow to change.

Dysfunctions: unintended consequences of behavioral patterns.

Ecolabel: indicates the superior environmental standards of a particular product.

Ecological footprint: the productive area required to provide the resources humanity is using and to absorb its waste.

Ecological modernization theory: The idea that material conditions—the challenges of sustainability—have led us to reshape our social institutions and to adapt to environmental changes.

Economic inequality: unequal distribution of economic resources.

Education: process through which a society transmits its culture and history and teaches social, intellectual, and specific work skills that result in productive works and citizens.

Emergence: during this stage of mobilizing a social movement, people who share the same grievance get together and find others who support their goals.

Empirical: empirical statements are those that could hypothetically be proven true or false.

Environmental justice: term used to document the social inequality in the environmental realm.

Environmental justice movement: has the goal of ending the practice of using poor and racial and ethnic minority areas as dumping grounds for environmental hazards.

Environmental racism: when environmental hazards are disproportionally borne by racial and ethnic minority groups.

Environmental sociology: focuses on the interaction between the social and natural systems.

Estates: in an estate system, there is very limited social mobility, but those with the lowest standing have more freedom than slaves. In this system, laws distribute power and rights based on social standing.

Ethnic group: consists of those who share the same cultural heritage, including languages, nation or origin, and religion.

Ethnocentrism: the belief that one's own culture is superior to others.

Ethnography: research that systematically studies how groups of people live and make meaning by understanding the group from its own point of view.

Ethnomethodology: the study of the "ethno" (meaning ordinary or everyday) methods people use to make sense of their social interactions.

Experiment: used to find out how people are likely to act in particular and potentially controlled situations.

Explanatory statistics: statistics used to measure the relationship between different elements within the data.

Externalities: externalities are all the side effects—things that people fail to incorporate in their decision making—of economic activities.

False consciousness: Marx's theory that the proletariat did not understand how they were being mistreated and misled by the owners of the means of production.

Family: a group of people who take responsibility for meeting each other's needs.

Family violence: when someone in a family hurts or controls someone else. It can take on many forms, such as sexual abuse, financial abuse, emotional mistreatment, and physical violence.

Family wage: earnings that are enough to support an entire family.

Feminist: someone who is committed to gender equality.

Feminist organization: organization working to end women's oppression.

Feral children: raised in isolation and do not have the opportunity to interact with others and become socialized.

Field experiment: experiments conducted in the real world, not in a laboratory setting.

Folk devils: those blamed for the collapse of public morality and therefore treated as threats to the social order.

Folkways: rules of behavior for common and routine interactions.

Frame competition: when organizations use another group's frames to discredit or ridicule their position.

Framing: how leaders influence how people think about an issue by highlighting certain facts and themes while making others invisible.

Front: the "expressive equipment" the individual uses to define the situation and convince others of the sincerity of his or her performance.

Front stage: where an interaction actually takes place.

Fundamentalists: those who resist societal changes and hold on to idealized, conservative, traditional religious practices.

Gender: a social concept associated with being male or female that is taught to us and continually created by us through interactions with others.

Gender as social structure: emphasizes that gender incorporates socialization, social interactions, and organizational structures and that these are all dimensions of every society's gender structure.

Gender roles: expectations and understandings about gender.

Gender scripts: expectations for behavior appropriate for our assigned genders.

Gender segregation: extent to which women and men are separated into different jobs.

Gender socialization: the process by which we learn to be a man or woman in our particular place and time.

Gender wage gap: the gap between the wages women and men earn.

General strain theory: contends that three types of strain lead to deviance and crime: (1) failure to achieve positively valued goals, (2) removal of positively valued stimuli, and (3) presentation of negatively valued stimuli.

Generalizability: whether it is possible to assume that the patterns and relationships observed among the sample in the research study would also hold true for the broader population.

Generalizations: statements used to describe groups of people or things in general terms, with the understanding that there can always be exceptions.

Generalized other: our perceptions of the attitudes of a whole community.

Gentlemen's Agreement of 1907: halted Japanese immigration.

Glass ceiling: the unofficial barrier that women and minorities face when trying to advance to the upper levels of an organization.

Glass escalator: the unfair advantage that men who work in a female-dominated occupations can receive over women in the same job.

Green consumption: allows consumers to "vote with their pockets" and to engage in social change through the marketplace.

Greenwashing: a green PR campaign that promotes an environmentally friendly, positive image of an organization, while its environmental practices are not line with the image.

Hayes-Tilden Compromise of 1877: agreement between the presidential candidates of 1877 where Hayes, the Northern candidate, won the Electoral College, but Tilden, the Southern candidate, won more of the popular vote. The compromise, where Hayes would become president, was reached provided that federal troops were withdrawn from the former confederacy and Whites were once again able to dominate political power in the South. After this, Jim Crow laws began to be established in the South.

Hidden curriculum: Implicit messages learned in school.

High culture: the culture of elites.

Homogamy: marrying within your social class.

Hooking up: generally means getting together at the end of an evening for the purposes of an intimate, no-strings-attached encounter.

Human capital: knowledge, skills, habits, and attributes necessary to succeed in work and in life.

Hypotheses: predictions about the expected findings of research, typically about the relationships between specific phenomena under study in the research project.

Identity: the characteristics by which we are known.

Ideology: set of beliefs.

Immigration Act of 1924: established 2 percent immigration quotas per nation, based on the 1890 U.S. Census (when relatively few Southern and Eastern Europeans were in the United States); this was done because Southern and Eastern Europeans were considered "less than White" at the time.

Immigration Act of 1965: abolished national quotas, replacing them with quotas for the Eastern and Western Hemispheres, and aimed to increase immigration and alter the racial makeup of the United States during the civil rights movement and worldwide pressure to address racial discrimination in the United States.

Impression management: trying to control others' evaluations of ourselves.

Income: earnings coming from employment, government programs, investments, or inheritances.

Inductive research: research where the data are gathered first to then be used to generate new ideas and understandings.

Informed consent: requires that the participants be told the purpose of the research, what they will be asked to do, and any risks of harm prior to participating. They must be given the chance to withdraw their participation at any time.

Institutional discrimination: happens as a result of how institutions operate.

Institutional review board: reviews experiments and was established to protect human subjects.

Institutionalized: encoded in laws, policies, and widely accepted practices.

Intensive mothering: exhausting child-centered style of parenting that requires women to copiously devote emotions, money, and time to raising children.

Interdependent power: the ties that bind institutions and individuals together and help to explain how social change can come from poor or powerless individuals.

Intergenerational mobility: moving from the social class in which one was born.

Internal colonialism: results from one ethnic or racial group (White Americans) subordinating and exploiting the resources of other racial and ethnic groups.

Interrater reliability: an assessment of the degree to which different people who are coding or rating the same data do so in the same ways.

Intersex: not clearly biologically male or female.

Interviews: research design where the researcher talks to the participant (in person, over the phone, through video chat), using an interview guide (list of questions or topics to cover).

Intimate partner violence: violence between partners who are or were involved in a romantic or sexual relationship.

Intimate terrorism: physical violence and other tactics that are used for overall control of an intimate partner.

Inverted quarantine: quarantining ourselves from the unsafe environment, rather than quarantining the bad thing.

Islamophobia: the fear/dislike of all or most Muslims.

Labeling: how certain individuals or groups come to be regarded as deviant; who is defined or labeled as deviant is the result of a social process in which others react as though the person is deviant.

Language: series of symbols used to communicate meaning among people.

Latent functions: unintended consequences of an institution.

Learning theories: assert that deviant and criminal behaviors are developed no differently than other social behaviors.

Legalistic approach: deviance defined as violation of the law.

Life course: various stages of one's life, from birth to death.

Life expectancy: the average number of years an individual is expected to live.

Literature review: finding out what is already known about a topic by reading prior scholarly literature.

Locations: places where interactions occur, namely, front stage and backstage.

Longitudinal: studies that are carried out over a longer period of time, with the research collecting more data from the same respondents or different ones at multiple points in time.

Lower class: the poor, with household incomes of less than $17,000 a year.

Lumpenproletariat: the perpetually unemployed.

Macro level of analysis (macro): focuses on the overall social structure of society and large-scale societal forces.

Manifest functions: obvious and stated reasons that a social institution exists.

Manner: the attitude conveyed by an individual in his or her particular social role.

Margin of error: a measure of the extent to which the results of the survey or poll are likely to differ from the real views of the population.

Mass society theory: understands social movement collective action as a response to social isolation.

Master frames: frames that have near-universal appeal.

Master status: the primary status by which others interact with a person.

Material culture: consists of artifacts ranging from tools to products designed for leisure. Reflects the values and beliefs of the people who live in a culture.

Means of production: the technology and materials needed to product products.

Mechanical solidarity: solidarity derived from the similarity of its members.

Medicalization of deviance: the transition from viewing behaviors, conditions, and beliefs as attributed to the deviant's evil character, or "badness," due to a pathology of the mind, or "madness."

Meritocracy: a society in which those with the most talent rise to the top and are appropriately rewarded for their contributions.

Microaggressions: everyday slights aimed, intentionally or unintentionally, at racial and ethnic minority groups.

Micro level of analysis (micro): focuses on either an individual or small groups.

Mobilizing: beginning a social movement.

Modernization: occurs as countries undergo the process of industrialization and decisions begin to be based more on reason and logic than tradition.

Moral entrepreneurs: individuals or groups who actively seek to change norms to align with their own moral worldview, often while taking part in social movements.

Moral panic: an exaggerated, widespread fear regarding the collapse of public morality.

Mores: widely held beliefs about what is considered moral and just behavior in society.

Multiculturalism: ideal of multiculturalism is that people respect differing cultures in a society and honor their unique contributions to a larger, "umbrella" culture that incorporates multiple subcultures.

Nature: biology, how we are born.

New social movement theory: explains why New social movements tend to mobilize around issues of rights and collective social identities.

Nonmaterial culture: concepts such as norms, values, beliefs, symbols, and language.

Norm of reciprocity: expectation that we give and take with others in relatively equal ways.

Normative: commonly accepted as the appropriate.

Normative approach: deviance defined as evoking disapproval from others.

Norms: expectations about the appropriate thoughts, feelings, and behaviors of people in a variety of situations.

Nuclear family: parents and their children.

Nurture: our cultural and social learning.

Observation: studying a phenomenon as a spectator.

Operationalize: turning an abstract concept into a concrete measure.

Organic solidarity: solidarity where societies operate like a living organism, with various parts, each specializing in only certain tasks but dependent on the others for survival.

Organizing: or coalescence, when people come together more formally toward a shared goal.

Overshoot: using resources at a pace more than the Earth's regenerative capacity.

Overworked: devoting more time to paid work, leaving less time for leisure and home life.

Paradigm shift theory: the shift in views toward the environment from the human exemptionalist paradigm that reflects an anthropocentric relationship to the new environmental paradigm, which views humans as only part of the complex ecosystem.

Participant-observation: observing action and interaction while participating as part of the social context being studied.

Participatory action research: starts with the idea people are the experts in their own lives and can participate in the research process. The people who live in a community participate in the research process and help produce the knowledge collectively.

Peer pressure: pressure to conform to the norms of one's peers.

Peers: others in one's age group.

Popular culture: culture that exists among common people in a society.

Power elite: members of the corporate community that dominate politics.

Prejudice: irrational feelings toward members of a particular group.

Presentation of self skills: efforts to shape the physical, verbal, visual, and gestural messages that we give to others to achieve impression management.

Primary deviance: rule breaking that individuals engage in without a deviant label.

Primary groups: small collections of people of which a person is a member, usually for life, and in which deep emotional ties develop.

Primary socialization: socialization that occurs in childhood, the most intense time for socialization.

Private sphere: the nonexposed sphere, an example being how wives stay at home to specialize in domesticity, staying in the private sphere.

Profane: a sphere of everyday life, not sacred.

Proletariat: the workers, those who do not own the means of production.

Props: material objects.

Protest: an individual or group act of challenging, resisting, or making demands toward social change.

Public sphere: the exposed sphere, an example being how men left the home to work and be the family breadwinner, leaving the private sphere of the home for the public sphere.

Qualitative methods: methods that rely primarily on information that is not numerical, such as words or images.

Quantitative methods: methods that rely on numerical information.

Race: a group of people perceived to be distinct on the basis of physical appearance.

Racism: belief in the superiority of one or more racial groups that creates and maintains a racial hierarchy.

Racism evasiveness: ignoring issues of racism.

Random: a sample where everyone who meets the criteria for participation in a study has an equal chance of being selected.

Redemptive social movements: seek radical change in individual behavior.

Reference group theory: where people evaluate and define themselves compared to others, which in turn affects their self-definition and self-esteem.

Reformative social movements: work for specific change across society.

Relative deprivation theory: holds that people join social movements when they feel dissatisfied with their current position in society.

Relative poverty: poverty of a household relative to others, such as being the poorest house on the block.

Relativist perspective: behaviors, conditions, and beliefs are deviant only to the extent that cultures regard them as deviant.

Reliability: the extent to which research results are consistent.

Religion: a social institution that involves the beliefs and practices of what has been socially constructed as sacred in a given society.

Religiosity: religiousness, measured through looking at a range of religious beliefs, activities, and practices in which people participate.

Religious pluralism: arises when different religious belief systems coexist within a society.

Representative: the people in the sample have characteristics typical of people in the broader population.

Repression: takes place when people and/or institutions with power use that power to control or destroy a movement.

Reproduction: people creating and raising members of the next generation.

Research: systematic process of data collection for the purpose of producing knowledge.

Research questions: what it is that the researcher plans to study.

Resocialization: learning to adapt to new social norms and values.

Resource mobilization theory: looks to the resources needed to mobilize and sustain a social movement. The presence of resources, such as followers and money, predicts whether or not a movement will be successful.

Revolutionary social movements: aims to achieve a radical reorganization of society.

Risk perception: the tendency to evaluate the danger of a situation in not purely rational terms but through the lens of individual biases and cultures.

Ritual: ceremonial behaviors.

Role conflict: when one's different social roles conflict with each other.

Role engulfment: occurs when the deviant role takes over people's other social roles due to others relating to them in response to their spoiled identity.

Role strain: competing demands within a particular social role and status.

Roles: the expectations about how people of a given status should think, feel, and behave.

Sacred: that which inspires reverence and devotion.

Sacrifice zones: the areas in developing countries where companies have moved the dirty parts of their business to appear to make progress in developed countries.

Sampling: the process of selecting respondents for inclusion in the research project.

Sanctions: punishments or penalties.

Sandwich generation: those with double caretaking duties where they are raising children and caring for aging parents at the same time.

Sapir-Whorf hypothesis: also known as linguistic relativism, notes that language influences our understanding of reality above and beyond the meaning of its symbols.

School choice: can include the ability to attend the public school of the family's choosing, attend a charter school, or use a voucher to subsidize attendance at a private school.

Scientific method: systematic process of steps that takes researchers from the development of a research question through the collection and analysis of data.

Second shift: the phenomenon wherein women return from their jobs to then begin their "second shift" where they do the housework and childcare.

Secondary deviance: rule-breaking behavior that occurs as a result of a deviant label.

Secondary socialization: teaching us how to behave appropriately in small groups and structured situations.

Sects: subgroups of larger religions that have some of their own distinct beliefs and practices.

Secular: nonreligious.

Secular humanists: believe that humans have the capability of being just without religion or a divine God.

Secularization: a society's movement away from identification with religious values and institutions.

Secularization theory: suggests that modernization encourages the demystifying of the world and undermines the influence of religion.

Self: sense of self, the knowledge that she or he is unique, separate from every other human.

Self-consciousness: an individual's awareness of how others see her or him.

Self-control theory: claims that stable, lifelong traits such as impulsivity, risk seeking, preference for simple and physical tasks, and self-centeredness predispose some individuals toward engaging in "acts of force or fraud undertaken in pursuit of self-interest."

Self-identity: our own understanding of who we are that is shaped by our interactions with others.

Setting: location of the "performance" or social interaction.

Sex: biological construct that is defined by external genitalia, chromosomes, and internal reproductive organs.

Sexual assault: nonconsensual sexual contact, including physical force, threats of physical force, or incapacitation that generally meets legal definitions of rape (penetration) and sexual battery (sexual touching).

Sexuality: our emotional and physical attraction to a particular sex.

Situational couple violence: violence that results when arguments escalate.

Slavery: where individuals own other individuals as property and have the legal right to dispense with that property as they wish.

Social actors: individuals involved in interactions.

Social capital: network of relationships that allows one to advance in society.

Social change: large-scale, macroscopic, structural shifts in society.

Social class: distinctions among groups of people in terms of income, education, and occupation or access to means of success.

Social class reproduction: how members of the upper class ensure that their children maintain their status.

Social cohesion: willingness of members of a society to work together to survive and prosper.

Social constructionism: holds that every society creates norms, values, objects, and symbols that it finds meaningful and useful.

Social control: the enforcement of conformity to the norms through either the threat or experience of formal or informal sanctions.

Social disorganization: argues that the reason some neighborhoods have more crime than others is that their structural conditions make it difficult for the community members to achieve collective efficacy.

Social exchange theory: presumes that individual family members, as rational actors, make decisions by weighing the benefits and costs of various actions and then pick the action/arrangement with the biggest reward or least cost.

Social harmony: occurs when a society with organic solidarity is "healthy," where the parts of the society are working well together.

Social identities: unique set of statuses, roles, and traits that each of us has.

Social institutions: sets of statuses and roles that focus on one central aspect of society.

Social intelligence: our ability to understand social relationships and get along with others.

Social interactions: the way individuals behave and interact with other people.

Social movement: forms when people who want social change create an organization that is collective, organized, and sustained and challenges authorities, powerholders, or cultural beliefs and practices in noninstitutional ways.

Social order: how the components of a society work together to maintain the society.

Social reproduction: the continuation of society's culture across generation.

Social scripts: the interactional rules that people use to guide an interaction.

Social solidarity: moral order of society.

Social stratification: the way valuable goods and desired intangibles are distributed in society.

Socialization: learning through social interaction how to follow the social norms and expectations of your society.

Socially constructed: meaning created through interactions among people.

Socioeconomic status: status determined by class, status/prestige, and power.

Sociological eye: enables you to see what others may not notice. It allows you to peer beneath the surface of a situation and discern social patterns.

Sociological imagination: the ability to connect what is happening in your own life and in the lives of other individuals to social patterns in the larger society.

Sociology: the scientific study of society, including how individuals both *shape* and *are shaped* by society.

Species being: the unique potential to imagine and then create what is imagined.

Spirituality: the search for the sacred, which involves finding meaning or purpose in your life and trusting in some higher power.

Stalled revolution: period during the 1960s and 1970s when divorce rates rose as women began to work at home and men had differing expectations about household responsibilities and earning income.

Statistical approach: treats anything that is statistically unusual, or anything that has a low probability or likelihood, as deviant.

Status: position or rank in a social hierarchy, based on prestige.

Stereotypes: predetermined ideas about particular groups of people that are passed on through hearsay or small samples and held regardless of evidence.

Stigma: a mark of disgrace and interactions that communicate that one is disgraced, dishonorable, or otherwise deviant.

Structural functionalism: view of modern societies as consisting of interdependent parts of working together for the good of the whole.

Structural mobility: occurs when changes in the economy create or destroy jobs for workers.

Structured inequalities: advantages and disadvantages built into social institutions.

Subcultural identity theory: suggests that individuals seek a collective identity that helps provide them with a strong moral code.

Subculture: cultural groups that exist within another, larger culture.

Surveys: a set of prewritten questions that respondents are asked to answer.

Sustainability: a social-economic system that can function within the Earth's ecological constraint.

Sustainable development: the development that meets the needs of the present without compromising the ability of future generations to meet their own needs.

Symbol: anything that has the same meaning for two or more people.

Symbolic interactionism: viewing society as a social construction, continually constructed and reconstructed by individuals through their use of shared symbols.

Taking the role of the other: imitating those around them.

Teams: groups of people involved in an interaction.

Techniques of neutralization: strategies that deviants use to maintain a positive self-concept.

The "I": the unsocialized response to the attitudes of others.

The "me": the side of our self that follows the norms and expectations of society and works to control our behavior accordingly.

Theoretical perspective: groups of theories that share certain common ways of "seeing" how society works.

Theory: a set of ideas used to explain how or why certain social patterns occur.

Three-Fifths Compromise: treated slaves as three-fifths of a person for the purposes of representation in the House of Representatives and taxation.

Total institution: an institution that is closed to external influences in which a group of people live together, following a strictly structured routine.

Tracking: involves placing students in classes based on "ability," which is usually measured by classroom behavior, academic performance, and academic aspiration.

Transgender: people who see themselves as a gender other than the one assigned to them at birth.

Treadmill of production: on the capitalist treadmill, firms have to use and degrade natural resources to sustain their profits. Because of the constant pressure to expand profits, they are forced to compete with others by running faster and faster, producing more and more, and drawing ever more resources. If they don't, they will go bankrupt and "fall off the treadmill."

True consciousness: when the proletariat are no longer in false consciousness and are aware of how they are being mistreated and misled.

Undeserving poor: those who are lazy and fail to try to lift themselves up by their own bootstraps; people whose poverty we believe is the result of their own making.

Unit of analysis: what is being examined.

Upper class: highest social class with the most resources.

Upward mobility: when one climbs up the economic ladder.

Validity: whether the research results accurately reflect the phenomena being studied.

Value coercion: the haves use their power over the major institutions to force their values onto the have-nots as part of their effort to maintain their higher-status positions in society.

Values: what a society holds to be desirable, good, and important.

Variables: factors that are likely to change or vary within the context of the study.

Veil of ignorance: a theory of justice that would require us to create rules for society without knowing our own social position.

Veil of opulence: being unable to understand the struggles faced by those who do not have the privileges of being in a higher social class and assuming others of lower social classes surely have these same resources.

Virtual environmentalism: seeks to create social conditions that lead people to help preserve the environment without thinking much about it.

Vouchers: certificates of government funding that make each pupil's state funds portable, allowing parents to choose to use their child's fund at a public or private school of their choice.

Wealth: assets one owns minus debts.

Wilderness: the highest ideal of nature and is a product of America's frontier mentality.

Women's movement: brought women together as women to fight for rights and equality.

Working class: those who work at manual, low-skilled jobs.

References

Chapter 1

American Sociological Association. 2014. *21st century careers with an undergraduate degree in sociology.* Washington, DC: American Sociological Association.

Berman, Jillian. 2015. Class of 2015 has the most student debt in U.S. history. *MarketWatch,* May 9.

Collins, Randall. 1998. The sociological eye and its blinders. *Contemporary Sociology 27* (1): 2–7.

Fisher, Marc, John Woodrow Cox, and Peter Hermann. 2016. Pizzagate: From rumor, to hashtag, to gunfire in D.C. *Washington Post*, December 6. https://www.washingtonpost.com/local/pizzagate-from-rumor-to-hashtag-to-gunfire-in-dc/2016/12/06/4c7def50-bbd4-11e6-94ac-3d324840106c_story.html?utm_term=.3002952c77d1 (accessed May 16, 2017)

Gamble, Teri, and Michael Gamble. 2015. *The gender communication connection.* New York: Routledge.

Mills, Wright C. 1959. *The sociological imagination.* Oxford, England: Oxford University Press.

Morris, Aldion. 2015. *The scholar denied: W. E. B. Du Bois and the birth of modern sociology.* Oakland: University of California Press.

Shane, Scott. 2017. From headline to photograph, a fake news masterpiece. *New York Times,* January 18. https://www.nytimes.com/2017/01/18/us/fake-news-hillary-clinton-cameron-harris.html?hp&action=click&pgtype=Homepage&clickSource=story-heading&module=b-lede-package-region&region=top-news&WT.nav=top-news&_r=0 (accessed May 16, 2017)

Small, Albion W. 1896. Scholarship and social agitation. *The American Journal of Sociology 1* (March): 564–82.

Sparshot, Jeffrey. 2015. Congratulations, class of 2015. You're the most indebted ever (for now). *Wall Street Journal,* May 8. http://blogs.wsj.com/economics/2015/05/08/congratulations-class-of-2015-youre-the-most-indebted-ever-for-now

Chapter 2

Best, Joel. 2012. *Social problems.* 2nd ed. New York: W. W. Norton.

Cahill, Spencer E. 1999. Emotional capital and professional socialization: The case of mortuary social students (and me). *Social Psychology Quarterly 62* (2): 101–16.

CBS News. 2014. S.C. mom's arrest over daughter alone in park sparks debate. *CBS News,* July 28. http://www.cbsnews.com/news/south-carolina-moms-arrest-over-daughter-alone-in-park-sparks-debate/ (accessed July 11, 2017)

Friedersdorf, Conor. 2014. Working mon arrested for letting her 9-year-old play alone at park. *The Atlantic,* July 15. https://www.theatlantic.com/national/archive/2014/07/arrested-for-letting-a-9-year-old-play-at-the-park-alone/374436/ (accessed May 28, 2017)

Goffman, Erving. 1959. *The presentation in everyday life.* New York: Anchor.

Mastro, Dana, Maria Knight Lapinski, Maria A. Kopacz, and Elizabeth Behm-Morawitz. 2009. The influence of exposure to depictions of race and crime in TV news on viewers' social judgments. *Journal of Broadcasting & Electronic Media 53* (4): 615–35.

Meitiv, Danielle. 2015. When letting your kids out of your sight becomes a crime. *The Washington Post*, February 13. https://www.washingtonpost.com/opinions/raising-children-on-fear/2015/02/13/9d9db67e-b2e7-11e4-827f-93f454140e2b_story.html (accessed December 27, 2015)

Reese, Diana. 2014. South Carolina mom who left daughter at park sues station. *The Washington Post,* August 14. https://www.washingtonpost.com/blogs/she-the-people/wp/2014/08/14/south-carolina-mom-who-left-daughter-at-park-sues-tv-station/?utm_term=.3d4b2c482243 (accessed July 11, 2017)

St. George, Donna. 2015a. "Free range" parents cleared in second neglect case after kids walked alone. *Washington Post*, June 22. https://www.washingtonpost.com/local/education/free-range-parents-cleared-in-second-neglect-case-after-children-walked-alone/2015/06/22/82283c24-188c-11e5-bd7f-4611a60dd8e5_story.html (accessed December 27, 2015)

St. George, Donna. 2015b. Parents investigated for neglect after letting kids walk home alone. *The Washington Post,* January 14. https://www.washingtonpost.com/local/education/maryland-couple-want-free-range-kids-but-not-all-do/2015/01/14/d406c0be-9c0f-11e4-bcfb-059ec7a93ddc_story.html (accessed December 27, 2015)

St. George, Donna. 2015c. "Unsubstantiated" child neglect finding for free-range parents. *Washington Post,* March 2. https://www.washingtonpost.com/local/education/decision-in-free-range-case-does-not-end-debate-about-parenting-and-safety/2015/03/02/5a919454-c04d-11e4-ad5c-3b8ce89f1b89_story.html) (video included) (accessed December 27, 2015)

St. George, Donna, and Brigid Schulte. 2015. Parents rally around "free-range family" with petitions, protest plans. *Washington Post,* April 15. https://www.washingtonpost.com/local/education/parents-rally-around-free-range-family-with-petitions-protest-plans/2015/04/15/1e96963c-e381-11e4-b510-962fcfabc310_story.html (accessed December 27, 2015)

immigration in the United States. American Immigration Council, Washington, D.C. http://immigrationpolicy.org/sites/default/files/docs/the_criminalization_of_immigration_in_the_united_states_final.pdf

Organization for Economic Co-operation and Development. 2014. OECD Health Statistics 2014: How does the United States compare? http://www.oecd.org/unitedstates/Briefing-Note-UNITED-STATES-2014.pdf (accessed May 16, 2016)

Organization for Economic Co-operation and Development. 2016. OECD data. https://data.oecd.org/ (accessed May 24, 2016)

Pager, Deva. 2003. The mark of a criminal record. *American Journal of Sociology* 108 (5): 937–75.

Peltier, Jon. 2009. Graphing the cost of health care. *Peltier Tech Blog.* http://peltiertech.com/graphing-the-cost-of-health-care/ (accessed May 16, 2016)

Porter, J. R. 1976. Antony van Leeuwenhoekl: Tercentenary of his discovery of bacteria. *Bacteriological Reviews* 40 (2): 260–69.

Sampson, Robert J. 2008. Rethinking crime and immigration. *Contexts* 7 (1): 28–33.

Spalter-Roth, Roberta, and Nicole Van Vooren. 2008. Pathways to job satisfaction: What happened to the class of 2005? American Sociological Association Department of Research and Development. http://www.asanet.org/research/PathJobSatisfaction.pdf (accessed March 28, 2016)

Chapter 3

Arum, Richard, and Josipa Roksa. 2011. *Academically adrift: Limited learning on college campuses.* Chicago: University of Chicago Press.

Bennett, Joan W., and King-Thom Chung. 2001. Alexander Fleming and the discovery of penicillin. In *Advances in applied microbiology*, vol. 49, edited by Allen I. Laskin, Joan W. Bennett, and Geoffrey M. Gadd, 163–84. San Diego, CA: Academic Press.

Brown, Anna. 2015. Chapter 4: U.S. public has mixed views of immigrants and immigration. Pew Research Center, Washington, D.C. http://www.pewhispanic.org/2015/09/28/chapter-4-u-s-public-has-mixed-views-of-immigrants-and-immigration/#fn-22980-20

Desmond, Matthew. 2016. *Evicted: Poverty and profit in the American city.* New York: Crown.

Ewing, Walter A., Daniel E. Martínez, and Rubén G. Rumbaut. 2015. The criminalization of

Chapter 4

Baker, Al. 2012. Baring shoulders and knees, students protest a dress code. *New York Times,* June 6. http://www.nytimes.com/2012/06/07/nyregion/stuyvesant-high-school-students-protest-dress-code.html?_r=0 (accessed December 17, 2015)

Berger, Peter L., and Thomas Luckmann. 1966. *The social construction of reality: A treatise in the sociology of knowledge.* New York: Doubleday.

Bourdieu, Pierre. 1984. *Distinction: A social critique of the subject of taste.* Cambridge, MA: Harvard University Press.

Bourdieu, Pierre, and Jean Claude Passeron. 1990. *Reproduction in education, society and culture.* Thousand Oaks, CA: Sage.

Brown, Donald. 1991. *Human universals.* Philadelphia: Temple University Press.

Carson, E. Ann. 2014. Prisoners in 2013. Bureau of Justice Statistics. https://www.bjs.gov/index.cfm?ty=pbdetail&iid=5109 (accessed October 14, 2017)

Davies, Alex. 2013. Painting with a private jet engine makes very cool abstract art. *Business Insider.* http://www.businessinsider.com/learjet-used-to-make-abstract-art-2013-5 (accessed June 10, 2017)

Duncan, Lauren E., and Abigail Stewart. 1995. Still bringing the Vietnam War home: Sources of contemporary student activism. *Personality and Social Psychology Bulletin* 21:914–924.

Elder, Glen H., Jr. 1999. *Children of the Great Depression, 25th anniversary edition.* Boulder, CO: Westview. (Original work published 1974)

Goleman, Daniel. 2006. *Social intelligence: The new science of human relationships.* New York: Bantam.

Kidder, Tracy. 2009. *Mountains beyond mountains: The quest of Dr. Paul Farmer, a man who would cure the world.* New York: Random House.

Lichtblau, Eric. 2016. Orlando gunman told police that U.S. should "stop bombing" Syria and Iraq. *New York Times,* June 20. http://www.nytimes.com/2016/06/21/us/fbi-transcripts-orlando-shooting-omar-mateen.html?rref=collection%2Fnewseventcollection%2F2016-orlando-shooting&action=click&contentCollection=us&region=stream&module=stream_unit&version=latest&contentPlacement=2&pgtype=collection (accessed June 20, 2016)

Mark, Noah P. 2003. Culture and competition: Homophily and distancing explanations for cultural niches. *American Sociological Review* 68 (3): 319–45.

Mazzola, Jessica. 2015. N.J. high schoolers protest "sexist" dress code. *NJ.Com,* May 14. http://www.nj.com/essex/index.ssf/2015/05/nj_high_schoolers_protest_sexist_dress_code.html (accessed December 17, 2015)

Mead, George Herbert. 1934. *Mind, self, and society from the standpoint of a social behaviorist.* Chicago: Chicago University Press.

Murdock, George P. 1945. The common denominator of culture. In *The science of man in the world crisis,* edited by Ralph Linton. New York: Columbia University Press.

Musolf, Gil Richard. 2003. The Chicago school. In *Handbook of symbolic interactionism,* edited by L. T. Reynolds and N. J. Herman-Kinney, 91–118. Lanham, MD: Rowman & Littlefield.

Nolan, Patrick, and Gerhard Lenski. 2010. *Human societies: An introduction to macrosociology.* 11th ed. Boulder, CO: Paradigm.

Sapir, Edward. 1958. *Culture, language and personality.* Berkeley: University of California Press.

Swidler, Ann. 1986. Culture in action: Symbols and strategies. *American Sociological Review* 51:273–86.

Varkey GEMS Foundation. October 2013. *2013 Global Teacher Status Index.* London: Varkey GEMS Foundation.

Williams, Robin M., Jr. 1970. *American society: A sociological interpretation.* 3rd ed. New York: Knopf.

World Bank. 2017. Rural population (% of total population). http://data.worldbank.org/indicator/SP.RUR.TOTL.ZS (accessed October 14, 2017)

Chapter 5

Anderson, Craig A., Leonard Berkowitz, Edward Donnerstein, L. Rowell Huesmann, James D. Johnson, Daniel Linz, Neil M. Malamuth, and Ellen Wartella. 2003. The influence of media violence on youth. *Psychological Science in the Public Interest* 4 (3): 81–110.

Anderson, Craig A., Akiko Shibuya, Nobuko Ihori, Edward L. Swing, Brad J. Bushman, Akira Sakamoto, Hannah R. Rothstein, and Muniba Saleem. 2010. Violent video game effects on aggression, empathy, and prosocial behavior in Eastern and Western Countries: A meta-analytic review. *Psychological Bulletin* 136 (2): 151–73.

Bellis, Rich. 2016. Here's everywhere in America you can still get fired for being gay or trans. *fastcompany.com,* March 3. http://www.fastcompany.com/3057357/the-future-of-work/heres-everywhere-in-america-you-can-still-get-fired-for-being-lgbt (accessed July 6, 2016)

Birkett, Michelle, and Dorothy L. Espelage. 2014. Homophobic name-calling, peer-groups, and masculinity: The socialization of homophobic behavior in adolescents. *Social Development* 24 (1): 184–205.

Bushman, Brad J., and L. Rowell Huesmann. 2012. Effects of violent media on aggression. In *Handbook of children and the media,* 2nd ed., edited by D. G. Singer and J. L. Singer, 231–48. Thousand Oaks, CA: Sage.

Chodorow, Nancy. 1978. *The reproduction of mothering.* Oakland: University of California Press.

Common Sense Media. 2015. The common sense census: Media use by tweens and teens. https://www.commonsensemedia.org/research/the-common-sense-census-media-use-by-tweens-and-teens (accessed July 5, 2016)

Garfinkel, Harold. 1967. *Studies in ethnomethodology*. Cambridge, UK: Polity.

Gentile, Douglas A., Craig A. Anderson, Shintaro Yukawa, Nobuko Ihori, Muniba Saleem, Lim Kam Ming, Akiko Shibuya, Albert K. Liau, Angeline Khoo, Brad J. Bushman, L. Rowell Huesmann, and Akira Sakamoto. 2009. The effects of prosocial video games on prosocial behaviors: International evidence from correlational, longitudinal, and experimental studies. *Personality and Social Psychology Bulletin* 35 (6): 752–63.

Goffman, Erving. 1959. *The presentation in everyday life*. New York: Anchor.

Goffman, Erving. 1961. *Asylums: Essays on the social situation of mental patients and other inmates*. Garden City, NY: Anchor.

Greitemeyer, Tobias, Silvia Osswald, and Markus Brauer. 2010. Playing prosocial video games increases empathy and decreases schadenfreude. *Emotion* 10 (6): 796–802.

Hannon, Lance, Robert DeFina, and Sarah Bruch. 2013. The relationship between skin tone and school suspension for African Americans. *Race and Social Problems* 5 (4): 281–95.

Huesmann, L. Rowell, Jessica Moise-Titus, Cheryl-Lynn Podolski, and Leonard D. Eron. 2003. Longitudinal relations between children's exposure to TV violence and their aggressive and violent behavior in young adulthood: 1977–1992. *Developmental Psychology* 39 (2): 201–21.

Jackson, Philip W. 1968. *Life in classrooms*. New York: Teachers College Press.

Karabel, Jerome, and Albert Henry Halsey, eds. 1978. *Power and ideology in education*. New York: Oxford University Press.

Lareau, Annette. 2002. *Unequal childhoods: Class, race and family life*. Oakland: University of California Press.

Mead, George Herbert. 1964. *On social psychology*. Chicago: University of Chicago Press.

Parsons, Talcott. 1959. The school class as a social system: Some of its functions in American society. *Harvard Educational Review* 29 (4): 297–318.

Patchin, Justin W., and Sameer Hinduja. 2013. Cyberbullying among adolescents: Implications for empirical research. *Journal of Adolescent Health* 53 (4): 431–32.

Pew Research Center. 2015. Gay marriage. http://www.pewresearch.org/data-trend/domestic-issues/attitudes-on-gay-marriage (accessed July 6, 2016)

Short, James E. 2013. How much media? Report on American consumers. Institute for Communications Technology Management, Marshall School of Business. http://www.marshall.usc.edu/faculty/centers/ctm/research/how-much-media (accessed July 6, 2016)

Vega, Tanzina. 2014. Schools' discipline for girls differs by race and hue. *New York Times*, December 10. http://www.nytimes.com/2014/12/11/us/school-discipline-to-girls-differs-between-and-within-races.html (accessed June 23, 2016)

Vespa, Jonathan, Jamie M. Lewis, and Rose M. Kreider. 2013. America's families and living arrangements: 2012. US Census Bureau. https://www.census.gov/prod/2013pubs/p20-570.pdf (accessed July 6, 2016)

Wentzel, Kathryn R. 2005. Peer relationships, motivation, and academic performance at school. In *Handbook of competence and motivation*, edited by A. Elliot and C. Dweck, 279–96. New York: Guilford.

Wentzel, Kathryn R., and Katherine Muenks. 2016. Peer influence on students' motivation, academic achievement and social behavior. In *Handbook of social influences in school contexts: social-emotional motivation and cognitive outcomes*, edited by K. R. Wentzel and G. B. Ramani, 13–20. New York: Routledge.

Will, Jerri Ann, Patricia A. Self, and Nancy Datan. 1976. Maternal behavior and perceived sex of infant. *American Journal of Orthopsychiatry* 46 (1): 135–39.

Wilson, Barbara J. 2008. Media and children's aggression, fear, and altruism. *The Future of Children* 18 (1): 87–118.

Chapter 6

Agnew, Robert. 1992. Foundation for a general strain theory of crime and delinquency. *Criminology* 30: 47–87.

American Psychiatric Association. 2013. *Diagnostic and statistical manual of mental disorders*. 5th ed. Arlington, VA: American Psychiatric Association.

Becker, Howard. 1973. *Outsiders*. New York: Free Press. (Original work published 1963)

Bourgois, Philippe I., and Jeffrey Schonberg. 2009. *Righteous dopefiend*. Berkeley: University of California Press.

Centers for Disease Control and Prevention. 2000. CDC growth charts: United States. http://www

.cdc.gov/growthcharts/data/set2/chart-08.pdf (accessed December 15, 2015)

Cohen, Stanley. 1972. *Folk devils and moral panics: The creation of the mods and the rockers.* London: MacGibbon and Kee.

Contreras, Randol. 2012. *The stickup kids: Race, drugs, violence, and the American Dream.* Berkeley: University of California Press.

Copes, Heith, and Lynne Vieraitis. 2012. *Identity thieves: Motives and methods.* Boston: Northeastern University Press.

de Young, Mary. 1997. The devil goes to day care: McMartin and the making of a moral panic. *Journal of American Culture* 20:9–25.

Durkheim, Émile. 1951. *Suicide.* New York: Free Press. (Original work published 1897)

Erikson, Kai T. 1966. *Wayward Puritans: A study in the sociology of deviance.* New York: John Wiley.

Goffman, Erving. 1963. *Stigma: Notes on the management of spoiled identity.* Englewood Cliffs, NJ: Prentice Hall.

Gottfredson, Michael, and Travis Hirschi. 1990. *A general theory of crime.* Stanford, CA: Stanford University Press.

Grealy, Lucy. 1994. *Autobiography of a face.* New York: Harper Perennial-Harper Collins.

Hirschi, Travis. 1969. *Causes of delinquency.* Berkeley: University of California Press.

Jacques, Scott, and Richard Wright. 2015. *Code of the suburb: Inside the world of young, middle-class drug dealers.* Chicago: University of Chicago Press.

Kershaw, Sarah. 2009. Shaking off the shame. *New York Times,* November 25.

Lemert, Edwin. 1951. *Social pathology: A systematic approach to the theory of sociopathic behavior.* New York: McGraw-Hill.

Liazos, Alexander. 1972. The poverty of the sociology of deviance: Nuts, sluts, and perverts. *Social Problems* 20:103–20.

Lombroso, Cesare. 1876. *On criminal man.* Milan, Italy: Hoepli.

Merton, Robert K. 1938. Social structure and anomie. *American Sociological Review* 35:672–82.

Merton, Robert K. 1957. *Social theory and social structure.* Revised and enlarged edition. New York: Free Press of Glencoe.

Reiman, Jeffrey, and Paul Leighton. 2012. *The rich get richer and the poor get prison: Ideology, class, and criminal justice.* 10th ed. New York: Routledge.

Reinarman, Craig. 1994. The social construction of drug scares. In *Constructions of deviance: Social power, context, and interaction,* edited by P. Adler and P. Adler, 92–105. Belmont, CA: Wadsworth.

Rios, Victor. 2012. *Punished: Policing the lives of Black and Latino boys.* New York: NYU Press.

Roschelle, Anne, and Peter Kaufmann. 2004. Fitting in and fighting back: Stigma management strategies among homeless kids. *Symbolic Interaction* 27:23–46.

Saguy, Abigail C. 2013. *What's wrong with fat?* Oxford, UK: Oxford University Press.

Sampson, Robert, Stephen Raudenbush, and Felton Earls. 1997. Neighborhoods and violent crime: A multilevel study of collective efficacy. *Science* 277:918–24.

Smith, Alexander, and Harriet Pollack. 1976. Deviance as a method of coping. *Crime and Delinquency* 22:3–16.

Spector, Malcolm, and John Kitsuse. 1977. *Constructing social problems.* Menlo Park, CA: Cummings.

Sumner, William G. 1907. *Folkways: A study of the sociological importance of usages, manners, customs, mores, and morals.* Boston: Ginn & Company.

Sykes, Gresham, and David Matza. 1957. Techniques of neutralization: A theory of delinquency. *American Sociological Review* 22:664–70.

Tannenbaum, Frank. 1938. *Crime and community.* New York: Columbia University Press.

Thomas, W. I., and Dorothy Thomas. 1928. *The child in America: Behavior problems and programs.* New York: Knopf.

Wolf, Brian, and Phil Zuckerman. 2012. Deviant heroes: Nonconformists as agents of justice and social change. *Deviant Behavior* 33:639–54.

Chapter 7

Alexander, Karl L., Linda Steffel Olson, and Doris R. Enwistle. 2007. Lasting consequences of the summer learning gap. *American Sociological Review* 72:167–80.

Americans for Tax Fairness. 2014. Walmart on Tax Day: How taypayers subsidize America's biggest employer and richest family. http://www.americansfortaxfairness.org/files/Walmart-on-Tax-Day-Americans-for-Tax-Fairness (accessed January 29, 2016)

Bruze, Gustaf. 2015. Male and female marriage returns to schooling. *International Economic Review* 56 (1): 207–34.

Carlozo, Lou. 2012. Why college students stop short of a degree. *Reuters,* March 27. http://reut.rs/HbsPlg (accessed June 2, 2017)

Carnevale, Anthony P., Stephen J. Rose, and Ban Cheah. 2014. The college payoff: Education, occupations, lifetime earnings. Georgetown University Center on Education and the Workforce. https://cew.georgetown.edu/wp-content/uploads/2014/11/collegepayoff-complete.pdf (accessed April 1, 2016)

Case, Ann, and Angus Deaton. 2015. Rising morbidity and mortality in midlife among White non-Hispanic Americans in the 21st century. *Proceedings of the National Academy of Science,* December 8. http://www.pnas.org/cgi/doi/10.1073/pnas.1518393112 (accessed January 11, 2016)

Cherlin, Andrew J. 2016. Why are death rates rising? *New York Times,* February 22, A19.

Chetty, Raj, and Nathaniel Hendren. 2015. The impacts of neighborhoods on intergenerational poverty. Equality of Opportunity. http://www.equality-of-opportunity.org/images/nbhds_exec_summary.pdf (accessed September 5, 2015)

Chetty, Raj, Michael Stepner, Sarah Abraham, Shelby Lin, Benjamin Scuderi, Nicholas Turner, Augustin Bergeron, and David Cutler. 2016. The association between income and life expectancy in the United States, 2001–2014. *Journal of the American Medical Association* 315 (16): 1750–1766.

Chyn, Eric. 2016. Moved to opportunity: The long-run effects of public housing demolition on labor market outcomes of children. http://www-personal.umich.edu/~ericchyn/Chyn_Moved-to_Opportunity.pdf (accessed April 20, 2016)

Corak, Miles. 2006. *Do poor children become poor adults? Lessons from a cross country comparison of generational earnings mobility.* IZA Discussion Paper No. 1933. Bonn, Germany: Institute for the Study of Labor.

Cowen, Tyler. 2015. The marriages of power couples reinforce income inequality. *New York Times,* December 24, BU6.

Cuddy, Emily, Joana Venator, and Richard V. Reeves. 2015. In a land of dollars: Deep poverty and its consequences. http://brookings.edu/blogs/social-mobility-memos/posts/2015/05/07-deep-poverty-income-spending-reeves (accessed June 1, 2016)

Daniels, Alex. 2014. As wealthy give smaller share of income to charity, middle class digs deeper. *Chronicle of Philanthropy,* October 5. http://www.philanthropy.com/article/As-Wealthy-Give-Smaller-Share/152481 (accessed July 15, 2016)

Davidai, Shai, and Thomas Gilovich. 2015. Building a more mobile America—one income quntile at a time. *Perspectives on Psychological Science* 10:60–71.

Davis, Kingsley, and Wilbert Moore. 1945. Some principles of stratification. *American Sociological Review* 10 (2): 242–49.

Desai, Raj M. 2007. The political economy of poverty reduction: Scaling up antipoverty programs in the developing world. http://brookings.edu/~/media/research/files/papers/2007/11/poverty-desai/11_poverty-desai.pdg (accessed June 23, 2016)

DeSilver, Drew. 2015. The many ways to measure economic inequality. http://www.pewcenter.org/fact-tank/2015/09/22/the-many-ways-to-measure-economic-inequality (accessed January 8, 2016)

Desmond, Matthew. 2015. Severe deprivation in America: An introduction. *Russell Sage Foundation Journal of Social Science* 1 (2):1–11.

Desmond, Matthew. 2016. *Evicted: Poverty and profit in the American city.* New York: Crown.

Domhoff, G. William. 2000. *Who rules America? Power and politics in the year 2000.* 3rd ed. New York: McGraw-Hill.

Dynarski, Susan. 2015. For the poor, the graduation gap is even wider than the enrollment gap. *New York Times,* June 2, A3.

Edelman, Peter. 2012. *So rich, so poor: Why it's so hard to end poverty in America.* New York: New Press.

FamiliesUSA. 2017. *A 50-state look at Medicaid expansion.* http://familiesusa.org/product/50-state-look-medicaid-expansion (accessed June 6, 2017)

Fox, Liana, Wimer, Christopher, Irwin Garfinkel, Neeraj Kaushal, Jaehyun Nam, and Jane Waldfogel. 2015. Trends in deep poverty from 1968 to 2011: The influence of family structure, employment patterns, and the safety net. *Russell Sage Foundation Journal of Social Science* 1 (2): 14–34.

Gavett, Gretchen. 2014. CEOs get paid too much according to pretty much everyone in the world. *Harvard Business Review,* September 23.

Goldfarb, Jeffrey. 2014. These four charts show how the SAT favors the rich, educated families. *Washington Post,* March 3. http://

www.washingtonpost.com/news/wonkblog/wp/2014/03/05/these-four-charts-show-how-the-sat-favors-the-rich-educated-families (accessed September 18, 2015)

Greenwood, Jeffrey, Nezih Guner, Georgi Kocharkov, and Cesar Santos. 2014. *Marry your like: Assortative mating and income inequality.* Working Paper 19829. Cambridge, MA: National Bureau of Economic Research.

Hale, Benjamin. 2012. The veil of ignorance. *New York Times,* August 12.

Hardoon, Deborah. 2017. *An economy for the 99%.* https://www.oxfam.org/en/research/economy-99 (accessed January 19, 2017)

Harris Poll. 2014. Doctors, military officers, engineers and scientists seen as among America's most prestigious occupations. http://www.theharrispoll.com/politics/Doctors__Military_Officers__Firefighters__and_Scientists_Seen_as_Among_America_s_Most_Prestigious_Occupations.html# (accessed June 1, 2017)

Hasset, Kevin A., and Aparna Mathur. 2012. *A new measure of consumption inequality.* Washington, DC: American Enterprise Institute.

Hochschild, Arlie Russell. 2016. *Strangers in their own land: Anger and mourning on the American right.* New York: New Press.

Irwin, Neil. 2015. As Walmart gives raises, other employers may have to go above minimum wage. *New York Times,* February 10, BU6.

Isaacs, Julia A. 2007. International comparisons of economic mobility. https://www.brookings.edu/wp-content/uploads/2016/07/02_economic_mobility_sawhill_ch3.pdf (accessed June 7, 2017)

Jacobs, Ken, Ian Perry, and Jenifer MacGillvary. 2015. *The high public cost of low wages.* Berkeley, CA: Berkeley Labor Center.

Jantti, Markus, Brent Bratsberg, Knut Røed, Oddbjørn Raaum, Robin Naylor, Eva Österbacka, Anders Björklund, and Torr Eriksson. 2006. *American exceptionalism in a new light: A comparison of intergenerational earnings mobility in the Nordic countries, the United Kingdom and the United States.* IZA Discussion Paper No. 1938. Bonn, Germany: Institute for the Study of Labor.

Katz, Lawrence F., and Alan B. Krueger. 2016. The rise and nature of alternative work arrangements in the United States, 1995–2015. http://krueger.princeton.edu/sites/default/files/akrueger/files/katz_krueger_cws_-_march_29_20165.pdf (accessed May 2, 2016)

Khalid, Amrita. 2016. Here are the cities and states that will soon have a $15 minimum wage. *Daily Dot Politics,* April 15. http://bit.ly/iXzi115 (accessed June 24, 2016)

Kiatpongsan, Sorapop, and Michael I. Norton. 2014. How much (more) should CEOs make? A universal desire for more equal pay. *Perspectives on Psychological Science* 9 (6): 587–93.

Kochar, Rakesh, and Richard Fry. 2014. Wealth inequality has widened along racial, ethnic lines since end of Great Recession. http://www.pewresearch.org/staff/rakesh-kochhar (accessed December 2, 2015)

Kolata, Gina, and Sarah Cohen. 2016. Drug overdoses propel rise in mortality rates of young Whites. *New York Times,* January 17, A1.

Kraus, Michael W., Paul K. Piff, Rodolfo Mendoza-Denton, Michelle L. Rheinschmidt, and Dacher Keltner. 2012. Social class, solipsism, and contextualism: How the rich are different from the poor. *Psychological Review* 119 (3): 546–72.

Krogstad, Jens Manuel, and Kim Parker. 2014. Public is sharply divided in views of Americans in poverty. http://pewresearch.org/fact-tank/2014/09/16/public-is-sharply-divided-in-views-of-americans-in=poverty (accessed February 10, 2016)

Kuziemko, Ilyana, Michael I. Norton, Emmanuel Saez, and Stephanie Stantcheva. 2015. How elastic are preferences for redistribution? Evidence from randomized survey experiments. *American Economic Review* 105 (4): 1478–508.

Malthus, Thomas R. 1951. *An essay on population.* London: J. M. Dent & Sons.

Marx, Karl, Frederich Engels, and Frederic L. Bender. 1988. *The Communist manifesto: Annotated text.* New York: W. W. Norton.

McNamee, Stephen J., and Robert K. Miller Jr. 2004. *The meritocracy myth.* Lanham, MD: Rowman & Littlefield.

Morath, Eric. 2016. Minimum wages set to increase in many states in 2017. *Wall Street Journal,* December 30. http://www.wsj.com/articles/minimum-wages-set-to-increase-in-many-states-in-2017-1483093806 (accessed January 7, 2017)

Morath, Eric, and Julie Jargon. 2016. Across the U.S., workers at the bottom of the ladder get pay raises. *Wall Street Journal,* August 23. http://www.wsj.com/articles/pay-rises-for-workers-at-the-bottom-of-the-ladder-1471944604 (accessed January 7, 2017)

Moynihan, Daniel Patrick. 1965. *The Negro family: The case for national action.* Washington, DC: Office of Policy Planning and Research, U.S. Department of Labor.

National Academy of Sciences. 2015. New report examines implications of growing gap in life span by income for entitlement programs. *Science Daily,* September. http://www.science-daily.com/releases/2015/09/1509171418.htm (accessed January 11, 2016)

National Employment Law Project. 2015. Super-sizing public costs: How low wages at top fast-food chains leave taxpayers footing the bill. http://www.nelp.org/content/uploads/2015/03/NELP-Super-Sizing-Public-Costs-Fast-Food-Report.pdf (accessed May 2, 2016)

Office of Disease Prevention and Health Promotion. n.d. Determinants of health. https://www.healthypeople.gov/2020/about/foundation-health-measures/Determinants-of-Health#.WTGxnEq15bU.email (accessed June 2, 2017)

Oxfam. 2016. An economy for the 1%. http://www.oxfamamerica.org/static/media/files/bp210-economy-one-percent-tax-havens-180116-en_0.pdf (accessed January 25, 2016)

Pew Research Center. 2015. The American middle class is losing ground. *Social & Demographic Trends,* December 9. http://www.pewsocialtrends.org/2015/12/09/the-american-middle-class-is-losing-ground (accessed January 13, 2016)

Piff, Paul K., Daniel M. Stancato, Stephanie Cote, Rodolfo Mendoza-Denton, and Dacher Keltner. 2012. Higher social class predicts increased unethical behavior. *PNAS* 109 (11): 4086–91.

Pink, Dan. 2012. How to predict a student's SAT score: Look at the parent's tax return. http://www.danpink.com/2012/02/how-to-predict-a-students-SAT-score-look-at-the-parents-tax-return (accessed November 15, 2015)

Proctor, Bernadette D., Jessica L. Semega, and Melissa A. Kollar. 2016. *U.S. Census Bureau, Current Population Reports, P60-256(RV), income and poverty in the United States: 2015.* Washington, DC: Government Printing Office.

Rank, Mark R., and Thomas A. Hirschl. 2016. Calculate your economic risk. *New York Times,* March 18, SR9.

Rawls, John. 1971. *A theory of justice.* Cambridge, MA: Harvard University Press.

Rousseau, Jean-Jacques, and Donald A. Cress. 1983. *On the social contract: Discourse on the origin of inequality: Discourse on political economy.* Indianapolis, IN: Hackett.

Saez, Emmanuel. 2013. Strike it richer: The evolution of top incomes in the United States. https://eml.berkeley.edu/~saez/Saez-UStopincome-2003.pdf (accessed April 22, 2016)

Saez, Emmanuel, and Gabriel Zucman. 2014. Wealth inequality in the United States since 1913: Evidence from capitalized income tax data. http://gabriel-zucman.eu/files/SaezZucman2014.pdf

Shulevitz, Judith. 2016. It's payback time for women. *New York Times,* January 10, SR1.

Silva, Jennifer. 2013. *Coming up short: Working class adulthood in an age of uncertainty.* London: Oxford University Press.

Silver, Nate. 2016. Was the Democratic primary a close call or a landslide? *FiveThirtyEight,* July 27. http://fivethirtyeight.com/features/was-the-democratic-primary-a-close-call-or-a-landslide/ (accessed January 7, 2017)

Starbucks. 2015. College achievement plan FAQs. https://news.starbucks.com/views/starbucks-college-achievement-plan-frequently-asked-questions (accessed June 23, 2016)

Steele, James B., and Lance Williams. 2016. Who got rich off the student debt crisis. *Reveal,* June 28. https://www.revealnews.org/article/who-got-rich-off-the-student-debt-crisis/ (accessed June 2, 2017)

Stiglitz, Joseph E. 2013. A tax system stacked against the 99 percent. *New York Times,* April 14.

U.S. Census Bureau. 2014a. *Share of aggregate income received by each fifth and top 5 percent of all households: Current Population Survey: Annual social and economic supplements.* Washington, DC: Commerce Department.

U.S. Census Bureau. 2014b. *Share of income limits for each fifth and top 5 percent of households, all races: Current Population Survey: Annual social and economic supplements.* Washington, DC: Commerce Department.

U.S. Department of Health and Human Services. 2016. *Federal Register:* Annual update of the HHS poverty guideline. http://www.federalregister.gov/articles/2015/01/22/-01120/annual-udpate-of-the-hhs-poverty-guidelines#1-1 (accessed May 1, 2016)

U.S. Government Accountability Office. 2015. Contingent workforce: Size, characteristics, earnings and benefits. http://www.gao.gov/assets/670/669899.pdf (accessed May 1, 2016)

Weber, Max, Hans Gerth, and C. Wright Mills. 1958. *From Max Weber: Essays in sociology.* New York: Oxford University Press.

Wilkinson, Richard, and Kate Pickett. 2009. *The spirit level: Why greater equality makes societies stronger.* New York: Bloomsbury.

Wolff, Edward N. 2014. *Household wealth trends in the United States, 1926–2013: What happened over the Great Recession?* NBER Working Paper 20733. Cambridge, MA: National Bureau of Economic Research.

World Bank. 2015. World development indicators 2015. http://www.worldbank.org/worlddevelopmentindicatiors2015.pdf (accessed January 27, 2016)

Zucman, Gabriel, with Emmanuel Saez. 2016. Wealth inequality in the United States since 1913: Evidence from capitalized income tax data, *Quarterly Journal of Economics* 13 (2): 519–78.

Chapter 8

AAUW. 2016. Best feminist Super Bowl commercials. http://www.aauw.org/2016/01/28/super-bowl-ads/ (accessed April 1, 2016)

Allison, Rachel, and Barbara J. Risman. 2013. A double standard for "hooking up": How far have we come toward equality? *Social Science Research* 42:1191–206.

American Bar Association. 2016. Lawyer demographics.http://www.americanbar.org/content/dam/aba/administrative/market_research/lawyer-demographics-tables-2016.authcheckdam.pdf (accessed July 1, 2016)

American Psychological Association. n.d. Answers to your questions about individuals with intersex conditions. http://www.apa.org/topics/lgbt/intersex.pdf (accessed October 12, 2017)

Anderson, Hans Christian. 1844. *The ugly duckling.* http://hca.gilead.org.il/ugly_duc.html (accessed March 30, 2016)

Anderson, Kristin L. 2010. Conflict, power and violence in families. *Journal of Marriage and the Family* 72:726–42.

Armstrong, Elizabeth, Laura Hamilton, and Paula England 2010. Is hooking up bad for young women? *Contexts* 9 (3): 22–27.

Associated Press and Natasha Bertrand. 2015. Here are all the countries where its still illegal to be gay. http://www.businessinsider.com/countries-where-its-illegal-to-be-gay-2015-5 (accessed June 14, 2016)

Association of American Universities. 2015. Campus climate survey on sexual assault and sexual misconduct. https://www.aau.edu/key-issues/aau-climate-survey-sexual-assault-and-sexual-misconduct-2015

Atkinson, Maxine P., Theodore N. Greenstein, and Molly Monahan Lang. 2005. For women, breadwinning can be dangerous: Gendered resource theory and wife abuse. *Journal of Marriage and the Family* 67:1137–48.

Bailey, Beth. 2004. From front porch to back seat: A history of the date. *OAH Magazine of History* 18 (4): 23–26.

Baker-Sperry, Lori, and Liz Grauerholz. 2003. The pervasiveness and persistence of the feminine beauty ideal in children's fairy tales. *Gender & Society* 15 (5): 711–26.

Bernard, Tara Siegel. 2014. For workers, less flexible companies. *New York Times,* May 19. http://www.nytimes.com/2014/05/20/business/for-workers-less-flexible-companies.html?_r=0 (accessed June 6, 2014)

Bianchi, Suzanne M. 2011. Family change and time allocation in American families. *Annals of the American Academy of Political and Social Science* 638:21–44.

Bianchi, Suzanne M., Liana C. Sayer, Melissa A. Milkie, and John P. Robinson. 2012. Housework: Who did, does or will do it, and how much does it matter? *Social Forces* 91 (1): 55–63.

Boushey, Heather, and Sarah Jane Glynn. 2012. There are significant business costs to replacing employees. Center for American Progress. https://www.americanprogress.org/issues/economy/reports/2012/11/16/44464/there-are-significant-business-costs-to-replacing-employees (accessed July 6, 2016)

Bridges, Tristan. 2017. Shifts in the U.S. LGBT population. https://thesocietypages.org/socimages/2017/01/16/shifts-in-the-us-lgbt-population (accessed September 4, 2017)

Brown, Anna, and Eileen Patten. 2017. The narrowing, but persistent, gender gap in pay. http://www.pewresearch.org/fact-tank/2017/04/03/gender-pay-gap-facts/

Bureau of Labor Statistics. 2015. Highlights of women's earnings in 2014. http://www.bls.gov/opub/reports/womens-earnings/archive/highlights-of-womens-earnings-in-2014.pdf (accessed March 30, 2016)

Bureau of Labor Statistics. 2016. Labor force participation by gender 1972–2015, US Bureau of Labor Statistics Civilian, noninstitutionalized population 16 years and older. Statistics from the Current Population Survey. http://www.bls.gov/cps/cpsaat02.htm (accessed June 15, 2016)

Bureau of Labor Statistics. 2017. Labor force statistics from the Current Population Survey. http://www.bls.gov/cps/cpsaat02.htm (accessed September 19, 2017)

Cameron, Darla, and Bonnie Berkowitz. 2016. The state of gay rights around the world. *Washington Post,* June 14. https://www.washingtonpost.com/graphics/world/gay-rights (accessed February 2, 2017)

Cantor, David, Bonnie Fisher, Susan Chibnall, Reanne Townsend, Hyunshik Lee, Carol Bruce, and Gail Thomas. 2015. *Report on the AAU Campus Climate Survey on Sexual Assault and Sexual Misconduct.* Rockville, MD: Westat. https://www.aau.edu/sites/default/files/%40%20Files/Climate%20Survey/AAU_Campus_Climate_Survey_12_14_15.pdf (accessed June 8, 2017)

Cha, Youngjoo. 2013. Overwork and the persistence of gender segregation in occupations. *Gender & Society* 27 (2): 158–84.

Clark, Jacqueline, and Maxine P. Atkinson. 2008. Analyzing the social construction of gender in birth announcement cards. In *Sociology through active learning,* edited by Kathleen McKinney, Frank Beck, and Barbara Heyl, 177–81. Thousand Oaks, CA: Pine Forge Press.

Cohen, Philip N. 2013. The persistence of workplace gender segregation in the U.S. *Sociology Compass* 7 (11): 889–99.

Cohen, Philip N., and Matt L. Huffman. 2007. Working for the woman? Female managers and the gender wage gap. *American Sociological Review* 72 (5): 681–704.

Connell, R. W. 1995. *Masculinities.* Berkeley: University of California Press.

Coontz, Stephanie. 1992. *The way we never were.* New York: Basic Books.

Darves, Bonnie. September 19, 2012. Women physicians in the specialties: Making gains. NEJM Career Center. http://www.nejmcareercenter.org/article/women-physicians-in-the-specialties-making-gains/ (accessed October 12, 2017)

Dau-Schmidt, Kenneth G., Marc S. Galanter, Kaushik Mukhopadhaya, and Kathleen E. Hull. 2008. Gender and the legal profession 1967–2000. http://www.lsac.org/docs/default-source/research-(lsac-resources)/gr-08-01.pdf (accessed May 10, 2016)

Davos-Klosters. 2014. Matching skills and labour market needs: Building social partnerships for better skills and better jobs. World Economic Forum Global Agenda Council on Employment. http://www3.weforum.org/docs/GAC/2014/WEF_GAC_Employment_MatchingSkillsLabourMarket_Report_2014.pdf (accessed September 4, 2017)

DeLoache, Judy S., Deborah J. Cassidy, and C. Jan Carpenter. 1987. The three bears are all boys: Mothers' gender labeling of neutral picture book characters. *Sex Roles* 17 (3): 163–78.

Deutsch, Francine M. 2007. Undoing gender. *Gender & Society* 2 (1): 106–27.

Dill, Kathryn. 2015. The best paying jobs for doctors in 2015. *Forbes.* http://www.forbes.com/sites/kathryndill/2015/07/22/the-best-paying-in-demand-jobs-for-doctors-in-2015/#1da4a08b7da3 (accessed June 15, 2016)

DiPrete, Thomas A., and Claudia Buchmann. 2014. Gender disparities in educational attainment in the new century: Trends, causes, and consequences. In *Diversity and disparities,* edited by John R. Logan. New York: Russell Sage Foundation.

Eliot, Lise. 2009. *Pink brain blue brain.* Boston, MA: Houghton Mifflin Harcourt.

England, Paula. 2015. Online College Social Life Survey. http://www.nyu.edu/projects/england/ocsls/ (accessed May 1, 2016)

England, Paula, and Jonathan Bearak. 2014. The sexual double standard and gender differences in attitudes towards casual sex among U.S. university students. *Demographic Research* 30:1327–38.

Eustace, Nicole. 2001. "The cornerstone of a copious work": Courtship, love and power in eighteenth-century Philadelphia. *Journal of Social History* 34 (3): 517–46.

Fausto-Sterling, Anne. 2000. *Sexing the body: Gender politics and the construction of sexuality.* New York: Basic Books.

Ford, Jessie, Paula England, and Jonathan Bearak. 2015. The American college hookup scene: Findings from the Online College Social Life Survey. *TRAILS: Teaching Resources and Innovations Library for Sociology.* http://trails.asanet.org/Pages/Resource.aspx?ResourceID=12959

Gardner, Andrew. 2007. Courtship, sex, and the single colonist. *Colonial Williamsburg Journal.* https://www.history.org/Foundation/journal/Holiday07/court.cfm

Gates, Gary J. 2017. In US, more adults identifying as LGBT. http://www.gallup.com/poll/201731/lgbt-identification-rises.aspx (accessed September 4, 2017)

Gill, Rosalind. 2007. *Gender and the media.* Cambridge, UK: Polity.

GLAAD. 2016. *Where we are on TV '16–'17.* http://glaad.org/files/WWAT/WWAT_GLAAD_2016–2017.pdf (accessed June 14, 2017)

Godbeer, Richard. 2004. Courtship and sexual freedom in eighteenth-century America. *OAH Magazine of History* 18 (4): 9–13.

Goldin, Claudia. 2014. A grand gender convergence: Its last chapter. *American Economic Review* 104 (4): 1091–119.

Greenstein, Theodore A. 2000. Economic dependence, gender, and the division of labor in the home: A replication and extension. *Journal of Marriage and the Family* 62:322–35.

Harvey Wingfield, Adia. 2009. Racializing the glass escalator: Reconsidering men's experiences with women's work. *Gender & Society* (23) 1: 5–26.

Hegewisch, Ariane, Hannah Liepmann, Jeffrey Hayes, and Heidi Hartmann. 2010. Separate and not equal? Gender segregation in the labor market and the gender wage gap. http://www.iwpr.org/publications/pubs/separate-and-not-equal-gender-segregation-in-the-labor-market-and-the-gender-wage-gap (accessed May 15, 2016)

International Lesbian, Gay, Bisexual, Trans and Intersex Association. 2016. *Lesbian and gay rights in the world.* http://ilga .org/downloads/2017/ILGA_WorldMap_ ENGLISH_Overview_2017.pdf

Johnson, Michael P. 2008. *A typology of domestic violence: Intimate terrorism, violent resistance, and situational couple violence.* Boston, MA: Northeastern University Press.

Johnson, Michael P., Janel M. Leone, and Yili Xu. 2014. Intimate terrorism and situational couple violence in general surveys: Ex-spouses required. *Violence Against Women* 20 (2): 186–207.

Kane, Emily W. 2006. "No way my boys are going to be like that!" Parents responses to children's gender nonconformity. *Gender & Society* 20:149–76.

Kimmel, Michael S. 1994. Masculinity as homophobia: Fear, shame and silence in the construction of gender identity. In *Theorizing masculinities,* edited by Harry Brod, 119–41. Thousand Oaks, CA: Sage.

Kreps, Daniel. 2016. Taylor Swift: Kanye West's 'Pablo' lyric about me is misogynistic. http:// www.rollingstone.com/music/news/taylor-swift-kanye-wests-pablo-lyric-about-me-is-misogynistic-20160212 (accessed June 8, 2016)

Livingston, Gretchen. 2014. Growing number of dads home with the kids. Pew Research Center. http://www.pewsocialtrends.org/2014/06/05/growing-number-of-dads-home-with-the-kids/ (accessed October 12, 2017)

Martinez, Gladys M., and Joyce C. Abma. 2015. *Sexual activity, contraceptive use, and childbearing teenagers 15-19 in the United States.* Atlanta, GA: National Center for Health Statistics.

McCabe, Janice, Emily Fairchild, Liz Grauerholz, Bernice A. Pescosolido, and Daniel Tope. 2011. Gender in twentieth century children's books: Patterns of disparity in titles and central characters. *Gender & Society* 25 (2): 197–226.

Moss-Racusina, Corinne A., John F. Dovidiob, Victoria L. Brescollc, Mark J. Grahama, and Jo Handelsmana. 2012. Science faculty's subtle gender biases favor male students. *Proceedings from the National Academy of Science* 109 (41): 16474–79.

Obergefell v. Hodges, 576 U.S. ___ (2015).

Park, Haeyoun, and Laryna Mykhyalyshyn. 2016. L.G.B.T. people are more likely to be targets of hate crimes than any other minority group. *New York Times,* June 15. http://www .nytimes.com/interactive/2016/06/16/us/ hate-crimes-against-lgbt.html?hp&action=-click&pgtype=Homepage&clickSource= story-heading&module=photo-spot-region& region=top-news&WT.nav=top-news&_r=0 (accessed June 22, 2016)

Parker, Kim, and Wendy Wang. 2013. Modern parenthood: Roles of moms and dads converge as they balance work and family. http://www .pewsocialtrends.org/2013/03/14/modern-parenthood-roles-of-moms-and-dads-con verge-as-they-balance-work-and-family/7/ (accessed June 17, 2016)

Pascoe, C. J. 2007. *Dude, you're a fag: Masculinity and sexuality in high school.* Berkeley: University of California Press.

Peiss, Kathy. 2004. Charity girls and city pleasures. *OAH Magazine of History* 18 (4): 14–16.

Pew Research Center. 2013. Growing support for gay marriage: Changed minds and changing demographics. http://www.people-press .org/2013/03/20/growing-support-for-gay-marriage-changed-minds-and-changing-demographics (accessed April 7, 2014)

Risman, Barbara J. 2004. Gender as a social structure: Theory wrestling with activism. *Gender & Society* 18 (4): 429–51.

Risman, Barbara J., and Georgiann Davis. 2012. From sex roles to gender structure. *Current Sociology* 61 (5–6). DOI: 10.1177/205684601271

Rothman, Ellen K. 1984. *Hands and hearts: A history of courtship in America.* New York: Basic Books.

Schilt, Kristen. 2006. Just one of the guys: How transmen make gender visible at work. *Gender & Society* 20:465–90.

Schwartz, Pepper, and Virginia Rutter. 1998. *Gender of sexuality.* Thousand Oaks, CA: Pine Forge Press.

Segal, Corrine. 2017. What the North Carolina legislation to repeal the HB2 'bathroom bill' actually says. PBS. http://www.pbs.org/newshour/rundown/watch-live-nc-legislature-debates-repeal-hb2-bathroom-bill (accessed June 12, 2017)

Sendak, Maurice. 1963. *Where the wild things are.* New York: Harper & Row.

Smith, S. G., J. Chen, K. C. Basile, L. K. Gilbert, M. T. Merrick, N. Patel, M. Walling, and A. Jain. 2017. *The National Intimate Partner and Sexual Violence Survey (NISVS): 2010–2012 state report.* Atlanta, GA: National Center for Injury Prevention and Control, Centers for Disease Control and Prevention.

Solebello, Nicholas, and Sinikka Elliott. 2011. We want them to be as heterosexual as possible: Fathers talk about their teen children's sexuality. *Gender & Society* 25:293–315.

Steinmetz, Katy. 2014. Laverne Cox talks to TIME about the transgender movement. http://time.com/132769/transgender-orange-is-the-new-black-laverne-cox-interview (accessed June 12, 2017)

Sweet, Stephen, Marcie Pitt-Catsouphes, Elyssa Besen, and Lonnie Golden. 2014. Explaining organizational variation in flexible work arrangements: why the pattern and scale of availability matter. *Community, Work & Family* 17 (2): 115–41.

Vassar, Lyndra. 2015. How medical specialties vary by gender. http://www.ama-assn.org/ama/ama-wire/post/medical-specialties-vary-gender (accessed June 15, 2016)

Wade, Lisa. 2017. *American hookup: The new culture of sex on campus.* New York: W. W. Norton.

Wallis, Cara. 2011. Performing gender: A content analysis of gender display in music videos. *Sex Roles* 64:160–72.

Weiser, Dana A. 2017. Confronting myths about sexual assault: A feminist analysis of the false report literature. *Family Relations* 66 (February): 46–60.

Welter, Barbara. 1966. The cult of true womanhood: 1820–1860. *American Quarterly* 18 (2): 151–74.

West, Candace, and Don H. Zimmerman. 1987. Doing gender. *Gender & Society* 1 (2): 125–51.

Williams, Christine L. 2013. The glass escalator, revisited. *Gender & Society* 27 (5): 609–29.

Williams, Joan. 2000. *Unbending gender: Why family and work conflict and what to do about it.* New York: Oxford University Press.

Wood, Julie T. 1994. *Gendered lives: Communication, gender, and culture.* Stamford, CT: Cenage Learning.

Women's Media Center. 2017. The status of women in the U.S. media 2017. http://wmc.3cdn.net/10c550d19ef9f3688f_mlbres2jd.pdf (accessed June 14, 2017)

Worthen, Meredith G. F., and Samantha A. Wallace. 2017. Intersectionality and perceptions about sexual assault education and reporting on college campuses. *Family Relations* 66 (February): 180–96.

Yamawaki, Niwako, Monica Ochoa-Shipp, Craig Pulsipher, Andrew Harlos, and Scott Swindler. 2012. Perceptions of domestic violence: The effects of domestic violence myths, victim's relationship with her abuser, and the decision to return to her abuser. *Journal of Interpersonal Violence* 27 (16): 3195–3212.

Chapter 9

Alcindor, Yamiche. 2016. Minorities worry what a "law and order" Donald Trump presidency will mean. *New York Times,* November 11. http://www.nytimes.com/2016/11/12/us/politics/minorities-worry-what-a-law-and-order-donald-trump-presidency-will-mean.html (accessed January 9, 2017)

Beeman, Angie. 2015. Walk the walk but don't talk the talk: The strategic use of color-blind ideology in an interracial social movement organization. *Sociological Forum* 30 (1): 127–147.

Blauner, Robert. 1972. *Racial oppression in America.* New York: Harper & Row.

Botsford, Jon D., Dwight L. Hamilton, Randall E. Mehrberg, and Deanne E. Maynard. 2000. Amicus brief in the United States District Court for the Eastern District of Michigan. http://www.umich.edu/~bhlumrec/a/admissions/legal/gratz/amici.html

Bradner, Eric, and Ted Barrett. 2015. Republicans to Obama: Keep Syrian refugees out. http://www.cnn.com/2015/11/16/politics/republicans-syrian-refugees-2016-elections-obama/ (accessed June 1, 2017)

Bureau of Labor Statistics. 2016. Table 15 (page 1 of 2). Life expectancy at birth, at age 65, and at age

75, by sex, race, and Hispanic origin: United States, selected years 1900–2014. http://www.cdc.gov/nchs/data/hus/hus15.pdf#015

Bureau of Labor Statistics. 2017. Labor force statistics from the Current Population Survey: Household data not seasonally adjusted quarterly averages E-16. Unemployment rates by age, sex, race, and Hispanic or Latino ethnicity. https://www.bls.gov/web/empsit/cpsee_e16.htm (accessed September 6, 2017)

Cohn, D'Vera. 2017. Seeking better data on Hispanics, Census Bureau may change how it asks about race. http://www.pewresearch.org/fact-tank/2017/04/20/seeking-better-data-on-hispanics-census-bureau-may-change-how-it-asks-about-race/ (accessed May 28, 2017)

Crenshaw, Kimberlé, Neil T. Gotanda, Gary Peller, and Kendall Thomas, editors. 1995. *Critical race theory: The key writings that formed the movement.* New York: Free Press.

Davis, Julie Hirschfeld. 2016. U.S. could exceed goal of accepting 10,000 Syrian refugees. *New York Times,* August 5. http://syrianrefugees.eu/ (accessed September 6, 2016)

DelReal, Jose A. 2016, November 10. Trump campaign staff redirects, then restores, mention of Muslim ban from website. *Washington Post,* November 10. https://www.washington-post.com/news/post-politics/wp/2016/11/10/trump-campaign-staff-deletes-mention-of-muslim-ban-from-website/?utm_term=.6fa81b24e3b6 (accessed January 9, 2017)

Desilver, Drew. 2013. Black unemployment is consistently twice that of Whites. http://www.pewresearch.org/fact-tank/2013/08/21/through-good-times-and-bad-black-unem-ployment-is-consistently-double-that-of-whites/ (accessed September 3, 2016)

Desmond, Matthew, and Mustafa Emirbayer. 2009. *Racial domination, racial progress.* New York: McGraw-Hill.

deVuono-Powell, Saneta, Chris Schweidler, Alicia Walters, and Azadeh Zohrabi. 2015. *Who pays? The true cost of incarceration on families.* Oakland, CA: Ella Baker Center, Forward Together, Research Action Design.

Domonoske, Camila. 2016. Denying housing over criminal record may be discrimination, Feds say. NPR. http://www.npr.org/sections/thetwo-way/2016/04/04/472878724/denying-housing-over-criminal-record-may-be-dis-crimination-feds-say (accessed May 30, 2017)

Dovey, Dana. 2016. Healthcare on Native American reservations is "horrifying": In the US, who you are affects how you're treated. *Medical Daily.* http://www.medicaldaily.com/native-american-reservations-healthcare-terrible-372442 (accessed September 5, 2016)

Douglass, Frederick. 1857. If there is no struggle, there is no progress. http://www.blackpast.org/1857-frederick-douglass-if-there-no-struggle-there-no-progress (accessed January 9, 2017)

Du Bois, W. E. B. 1948. Is man free? *Scientific Monthly* 66:432–33.

Du Bois, W. E. B. 1961. Application for membership in the Communist Party by W. E. B. Du Bois. http://www.cpusa.org/party_info/application-to-join-the-cpusa-by-w-e-b-du-bois-1961 (accessed September 8, 2016)

Durkheim, Émile. 1997. *The division of labor in society.* New York: Simon & Schuster. (Original work published 1892)

Feisthamel, Kevin, and Robert Schwartz. 2009. Differences in mental health counselors' diagnoses based on client race: An investigation of adjustment, childhood, and substance-related disorders. *Journal of Mental Health Counseling* 31 (1): 47–59.

FindLaw.com. 2016. Fair housing: Race discrimination. http://civilrights.findlaw.com/discrimination/fair-housing-race-discrimination.html (accessed September 3, 2016)

Flake, Dallan F. 2015. When any sentence is a life sentence: Employment discrimination against ex-offenders. *Washington University Law Review* 93 (1): 45–102.

Ford, Richard Thomas. 2008. *The race card: How bluffing about bias makes race relations worse.* New York: Farrar, Straus and Giroux.

Frey, William H. 2014. *Diversity explosion.* http://www.brookings.edu/research/reports2/2014/11/diversity-explosion (accessed May 23, 2016)

Gibson, Campbell J., and Emily Lennon. 1999. *Historical census statistics on the foreign-born population of the United States: 1850–1990.* Washington, DC: U.S. Census Bureau.

Goodstein, Laurie. 2016. Jimmy Carter, seeing resurgence of racism, plans Baptist conference for unity. *New York Times,* May 23. http://www.nytimes.com/2016/05/24/us/jimmy-carter-racism-baptist-conference-unity-donald-trump.html (accessed September 5, 2016)

Goyal, Monika K., Nathan Kuppermann, Sean D. Cleary, Stephen J. Teach, and James M. Chamberlain. 2015. Racial disparities in pain management of children with appendicitis in emergency departments. *JAMA Pediatrics* 169 (11): 996–1002.

Griffin, John D. 2014. When and why minority legislators matter. *Annual Review of Political Science* 17:327–36.

Gross, Daniel A. 2015. The U.S. government turned away thousands of Jewish refugees, fearing that they were Nazi spies. *Smithsonian Magazine,* November 18. http://www.smithsonianmag.com/history/us-government-turned-away-thousands-jewish-refugees-fearing-they-were-nazi-spies-180957324/ (accessed January 9, 2017)

Harris, Art. 1983. Louisiana court sees no shades of gray in woman's request. *Washington Post,* May 21. https://www.washingtonpost.com/archive/politics/1983/05/21/louisiana-court-sees-no-shades-of-gray-in-womans-request/ddb0f1df-ba5d-4141-9aa0-6347e60ce52d/ (accessed August 28, 2016)

Hsin, Amy, and Yu Xie. 2017. Explaining Asian Americans' academic advantage over Whites. *PNAS* 111 (23): 8416–21.

Ignatiev, Noel. 1995. *How the Irish became White.* New York: Routledge.

Indian Health Service. 2016. Disparities. https://www.ihs.gov/newsroom/factsheets/disparities/ (accessed September 5, 2016)

Jaynes, Gregory. 1982. Suit on race recalls lines drawn under slavery. *New York Times*, September 30. http://www.nytimes.com/1982/09/30/us/suit-on-race-recalls-lines-drawn-under-slavery.html?pagewanted=all (accessed August 28, 2016)

Jorde, Lynn B., and Stephen P. Wooding. 2004. Genetic variation, classification, and race. *Nature Genetics* 36:S28–S33.

Kahn, Andrew, and Chris Kirk. 2015. There's blatant inequality at nearly every phase of the criminal justice system. *Business Insider,* August 9. www.businessinsider.com/theres-blatant-inequality-at-nearly-every-phase-of-the-criminal-justice-system-2015-8

Khanna, Nikki. 2013. *Biracial in America: Forming and performing racial identity.* Lanham, MD: Lexington Books.

King, Gilbert. 2012. The ugliest, most contentious election ever. *Smithsonian Magazine,* September 7. http://www.smithsonianmag.com/history/the-ugliest-most-contentious-presidential-election-ever-28429530/?no-ist (accessed September 1, 2016)

Korgen, Kathleen Odell, editor. 2010. *Multiracial Americans and social class.* Abingdon, England: Routledge.

Korgen, Kathleen Odell, editor. 2016. *Race policy and multiracial Americans.* Bristol, England: Policy.

Krogstad, Jens Manuel. 2016. 5 facts about Latinos and education. http://www.pewresearch.org/fact-tank/2016/07/28/5-facts-about-latinos-and-education (accessed August 30, 2016)

Krogstad, Jens Manuel. 2016. 2016 electorate will be most diverse in U.S. history. Pew Research Center. http://www.pewresearch.org/fact-tank/2016/02/03/2016-electorate-will-be-the-most-diverse-in-u-s-history/ (accessed August 30, 2016)

Krogstad, Jens Manuel, and Mark Hugo Lopez. 2017. Black voter turnout fell in 2016, even as a record number of Americans cast ballots. http://www.pewresearch.org/fact-tank/2017/05/12/black-voter-turnout-fell-in-2016-even-as-a-record-number-of-americans-cast-ballots (accessed September 4, 2017)

LaFraniere, Sharon, and Andrew W. Lehren. 2015. The disproportionate risks of driving while Black. *New York Times,* October 24. http://www.nytimes.com/2015/10/25/us/racial-disparity-traffic-stops-driving-black.html?_r=0 (accessed September 4, 2016)

Levin, Brian H. 2017. Hate crimes rise in major American localities in 2016. Center for the Study of Hate and Extremism, California State University, San Bernardino. https://csbs.csusb.edu/sites/csusb_csbs/files/Levin%20DOJ%20Summit%202.pdf (accessed September 4, 2017)

Marshall, Michael. 2012. Climate change determined humanity's global conquest. *New Scientist,* September 19. http://www.newscientist.com/article/mg21528834-600-climate-change-determined-humanitys-global-conquest/

Marte, Janelle. 2017. Wells Fargo steered Blacks and Latinos toward costlier mortgages, Philadelphia lawsuit alleges. *Washington Post,* May 16. http://www.latimes.com/business/la-fi-wells-fargo-philadelphia-20170516-story.html (accessed May 30, 2017)

McWhorter, John. 2008. Racism in America is over. *Forbes,* December 30. http://www.forbes.com/2008/12/30/end-of-racism-oped-cx_jm_1230mcwhorter.html (accessed September 2, 2016)

National Center for Education Statistics. 2017. Public high school graduation rates. http://nces.ed.gov/programs/coe/indicator_coi.asp

National Center for Health Statistics. 2015. Health, United States, 2015—American Indian or Alaska Native population. Figure 26: No health insurance coverage among persons under age 65, by age and race and Hispanic Origin: United States, 1999–June 2015. https://www.cdc.gov/nchs/data/hus/2015/fig26.pdf (accessed September 6, 2017)

National Conference of State Legislatures. 2016. Felon voting rights. http://www.ncsl.org/research/elections-and-campaigns/felon-voting-rights.aspx (accessed May 30, 2017)

National Research Council. 2014. *The growth of incarceration in the United States: Exploring causes and consequences.* Edited by Committee on Causes and Consequences of High Rates of Incarceration, J. Travis, B. Western, and S. Redburn. Committee on Law and Justice, Division of Behavioral and Social Sciences and Education. Washington, DC: National Academies Press.

NPR. 2014. Black preschoolers far more likely to be suspended. http://www.npr.org/sections/codeswitch/2014/03/21/292456211/black-preschoolers-far-more-likely-to-be-suspended (accessed August 29, 2016)

Pager, Devah, Bruce Western, and Naomi Sugie. 2009. Sequencing disadvantage: Barriers to employment facing young Black and White men with criminal records. *Annals of the American Academy of Political and Social Sciences* 623:195–213.

Pearson, Rachel. 2015. Bias in medicine. *Scientific American,* November 1. http://www.scientificamerican.com/article/how-doctors-can-confront-racial-bias-in-medicine (accessed September 5, 2016)

Pettigrew, Thomas F., and Linda R. Tropp. 2008. How does intergroup contact reduce prejudice? Meta-analytic tests of three mediators. *European Journal of Social Psychology* 38:922–934.

Pew Research Center. 2015a. *Multiracial in America: Proud, diverse, and growing in numbers.* http://www.pewsocialtrends.org/files/2015/06/2015-06-11_multiracial-in-america_final-updated.pdf (accessed February 15, 2016)

Pew Research Center. 2015b. *Modern immigration wave brings 59 million to U.S., driving population growth and change through 2065: Views of immigration's impact on U.S. society mixed.* Washington, DC: Pew Research Center.

Plessy v. Ferguson, 163 U.S. 537 (1896).

Poyhonen, Sofia. 2015. Glass ceiling for Asian Americans is 3.7x times harder to crack. http://www.ascendleadership.org/news/230114 (accessed September 5, 2016)

Rockquemore, Kerry, and David L. Brunsma. 2008. *Beyond Black: Biracial identity in America.* New York: Rowman & Littlefield.

Rodriguez, Clara. E. 2000. *Changing race: Latinos, the Census and the history of ethnicity.* New York: NYU Press.

Rothwell, Jonathan. 2014. How the war on drugs damages Black social mobility. https://www.brookings.edu/blog/social-mobility-memos/2014/09/30/how-the-war-on-drugs-damages-black-social-mobility (accessed May 30, 3017)

Rutherford, Adam. 2015. Why racism is not backed by science. *The Guardian.* https://www.theguardian.com/science/2015/mar/01/racism-science-human-genomes-darwin (accessed August 28, 2016)

Sacks, David, and Peter Thiel. 1996. The case against affirmative action. *Stanford Magazine,* September/October. https://alumni.stanford.edu/get/page/magazine/article/?article_id=43448

Schwartz, Robert C., and David M. Blankenship. 2014. Racial disparities in psychotic disorder diagnosis: A review of empirical literature. *World Journal of Psychiatry* 4 (4): 133–40.

ScienceDaily. 2015. Young Whites usually more optimistic than minority peers about likelihood of living to 35. https://www.sciencedaily.com/releases/2015/11/151118070804.htm (accessed September 5, 2016)

Singhal Astha, Yu Yu Tien, and Renee Y. Hsia. 2016. Racial-ethnic disparities in opioid prescriptions at emergency department visits for conditions commonly associated with prescription drug abuse. *PLoS ONE* 11 (8).

Smithsonian Institute. 2016. Genetics. http://humanorigins.si.edu/evidence/genetics (accessed September 8, 2016)

Spickard, Paul. 2009. *Japanese Americans: the formation and transformations of an ethnic group.* Piscataway, NJ: Rutgers University Press.

Swarns, Rachel L. 2015. Biased lending evolves, and Blacks face trouble getting mortgages. *New York Times,* October 30. http://www.nytimes.com/2015/10/31/nyregion/hudson-city-bank-settlement.html (accessed September 3, 2016)

Syrianrefugees.eu. 2016. Syrian refugees: A snapshot of the crisis—in the Middle East and Europe. http://syrianrefugees.eu (accessed September 6, 2016)

Thompson, Krissa, and Scott Clement. 2016. Poll: Majority of Americans are thinking race relations are getting worse. *The Washington Post,* July 16. https://www.washingtonpost.com/national/more-than-6-in-10-adults-say-us-race-relations-are-generally-bad-poll-indicates/2016/07/16/66548936-4aa8-

11e6-90a8-fb84201e0645_story.html (accessed September 7, 2016)

Torimoto, Ikuko. 2017. *Okina Kyūin and the politics of early Japanese immigration to the United States 1868–1924.* Jefferson, NC: McFarland.

Ueda, Michiko. 2008. Does minority representation matter for policy outcomes? Evidence from the U.S. states. California Institute of Technology, Working Paper. http://s3-us-west-1.amazonaws.com/hss-prod-storage.cloud.caltech.edu/hss_working_papers/sswp1284.pdf (accessed May 31, 2017)

U.S. Census Bureau. 2012. 2010 Census shows interracial and interethnic married couples grew by 28 percent over decade. http://www.census.gov/newsroom/releases/archives/2010_census/cb12-68.html (accessed February 15, 2016)

U.S. Department of Housing and Urban Development. 2013. *Housing discrimination against racial and ethnic minorities 2012.* http://www.huduser.gov/portal/Publications/pdf/HUD-514_HDS2012_execsumm.pdf (accessed September 3, 2016)

Valverde, Miriam. 2017. For Trump, no signal yet refugee policy will change after U.S. airstrike in Syria. *Politifact,* April 7. http://www.politifact.com/truth-o-meter/article/2017/apr/07/after-syrian-missile-airstrikes-will-trump-change-/ (accessed June 1, 2017)

Wike, Richard, Bruce Stokes, and Katie Simmons. 2016. Europeans fear wave of refugees will mean more terrorism, fewer jobs. http://www.pewglobal.org/2016/07/11/europeans-fear-wave-of-refugees-will-mean-more-terrorism-fewer-jobs (accessed September 6, 2016)

Wiltz, Teresa. 2015. Legislative boundaries, lack of connections lead to few minority lawmakers. The Pew Charitable Trusts. http://www.pewtrusts.org/en/research-and-analysis/blogs/stateline/2015/12/09/legislative-boundaries-lack-of-connections-lead-to-few-minority-lawmakers (accessed August 30, 2016)

Ye He Lee, Michelle. 2015. Donald Trump's false comments connecting Mexican immigrants and crime. *Washington Post,* July 8. https://www.washingtonpost.com/news/fact-checker/wp/2015/07/08/donald-trumps-false-comments-connecting-mexican-immigrants-and-crime/?utm_term=.70b090b9add6 (accessed January 9, 2017)

Zucchino, David. 2016. "I've become a racist": Migrant wave unleashes Danish tensions over identity. *New York Times,* September 5. http://www.nytimes.com/2016/09/06/world/europe/denmark-migrants-refugees-racism.html (accessed September 6, 2016)

Chapter 10

Amato, Paul R. 2010. Research on divorce: Continuing trends and new developments. *Journal of Marriage and Family* 72 (3): 650–66.

Amato, Paul R., and Christopher J. Anthony. 2014. Estimating the effects of parental divorce and death with fixed effects models. *Journal of Marriage and Family* 76 (2):370–86.

Amato, Paul R., and Bryndl Hohmann-Marriott. 2007. A comparison of high-and low-distress marriages that end in divorce. *Journal of Marriage and Family* 69 (3): 621–38.

Bartel, Ann, Charles Baum, Maya Rossin-Slater, Christopher Ruhm, and Jane Waldfogel. 2014. *California's paid leave law: Lessons from the first decade.* Washington, DC: U.S. Department of Labor.

Berk, Sarah Fenstermaker. 1985. *The gender factory: The apportionment of work in American households.* New York: Plenum.

Bernstein, Basil. 2003. *Class, codes, and control: Towards a theory of educational transmission.* New York: Routledge & Kegan Paul.

Bianchi, Suzanne M. 2011. Family change and time allocation in American families. *The Annals of the American Academy of Political and Social Science* 638:21–44.

Biblarz, Timothy J., and Evren Savci. 2010. Lesbian, gay, bisexual, and transgender families. *Journal of Marriage and Family* 72 (3): 480–97.

Bloom, Nick, and John Van Reenen. 2006. *Measuring and explaining management practices across firms and countries.* Cambridge, MA: National Bureau of Economic Research.

Carrington, Christopher. 1999. *No place like home: Relationships and family life among lesbians and gay men.* Chicago: University of Chicago Press.

Cherlin, Andrew. 1983. Changing family and household: Contemporary lessons from historical research. *Annual Review of Sociology* 9:51–66.

Cherlin, Andrew J. 2009. *The marriage-go-round.* New York: Knopf.

Collins, Patricia Hill. 2000. *Black feminist thought: Knowledge, consciousness, and the politics of empowerment.* New York: Routledge.

Coontz, Stephanie. 1992. *The way we never were: American families and the nostalgia trap.* New York: Basic Books.

Coontz, Stephanie. 2005. *Marriage, a history: How love conquered marriage.* New York: Viking.

Coontz, Stephanie. 2010. The evolution of American families. In *Families as they really are,* edited by B. Risman. New York: W. W. Norton.

Corsaro, William A. 2005. *The sociology of childhood.* Thousand Oaks, CA: Pine Forge.

The Council of Economic Advisers. 2014. Work-life balance and the economics of workplace flexibility. https://obamawhitehouse.archives.gov/sites/default/files/docs/updated_workplace_flex_report_final_0.pdf

Creighton, Mathew J., Hyunjoon Park, and Graciela M. Teruel. 2009. The role of migration and single motherhood in upper secondary education in Mexico. *Journal of Marriage and Family* 71 (5): 1325–39.

Dill, Bonnie Thornton. 1988. Our mothers' grief: Racial ethnic women and the maintenance of families. *Journal of Family History* 13 (4): 415–31.

Edin, Kathryn, and Maria Kefalas. 2005. *Promises I can keep: Why poor women put motherhood before marriage.* Berkeley: University of California Press.

Edin, Kathryn, and Timothy J. Nelson. 2013. *Doing the best I can: Fatherhood in the inner city.* Berkeley: University of California Press.

Elliott, Sinikka, Rachel Powell, and Joslyn Brenton. 2015. Being a good mom. *Journal of Family Issues* 36 (3): 351–70.

Finkelhor, David. 2008. *Childhood victimization: Violence, crime, and abuse in the lives of young people.* Oxford, UK: Oxford University Press.

Finkelhor, David, Richard K. Ormrod, and Heather A. Turner. 2007. Poly-victimization: A neglected component in child victimization. *Child Abuse & Neglect* 31 (1): 7–26.

Finkelhor, David, Heather Turner, Richard Ormrod, and Sherry L. Hamby. 2009. Violence, abuse, and crime exposure in a national sample of children and youth. *Pediatrics* 124 (5): 1411–23.

Gorman, Gregory H., Matilda Eide, and Elizabeth Hisle-Gorman. 2009. Wartime military deployment and increased pediatric mental and behavioral health complaints. *Pediatrics* 136 (6): 1058–66.

Hays, Sharon. 1996. *The cultural contradictions of motherhood.* New Haven, CT: Yale University Press.

Hill, Shirley A. 2005. *Black intimacies: A gender perspective on families and relationships.* New York: Rowman Altamira.

Hill, Shirley A. 2012. *Families: A social class perspective.* Thousand Oaks, CA: Pine Forge Press.

Hochschild, Arlie, and Anne Machung. 2012. *The second shift: Working families and the revolution at home.* New York: Penguin.

Jacobs, Jerry A., and Kathleen Gerson. 2004. *The time divide.* Cambridge, MA: Harvard University Press.

Kamo, Yoshinori, and Ellen L. Cohen. 1998. Division of household work between partners: A comparison of Black and White couples. *Journal of Comparative Family Studies* 29:131–45.

Kohn, Melvin L. 1977. *Class and conformity: A study in values.* Chicago: University of Chicago Press.

Lareau, Annette. 2002. Invisible inequality: Social class and childrearing in Black families and White families. *American Sociological Review* 67 (3): 747–76.

Loving v. Virginia, 388 U.S. 1 (1967).

Mintz, Steven. 2001. Introduction: Does the American family have a history? Family images and realities. *OAH Magazine of History* 15 (4): 4–10.

Mintz, Steven. 2004. *Huck's raft: A history of American childhood.* Cambridge, MA: Harvard University Press.

Moore, Mignon. 2011. *Invisible families: Gay identities, relationships, and motherhood among Black women.* Berkeley: University of California Press.

Obergefell v. Hodges, 576 U.S. ___ (2015).

Parsons, Talcott, and Robert F. Bales. 1956. *Family socialization and interaction processes.* London: Routledge and Kegan Paul.

Pear, Robert, and David D. Kirkpatrick. 2004. Bush plans 1.5 billion drive for promotion of marriage. *New York Times,* January 14. http://www.nytimes.com/2004/01/14/us/bush-plans-1.5-billion-drive-for-promotion-of-marriage.html (accessed September 10, 2017)

Pemberton, David. 2015. Statistical definition of "family" unchanged since 1930. United States Census Bureau. https://www.censusnewsroom/blogs/random-samplings/2015/01/statistical-definition-of-family-unchanged-since-1930.html (accessed September 10, 2017)

Ray, Rebecca, Janet C. Gornick, and John Schmitt. 2009. *Parental leave policies in 21 countries.* Washington, DC: Center for Economic and Policy Research.

Schneider, Daniel. 2011. Market earnings and household work: New tests of gender performance theory. *Journal of Marriage and Family* 73 (4): 845–60.

Shows, Carla, and Naomi Gerstel. 2009. Fathering, class, and gender: A comparison of physicians and emergency medical technicians. *Gender & Society* 23 (2): 161–87.

Staples, Robert, and Leanor Boulin Johnson. 1993. *Black families at the crossroads: Challenges and prospects.* San Francisco: Jossey-Bass.

Supreme Court of the United States. 2014. Obergefell et al. v. Hodges, Director, Ohio department of Health, et al., Syllabus. https://www.supremecourt.gov/opinions/14pdf/14-556_3204.pdf (accessed September 10, 2017)

Turner, Heather A., David Finkelhor, and Richard Ormrod. 2007. Family structure variations in patterns and predictors of child victimization. *American Journal of Orthopsychiatry* 77 (2): 282–95.

Turner, Heather A., David Finkelhor, Richard Ormrod, Sherry Hamby, Rebecca T. Leeb, James A. Mercy, and Melissa Holt. 2012. Family context, victimization, and child trauma symptoms: Variations in safe, stable, and nurturing relationships during early and middle childhood. *American Journal of Orthopsychiatry* 82 (2): 209–19.

Turner v. Safley, 482 U.S. 78 (1987).

Turney, Kristin, Jason Schnittker, and Christopher Wildeman. 2012. Those they leave behind: Paternal incarceration and maternal instrumental support. *Journal of Marriage and Family* 74 (5): 1149–65.

U.S. Department of Labor. 2015. DOL factsheet: Paid family and medical leave. https://www.dol.gov/wb/resources/paid_leave_fact_sheet.pdf (accessed June 19, 2017)

Chapter 11

Alwin, Duane F., Michael Braun, and Jacqueline Scott. 1992. The separation of work and the family: Attitudes towards women's labour-force participation in Germany, Great Britain, and the United States. *European Sociological Review* 8 (1): 13–37.

Amurao, Carla. 2013. Fact sheet: How bad is the school-to-prison pipeline? http://www.pbs.org/wnet/tavissmiley/tsr/education-under-arrest/school-to-prison-pipeline-fact-sheet (accessed March 31, 2016)

BenTsvi-Mayer, Shoshanna, Rachel Hertz-Lazarowitz, and Marilyn Safir. 1989. Teachers' selections of boys and girls as prominent pupils. *Sex Roles* 21 (3/4): 231–46.

Berends, Mark. 2015. Sociology and school choice: What we know after two decades of charter schools. *Annual Review of Sociology* 41:159–80.

Blau, Peter, and Otis Duncan. 1967. *The American occupational structure.* New York: Academic Press.

Bourdieu, Pierre, and Jean-Claude Passeron. 1977. *Reproduction in education, society and culture.* London: Sage.

Bowles, Samuel, and Herbert Gintis. 1976. *Schooling in capitalist America.* New York: Basic Books.

Brown, Emma. 2007. New federal civil rights data show persistent racial gaps in discipline, access to advanced coursework. *Washington Post,* June 7. https://www.washingtonpost.com/local/education/new-federal-civil-rights-data-show-persistent-racial-gaps-in-discipline-access-to-advanced-coursework/2016/06/06/e95a4386-2bf2-11e6-9b37-42985f6a265c_story.html (accessed June 7, 2016)

Brown v. Board of Education of Topeka, 347 U.S. 483 (1954).

Bureau of Labor Statistics. 2017. Economics news release: Employment characteristics of families summary. https://www.bls.gov/news.release/famee.nr0.htm (accessed September 10, 2017)

California Newsreel. 2014. Are we crazy about our kids? *The Raising of America.* http://www.raisingofamerica.org/are-we-crazy-about-our-kids

Carnevale, Anthony P., Tamara Jayasundera, and Artem Gulish. 2015. *Good jobs are back: College graduates are first in line.* Washington, DC: Georgetown University Center on Education and the Workforce.

Center on the Developing Child at Harvard University. 2016. From best practices to breakthrough impacts: A science-based approach to building a more promising future for young children and families. http://www.developingchild.harvard.edu

Cherry, Louise. 1975. The preschool teacher-child dyad: Sex differences in verbal interaction. *Child Development* 46 (2): 532–35.

Chubb, John E., and Terry M. Moe. 1990. *Politics, markets, and America's schools.* Washington, DC: The Brookings Institution.

Coleman, James S., Ernest Q. Campbell, Carol J. Hobson, James McPartland, Alexander M. Mood, Frederic D. Weinfeld, and Robert L. York. 1966. *Equality of educational opportunity.* Washington, DC: U.S. Department of Health, Education, and Welfare.

Curtis, Aaron J. 2014. Tracing the school-to-prison pipeline from zero-tolerance policies to juvenile justice disposition. *Georgetown Law Journal* 102:1251–78.

Daniel, Shirley J., Fujiao Xie, and Ben Kedia. 2014. 2014 U.S. business needs for employees with international expertise. Prepared for the Internationalization of U.S. Education in the 21st Century, The Future of International and Foreign Language Studies: A Research Conference on National Needs and Policy Implications, April 11–13, 2014, Williamsburg, VA.

Davis, Kingsley, and Wilbert Moore. 1945. Some principles of stratification. *American Sociological Review* 10:242–49.

Douthat, Ross. 2005. Does meritocracy work? *The Atlantic,* November. http://www.theatlantic.com/magazine/archive/2005/11/does-meritocracy-work/304305 (accessed March 20, 2016)

Durkheim, Émile. 1912. *The elementary forms of religious life.* New York: Free Press, 1995.

Elman, Cheryl, and Angela M. O'Rand. 2007. The effects of social origins, life events, and institutional sorting on adults' school transitions, 1987–1994. *Social Science Research* 36 (3): 1276–99.

Equal Justice Initiative. 2017. Lynching in America: Confronting the legacy of racial terror. *Equal Justice Initiative Reports.* http://eji.org/reports/lynching-in-america (accessed June 5, 2017)

Fabelo, Tony, Michael D. Thompson, Martha Plotkin, Dottie Carmichael, Miner P. Marchbanks III, and Eric A. Booth. 2011. *Breaking schools' rules: A statewide study of how school discipline relates to students' success and juvenile justice involvement.* New York: Council of State Governments Justice Center.

Farkas, George. 2003. Cognitive and non-cognitive traits and behaviors in stratification processes. *Annual Review of Sociology* 29:541–62.

Featherman, David, and Robert Hauser. 1978. *Opportunity and change.* New York: Academic Press.

Finn, Chester, Bruno V. Manno, and Greg Vanourek. 2000. *Charter schools in action: Renewing public education.* Princeton, NJ: Princeton University Press.

Gamoran, Adam. 2001. American schooling and educational inequality: A forecast for the 21st Century. *Sociology of Education* 74:135–153.

Global Monitoring Report. 2015. *Education for all 2000–2015: Achievements and challenges.* Paris, France: United Nations Educational, Scientific and Cultural Organization.

Glock, Sabine, Sabine Krolak-Schwerdt, and Ineke Pit-ten Cate. 2015. Are school placement recommendations accurate? The effect of students' ethnicity on teachers' judgments and recognition memory. *European Journal of Psychology of Education* 30 (2): 169–88.

Gould, Elise, and Tanyell Cooke. 2015. *High quality child care is out of reach for working families.* Washington, DC: Economic Policy Institute. www.epi.org/publication/child-care-affordability

Government Accountability Office. 2016. Better use of information could help agencies identify disparities and address racial discrimination. http://www.gao.gov/assets/680/676744.pdf (accessed August 18, 2016)

Hanson, Jamie L., Nicole Hair, Dinggang G. Shen, Feng Shi, John H. Gilmore, Barbara Wolfe, and Seth D. Pollack. 2013. Family poverty affects the rate of human infant brain growth. *PLoS One* 8 (12): 1–9.

Harper, Shannon, and Barbara Reskin. 2005. Affirmative action at school and on the job. *Annual Review of Sociology* 31:357–79.

Heckman, James J. 2006. Skill formation and the economics of investing in disadvantaged children. *Science* 312:1900–2.

Hertel, Florian R., and Olaf Groh-Samberg. 2014. Class mobility across three generations in the U.S. and Germany. *Research in Social Stratification and Mobility* 35:35–52.

Hillemeier, Marianne M., Paul L. Morgan, George Farkas, and Steven A. Maczuga. 2013. Quality disparities in child care for at-risk children: Comparing Head Start and non-Head Start Settings. *Maternal Child Health Journal* 17 (1): 180–88.

Jonsson, Jan O., David B. Grusky, Matthew Di Carlo, and Reinhard Pollack. 2011. It's a decent bet that our children will be professors too. In *The inequality reader: Contemporary and foundational readings in race, class, and gender,* edited by David B. Grusky and Szonja Szelenyi, 2nd ed., 499–516. Boulder, CO: Westview.

Kozol, Jonathan. 1991. *Savage inequalities.* New York: Crown.

Kozol, Jonathan. 2005. *Shame of a nation: The restoration of apartheid schooling in America.* New York: Three Rivers Press.

Kristof, Nicholas. 2016. So little to ask for: A home. *New York Times Opinion Pages.* http://www.nytimes.com/2016/04/07/opinion/so-little-to-ask-for-a-home.html?_r=0 (accessed April 7, 2016)

Lareau, Annette. 2003. *Unequal childhoods: Class, race and family life.* Berkeley: University of California Press.

Layton, Lindsey. 2015. U.S. schools are too focused on standardized tests, poll says. *Washington Post,* August 23. https://www .washingtonpost.com/local/education/ us-schools-are-too-focused-on-standardized-tests-poll-finds/2015/08/22/4a954396-47b3-11e5-8e7d-9c033e6745d8_story.html

Liu, Meirong. 2015. An ecological review of literature on factors influencing working mothers' child care arrangements. *Journal of Child and Family Studies* 24:161–71.

Loewen, James W. 2007. *Lies my teacher told me: Everything your American history textbook got wrong.* New York: Touchstone. (Original work published 1995)

Map: The average cost for child care by state. 2014. *The Boston Globe,* July 2. https://www .bostonglobe.com/2014/07/02/map-the-ave rage-cost-for-child-care-state/LN65rSHXKN jr4eypyxT0WM/story.html (accessed September 10, 2017)

Marx, Karl, and Friedrich Engels. 1979. The German Ideology. In *The Marx-Engels reader,* edited by Robert C. Tucker, 2nd ed., XX. New York: W. W. Norton. (Original work published 1844)

Mitchell, Michael, Michael Leachman, and Kathleen Masterson. 2016. *Funding down, tuition up: State cuts to higher education threaten quality and affordability at public colleges.* Washington, DC: Center on Budget and Policy Priorities. http:// www.cbpp.org/research/state-budget-and-tax/ funding-down-tuition-up#_ftn1

Moodie-Dyer, Amber. 2011. A policy analysis of child care subsidies: Increasing quality, access, and affordability. *Children & Schools* 33 (1): 37–45.

NAFSA. 2015. Trends in U.S. study abroad. *Explore International Education.* http://www.nafsa. org/Explore_International_Education/Advo-cacy_And_Public_Policy/Study_Abroad/ Trends_in_U_S__Study_Abroad (accessed April 6, 2016)

National Center for Education Statistics. 2014. Table 202.10. Enrollment of 3-, 4-, 5-year-old children in preprimary programs, by age of child, level of program, control of program, and attendance status: Selected years, 1970–2013. *Digest of Education Statistics.* https:// nces.ed.gov/programs/digest/d14/tables/ dt14_202.10.asp (accessed March 20, 2016)

National Commission on Excellence in Education. 1983. *A nation at risk: The imperative for educational reform.* http://www2.ed.gov/pubs/ NatAtRisk/index.html (accessed October 2, 2011)

The Nation's Report Card. 2016. Report highlights. *U.S. History, Geography, and Civics.* http://www .nationsreportcard.gov/hgc_2014/# (accessed August 4, 2016)

Oakes, Jeannie. 1994a. More than misapplied technology: A normative and political response to Hallinan on tracking. *Sociology of Education* 67:84–89.

Oakes, Jeannie. 1994b. One more thought. *Sociology of Education* 67:91.

Oprah's Lifeclass. 2009. Khadija Williams' story. *Oprah Winfrey Show.* http://www.oprah .com/oprahs-lifeclass/Khadijah-Williams-Story-Video (accessed February 22, 2016)

Organization for Economic Cooperation and Development. 2010. Finland: Slow and steady reform for consistently high results. https://www.oecd .org/pisa/pisaproducts/46581035.pdf

OWN Videos. 2013. From homeless to Harvard (and beyond): Khadijah Williams starts new life in NYC. http://www.huffingtonpost .com/2013/12/24/khadijah-williams-homeless-harvard_n_4493490.html (accessed February 22, 2016)

Palardy, Gregory, Russell Rumberger, and Truman Butler. 2015. The effect of high school socio-economic, racial, and linguistic segregation on academic performance and school behaviors. *Teachers College Record* 117 (12): 1–52.

Pfeffer, Fabian T., and Florian R. Hertel. 2015. How has educational expansion shaped social mobility trends in the United States. *Social Forces* 94 (1): 143–80.

Podesta, Jennifer. 2014. Habitus and the accomplishment of natural growth: Maternal parenting practices and the achievement of 'school-readiness'. *Australasian Journal of Early Childhood* 39 (4): Online Annex.

Porter, Michael E., and Jan W. Rivkin. 2012. The looming challenge to U.S. competitiveness. *Harvard Business Review,* March. https://hbr.org/2012/03/the-looming-challenge-to-us-competitiveness

Rauscher, Emily. 2015. Educational expansion and occupational change: US compulsory schooling laws and the occupational structure 1850–1930. *Social Forces* 93 (4): 1397–422.

Ravitch, Diane. 2010. *The death and life of the great American school system: How testing and choice are undermining education.* Philadelphia, PA: Basic Books.

Ripley, Amanda. 2014. *The smartest kids in the world and how they got that way.* New York: Simon & Schuster.

Rivera, Lauren. 2011. Ivies, extracurriculars, and exclusion: Elite employers' use of educational credentials. *Research in Social Stratification & Mobility* 29 (1): 71–90.

Robertson, Susan L. 2005. Re-imagining and rescripting the future of education: Global knowledge economy discourses and the challenge to education systems. *Comparative Education* 41 (2): 151–70.

Rosenbaum, James E. 2001. *Beyond college for all: Career paths for the forgotten half.* New York: Russell Sage Foundation.

Rosenbaum, James E. 2007. College-for-all: Do students understand what college demands? In *Sociology of education: A critical reader,* edited by Alan R. Sadovnik, 2nd ed., 271–88. New York: Routledge.

Rosling, Hans. 2007. New insights on poverty. *TED: Ideas Worth Spreading.* https://www.ted.com/talks/hans_rosling_reveals_new_insights_on_poverty?language=en (accessed October 13, 2015)

Rudd, Tom. 2014. *Racial disproportionality in school discipline: Implicit bias is heavily implicated.* Columbus: Kirwan Institute for the Study of Race and Ethnicity, The Ohio State University.

Sadovnik, Alan R. 2007. Theory and research in the sociology of education. In *Sociology of education: A critical reader*, edited by Alan R. Sadovnik, 2nd ed., 3–21. New York: Routledge.

Saxenian, Annalee. 1996. *Regional advantage: Culture and competition in Silicon Valley and Route 128.* Cambridge, MA: Harvard University Press.

Siegel-Hawley, Genevieve, and Erica Frankenberg. 2012. *Reviving magnet schools: Strengthening a successful choice option.* Los Angeles: The Civil Rights Project at UCLA. https://civilrightsproject.ucla.edu/research/k-12-education/integration-and-diversity/reviving-magnet-schools-strengthening-a-successful-choice-option/MSAPbrief-02-02-12.pdf (accessed August 12, 2016)

Stokes, Randall, and Albert Chevan. 1996. Female-headed families: Social and economic context of racial differences. *Journal of Urban Affairs* 18 (3): 245–68.

Stoltzfus, Emilie. 2000. *Child care: The federal role during World War II.* Washington, DC: United States Congressional Research Service.

Strauss, Valerie. 2015. No Child Left Behind: What standardized test scores reveal about its legacy. *Washington Post,* March 10. https://www.washingtonpost.com/news/answer-sheet/wp/2015/03/10/no-child-left-behind-what-standardized-test-scores-reveal-about-its-legacy (accessed August 20, 2016)

Supovitz, Jonathan. 2016. Is high-stakes testing working? University of Pennsylvania Graduate School of Education. https://www.gse.upenn.edu/review/feature/supovitz

Szafran, Robert F. 2002. Age-adjusted labor force participation rates, 1960–2045. *Monthly Labor Review* 125 (9): 25–39.

Teachman, Jay D. 1987. Family background, educational resources, and educational attainment. *American Sociological Review* 52:548–57.

Temple, Judy A., and Arthur J. Reynolds. 2007. Benefits and costs of investments in preschool education: Evidence from the Child-Parent Centers and related programs. *Economics of Education Review* 26:126–44.

Turner, Corey, Reema Khrais, Tim Lloyd, Alexandra Olgin, Laura Isensee, Beckey Vevea, and Ben Carson. 2016. Why America's schools have a money problem. NPR.org. http://www.npr.org/2016/04/18/474256366/why-americas-schools-have-a-money-problem (accessed September 14, 2016)

U.S. Census Bureau. 2011. *The Hispanic population: 2010.* http://www.census.gov/prod/cen2010/briefs/c2010br-04.pdf (accessed May 27, 2016)

U.S. Census Bureau. 2015a. Educational attainment of the population 18 years and over, by age, sex, race, and Hispanic origin. American Community Survey 2014, 5 Year Estimates, Tables 01-1 through 01-6. www.census.gov

U.S. Census Bureau. 2015b. Table 8: Per pupil amounts for current spending of public elementary-secondary school systems by state: Fiscal year 2013. Public Elementary-Secondary Education Finance Data. https://www.census.gov/content/dam/Census/library/publications/2015/econ/g13-aspef.pdf

U.S. Department of Education. 2013. Education matters: Children's brain development, fact sheet. U.S. Department of Education Center for Faith-based and Neighborhood Partnerships. http://sites.ed.gov/fbnp/files/2013/07/Education-Matters-CFBNP-Childrens-Brain-Development.pdf

U.S. Department of Veterans Affairs. 2013. History and timeline. Veterans Benefits Administration Education and Training. www.benefits.va.gov/gibill/history.asp (accessed March 27, 2016)

U.S. House of Representatives. 2001. H.R. 1-No Child Left Behind Act of 2001. https://www.gpo.gov/fdsys/pkg/CRPT-107hrpt334/pdf/CRPT-107hrpt334.pdf (accessed March 15, 2016)

U.S. House of Representatives. 2015. ESEA Conference Report Summary: S. 1177, The Every Student Succeeds Act. http://edworkforce .house.gov/uploadedfiles/esea_conference_ report_summary.pdf (accessed March 15, 2016)

U.S. Immigration and Customs Reinforcement. 2016. Student and exchange visitor program: ICE releases quarterly international student data. https://www.ice.gov/news/releases/ice-releases-quarterly-international-student-data (accessed September 10, 2017)

Warner, Mildred E. 2009. (Not) valuing care: A review of recent popular economic reports on preschool in the U.S. *Feminist Economics* 15 (2): 73–95.

Wexler, Jade, and Nicole Pyle. 2012. Dropout prevention and the model-minority stereotype: Reflections from an Asian American high school dropout. *Urban Review* 44 (5): 551–70.

The White House. 2015. Fact sheet: Congress acts to Fix No Child Left Behind. Briefing Room Statements and Releases. https://www .whitehouse.gov/the-press-office/2015/12/03/ fact-sheet-congress-acts-fix-no-child-left-behind (accessed March 15, 2016)

Wilson, William Julius. 1999. *Bridge over the racial divide*. Berkeley: University of California Press.

Wing, Jean. 2007. Beyond black and white: The model minority myth and the invisibility of Asian American students. *Urban Review* 39 (4): 455–87.

Worthy, Jo. 2010. Only the names have been changed: Ability grouping revisited. *Urban Review* 42:271–95.

Zinn, Howard. 2003. *A people's history of the United States*. New York: HarperCollins. (Original work published 1980)

Chapter 12

Altemeyer, Bob, and Bruce Hunsberger. 2004. A revised religious fundamentalism scale: The short and sweet of it. *The International Journal for the Psychology of Religion* 14 (1): 47–54.

Berger, Peter. 1992. *A far glory: The quest for faith in the age of credulity*. New York: Free Press.

Berger, Peter. 2008. Secularization falsified. *First Things*. http://www.firstthings.com/article/ 2008/02/002-secularization-falsified (accessed March 20, 2016)

Blumer, Herbert. 1969. *Symbolic interaction: Perspective and method*. Englewood Cliffs, NJ: Prentice-Hall.

Cadge, Wendy, Peggy Levitt, and David Smilde. 2011. De-centering and re-centering: Rethinking concepts and methods in the sociological study of religion. *Journal for the Scientific Study of Religion* 50 (3): 437–49.

Campbell, Heidi A. 2013. Religion and the Internet: A microcosm for studying internet trends and implications. *New Media & Society* 15 (5): 680–94.

Chaves, Mark. 2011. *American religion: Contemporary trends*. Princeton, NJ: Princeton University Press.

Chaves, Mark, and Philip S. Gorski. 2001. Religious pluralism and religious participation. *Annual Review of Sociology* 27:261–81.

Durkheim, Émile. 1951. *Suicide*. New York: Free Press. (Original work published 1897)

Durkheim, Émile. 1995. *The elementary forms of religious life*. Translated by K. E. Fields. New York: Free Press. (Original work published 1912)

Emerson, Michael O., and David Hartman. 2006. The rise of religious fundamentalism. *Annual Review of Sociology* 32:127–44.

Jenkins, Willis, and Christopher Key Chapple. 2011. Religion and environment. *Annual Review of Environment and Resources* 36:441–63.

Levitt, Perry, Kristen Lucken, and Melissa Barnett. 2011. Beyond home and return: Negotiating religious identity across time and space through the prism of the American experience. *Mobilities* 6 (4): 467–82.

Loving v. Virginia, 388 U.S. 1 (1967).

Mankowski, Eric S., and Elizabeth Thomas. 2000. The relationship between personal and collective identity: A narrative analysis of a campus ministry community. *Journal of Community Psychology* 28 (5): 517–28.

Marx, Karl. 1970. A contribution to the critique of Hegel's philosophy of right. In *Marx/Engels collected works,* Vol. 3, 3–129. New York: International Publishers. (Original work published 1843)

Nosich, Gerald M. 2009. *Learning to think things through: A guide to critical thinking across the curriculum*. 3rd ed. Upper Saddle River, NJ: Pearson.

Pew Research Center. 2012. The global religious landscape. http://www.pewforum.org/global-religious-landscape.aspx (accessed April 10, 2016)

Pew Research Center. 2015a. The future of world religions: Population growth projections, 2010–2050. http://www.pewforum.org/2015/ 04/02/religious-projections-2010-2050 (accessed April 10, 2016)

Pew Research Center. 2015b. America's changing religious landscape. http://www.pewforum.org/files/2015/05/RLS-08-26-full-report.pdf (accessed April 10, 2016)

Pew Research Center. 2016. The gender gap in religion around the world. http://www.pewforum.org/2016/03/22/the-gender-gap-in-religion-around-the-world (accessed September 10, 2017)

Roberts, Keith A., and David Yamane. 2016. *Religion in sociological perspective.* 6th ed. Los Angeles, CA: Sage.

Smith, Christian. 2008. Future directions in the sociology of religion. *Social Forces* 86 (4): 1561–89.

Smith, Christian, Michael Emerson, Sally Gallagher, Paul Kennedy, and David Sikkink. 1998. *American evangelicalism: Embattled and thriving.* Chicago: Chicago University Press.

Stanczak, Gregory C. 2006. *Engaged spirituality: Social change and American religion.* New Brunswick, NJ: Rutgers University Press.

Sullins, D. Paul. 2006. Gender and religion: Deconstructing universality, constructing complexity. *American Journal of Sociology* 112 (3): 838–80.

Taniguchi, Hiromi, and Leonard D. Thomas. 2011. The influences of religious attitudes on volunteering. *Voluntas* 22:335–55.

Vatican Press Office. 2016. Francis greets the population of Lesbos: Immigrants are not numbers, but people, faces, names and stories. https://press.vatican.va/content/salastampa/en/bollettino/pubblico/2016/04/16/160416c.html (accessed August 25, 2016)

Weber, Max. 1958. *The Protestant ethic and the spirit of capitalism.* New York: Scribner's. (Original work published 1904)

Wuthnow, Robert, and Stephen Offutt. 2008. Transnational religious connections. *Sociology of Religion* 69:209–32.

Zwissler, Laurel. 2012. Feminism and religion: Intersections between Western activism, theology and theory. *Religion Compass* 6 (7): 354–68.

Chapter 13

Anderegg, William R., James W. Prall, Jacob Harold, and Stephen H. Schneider. 2010. Expert credibility in climate change. *Proceedings of the National Academy of Sciences* 107 (27): 12107–9.

Bartley, Tim. 2007. Institutional emergence in an era of globalization: The rise of transnational private regulation of labor and environmental conditions. *American Journal of Sociology* 113 (2): 297–351.

Bell, Michael Mayerfeld. 1994. *Childerley: Nature and mortality in a country village.* Chicago: University of Chicago Press.

Bell, Michael Mayerfeld, and Loka Ashwood. 2015. *An invitation to environmental sociology.* Los Angeles: Sage.

Bullard, Robert D. 1990. *Dumping in Dixie: Race, class, and environmental quality.* Vol. 3. Boulder, CO: Westview.

Bullard, Robert D. 1993. *Confronting environmental racism: Voices from the grassroots.* New York: South End Press.

Catton, Willian R., Jr., and Riley E. Dunlap. 1978. Environmental sociology: A new paradigm. *The American Sociologist* 13:41–49.

Cronon, William. 1996. The trouble with wilderness: Or, getting back to the wrong nature. *Environmental History* 1 (1): 7–28.

Daly, Herman E. 1991. *Steady-state economics: With new essays.* New York: Island Press.

Douglas, Mary, and Aaron Wildavsky. 1983. *Risk and culture: An essay on the selection of technological and environmental dangers.* Berkeley: University of California Press.

Economy, Elizabeth C. 2011. *The river runs black: The environmental challenge to China's future.* Ithaca, NY: Cornell University Press.

Ehrlich, Paul R. 1968. *The population bomb.* Cutchogue, NY: Buccaneer.

Flint Water Advisory Task Force. 2016 *Flint water advisory task force final report.* http://mediad.publicbroadcasting.net/p/michigan/files/201603/taskforce_report.pdf?_ga=1.147700144.609033213.1458749402 (accessed October 8, 2016)

Funk, Cary, and Brian Kennedy. 2016. The politics of climate. http://www.pewinternet.org/2016/10/04/the-politics-of-climate (accessed October 8, 2016)

Hatanaka, Maki, Carmen Bain, and Lawrence Busch. 2005. Third-party certification in the global agrifood system. *Food Policy* 30 (3): 354–69.

Hohn, Donovan. 2016. Flint's water crisis and the "troublemaker" scientist. *New York Times,* August 16. http://www.nytimes.com/2016/08/21/magazine/flints-water-crisis-and-the-troublemaker-scientist.html (accessed October 8, 2016)

Jacques, Peter J., Riley E. Dunlap, and Mark Freeman. 2008. The organisation of denial: Conservative think tanks and environmental scepticism. *Environmental Politics* 17 (3): 349–85.

Jerolmack, Colin. 2007. Animal practices, ethnicity, and community: The Turkish pigeon handlers of Berlin. *American Sociological Review* 72 (6): 874–94.

Jerolmack, Colin, and Iddo Tavory. 2014. Molds and totems nonhumans and the constitution of the social self. *Sociological Theory* 32 (1): 64–77.

Kahan, Dan M., Donald Braman, John Gastil, Paul Slovic, and C. K. Mertz. 2007. Culture and identity-protective cognition: Explaining the white-male effect in risk perception. *Journal of Empirical Legal Studies* 4 (3): 465–505.

Laufer, William S. 2003. Social accountability and corporate greenwashing. *Journal of Business Ethics* 43 (3): 253–61.

Magdoff, Fred, and John Bellamy Foster. 2011. *What every environmentalist needs to know about capitalism: A citizen's guide to capitalism and the environment.* New York: NYU Press.

Malthus, T. R. 1798. *An essay on the principle of population.* Mineola, NY: Dover.

Maniates, Micahel F. 2001. Individualization: Plant a tree, buy a bike, save the world? *Global Environmental Politics* 1 (3): 31–52.

Martinez-Alier, Joan. 2003. *The environmentalism of the poor: A study of ecological conflicts and valuation.* Cheltenham, UK: Edward Elgar Publishing.

McCright, Aaron M., and Riley E. Dunlap. 2003. Defeating Kyoto: The conservative movement's impact on US climate change policy. *Social Problems* 50 (3): 348–73.

McCright, Aaron M., and Riley E. Dunlap. 2011. Cool dudes: The denial of climate change among conservative white males in the United States. *Global Environmental Change* 21 (4): 1163–72.

McGurty, Eileen Maura. 2000. Warren County, NC, and the emergence of the environmental justice movement: Unlikely coalitions and shared meanings in local collective action. *Society & Natural Resources* 13 (4): 373–87.

Meadows, Donella H., Dennis L. Meadows, Jorgen Randers, and William W. Behrens III. 1972. *The limits to growth: A report for the Club of Rome's project on the predicament of mankind.* https://www.clubofrome.org/report/the-limits-to-growth

Mohai, Paul, David Pellow, and J. Timmons Roberts. 2009. Environmental justice. *Annual Review of Environment and Resources* 34:405–30.

Mol, Arthur P. J., Gert Spaargaren, and David A. Sonnenfeld. 2014. Ecological modernisation theory: Taking stock, moving forward. In *Routledge international handbook on social and environmental change,* edited by Stewart Lockie, David A. Sonnenfeld, and Dana R. Fisher, 15–30. New York: Routledge.

National Centers for Environmental Information. 2016. *Global analysis, December 2016.* https://www.ncdc.noaa.gov/sotc/global/201612 (accessed January 28, 2017)

Oreskes, Naomi, and Eric M. Conway. 2010. *Merchants of doubt: How a handful of scientists obscured the truth on issues from tobacco smoke to global warming.* New York: Bloomsbury.

Pellow, David N. 2000. Environmental inequality formation toward a theory of environmental injustice. *American Behavioral Scientist* 43 (4): 581–601.

Pellow, David N. 2007. *Resisting global toxics: Transnational movements for environmental justice.* Cambridge: MIT Press.

Rice, James. 2007. Ecological unequal exchange: Consumption, equity, and unsustainable structural relationships within the global economy. *International Journal of Comparative Sociology* 48 (1): 43–72.

Ringquist, Evan J. 2005. Assessing evidence of environmental inequities: A meta-analysis. *Journal of Policy Analysis and Management* 24 (2): 223–47.

Roberts, J. Timmons, and Bradley Parks. 2006. *A climate of injustice: Global inequality, North-South politics, and climate policy.* Cambridge: MIT Press.

Roberts, J. Timmons, and Bradley Parks. 2009. Ecologically unequal exchange, ecological debt, and climate justice the history and implications of three related ideas for a new social movement. *International Journal of Comparative Sociology* 50 (3–4): 385–409.

Schnaiberg, Allan. 1980. Environment: From surplus to scarcity. In *Environment: From surplus to scarcity.* Oxford, UK: Oxford University Press.

Schnaiberg, Allan, and Kenneth A. Gould. 2000. *Environment and society: The enduring conflict.* Caldwell, NJ: Blackburn.

Schor, Juliet B. 2011. *True wealth: How and why millions of Americans are creating a time-rich, ecologically light, small-scale, high-satisfaction economy.* New York: Penguin.

Schwarz, M., and M. Thompson. 1990. *Divided we stand: Redefining politics, technology, and social choice.* Philadelphia: University of Pennsylvania Press.

Sen, Amartya. 1981. *Poverty and famines: An essay on entitlement and deprivation.* Oxford, UK: Oxford University Press.

Shapiro, Judith. 2001. *Mao's war against nature: Politics and the environment in revolutionary China.* Cambridge, UK: Cambridge University Press.

Spaargaren, Gert, and Arthur P. Mol. 1992. Sociology, environment, and modernity: Ecological modernization as a theory of social change. *Society & Natural Resources* 5 (4): 323–44.

Szasz, Andrew. 2007. *Shopping our way to safety: How we changed from protecting the environment to protecting ourselves.* Minneapolis: University of Minnesota Press.

Taylor, Dorceta E. 2000. The rise of the environmental justice paradigm injustice framing and the social construction of environmental discourses. *American Behavioral Scientist* 43 (4): 508–80.

United Church of Christ, Commission for Racial Justice. 1987. *Toxic wastes and race in the United States: A national report on the racial and socio-economic characteristics of communities with hazardous waste sites.* New York: United Church of Christ Commission for Racial Justice.

United Nations Commission on Environment and Development. 1987. *Our common future: Chapter 2: Towards sustainable development.* http://www.un-documents.net/ocf-02.htm#I (accessed January 28, 2017)

Veblen, Thorstein. 1899. *The theory of the leisure class.* New York: Macmillan.

Wackernagel, Mathis, and William Rees. 1998. *Our ecological footprint: Reducing human impact on the earth* (No. 9). Gabriola Island, Canada: New Society Publishers.

Weller, Robert P. 2006. *Discovering nature: Globalization and environmental culture in China and Taiwan.* Cambridge, UK: Cambridge University Press.

Chapter 14

Barnett, Bernice McNair. 1993. Invisible Southern Black women leaders in the civil rights movement: The triple constraints of gender, race, and class. *Gender & Society* 7 (2): 162–82.

Beamish, Thomas D., Harvey Molotch, and Richard Flacks. 1995. Who supports the troops? Vietnam, the Gulf War, and the making of collective memory. *Social Problems* 42 (3): 344–60.

Benford, Robert D., and Scott A. Hunt. 1992. Dramaturgy and social movements: The social construction and communication of power. *Sociological Inquiry* 62 (1): 36–55.

Bloom, Joshua, and Waldo E. Martin Jr. 2013. *Black against empire: The history and politics of the Black Panther Party.* Berkeley: University of California Press.

Blow, Charles M. 2012. The curious case of Trayvon Martin. *New York Times,* March 16.

Blumer, Herbert. 1995. Social movements. In *Social movements, main trends of the modern world,* edited by S. M. Lyman, 60–83. London: Palgrave Macmillan UK.

Carlson, Jennifer, and David Pettinicchio. 2016. The gay rights movement could take on the NRA—and actually win. *Washington Post,* June 17.

Carter, David. 2005. *Stonewall: The riots that sparked the gay revolution.* New York: Macmillan.

Clark, Rosemary. 2014. #NotBuyingIt: Hashtag feminists expand the commercial media conversation. *Feminist Media Studies* 14 (6): 1108–10.

Cress, Daniel M., and David A. Snow. 1996. Mobilization at the margins: Resources, benefactors, and the viability of homeless social movement organizations. *American Sociological Review* 61 (6): 1089–109.

Dewey, Caitlin. 2015. More than 26 million people have changed their Facebook picture to a rainbow flag. Here's why that matters. *Washington Post,* June 29.

Faludi, Susan. 1994. *Backlash: The undeclared war against American women.* New York: Crown/Archetype.

Fetner, Tina. 2016. U.S. attitudes toward lesbian and gay people are better than ever. *Contexts* 15 (2): 20–27.

Fox-Genovese, Elizabeth. 1994. Difference, diversity, and divisions in an agenda for the women's movement. In *Color, class & country: Experiences of gender,* edited by G. Young and B. Dickerson. London: Zed Books.

Friedan, Betty. 1963. *The feminine mystique.* New York: W. W. Norton.

Greenwood, Davydd J., and Morten Levin. 2006. *Introduction to action research: Social research for social change.* Thousand Oaks, CA: Sage.

Gurney, Joan Neff, and Kathleen J. Tierney. 1982. Relative deprivation and social movements: A Critical look at twenty years of theory and research. *Sociological Quarterly* 23 (1): 33–47.

Gusfield, Joseph R. 2009. *New social movements: From ideology to identity.* Philadelphia: Temple University Press.

hooks, bell. 1984. *Feminist theory from margin to center*. Boston: South End Press.

Industrial Areas Foundation (IAF). 2017. Impact. http://www.industrialareasfoundation.org (accessed February 1, 2017)

Lembcke, Jerry. 1998. *The spitting image: Myth, memory, and the legacy of Vietnam*. New York: New York University Press.

Levy, Brian L., and Denise L. Levy. 2017. When love meets hate: The relationship between state policies on gay and lesbian rights and hate crime incidence. *Social Science Research* 61:142–59.

Loving v. Virginia, 388 U.S. 1 (1967).

McAdam, Doug. 1990. *Freedom summer*. Oxford, UK: Oxford University Press.

McCarthy, John D., and Mayer N. Zald. 1977. Resource mobilization and social movements: A partial theory. *American Journal of Sociology* 82 (6): 1212–41.

Morgan, Robin. 1984. *Sisterhood is global: The international women's movement anthology*. New York: Feminist Press at City University of New York.

Morris, Aldon. 1981. Black Southern student sit-in movement: An analysis of internal organization. *American Sociological Review* 46 (6): 744–67.

Obergefell v. Hodges, 576 U.S. ___ (2015).

Oliver, Pam, and Hank Johnston. 2000. What a good idea: Frames and ideology in social movement research. *Mobilization* 5:37–54.

Oliver, Pamela E. 1993. Formal models of collective action. *Annual Review of Sociology* 19:271–300.

Piven, Frances Fox. 2006. *Challenging authority: How ordinary people change America*. New York: Rowman & Littlefield.

Porta, Donatella Della, and Mario Diani. 2008. *Social movements: An introduction*. 2nd ed. New York: Wiley-Blackwell.

Read, Jen'Nan Ghazal, and John P. Bartkowski. 2000. To veil or not to veil? A case study of identity negotiation among Muslim women in Austin, Texas. *Gender & Society* 14 (3):395–417.

Rosenberg, Jessica, and Gitana Garofalo. 1998. Riot Grrrl: Revolutions from within. *Signs* 23 (3): 809–41.

Rupp, Leila J. 1997. *Worlds of women: The making of an international women's movement*. Princeton, NJ: Princeton University Press.

Smelser, Neil J. 1962. *Theory of collective behavior*. New York: Free Press.

Snow, David A., and Robert D. Benford. 1988. Ideology, frame resonance and participant mobilization. *International Social Movement Research* 1:197–219.

Snow, David A., E. B. Rochford Jr., S. K. Worden, and R. D. Benford. 1986. Frame alignment processes, micromobilization, and movement participation. *American Sociological Review* 51 (4): 464–81.

Stein, Arlene. 2001. *The stranger next door: The story of a small community's battle over sex, faith, and civil rights*. Boston: Beacon.

Weeber, Stanley C., and Daniel Gilbert Rodeheaver. 2004. *Militias in the new millennium: A Test of Smelser's theory of collective behavior*. Lanham, MD: University Press of America.

National Organization for Women (NOW), 306, 310
National parks, 278
Nation's Report Card, The, 230
Nature, social construction of, 278–279
Nature versus nurture, 80
Neighborhood quality, 127–128
Neutralization technique, 115–116
New ecological paradigm, 280
New social movement theory, 304
News media, sex and gender messages, 158–159. *See also* Media
Nigeria, 298
Nineteenth Amendment, 306
No Child Left Behind (NCLB), 246–247
Nonmaterial culture, 59
Nonrandom samples, 49
Norm of reciprocity, 214
Normal schools, 227
Normalizing, 117
Normative approach to defining deviance, 101
Normative statements, 38
Norms, 62–63
    conceptualizing deviance, 100. *See also* Deviance
    gender, 153–154
    moral entrepreneurs and changing, 107–108
    religious affiliation and attitudes, 269–270
    socialization of, 79–80. *See also* Socialization
    state of anomie, 104, 106
    structural functionalism perspective, 19–20
    See also Social construction
North Carolina's bathroom law, 161
"Not In My Backyard" (NIMBY), 288
Nuclear family, 83, 205, 210
Nurture versus nature, 80

Obergefell v. Hodges (2015), 206*n*, 207, 312
Obesity, 109–110, 111
Observation, 43
Occupational gender segregation, 162–166
One-drop rule, 180, 182
Operationalization of concepts, 50
Organic solidarity, 18
Organizing, 298, 306–308, 309
Overshoot, 276–277
Overwork, 218

Pager, Devah, 44
Pakistan, 270
Paradigm shift theory, 280
Parenting, 214–215
    discipline approaches, 215
    "free range parenting" case, 22–24, 27–28, 31–32

gendered roles, 170, 215
single parenthood, 211
Paris Agreement on climate change (2015), 279
Participant-observation research, 43, 266
Participatory action research (PAR), 313–314
Passing, 117
Peer pressure, 84
Peers as agents of socialization, 84–85
People for the Ethical Treatment of Animals (PETA), 300
People Improving Communities through Organizing (PICO), 298
Performance of social roles, 92
Phipps, Susie Guillory, 182
Pivens, Francis, 313
Play and socialization, 81–82
Pluralism, religious, 256
Police violence, 93, 199, 200, 302
Political party affiliation trends, 257–258
Polls, 52–53
Popular culture, 68
Population and the environment, 283–284
Postindustrial economy and education, 228
Poverty, 133–134
    absolute and relative, 133
    culture of poverty theories, 134
    deserving and undeserving poor, 134
    educational consequences, 136–139
    housing issues, 141
    population growth and, 284
    religious institutions and, 267
    social constructionism perspective, 31
    University of the Poor, 299
    See also Economic inequality
Power
    determinants of socioeconomic status, 126
    independent, 313
    social movement success and, 309–310
Power elite, 131
Prayer in school, 254
Preindustrial societies, education in, 227
Prejudice, 183
Preschool programs, 233, 246
Presentation of self skills, 30
Primary deviance, 111
Primary groups, 29
Primary socialization, 29, 82–83
Prisons, agents of socialization, 87
Private sphere, 209
Production and environmental change, 284–286
Profane, 253
Program evaluation, 147
Prohibition, 108, 109*f*
Proletariat, 24–25, 127–128, 131